Wh ... cob's
... ying

"Hassle Free Car Buying is one of the best books I have read in some time. It is marvelous. You have written an exceptional book Mr. Jacobs, a well thought out and very well written book, a no-nonsense book that everyone considering buying a car should read."

–Robert Boyce,
Editorial Director - Publisher
American Literary Services
Atlanta, Georgia

"To take the advice of a professional who is on your side when it comes to purchasing a car is a definate way to take the stress out of car buying and getting more value for your money and keeping more money in your pocket.

In our high tech world of today any time we can reduce financial stress we are ahead of the game and healthier for it."

–Dr. Diane Copeland,
Chiropractor
West Palm Beach, Florida

"I have been waiting years for this book. For me, it has cleared up the mystery of getting a good deal in buying a car, while putting money in my pocket."

–Paul Phillips,
Houston Texas

"This expanded and revised edition is the perfect companion for would-be car buyers. A book that delivers on its promise of big savings of time, energy and money."

–MID-CONTINENT PUBLIC LIBRARY Southern Book Service

i

"One idea will save you many times the price of the book. It is money in the bank....with a full refund!!

Buy this book and you can negotiate from a position of power!"

–Jack Cuthrell,
Author of "Letters to the Soul"
Tequesta, Florida

"Thanks, Jake! This is a simple and easy to read book, good for both new and experienced car buyers."

–Dr. Shiv Metha,
Sugarland, Texas

"Hassle Free Car Buying opened up my eyes! I never knew about the terms "closed end" and "open end", nor was I aware a purchase option was negotiable. In short, until I had read the book, I was a duck for my dealer. Now I am the one in control! Thanks Mr. Jacobs.

The price one pays for the book will certainly be given back to them many times over by the money they will save just by reading through the pages."

–Jack Kerman,
Advertising Executive
Williamsport, Pennsylvania

THE COMPLETE GUIDE TO
HASSLE FREE
CAR BUYING

Jake Jacobs

The Complete Guide to
Hassle Free
Car Buying

The Complete, Step-By-Step
Guide for Buying a New or Used Car or Truck
Without the Hassle.

The Complete Guide to Hassle Free Car Buying

published by:

Jacobs House
P.O. Box 740893
Boynton Beach, FL 33474
e-mail – jacobsh@bellsouth.net

expanded 2nd ed.   ISBN: 0-9639268-1-0

Library of Congress Catalog Card Number 98-91205

Publisher's Cataloging-in-Publication
(*Provided by Quality Books, Inc.*)

Jacobs, Jake, 1946-
    Hassle free car buying/by Jake Jacobs.--Expnaded updated 2nd ed.
    p. cm.
    Includes index.
    Preassigned LCCN: 98-91205
    ISBN: 0-9639268-1-0

    1. Automobilies--Purchasing.   I. Title.

TL162.J33 1998   629.222'029'6
                      QBI98-501

Printed in the United States of America

10 9 8 7 6 5 4 3 2

UNITED
GRAPHICS
INCORPORATED
An Employee-Owned Corporation

Printed on acid-free paper

"If a man empties his purse into his head, no man can take it away from him. An investment in knowledge always pays the best interest."

Benjamin Franklin.

Table of Contents

Acknowledgement

With my deep sentiments and gratitude, I dedicate this book to my dear parents and my children, Joseph and Megan, without whose love and support my venture in writing this book would not have been possible.

I would be failing in my duty, if I did not express my sincere thanks to Bruce, Prince, Byron, Carol and Kim their valuable suggestions, encouragement and, above all, their friendship. My thanks to New York Attorney General and his staff for supplying the information on the lemon laws and leasing information, and to Carleton Inc./Financial Publishing Company for their permission to re-print monthly payment tables.

I would also like to thank Sally and Peggy for their typing and valuable suggestions, in spite of their busy schedules, enabling me to send it to the press in time.

My sincere thanks also goes to those who have gone before, from the pioneers who first settled in this country to the designers and engineers who designed our highways and freeways, so that our motoring can be pleasant. And finally, to the consumers who bought this book wherever you are, my sincere thanks to you. Keep calling and asking for the **HASSLE FREE CAR-BUYING** book, and carry it with you whenever you go car buying.

Happy Motoring!

Preface

As a car dealer, I sold a brand new Ford Taurus for $1,325 below the invoice. Hard to believe? Right! But, then, it is a fact. How did I manage that? Well, life often may spell HASSLE, but buying a car, new or used, need not be. This book will demonstrate to you, step-by-step, in simple terms, how you can own your dream car, or any other type of vehicle, hassle-free.

Notwithstanding the fact that I often wondered why, yet, another book on buying should be written when several on the topic already exists by reputable authors, hardly any of them gives peek into the inner information. As an experienced car dealer, I ventured to launch on the project of writing this book solely to assist people who save their hard-earned money to buy their dream car. This book clearly shows the various strategies of hassle-free car buying, the various options that are open for adequate financing, and how to go about it.

Over the years, I have come across intelligent people from all walks of life and different ethnic backgrounds, including accountants, physicians, teachers and many others, who had rather frustrating and painful experiences while purchasing their car. Of course, when there are over three hundred and fifty models of cars in the U. S., making the right choice is a Herculean task. However, owning your dream car should not be a mind boggling matter, especially when it is a question of a big investment, second only to buying a dream home. Obviously, careful planning is of prime importance.

People quite often are confused in our fast-paced society when it comes to car buying. People lack the experience and knowledge on the subject because they do not buy cars or trucks often. I have put in writing, my vast experience as a car sales person, with several examples, for a better understanding of how to buy your dream car with confidence and hassle-free. A small slip could be a costly mistake. If one follows the suggestions and adopts the various strategies detailed in this book, one will avoid such costly errors. Thus, you will find the features of this book unique. The purpose of this book is to build confidence in dealing with sales people and dealers, so that you can be in control during the buying process. Also, most people don't want to be sold cars the old way.

You may not need to memorize all the information I have put in this book. Perhaps you are knowledgeable in some aspects of hassle-free car buying...then skip those pages. It might be helpful to highlight those lines which you don't want to skip or forget. You richly deserve the best for your money, which you earned in the old-fashioned way.

In these pages, you will read about three different families who found their dream cars at the right price and the right financing, because they had the confidence and knowledge they needed to get exactly what they wanted. They are real life stories.

For Megan

Chapter One

Selecting A New/Used Car or Truck

One of the most important things in selecting an automobile, whether new or used, is to keep in mind the size of your family. Are you single? Have children? A single person may be interested in driving a sleek sports car. A Young couple planning to have children may want to consider purchasing a family car. A station wagon or minivan may suit your family as your family grows. On the other hand, once your children have grown, may be right time to go in for a luxury sedan, an expensive sports car or a sports utility vehicle. Whatever automobile you intend to purchase, it is solely your decision. The above points may enhance your decision-making process.

Another thing to consider while making an investment in a car is making the right selection. In doing so, one should keep in mind the purpose of the vehicle. For example, will the vehicle be used mostly as a family car, for your grocery shopping, or for extracurricular activities? Or will it be used as a second car to commute to work? Or perhaps you may want a car for your children to commute to college. Then think about purchasing a used car because you intend to use it only for a few years and don't want to invest a lot of money. Purchasing a used car can have certain advantages in addition to the lower cost. Besides saving money on taxes and insurance, a used car may be the right option for you. When your children graduate, you may prefer to replace it for a brand new car, as a graduation gift, or get rid of the old car by selling it to someone else. There is more about purchasing a used car discussed in detail in chapters **fourteen** and **fifteen** of this book.

Needless to say, you should include all the family members in the decision making process and in assessing your family's needs. Make it fun. Decide on a body style that suits your taste...a four door. two door, sports car, station wagon, minivan, luxury car or sport utility vehicle, and so on and so forth. One should always keep in mind performance, comfort, handling, style and safety—these are also important factors to consider.

Necessary information one needs to know, is in the brochure normally displayed at the new car showroom. The auto makers will also provide you with brochures, if you call them on the toll free numbers provided in the appendix. Let the auto maker deliver it to you at your home. The brochure contains information on make, models, quality, technology, safety, trailering and warranty. You will also find information about colors that are available for both the interior and exterior of the vehicle, standard features, power teams, and preferred equipment groups. Individually available options are also listed in the brochure. Many of the brochures will have a color chart printed. If not, you may have to ask the salesperson for one.

Transmission

If you prefer a manual to automatic transmission, consider the pros and cons of your choice. A manual transmission will give you better gas mileage and is less expensive than an automatic transmission. On the other hand, many people prefer a car with automatic transmission because it is more convenient and easier to handle, especially in traffic.

Options

Do you want to purchase a fully loaded automobile with air conditioning, sunroof, AM-FM stereo cassette, power windows, power locks, power seats, and cruise control? Or do you want a basic car with manual or automatic transmission, air conditioning, and a radio? People often ask me, "just what is a good car?" I tell them there is no simple answer to their question. Cars are manufactured by some companies and people just buy them. Around thirteen to sixteen million new cars are sold in America each year. Making a choice is a Herculean task. The wise choice is yours. It is up to you to decide which car is best for you and your family. Therefore, it is up to you to make the wise decision on a car that suits the best interest of the whole family. Checking the consumer buyer's guide, which reviews cars from time to time would certainly be worthwhile. These publications are available at any public library. A master index will guide you to the issue of the publication.

There are currently nearly three hundred and fifty different models to choose from in the United States. As previously said, it is not a simple task. Most automobiles are manufactured in the United States. There are many that are imported from Japan, Germany, England and various other parts of the world. Furthermore, you may have to decide whether to purchase an imported or domestic car. There are quite a few cars made in America by foreign companies like Toyota, Honda and BMW as well as from their mother countries and exported to the United States.

Colors

One may find choosing a color for their car all the more complicated, as each member of the family may have their own favorite color. The question is the availability of cars in the color you prefer with the dealer you visited. I would suggest that you insist on the color you have in mind.

When it comes to the question of purchasing a car, one has to be very cautious. You are investing your hard earned cash; you certainly should have the best benefit for your money. Hence, your decision with regard to the make, model, color, and type of your vehicle depends on the amount of money you can afford to invest. Refer to Appendix "D" for complete details on options, benefits, and drawbacks.

EPA Gas Mileage

It is important to look into gas mileage, EPA estimated numbers, which are normally displayed on the window sticker. These numbers are often not even close to the EPA gas mileage per your driving habits. Remember your driving habits have its own effects on the gas mileage. Most demonstration models and used cars may not always have window stickers, in which case you may have to find out the EPA mileage from the owner's manual; do not take the salesperson's word for it, unless he checks the manual for you. The owner's manual is your best bet.

Selecting A Truck

Have you ever heard that the best selling car is not a car? It's a truck!! Most car makers are making trucks. In order to select a truck, I cannot stress enough the importance of your personal homework on the subject for the simple reason that the trucks have their own specialized workmanship, quite different than that of the cars. Two trucks may look like twins, but each one has their own individual specifications. Every truck, of course, comes with a window sticker with complete factory specifications. Do not even bother to look into a truck that does not display such a window sticker. The sticker should clearly state EPA gas mileage, size of the engine and other important specifications.

If you are a first-time truck buyer, I am sure that you would certainly be cautious, for it is a really big investment. Your personal homework will certainly come in handy. Of course, when it is a question of a big investment, one does not rush into it. One would certainly take time to look into various options before he makes a final decision. However, before arriving at a decision I would recommend that you do some shopping, to compare various models, price range, and the manufacturer's warranty. Do not hesitate to ask questions...shooting in the dark is a blind art. The more knowledgeable you are, the better position you will be in to make a well-informed decision. Don't let the salesperson talk you into something and take you for a ride, Remember, you have gone there to buy a car or truck that you want to buy, and not what the salesman wants to sell. A first-time truck buyer should know that the fuel consumption of the truck is higher than in a car. Trucks are not required to meet the Federal or NHTSA (National Highway Traffic Safety Administration) average fuel economy standard. Further, a truck should suit both your needs and your pocket. It is good for one to know the major cost of owning a vehicle is depreciation, financing, insurance, state fees, fuels, repairs, and maintenance.

Purchasing an R.V. (Recreational Vehicle)

Before you think about purchasing an R.V., you would do well to know what type of vehicle you would prefer to have. Recreational vehicles come in two categories:

Motorized:

Class A motor-home, custom coach, micro-mini motor home, mini motor home, van camper, van conversion.

Towables:

Pick-up camper, travel trailer, park trailer, fold-down trailer, fifth-wheel trailer. You can buy an R.V. anywhere from $5,000 to $500,000—perhaps even higher. There are several vehicles available in the market which can be used in connection with the trailer. Some of these vehicles can even be used for daily commuting, and are also designed for towing.

Decide what type of R.V. you want before you begin shopping. There is basic information you need to know regarding your trailer length, weight of the trailer, as well as the brakes they are equipped with. Most R.V. salespeople are mature and very knowledgeable about their product and will be able to answer all the questions you may have. Call R.V. manufacturers (see appendix) and ask for a brochure. In the comfort of your living room, you will be able to gather as much information as you need. Visit as many different dealers and auctions to check all that are available in the market, as well as prices. After you have done your homework you will know what type you'll need.

There are R.V.'s with diesel engines or gasoline engines. One would prefer a diesel engine R.V. for the simple reason that they are cheaper to operate and gives better mileage per gallon compared to a gasoline engine. In addition, diesel engines give longer service before it comes for an overhauling, which means an additional saving of cash in your pocket.

When you buy an R.V., of course, then you have to go in for R.V. insurance. Look for an insurance company or agent who specializes in R.V. insurance and will give you the necessary coverage. For one who is in need of an R.V. but does not intend to own one, one can always rent or lease an R.V. There are many dealers all over the country who specialize in R.V.'s. Shopping to compare, various sizes, models, and so forth, in order to find the R.V. that will suit your purpose is of great importance in order to be well-informed and knowledgeable on the said vehicles.

Quite often, if you have cash in your pocket, you are a king. You may be able to get into any auction, or go to a dealer who sells repossessed R.V.'s and be able to strike a good deal on an R.V.

Summary

Don't expect a salesperson, sales manager, or finance manager to work for you. They are there to make maximum profit for the dealer, because they are all paid on the percentage of the profit.

•

If you are buying a truck, make sure it has a rear bumper. If it is missing, check the window sticker to see whether it comes with the truck.

* * * * * * *

JAKE'S HOT TIP #101

If you're planning to purchase a European luxury car, ask about the tourist delivery program at your local dealer, or contact the European manufacturer. The money you save will be worth a trip abroad.

Chapter Two

Choosing A Dealership

Once you have made your decision about the kind of car you want to purchase, equipped with sufficient knowledge of the make, model, type, domestic or imported, and the purpose, you are now ready to venture into a dealership. The price tag on a new car, as you may be well aware, can be anywhere from $5,000 to $100,000. The price range for the vehicle you choose depends upon your financial capacity.

You would do well to keep in mind that the manufacturers will spend billions of dollars in advertising their products and mega dealers, too, spend millions of dollars each year on advertisements for so-called "sales" under different no-menclature such as *red tag sale*, national holiday sales like Memorial Day, Labor Day, or a president's birthday, director's birthday, and so forth—except on your birthday and mine—only to boost the foot traffic. In their promotions, they may offer free car phones, television sets, loaner cars, balloons and ice cream for the kids, along with a host of other things. The truth of the matter is that all these are aids of business psychology.

Why do they take so much trouble on those sundries in the name of promotion? "Sale," of course! "Come into my parlor said the spider to the fly..." to get you into the dealership and sell you their product. Who's paying for his, anyway? You, of course! All that smooth talk and tailoring of your unique taste is their goodwill bonus, perhaps.

You work hard for your money, so you deserve a good deal on your purchase and to enjoy your vehicle for years to come. All promotions and low-balling (quoting prices below the dealer cost) are but some of the gimmicks of the salesperson, just to get you into their dealership. They know how to get you to buy a vehicle. Beware of the advertisements, promotions, gimmicks, and other sales tactics used by the mega dealers and auto manufacturers. This book explains how to resist temptation and driving headlong in a hurry in the purchase of your vehicle, and fall victim to an unscrupulous salesperson with their smooth talk. Pay no attention to advertising hype such as "At near or below list," or "$6,000 below manufacturer's suggested retail price (MSRP)?" These are meaningless numbers which dealers can offer, which sound like huge price cuts. There are toll free numbers you can call (see Appendix) to find dealers close to your home. In a large city, of course, there are dealers "cheaper by the dozen" where you may shop. The reason for choosing a dealer near you is simple. It is easy to get there, and you don't have to drive tens of miles when it is time for the warranty work or maintenance. Why waste energy and fuel more than it is necessary?

Carefully study dealer's reputation with regard to service. The reputation of the dealer and his proximity to your home has its benefits. The color of the car and options you want should be available at the dealer you have chosen. If these items are not available, then you have no other option than to use the same revolving door that you came in, to get out and look for another dealer who is able to provide you with a vehicle with specifications you have in mind, or at least make arrangements for you from a fellow dealer. Do not settle for anything less, or compromise. It is your hard-earned money—you should get the best for it, and not something mediocre. Don't let the salesperson talk you into something that is not in keeping with your choice. Insist on exactly what you have in mind and would like to have. The dealer should be able to locate a vehicle of your choice from another dealer, using dealer-locating services, at no extra cost. If he is unable to oblige you—there are plenty of fish in the sea—choose another dealer, who will be able to deliver the goods according to your decisions.

It is good to visit several dealerships outside working hours, so that you can see an automobile without having to contest with high pressure salespeople. Most of the dealers are closed on Sundays, while some are open on Sunday and closed on Saturday. You should be able to walk through lots at your leisure and compare prices, models, options, types of cars, and so on, which will help you to arrive at a wise decision. This is the main point of *hassle-free shopping*.

Of course, you will not be able to get into a vehicle when the dealership is closed, but you will be doing very important homework. The time spent on such homework is certainly worthwhile, and will pay its own dividend. You will be able to check various models, and the specifications you need to know are on the window sticker. Sometimes there may be more than one placed by the dealer with additional specifications which the dealer has worked on; for example special tire, pin stripe, cellular phones, alarm system—these are but a few things to add to their profit. However, if you do like the vehicle, but don't want to pay extra for the so-called "special" things, you could ask the dealer to strip them all, or buy them at a reduced price, but make sure that the original tires and other basics are there, according to the factory specifications.

There is no limit to what one can add to one's car to feed one's fancy. Perhaps an alarm system, AM-FM radio, fancy wheels, cellular phone, pin stripping...many other tantalizing luxury items. But then, these things could be added later on by yourself for much less than the dealer would charge you for such installations. You would be much better off handling the project on your own, provided it is in keeping with the manufacturer's warranty Consult the dealer on the matter.

Don't hesitate to browse during regular business hours, if you feel more comfortable doing so. If the salesperson approaches, you could simply say that you are "just shopping." You wouldn't like to be pressured into anything, would you?

Dealers, in addition to making their own profits on the cars they sell, also get a sizable chunk of the profit from financing, and from the so-called extended warranties. Beware! Don't let them bush-whack you with these items. Dealers offer these so-called services to further fatten their profits.

One Price Selling

The Saturn Corporation, a subsidiary of General Motors, sells cars at only one price. They will not budge or renegotiate on a new Saturn. Compare prices of other models of different cars before you decide on the Saturn. Make sure you can negotiate on such things as financing, extended warranties and the like, if you decide to buy a Saturn. It is worth remembering the fact that very few other dealers across the country sell cars the Saturn way—NO DICKER STICKERS— A firm price that makes comparisons easier. Buying a new Saturn is one thing, but buying a used car is entirely different. For example, a Saturn dealer may have their own well-guarded reputation on their new cars. They seem to be more inclined to project the same image on the used cars.

"Caveat Emptor"

Do not get intimidated by attitude or, in any way, balled up. Negotiate. They may offer you 150 point inspection, along with limited warranty and a money-back guarantee. In other words, their used cars may be as good as other dealer's used cars. When you have a firm price, it makes it easier for you to compare. Try to get at least three different bids—then choose the lowest one.

Ordering a New Car or Truck

Visit any dealer of your choice and then ask for a fleet manager. Tell the fleet manager or the salesperson you want to order a vehicle, and give him the specifications. Inquire about the approximate date you could expect your vehicle to arrive. Dealers always prefer to sell from their stock, rather than take your order for the car. No doubt, it is a hassle negotiating on a car or truck, as well as time consuming, frustrating, and expensive. But negotiating is vital, even if you are placing an order for a vehicle you have decided upon. Carefully study the auto contract price, which is a written contract between the customer and the new car dealer. It is the final contract price, and the contract should note it clearly to prevent any change in the price subsequent to the signing of the contract agreement, regardless of any price increase by the manufacturer.

CAR BUYING SERVICES

Car Brokers: These people take your order and locate the car for you with a dealer who may be close to you, or find one several hundreds of miles away. These brokers may even be able to obtain the car for you, if you are willing to buy it from them. It is a good idea to check with a local Better Business Bureau before you hire their services. Some of these car brokers will be like a shopping friend. They will accompany you to the dealership and do all the negotiating on your behalf. The broker then will charge you a flat fee for his services.

Locating Services: Many credit unions, banks, discount clubs and auto clubs offer locating services at no cost or for a minimal cost. They can steer you to a dealer who will offer you a car you want at a competitive price. It is up to you to decide if the price is really a bargain. You may arrange the financing from the dealer, or pay in cash and take delivery of the vehicle from the dealer after negotiating the financing, as well as the warranty aspects.

Some locating services, for a fee, will collect several bids from dealers in your area. You may have to approach the dealer who gives you the lowest bid to buy your vehicle. It may happen that by the time you get to the dealer with the lowest bid you received from the locating service, the dealer may not have the exact car you had bid for in the inventory. Then, of course, again, you are in square one, and you may have to do negotiating anew to find a car with the similar bid price, as well as financing and warranty.

Credit Unit Program: The price quote obtained from the above said program, may not match, or sometimes, even come close to the price you gathered on your own during your shopping expedition. You will be better off to plan on your own with the help of the checklist given at the end of this book.

There are hundreds of auto services that have opened in recent years, and more new ones keep mushrooming year after year. You may be able to access them through your home computer. You are well advised to compare prices, as well as check their service record and reputation with the local Better Business Bureau before you decide.

There are newsletters published by non-profit organizations that you could refer to for information about cars, their rebates, and about low-point financing, but the service could cost you a bundle. No matter what services you use, you must not underestimate your own homework on your own best interest.

Car Buying Guide on the World Wide Web

The Internet offers a great deal of information to prospective buyers. Today, one can get up-to-date information right at home using a personal computer and your favorite on-line service. The sky is the limit, as to the volume of information you can access!

There are also a number of car buying services available through the Internet. These services, which are growing rapidly in number, can provide information such as dealer costs, options, and so forth. Many retail stores carry software with which you can compare vehicle prices, models, and a host of other things.

Summary

Do your homework before you shop for a vehicle. Decide on the type of car, the model and color of the car you would like to buy. Compare price. Make sure you get three different bids before you make a final decision.

* * * * * * *

Jake's Hot Tip #102

Choose a dealer near you, if he is reputable. To find a dealer near you, call the manufacturer's toll free number which you will find in the Appendix. Remember, a good deal is only when you get both a good car price and financing with low interest rates.

Chapter Three

Inside Information

Option Package/Value Pricing

On certain fully loaded models, and sometimes in certain locations, the car makers equip the value-priced vehicles with all possible options such as air conditioning, automatic transmission, sunroof, AM-FM radio cum cassette player, power windows, power locks, rear defrosters, and so on and so forth. Then, the car maker prices the vehicle as low as possible. Even though when charged separately for each individual item, it may cost one an arm and a leg, no doubt. But to attract consumers, they consider it a *no-dicker sticker price*. One would wonder how a car manufacturer could afford such a deal. Well, the secret is mass production. It brings down the cost price of the items. As a customer, you have to decide the options you want in your vehicle. If the dealer offers you a price you can't refuse with all the above options, then by all means, buy it. But then, you would unnecessarily waste money if you pay for all the options, which you really do not need or hardly use. If the salespersons quotes you a price including all these extra fittings, let him know that you are not interested in all those options and that you would prefer a basic vehicle. Negotiate. Compare prices and various models.

Hold Back

The dealers have multiple ways of making money. "Hold Back" is one of them. It is the hidden profit the dealer makes when he sells you a car. A dealer can sell you a car for the invoice price and make a profit of anywhere from two to three percent of the sticker price. Most salespersons do not know about it. The dealer may not reveal it to the salesperson, either, because of the fear that if the salesperson finds out about it, he may negotiate this at the end of the sale. As a customer, you must use this as a negotiating tool (Refer to Chapter 7). When negotiating, ask for the invoice. If the dealer says that he is selling the vehicle for the invoice price and not making any profit, ask him about the "hold back." You can figure the amount from the sticker price. From time to time, car makers send the money to the dealer per number of cars sold.

Cash Rebates or Low Interest Rate Financing

Major manufacturers may present you with a choice of cash incentives such as cash or low interest rate financing. If you prefer to choose the cash rebate they will mail you a check for the amount, or you can use that cash to reduce the price of the car which, in turn, reduces your sales tax, too. However, if you prefer, you could opt for low interest rate financing. Some car makers may not offer you a choice—it is either cash rebate or low interest rate financing (see Chapter six). When a certain lady named Theresa bought a Hyundai car, the dealer offered her only the cash rebate. Of course, Theresa was smart enough to take advantage of it, using the rebate for the down payment. Whether it is a cash rebate or low interest rate financing, the dealer will let you know of these options, even if you forget to ask about it, since you are entitled to any of those options.

Factory to Dealer Cash Incentive Program

This cash incentive to dealer varies anywhere between $400 to $1,000, depending upon the volume of cars sold by the dealer during the program period. Manufacturers may sometimes advertise these cash incentive programs, but most of the time, it is kept a secret. The dealer may use this money for advertising, to pay a bonus to salespeople, or pocket the extra profit for himself. As a customer, do not hesitate to negotiate and claim a share of that profit derived by the dealer from the program. Don't expect the dealer to reveal the program to you. You should find out about the factory to dealer cash incentive program on your own. It is part of your homework. Use this information to negotiate a lower price for the car.

Carry-Over Allowance/Special Sale

Auto manufacturers will offer cash incentives to dealers in order to curtail the enormous expense of the inventory. So the dealers advertise on local news, papers or local weekly papers for year-end clearance. They may also call it a "reduction of inventory." Sometimes, bad weather can trigger a move for a mid-year clearance sale. Well, here is an opportunity for one to make hay when the sun shines! If you plan to buy a car at this point, you may be able to claim a share of that dealer's "cash incentive" by negotiating for some additional discount, a double in brass, on your purchase.

Luxury Tax

If you are thinking about buying an upscale model car or an expensive car, remember, there is ten-percent tax on the portion of the vehicle price which exceeds $34,000. For example, if you buy a $64,000 car, the price tag would show the $3,000 tax, which is ten percent of $30,000. Federal taxes may effect the price of the vehicle, as well. Automakers are required to meet the minimum E.P.A. gas mileage. Some cars do not. These are called "gas guzzlers." If you buy a gas guzzler car, it may cost you an additional $1,000 to $3,000. However, the federal luxury tax rule does not apply to trucks with gross weight over 6,000 pounds. The same rule applies to sport utility vehicles, too.

Ladies, Stop Paying More!

Women end up paying more for their car than their male counterparts. Sounds rather strange, but it is true. Why should you pay more? You are aware that the salesperson is out there looking for the maximum profit they can possibly make on their merchandise. It is not because you are of a different gender, but because of their greed for profit. Ladies become easy victims to the greed of the salesperson, if you have not done your homework and are not familiar with the car buying procedure.

It is a known fact that over 50% of the car buyers are female. Does that mean that they should pay more for their cars than the rest of the world? The only way to cut a good deal is to do your homework and find out the cost of the vehicle (the price the dealer pays for the vehicle), without paying attention to the sticker price or manufacturer's suggested retail price (MSRP). Once you have a figure in mind, you can begin to negotiate. Negotiate on discounts such as first-time car buyer, college graduate rebates, cash rebate, hold back, year-end clearance, special sale, and so on (see Chapter-three for low interest rates). When finished negotiating on various discounts, buckle down to negotiate on financing and extended warranties. While you are working on your homework, you will do well to refer to *Automotive News*, which is available in most libraries. The dealer will most likely not give you this information about the various discounts that are offered by the manufacturer.

The above mentioned information is available to everyone. If you are equipped with sufficient knowledge regarding the price of the car and the various discounts, the salesperson will lower his price in order not to lose a customer. If he will not compromise, there are many others who will be eager to do business with you.

Summary

Look for cash rebates or low interest rate financing that are offered through manufacturers! If you are buying an Escort, for example, the manufacturer is Ford. Financing and rebates are offered through Ford Motor Company.

Finding out dealer true cost is the first step. Calculate the *hold back* and use this amount as a tool when negotiating. Hold back is usually 2% to 3% of the sticker price.

* * * * * * *

Jake's Hot Tip #103

Read the <u>Automotive News</u> from time to time, as well as other newsletters, to find out about current rebates, especially the cash rebates/low interest rate financing, factory to dealer incentives, customer incentives, carry-over allowance, and so forth. Ask the dealer about first-time car buyer or college graduates rebate programs. A dealer may keep you in the dark about such matters. It is up to you to keep abreast with available discounts and rebate programs.

Chapter Four

Test Driving A New Car

Car super-stars rattle an industry. New and used car dealers dispute the impact of the industry's new kid on the block, but the customer may end up the winner. Ladies and gentlemen, start your engines—A new race for auto sales is about to begin!

One by one, used car supporters have announced their entry into the national competition already fierce among veteran dealers and "mom and pop" auto-shops. The powerful dealers and their road maps for success have not been lost on used or new auto-dealers in the country. if anything, it will stimulate business says many a small dealer. The arrival of used-car supporters may stimulate the industry, but also hurt mom and pop lots. Nevertheless, the supporters may bring in new business for the old players in the market they enter. At the same time, the existing dealers may shift gears and adopt the consumer kind of sales techniques the new players employ. They may offer a bigger selection of cars to compete with in the mega-lots. They may haggle less over the price, and even pick up high tech sales tools quickly.

But some guest independent dealers and small mom an pop lots may get sideswiped by the new competitors, while others say new car sales could feel the impact. Under such circumstances you, as a car buyer, is in the driver's seat. Equipped with this knowledge for your personal consumption, proceed to test drive a car of your choice. You may like to test drive a few other cars of different makes and models to compare their performance and the package amenities.

It would be a good idea to test drive several different cars, so as to enable you to compare various aspects of the car. If you are interested in Ford, Toyota, Honda, or any other make, test drive their various models. Visit various dealerships—at least three, if not more—in order to have a fairly good knowledge of the over-all performance of the different models of various makes. You may approach a salesperson and express your intention of purchasing a new car, and your desire to test drive a few different models which are available. Normally, the salesperson will oblige you. You may have to provide him with a photocopy of your driving license. Thereafter, he may either accompany you on a test drive, or he may allow you to test drive a car on your own. Make sure that you have sufficient gas in the car, because you may want to drive long enough to get a proper feel of the performance of the vehicle. Test drive it on a highway if you like to study it's pick up, as well as its road grip and its over-all performance.

As a salesperson, I always accompanied my customer during the test drive, which facilitated getting to know the customer better and explain to him or her some of the good features of the car, while answering questions on friendly terms, and showing the customer that I am equally interested in him as I am in selling a car. Do not hesitate to test drive a car a second time, if you have decided on the particular make and model, so as to make sure that you have made a right choice.

Trading Your Old Car

If you have your old car, you may want to trade it in for a new one. You may have to discuss it with the dealer, or sell it on your own. When you purchase a new car, it does not matter to the salesperson whether you give him your old car as a trade-in. He will make his commission either way, no doubt. For the dealer, however, it does make a difference if the vehicle is well maintained and a late model (see Chapter 15).

However, if you intend to dispose of your old car on your own, it is a good plan to put an ad in your local newspapers. The advantage of such a move is that you would certainly get a better price for your old vehicle that the dealer offers you for the trade-in. But then, you may have to face some aggravating situations, such a strangers calling you at odd hours of the day and night. If this nuisance is in proportion to the extra money you would make by selling your car on your own, and you are able to put up with the annoying calls, then perhaps there would be no problem. However, if it proves otherwise, it is better that you trade it in to avoid all the headaches. In either case, give a thorough cleaning, both inside and out. A clean and neat appearance of your car cannot be stressed enough. A clean and well-maintained car will certainly fetch you a much better price—at least an additional couple of hundred dollars in your pocket.

Your trade-in is often appraised by the manager for the used cars, and decide on the allowance that would be applied towards the purchase of a new car. While you are across the negotiating table for your new car with the salesperson, find out the manager's offer on your trade-in as part of your negotiation. But if the offer on your car is not satisfactory and does not even come close to the fair price you have on your check-list which you gathered through your research work, then you may have to bargain harder (see checklist.) The subject on fair value on trade-ins is explained more elaborately in Chapter Seven. Keep in mind the dealer has his own margin of profit on your trade-in.

It is possible that the dealer may not budge from the original offer. Well, then you have no other option than to dispose of your car on your own. There are plenty of buyers out there, looking for a clean and well-maintained car. You would certainly get the price you expect on your old car. In any case, the trade-in option will always be open to you when you return to negotiate for your new car if you have any second thoughts about your old car.

How Much is a Trade-In Worth?

NADA GUIDE or THE BLUE BOOK are the best reference guides for you. You will find a list of used cars and their fair market value. Almost all the dealers have these guides. Most banks and insurance companies carry copies of the guides. The guides provide up-to-date and comprehensive information regarding the price of used cars. It is a useful reference guide for day-to-day business for the car dealers. One should not have any difficulty in getting hold of a copy for one's personal reference. The average value listed in the above mentioned official used car guide are based on the reports of actual transactions throughout the area. These guides would help you to determine the value of your car and the extra equipment therein.

Familiarize yourself with the meaning of certain business terminology: *Price*—it is the latest average retail value based on the actual sales reports from the new and used car dealers; *Wholesale price* or *Trade-in*—this means the latest average of wholesale value based on auction reports and dealer wholesale reports through a given area.

Demo Sales

Often you may read newspaper advertisements about car demo sales. From time to time, car dealers put on sale the cars used by the employees of the dealership such as salespersons or the owner. A demo vehicle may have been driven about 5,000 to 10,000 miles or less during the year. Demonstration vehicles are untitled cars. However, the factory warranty and everything else remains the same as that of a new car.

As a salesperson, I was rather hesitant to sell a demo car with so many miles on it. Of course, a salesperson selling such a vehicle usually gets paid a flat rate, since the dealer does not make a big profit. No doubt, it is more rewarding for the salesperson to sell a demo vehicle to you. But, then, why would you go for a demo when you are most likely to get a brand new car for the same price?

However, if the salesperson wants to sell you a demo, compare the price with the price of a new car, taking into account the mileage, the wear and tear, and the length of time it was used as a demo. If, however, the salesperson offers a price which you think quite attractive, and you feel deep inside you that you should not refuse, go ahead— strike a deal and come out a winner!

A word of caution may be in order here. Please note that *demo* is a vehicle driven by someone else from the salesperson to the owner. It is a demonstration model. So look into the wear and tear of the vehicle.

Summary

If you want to trade in your car for a new one, have your car well cleaned. Use the trade-in as your only down payment. If it is worth more than you want to put down, ask for the difference in cash.

•

If you are planning to sell your old car on your own, ask for retail value. To find out the retail value you need to check NADA guide book or from blue book.

* * * * * * *

Jake's Hot Tip #104

Get your car cleaned. A neat and clean car puts extra money in your pocket. Fill gas on your own—it may save a few more dollars. Do not use high octane gas unless your owner's manual specifically recommends it. Do not go in for a four-wheel drive unless you need it. You will unnecessarily end up paying extra on the car, tires, gas, and insurance.

Chapter Five

Buying vs. Leasing

You may either buy or lease a new vehicle. There are pros and cons to be considered on the above option. You, as a customer, will have to make the decision as to which choice is right for you. The information in this chapter will help you arrive at the right choice.

Buying

When you buy a car, you purchase it from the dealer, whether on an all-cash down terms or with a small down payment and the balance financed. Once you purchase the vehicle, you are responsible for insurance coverage, maintenance, and everything else that goes along with the car ownership. The car, however, is yours, so you are free to sell it or trade it in any time you want. If your auto is financed, you would have a lien on it. Once your loan is totally paid off, you have the clear title to the car.

Leasing

Some dealers feel that it is a smart way to purchase a new car. You can lease a car for a certain period of time— usually twelve to seventy-two months. The pride of ownership is only during the lease period. At the end of the contract, you are required to return the car to the dealer. However, you could also buy it out-right at the end of your lease period, or finance it if you wish to do so.

One advantage in leasing a car is that your monthly payments are lower than in the conventional financing, because you are only paying the loan down to the estimated residual value. You may be required to pay sales tax and fees for title and license. You are responsible for the full insurance coverage and maintenance of your leased vehicle.

When you lease a vehicle you will get a Guaranteed Trade Value. That means you would know the worth of the car at the end of the lease contract. Often, when you lease a vehicle, the dealer might tell you that no down payment is required, in which case your money is free with you to be invested in your own time, if you prefer to do so. When you lease a vehicle, the lessee is required to place a security deposit besides the first month's lease payment. The security is refundable only at the end of the lease period. The terms of the contract will tell you that you can drive only a certain number of miles. Over and above that mileage allowed, you are charged extra for the additional miles you have put on the car.

The following is an example of a lease agreement based on a $14,000 MSRP[1] vehicle:

Number of months	48
Monthly Lease Payment[2]	$296.07
Refundable Security Deposit	300.00
Total Cash Due at Beginning of Lease	596.07
Total Payment	$14,211.00
Purchase Option Price[3]	4,928.00
Total Mileage Penalty over 60,000 Miles	$ 8 per mile

Most dealers and manufacturers have heavy promotions on leasing. Sales people usually make a higher commission on a leased vehicle than on a sale. Most dealers

---

1   Manufacturer's Suggested Retail Price.
2   Does not include license and title fees, sales/use tax, or insurance.
3   Varies by vehicle model, usage, and length of lease.

have leasing agents who would be happy to lease you a car. The salesperson in the dealership does most of the work for you and then turns it over to a leasing agent. If the salesperson asks you whether you are interested in leasing and you do not want to consider it, you may plainly tell him that you're not interested in such a deal.

As a car salesman, my sales manager once asked me to suggest a lease to a customer who asked for a lower monthly payment. I was expected to convince the buyer of the advantages of leasing or direct him to the leasing agent in the sales office. The manager advised me that my commission would be larger if the buyer leased the vehicle he wanted. I was, however, more concerned about my customer than the supposed large commission I might have earned by leasing him a vehicle. The customer, an honest, hardworking person, did not want a lease. He preferred to purchase the vehicle outright. Nevertheless, the leasing agent spoke to my customer and convinced him to lease instead of the outright purchase I proposed. Do not allow yourself to be talked out of buying the vehicle if, indeed, that is what you really want. Firmly insist on your intention—whether on buying or leasing a vehicle.

You may lease a new car or a used car, if you so desire. No doubt, the new car prices are skyrocketing steadily. More and more vehicles are being leased. Nowadays, many prospective buyers may prefer to lease either a new or used one because of the skyrocketing prices, which is a heavy strain on an ordinary man's budget.

You may have to shop around for the best deal, if you intend to lease a vehicle. Your leasing rights are a "capital" idea—you have the right to know the full selling price or "capitalized" cost of a leased vehicle. This will help you to know which leasing company can offer you the best deal.

Worth a second opinion? You have the right to an independent damage appraisal prior to or following termination of the lease. *Please "release" me*—you have the right to terminate the lease at any time after fifty percent of the lease term, or earlier, if such provision is entered in the lease.

There is a limit to the early termination charges based on the terms of the law. *"Keep covered"*—a "gap" is the difference between an insurance company's coverage on the theft or damage on your leased vehicle, and what you owe on the vehicle. You have a right to a "gap" insurance with no additional charges.

Consumers in New York are now protected by the strict auto leasing laws in the country. If you are planning to lease a vehicle in New York, you may contact the New York Attorney General's office to obtain a copy of *Consumer's Guide to Automobile Leasing*. Residents of other states may contact the Attorney General's office in their respective state or local consumer agency. Keep in mind that the lemon law covers both new, as well as leased cars. The lessee is, of course, responsible for repairs and maintenance of the car (see Chapter twelve on lemon laws.) When you lease a vehicle your obligations are, as follows: all manufacturer recommended maintenance, oil changes and usage of the vehicle in compliance with the terms of the lease, but never for any illegal purpose. The lessee is required to maintain automobile insurance, as specified in the terms of the lease agreement.

A note of caution—avoid leasing a car at year-end, as new models for the forthcoming year are already on the market. Why should you take an old model when a new model is available; besides, you would be a year ahead.

Some of the Commonly Asked Questions in the Leasing of a Vehicle

Q: Can I lease a car with no money down?
A: Yes, you can.

Q: If leasing companies need a down payment, how much would it be?
A: Yes and no. Usually, the first month payment as a security deposit, in addition to taxes and fees will have to be paid in advance. However, you could negotiate for zero money down leasing.

Q: How long can one lease a vehicle?
A: From twelve to seventy-two months. The terms, however, may vary. The popular terms are 24 months, 36 months, or 48 months.

Q: Who is responsible for the maintenance?
A: You are, along with all the manufacturer's recommended servicing and oil changes.

Q: Who is responsible for maintaining the auto insurance?
A: You are. Maintenance of required automobile insurance is specified in your lease agreement.

Q: What will I do with my car after the lease expires?
A: Return the vehicle to the lessor and walk away, or you may purchase the vehicle at a predetermined price, if such option is offered to you in the lease agreement.

Q: If I am only leasing a vehicle for 24 months, why should I pay full sales tax?

A: You may have to find out about it from the lessor.

Q: What is the difference between a closed-end and an open-end lease?

A: In a "closed-end" lease the lessor bears the market valuation risk. In an "open-end" lease the lessee shares in the responsibility for the vehicle's worth at lease end. However, most manufacturers prefer a "close-end" lease.

Q: Who is the lessee?

A: You, the person who leases the vehicle.

Q: Who is the lessor?

A: The dealer or the leasing company who leases the vehicle to you, the lessee.

Q: What is "lease end residual value," "lease end value," or "guaranteed future value"?

A: They are the same. This value is set by the lessor at the start of the lease. It varies according to the lease term, mileage allowance and the make/model of the vehicle. This value is estimated at fair market value of the leased vehicle at the scheduled end of the lease.

Q: What is the "purchase option"?

A: This gives you the option to buy the vehicle at the lease end for a predetermined price. The purchase option is always negotiable.

Q: What is a "lease charge"?

A: It is a finance charge, including other administrative expenses, paid when leasing a vehicle.

Q: What is "capitalized cost"?

A: It is cash amount agreed upon by both parties. This may include taxes, fees, and other charges.

Q: Where can I lease a vehicle?

A: One can lease a vehicle from a dealer, a manufacturer, or from a leasing company.

Q: What should I do if I have a problem with "wearing thin"?

A: Contact the attorney general's office to mediate a "wear and tear" dispute. The attorney general's office has civil enforcement authority.

Q: Am I entitled to a second opinion?

A: You have the right to an independent damage appraisal prior to, or following, termination of the lease.

Q: Can I lease a used car?

A: Of course, you can.

Q: Is a leased car covered by the lemon laws and secret warranty?

A: You are covered on both items.

Q: Is a security deposit necessary?

A: Yes and no. If you have placed a security deposit, which is refundable at the lease end. However, the allowable charges for the excess mileage put on the car would be deducted before final disbursement of the security deposit.

Q: Is there any penalty for excess mileage?

A: Yes. You may incur extra charges for the additional mileage over and above the mileage allowed in the lease contract.

Q: If I lease a vehicle for three years or 36,000 miles, and drive 44,000 miles, am I responsible for the additional 8,000 miles?

A: Yes, you are. If the warranty is only for three years or 36,000 miles anything over and above those miles is your responsibility.

Q: Do they charge for wear and tear?

A: You are supposed to keep the vehicle in good operating condition. However, each leasing company or dealer may have its own governing terms.

Q: Who pays for "GAP" protection?

A: You may have to consult the lessor. You have the right to "GAP" insurance with no additional charges.

Summary

If you want to lease instead of buy, obtain a leasing guide from the Attorney General's office, or from your local consumer agency.

* * * * * * *

Jake's Hot Tip #105

Keep a sharp eye on the fine print. If you have a problem or complaint, always speak to someone in authority at the dealership. As a business person, you may be enti-

tled to a tax deduction-on your lease payments. Perhaps, if you buy a car for your business, it could go under your business expenses for tax purposes. If you put your auto insurance under your company name, you may also be able to deduct the expense. Consult your tax advisor. He may be able to enlighten you on this matter further.

Chapter Six

Cash Buyer/Payment Buyer

Cash Buyer

Whether you pay all cash or finance part of it, you are called a cash buyer, as long as you are negotiating on a selling price.

Mr. and Mrs. P were cash buyers. They were an average family who knew exactly which model they wanted. They liked everything about the Ford Taurus I showed them, including the color, and the various options that were offered.

Mr. P alone earned more than $5,400 a month. The couple had no financial problems. They wanted to put $5,000 down payment and finance the balance. They also wanted a good deal on a 1991 Ford Taurus.

Total before discount	$16,058.00
Special added discount	1,050.00
Suggested Retail Price	$15,008.00
Dealer's Cost	13,212.00
Dealer's Profit Per Invoice	$ 1,796.00

I sat down with Mr. and Mrs. P and worked out a good deal for them. I sold them the car for $11,887 with the following breakdown:

Dealer's Cost Per Invoice	$13,212.00
Selling Price	11,887.00
	$1,325.00 below dealer's invoice
Suggested Retail Price	$15,008.00
Final Selling Price	11,887.00
Total Savings	$3,121.00

The special added discount of $1,050 was from the manufacturer. The total price before the discount was $16,058. Mr. and Mrs. P bought the car for $11,887.

Any other salesperson, perhaps, would negotiate with Mr. and Mrs. P on the amount of $16,058 price. He would have told them about the $1,050 special added discount and sold them the car for $15,008; although the actual dealer's cost was $13,212, the dealer would have made a clean profit of $1,796 on the vehicle, at that selling price.

Mr. and Mrs. P, however, paid $11,887 for a brand new Ford Taurus, fully loaded with options such as a V-6 engine, air conditioning, cruise control and power door locks. They saved cash of $3,121 on their vehicle and drove off happily.

The total "drive-out" price on their new automobile was as follows:

Selling Price	$11,887.00
Sales Tax	713.22
Documentary Fee	25.00
License Fee	63.80
Title Fee	10.00
State Inspection Fee	15.75
Total Price	**$12,714.77**

After we worked out the best possible deal, I sent the couple to the finance office where they could negotiate for a good interest rate.

They picked up the new Ford Taurus with a full tank of gas, about two hours later. While Mr. and Mrs. P were very happy with the deal they got on their dream car, I received my paltry commission voucher for $50 the next day.

Sales people are paid on straight commission, which is usually 25% of the dealer's gross profit. The dealer's gross profit would have been $1,796 from the $15,008 sales price, and the sales person's commission $449.00.

Most sales people want to keep the profit high, so they can earn a higher commission. In order to do this, they may try to sell you a lot of extras on the car. As a customer, however, you want to get the best deal possible.

Payment Buyer

Mr. and Mrs. M, a young couple with a baby from Houston, Texas, wanted to replace their sports car with a family car to accommodate a small family. They were interested in a used car because of their tight budget. They could only afford payments of $300 a month. I was able to sit down with them to strike a deal. Subsequently, we walked through the lot and found a car to their tastes and specifications. Mr. M took the car for a test drive and was fully satisfied with the automobile.

I needed the approval of my manager before I could sell the car on monthly payments. I managed to obtain this from the manager. I was able to furnish the required paper work in an hour or so. Mr. and Mrs. M got the car they wanted and decided to sell their sports car themselves, rather than trade it in. As a salesperson, I did very little work on that deal, and there was not much negotiation.

Nevertheless, I received my commission the next day—a voucher for over $550. How about that? A good commission, indeed! But, imagine the profit made by the finance manager and the dealer.

By the same token, if the couple had done some shopping, compared prices, and buckled down to negotiate, they could have gotten a brand new car at a lower monthly payment than they are paying for their used vehicle. A little homework can go a long way.

When a salesperson asks you what you can afford to pay on a monthly basis, do not name a figure just ask him the selling price. Then, go to the finance office to discuss the interest rate on the loan you wish to take. However, if the interest rate is higher than you expected, then negotiate. If they will not work with you, you can always try to get a better deal on your car loan through a bank or credit union, which takes only a day or two to obtain on your own. Chances are that the finance manager will then offer you a good rate, so that he does not lose a prospective customer.

No Money Down

Another customer, Theresa of Sugarland, Texas, came in to buy a new car. She knew exactly what model and options she wanted. Her choice of color was either black or white, but those colors were not available in stock at the time. The customer decided to wait until the car with the color or her choice was available. I assured her that I would check the incoming car list and find out when the next consignment of cars with colors the customer had chosen would be in, and that I would give her a call as soon as they arrived. It wasn't long before the vehicle she wanted arrived at our lot. I gave her a call and informed her about it. She came down immediately to see the car. After test driving the auto, she decided to purchase the car right away. Notwithstanding the fact, Theresa had two offers from other car dealers. She said she would do business with me, if I could give her a better price than the offers she had. I realized that this smart lady had done some good homework, and knew exactly what she wanted, so we could sit down and negotiate to complete the deal to her satisfaction.

At this point, she told me she does not have any money for the down payment on the car. Furthermore, she requested that I find out if I could apply the rebate towards the down payment...a smart move! Theresa had a young child and financial problems—a problem that many a young parent faces today. The rebate for the fourdoor Hyundai Excel was $750. The best thing I liked about this lady was that she had done her homework, and had come well prepared, and was well acquainted with all the necessary information, and had figured out the price of the car, as well as the lowest interest rate.

I approached the sales manager with the buyer's order the customer had brought with her, along with the worksheet I had completed with all the information about the new car, for approval. The manager agreed on the selling price, but said that the customer should pay at least $500 as a down payment. I wanted to help this good lady, and requested that the manager forward her credit application to the finance company or to the bank to process her application, with the rebate she was entitled to as the down payment.[4]

Two days later, the finance company approved the loan and Theresa came down to sign the appropriate papers and pick up her new car. The sales manager, somehow wanted some cash from my customer, but she was not prepared to

---

4   *Down Payment*: A portion of the car purchase price that borrowers pay.

pay a single red cent extra, not even for a protection plan. Theresa got what she wanted.

Although the salesmanager and finance managers tried to pressure her into providing a down payment of $500, she had been successful in the purchase of her new Hyundai Excel without cash in her hand, because she stood her ground and knew how to negotiate

The down payment is normally the part of the dealer's profit. Finance companies usually only fund the cost of the vehicle. They do not finance the *profit*. So, if the dealer offers a rebate[5], why not use it for a down payment instead of cash from your pocket? You pay only the taxes, title, and license. That way, you would make your purchase with a minimum amount of cash in hand. If no rebate is offered, then, of course, negotiate for as little cash down as possible towards the down payment.

If you purchase the car with only the rebate as down payment, then the dealer may not make as much money up front. He may then try to compensate the former at the back end, by financing. Well, make sure that you negotiate on the interest at the bank rate. You will have secured a good deal when you get both a good price and a good interest rate. Only then you will have come out a smart buyer. That is why I call Theresa a smart buyer, when she bought her brand new Hyundai Excel. The manufacturer did give her the option of a cash rebate, but not on the low interest rate financing. She could only get a cash rebate of $750. However, Theresa did have the option to keep the rebate or use it as part of the down payment. Being a smart customer, she used her $750 towards the down payment. She did not have to come up with any cash in hand. On the other hand, she saved some cash on the sales tax. How could she do that? Let me give you the rundown:

---

5   Cash back

Assume the price of the car is $10,000. Eight percent tax on $10,000=

$10,000 x 8% = $800.00 sales tax
Factory rebate $750.00
Final cost of car—
         $10,000
    -       750
         $9,250
Tax on $9,250 $740
Sales Tax Saved $60

Summary

Call various sources to check interest rates (see check-list) before making any commitment or accepting the dealer's financing.

•

Make sure the dealer does not increase the price of the car when he "applies" the rebate.

* * * * * * *

Jake's Hot Tip #106

Avoid using home equity loans to pay for your vehicle. The interest rate may be competitive and the interest you pay is usually a tax write-off on your income taxes, on creative car financing, such as a second mortgage on your home. Some dealers do this to get out of "auto loan interest rate ceiling." Beware of the combo loan (one payment plan), such as your home, car, and the credit card payments that would entrap you with a huge, one monthly payment.

If you miss, you lose your home!

Chapter Seven

Negotiation

Once you have decided on the model and color of the vehicle you are interested in and plan to purchase, presumably you are well acquainted with the various options that are available to you, checked the vehicle in detail to your satisfaction, both inside and out, have chosen a dealer you prefer to do business with, you are ready to venture on making a deal. At this juncture, you might be in a dilemma as to what to do with your old car.

There are several options. If you would not like to keep your old car as a second car, you could trade it in. If you prefer, you can sell it on your own. That will save you maintenance and insurance costs (see chapter on trade-ins.)

Now you come to the hard part. You are across the negotiating table with the dealer to seriously negotiate the final price for the vehicle you have in mind. You would do well to keep in mind that there are two types of buyers: (1) Cash buyers and (2) Payment buyers. As explained in the previous chapter, do not get confused or be intimidated by these jaw-breaking terminology. You are a cash buyer regardless of how you pay for your new vehicle—whether you pay all cash down or finance it through a bank or dealer or the manufacturer. Do not be concerned about the payment procedure at this point. Let your first priority be to negotiate the final price of the vehicle you are interested in. Once the final price of the vehicle is settled, then you could look into the various options that are available to you with regard to payment. Refer to Chapter Six for a detailed explanation on *cash buyers* and *payment buyers*. An example might help for a clear understanding of the rather subtle point. Well, let us assume that a certain payment buyer customer has a certain amount of cash available for an initial down payment. Thereafter, all that the customer is worried about is his monthly payments, and not the final price of the vehicle or the interest rate on the loan he would obtain towards the purchase of the vehicle. You would know that while you make your monthly payments for a specific period of time, the interest rate on the loan can make a sizable difference in what you pay for your new vehicle in the long run.

By this time, you will have reached the second stage of your negotiation. After you have test driven the car to your satisfaction and have decided on your new vehicle you are in the sales person's office to complete paper work. While you are there, the salesperson will complete the necessary paper work, such as filling out a *buyer's order* or *worksheet*[6] with your name, address, telephone number, and other required details.

In the next stage, you enter a tricky part. Your alertness is of importance when the salesperson is trying to negotiate for your trade-in, if you have one. If you do, then you may give him the necessary particulars of your vehicle, such as the model, type of car, the mileage on the meters, and so on and so forth. The salesperson, of course, will jot down those particulars you supplied for your trade-in on his work sheet known as *Appraisal Form Slip*,[7] when you opt for your trade-in to the dealer with whom you are negotiating for your new car. You should have a clear title for your car while you are trading your old car. In the event that you do not have the clear title, then that would necessitate some

---

6   See the back of this book for a Work Sheet.
7   See the back of this book for Appraisal Form Slip.

additional forms to be filled out. You are required to provide the necessary information of the lien-holder on your vehicle and to facilitate the salesperson in verifying the outstanding balance you owe on your car. Finally, the salesperson would certainly like to know the price you expect for your trade in. Do not give the figures that you have on your personal check list, as you would know the worth of your old vehicle you want to trade in, since you have done some good "homework" on your own and you may have all the necessary information at hand. On the contrary, ask the salesperson for his quotation for your trade-in.[8] On having his estimate price for your car against yours, you will be in a better position to negotiate for a better price. Remember, the idea is that you should get the maximum cash for your trade-in while you bring down the price of your new vehicle to the lowest possible minimum (buy low, sell high). But then, perhaps, it is easier said than done.

Well, that's what negotiation is all about. If you do not have a trade-in, however, then, of course, you will restrict your negotiation to the price of the vehicle you intend to purchase. The salesperson might quote a rough estimate for your trade-in, or he may pass over your car to the manager for the used cars. The manager may check your vehicle, inside and out, test drive it to see the performance to determine the fair value of your trade-in. The procedure might take some time. Perhaps you will have ample time to relax; you could, as well, walk across the street to enjoy a good cup of coffee. Don't expect the salesperson to provide you with one. Remember that you are there to do business, and not on a friendly social visit!

---

8   You already know the value of your car because you called the bank or checked in NADA Guidebook and gotten the retail wholesale price and loan value.

When the salesperson returns with the estimate for your trade-in in hand, he might sit down with you to seriously discuss the method of payment on your new car. Whether you pay in cash or finance through a dealer, bank, or through manufacturer's discount financing (see chapter on financing), under no circumstances discuss about financing at this point. You have not yet come to that stage. Just restrict your negotiation only on the final price of the car. A note of caution would be worthwhile at this juncture. DO NOT fill out any credit applications if you plan to visit several dealerships to negotiate a good price on your new vehicle. Every time you apply for a credit check it will show on your credit report.[9] This may work against you. Besides, you wouldn't want every dealer to have a peek into your credit history when they run a credit check on you, would you? However, it may be necessary to fill one in at one or two dealerships where you are comfortable.

Finally, the salesperson will have before him the price for the new car and the allowance for your trade-in. Make sure that the salesperson works with you and that you are in control. You should be able to leave happy with a good deal. By the same token, if you are not satisfied with the price of the vehicle you intend to purchase or the trade-in, or both, then the manager will send the floor manager, or the manager himself comes down for a satisfactory negotiation. The floor manager has the power to use his discretion to override the decision of the salesperson, as it is the manager who makes the final decision on the deal. As far as you are concerned, it matters very little to you to whom you speak, insofar as you get the best deal on your purchase and on your trade-in and come out a winner.

---

9   *Credit Report:* A borrower's history of meeting financial obligations on a timely basis which most lenders report to credit bureaus.

After all that is said and done, you may realize that it is easier said than done. Well, if you are not satisfied with the allowance quoted by the salesperson, then reveal to him the price you have gotten from the bank, which you have on your personal check list.[10] Let him also know that you mean business, and that you would not hesitate to take your business elsewhere, where you can strike a good deal to your satisfaction. Let nothing intimidate you or cause you to become over-anxious. Be in total control during negotiation. However, total control would be rather difficult, if not impossible, if your concentration is encumbered with distraction which may, in turn, undermine your negotiation. Do not have your little children tag along. Much as we love them they are, unfortunately, of no help to you in a serious business deal. But, on the contrary, they would be a source of distraction which would undermine your negotiation.

You would do well to keep in mind that the salesperson or the manager will use every smart trick in the world to derive the maximum profits. Be equally smart, so that they do not outwit you. You are investing your hard-earned money on your dream car. Hang tough! It may be the biggest investment you ever make. So spending a couple of hours at the dealership to negotiate and plan your purchase in detail, would certainly prove worthwhile and pay its own dividend of which you would be proud.

Once you are able to settle on the price of the vehicle you're looking for, the manager or salesperson may talk you into the urgency of a deposit to reserve your vehicle stating that particular model, being hot and in great demand, are in short supply, and so forth. Stick to your ground and pay no deposit either in cash or by check. You can imagine the hassle, the time, and the energy wasted to get a refund of your

---

10   Refer to checklist

deposit in the event the deal falls into the cracks. Why walk through such tight corners? However, if you judge a deposit is a wise move for reasons of your own then, as most of the dealers accept credit cards, you would do well to use that facility to his advantage and obtain a receipt for the amount paid, which may help you to a quick refund of your deposit, if the deal does not materialize.

Sometimes it is good to do negotiations over the phone when you have all the necessary information ready at hand, when you have test driven the car and are satisfied with its performance, and other details. Negotiate for the lowest price possible with the salesperson with conjunction with the manager, as he has the final word on all sales. Jot down the final price agreed upon on your check list. This might come in handy, if there happens to be a discrepancy on the price agreed on in the later stage. Chances are that when the manager is too busy with his responsibilities, the salesperson, himself, may low-ball[11] the price to his advantage to keep your interest going and keep you in his dealership for the sale. A few dollars here and there can add up to your benefit and lower your final cost and come out a winner.

Another interesting "game" a salesperson may play to boost his profit is to wet your appetite with sweet talk on various extras in the car, impressing on you the importance of such extras, such as rust-proofing, paint-sealing and whatnot. The price of these sundries may add up to anywhere from $500 to $1,000. The dealer may use this figure to leverage the negotiation on the final price, with ample room for a better profit for himself. *Local Dealer Service* is yet another game of the salesperson to boast his personal gain, which may drain your purse for about $300—I should say

---

11   Low-ball quoting priced over the phone below dealer cost is usually done by the sales person to get you into the dealership.

$299.95 to be more accurate. Very attractive and necessary as it may sound, just resist the temptation and spell it out to him emphatically—NO extras!

Hard as it is to believe, in this country of ours, women-folk end up paying more for their dream vehicle than the white male. Yet, it is a well known fact according to a recent survey. The same applies to the minority group of car-buyers. It almost sounds like discrimination, but the fact of the matter is that an Afro-American female ends up paying the highest. This book will be of great help to you, if you adhere to the suggestions therein. Discrimination of whatever sort will have no place. Remember—USE OF KNOWLEDGE IS POWER.

At this point, a few words of advice may not be out of place. As far as possible, avoid weekend shopping for cars. The dealership may be overcrowded, and you may find it difficult to locate a salesperson to talk to, much less test drive a car. It may prove that you have wasted your time and energy for nothing.

Summary

Stay in control during negotiation. Remember a large investment is involved. The more you know about the strategies, the better your chances are to strike a good deal. The dealership sells cars every day, so their salespeople are well-trained in the business.

* * * * * * *

Jake's Hot Tip #107
Remember, the basic principle of dealing with the dealer is to negotiate, and to be polite, but firm. Don't display

too much emotion or anxiety. Never give out cash figures you can afford per month. Do not hesitate to walk out through same revolving door that you came in, if you are not satisfied with the deal. Another thing to remember is that you should not buy on impulse or accept spot delivery, unless it is completely acceptable to you.

Chapter Eight

How Much Down Payment is Required?

The amount of down payment on a car usually depends on you, banks, credit unions, insurance companies, dealers, and manufacturers require you to put down at least twenty percent of the total price of the vehicle. Some consumers put down as little as five hundred dollars, while others may provide as much as fifty percent of the total price.

You may negotiate on the down payment, especially when you are getting a low interest rate. The money you save on your down payment can then be used for other investments such as a money market fund, where you can earn maximum interest and have the money available to you. One can always use some extra cash in hand. As they say, a bird in the hand is worth two in the bush.

If you do save up a little money, don't use it all for your down payment; you may need it for an emergency. Besides, why use your money when you can use other people's money. How would one use other people's money? Well, what I mean by *other people's money* is that you can finance the entire automobile through an auto loan. It is advisable to take an auto loan rather than a personal loan for your car payment, for the simple reason that it is difficult to secure a loan without collateral. Besides, the interest rate is higher on personal loans than on auto loans.

If you have a trade-in, you could use that as a down payment. If, however, the trade-in is worth more than the required down payment, you could claim the difference in cash. If, for example. your trade-in is worth $3,000 and you want to put only $1,000 down, the difference is $2,000. You should get that amount back from the dealer.

Manufacturers often offer rebates or cash back offers if their sales are slow. Watch for these special offers. You can use the rebate as a down payment towards your new car, which is anywhere between $500 to $2,000, depending on the manufacturer and the model of the vehicle.

The car manufacturers offer rebates from time to time through dealers. Find out from the salesperson the amount of such rebate. That amount could be used as a down payment. It is as simple as that! The rebate given does not effect the selling price of the vehicle, so you can negotiate the amount, as explained earlier. Remember—the rebate the dealer offers you comes from the manufacturer and not from the dealer, so it is not subject to negotiation.

Sometimes the manufacturer may offer a low interest rate on financing. It could be as low as 2.9% for 36 months or 3.9% for 48 months. It is a good offer and it is worthwhile to accept the dealer's financing. Put as little money down as possible. Be aware that the dealer usually instructs the salesperson to get the maximum down payment from the customer.

During the negotiation, you might notice the sales manager write $3,000 payable cash down on the buyer's order, with $350 as a monthly payment for 48 months. This is done deliberately in order to surprise you and get you thinking on the high side. However, if you want to put $500 down or pay just enough to cover the tax, title, and licensing fees, don't hesitate to tell the salesperson the exact amount you are comfortable with.

Don't be concerned with the monthly payment at this point. Your concern should now be the selling price.

Subsequently, you can ask the finance manager about your monthly payment and interest rates. Remember how Theresa bought her car—everyone at the dealership, including the sales manager and finance manager, tried to pressure her into a cash down payment. She refused to budge or compromise her plan. She managed to get her dream car using only the rebate of $750 as her down payment.

Summary

In order to find out about the various incentives such as cash rebates, low interest rate financing, factory-to-dealer cash program, carry-over allowance, special sales, and rebates for first-time car buyers and college students, check with Automotive News. To obtain a copy of this publication, write to:

**Automotive News
965 East Jefferson Avenue
Detroit, Ml 48207**

**For *Hemmings Motor News*,
call 1-800-227-4373.**

* * * * * * *

Jake's Hot Tip #108
Use as little cash as possible for your down payment, especially when you are getting the manufacturer's low interest rate financing.

Chapter Nine

Where Can You Find the Lowest Interest Rate?

1. Banks
2. Credit Unions
3. Dealers/Manufacturers

You need to check with all the above sources for the lowest interest rate available. Call at least three different banks. Compare the interest rates, the terms of the loan and its repayment, which will help you arrive at a decision.

Bank Loan

It is not always necessary to have your account with a particular bank in order to obtain an auto loan. Most banks will want to accommodate you. Note down on your check list the lowest quote you received, including the name, telephone number of the bank and the loan officer.

It is very important that you have this information at hand when you visit the dealership, so that you are able to negotiate with the finance manager for a competitive rate. If, for some reason, he cannot accommodate you, get the auto loan from a bank.

Some banks may offer pre-approved loans. You may lock in the interest rate, if you think it is quite reasonable. The banks usually give you three to six weeks time to consider. That will give you sufficient time to shop around for a vehicle of your choice.

The following is an example of a typical automobile loan:

Amount of loan	$15,000.00
Annual percentage rate	10%
Monthly payments	$380.44
Number of months	48

The figures of $15,000 shown above as the loan, is being borrowed from a bank. At the end of four years, the borrower has paid a total of $18,261.12, including the principal, which is $15,000. The interest amount of $3,261.12 at the rate of 10%. You might have noticed the advantage to this is that you know exactly the amount of your monthly payments, so you will be able to adjust your budget accordingly.

Credit Union

This is another desirable source for an automobile loan. Their rate is sometimes lower than that of the bank. If you have a credit union where you work, you could visit or call to inquire about the loan you intend to take. Perhaps it would be easy for you to work with a credit union, since they know about you and your credit history. It is very important that you jot down all the information you gathered on your checklist.

Company 401(K) Plan

Borrowing money is always a painful task, but some time or another, borrowing may be a necessity in certain situations. There are various options and more lending institutions with competitive interest rates on the loans. But the conditions of repayment may differ from institution to institution or bank to bank. Hence, careful personal research on the matter is a wise idea.

However, if you have the privilege of a (401)K plan, taking advantage of that facility would be in your best interest. You can borrow a maximum of $50,000, depending on the amount you have in your account. Usually you can borrow half of what you have in your account and you will have five years to repay. Your firm may determine the method of repayment, the interest rate and the amount of monthly payment. The said monthly payments are attached to your payroll and deducted monthly at the source. The aforesaid method of borrowing and repayment has its own advantages and, of course, its own disadvantages, too. Any defaulting on your part in repayment may incur tax on the balance you owe, in addition to a penalty. But then. the advantage is that your vehicle will not be repossessed and deprive you of your personal transportation. Furthermore, since it is your own money, a credit check does not come into the picture. As a matter of fact, by and large, it is a good option. Plan ahead. It takes time to close a deal. Consult your accountant with regard to tax deductions before making your final commitment.

Major Insurance Companies

This is another reliable source for useful information. The insurance agent may be able to provide you with necessary information and the competitive interest rate. Write it down on your checklist and keep it handy. Insurance agents work through the local banks. You should be able to do the work over the telephone at your convenience. If you find a lower rate than that of your bank and credit union, then it is certainly worthwhile to go for it without any hesitation or delay.

I called my automobile insurance agent when I purchased my new BMW. When I told him that I was shopping for the best rate, he offered me a loan at 9.75% through the same bank which had offered me a 10.5% annual percentage rate.

He already had all the information he needed. All I had to do was to visit his office and sign some documents and the security agreement. So, my car was financed for $14,000 with an annual percentage rate of 9.75% and a monthly payment of $353.40 for 48 months A very good deal indeed!

Dealers

Most dealers can provide automobile financing. They make all the arrangements with local banks. He will take your credit application and send it to various lending institutions. Some of these may be banks which you had contacted. The banks, however, will give the dealer a better rate than they would give an individual. If you apply for financing through a dealer, it may, perhaps, cost you less than bank financing. Since the dealership buys in bulk, this dealer gets a bulk rate. Besides, the dealers do all the paper work.

The difference between what the dealer charges you and what he pays to a bank is called *spread*. It is their profit on the financing. It is very important that you negotiate on the interest rate. If the finance manager charges you more than the bank, credit union or insurance agent, let them know that you have done your homework, and their rates do not tally with the one you have gotten as a competitive rate of interest.

Manufacturer's Financing

Most major manufacturers have their own financing. The arrangements can be made through the dealer. Manufacturers, from time to time, do offer a low annual interest rate in order to sell their cars fast and reduce their inventory. They may offer 1.9% for 24 months, or 2.9% for 36 months, or 3.9% for 48 months, the lowest financing that would be available. One major foreign car manufacturer offers 3.5% annual percentage rate for 48 months. Keep in mind that when they offer such a low rate, you will put down a very minimum down payment. The following are major automobile manufacturers who offer a rate quite competitive, and is worth giving a try:

General Motors
Ford
Chrysler

Their financing is through General Motors Acceptance Corporation, Ford Motor Credit Corporation, and Chrysler Credit Corporation respectively.

It is extremely important that you look for manufacturer's low interest rates. The money you save on finance charges could be quite substantial, so why not take advantage of the lowest interest rate you can possibly get.

Summary

Keep your checklist handy all the time.

* * * * * * *

Jake's Hot Tip #109

Look for manufacturer's offers of low interest rate financing.

Chapter Ten

Financing

There are many different sources for financing available to new car buyers, such as a bank, credit union, the dealer/manufacturer where the vehicle was purchased, and so on. When financing through a dealer, he and the manufacturers which offer financing are required to guarantee that the rate of interest of loans will not increase once the car is ordered. If a trade-in allowance is agreed upon, it must be written in the contract. The said allowance cannot be reduced at a later date unless the value of the vehicle has decreased, due to normal wear and tear.

Manufacturers may offer low interest rate financing from time to time. When they do, the savings on interest rates are enormous. Now, if you accept the dealer/manufacturer financing, the salesperson might ask you to fill out a complete credit application after you have settled on the final selling price. The salesperson will take all paper work to the sales manager for his approval, and then to the finance manager. While you are waiting, the finance manager will look into the buyer's order, credit report, and other relevant data. The salesperson will then bring you into the finance office to gather additional information. All this information will be fed into a computer. Thereafter, you may be asked to fill in the following, duly signed by you:

1. Buyer's order
2. Title form[12]

---

12   Title: A document that shows evidence of ownership of an automobile.

3. Power of attorney
4. Odometer form
5. Security agreement

Do not sign any forms if anything is left blank; unless you are certain of what you attach your signature to. You must receive a copy of all documents you have signed. You would not sign your death bond, would you?

You will be told how much you are financing, what your monthly payments would be, and the percentage of interest rate. If the interest rate quoted is too high, look squarely at the finance manager's eyes and let him know that your bank or credit union has given you a much better rate. Show him your check list on which you have written all the pertinent information. Then the finance manager is very likely to match that amount. Most dealers work with local banks and they know the going rate. If he charges you more than the going rate, don't hesitate to say, "OH, NO!!!"

It is always good to finance through the dealer from whom you purchase your car, because it saves you both time and energy. But, if the finance manager does not match the rate on your checklist, then you have no other choice than to obtain the loan from the institution which quoted you a better rate. Now consider the fact that you succeeded in getting a car you wanted at a good price, because you negotiated well. You may have to negotiate hard to get a good interest rate, too. Only then will your homework and your hard work pay off.

People are often too enthusiastic about their new car, and are in a hurry to drive it home. Do not exhibit to the finance manager your eagerness in your purchase, or give any clue of being tired negotiating a good rate. Take the new car home only if and when you get the right deal. You may be in the finance office from 30 to 45 minutes, depending on how fast the manager can work with you.

The finance manager might try to raise your payments by adding expensive extras like payment protection (credit insurance), extended service or warranty contracts to your car payments. Credit insurance is almost never required for financing. When the finance manager suggests that, just say *thank you, but no thanks*. However, you may like to consider the extended warranty providing you get a good price. Shop and compare it with direct marketers like Geico. You would also do well to compare it with major warranty companies such as Ryon Warranty Services, Western National Corporation (see Appendix). Refer to Chapter Eleven for further information on new car warranties. Many independent service contract companies have gone broke and left customers holding the bag. If you want the security of a service contract, look at what the manufacturers and major insurance companies have to offer. You may want to make sure you have proper insurance coverage. Before you pick up the vehicle, call your insurance agent and request coverage for your car. If you financed the car through the dealer, ask the insurance agent to call the finance manager so that he can verify the coverage, since the dealer will not deliver the vehicle to you unless he knows the car is covered by an insurance policy.

Co-Signature

If you are a first-time car buyer and do not have established credit, the bank or dealer from whom you are getting your financing may ask you for a co-signature—usually from your parents or guardian, who would guarantee the payment if you default. If you are under age, of course, you will be required to have a parent or guardian co-sign. Check with the vendor, since requirements may vary.

Credit Cards

One of the many ways of saving is by using credit cards. General Motors has their own credit card, but other major manufacturers have credit through various banks. Credit cards can be used like any other bank credit cards such as Visa and Master Card. The advantage of having an auto-maker's credit card even though you have your own card, is that the automaker's card will give you the power to purchase things at discount rates, as well as gain bonus points towards the purchase of a new vehicle down the line.

Application forms may be obtained either from the manufacturer or from the bank. Your card may be issued to you on approval of the bank. However, the interest rate and payment procedure may vary from bank to bank. Why not take advantage of the credit cards when the going is good? Ford Motor Company has a credit card through CitiBank. Presently, you may obtain one with a 5% rebate for every purchase you make on a Ford or Lincoln-Mercury car, besides earning an additional 5% promotional rate at participating rental companies, such as Hertz and Texaco. You may also get rebates on the rental of luxury cars such as Lincoln or Jaguar.

To obtain a Visa or Master Card from General Motors, write to the following address:

General Motors Card
P.O. Box 80082
Salinas, CA 93912-0082

Credit application: 1 /800-846-2273
Customer service: 1/800-947-1000

To obtain a Ford credit card write to the following address:

CitiBank
New Card Member Service
14700 Citicorp Drive
Hagerstown, MD 21749-9723

Telephone: 1/800-374-7777, ext. 83

At present, there are no annual fees for auto-maker's credit cards. Please note that credit cards are as good as cash reserve. Obtain as many as you need. They will certainly come in handy in the event you lose your job or become disabled. You will know that you have some money in the bank; even though it is not your own, you have the power to use it.

If you are accustomed to paying your credit card bills in full each month within the grace period (normally 25 days), you will be paying no interest (finance charge) on your payments. Meanwhile, your money is earning interest for that duration. However, if you are carrying credit cards from American Express, Chemical Bank, Discover Card and the like, you would be paying a high interest rate besides their annual fee. It would be worthwhile for you to replace the above mentioned cards with the credit card that would offer, besides lower rate of interest, but also no annual fee. You would do well to take advantage of bonuses offered from the auto manufacturer's credit card. However, settle those bills of auto manufacturer with low interest personalized checks acquired from the low interest rate banks. Make sure monthly payments are made regularly; however; not more than you could afford each month.

Similarly, you could also settle the bills of whatever charge cards you carry with personalized checks from the above-mentioned banks. The grace period has double advantage, so to say, "killing two birds with one stone," while you use other people's money, you will be earning interest on your money for the said grace period.

Some credit card companies and some banks do not credit your account the day they receive the payments, which they should do. If such a problem arises that you have not been given credit to the payment on the date of receipt of payment check, you could recourse to the Federal regulators which oversees the activities of the bank. The credit cards and charge cards are for your convenience, so make good use of them to your advantage, while not paying a single red cent on finance charges. To obtain credit cards with no annual fee and low interest, call the following banks:

1. USAA Federal Savings Bank
   10750 McDermott Freeway
   San Antonio, TX 78288
   1 /800-922-9092

2. AFBA Industrial Bank
   P.O. Box 14108
   Colorado Springs, CO 80914
   1/800-776-2265

3. Pullman Bank
   P.O. Box 94855
   Chicago, IL 60690
   1/800-PULLMAN

4. Huntington National Bank
    P.O. Box 1558
    Columbus, OH 43216
    1/800-480-2265

5. Wachovia Bank Card Services
    P.O. Box 105336
    Atlanta, GA 30348
    1 /800-842-3262

* * * * * * *

Jake's Hot Tip #110

Shop around and compare, whether it is a product, a service, or credit.

Chapter Eleven

New Car Warranty

Every new car comes with a warranty. Some manufacturers offer bumper-to-bumper in addition to a three year or 36,000 mile limited warranty. It all depends on the individual manufacturer. For example, some manufacturers' new car limited warranty involves the application of a $100 deductible. This is similar to the deductibles applied under many other insurance policies. It represents the highest amount that you would be required to pay for any covered repair. It does not mean that you will have to pay $100 for each repair visit, but rather that you are obliged to pay up to the first $100 on any repair. This deductible amount does not apply to corrosion or repeat repairs. Manufacturers warranties may vary in accordance to the company policy.

What is Covered?
Repairs—This warranty covers repairs to correct any vehicle defect related to material or workmanship during the warranty period.

Warranty Period
The warranty period for all coverage begins on the date the vehicle is first delivered or put into use, and ends at the expiration of the bumper-to-bumper plus coverage.

Bumper-to-Bumper Plus Coverage
The entire vehicle is covered for three years or 36,000 miles, whichever comes first. After the first year, or 12,000

miles, repairs are totally covered—parts and labor with a deductible of $100 for each repair visit.

Battery Coverage

If a battery replacement is required within the first year from the date of delivery or 12,000 miles, whichever comes first, it is covered by the warranty with no deduction, and will be free of charges. Replacement after the first year, but before the third year or 36,000 miles, will be subjected to a pro-rated charge. Please consult the car dealer about the pro-rated charges.

Corrosion

A major manufacturer will guarantee any body sheet metal that rusts through corrosion within six years or 100,000 miles, whichever comes first, with no deductibles. Sheet panels may be repaired or replaced.

Towing

Towing to the nearest dealership is covered if the vehicle cannot be driven because of a warranty defect. If you purchased a GM car, then towing would be to the nearest Chevrolet dealer.

No Charge

Warranty repairs, including towing, parts and labor, will be made at no charge, over and above the applicable $100 deductible per repair visit after the first year or 12,000 miles, whichever comes first.

Warranty Coverage Extension

A new car limited warranty will be extended for one day for each day beyond the first 24-hour period your vehicle was with an authorized dealer for warranty service. You may be asked to show repair orders in order to verify the period of time the warranty is to be extended. It is a good idea to take your car to the same dealership where you bought it for warranty or repairs. But if you are touring, or if you moved, then you may take it anywhere in the USA or Canada. Warranty may vary, depending on the manufacturer and the state in which you reside.

Vehicle Mileage at Delivery

Sometimes, you may find some mileage is put on your vehicle during testing, but that does not mean it is a used car. They are normally the testing mileage at the assembly plant, or during shipping or while moving the cars at the dealership. Most dealerships record this mileage at delivery in the warranty booklet. Make sure this mileage is added to the mileage limits in your new car. As mentioned earlier, when you buy your new car, you have a warranty and the owner assistance information booklet. This booklet will tell you exactly what is covered and what is not covered under the warranty.

Warranties

The basic manufacturer's warranty on a new car is normally good for 12 months or 36 months/36,000 miles, depending on the car manufacturer. Once this warranty ends, you can buy an extended warranty even if you forget to ask for this protection at the time you purchased the vehicle. The dealer will be happy to sell you one. You can purchase this extended warranty for five years or 60,000 miles or even seven years or 70,000 miles, depending upon who is backing the warranty and how much it costs. If the warranty is backed by an obscure company it may not be worth the paper it is written on, so make sure you read the fine print. The cost of the extended warranty is set by the dealer. The extended warranty promises to pick up a list of certain repairs after the manufacturer's original warranty expires.

You may purchase an extended warranty from the dealer, which is backed by major manufacturers such as GM, Ford, and Chrysler. Some major insurance companies also sell extended warranties, which are called Mechanical Breakdown Insurance. This is sold directly to car owners all across the United States. Since the dealer sets the price of the warranty, he may offer it at a reduced price as an incentive when sales are slow. If your checklist shows a lower price than the dealer offers you and you don't like it, you dump it. Now you have a choice. The dealer markups are usually higher than elsewhere. Buy the extended warranty from the dealer, only if he offers a reduced price or a rate that is equal to the quote you received from an insurance company. The cost of the warranty is as important as the warranty itself. Make sure that it is backed by the manufacturer.

You can buy your extended warranty at the time you purchase your car, although you may not need it until two or three years later. Major insurance companies will allow you to buy Mechanical Breakdown Insurance several months after you purchase the new vehicle. Direct marketers, such as Geico, are not always cheap and may not provide you with too many services, but they are easy to get a quote from the privacy of your home. Get their bid for auto, home, or other personal insurance needs and then compare with other insurance companies. While you are at it, it is also a good time to check on your automobile insurance. You can compare your current insurance policy with the one they have to offer or review every time you get a bill.

You may be allowed to pay monthly for the warranty. When you buy from the dealer, this payment can be added to the car payments.

Before you buy, sign, or accept any extended warranty or Mechanical Breakdown Insurance, make sure you know who is backing it up and get that backing in writing. If it is backed by the manufacturer, you know it is good. You can trust the warranty if it is through a major insurance company such as Prudential Insurance Company of America or Government Employees Insurance Company in Washington, D.C. For information on mechanical breakdown insurance at GEICO, call 1/800-8413000.

Used Car Warranty

You can purchase a warranty for most used cars. Sometimes a dealer may offer you a free 30-day or 1,000 mile warranty. Check with your dealer. Most used cars are sold "as is." As explained in the above paragraph, make sure before you buy, sign, or accept any extended warranty that it is legal and backed up by reputable companies.

A Note of Caution

Please remember that damages caused due to negligence or failure to follow the requirements of the maintenance schedule, and failure to maintain proper levels of fluids, fuel, oil, and lubricant as recommended in the owner's manual is not covered in your warranty.

Proper maintenance is the owner's responsibility. Make sure you keep all receipts of maintenance performed on your car.

The Owner's Manual

The owner's manual is the natural reference for your vehicle's maintenance requirements. The manual's maintenance schedule clearly maps out all the required services and supply time and mileage intervals between each service task. Much of the work should be performed, even if your car accumulates mileage slowly.

Most owner's manuals provide different maintenance schedules based on the type of use your vehicle gets. The temptation is to assume that your vehicle gets normal use and longer service intervals.

All the information regarding warranties, as well as other instructions, are contained in the owner's manual or the warranty booklet. Refer to them for details, and be sure you keep them in your car at all times. You should also receive a warranty card which you will need to show to the service adjuster any time you visit the dealer to have any work done.

For annual summary coverage each year, refer to the car book by Jack Gilles.

Secret Warranty/Service Bulletin

The secret warranty or service bulletin is neither a secret nor an actual warranty. When an auto-maker has a major defect that is not covered by the written warranty or that occurs after its factory warranty lapses, it establishes an adjustment policy to pay for the repair, rather than deal with thousands of complaints on a case-by-case basis. Service bulletins are sent from the manufacturer to the dealer for use by the service department in order to assist them in diagnosing and repairing problems on the vehicles they service. The bulletins contain information such as consumer complaints, safety defects, and docket materials. The manufacturer communicates only to their regional offices and dealers. They never notify the customer, naturally. Only those who complain loudly enough get covered by the secret warranty. Finding the right bulletin can save you thousands of dollars. To find out about secret warranties you must check the technical service bulletin at your dealer's office. The more you know, the more persuasive you become in arguing your rights with a dealer/automakers. Only then, your chances of getting through the secret warranty are better.

Automakers often stonewall the consumers over warranties, knowing that many customers will give up in utter frustration and go away. Don't! Take the documentation on the secret warranty and your repair efforts to small claim's court. At this point, it is the automakers who often give in, knowing that the courts favor the consumer. The auto-makers rely on its own length claim-handling mechanism to wear down consumers—a kind of delay tactic. Once you show you won't be beat by this mechanism, you should succeed in your effort to get the auto-maker to pay.

For further details regarding secret warranty/service bulletin write or call the Technical Reference Division of the National High Traffic Safety Administration (NHTSA).

> National Highway Traffic Safety Administration
> Technical Reference Division
> NAD-52
> 407th Street S.W.
> Washington, DC 20590
> 1/800-445-01 97

When you call, you will get a recorded message. Follow the instructions step-by-step. That may be one of the ways of solving the problem. Don't give up. Remember the old saying, "The squeaky wheel gets the grease."

Alarm/Security System

A Three-way alarm system can become part of your vehicle.

Factory Installed—Car makers either design and build security systems that are installed in the vehicles while cars are being assembled in the factory.

Dealers may install a factory authorized system in their facility through a technician. A dealership mechanic may install on its own, the said security system purchased from other companies in the vehicle, where the factory alarm system is not available. Installing such an after-market item, the dealer may enhance the vehicle's option package. Most dealers prefer this because they can control the cost, not only by choosing the product themselves but, also, by having the work done on their premises.

Dealer installed system is added to the vehicle in a way that does not actually have much to do with the dealer at all. This is where the dealer contacts an outside company to install an after-market system, either at the dealership or by contractors done outside the dealership.

After-market security products are available on the market. There are many varieties of security systems such as just a rod, to state of the art high tech, with the price bracket of $50-$500. You can purchase them anywhere from department stores, mass merchandisers, mail order, network marketing companies, some exclusive car shops dealing with car accessories, and hundreds of other places. The effectiveness of such security system depends on quality of the product, as well as on the diversity and the skill of their installation. No matter how sophisticated equipment one may have installed in the vehicle, one can still be apprehensive about its cent-per-cent safety. However, it is up to you to choose a system that will serve the best purpose with regard to safety and maximum protection of your property. But then, if you don't know a hawk from a hand saw, it may cost you an arm and a leg for such equipment.

Summary

Did the salesperson promise certain items such as floor mats, spare tire, rear bumper for the truck? Make sure you get a written statement to that effect.

* * * * * * *

Jake's Hot Tip #111

In the event of an accident, instruct the tow truck driver to take the car to the dealer. The insurance adjuster would be able to inspect your vehicle. Besides, you are able to pick up a rental car if your car is damaged and needs repairs. When the repair work is finished, you can return the rental car at the same place without having to run from pillar to post. Remember to use the dealer's tow truck and negotiate on the towing charges. Insurance companies do not insist or suggest that accident repair work be done at any particular shop.

Chapter Twelve

Payment Protection Plan/Lemon Laws

You may wonder what a payment protection plan is. It is a life, accident, and health insurance policy which will make your loan payment when you cannot. It is protection you can buy.

But think for a moment—do you really need this kind of protection? If you are married you may need it, for if your spouse dies, the plan may pay off the loan if the survivor is unable to do so. It may also make your monthly finance payments if you become disabled as a result of an accident or illness. Your family would not be financially burdened during such difficult circumstances.

But what will it cost you? Whatever that cost may be, it would normally be added to your monthly car payments. Think about term life insurance. Think about home owners insurance. Think about other insurance plans which you may have with your employer, such as health, disability or life insurance. If you have all of these, you may not need another protection plan. It is an unnecessary additional cost that will be added to your car payments.

The smooth-talking finance manager may try to convince you to buy such an insurance plan. He will tell you that it only costs a few extra dollars a month and that it will give you peace of mind. Remember, however, that you are trying to save money. If you say yes to the plan, the coverage will go into effect immediately on the date you secure your loan.

Make a decision about the protection plan. You may have life insurance. If you don't, then give this protection plan some thought. Buy the payment protection plan from a car dealer or a term-life plan from the insurance company. This alternative would, perhaps, cost you less in the long run.

Before you say *yes* to the payment protection plan, think about your insurance needs. For example, you may have $100,000 in term life insurance. If you die in an accident, this amount may be doubled. If you do not have sufficient coverage on your current policy. It would be worthwhile to consider some additional coverage.

Several books have been written on the subject of insurance such as *The Life Insurance Game* by Ronald Kessler, which explains how the industry has amassed over $600 billion at the expense of the American public. The book, *How Life Insurance Companies Rob You* by Walter S. Kenton, Jr., CLU, shows how you can pay less for more protection and make money on the insurance you already own.

While you are checking on automobile insurance, look into the following discounts:

1. Multi-car discount
2. Mature motorist discount
3. Air bag or automatic seat belt discount
4. Anti-theft device discount
5. Anti-lock brake discount
6. Defensive driving course discount
7. Five years or more of a good driving record

Every time you receive your insurance bill, review your coverage. If your car is old (five or six years), consider eliminating your collision coverage. Shop around, contact an independent agent who can query other companies for you. If you have your own business, put your car in the company's name. You may be able to persuade the insurer who writes your business policy to cover the car as a company vehicle at a lower rate than you would receive on a personal policy.

If you do this, you will be surprised to find that the premium prices can differ as much as 30% to 50% for the same coverage. Remember to compare insurance plans to see which one will cost you the least and give you maximum protection. However, you should also study each company's claim record. A cheap insurance policy is not a good bargain if the insurer can't pay your claim, or is not there to service your claim when you need help. Would the policy then be worth the paper it was written on? I think not!

Rental Cars

If you are thinking about renting a car or van, consider a car dealership instead of a rental agency. It will cost you 20% to 30% less, and will sometimes be as much as 50% less than renting a car from a rental agency.

Nearly all dealerships rent cars. If the vehicle of your choice is not readily available, some dealerships may be able to assist you in locating the car for you. It's another way of saving money if you need a rented vehicle while your own car is being repaired. If you rent a vehicle from the dealer you purchased the car, it may be more convenient since they already know you.

You can add coverage for a rental car to your personal automobile insurance policy. It may cost you a few extra dollars, but that can save you money when you need a rental. Some policies may include this coverage at no extra charge. It's a good idea to check with your insurance agent from time to time to up-date your coverage.

Towing

If your car breaks down, call the dealer. Most of them provide emergency tow trucks for their customers. They may be willing to tow your car at no charge; otherwise, you can negotiate the cost. Your car will, most likely, be repaired at the dealership, so you can pay both charges in one bill. If you call a regular towing service, you will have to pay more. They will also demand payment on the spot.

Check your automobile insurance. If emergency road service is not already included in the policy, you can have it added for just a few extra dollars. Some insurance companies will limit the amount of money they will pay for towing.

New Car Lemon Laws

The lemon law provides a legal remedy for consumers for a refund when you buy or lease a new car with a defect that cannot be fixed within a reasonable period. If you have a problem and need repairs, have tried three different times and have not been successful, then you are covered by the lemon law. The lemon law may differ from state to state.

In most states, a dealer is required by the Department of Motor Vehicles' (DMV) regulations to provide a legible and correct written work order on consumer's demand every time any work is done on your car, including warranty work. If the dealer does not comply with the said document, you may contact the Department of Motor Vehicles and ask for their guidance.

If you bought a car in New York, then the New York law imposes a duty upon the manufacturer to repair, free of charge and without any deductible, any defect covered by the warranty within 18,000 miles or two years from the original delivery date, whichever comes first. Once timely notice of the defect is given, the manufacturer may not charge for the repairs, regardless of when the repairs are performed. The consumer should report any defect, either directly to the manufacturer or its authorized dealer. A general problem such as difficulty in starting, repeated stalling, or malfunctioning transmission can result from a defect of one or more parts. If your vehicle qualifies for the lemon law of your state, you are obliged to notify the manufacturer in writing with a copy to the dealer requesting to rectify the defects.

Before you consider buying a new car, it is advisable for you to obtain a new car lemon law guide from the Attorney General's office. In New York State the guide is free. Write to the following address

Office of Public Information
New York State Department of Law
120 Broadway
New York, NY 10271

or call the Attorney General's office at 1/800-771-7755.

If, however, you are not satisfied with repair work done, then you have a cause for arbitration. *The Lemon Law Guide* explains in clear terms the procedure on how to make your claims. In the rest of the forty-nine states, including the District of Columbia, contact your Attorney General's office dealing with the lemon law.

When you buy a new car, you certainly do not expect it to be a lemon. But, in the event it does happen, remember that you are protected by the state lemon law. However, most arbitration is run by the manufacturer. Make sure you follow the guidelines provided in your owner's manual regarding the routine maintenance. Keeping all the documents of the repeated repair attempts of the defect is important, such as correspondence, work orders, relevant receipts, including any warranty work performed on your vehicle. Keep all other records you may have regarding the visits you make to the dealer.

Some of the laws are quite complex and difficult to comprehend, in which case, you may have to hire an attorney to represent you. Most of the problems are settled through an arbitration. If not, hire an attorney who is familiar with lemon laws. Consumers have the choice of either participating in an arbitration program or suing the manufacturer directly in a court of your jurisdiction. If the manufacturer has established an arbitration procedure which complies with federal regulations and the state lemon law, the manufacturers may refuse to provide a refund until the consumer first participates in such a procedure, or in the state run arbitration program. Any action under the lemon law must be commenced within four years of the date of original delivery. An arbitration proceeding is much less complicated, time consuming, and expensive than going to court. The arbitration hearing is informal. The strict rules of evidence do not apply. Arbitrators, rather than judges, listen to each side, review the evidence, and render a decision. Consumers may participate in the New York State lemon law. The New York program is administered by the American Arbitration Association (AAA) under regulations issued by the Attorney General. Decisions under the New York program are binding by both parties. Consumers may also choose to participate in an arbitration program established by the auto manufacturer (see Appendix).

Decisions under the manufacturer's program are not binding on consumers. Consequently, consumers who have gone through the manufacturer's program and are not satisfied, may still apply for arbitration under the New York program. However, any prior arbitration decision may be considered at any subsequent arbitration or court proceeding. The law permits manufacturers to require that consumers first participate in the manufacturer's program if it complies with federal regulations and the state lemon law, before going to court for relief under the lemon law.

If you want to participate in the New York program, first complete a *Request for Arbitration* form. Complete the form and send it to the Attorney General's office. Once they receive information, they will review it and determine whether the consumer's claim is eligible under the lemon law to be heard by an arbitrator. If accepted, the form will be forwarded to AAA, the program administrator, for processing. The new lemon law guide is quite comprehensive. Complete step-by-step descriptions, including the forms, are in the New Cars Lemon Law Guide for Consumers booklet.

Motor homes (RV) are covered under the law, except for defects in the system, fixtures, appliances, or other parts that are residential in character.

Used Car Lemon Laws

The used car lemon law provides a legal remedy for consumers who are buyers or lessees of used cars that turn out to be lemons. The law requires dealers to give consumers a written warranty. Under this warranty, dealers must repair, free of charge, any defects and covered parts. If the dealer is unable to repair the car after a reasonable number of attempts, then the consumer is entitled to a full refund. The lemon law may differ from state to state. In New York State the following used cars are covered by the lemon law:

1. Cars purchased or leased, transferred after the earlier of 18,000 miles of operation or two years from the date of delivery.
2. It was purchased or leased from a New York dealer.

3. It has a purchase price or lease amount of not less than $1,500.
4. It has been driven less than 100,000 miles at the time of purchase or lease.

Any person to whom a used car was transferred by the purchaser during the used car lemon law warranty is covered. You would do well to know that if you purchased a used car from a private sale (classified ad), it will not be protected by the used car lemon law. You should then consult a lawyer for advice as to other possible remedies. If the purchase price of the used car is less than $2,000 then small claim's court is your best bet. Refer to appendix.

If you purchase a used car at retail auto auction, the auction company must be a used car dealer registered with the Department of Motor Vehicles (DMV), and it must provide you with your lemon law rights.

The dealer who sells or leases a used car to a consumer is required to give a written warranty to the customer, the terms of which are specified in the law. The warranty may be referred to at times as a "statutory warranty" because it is honored by the dealer. The statutory warranty must specify that while it is in effect, the dealer or his agent will repair, free of charge, any part covered by the warranty. The dealer may elect to reimburse the consumer for a reasonable cost of repairing any covered part. The warranty may be included in the sales contract or lease, or on a separate sheet of paper. If it is part of the sales contract or lease, it must be separate from the other contract provisions and headed by a conspicuous title. A dealer may agree, as part of the sale or lease, to give consumer more warranty protection than the law requires. Many dealers will offer extended service contracts. Of course, you must always negotiate on such extended service contracts for a good price. If you have a problem immediately, report any malfunction or defect of a covered part to the dealer and request the necessary repair. If you have informed the dealer of a problem within the warranty period, the dealer must make the repair even if the warranty has subsequently expired. The warranty is extended for each day the car is in the shop for repairs. If the dealer fails to repair the problem within a reasonable period of time, and if the problem substantially impairs the value of the used car, the dealer must accept the return of the car and refund the full purchase price, The dealer may deduct a reasonable amount for any damage beyond normal wear or use.

An adjustment may also be made for any modification to the car which either increases or decreases its market value. There is, however, no deduction for mileage.

In order to prove your car is a lemon, you must keep all the documents regarding the required repair work, copies of work orders, and all relevant correspondence. Contact the Attorney General's office and follow the same procedure, as explained earlier, and request a Used Car Lemon Law Guide. Contact your local consumer office or Attorney General's office to find out more details of your respective state for additional information.

Summary

You would do well to rent any vehicle with your personal auto insurance or with a credit card that covers collision damage waiver.

* * * * * * *

HOT TIP #112

Obtain Lemon Law Guide booklet for new cars or used cars from New York Attorney General's office. All other states call your respective states Attorney General's office.

Chapter Thirteen

Vehicle Delivery

By now, you will have done all the necessary paper work at the finance office, and the vehicle has been washed neat and clean and prepared for delivery. You are probably eager to drive your new car home. You need not be in a hurry. One cannot swap horses in the middle of the storm. Therefore, before you drive off with your new car, familiarize yourself with the automobile and ask yourself the following questions, as you check out your new car: *Has the vehicle been well cleaned? Has it been inspected for proper paint, appearance and body components? Do the body components fit properly? Is the general appearance of the automobile satisfactory?*

Interior

Make sure that the interior of your vehicle has been inspected for a neat and clean appearance, and that the components have been checked to verify their normal function and operation.

Mechanical

Ensure that each mechanical system has been checked for proper operation and fluids have been checked for proper levels.

Familiarize yourself with the operation of the vehicle, its starting procedure, seat adjustments, child safety locks, and other features, not forgetting to inquire about the maintenance schedule that is needed for your car. Some dealers offer a free 3,000 mile oil change.

Defects or damage to the mechanical, electrical, sheet metal, paint, trim, and other components of your vehicle is inevitable. They may occur anywhere between the factory and the dealership while it is being transported. Make a list of them for necessary claims for damages. Any defects still present at the time the vehicle is delivered to you are covered by the warranty.

If you notice such defects when you take delivery of the car, please show it to the salesperson immediately. If there is a problem that requires the vehicle to be in the dealership's repair shop for a couple of days, ask for a loaner. Keep in mind, too, that even though you signed a contract you can still change your mind if you are unsatisfied, as long as you have not driven the vehicle out of the dealership's car lot. For instance, if the new car is defective or requires major repair, you may want to ask them to order a new vehicle for you instead of having it repaired. Make sure that your new car meets with your approval in every way. You may find, for instance, that the spare tire is missing. Don't be satisfied with only a promise to remedy your problem. Ask the salesperson for a written statement. It will save you from hassle and embarrassment when you return to the dealership to pick up the aforesaid missing spare tire. The salesperson or manager who verbalized the promise to you might not be there for more than one reason, in which case the written statement with the sales person's or manager's signature would certainly come to your rescue and would avoid all misunderstanding.

Check the vehicle for floor mats before you take delivery of the car. If they are missing, look at the window sticker to verify whether they come with the car. If they do not, you could ask the salesperson whether you could buy the mats from the dealer's parts department at cost price.

If you are purchasing a small pick-up truck, see that it has a rear bumper. If it does not come with one you will have to buy it. The window sticker should give you an understanding as to whether it is part of the deal.

Be sure that you receive a set of spare keys. Find out the days and hours that the dealer's service and parts departments are open. Get to know the service adjuster, and ask for his business card—sooner or later you may need him!

Most dealerships will ask you to sign a *Vehicle Delivery Presentation*. They will ask you if you have checked all the items and are satisfied with the delivery conditions. When you accept delivery of your new vehicle, you should be satisfied that it is in perfect condition.

Check and re-check to make sure that everything works before you drive home your new car. Collect copies of all documents you have signed including the vehicle warranty booklet, warranty card, and owner's manual. Ask if the salesperson can provide you with an extra set of keys. You should have a full tank of gas. Demand it, if it is not provided, as it should be.

License Plates

When you purchase a new car, the dealer will place a temporary paper plate on your car, which is good for twenty days. This period of time should be sufficient for your metal plate to be ready. The dealer will usually telephone you when the plate is ready, so you can pick it up. If you do not hear from him before the expiration date, you better give him a call and remind him.

If you would like to have a personalized license plate, indicate this to the salesperson, so that he can complete the necessary paper work. You may have to pay a little more for this type of plate. If you decide on this after you've gotten your regular plates and picked up the car, you may have to inform the Department of Motor Vehicles.

Summary

Some manufacturers offer toll-free numbers for emergency road service assistance. Keep those numbers handy in your car at all times.

* * * * * * *

Jake's Hot Tip #113

Pick up your car during daylight hours so that you can inspect it more easily. As it is often said, "Crying babies get the feed"—the consumer who complains the loudest gets reimbursed. A quiet customer usually gets ripped.

Chapter Fourteen

How to Look for a Used Car

More than a hundred billion dollars a year is spent on used cars. These cars are purchased from hundreds of different outlets across the country. Before you begin looking for a good used car, you will have to do some homework. For example, you will want to know about financing, the going price of the used car you are considering, how much you would like to invest, and the primary reason you are buying such a vehicle.

One way to determine the price of a used car is by checking the NADA guide book which may help you determine the most up-to-date price for a particular model you intend to purchase. For example, if you are interested in a 1995 Toyota Camry, check the wholesale and retail prices in the NADA BOOK. You may also want to look through the classified ads in your local newspaper to help you determine the current average selling price of the car in which you are interested.

When you are at the library, you can locate other reference books for technical information on the vehicle you are considering, or to compare several models. You will then be a more knowledgeable customer when you approach the dealer.

One of the important things you should consider in the automobile you are purchasing is the number of miles it has been driven. The average car is driven about 12,000 miles a year. A vehicle that is three years old will usually have been driven about 36,000 miles. Anything beyond that is considered to be high mileage. If a car has been driven less than the average figures, it is considered to have low mileage.

You will also want to check the condition of the vehicle, the number of previous owners, and the place where the car came from. When you are test driving the automobile, listen for unusual noises, misfiring, and other possible problems. You should also check the odometer for any signs of tampering, such as misaligned numbers on an analog mileage gauge, scratches, or missing screws on the dashboard. Finally, take the car to a reliable mechanic for a complete check up. Sometimes, you may not be able to detect signs of abuse and misuse. It is crucial that an independent mechanic of your choice inspect the car before you make a deposit or any other kind of commitment to buy it.

Odometer (speedometer) tampering is against the law, but it happens. Federal law requires odometer readings on auto titles whenever the car is sold and re-titled. Check the title and look for excessive wear and tear, not forgetting the mileage reading on the car.

If you are suspect that the car you are buying may have been stolen, the Vehicle Identification Number (YIN) can be checked by your insurance company or with a national registry of stolen cars.

Locating a quality used car requires a different kind of thinking than most of us are accustomed to. It's not an easy task—remember, it's a jungle out there! It may take a lot of wheeling and dealing to get exactly what you want. Keep your eyes and ears open and check around carefully until you find a vehicle with which you are thoroughly satisfied.

Regardless of whether you purchase a new or a used car, a regular maintenance is very essential. Needless to say, sooner or later, it will need some repair. The advantage of letting the dealer handle this work is that he has trained mechanics with the right tools, dependable equipment, and the service parts needed for your particular vehicle. Select a dealership conveniently located, and stay in touch with the service adjuster. Compare prices with other dealers. If he charges you too much for repairs, negotiate. Always make sure you get a pre-estimate before any repair work on your car is indicated. One should realize that it would take some time to service your car, so always plan ahead. If you need to leave the vehicle at the dealership for a day or two, you may want to make arrangements for a loaner car or make alternate plans.

If your automobile requires wheel balancing, the best place to have this done would be at a garage that sells tires such as Goodyear, Firestone, or Sears. They can usually service your car in about an hour or so. Check your local newspaper for sales. When it comes to repairs, major or minor, use conventional wisdom in selecting a garage or a dealer. Use a credit card when you pay for car service, as explained in the preceding chapters.

* * * * * * *

Jake's Hot Tip #114

Consider purchasing a late model used car rather than a fully-loaded new car. Compare the price difference, interest rate, and warranty cost.

Chapter Fifteen

Where to Find Quality Used Cars

Dealers

Twelve to eighteen million used cars are sold each year. One of the best places to buy a used car is from a major dealership. It may cost a little more than elsewhere, but you will not only have the advantage of choosing from a wide variety of vehicles, but also the dealer can offer a warranty and help you with financing. The dealer will work with you so that you can get nearly everything done in one place.

Where do dealers get their cars? Most of them come from trade-ins, and the rest are bought from wholesalers and from various auctions. Once dealers get their cars, they are well serviced and get them ready for resale. If a customer brings in a vehicle which is not a late model, or not so clean, the car may be sent to auction or sold to a wholesaler.

A reputable dealer will sell only quality used cars, because customer satisfaction is important to them. If you have a problem or complaint, you can take it up with the used car manager. He will try to resolve problems for you because his reputation is at stake. If he cannot solve that problem for you, you may as well take the matter to higher ups.

When you find a car you like, take it for a test drive on a freeway or a highway. Check out the car, both inside and outside. You must do your homework—don't depend on the salesperson to do it for you. Once you have finished checking out your prospective purchase, have taken it for a test drive, and are completely satisfied with the vehicle, you are ready for the critical part of your purchase—negotiation!

How much does a dealer mark up on the used car he sells? Most dealers mark up their automobiles from $1,000 to $3,000, depending on the mileage, model, and condition of the car. If you have done your homework and checked the NADA Guide Book, you would know the fair retail and the wholesale prices of various cars.

Negotiating with a salesperson is an art. After you have read this book, you will have acquired the art sufficiently and would be a smart customer and can negotiate hard. The salesperson dislikes a knowledgeable customer.

Try to obtain a good deal on the vehicle of your choice! If you can't buy the vehicle on your own terms, go and find another dealer. You are not committed to any particular dealer, are you? Find out from the salesperson how long he had the car or truck with him. Look at the yellow tag on the windshield, which you will find above the state inspection sticker. If the vehicle has been on the dealer's lot more than 60 days, chances are he wants to sell it fast. He usually doesn't want a vehicle to sit on his grounds too long, for he has to pay interest on the inventory. He would rather sell it to you with a small margin of profit. If he fails, he would have to send it for auction or sell it to a wholesaler. Used car managers are under pressure to meet their monthly quotas.

Many of the used cars that are sold, are vehicles which had been leased for a particular period of time. These cars may not have a lot of mileage, because a surcharge is imposed on the lessee over and above the prescribed number of miles on the contract The typical leased car is driven about two or three years. You may be able to purchase one for as little as half the sticker price, if such option was offered. These are good vehicles to buy. You may also want to consider purchasing a used car from one of the following sources:

Independent Small Car Dealers/Used Car Lots

You will find these dealers on the corners of many streets. They carry all types of used vehicles including taxi cabs, police cars, vans, and ambulances. These dealers obtain their goods from auctions and wholesalers. They may also purchase cars that are *totaled* or destroyed in accidents, which are sometimes rebuilt and sold as used cars.

Some, but not all states, are required to meet the title designation or *brand* requirement. Two totaled cars may be cut in half, spot-welded together, retitled in a non-branding state, and sold to an unsuspecting consumer. To know about it, contact your state or local consumer protection office or Department of Motor Vehicles (DMV) to find out if branding is required. If not, look for extensive body work, and try to get as much information as possible about the car's history.

There are some who sell older model cars for cash. Be very careful with such deals. Getting financing on an older model car can be difficult. Check with your banker.

A word about wholesalers—they purchase automobiles from major dealers and from the auctions, and then sell them to small dealers. They make some fast cash, but comparatively a meager profit—mostly same day transactions.

Pre-Owned Vehicles

Every year corporations, major companies, and lending institutions purchase new cars from manufacturers or dealers on fleet price, as incentive for the employees. The PGA Golf Tournament, for example, buys new cars in bulk from certain car makers for transportation purposes. When these vehicles are no longer needed, they are auctioned off to dealers.

These automobiles may have a mileage of 5,000 to 10,000 miles or more. Once a dealer gets such a car, he services the vehicle and sells it as a pre-owned car. Some manufacturers will offer a pre-owned limited warranty for twelve months or 12,000 miles, including 24-hour road service. Nissan is currently offering a manufacturer-backed warranty on its used cars and trucks. Lexus, the upscale model of Toyota offer the same, and other car manufacturers will soon follow. Compare the prices and consider the model, year, interest rate, cost of warranty, and other factors against a stripped-down new car. Keep in mind that a new car warranty is free for three years or 36,000 miles, the interest rates are lower, and it can be financed for a longer term.[13] The bottom line is how much down payment would be required, and what would your monthly payment be.

Keep in mind the mileage and the wear and tear these cars have been subjected to which, perhaps, are similar to that of the rental and demonstration vehicles.

A word of caution may not be out of place here. If you are considering the purchase of a pre-owned car, ask the salesperson where the dealer got the car from. Some dealers sell used cars as pre-owned.

Rental Companies

Most major car rental services such as Avis, Budget, Hertz, sell their vehicles to the public. The cars they sell have been used as rental cars. Since these autos had been rented by many different people on a daily or weekly basis, they will usually have higher mileage than other late model used car. Besides, they may be abused vehicles. Avoid purchasing an automobile from a car rental service, if possible.

---

13   Five to six years.

Banks

Some major banks auction off repossessed cars on a daily basis. These automobiles have been repossessed by the bank because their owners defaulted on their car loans. You can find late model cars and purchase them for wholesale prices. The banks are not trying to make large profits, they simply want to recover their money as soon as they can. You may be able to buy a late model car at enormous savings. A new car begins to depreciate as soon as it is driven away by its new owner. The longer a bank keeps the car it repossessed, the greater is its loss, because the longer the car sits it depreciates, and the bank is losing interest on its money. People may default on their loans for various reasons such as divorce, loss of job, or illness. They are usually good people, but unfortunately, may be experiencing life during difficult times.

Call various banks for more information and location of their auctions. Stay in touch with the individual who is in charge of them. Call periodically, and find out about their forthcoming auctions. Request that they put you on their mailing lists, so that you receive information about upcoming auctions.

Individual Sales

Nearly forty percent of used car sales are through private sales, such as neighbors, friends, or through classified ads. Other places you may look for cars are through bulletin boards at churches, synagogue, or temples, or at work. Sooner or later, you may find some individual who wants to sell a car. If you have the time and patience, you may be able to find a quality used car from such individuals. When you buy such a car, remember the cliche, "buy low, sell high" and offer to purchase at a wholesale price.

If you are answering a classified ad, you may as well ask the following questions before you decide whether further investigation is worth your while: How long have you had the car? Did you buy the car new? What is the mileage on the car? Why are you selling? If you are satisfied with the answers, then investigate the car further.

Once you buy a car from a private individual you are stuck with it. You do not receive a warranty or financing for this type of sale. You can, however, get a good price.

Public Auctions

Public auctions are listed in newspapers. Auctions are held practically in every major city across America. Auctioneers most often get their vehicles from new car dealers who were not able to sell them anywhere else. Buying from a public auction is rather risky for the average consumer. Not only is it time consuming, but it is also possible to end up with a lemon in your hand. Auction reports are sent to dealers only. If you can get hold of a copy from the dealer, it may be worthwhile for you to check on the prices.

Government Auctions

Various agencies of the federal government hold auctions from time to time. The U.S. Customs Service, for example, will auction seized vehicles. There are more than forty custom districts where you may be able to locate late model cars, sports cars, or expensive imports far below wholesale prices. If you're looking for a good bargain, this is the place to go. You can never tell what you will find.

Government auctions usually require cash on the spot, but may sometimes give you several days to come up with the money. At the end of this section, you will find the address of the U. S. Customs Service. Contact them and request the location of the district headquarters that is clos-est to you. Once you receive this information, you can write to the district and ask for information regarding their auc-tions. Auctions are also conducted by the Department of Defense and the U.S. Postal Service which auctions nearly any type of vehicle. The General Service Administration (GSA) also holds auctions. It is a division of the Government Civil Procurement Agency. Contact the fol-lowing government agencies and ask them to place you on their mailing lists. You will then know when and where their auctions are being conducted.

U. S. Customs Service
Attention Dept. MS2300
Clarendon Boulevard, Room 105
Arlington, VA 22201
Telephone 703/273-3441

U.S. Postal Service
Office of Material Management
475 L'Enfant Plaza, Room 1221
Washington, D.C. 20260-6226

General Service Administration
Surplus Sales Information
26 Federal Plaza
New York, NY 11027
Telephone 212/264-4824

Defense Reutilization Marketing Service
P.O. Box 5275
2163 Airways Boulevard
Memphis, TN 38224-5210
Telephone 1/800-468-8289

Summary

For the Federal Information Center, call toll free 1/800-688-9889

* * * * * * *

Jake's Hot Tip #115

Always pre-inspect a vehicle before the auction starts. Do not try to out-guess your fellow bidders, much less get caught up in the excitement of bidding and end up over-paying. Obtain an auction report, if possible.

Last Word

Sooner or later every car needs work. Few customers are mechanics, but there are ways to protect yourself from car rip-offs.

1. Get recommendations from family, friends, and check complaint records with your local consumer protection office or local Better Business Bureau.

2. When you take the car to the shop, describe the symptoms—don't diagnose the problem.

3. Make it clear that no work can be done until it has been authorized by you.

4. Do not authorize any work without a written estimate.

5. Get all warranties in writing.

When you are on a trip some of these steps are obviously impossible, but make sure everything done is reflected in your receipt and warranties. If work is substandard, or you feel you were treated unfairly, you have recourse to the manufacturer if the shop was a franchised dealer, the parent company if it was part of a regional or national chain.

The following are a few common repair tips:

Alternator: Loose wiring can make your alternator appear defective. Make sure the technician checks for loose connections and performs an output test before replacing it.

Battery: Corroded or loose battery terminals can make the battery appear dead or defective. Make sure the technicians clean the terminals and test battery functions before replacing it.

Starter: What appears to be a defective starter may actually be a dead battery or poor connection. Ask your technician to check all connections and test the battery connections before replacing the starter.

Muffler: A loud rumbling noise under your vehicle indicates the need for a new muffler or exhaust pipe. Quality replacement parts obviously cost more. Low priced parts are seldom a good buy unless you keep the vehicle less than a year. Make sure you understand exactly what the warranty covers, because many exhaust system warranties have exceptions and limitations.

Tune-up: The old fashioned "tune-up" may not apply to your vehicle. Fewer parts need to be replaced on newer vehicles other than belts, spark plugs, hoses, and filters.

Check tire pressure periodically with a good tire pressure gauge. It only takes a few minutes to check all four tires. This should be done once a month. Also make sure to check the pressure when they are cold.

The automakers recommended pressure is printed either in the owner's manual or on an information sticker, usually located on a front door jam or in the glove box.

Car Care and the Environment

Remember that a properly maintained and operated vehicle runs better, safer, and lasts longer.

> Check your tires for proper air
> Tune up the engine, as suggested
> Observe speed limits
> Drive carefully
> Make certain that you dispose of waste properly
> Never dump waste on the street

THINK ABOUT OUR ENVIRONMENT

Abbreviations

2 DR	Two door
4 DR	Four door
4 x 4 or 4 W.D.	Four wheel drive
A.A.A.	American Automobile Association
AAA	American Arbitration Association
A/C	Air conditioning
ACV	Actual cash value
ACVL	Association of Consumer Vehicle Leases
ADP	Added dealer profit
AIA	Automobile Importers of America
AIC	Additional injector controller
ALAS	Association Latino Auto Sonido
Amt.	Amount
AMU	Additional mark-up
APA	American Protection Association
APIP	Additional personal injury protection
APP	Advance payment plan
Approx.	Approximately
ATAM	Automotive Trade Association Management
Av.	Average
B.M.W.	Bayerische Motoren Werke—AG
BAC	Blood alcohol content
BPIP	Basic personal injury protection
CAFE	Corporate Average Fuel Economy
CART	Championship auto racing teams
CAS	California audio system
CCMC	Cross-country Motor Club
CDL	Commercial driver's license
CDW	Collision damage waiver
CEPA	Consumer Education and Protection Association
CFA	Consumer Federation of America
CNG	Compressed natural gas

CSI	Customer satisfaction index
DAB	Driver's air bag
DMA	Digital model assembly
DOHC	Duel overhead camshift
DRL	Daytime running lights
DSE	Dynamic stability control
DUI	Driving under the influence
DWAI	Driving while ability impaired
DWI	Driving while intoxicated
E.P.A.	Environmental Protection Agency
E.V.	Electronic vehicle
ECD	Energy conversion devices
EFL	Electronic fuel injection
Enviro.	Environmental
ERS	Emergency road service
ESP	Electronic Stability program
ESP	Electronic shock protection
ETC	Electronic touring coupe
Fed.	Federal
F&I	Finance and Insurance
F.M.C.C.	Ford Motors Credit Corporation
F.W.D.	Front wheel drive
GBL	General business law
GCC	Graphic computer controller
GCWR	Gross combination weight rating
G.M.	General Motors
GMAC	General Motors Acceptance Corporation
GNYADA	Greater New York Automobile Dealers Association
GSA	General Service Administration
GTP	Grand touring prototype
GVW	Gross vehicle weight
GVWR	Gross vehicle weight rating
HDS	Honda Drop Shop
HPD	High performance driving

ICCS	Integrated chassis control system
ICP	Integrated control panel
IIHS	Insurance Institute for Highway Safety
IMSA	International Motor Sport Association
LDW	Loss damage waiver
LPT	Light pressure turbo
M.G.	Moris Garage
MSRP	Manufacturer's suggested retail price
M.V.R.	Motor vehicle report
MPG	Miles per gallon
MPH	Miles per hour
MTC	Melling torque cams
MVA	Market value adjustment
MVMA	Motor Vehicle Manufacturers Association
MVRLA	Motor Vehicle Retail Leasing Association
N/A	Not applicable
NADA	National Automobile Dealers Association
NAIC	National Association of Insurance Commission
NCAP	New Car Assessment Program
NHRA	National Hot Rod Association
NHTSA	National Highway Traffic Safety Administration
NIRA	National Import Raising Association
NMCA	National Muscle Car Association
NSPL	National Sounds Pressure League
NVH	Noise/vibration/harshness
OBEL	Optional basic economic loss
OHV	Overhead valve
OTB	Overtake boost
OXC	Overhead cam
P&H	Postage and handling

P/B	Power brakes
PCHRA	Pearl City Hot Rod Association
PDI	Pre-delivery inspection
PFI	Port fuel injection
PGA	Professional Golf Association
PIP	Personal injury protection
P/S	Power steering
P/W	Power windows
R.V.	Recreational vehicle
RDS	Radio Data System
RMA	Rubber Manufacturers of America
RPM	Revolutions per minute
SCCA	Sports Car Club of America
SFI	Sequential fuel injection
SOA	Society of Automobiles
SOHC	Single overhead camshift
SST	Synthesis of simulation technology
STS	Service Technicians Society
SUM	Supplementary uninsured motorist
SUV	Sports utility vehicle
TMCC	Toyota Motors Credit Corporation
TO	Turnover
UKC	Ubiquitous Korean car
Univ.	University
USAA	United Services Automobile Association
VIN	Vehicle identification number
VPC	Vein pressure converter
VTEC	Valve Timing Electronically controlled
VW	Volkswagon
Wt.	Weight
Yr.	Year

Appendix "A"

The "Big Three" car manufacturers:

General Motors Corporation
General Motors Building
3044 West Grand Boulevard
Detroit, Michigan 48202
(313) 556-5000

Ford Motor Company
P.O. Box 1399
Dearborn, Ml 48121
(313) 322-3000

Chrysler Corporation
12000 T Chrysler Drive
Highland Park, Ml 48288
(313) 956-5741

You can also contact the following manufacturers for brochures or for the name of your nearest dealer:

American Honda
ACURA Division
1919 Torrance Blvd.
Torrance, CA 90501
Customer service 1/800 382-2238
Roadside assistance 1/800 594-8500

Audi of America
3800 Hamlin Road
Auburn Hill, Ml 48326
Customer service 1/800 367-2834
Roadside assistance 1/800 411-9988

BMW
P.O. Box 1227
Westwood, NJ 07675-1227
1/800-831-1117
201/307-4000

Buick Motor Division
902 East Hamilton Avenue
Flint, Ml 48550
RSA: 1/800-252-1112
CS: 1/800-422-8425

Cadillac, Inc.
P.O. Box 9025
Warren, Ml 48090
RSA: 1 /800-882-1112
CS: 1/800458-8006

Chrysler Corporation
P.O. Box 218004
Auburn Hill, Ml 48321-8004
(Chrysler/Dodge/Plymouth)
1 /800-992-1997

Chevrolet Motor Division
P.O. Box 7047
Troy, Ml 48007-7047
(Chevrolet/Geo)
1 /800-222-1020

Daihatsu of America
4422 Corporate Center Drive
Los Alamitos, CA 90720
1 /800-777-7070
1.800-552-7070

Honda Motors
700 Ven Ness Avenue
Torrance, CA 90501-1490
Customer service 1/800 247-8479
Credit information 1/800 445-1358

Hyundai Motor America
10550 Talbert Ave.
P.O. Box 20850
Fountain Valley, CA 92728-0850
1/800-633-5151
1/800-826-CARS

Infiniti Division
P.O. Box 191
Gardena, CA 90248-0191
Customer service 1/800 826-6500
Roadside assistance 1/800 662-6200
Credit information 1/800 627-4437

KIA Motors of America
P.O. Box 52410
Irvine, CA 92619
C.S. 1/800-333-4542

Lamborghini USA
7601 Centurion Parkway South
Jacksonville, FL 32256
1 /800-882-5872

Lexus Division
Toyota Motor Sales, USA, Inc.
19001 Southwestern Avenue
Torrance, CA 90509
1/800 255-3987

Mazda Motors of America
P.O. Box 19734
Irvine, CA 92713-9734
1/800 222-5500

Mercedes Benz
North America
1 Mercedes Drive
Montvale, NJ 07645
1-800-634-6262

Mitsubishi Motor Service
Customer service 1/800 222-0037
Credit information 1/800 426-7038

Nissan Motor Corporation
P.O. Box 191
Gardena, CA 90248-0191
1 /800-255-3987

Pontiac Division
1 Pontiac Plaza
Pontiac, Ml 48340
RSA: 1/800-762-3743
CS: 1/800-762-2737

Rolls Royce
140 East Ridgewood Ave.
Paramus, NJ 07652
1/800 487-6557

SAAB Cars
P.O. Box 9000
Norcross, GA 30091
1/800 955-9007

Suzuki of America Auto Corporation
3251 East Imperial Highway
Brea, CA 92621
CS 1/800-934-0934
1 /800-447-4700

Toyota Motor Sales, USA, Inc.
19001 Southwestern Avenue
Torrance, CA 90509
1/800-331-4331
310/618-4000

Volkswagen of America
3800 Hamlin Road
Auburn Hill, Ml 48326
1/800 822-8987

Volvo Cars of North America
P.O. Box 914
Rockleigh, NJ 07647
Customer service 1/800 458-1552
Roadside assistance 1/800 638-6586

Major Car Rental Companies:

Alamo Rent A Car
110 S.E. 6th Street
Fort Lauderdale, FL 33301
1/800-327-9633

Avis, Inc.
World Headquarters
900 Old Country Road
Garden City, NY 11530
RSA: 1/800-354-2847

Budget Rental Car Corp.
4225 Naperville Road
Lisle, IL 60532
1/800-621 -2844

Hertz Rental Cars
Worldwide Customer Relations
P.O. Box 26120
Oklahoma City, Oklahoma 73126
1/800-654-4173

Enterprise Rental Cars
600 Corporate Park Drive
St. Louis, MO 63105
1/800-325-8007
RSA: 1/800-207-6666

National Car Rental
7700 France Avenue South
Minneapolis, MN 55435
RSA: 1/800-367-6767
CS: 1/800-468-3334

Major R.V. Manufacturers:

Carriage, Inc.
P.O. Box 246
Millersburg, IN 46543
1/800-832-3632

Gulf Stream
P.O. Box 1005
Nappance, IN 46550
1/800-289-8787

Fleet Wood
Reed Industrial Park
P.O. Box 106
Paxinos, PA 17860
1/800-322-8216

Jayco, Inc.
P.O. Box 460
Middlebury, IND 46540
1/800-283-8267

King of the Road
P. O. Box 553
Russell, KS 67665
1/800-255-0521
(only manufacturer 5th wheel)

Appendix "B"

Auto Safety Hot Line

If you are calling from Washington, D. C.
1-800/366-0123
If you are calling from any other state
1-800/424-9393

For consumer disputes, write to the following:

Automotive Consumer Action Program
Attention: Lesley J. Hardesty
8400 West Park Drive
McLean, Virginia 22102
(703) 821-7144

For assistance with unresolved disputes between car owners and automobile manufacturers:

Council of Better Business Bureau
Alternative Dispute Resolution
4200 Wilson Blvd., #800
Arlington, Virginia 22203
(703) 247-9361

Federal Trade Commission
6th and Pennsylvania Avenue, NW
Room 130
Washington, D. C. 20580
202/326-2222

If you live in New York state and have any insurance problems or complaints, write to the address shown below.

Consumer Service Bureau
New York State
160 West Broadway
New York, NY 10013
212/602-0203/0525

For your guide to more than 200 free or low-cost government publications about getting federal benefits, finding jobs, staying healthy, buying a house, educating your children, saving and investing, as well as buying a safer car, buying a used car, glove box tips, how to find your way under the hood and around the car, the motorist tire care and safety guide, new car buying guide, nine ways to lower your auto insurance cost, underhood tips to keep you cool, write to:

Woods
Consumer Information Center
6C
P.O. Box 100
Pueblo, CO

Appendix "C"

Auto Loan Institutions

Some of the lowest rate auto loans are available through banks. If you live near one, contact them.

First National Bank of Commerce
New Orleans, LA
1/800-228-3265

Liberty National Bank
Los Angeles, CA

Maryland Federal Savings
Washington, D. C.

Norwalk Savings Society
Southwest Connecticut

Mainline Federal
Detroit, Ml

Broadway National Bank
San Antonió, TX
1/800-531-7650

Columbia Savings Bank
Newark, NJ
1/800-962-4989

Jamaica Savings Bank
303 Merrick Road
Lynbrook, NY 11563

Major Credit Reporting Agencies:

TRW
P. O. Box 8030
Layton, UT 840441-8030
1/800-392-1122
TRW offers a free credit report every year upon request.
Waiting time is usually 2-3 weeks.

Equifax
P.O. Box 105873
Atlanta, GA 30348
1/800-685-1111

Trans Union Corp.
P.O. Box 390
Springfield, PA 19064
1/800-888-4213

Contact your local Better Business Bureau or write to them if you have a problem or complaint.

Council of Better Business Bureaus, Inc.
4220 Wilson Boulevard
Suite 800
Arlington, VA 22203
703/276-0100

Major Insurance and Service Contract Companies:

Nationwide Insurance
One Nationwide Plaza
Columbus, OH 43215

Liberty Mutual Insurance Groups
175 Berkeley Street
Boston, MA 02117
1/800-225-2390
617/357-9500

Travelers/Aetna Insurance and Casualty
1/800-243-0185

USAA
9800 Fredericksburg Road
San Antonio, TX 78288
1/800-531 -8080

Insurance Specialist
3885 Upham Street
Wheat Ridge, CO 80034
1/800-445-4065

Western General Insurance
16501 Ventura Boulevard, Suite 200
Encino, CA 91436
1/800-345-0191

Ryan Warranty Services:

GEICO
One Geico Plaza
Washington, DC 20076
202/364-9000

Cigna Group
1601 Chestnut Street
P.O. Box 7716
Philadelphia, PA 19192
215/761-1000

Metropolitan Life Insurance Company
One Madison Avenue
New York, NY 10010
212/578-2211

The Prudential Insurance Company of America
Prudential Plaza
Newark, NJ 07102
201/802-6000

State Farm Group
One State Farm Plaza
Bloomington, IL 61710
309/766-2311

Further insurance questions, contact the Insurance Help Line at 1/800-942-4242 This is a non-profit organization funded by major insurance companies.

Worksheet Sample

DELIVERY DATE _____

STOCK NO. _____

SALESMAN _____

SOURCE _____

PURCHASER _____

ADDRESS _____

CITY, STATE, ZIP _____

HOME TELE. NO. _____

BUSINESS TELE. _____

SOC. SEC. NO. _____

NEW	USED	DEMO	YEAR	MAKE	MODEL	BODY STYLE

COLOR	SERIAL NO.	MILEAGE

FACTORY EQUIPMENT	DEALER & EQUIPMENT	TRADE–IN DESCRIPTION
		MAKE ————
		YEAR ————
		MODEL ————
		BODY ————
		SER. NO. ————
		MILEAGE ————
		PAYOFF AMT._____
		LIEN HOLDER_____
		MO. PAYMENT_____
		CONDITION ————
		Excellent ____ Good ____ Fair ____

SELLING PRICE _____

TRADE–IN ALLOWANCE _____

PRICE DIFFERENCE _____

APPROXIMATE TOTAL _____

CASH DOWN _____

MONTHLY PAYMENT _____

Customer will take delivery today if terms are agreeable.

CUSTOMER'S OKAY _____   DEALERSHIP APPROVAL _____

Appendix "D"

Auto Loan Monthly Payment Tables

1.90% ANNUAL PERCENTAGE RATE

LOAN AMT	12 MONTHS TOTAL NOTE	12 MONTHS MONTHLY PAYMENT	18 MONTHS TOTAL NOTE	18 MONTHS MONTHLY PAYMENT	24 MONTHS TOTAL NOTE	24 MONTHS MONTHLY PAYMENT	30 MONTHS TOTAL NOTE	30 MONTHS MONTHLY PAYMENT
1	.96	.08	.90	.05	.96	.04	.90	.03
2	1.92	.16	1.98	.11	1.92	.08	1.80	.06
3	3.00	.25	2.88	.16	2.88	.12	3.00	.10
4	3.96	.33	3.96	.22	3.84	.16	3.90	.13
5	5.04	.42	5.04	.28	5.04	.21	5.10	.17
6	6.00	.50	5.94	.33	6.00	.25	6.00	.20
7	6.96	.58	7.02	.39	6.96	.29	6.90	.23
8	8.04	.67	8.10	.45	7.92	.33	8.10	.27
9	9.00	.75	9.00	.50	9.12	.38	9.00	.30
10	10.08	.84	10.08	.56	10.08	.42	10.20	.34
20	20.16	1.68	20.16	1.12	20.16	.84	20.40	.68
30	30.24	2.52	30.42	1.69	30.48	1.27	30.60	1.02
40	40.32	3.36	40.50	2.25	40.56	1.69	40.80	1.36
50	50.40	4.20	50.58	2.81	50.88	2.12	51.00	1.70
60	60.60	5.05	60.84	3.38	60.96	2.54	61.20	2.04
70	70.68	5.89	70.92	3.94	71.28	2.97	71.70	2.39
80	80.76	6.73	81.18	4.51	81.36	3.39	81.90	2.73
90	90.84	7.57	91.26	5.07	91.68	3.82	92.10	3.07
100	100.92	8.41	101.34	5.63	101.76	4.24	102.30	3.41
200	201.96	16.83	202.86	11.27	203.76	8.49	204.90	6.83
300	303.00	25.25	304.38	16.91	305.76	12.74	307.20	10.24
400	404.04	33.67	405.90	22.55	407.76	16.99	409.80	13.66
500	505.08	42.09	507.42	28.19	509.76	21.24	512.10	17.07
600	606.12	50.51	608.94	33.83	611.76	25.49	614.70	20.49
700	707.16	58.93	710.46	39.47	713.76	29.74	717.30	23.91
800	808.20	67.35	811.98	45.11	815.76	33.99	819.60	27.32
900	909.24	75.77	913.50	50.75	917.76	38.24	922.20	30.74
1000	1010.28	84.19	1015.02	56.39	1019.76	42.49	1024.50	34.15
1500	1515.48	126.29	1522.62	84.59	1529.76	63.74	1536.90	51.23
2000	2020.56	168.38	2030.04	112.78	2039.76	84.99	2049.30	68.31
2500	2525.76	210.48	2537.64	140.98	2549.76	106.24	2561.70	85.39
3000	3030.96	252.58	3045.24	169.18	3059.52	127.48	3074.10	102.47
3500	3536.04	294.67	3552.84	197.38	3569.52	148.73	3586.50	119.55
4000	4041.24	336.77	4060.26	225.57	4079.52	169.98	4098.90	136.63
4500	4546.44	378.87	4567.86	253.77	4589.52	191.23	4611.00	153.70
5000	5051.52	420.96	5075.46	281.97	5099.52	212.48	5123.40	170.78
5500	5556.72	463.06	5583.06	310.17	5609.28	233.72	5635.80	187.86
6000	6061.92	505.16	6090.48	338.36	6119.28	254.97	6148.20	204.94
6500	6567.00	547.25	6598.08	366.56	6629.28	276.22	6660.60	222.02
7000	7072.20	589.35	7105.68	394.76	7139.28	297.47	7173.00	239.10
7500	7577.40	631.45	7613.28	422.96	7649.28	318.72	7685.40	256.18
8000	8082.48	673.54	8120.70	451.15	8159.28	339.97	8197.80	273.26
8500	8587.68	715.64	8628.30	479.35	8669.04	361.21	8709.90	290.33
9000	9092.88	757.74	9135.90	507.55	9179.04	382.46	9222.30	307.41
10000	10103.16	841.93	10150.92	563.94	10199.04	424.96	10247.10	341.57
11000	11113.44	926.12	11166.12	620.34	11218.80	467.45	11271.90	375.73
12000	12123.84	1010.32	12181.14	676.73	12238.80	509.95	12296.70	409.89
13000	13134.12	1094.51	13196.34	733.13	13258.80	552.45	13321.20	444.04
14000	14144.40	1178.70	14211.36	789.52	14278.56	594.94	14346.00	478.20
15000	15154.80	1262.90	15226.56	845.92	15298.56	637.44	15370.80	512.36
16000	16165.08	1347.09	16241.58	902.31	16318.56	679.94	16395.60	546.52
17000	17175.36	1431.28	17256.78	958.71	17338.32	722.43	17420.10	580.67
18000	18185.76	1515.48	18271.80	1015.10	18358.32	764.93	18444.90	614.83
19000	19196.04	1599.67	19287.00	1071.50	19378.32	807.43	19469.70	648.99
20000	20206.32	1683.86	20302.02	1127.89	20398.08	849.92	20494.50	683.15
21000	21216.72	1768.06	21317.22	1184.29	21418.08	892.42	21519.30	717.31
22000	22227.00	1852.25	22332.24	1240.68	22437.84	934.91	22543.80	751.46
23000	23237.28	1936.44	23347.44	1297.08	23457.84	977.41	23568.60	785.62
24000	24247.68	2020.64	24362.46	1353.47	24477.84	1019.91	24593.40	819.78
25000	25257.96	2104.83	25377.66	1409.87	25497.60	1062.40	25618.20	853.94

ANNUAL PERCENTAGE RATE **1.90%**

LOAN AMT	36 MONTHS TOTAL NOTE	36 MONTHS MONTHLY PAYMENT	42 MONTHS TOTAL NOTE	42 MONTHS MONTHLY PAYMENT	48 MONTHS TOTAL NOTE	48 MONTHS MONTHLY PAYMENT	60 MONTHS TOTAL NOTE	60 MONTHS MONTHLY PAYMENT
1	.72	.02	.84	.02	.96	.02	.60	.01
2	1.80	.05	1.68	.04	1.92	.04	1.80	.03
3	2.88	.08	2.94	.07	2.88	.06	3.00	.05
4	3.96	.11	3.78	.09	3.84	.08	3.60	.06
5	5.04	.14	5.04	.12	4.80	.10	4.80	.08
6	6.12	.17	5.88	.14	5.76	.12	6.00	.10
7	7.20	.20	7.14	.17	7.20	.15	7.20	.12
8	7.92	.22	7.98	.19	8.16	.17	7.80	.13
9	9.00	.25	9.24	.22	9.12	.19	9.00	.15
10	10.08	.28	10.08	.24	10.08	.21	10.20	.17
20	20.52	.57	20.58	.49	20.64	.43	20.40	.34
30	30.60	.85	30.66	.73	30.72	.64	31.20	.52
40	41.04	1.14	41.16	.98	41.28	.86	41.40	.69
50	51.12	1.42	51.66	1.23	51.84	1.08	52.20	.87
60	61.56	1.71	61.74	1.47	61.92	1.29	62.40	1.04
70	72.00	2.00	72.24	1.72	72.48	1.51	73.20	1.22
80	82.08	2.28	82.74	1.97	83.04	1.73	83.40	1.39
90	92.52	2.57	92.82	2.21	93.12	1.94	94.20	1.57
100	102.60	2.85	103.32	2.46	103.68	2.16	104.40	1.74
200	205.56	5.71	206.64	4.92	207.84	4.33	209.40	3.49
300	308.52	8.57	309.96	7.38	311.52	6.49	314.40	5.24
400	411.48	11.43	413.70	9.85	415.68	8.66	419.40	6.99
500	514.44	14.29	517.02	12.31	519.36	10.82	524.40	8.74
600	617.40	17.15	620.34	14.77	623.52	12.99	629.40	10.49
700	720.36	20.01	724.08	17.24	727.20	15.15	733.80	12.23
800	823.32	22.87	827.40	19.70	831.36	17.32	838.80	13.98
900	926.28	25.73	930.72	22.16	935.04	19.48	943.80	15.73
1000	1029.24	28.59	1034.04	24.62	1039.20	21.65	1048.80	17.48
1500	1544.04	42.89	1551.48	36.94	1558.56	32.47	1573.20	26.22
2000	2058.84	57.19	2068.50	49.25	2078.40	43.30	2097.60	34.96
2500	2573.64	71.49	2585.94	61.57	2597.76	54.12	2622.60	43.71
3000	3088.44	85.79	3102.96	73.88	3117.60	64.95	3147.00	52.45
3500	3603.24	100.09	3620.40	86.20	3637.44	75.78	3671.40	61.19
4000	4118.04	114.39	4137.42	98.51	4156.80	86.60	4195.80	69.93
4500	4632.84	128.69	4654.44	110.82	4676.64	97.43	4720.20	78.67
5000	5147.64	142.99	5171.88	123.14	5196.00	108.25	5245.20	87.42
5500	5662.44	157.29	5688.90	135.45	5715.84	119.08	5769.60	96.16
6000	6177.24	171.59	6206.34	147.77	6235.20	129.90	6294.00	104.90
6500	6692.04	185.89	6723.36	160.08	6755.04	140.73	6818.40	113.64
7000	7206.84	200.19	7240.80	172.40	7274.88	151.56	7342.80	122.38
7500	7721.64	214.49	7757.82	184.71	7794.24	162.38	7867.80	131.13
8000	8236.44	228.79	8275.26	197.03	8314.08	173.21	8392.20	139.87
8500	8751.24	243.09	8792.28	209.34	8833.44	184.03	8916.60	148.61
9000	9266.04	257.39	9309.30	221.65	9353.28	194.86	9441.00	157.35
10000	10295.28	285.98	10343.76	246.28	10392.48	216.51	10490.40	174.84
11000	11324.88	314.58	11378.22	270.91	11431.68	238.16	11539.20	192.32
12000	12354.48	343.18	12412.68	295.54	12470.88	259.81	12588.00	209.80
13000	13384.08	371.78	13447.14	320.17	13510.08	281.46	13637.40	227.29
14000	14413.68	400.38	14481.60	344.80	14549.76	303.12	14686.20	244.77
15000	15443.28	428.98	15516.06	369.43	15588.96	324.77	15735.60	262.26
16000	16472.88	457.58	16550.52	394.06	16628.16	346.42	16784.40	279.74
17000	17502.48	486.18	17584.56	418.68	17667.36	368.07	17833.20	297.22
18000	18532.08	514.78	18619.02	443.31	18706.56	389.72	18882.60	314.71
19000	19561.32	543.37	19653.48	467.94	19745.76	411.37	19931.40	332.19
20000	20590.92	571.97	20687.94	492.57	20785.44	433.03	20980.80	349.68
21000	21620.52	600.57	21722.40	517.20	21824.64	454.68	22029.60	367.16
22000	22650.12	629.17	22756.86	541.83	22863.84	476.33	23078.40	384.64
23000	23679.72	657.77	23791.32	566.46	23903.04	497.98	24127.80	402.13
24000	24709.32	686.37	24825.78	591.09	24942.24	519.63	25176.60	419.61
25000	25738.92	714.97	25860.24	615.72	25981.44	541.28	26226.00	437.10

2.90% ANNUAL PERCENTAGE RATE

LOAN AMT	12 MONTHS TOTAL NOTE	12 MONTHS MONTHLY PAYMENT	18 MONTHS TOTAL NOTE	18 MONTHS MONTHLY PAYMENT	24 MONTHS TOTAL NOTE	24 MONTHS MONTHLY PAYMENT	30 MONTHS TOTAL NOTE	30 MONTHS MONTHLY PAYMENT
1	.96	.08	.90	.05	.96	.04	.90	.03
2	1.92	.16	1.98	.11	1.92	.08	1.80	.06
3	3.00	.25	3.06	.17	2.88	.12	3.00	.10
4	3.96	.33	3.96	.22	4.08	.17	3.90	.13
5	5.04	.42	5.04	.28	5.04	.21	5.10	.17
6	6.00	.50	6.12	.34	6.00	.25	6.00	.20
7	7.08	.59	7.02	.39	7.20	.30	7.20	.24
8	8.04	.67	8.10	.45	8.16	.34	8.10	.27
9	9.12	.76	9.18	.51	9.12	.38	9.30	.31
10	10.08	.84	10.08	.56	10.08	.42	10.20	.34
20	20.28	1.69	20.34	1.13	20.40	.85	20.70	.69
30	30.36	2.53	30.60	1.70	30.72	1.28	30.90	1.03
40	40.56	3.38	40.86	2.27	41.04	1.71	41.40	1.38
50	50.76	4.23	51.12	2.84	51.36	2.14	51.60	1.72
60	60.84	5.07	61.38	3.41	61.68	2.57	62.10	2.07
70	71.04	5.92	71.46	3.97	72.00	3.00	72.60	2.42
80	81.24	6.77	81.72	4.54	82.32	3.43	82.80	2.76
90	91.32	7.61	91.98	5.11	92.64	3.86	93.30	3.11
100	101.52	8.46	102.24	5.68	102.96	4.29	103.50	3.45
200	203.04	16.92	204.48	11.36	205.92	8.58	207.30	6.91
300	304.68	25.39	306.90	17.05	309.12	12.88	311.10	10.37
400	406.20	33.85	409.14	22.73	412.08	17.17	414.90	13.83
500	507.84	42.32	511.38	28.41	515.04	21.46	518.70	17.29
600	609.36	50.78	613.80	34.10	618.24	25.76	622.50	20.75
700	711.00	59.25	716.04	39.78	721.20	30.05	726.30	24.21
800	812.52	67.71	818.46	45.47	824.16	34.34	830.10	27.67
900	914.16	76.18	920.70	51.15	927.36	38.64	933.90	31.13
1000	1015.68	84.64	1022.94	56.83	1030.32	42.93	1037.70	34.59
1500	1523.64	126.97	1534.50	85.25	1545.60	64.40	1556.70	51.89
2000	2031.48	169.29	2046.06	113.67	2060.88	85.87	2075.70	69.19
2500	2539.44	211.62	2557.62	142.09	2576.16	107.34	2594.70	86.49
3000	3047.28	253.94	3069.18	170.51	3091.44	128.81	3113.40	103.78
3500	3555.12	296.26	3580.74	198.93	3606.48	150.27	3632.40	121.08
4000	4063.08	338.59	4092.30	227.35	4121.76	171.74	4151.40	138.38
4500	4570.92	380.91	4603.86	255.77	4637.04	193.21	4670.40	155.68
5000	5078.88	423.24	5115.42	284.19	5152.32	214.68	5189.40	172.98
5500	5586.72	465.56	5626.98	312.61	5667.60	236.15	5708.40	190.28
6000	6094.56	507.88	6138.54	341.03	6182.88	257.62	6227.10	207.57
6500	6602.52	550.21	6650.10	369.45	6698.16	279.09	6746.10	224.87
7000	7110.36	592.53	7161.66	397.87	7213.20	300.55	7265.10	242.17
7500	7618.32	634.86	7673.22	426.29	7728.48	322.02	7784.10	259.47
8000	8126.16	677.18	8184.78	454.71	8243.76	343.49	8303.10	276.77
8500	8634.00	719.50	8696.34	483.13	8759.04	364.96	8822.10	294.07
9000	9141.96	761.83	9207.90	511.55	9274.32	386.43	9340.80	311.36
10000	10157.76	846.48	10231.02	568.39	10304.64	429.36	10378.80	345.96
11000	11173.44	931.12	11254.14	625.23	11335.20	472.30	11416.80	380.56
12000	12189.24	1015.77	12277.26	682.07	12365.76	515.24	12454.50	415.15
13000	13205.04	1100.42	13300.38	738.91	13396.32	558.18	13492.50	449.75
14000	14220.84	1185.07	14323.50	795.75	14426.64	601.11	14530.50	484.35
15000	15236.64	1269.72	15346.62	852.59	15457.20	644.05	15568.20	518.94
16000	16252.44	1354.37	16369.74	909.43	16487.76	686.99	16606.20	553.54
17000	17268.12	1439.01	17392.86	966.27	17518.08	729.92	17644.20	588.14
18000	18283.92	1523.66	18415.98	1023.11	18548.64	772.86	18681.90	622.73
19000	19299.72	1608.31	19439.10	1079.95	19579.20	815.80	19719.90	657.33
20000	20315.52	1692.96	20462.22	1136.79	20609.52	858.73	20757.90	691.93
21000	21331.32	1777.61	21485.34	1193.63	21640.08	901.67	21795.60	726.52
22000	22347.00	1862.25	22508.46	1250.47	22670.64	944.61	22833.60	761.12
23000	23362.80	1946.90	23531.58	1307.31	23701.20	987.55	23871.30	795.71
24000	24378.60	2031.55	24554.70	1364.15	24731.52	1030.48	24909.30	830.31
25000	25394.40	2116.20	25577.82	1420.99	25762.08	1073.42	25947.30	864.91

ANNUAL PERCENTAGE RATE **2.90%**

	36 MONTHS		42 MONTHS		48 MONTHS		60 MONTHS	
LOAN AMT	TOTAL NOTE	MONTHLY PAYMENT	TOTAL NOTE	MONTHLY PAYMENT	TOTAL NOTE	MONTHLY PAYMENT	TOTAL NOTE	MONTHLY PAYMENT
1	.72	.02	.84	.02	.96	.02	.60	.01
2	1.80	.05	2.10	.05	1.92	.04	1.80	.03
3	2.88	.08	2.94	.07	2.88	.06	3.00	.05
4	3.96	.11	4.20	.10	3.84	.08	4.20	.07
5	5.04	.14	5.04	.12	5.28	.11	4.80	.08
6	6.12	.17	6.30	.15	6.24	.13	6.00	.10
7	7.20	.20	7.14	.17	7.20	.15	7.20	.12
8	8.28	.23	8.40	.20	8.16	.17	8.40	.14
9	9.36	.26	9.24	.22	9.12	.19	9.60	.16
10	10.44	.29	10.50	.25	10.56	.22	10.20	.17
20	20.88	.58	21.00	.50	21.12	.44	21.00	.35
30	31.32	.87	31.50	.75	31.68	.66	31.80	.53
40	41.76	1.16	42.00	1.00	42.24	.88	42.60	.71
50	52.20	1.45	52.50	1.25	52.80	1.10	53.40	.89
60	62.64	1.74	63.00	1.50	63.36	1.32	64.20	1.07
70	73.08	2.03	73.50	1.75	73.92	1.54	75.00	1.25
80	83.52	2.32	84.00	2.00	84.48	1.76	85.80	1.43
90	93.96	2.61	94.50	2.25	95.04	1.98	96.60	1.61
100	104.40	2.90	105.00	2.50	105.60	2.20	107.40	1.79
200	208.80	5.80	210.42	5.01	211.68	4.41	214.80	3.58
300	313.56	8.71	315.84	7.52	317.76	6.62	322.20	5.37
400	417.96	11.61	420.84	10.02	423.84	8.83	429.60	7.16
500	522.36	14.51	526.26	12.53	529.92	11.04	537.60	8.96
600	627.12	17.42	631.68	15.04	636.00	13.25	645.00	10.75
700	731.52	20.32	736.68	17.54	742.08	15.46	752.40	12.54
800	835.92	23.22	842.10	20.05	848.16	17.67	859.80	14.33
900	940.68	26.13	947.52	22.56	954.24	19.88	967.80	16.13
1000	1045.08	29.03	1052.52	25.06	1060.32	22.09	1075.20	17.92
1500	1567.80	43.55	1579.20	37.60	1590.24	33.13	1612.80	26.88
2000	2090.52	58.07	2105.46	50.13	2120.64	44.18	2150.40	35.84
2500	2613.24	72.59	2631.72	62.66	2650.56	55.22	2688.60	44.81
3000	3135.96	87.11	3158.40	75.20	3180.96	66.27	3226.20	53.77
3500	3658.68	101.63	3684.66	87.73	3710.88	77.31	3763.80	62.73
4000	4181.04	116.14	4210.92	100.26	4241.28	88.36	4301.40	71.69
4500	4703.76	130.66	4737.60	112.80	4771.20	99.40	4839.00	80.65
5000	5226.48	145.18	5263.86	125.33	5301.60	110.45	5377.20	89.62
5500	5749.20	159.70	5790.12	137.86	5831.52	121.49	5914.80	98.58
6000	6271.92	174.22	6316.80	150.40	6361.92	132.54	6452.40	107.54
6500	6794.64	188.74	6843.06	162.93	6891.84	143.58	6990.00	116.50
7000	7317.36	203.26	7369.32	175.46	7422.24	154.63	7528.20	125.47
7500	7839.72	217.77	7896.00	188.00	7952.16	165.67	8065.80	134.43
8000	8362.44	232.29	8422.26	200.53	8482.56	176.72	8603.40	143.39
8500	8885.16	246.81	8948.52	213.06	9012.48	187.76	9141.00	152.35
9000	9407.88	261.33	9475.20	225.60	9542.88	198.81	9678.60	161.31
10000	10453.32	290.37	10528.14	250.67	10603.20	220.90	10754.40	179.24
11000	11498.40	319.40	11580.66	275.73	11663.52	242.99	11829.60	197.16
12000	12543.84	348.44	12633.60	300.80	12723.84	265.08	12905.40	215.09
13000	13589.28	377.48	13686.54	325.87	13784.16	287.17	13980.60	233.01
14000	14634.72	406.52	14739.06	350.93	14844.48	309.26	15056.40	250.94
15000	15679.80	435.55	15792.00	376.00	15904.80	331.35	16131.60	268.86
16000	16725.24	464.59	16844.94	401.07	16965.12	353.44	17206.80	286.78
17000	17770.68	493.63	17897.46	426.13	18025.44	375.53	18282.60	304.71
18000	18815.76	522.66	18950.40	451.20	19085.76	397.62	19357.80	322.63
19000	19861.20	551.70	20003.34	476.27	20146.08	419.71	20433.60	340.56
20000	20906.64	580.74	21056.28	501.34	21206.40	441.80	21508.80	358.48
21000	21952.08	609.78	22108.80	526.40	22266.72	463.89	22584.60	376.41
22000	22997.16	638.81	23161.74	551.47	23327.04	485.98	23659.80	394.33
23000	24042.60	667.85	24214.68	576.54	24387.36	508.07	24735.00	412.25
24000	25088.04	696.89	25267.20	601.60	25447.68	530.16	25810.80	430.18
25000	26133.12	725.92	26320.14	626.67	26508.00	552.25	26886.00	448.10

3.90% ANNUAL PERCENTAGE RATE

LOAN AMT	12 MONTHS TOTAL NOTE	12 MONTHS MONTHLY PAYMENT	18 MONTHS TOTAL NOTE	18 MONTHS MONTHLY PAYMENT	24 MONTHS TOTAL NOTE	24 MONTHS MONTHLY PAYMENT	30 MONTHS TOTAL NOTE	30 MONTHS MONTHLY PAYMENT
1	.96	.08	.90	.05	.96	.04	.90	.03
2	2.04	.17	1.98	.11	1.92	.08	2.10	.07
3	3.00	.25	3.06	.17	3.12	.13	3.00	.10
4	4.08	.34	3.96	.22	4.08	.17	4.20	.14
5	5.04	.42	5.04	.28	5.04	.21	5.10	.17
6	6.12	.51	6.12	.34	6.24	.26	6.30	.21
7	7.08	.59	7.20	.40	7.20	.30	7.20	.24
8	8.16	.68	8.10	.45	8.16	.34	8.40	.28
9	9.12	.76	9.18	.51	9.36	.39	9.30	.31
10	10.20	.85	10.26	.57	10.32	.43	10.50	.35
20	20.40	1.70	20.52	1.14	20.64	.86	21.00	.70
30	30.60	2.55	30.78	1.71	31.20	1.30	31.50	1.05
40	40.80	3.40	41.22	2.29	41.52	1.73	42.00	1.40
50	51.00	4.25	51.48	2.86	51.84	2.16	52.50	1.75
60	61.20	5.10	61.74	3.43	62.40	2.60	63.00	2.10
70	71.40	5.95	72.18	4.01	72.72	3.03	73.50	2.45
80	81.60	6.80	82.44	4.58	83.28	3.47	84.00	2.80
90	91.80	7.65	92.70	5.15	93.60	3.90	94.50	3.15
100	102.12	8.51	102.96	5.72	103.92	4.33	105.00	3.50
200	204.24	17.02	206.10	11.45	208.08	8.67	210.00	7.00
300	306.36	25.53	309.24	17.18	312.24	13.01	315.30	10.51
400	408.48	34.04	412.38	22.91	416.40	17.35	420.30	14.01
500	510.60	42.55	515.52	28.64	520.56	21.69	525.30	17.51
600	612.72	51.06	618.66	34.37	624.48	26.02	630.60	21.02
700	714.84	59.57	721.80	40.10	728.64	30.36	735.60	24.52
800	816.96	68.08	824.76	45.82	832.80	34.70	840.90	28.03
900	919.08	76.59	927.90	51.55	936.96	39.04	945.90	31.53
1000	1021.20	85.10	1031.04	57.28	1041.12	43.38	1050.90	35.03
1500	1531.80	127.65	1546.56	85.92	1561.68	65.07	1576.50	52.55
2000	2042.40	170.20	2062.26	114.57	2082.24	86.76	2102.10	70.07
2500	2553.12	212.76	2577.78	143.21	2602.80	108.45	2627.70	87.59
3000	3063.72	255.31	3093.30	171.85	3123.36	130.14	3153.30	105.11
3500	3574.32	297.86	3609.00	200.50	3643.92	151.83	3678.90	122.63
4000	4084.92	340.41	4124.52	229.14	4164.48	173.52	4204.50	140.15
4500	4595.52	382.96	4640.04	257.78	4685.04	195.21	4730.10	157.67
5000	5106.24	425.52	5155.74	286.43	5205.60	216.90	5255.70	175.19
5500	5616.84	468.07	5671.26	315.07	5726.16	238.59	5781.30	192.71
6000	6127.44	510.62	6186.78	343.71	6246.72	260.28	6306.90	210.23
6500	6638.04	553.17	6702.48	372.36	6767.28	281.97	6832.50	227.75
7000	7148.64	595.72	7218.00	401.00	7287.84	303.66	7358.10	245.27
7500	7659.36	638.28	7733.52	429.64	7808.40	325.35	7883.70	262.79
8000	8169.96	680.83	8249.22	458.29	8328.96	347.04	8409.30	280.31
8500	8680.56	723.38	8764.74	486.93	8849.52	368.73	8934.90	297.83
9000	9191.16	765.93	9280.26	515.57	9370.08	390.42	9460.20	315.34
10000	10212.48	851.04	10311.48	572.86	10411.20	433.80	10511.40	350.38
11000	11233.68	936.14	11342.70	630.15	11452.32	477.18	11562.60	385.42
12000	12255.00	1021.25	12373.74	687.43	12493.44	520.56	12613.80	420.46
13000	13276.20	1106.35	13404.96	744.72	13534.56	563.94	13665.00	455.50
14000	14297.40	1191.45	14436.18	802.01	14575.68	607.32	14716.20	490.54
15000	15318.72	1276.56	15467.22	859.29	15616.80	650.70	15767.40	525.58
16000	16339.92	1361.66	16498.44	916.58	16657.92	694.08	16818.60	560.62
17000	17361.24	1446.77	17529.66	973.87	17699.04	737.46	17869.80	595.66
18000	18382.44	1531.87	18560.70	1031.15	18740.16	780.84	18920.70	630.69
19000	19403.76	1616.98	19591.92	1088.44	19781.28	824.22	19971.90	665.73
20000	20424.96	1702.08	20623.14	1145.73	20822.40	867.60	21023.10	700.77
21000	21446.16	1787.18	21654.18	1203.01	21863.52	910.98	22074.30	735.81
22000	22467.48	1872.29	22685.40	1260.30	22904.64	954.36	23125.50	770.85
23000	23488.68	1957.39	23716.62	1317.59	23945.76	997.74	24176.70	805.89
24000	24510.00	2042.50	24747.66	1374.87	24987.12	1041.13	25227.90	840.93
25000	25531.20	2127.60	25778.88	1432.16	26028.24	1084.51	26279.10	875.97

ANNUAL PERCENTAGE RATE **3.90%**

LOAN AMT	36 MONTHS TOTAL NOTE	36 MONTHS MONTHLY PAYMENT	42 MONTHS TOTAL NOTE	42 MONTHS MONTHLY PAYMENT	48 MONTHS TOTAL NOTE	48 MONTHS MONTHLY PAYMENT	60 MONTHS TOTAL NOTE	60 MONTHS MONTHLY PAYMENT
1	.72	.02	.84	.02	.96	.02	.60	.01
2	1.80	.05	2.10	.05	1.92	.04	1.80	.03
3	2.88	.08	2.94	.07	2.88	.06	3.00	.05
4	3.96	.11	4.20	.10	4.32	.09	4.20	.07
5	5.04	.14	5.04	.12	5.28	.11	5.40	.09
6	6.12	.17	6.30	.15	6.24	.13	6.60	.11
7	7.20	.20	7.14	.17	7.20	.15	7.20	.12
8	8.28	.23	8.40	.20	8.64	.18	8.40	.14
9	9.36	.26	9.24	.22	9.60	.20	9.60	.16
10	10.44	.29	10.50	.25	10.56	.22	10.80	.18
20	20.88	.58	21.42	.51	21.60	.45	21.60	.36
30	31.68	.88	31.92	.76	32.16	.67	33.00	.55
40	42.12	1.17	42.84	1.02	43.20	.90	43.80	.73
50	52.92	1.47	53.34	1.27	53.76	1.12	54.60	.91
60	63.36	1.76	64.26	1.53	64.80	1.35	66.00	1.10
70	74.16	2.06	74.76	1.78	75.36	1.57	76.80	1.28
80	84.60	2.35	85.68	2.04	86.40	1.80	87.60	1.46
90	95.40	2.65	96.18	2.29	96.96	2.02	99.00	1.65
100	105.84	2.94	107.10	2.55	108.00	2.25	109.80	1.83
200	212.04	5.89	214.20	5.10	216.00	4.50	220.20	3.67
300	318.24	8.84	321.30	7.65	324.48	6.76	330.60	5.51
400	424.44	11.79	428.40	10.20	432.48	9.01	440.40	7.34
500	530.28	14.73	535.50	12.75	540.48	11.26	550.80	9.18
600	636.48	17.68	642.60	15.30	648.96	13.52	661.20	11.02
700	742.68	20.63	749.70	17.85	756.96	15.77	771.60	12.86
800	848.88	23.58	856.80	20.40	864.96	18.02	881.40	14.69
900	955.08	26.53	963.90	22.95	973.44	20.28	991.80	16.53
1000	1060.92	29.47	1071.42	25.51	1081.44	22.53	1102.20	18.37
1500	1591.56	44.21	1606.92	38.26	1622.40	33.80	1653.00	27.55
2000	2122.20	58.95	2142.84	51.02	2162.88	45.06	2204.40	36.74
2500	2652.84	73.69	2678.34	63.77	2703.84	56.33	2755.20	45.92
3000	3183.48	88.43	3214.26	76.53	3244.80	67.60	3306.60	55.11
3500	3714.12	103.17	3749.76	89.28	3785.76	78.87	3858.00	64.30
4000	4244.76	117.91	4285.68	102.04	4326.24	90.13	4408.80	73.48
4500	4775.40	132.65	4821.18	114.79	4867.20	101.40	4960.20	82.67
5000	5306.04	147.39	5357.10	127.55	5408.16	112.67	5511.00	91.85
5500	5836.68	162.13	5892.60	140.30	5948.64	123.93	6062.40	101.04
6000	6367.32	176.87	6428.52	153.06	6489.60	135.20	6613.20	110.22
6500	6897.96	191.61	6964.02	165.81	7030.56	146.47	7164.60	119.41
7000	7428.60	206.35	7499.94	178.57	7571.52	157.74	7716.00	128.60
7500	7959.24	221.09	8035.44	191.32	8112.00	169.00	8266.80	137.78
8000	8489.88	235.83	8571.36	204.08	8652.96	180.27	8818.20	146.97
8500	9020.52	250.57	9106.86	216.83	9193.92	191.54	9369.00	156.15
9000	9551.16	265.31	9642.78	229.59	9734.40	202.80	9920.40	165.34
10000	10612.44	294.79	10714.20	255.10	10816.32	225.34	11022.60	183.71
11000	11673.72	324.27	11785.62	280.61	11897.76	247.87	12124.80	202.08
12000	12735.00	353.75	12857.04	306.12	12979.68	270.41	13227.00	220.45
13000	13796.28	383.23	13928.46	331.63	14061.12	292.94	14329.20	238.82
14000	14857.56	412.71	14999.88	357.14	15143.04	315.48	15432.00	257.20
15000	15918.84	442.19	16071.30	382.65	16224.48	338.01	16534.20	275.57
16000	16980.12	471.67	17142.72	408.16	17305.92	360.54	17636.40	293.94
17000	18041.40	501.15	18214.14	433.67	18387.84	383.08	18738.60	312.31
18000	19102.68	530.63	19285.56	459.18	19469.28	405.61	19840.80	330.68
19000	20163.96	560.11	20356.98	484.69	20551.20	428.15	20943.00	349.05
20000	21225.24	589.59	21428.40	510.20	21632.64	450.68	22045.20	367.42
21000	22286.16	619.06	22499.82	535.71	22714.56	473.22	23148.00	385.80
22000	23347.44	648.54	23571.24	561.22	23796.00	495.75	24250.20	404.17
23000	24408.72	678.02	24642.66	586.73	24877.44	518.28	25352.40	422.54
24000	25470.00	707.50	25714.08	612.24	25959.36	540.82	26454.60	440.91
25000	26531.28	736.98	26785.50	637.75	27040.80	563.35	27556.80	459.28

4.90% ANNUAL PERCENTAGE RATE

LOAN AMT	12 MONTHS TOTAL NOTE	MONTHLY PAYMENT	18 MONTHS TOTAL NOTE	MONTHLY PAYMENT	24 MONTHS TOTAL NOTE	MONTHLY PAYMENT	30 MONTHS TOTAL NOTE	MONTHLY PAYMENT
1	.96	.08	.90	.05	.96	.04	.90	.03
2	2.04	.17	1.98	.11	1.92	.08	2.10	.07
3	3.00	.25	3.06	.17	3.12	.13	3.00	.10
4	4.08	.34	4.14	.23	4.08	.17	4.20	.14
5	5.04	.42	5.04	.28	5.04	.21	5.10	.17
6	6.12	.51	6.12	.34	6.24	.26	6.30	.21
7	7.08	.59	7.20	.40	7.20	.30	7.20	.24
8	8.16	.68	8.28	.46	8.40	.35	8.40	.28
9	9.24	.77	9.18	.51	9.36	.39	9.30	.31
10	10.20	.85	10.26	.57	10.32	.43	10.50	.35
20	20.52	1.71	20.70	1.15	20.88	.87	21.00	.70
30	30.72	2.56	31.14	1.73	31.44	1.31	31.80	1.06
40	41.04	3.42	41.40	2.30	42.00	1.75	42.30	1.41
50	51.24	4.27	51.84	2.88	52.56	2.19	53.10	1.77
60	61.56	5.13	62.28	3.46	62.88	2.62	63.60	2.12
70	71.76	5.98	72.72	4.04	73.44	3.06	74.40	2.48
80	82.08	6.84	82.98	4.61	84.00	3.50	84.90	2.83
90	92.40	7.70	93.42	5.19	94.56	3.94	95.70	3.19
100	102.60	8.55	103.86	5.77	105.12	4.38	106.20	3.54
200	205.32	17.11	207.72	11.54	210.24	8.76	212.70	7.09
300	307.92	25.66	311.76	17.32	315.36	13.14	319.20	10.64
400	410.64	34.22	415.62	23.09	420.72	17.53	425.70	14.19
500	513.36	42.78	519.48	28.86	525.84	21.91	532.20	17.74
600	615.96	51.33	623.52	34.64	630.96	26.29	638.70	21.29
700	718.68	59.89	727.38	40.41	736.08	30.67	744.90	24.83
800	821.28	68.44	831.24	46.18	841.44	35.06	851.40	28.38
900	924.00	77.00	935.28	51.96	946.56	39.44	957.90	31.93
1000	1026.72	85.56	1039.14	57.73	1051.68	43.82	1064.40	35.48
1500	1540.08	128.34	1558.80	86.60	1577.52	65.73	1596.60	53.22
2000	2053.44	171.12	2078.46	115.47	2103.60	87.65	2128.80	70.96
2500	2566.80	213.90	2597.94	144.33	2629.44	109.56	2661.30	88.71
3000	3080.16	256.68	3117.60	173.20	3155.28	131.47	3193.50	106.45
3500	3593.52	299.46	3637.26	202.07	3681.36	153.39	3725.70	124.19
4000	4106.88	342.24	4156.92	230.94	4207.20	175.30	4257.90	141.93
4500	4620.24	385.02	4676.40	259.80	4733.04	197.21	4790.40	159.68
5000	5133.60	427.80	5196.06	288.67	5259.12	219.13	5322.60	177.42
5500	5646.96	470.58	5715.72	317.54	5784.96	241.04	5854.80	195.16
6000	6160.32	513.36	6235.38	346.41	6310.80	262.95	6387.00	212.90
6500	6673.80	556.15	6755.04	375.28	6836.88	284.87	6919.20	230.64
7000	7187.16	598.93	7274.52	404.14	7362.72	306.78	7451.70	248.39
7500	7700.52	641.71	7794.18	433.01	7888.56	328.69	7983.90	266.13
8000	8213.88	684.49	8313.84	461.88	8414.64	350.61	8516.10	283.87
8500	8727.24	727.27	8833.50	490.75	8940.48	372.52	9048.30	301.61
9000	9240.60	770.05	9352.98	519.61	9466.32	394.43	9580.80	319.36
10000	10267.32	855.61	10392.30	577.35	10518.24	438.26	10645.20	354.84
11000	11294.04	941.17	11431.62	635.09	11570.16	482.09	11709.90	390.33
12000	12320.76	1026.73	12470.76	692.82	12621.84	525.91	12774.30	425.81
13000	13347.60	1112.30	13510.08	750.56	13673.76	569.74	13838.70	461.29
14000	14374.32	1197.86	14549.22	808.29	14725.68	613.57	14903.40	496.78
15000	15401.04	1283.42	15588.54	866.03	15777.36	657.39	15967.80	532.26
16000	16427.76	1368.98	16627.68	923.76	16829.28	701.22	17032.50	567.75
17000	17454.48	1454.54	17667.00	981.50	17881.20	745.05	18096.90	603.23
18000	18481.20	1540.10	18706.14	1039.23	18932.88	788.87	19161.60	638.72
19000	19508.04	1625.67	19745.46	1096.97	19984.80	832.70	20226.00	674.20
20000	20534.76	1711.23	20784.78	1154.71	21036.72	876.53	21290.70	709.69
21000	21561.48	1796.79	21823.92	1212.44	22088.40	920.35	22355.10	745.17
22000	22588.20	1882.35	22863.24	1270.18	23140.32	964.18	23419.80	780.66
23000	23614.92	1967.91	23902.38	1327.91	24192.24	1008.01	24484.20	816.14
24000	24641.64	2053.47	24941.70	1385.65	25243.92	1051.83	25548.90	851.63
25000	25668.48	2139.04	25980.84	1443.38	26295.84	1095.66	26613.30	887.11

ANNUAL PERCENTAGE RATE **4.90%**

LOAN AMT	36 MONTHS TOTAL NOTE	MONTHLY PAYMENT	42 MONTHS TOTAL NOTE	MONTHLY PAYMENT	48 MONTHS TOTAL NOTE	MONTHLY PAYMENT	60 MONTHS TOTAL NOTE	MONTHLY PAYMENT
1	.72	.02	.84	.02	.96	.02	.60	.01
2	1.80	.05	2.10	.05	1.92	.04	1.80	.03
3	2.88	.08	2.94	.07	2.88	.06	3.00	.05
4	3.96	.11	4.20	.10	4.32	.09	4.20	.07
5	5.04	.14	5.04	.12	5.28	.11	5.40	.09
6	6.12	.17	6.30	.15	6.24	.13	6.60	.11
7	7.20	.20	7.56	.18	7.68	.16	7.80	.13
8	8.28	.23	8.40	.20	8.64	.18	9.00	.15
9	9.36	.26	9.66	.23	9.60	.20	9.60	.16
10	10.44	.29	10.50	.25	10.56	.22	10.80	.18
20	21.24	.59	21.42	.51	21.60	.45	22.20	.37
30	32.04	.89	32.34	.77	32.64	.68	33.60	.56
40	42.84	1.19	43.26	1.03	43.68	.91	45.00	.75
50	53.64	1.49	54.18	1.29	54.72	1.14	56.40	.94
60	64.44	1.79	65.10	1.55	65.76	1.37	67.20	1.12
70	75.24	2.09	76.02	1.81	76.80	1.60	78.60	1.31
80	86.04	2.39	86.94	2.07	87.84	1.83	90.00	1.50
90	96.84	2.69	97.86	2.33	98.88	2.06	101.40	1.69
100	107.64	2.99	108.78	2.59	109.92	2.29	112.80	1.88
200	215.28	5.98	217.98	5.19	220.32	4.59	225.60	3.76
300	322.92	8.97	326.76	7.78	330.72	6.89	338.40	5.64
400	430.92	11.97	435.96	10.38	441.12	9.19	451.80	7.53
500	538.56	14.96	544.74	12.97	551.52	11.49	564.60	9.41
600	646.20	17.95	653.94	15.57	661.92	13.79	677.40	11.29
700	753.84	20.94	763.14	18.17	771.84	16.08	790.20	13.17
800	861.84	23.94	871.92	20.76	882.24	18.38	903.60	15.06
900	969.48	26.93	981.12	23.36	992.64	20.68	1016.40	16.94
1000	1077.12	29.92	1089.90	25.95	1103.04	22.98	1129.20	18.82
1500	1615.68	44.88	1635.06	38.93	1654.56	34.47	1693.80	28.23
2000	2154.60	59.85	2180.22	51.91	2206.08	45.96	2259.00	37.65
2500	2693.16	74.81	2725.38	64.89	2758.08	57.46	2823.60	47.06
3000	3231.72	89.77	3270.54	77.87	3309.60	68.95	3388.20	56.47
3500	3770.64	104.74	3815.70	90.85	3861.12	80.44	3952.80	65.88
4000	4309.20	119.70	4360.86	103.83	4412.64	91.93	4518.00	75.30
4500	4847.76	134.66	4906.02	116.81	4964.16	103.42	5082.60	84.71
5000	5386.68	149.63	5450.76	129.78	5516.16	114.92	5647.20	94.12
5500	5925.24	164.59	5995.92	142.76	6067.68	126.41	6211.80	103.53
6000	6463.80	179.55	6541.08	155.74	6619.20	137.90	6777.00	112.95
6500	7002.36	194.51	7086.24	168.72	7170.72	149.39	7341.60	122.36
7000	7541.28	209.48	7631.40	181.70	7722.24	160.88	7906.20	131.77
7500	8079.84	224.44	8176.56	194.68	8274.24	172.38	8471.40	141.19
8000	8618.40	239.40	8721.72	207.66	8825.76	183.87	9036.00	150.60
8500	9157.32	254.37	9266.88	220.64	9377.28	195.36	9600.60	160.01
9000	9695.88	269.33	9812.04	233.62	9928.80	206.85	10165.20	169.42
10000	10773.36	299.26	10901.94	259.57	11032.32	229.84	11295.00	188.25
11000	11850.48	329.18	11992.26	285.53	12135.36	252.82	12424.20	207.07
12000	12927.96	359.11	13082.58	311.49	13238.40	275.80	13554.00	225.90
13000	14005.08	389.03	14172.90	337.45	14341.92	298.79	14683.80	244.73
14000	15082.56	418.96	15263.22	363.41	15444.96	321.77	15813.00	263.55
15000	16160.04	448.89	16353.12	389.36	16548.48	344.76	16942.80	282.38
16000	17237.16	478.81	17443.44	415.32	17651.52	367.74	18072.00	301.20
17000	18314.64	508.74	18533.76	441.28	18754.56	390.72	19201.80	320.03
18000	19391.76	538.66	19624.08	467.24	19858.08	413.71	20331.00	338.85
19000	20469.24	568.59	20714.40	493.20	20961.12	436.69	21460.80	357.68
20000	21546.72	598.52	21804.30	519.15	22064.64	459.68	22590.00	376.50
21000	22623.84	628.44	22894.62	545.11	23167.68	482.66	23719.80	395.33
22000	23701.32	658.37	23984.94	571.07	24270.72	505.64	24849.00	414.15
23000	24778.44	688.29	25075.26	597.03	25374.24	528.63	25978.80	432.98
24000	25855.92	718.22	26165.58	622.99	26477.28	551.61	27108.60	451.81
25000	26933.40	748.15	27255.48	648.94	27580.80	574.60	28237.80	470.63

5.00% ANNUAL PERCENTAGE RATE

LOAN AMT	12 MONTHS TOTAL NOTE	12 MONTHS MONTHLY PAYMENT	18 MONTHS TOTAL NOTE	18 MONTHS MONTHLY PAYMENT	24 MONTHS TOTAL NOTE	24 MONTHS MONTHLY PAYMENT	30 MONTHS TOTAL NOTE	30 MONTHS MONTHLY PAYMENT
1	.96	.08	.90	.05	.96	.04	.90	.03
2	2.04	.17	1.98	.11	1.92	.08	2.10	.07
3	3.00	.25	3.06	.17	3.12	.13	3.00	.10
4	4.08	.34	4.14	.23	4.08	.17	4.20	.14
5	5.04	.42	5.04	.28	5.04	.21	5.10	.17
6	6.12	.51	6.12	.34	6.24	.26	6.30	.21
7	7.08	.59	7.20	.40	7.20	.30	7.20	.24
8	8.16	.68	8.28	.46	8.40	.35	8.40	.28
9	9.24	.77	9.36	.52	9.36	.39	9.30	.31
10	10.20	.85	10.26	.57	10.32	.43	10.50	.35
20	20.52	1.71	20.70	1.15	20.88	.87	21.30	.71
30	30.72	2.56	31.14	1.73	31.44	1.31	31.80	1.06
40	41.04	3.42	41.58	2.31	42.00	1.75	42.60	1.42
50	51.36	4.28	51.84	2.88	52.56	2.19	53.10	1.77
60	61.56	5.13	62.28	3.46	63.12	2.63	63.90	2.13
70	71.88	5.99	72.72	4.04	73.68	3.07	74.40	2.48
80	82.08	6.84	83.16	4.62	84.00	3.50	85.20	2.84
90	92.40	7.70	93.60	5.20	94.56	3.94	95.70	3.19
100	102.72	8.56	103.86	5.77	105.12	4.38	106.50	3.55
200	205.44	17.12	207.90	11.55	210.48	8.77	213.00	7.10
300	308.16	25.68	311.94	17.33	315.84	13.16	319.50	10.65
400	410.88	34.24	415.98	23.11	420.96	17.54	426.30	14.21
500	513.60	42.80	520.02	28.89	526.32	21.93	532.80	17.76
600	616.32	51.36	623.88	34.66	631.68	26.32	639.30	21.31
700	719.04	59.92	727.92	40.44	736.80	30.70	746.10	24.87
800	821.76	68.48	831.96	46.22	842.16	35.09	852.60	28.42
900	924.48	77.04	936.00	52.00	947.52	39.48	959.10	31.97
1000	1027.20	85.60	1040.04	57.78	1052.88	43.87	1065.60	35.52
1500	1540.92	128.41	1560.06	86.67	1579.20	65.80	1598.70	53.29
2000	2054.52	171.21	2080.08	115.56	2105.76	87.74	2131.50	71.05
2500	2568.12	214.01	2600.10	144.45	2632.08	109.67	2664.60	88.82
3000	3081.84	256.82	3120.12	173.34	3158.64	131.61	3197.40	106.58
3500	3595.44	299.62	3640.14	202.23	3684.96	153.54	3730.50	124.35
4000	4109.04	342.42	4160.16	231.12	4211.52	175.48	4263.30	142.11
4500	4622.76	385.23	4680.18	260.01	4738.08	197.42	4796.40	159.88
5000	5136.36	428.03	5200.20	288.90	5264.40	219.35	5329.20	177.64
5500	5650.08	470.84	5720.22	317.79	5790.96	241.29	5862.30	195.41
6000	6163.68	513.64	6240.24	346.68	6317.28	263.22	6395.10	213.17
6500	6677.28	556.44	6760.26	375.57	6843.84	285.16	6928.20	230.94
7000	7191.00	599.25	7280.28	404.46	7370.16	307.09	7461.00	248.70
7500	7704.60	642.05	7800.30	433.35	7896.72	329.03	7994.10	266.47
8000	8218.20	684.85	8320.32	462.24	8423.28	350.97	8526.90	284.23
8500	8731.92	727.66	8840.34	491.13	8949.60	372.90	9059.70	301.99
9000	9245.52	770.46	9360.36	520.02	9476.16	394.84	9592.80	319.76
10000	10272.84	856.07	10400.40	577.80	10529.04	438.71	10658.70	355.29
11000	11300.16	941.68	11440.44	635.58	11581.92	482.58	11724.60	390.82
12000	12327.36	1027.28	12480.48	693.36	12634.80	526.45	12790.50	426.35
13000	13354.68	1112.89	13520.52	751.14	13687.68	570.32	13856.40	461.88
14000	14382.00	1198.50	14560.56	808.92	14740.56	614.19	14922.30	497.41
15000	15409.32	1284.11	15600.60	866.70	15793.68	658.07	15988.20	532.94
16000	16436.52	1369.71	16640.64	924.48	16846.56	701.94	17053.80	568.46
17000	17463.84	1455.32	17680.68	982.26	17899.44	745.81	18119.70	603.99
18000	18491.16	1540.93	18720.72	1040.04	18952.32	789.68	19185.60	639.52
19000	19518.48	1626.54	19760.94	1097.83	20005.20	833.55	20251.50	675.05
20000	20545.68	1712.14	20800.98	1155.61	21058.08	877.42	21317.40	710.58
21000	21573.00	1797.75	21841.02	1213.39	22110.96	921.29	22383.30	746.11
22000	22600.32	1883.36	22881.06	1271.17	23164.08	965.17	23449.20	781.64
23000	23627.64	1968.97	23921.10	1328.95	24216.96	1009.04	24515.10	817.17
24000	24654.84	2054.57	24961.14	1386.73	25269.84	1052.91	25581.00	852.70
25000	25682.16	2140.18	26001.18	1444.51	26322.72	1096.78	26646.90	888.23

ANNUAL PERCENTAGE RATE **5.00%**

LOAN AMT	36 MONTHS TOTAL NOTE	36 MONTHS MONTHLY PAYMENT	42 MONTHS TOTAL NOTE	42 MONTHS MONTHLY PAYMENT	48 MONTHS TOTAL NOTE	48 MONTHS MONTHLY PAYMENT	60 MONTHS TOTAL NOTE	60 MONTHS MONTHLY PAYMENT
1	.72	.02	.84	.02	.96	.02	.60	.01
2	1.80	.05	2.10	.05	1.92	.04	1.80	.03
3	2.88	.08	2.94	.07	2.88	.06	3.00	.05
4	3.96	.11	4.20	.10	4.32	.09	4.20	.07
5	5.04	.14	5.46	.13	5.28	.11	5.40	.09
6	6.12	.17	6.30	.15	6.24	.13	6.60	.11
7	7.20	.20	7.56	.18	7.68	.16	7.80	.13
8	8.28	.23	8.40	.20	8.64	.18	9.00	.15
9	9.36	.26	9.66	.23	9.60	.20	9.60	.16
10	10.44	.29	10.92	.26	11.04	.23	10.80	.18
20	21.24	.59	21.84	.52	22.08	.46	22.20	.37
30	32.04	.89	32.76	.78	33.12	.69	33.60	.56
40	42.84	1.19	43.68	1.04	44.16	.92	45.00	.75
50	53.64	1.49	54.60	1.30	55.20	1.15	56.40	.94
60	64.44	1.79	65.52	1.56	66.24	1.38	67.80	1.13
70	75.24	2.09	76.44	1.82	77.28	1.61	79.20	1.32
80	86.04	2.39	87.36	2.08	88.32	1.84	90.00	1.50
90	96.84	2.69	98.28	2.34	99.36	2.07	101.40	1.69
100	107.64	2.99	109.20	2.60	110.40	2.30	112.80	1.88
200	215.64	5.99	218.40	5.20	220.80	4.60	226.20	3.77
300	323.64	8.99	327.60	7.80	331.20	6.90	339.60	5.66
400	431.28	11.98	436.80	10.40	442.08	9.21	452.40	7.54
500	539.28	14.98	546.00	13.00	552.48	11.51	565.80	9.43
600	647.28	17.98	655.20	15.60	662.88	13.81	679.20	11.32
700	754.92	20.97	764.40	18.20	773.76	16.12	792.00	13.20
800	862.92	23.97	873.60	20.80	884.16	18.42	905.40	15.09
900	970.92	26.97	982.80	23.40	994.56	20.72	1018.80	16.98
1000	1078.92	29.97	1092.00	26.00	1104.96	23.02	1132.20	18.87
1500	1618.20	44.95	1638.00	39.00	1657.92	34.54	1698.00	28.30
2000	2157.84	59.94	2184.00	52.00	2210.40	46.05	2264.40	37.74
2500	2697.12	74.92	2730.00	65.00	2763.36	57.57	2830.20	47.17
3000	3236.76	89.91	3276.00	78.00	3315.84	69.08	3396.60	56.61
3500	3776.04	104.89	3822.42	91.01	3868.80	80.60	3962.40	66.04
4000	4315.68	119.88	4368.42	104.01	4421.28	92.11	4528.80	75.48
4500	4854.96	134.86	4914.42	117.01	4974.24	103.63	5095.20	84.92
5000	5394.60	149.85	5460.42	130.01	5526.72	115.14	5661.00	94.35
5500	5933.88	164.83	6006.42	143.01	6079.68	126.66	6227.40	103.79
6000	6473.52	179.82	6552.42	156.01	6632.16	138.17	6793.20	113.22
6500	7013.16	194.81	7098.42	169.01	7185.12	149.69	7359.60	122.66
7000	7552.44	209.79	7644.84	182.02	7737.60	161.20	7925.40	132.09
7500	8092.08	224.78	8190.84	195.02	8290.08	172.71	8491.80	141.53
8000	8631.36	239.76	8736.84	208.02	8843.04	184.23	9057.60	150.96
8500	9171.00	254.75	9282.84	221.02	9395.52	195.74	9624.00	160.40
9000	9710.28	269.73	9828.84	234.02	9948.48	207.26	10190.40	169.84
10000	10789.20	299.70	10921.26	260.03	11053.92	230.29	11322.60	188.71
11000	11868.12	329.67	12013.26	286.03	12159.36	253.32	12454.80	207.58
12000	12947.40	359.65	13105.26	312.03	13264.80	276.35	13587.00	226.45
13000	14026.32	389.62	14197.26	338.03	14370.24	299.38	14719.20	245.32
14000	15105.24	419.59	15289.68	364.04	15475.68	322.41	15851.40	264.19
15000	16184.16	449.56	16381.68	390.04	16580.64	345.43	16983.60	283.06
16000	17263.08	479.53	17473.68	416.04	17686.08	368.46	18115.80	301.93
17000	18342.00	509.50	18566.10	442.05	18791.52	391.49	19248.60	320.81
18000	19420.92	539.47	19658.10	468.05	19896.96	414.52	20380.80	339.68
19000	20499.84	569.44	20750.10	494.05	21002.40	437.55	21513.00	358.55
20000	21578.76	599.41	21842.52	520.06	22107.84	460.58	22645.20	377.42
21000	22657.68	629.38	22934.52	546.06	23213.28	483.61	23777.40	396.29
22000	23736.60	659.35	24026.52	572.06	24318.72	506.64	24909.60	415.16
23000	24815.88	689.33	25118.52	598.06	25424.16	529.67	26041.80	434.03
24000	25894.80	719.30	26210.94	624.07	26529.60	552.70	27174.00	452.90
25000	26973.72	749.27	27302.94	650.07	27635.04	575.73	28306.80	471.78

5.10% ANNUAL PERCENTAGE RATE

LOAN AMT	12 MONTHS TOTAL NOTE	MONTHLY PAYMENT	18 MONTHS TOTAL NOTE	MONTHLY PAYMENT	24 MONTHS TOTAL NOTE	MONTHLY PAYMENT	30 MONTHS TOTAL NOTE	MONTHLY PAYMENT
1	.96	.08	.90	.05	.96	.04	.90	.03
2	2.04	.17	1.98	.11	1.92	.08	2.10	.07
3	3.00	.25	3.06	.17	3.12	.13	3.00	.10
4	4.08	.34	4.14	.23	4.08	.17	4.20	.14
5	5.04	.42	5.04	.28	5.04	.21	5.10	.17
6	6.12	.51	6.12	.34	6.24	.26	6.30	.21
7	7.08	.59	7.20	.40	7.20	.30	7.20	.24
8	8.16	.68	8.28	.46	8.40	.35	8.40	.28
9	9.24	.77	9.36	.52	9.36	.39	9.60	.32
10	10.20	.85	10.26	.57	10.32	.43	10.50	.35
20	20.52	1.71	20.70	1.15	20.88	.87	21.30	.71
30	30.72	2.56	31.14	1.73	31.44	1.31	31.80	1.06
40	41.04	3.42	41.58	2.31	42.00	1.75	42.60	1.42
50	51.36	4.28	52.02	2.89	52.56	2.19	53.10	1.77
60	61.56	5.13	62.28	3.46	63.12	2.63	63.90	2.13
70	71.88	5.99	72.72	4.04	73.68	3.07	74.70	2.49
80	82.20	6.85	83.16	4.62	84.24	3.51	85.20	2.84
90	92.40	7.70	93.60	5.20	94.80	3.95	96.00	3.20
100	102.72	8.56	104.04	5.78	105.36	4.39	106.50	3.55
200	205.56	17.13	208.08	11.56	210.72	8.78	213.30	7.11
300	308.28	25.69	312.12	17.34	316.08	13.17	320.10	10.67
400	411.12	34.26	416.34	23.13	421.44	17.56	426.60	14.22
500	513.84	42.82	520.38	28.91	526.80	21.95	533.40	17.78
600	616.68	51.39	624.42	34.69	632.16	26.34	640.20	21.34
700	719.40	59.95	728.46	40.47	737.76	30.74	747.00	24.90
800	822.24	68.52	832.68	46.26	843.12	35.13	853.50	28.45
900	924.96	77.08	936.72	52.04	948.48	39.52	960.30	32.01
1000	1027.80	85.65	1040.76	57.82	1053.84	43.91	1067.10	35.57
1500	1541.64	128.47	1561.14	86.73	1580.88	65.87	1600.80	53.36
2000	2055.60	171.30	2081.70	115.65	2107.92	87.83	2134.20	71.14
2500	2569.56	214.13	2602.08	144.56	2634.96	109.79	2667.90	88.93
3000	3083.40	256.95	3122.46	173.47	3161.76	131.74	3201.60	106.72
3500	3597.36	299.78	3642.84	202.38	3688.80	153.70	3735.00	124.50
4000	4111.32	342.61	4163.40	231.30	4215.84	175.66	4268.70	142.29
4500	4625.16	385.43	4683.78	260.21	4742.88	197.62	4802.40	160.08
5000	5139.12	428.26	5204.16	289.12	5269.92	219.58	5336.10	177.87
5500	5653.08	471.09	5724.72	318.04	5796.72	241.53	5869.50	195.65
6000	6166.92	513.91	6245.10	346.95	6323.76	263.49	6403.20	213.44
6500	6680.88	556.74	6765.48	375.86	6850.80	285.45	6936.90	231.23
7000	7194.84	599.57	7285.86	404.77	7377.84	307.41	7470.30	249.01
7500	7708.68	642.39	7806.42	433.69	7904.88	329.37	8004.00	266.80
8000	8222.64	685.22	8326.80	462.60	8431.68	351.32	8537.70	284.59
8500	8736.60	728.05	8847.18	491.51	8958.72	373.28	9071.40	302.38
9000	9250.44	770.87	9367.74	520.43	9485.76	395.24	9604.80	320.16
10000	10278.36	856.53	10408.50	578.25	10539.84	439.16	10672.20	355.74
11000	11306.16	942.18	11449.44	636.08	11593.68	483.07	11739.30	391.31
12000	12333.96	1027.83	12490.20	693.90	12647.76	526.99	12806.40	426.88
13000	13361.88	1113.49	13531.14	751.73	13701.84	570.91	13873.80	462.46
14000	14389.68	1199.14	14571.90	809.55	14755.68	614.82	14940.90	498.03
15000	15417.48	1284.79	15612.84	867.38	15809.76	658.74	16008.30	533.61
16000	16445.40	1370.45	16653.60	925.20	16863.60	702.65	17075.40	569.18
17000	17473.20	1456.10	17694.54	983.03	17917.68	746.57	18142.80	604.76
18000	18501.00	1541.75	18735.48	1040.86	18971.76	790.49	19209.90	640.33
19000	19528.92	1627.41	19776.24	1098.68	20025.60	834.40	20277.00	675.90
20000	20556.72	1713.06	20817.18	1156.51	21079.68	878.32	21344.40	711.48
21000	21584.52	1798.71	21857.94	1214.33	22133.52	922.23	22411.50	747.05
22000	22612.44	1884.37	22898.88	1272.16	23187.60	966.15	23478.90	782.63
23000	23640.24	1970.02	23939.64	1329.98	24241.68	1010.07	24546.00	818.20
24000	24668.04	2055.67	24980.58	1387.81	25295.52	1053.98	25613.10	853.77
25000	25695.96	2141.33	26021.34	1445.63	26349.60	1097.90	26680.50	889.35

ANNUAL PERCENTAGE RATE **5.10%**

LOAN AMT	36 MONTHS TOTAL NOTE	36 MONTHS MONTHLY PAYMENT	42 MONTHS TOTAL NOTE	42 MONTHS MONTHLY PAYMENT	48 MONTHS TOTAL NOTE	48 MONTHS MONTHLY PAYMENT	60 MONTHS TOTAL NOTE	60 MONTHS MONTHLY PAYMENT
1	1.08	.03	.84	.02	.96	.02	.60	.01
2	2.16	.06	2.10	.05	1.92	.04	1.80	.03
3	3.24	.09	2.94	.07	2.88	.06	3.00	.05
4	4.32	.12	4.20	.10	4.32	.09	4.20	.07
5	5.40	.15	5.46	.13	5.28	.11	5.40	.09
6	6.48	.18	6.30	.15	6.24	.13	6.60	.11
7	7.56	.21	7.56	.18	7.68	.16	7.80	.13
8	8.64	.24	8.40	.20	8.64	.18	9.00	.15
9	9.72	.27	9.66	.23	9.60	.20	10.20	.17
10	10.80	.30	10.92	.26	11.04	.23	10.80	.18
20	21.60	.60	21.84	.52	22.08	.46	22.20	.37
30	32.40	.90	32.76	.78	33.12	.69	33.60	.56
40	43.20	1.20	43.68	1.04	44.16	.92	45.00	.75
50	54.00	1.50	54.60	1.30	55.20	1.15	56.40	.94
60	64.80	1.80	65.52	1.56	66.24	1.38	67.80	1.13
70	75.60	2.10	76.44	1.82	77.28	1.61	79.20	1.32
80	86.40	2.40	87.36	2.08	88.32	1.84	90.60	1.51
90	97.20	2.70	98.28	2.34	99.36	2.07	102.00	1.70
100	108.00	3.00	109.20	2.60	110.40	2.30	113.40	1.89
200	216.00	6.00	218.40	5.20	221.28	4.61	226.80	3.78
300	324.00	9.00	328.02	7.81	332.16	6.92	340.20	5.67
400	432.00	12.00	437.22	10.41	442.56	9.22	453.60	7.56
500	540.00	15.00	546.84	13.02	553.44	11.53	567.00	9.45
600	648.00	18.00	656.04	15.62	664.32	13.84	681.00	11.35
700	756.36	21.01	765.66	18.23	775.20	16.15	794.40	13.24
800	864.36	24.01	874.86	20.83	885.60	18.45	907.80	15.13
900	972.36	27.01	984.48	23.44	996.48	20.76	1021.20	17.02
1000	1080.36	30.01	1093.68	26.04	1107.36	23.07	1134.60	18.91
1500	1620.72	45.02	1640.94	39.07	1661.28	34.61	1702.20	28.37
2000	2161.08	60.03	2187.78	52.09	2214.72	46.14	2269.80	37.83
2500	2701.08	75.03	2735.04	65.12	2768.64	57.68	2837.40	47.29
3000	3241.44	90.04	3281.88	78.14	3322.56	69.22	3405.00	56.75
3500	3781.80	105.05	3828.72	91.16	3876.48	80.76	3972.00	66.20
4000	4322.16	120.06	4375.98	104.19	4429.92	92.29	4539.60	75.66
4500	4862.52	135.07	4922.82	117.21	4983.84	103.83	5107.20	85.12
5000	5402.52	150.07	5470.08	130.24	5537.76	115.37	5674.80	94.58
5500	5942.88	165.08	6016.92	143.26	6091.68	126.91	6242.40	104.04
6000	6483.24	180.09	6563.76	156.28	6645.12	138.44	6810.00	113.50
6500	7023.60	195.10	7111.02	169.31	7199.04	149.98	7377.60	122.96
7000	7563.96	210.11	7657.86	182.33	7752.96	161.52	7944.60	132.41
7500	8103.96	225.11	8205.12	195.36	8306.40	173.05	8512.20	141.87
8000	8644.32	240.12	8751.96	208.38	8860.32	184.59	9079.80	151.33
8500	9184.68	255.13	9298.80	221.40	9414.24	196.13	9647.40	160.79
9000	9725.04	270.14	9846.06	234.43	9968.16	207.67	10215.00	170.25
10000	10805.40	300.15	10940.16	260.48	11075.52	230.74	11350.20	189.17
11000	11886.12	330.17	12033.84	286.52	12183.36	253.82	12484.80	208.08
12000	12966.48	360.18	13127.94	312.57	13290.72	276.89	13620.00	227.00
13000	14047.20	390.20	14222.04	338.62	14398.56	299.97	14755.20	245.92
14000	15127.92	420.22	15316.14	364.67	15505.92	323.04	15889.80	264.83
15000	16208.28	450.23	16410.24	390.72	16613.28	346.11	17025.00	283.75
16000	17289.00	480.25	17504.34	416.77	17721.12	369.19	18160.20	302.67
17000	18369.36	510.26	18598.02	442.81	18828.48	392.26	19295.40	321.59
18000	19450.08	540.28	19692.12	468.86	19936.32	415.34	20430.00	340.50
19000	20530.80	570.30	20786.22	494.91	21043.68	438.41	21565.20	359.42
20000	21611.16	600.31	21880.32	520.96	22151.52	461.49	22700.40	378.34
21000	22691.88	630.33	22974.42	547.01	23258.88	484.56	23835.00	397.25
22000	23772.24	660.34	24068.10	573.05	24366.72	507.64	24970.20	416.17
23000	24852.96	690.36	25162.20	599.10	25474.08	530.71	26105.40	435.09
24000	25933.32	720.37	26256.30	625.15	26581.92	553.79	27240.00	454.00
25000	27014.04	750.39	27350.40	651.20	27689.28	576.86	28375.20	472.92

5.20% ANNUAL PERCENTAGE RATE

LOAN AMT	12 MONTHS TOTAL NOTE	12 MONTHS MONTHLY PAYMENT	18 MONTHS TOTAL NOTE	18 MONTHS MONTHLY PAYMENT	24 MONTHS TOTAL NOTE	24 MONTHS MONTHLY PAYMENT	30 MONTHS TOTAL NOTE	30 MONTHS MONTHLY PAYMENT
1	.96	.08	.90	.05	.96	.04	.90	.03
2	2.04	.17	1.98	.11	1.92	.08	2.10	.07
3	3.00	.25	3.06	.17	3.12	.13	3.00	.10
4	4.08	.34	4.14	.23	4.08	.17	4.20	.14
5	5.04	.42	5.04	.28	5.04	.21	5.10	.17
6	6.12	.51	6.12	.34	6.24	.26	6.30	.21
7	7.08	.59	7.20	.40	7.20	.30	7.20	.24
8	8.16	.68	8.28	.46	8.40	.35	8.40	.28
9	9.24	.77	9.36	.52	9.36	.39	9.60	.32
10	10.20	.85	10.26	.57	10.32	.43	10.50	.35
20	20.52	1.71	20.70	1.15	20.88	.87	21.30	.71
30	30.84	2.57	31.14	1.73	31.44	1.31	31.80	1.06
40	41.04	3.42	41.58	2.31	42.00	1.75	42.60	1.42
50	51.36	4.28	52.02	2.89	52.56	2.19	53.40	1.78
60	61.68	5.14	62.46	3.47	63.12	2.63	63.90	2.13
70	71.88	5.99	72.90	4.05	73.68	3.07	74.70	2.49
80	82.20	6.85	83.16	4.62	84.24	3.51	85.20	2.84
90	92.52	7.71	93.60	5.20	94.80	3.95	96.00	3.20
100	102.72	8.56	104.04	5.78	105.36	4.39	106.80	3.56
200	205.56	17.13	208.26	11.57	210.96	8.79	213.60	7.12
300	308.40	25.70	312.48	17.36	316.32	13.18	320.40	10.68
400	411.24	34.27	416.52	23.14	421.92	17.58	427.20	14.24
500	514.08	42.84	520.74	28.93	527.52	21.98	534.00	17.80
600	616.92	51.41	624.96	34.72	632.88	26.37	641.10	21.37
700	719.76	59.98	729.00	40.50	738.48	30.77	747.90	24.93
800	822.60	68.55	833.22	46.29	843.84	35.16	854.70	28.49
900	925.44	77.12	937.44	52.08	949.44	39.56	961.50	32.05
1000	1028.28	85.69	1041.66	57.87	1055.04	43.96	1068.30	35.61
1500	1542.48	128.54	1562.40	86.80	1582.56	65.94	1602.60	53.42
2000	2056.68	171.39	2083.32	115.74	2110.08	87.92	2136.90	71.23
2500	2570.88	214.24	2604.06	144.67	2637.60	109.90	2671.20	89.04
3000	3085.08	257.09	3124.98	173.61	3165.12	131.88	3205.50	106.85
3500	3599.28	299.94	3645.72	202.54	3692.64	153.86	3739.80	124.66
4000	4113.48	342.79	4166.64	231.48	4220.16	175.84	4274.10	142.47
4500	4627.68	385.64	4687.38	260.41	4747.68	197.82	4808.40	160.28
5000	5141.88	428.49	5208.30	289.35	5275.20	219.80	5342.70	178.09
5500	5656.08	471.34	5729.04	318.28	5802.72	241.78	5877.00	195.90
6000	6170.28	514.19	6249.96	347.22	6330.24	263.76	6411.30	213.71
6500	6684.48	557.04	6770.70	376.15	6857.76	285.74	6945.60	231.52
7000	7198.68	599.89	7291.62	405.09	7385.28	307.72	7479.90	249.33
7500	7712.88	642.74	7812.36	434.02	7912.80	329.70	8014.20	267.14
8000	8227.08	685.59	8333.28	462.96	8440.32	351.68	8548.50	284.95
8500	8741.28	728.44	8854.20	491.90	8967.84	373.66	9082.80	302.76
9000	9255.48	771.29	9374.94	520.83	9495.36	395.64	9617.10	320.57
10000	10283.88	856.99	10416.60	578.70	10550.64	439.61	10685.70	356.19
11000	11312.28	942.69	11458.26	636.57	11605.68	483.57	11754.00	391.80
12000	12340.56	1028.38	12499.92	694.44	12660.72	527.53	12822.60	427.42
13000	13368.96	1114.08	13541.58	752.31	13715.76	571.49	13891.20	463.04
14000	14397.36	1199.78	14583.24	810.18	14770.80	615.45	14959.80	498.66
15000	15425.76	1285.48	15624.90	868.05	15825.84	659.41	16028.40	534.28
16000	16454.16	1371.18	16666.56	925.92	16880.88	703.37	17097.00	569.90
17000	17482.56	1456.88	17708.40	983.80	17935.92	747.33	18165.60	605.52
18000	18510.96	1542.58	18750.06	1041.67	18990.96	791.29	19234.20	641.14
19000	19539.36	1628.28	19791.72	1099.54	20046.00	835.25	20302.80	676.76
20000	20567.76	1713.98	20833.38	1157.41	21101.28	879.22	21371.40	712.38
21000	21596.16	1799.68	21875.04	1215.28	22156.32	923.18	22439.70	747.99
22000	22624.56	1885.38	22916.70	1273.15	23211.36	967.14	23508.30	783.61
23000	23652.96	1971.08	23958.36	1331.02	24266.40	1011.10	24576.90	819.23
24000	24681.24	2056.77	25000.02	1388.89	25321.44	1055.06	25645.50	854.85
25000	25709.64	2142.47	26041.68	1446.76	26376.48	1099.02	26714.10	890.47

ANNUAL PERCENTAGE RATE **5.20%**

LOAN AMT	36 MONTHS TOTAL NOTE	36 MONTHS MONTHLY PAYMENT	42 MONTHS TOTAL NOTE	42 MONTHS MONTHLY PAYMENT	48 MONTHS TOTAL NOTE	48 MONTHS MONTHLY PAYMENT	60 MONTHS TOTAL NOTE	60 MONTHS MONTHLY PAYMENT
1	1.08	.03	.84	.02	.96	.02	.60	.01
2	2.16	.06	2.10	.05	1.92	.04	1.80	.03
3	3.24	.09	2.94	.07	2.88	.06	3.00	.05
4	4.32	.12	4.20	.10	4.32	.09	4.20	.07
5	5.40	.15	5.46	.13	5.28	.11	5.40	.09
6	6.48	.18	6.30	.15	6.24	.13	6.60	.11
7	7.56	.21	7.56	.18	7.68	.16	7.80	.13
8	8.64	.24	8.40	.20	8.64	.18	9.00	.15
9	9.72	.27	9.66	.23	9.60	.20	10.20	.17
10	10.80	.30	10.92	.26	11.04	.23	10.80	.18
20	21.60	.60	21.84	.52	22.08	.46	22.20	.37
30	32.40	.90	32.76	.78	33.12	.69	33.60	.56
40	43.20	1.20	43.68	1.04	44.16	.92	45.00	.75
50	54.00	1.50	54.60	1.30	55.20	1.15	56.40	.94
60	64.80	1.80	65.52	1.56	66.24	1.38	67.80	1.13
70	75.60	2.10	76.44	1.82	77.28	1.61	79.20	1.32
80	86.40	2.40	87.36	2.08	88.32	1.84	90.60	1.51
90	97.20	2.70	98.28	2.34	99.84	2.08	102.00	1.70
100	108.00	3.00	109.20	2.60	110.88	2.31	113.40	1.89
200	216.36	6.01	218.82	5.21	221.76	4.62	227.40	3.79
300	324.36	9.01	328.44	7.82	332.64	6.93	340.80	5.68
400	432.72	12.02	438.06	10.43	443.52	9.24	454.80	7.58
500	541.08	15.03	547.68	13.04	554.88	11.56	568.80	9.48
600	649.08	18.03	657.30	15.65	665.76	13.87	682.20	11.37
700	757.44	21.04	766.92	18.26	776.64	16.18	796.20	13.27
800	865.44	24.04	876.54	20.87	887.52	18.49	910.20	15.17
900	973.80	27.05	986.16	23.48	998.40	20.80	1023.60	17.06
1000	1082.16	30.06	1095.78	26.09	1109.76	23.12	1137.60	18.96
1500	1623.24	45.09	1643.46	39.13	1664.64	34.68	1706.40	28.44
2000	2164.32	60.12	2191.56	52.18	2219.52	46.24	2275.20	37.92
2500	2705.40	75.15	2739.66	65.23	2774.40	57.80	2844.00	47.40
3000	3246.48	90.18	3287.34	78.27	3329.28	69.36	3412.80	56.88
3500	3787.56	105.21	3835.44	91.32	3884.16	80.92	3982.20	66.37
4000	4328.64	120.24	4383.54	104.37	4439.04	92.48	4551.00	75.85
4500	4869.72	135.27	4931.22	117.41	4993.92	104.04	5119.80	85.33
5000	5410.80	150.30	5479.32	130.46	5548.80	115.60	5688.60	94.81
5500	5951.88	165.33	6027.42	143.51	6103.68	127.16	6257.40	104.29
6000	6492.96	180.36	6575.10	156.55	6658.56	138.72	6826.20	113.77
6500	7034.04	195.39	7123.20	169.60	7213.44	150.28	7395.00	123.25
7000	7575.12	210.42	7671.30	182.65	7768.32	161.84	7964.40	132.74
7500	8116.20	225.45	8218.98	195.69	8323.20	173.40	8533.20	142.22
8000	8657.28	240.48	8767.08	208.74	8878.08	184.96	9102.00	151.70
8500	9198.36	255.51	9315.18	221.79	9432.96	196.52	9670.80	161.18
9000	9739.44	270.54	9862.86	234.83	9987.84	208.08	10239.60	170.66
10000	10821.60	300.60	10959.06	260.93	11097.60	231.20	11377.20	189.62
11000	11903.76	330.66	12054.84	287.02	12207.36	254.32	12515.40	208.59
12000	12985.92	360.72	13150.62	313.11	13317.12	277.44	13653.00	227.55
13000	14068.44	390.79	14246.82	339.21	14426.88	300.56	14790.60	246.51
14000	15150.60	420.85	15342.60	365.30	15536.64	323.68	15928.80	265.48
15000	16232.76	450.91	16438.38	391.39	16646.40	346.80	17066.40	284.44
16000	17314.92	480.97	17534.58	417.49	17756.16	369.92	18204.00	303.40
17000	18397.08	511.03	18630.36	443.58	18865.92	393.04	19342.20	322.37
18000	19479.24	541.09	19726.14	469.67	19975.68	416.16	20479.80	341.33
19000	20561.40	571.15	20822.34	495.77	21085.44	439.28	21617.40	360.29
20000	21643.56	601.21	21918.12	521.86	22195.20	462.40	22755.00	379.25
21000	22725.72	631.27	23013.90	547.95	23304.96	485.52	23893.20	398.22
22000	23807.88	661.33	24110.10	574.05	24414.72	508.64	25030.80	417.18
23000	24890.04	691.39	25205.88	600.14	25524.48	531.76	26168.40	436.14
24000	25972.20	721.45	26301.66	626.23	26634.24	554.88	27306.60	455.11
25000	27054.36	751.51	27397.86	652.33	27744.00	578.00	28444.20	474.07

5.25% ANNUAL PERCENTAGE RATE

LOAN	12 MONTHS		18 MONTHS		24 MONTHS		30 MONTHS	
AMT	TOTAL NOTE	MONTHLY PAYMENT	TOTAL NOTE	MONTHLY PAYMENT	TOTAL NOTE	MONTHLY PAYMENT	TOTAL NOTE	MONTHLY PAYMENT
1	.96	.08	.90	.05	.96	.04	.90	.03
2	2.04	.17	1.98	.11	1.92	.08	2.10	.07
3	3.00	.25	3.06	.17	3.12	.13	3.00	.10
4	4.08	.34	4.14	.23	4.08	.17	4.20	.14
5	5.04	.42	5.04	.28	5.04	.21	5.10	.17
6	6.12	.51	6.12	.34	6.24	.26	6.30	.21
7	7.20	.60	7.20	.40	7.20	.30	7.20	.24
8	8.16	.68	8.28	.46	8.40	.35	8.40	.28
9	9.24	.77	9.36	.52	9.36	.39	9.60	.32
10	10.20	.85	10.26	.57	10.32	.43	10.50	.35
20	20.52	1.71	20.70	1.15	20.88	.87	21.30	.71
30	30.84	2.57	31.14	1.73	31.44	1.31	31.80	1.06
40	41.04	3.42	41.58	2.31	42.00	1.75	42.60	1.42
50	51.36	4.28	52.02	2.89	52.56	2.19	53.40	1.78
60	61.68	5.14	62.46	3.47	63.12	2.63	63.90	2.13
70	72.00	6.00	72.90	4.05	73.68	3.07	74.70	2.49
80	82.20	6.85	83.34	4.63	84.24	3.51	85.50	2.85
90	92.52	7.71	93.78	5.21	94.80	3.95	96.00	3.20
100	102.84	8.57	104.04	5.78	105.36	4.39	106.80	3.56
200	205.68	17.14	208.26	11.57	210.96	8.79	213.60	7.12
300	308.52	25.71	312.48	17.36	316.56	13.19	320.70	10.69
400	411.36	34.28	416.70	23.15	422.16	17.59	427.50	14.25
500	514.32	42.86	520.92	28.94	527.76	21.99	534.60	17.82
600	617.16	51.43	625.14	34.73	633.36	26.39	641.40	21.38
700	720.00	60.00	729.36	40.52	738.72	30.78	748.20	24.94
800	822.84	68.57	833.58	46.31	844.32	35.18	855.30	28.51
900	925.68	77.14	937.80	52.10	949.92	39.58	962.10	32.07
1000	1028.64	85.72	1042.02	57.89	1055.52	43.98	1069.20	35.64
1500	1542.96	128.58	1562.94	86.83	1583.28	65.97	1603.80	53.46
2000	2057.28	171.44	2084.04	115.78	2111.04	87.96	2138.40	71.28
2500	2571.60	214.30	2605.14	144.73	2638.80	109.95	2673.00	89.10
3000	3085.92	257.16	3126.06	173.67	3166.80	131.95	3207.60	106.92
3500	3600.24	300.02	3647.16	202.62	3694.56	153.94	3742.20	124.74
4000	4114.56	342.88	4168.26	231.57	4222.32	175.93	4276.80	142.56
4500	4628.88	385.74	4689.18	260.51	4750.08	197.92	4811.40	160.38
5000	5143.32	428.61	5210.28	289.46	5277.84	219.91	5346.00	178.20
5500	5657.64	471.47	5731.38	318.41	5805.60	241.90	5880.60	196.02
6000	6171.96	514.33	6252.30	347.35	6333.60	263.90	6415.20	213.84
6500	6686.28	557.19	6773.40	376.30	6861.36	285.89	6949.80	231.66
7000	7200.60	600.05	7294.50	405.25	7389.12	307.88	7484.70	249.49
7500	7714.92	642.91	7815.42	434.19	7916.88	329.87	8019.30	267.31
8000	8229.24	685.77	8336.52	463.14	8444.64	351.86	8553.90	285.13
8500	8743.56	728.63	8857.62	492.09	8972.40	373.85	9088.50	302.95
9000	9257.88	771.49	9378.54	521.03	9500.40	395.85	9623.10	320.77
10000	10286.64	857.22	10420.74	578.93	10555.92	439.83	10692.30	356.41
11000	11315.28	942.94	11462.76	636.82	11611.44	483.81	11761.50	392.05
12000	12343.92	1028.66	12504.78	694.71	12667.20	527.80	12830.70	427.69
13000	13372.56	1114.38	13546.98	752.61	13722.72	571.78	13899.90	463.33
14000	14401.20	1200.10	14589.00	810.50	14778.24	615.76	14969.40	498.98
15000	15429.96	1285.83	15631.02	868.39	15834.00	659.75	16038.60	534.62
16000	16458.60	1371.55	16673.22	926.29	16889.52	703.73	17107.80	570.26
17000	17487.24	1457.27	17715.24	984.18	17945.04	747.71	18177.00	605.90
18000	18515.88	1542.99	18757.26	1042.07	19000.80	791.70	19246.20	641.54
19000	19544.52	1628.71	19799.28	1099.96	20056.32	835.68	20315.40	677.18
20000	20573.28	1714.44	20841.48	1157.86	21111.84	879.66	21384.60	712.82
21000	21601.92	1800.16	21883.50	1215.75	22167.60	923.65	22454.10	748.47
22000	22630.56	1885.88	22925.52	1273.64	23223.12	967.63	23523.30	784.11
23000	23659.20	1971.60	23967.72	1331.54	24278.64	1011.61	24592.50	819.75
24000	24687.96	2057.33	25009.74	1389.43	25334.40	1055.60	25661.70	855.39
25000	25716.60	2143.05	26051.76	1447.32	26389.92	1099.58	26730.90	891.03

ANNUAL PERCENTAGE RATE **5.25%**

LOAN AMT	36 MONTHS TOTAL NOTE	MONTHLY PAYMENT	42 MONTHS TOTAL NOTE	MONTHLY PAYMENT	48 MONTHS TOTAL NOTE	MONTHLY PAYMENT	60 MONTHS TOTAL NOTE	MONTHLY PAYMENT
1	1.08	.03	.84	.02	.96	.02	.60	.01
2	2.16	.06	2.10	.05	1.92	.04	1.80	.03
3	3.24	.09	2.94	.07	2.88	.06	3.00	.05
4	4.32	.12	4.20	.10	4.32	.09	4.20	.07
5	5.40	.15	5.46	.13	5.28	.11	5.40	.09
6	6.48	.18	6.30	.15	6.24	.13	6.60	.11
7	7.56	.21	7.56	.18	7.68	.16	7.80	.13
8	8.64	.24	8.40	.20	8.64	.18	9.00	.15
9	9.72	.27	9.66	.23	9.60	.20	10.20	.17
10	10.80	.30	10.92	.26	11.04	.23	10.80	.18
20	21.60	.60	21.84	.52	22.08	.46	22.20	37
30	32.40	.90	32.76	.78	33.12	.69	33.60	.56
40	43.20	1.20	43.68	1.04	44.16	.92	45.00	.75
50	54.00	1.50	54.60	1.30	55.20	1.15	56.40	94
60	64.80	1.80	65.52	1.56	66.24	1.38	67.80	1.13
70	75.60	2.10	76.44	1.82	77.28	1.61	79.20	1.32
80	86.40	2.40	87.36	2.08	88.80	1.85	90.60	1.51
90	97.20	2.70	98.70	2.35	99.84	2.08	102.00	1.70
100	108.00	3.00	109.62	2.61	110.88	2.31	113.40	1.89
200	216.36	6.01	219.24	5.22	221.76	4.62	227.40	3.79
300	324.72	9.02	328.86	7.83	333.12	6.94	341.40	5.69
400	433.08	12.03	438.48	10.44	444.00	9.25	455.40	7.59
500	541.44	15.04	548.10	13.05	555.36	11.57	569.40	9.49
600	649.44	18.04	657.72	15.66	666.24	13.88	683.40	11.39
700	757.80	21.05	767.76	18.28	777.12	16.19	797.40	13.29
800	866.16	24.06	877.38	20.89	888.48	18.51	910.80	15.18
900	974.52	27.07	987.00	23.50	999.36	20.82	1024.80	17.08
1000	1082.88	30.08	1096.62	26.11	1110.72	23.14	1138.80	18.98
1500	1624.32	45.12	1645.14	39.17	1666.08	34.71	1708.20	28.47
2000	2165.76	60.16	2193.66	52.23	2221.44	46.28	2278.20	37.97
2500	2707.20	75.20	2741.76	65.28	2776.80	57.85	2847.60	47.46
3000	3248.64	90.24	3290.28	78.34	3332.16	69.42	3417.00	56.95
3500	3790.44	105.29	3838.80	91.40	3887.52	80.99	3987.00	66.45
4000	4331.88	120.33	4387.32	104.46	4443.36	92.57	4556.40	75.94
4500	4873.32	135.37	4935.84	117.52	4998.72	104.14	5125.80	85.43
5000	5414.76	150.41	5483.94	130.57	5554.08	115.71	5695.20	94.92
5500	5956.20	165.45	6032.46	143.63	6109.44	127.28	6265.20	104.42
6000	6497.64	180.49	6580.98	156.69	6664.80	138.85	6834.60	113.91
6500	7039.44	195.54	7129.50	169.75	7220.16	150.42	7404.00	123.40
7000	7580.88	210.58	7678.02	182.81	7775.52	161.99	7974.00	132.90
7500	8122.32	225.62	8226.12	195.86	8331.36	173.57	8543.40	142.39
8000	8663.76	240.66	8774.64	208.92	8886.72	185.14	9112.80	151.88
8500	9205.20	255.70	9323.16	221.98	9442.08	196.71	9682.80	161.38
9000	9746.64	270.74	9871.68	235.04	9997.44	208.28	10252.20	170.87
10000	10829.88	300.83	10968.30	261.15	11108.16	231.42	11391.00	189.85
11000	11912.76	330.91	12065.34	287.27	12218.88	254.56	12530.40	208.84
12000	12995.64	360.99	13162.38	313.39	13330.08	277.71	13669.80	227.83
13000	14078.88	391.08	14259.00	339.50	14440.80	300.85	14808.60	246.81
14000	15161.76	421.16	15356.04	365.62	15551.52	323.99	15948.00	265.80
15000	16244.64	451.24	16452.66	391.73	16662.72	347.14	17086.80	284.78
16000	17327.88	481.33	17549.70	417.85	17773.44	370.28	18226.20	303.77
17000	18410.76	511.41	18646.32	443.96	18884.16	393.42	19365.60	322.76
18000	19493.64	541.49	19743.36	470.08	19994.88	416.56	20504.40	341.74
19000	20576.88	571.58	20840.40	496.20	21106.08	439.71	21643.80	360.73
20000	21659.76	601.66	21937.02	522.31	22216.80	462.85	22782.60	379.71
21000	22742.64	631.74	23034.06	548.43	23327.52	485.99	23922.00	398.70
22000	23825.88	661.83	24130.68	574.54	24438.24	509.13	25061.40	417.69
23000	24908.76	691.91	25227.72	600.66	25549.44	532.28	26200.20	436.67
24000	25991.64	721.99	26324.76	626.78	26660.16	555.42	27339.60	455.66
25000	27074.88	752.08	27421.38	652.89	27770.88	578.56	28478.40	474.64

5.30% ANNUAL PERCENTAGE RATE

	12 MONTHS		18 MONTHS		24 MONTHS		30 MONTHS	
LOAN AMT	TOTAL NOTE	MONTHLY PAYMENT	TOTAL NOTE	MONTHLY PAYMENT	TOTAL NOTE	MONTHLY PAYMENT	TOTAL NOTE	MONTHLY PAYMENT
1	.96	.08	.90	.05	.96	.04	.90	.03
2	2.04	.17	1.98	.11	1.92	.08	2.10	.07
3	3.00	.25	3.06	.17	3.12	.13	3.00	.10
4	4.08	.34	4.14	.23	4.08	.17	4.20	.14
5	5.04	.42	5.04	.28	5.28	.22	5.10	.17
6	6.12	.51	6.12	.34	6.24	.26	6.30	.21
7	7.20	.60	7.20	.40	7.20	.30	7.20	.24
8	8.16	.68	8.28	.46	8.40	.35	8.40	.28
9	9.24	.77	9.36	.52	9.36	.39	9.60	.32
10	10.20	.85	10.26	.57	10.56	.44	10.50	.35
20	20.52	1.71	20.70	1.15	21.12	.88	21.30	.71
30	30.84	2.57	31.14	1.73	31.68	1.32	31.80	1.06
40	41.04	3.42	41.58	2.31	42.24	1.76	42.60	1.42
50	51.36	4.28	52.02	2.89	52.80	2.20	53.40	1.78
60	61.68	5.14	62.46	3.47	63.36	2.64	63.90	2.13
70	72.00	6.00	72.90	4.05	73.92	3.08	74.70	2.49
80	82.20	6.85	83.34	4.63	84.48	3.52	85.50	2.85
90	92.52	7.71	93.78	5.21	95.04	3.96	96.00	3.20
100	102.84	8.57	104.22	5.79	105.60	4.40	106.80	3.56
200	205.68	17.14	208.44	11.58	211.20	8.80	213.90	7.13
300	308.64	25.72	312.66	17.37	316.80	13.20	320.70	10.69
400	411.48	34.29	416.88	23.16	422.40	17.60	427.80	14.26
500	514.44	42.87	521.10	28.95	528.00	22.00	534.90	17.83
600	617.28	51.44	625.32	34.74	633.60	26.40	641.70	21.39
700	720.24	60.02	729.72	40.54	739.20	30.80	748.80	24.96
800	823.08	68.59	833.94	46.33	844.80	35.20	855.90	28.53
900	926.04	77.17	938.16	52.12	950.40	39.60	962.70	32.09
1000	1028.88	85.74	1042.38	57.91	1056.00	44.00	1069.80	35.66
1500	1543.32	128.61	1563.66	86.87	1584.00	66.00	1604.70	53.49
2000	2057.88	171.49	2084.94	115.83	2112.24	88.01	2139.60	71.32
2500	2572.32	214.36	2606.04	144.78	2640.24	110.01	2674.50	89.15
3000	3086.76	257.23	3127.32	173.74	3168.24	132.01	3209.70	106.99
3500	3601.20	300.10	3648.60	202.70	3696.48	154.02	3744.60	124.82
4000	4115.76	342.98	4169.88	231.66	4224.48	176.02	4279.50	142.65
4500	4630.20	385.85	4691.16	260.62	4752.48	198.02	4814.40	160.48
5000	5144.64	428.72	5212.26	289.57	5280.48	220.02	5349.30	178.31
5500	5659.08	471.59	5733.54	318.53	5808.72	242.03	5884.50	196.15
6000	6173.64	514.47	6254.82	347.49	6336.72	264.03	6419.40	213.98
6500	6688.08	557.34	6776.10	376.45	6864.72	286.03	6954.30	231.81
7000	7202.52	600.21	7297.20	405.40	7392.96	308.04	7489.20	249.64
7500	7716.96	643.08	7818.48	434.36	7920.96	330.04	8024.10	267.47
8000	8231.52	685.96	8339.76	463.32	8448.96	352.04	8559.30	285.31
8500	8745.96	728.83	8861.04	492.28	8976.96	374.04	9094.20	303.14
9000	9260.40	771.70	9382.32	521.24	9505.20	396.05	9629.10	320.97
10000	10289.40	857.45	10424.70	579.15	10561.20	440.05	10698.90	356.63
11000	11318.28	943.19	11467.26	637.07	11617.44	484.06	11769.00	392.30
12000	12347.28	1028.94	12509.64	694.98	12673.68	528.07	12838.80	427.96
13000	13376.16	1114.68	13552.20	752.90	13729.68	572.07	13908.90	463.63
14000	14405.16	1200.43	14594.58	810.81	14785.92	616.08	14978.70	499.29
15000	15434.04	1286.17	15637.14	868.73	15841.92	660.08	16048.50	534.95
16000	16463.04	1371.92	16679.70	926.65	16898.16	704.09	17118.60	570.62
17000	17491.92	1457.66	17722.08	984.56	17954.16	748.09	18188.40	606.28
18000	18520.92	1543.41	18764.64	1042.48	19010.40	792.10	19258.20	641.94
19000	19549.80	1629.15	19807.02	1100.39	20066.64	836.11	20328.30	677.61
20000	20578.80	1714.90	20849.58	1158.31	21122.64	880.11	21398.10	713.27
21000	21607.68	1800.64	21891.96	1216.22	22178.88	924.12	22468.20	748.94
22000	22636.68	1886.39	22934.52	1274.14	23234.88	968.12	23538.00	784.60
23000	23665.56	1972.13	23977.08	1332.06	24291.12	1012.13	24607.80	820.26
24000	24694.56	2057.88	25019.46	1389.97	25347.36	1056.14	25677.90	855.93
25000	25723.44	2143.62	26062.02	1447.89	26403.36	1100.14	26747.70	891.59

ANNUAL PERCENTAGE RATE **5.30%**

LOAN AMT	36 MONTHS TOTAL NOTE	MONTHLY PAYMENT	42 MONTHS TOTAL NOTE	MONTHLY PAYMENT	48 MONTHS TOTAL NOTE	MONTHLY PAYMENT	60 MONTHS TOTAL NOTE	MONTHLY PAYMENT
1	1.08	.03	.84	.02	.96	.02	.60	.01
2	2.16	.06	2.10	.05	1.92	.04	1.80	.03
3	3.24	.09	2.94	.07	2.88	.06	3.00	.05
4	4.32	.12	4.20	.10	4.32	.09	4.20	.07
5	5.40	.15	5.46	.13	5.28	.11	5.40	.09
6	6.48	.18	6.30	.15	6.24	.13	6.60	.11
7	7.56	.21	7.56	.18	7.68	.16	7.80	.13
8	8.64	.24	8.40	.20	8.64	.18	9.00	.15
9	9.72	.27	9.66	.23	9.60	.20	10.20	.17
10	10.80	.30	10.92	.26	11.04	.23	11.40	.19
20	21.60	.60	21.84	.52	22.08	.46	22.80	.38
30	32.40	.90	32.76	.78	33.12	.69	34.20	.57
40	43.20	1.20	43.68	1.04	44.16	.92	45.60	.76
50	54.00	1.50	54.60	1.30	55.20	1.15	57.00	.95
60	64.80	1.80	65.52	1.56	66.24	1.38	68.40	1.14
70	75.60	2.10	76.44	1.82	77.76	1.62	79.80	1.33
80	86.40	2.40	87.78	2.09	88.80	1.85	91.20	1.52
90	97.20	2.70	98.70	2.35	99.84	2.08	102.60	1.71
100	108.36	3.01	109.62	2.61	110.88	2.31	114.00	1.90
200	216.72	6.02	219.24	5.22	222.24	4.63	228.00	3.80
300	325.08	9.03	329.28	7.84	333.12	6.94	342.00	5.70
400	433.44	12.04	438.90	10.45	444.48	9.26	456.00	7.60
500	541.80	15.05	548.52	13.06	555.84	11.58	570.00	9.50
600	650.16	18.06	658.56	15.68	666.72	13.89	684.00	11.40
700	758.52	21.07	768.18	18.29	778.08	16.21	798.00	13.30
800	866.88	24.08	878.22	20.91	889.44	18.53	912.00	15.20
900	975.24	27.09	987.84	23.52	1000.32	20.84	1026.00	17.10
1000	1083.60	30.10	1097.46	26.13	1111.68	23.16	1140.00	19.00
1500	1625.40	45.15	1646.40	39.20	1667.52	34.74	1710.60	28.51
2000	2167.56	60.21	2195.34	52.27	2223.84	46.33	2280.60	38.01
2500	2709.36	75.26	2744.28	65.34	2779.68	57.91	2851.20	47.52
3000	3251.16	90.31	3293.22	78.41	3335.52	69.49	3421.20	57.02
3500	3793.32	105.37	3842.16	91.48	3891.36	81.07	3991.80	66.53
4000	4335.12	120.42	4391.10	104.55	4447.68	92.66	4561.80	76.03
4500	4876.92	135.47	4940.04	117.62	5003.52	104.24	5132.40	85.54
5000	5418.72	150.52	5488.98	130.69	5559.36	115.82	5702.40	95.04
5500	5960.88	165.58	6037.92	143.76	6115.20	127.40	6272.40	104.54
6000	6502.68	180.63	6586.86	156.83	6671.52	138.99	6843.00	114.05
6500	7044.48	195.68	7135.80	169.90	7227.36	150.57	7413.00	123.55
7000	7586.64	210.74	7684.32	182.96	7783.20	162.15	7983.60	133.06
7500	8128.44	225.79	8233.26	196.03	8339.52	173.74	8553.60	142.56
8000	8670.24	240.84	8782.20	209.10	8895.36	185.32	9124.20	152.07
8500	9212.04	255.89	9331.14	222.17	9451.20	196.90	9694.20	161.57
9000	9754.20	270.95	9880.08	235.24	10007.04	208.48	10264.80	171.08
10000	10837.80	301.05	10977.96	261.38	11119.20	231.65	11404.80	190.08
11000	11921.76	331.16	12075.84	287.52	12230.88	254.81	12545.40	209.09
12000	13005.36	361.26	13173.72	313.66	13343.04	277.98	13686.00	228.10
13000	14089.32	391.37	14271.60	339.80	14455.20	301.15	14826.60	247.11
14000	15173.28	421.48	15369.06	365.93	15566.88	324.31	15967.20	266.12
15000	16256.88	451.58	16466.94	392.07	16679.04	347.48	17107.80	285.13
16000	17340.84	481.69	17564.82	418.21	17790.72	370.64	18248.40	304.14
17000	18424.44	511.79	18662.70	444.35	18902.88	393.81	19389.00	323.15
18000	19508.40	541.90	19760.58	470.49	20014.56	416.97	20529.60	342.16
19000	20592.00	572.00	20858.46	496.63	21126.72	440.14	21670.20	361.17
20000	21675.96	602.11	21955.92	522.76	22238.40	463.30	22810.20	380.17
21000	22759.92	632.22	23053.80	548.90	23350.56	486.47	23950.80	399.18
22000	23843.52	662.32	24151.68	575.04	24462.24	509.63	25091.40	418.19
23000	24927.48	692.43	25249.56	601.18	25574.40	532.80	26232.00	437.20
24000	26011.08	722.53	26347.44	627.32	26686.56	555.97	27372.60	456.21
25000	27095.04	752.64	27445.32	653.46	27798.24	579.13	28513.20	475.22

5.40% ANNUAL PERCENTAGE RATE

LOAN AMT	12 MONTHS TOTAL NOTE	12 MONTHS MONTHLY PAYMENT	18 MONTHS TOTAL NOTE	18 MONTHS MONTHLY PAYMENT	24 MONTHS TOTAL NOTE	24 MONTHS MONTHLY PAYMENT	30 MONTHS TOTAL NOTE	30 MONTHS MONTHLY PAYMENT
1	.96	.08	.90	.05	.96	.04	.90	.03
2	2.04	.17	1.98	.11	1.92	.08	2.10	.07
3	3.00	.25	3.06	.17	3.12	.13	3.00	.10
4	4.08	.34	4.14	.23	4.08	.17	4.20	.14
5	5.04	.42	5.04	.28	5.28	.22	5.10	.17
6	6.12	.51	6.12	.34	6.24	.26	6.30	.21
7	7.20	.60	7.20	.40	7.20	.30	7.20	.24
8	8.16	.68	8.28	.46	8.40	.35	8.40	.28
9	9.24	.77	9.36	.52	9.36	.39	9.60	.32
10	10.20	.85	10.26	.57	10.56	.44	10.50	.35
20	20.52	1.71	20.70	1.15	21.12	.88	21.30	.71
30	30.84	2.57	31.14	1.73	31.68	1.32	32.10	1.07
40	41.16	3.43	41.58	2.31	42.24	1.76	42.60	1.42
50	51.36	4.28	52.02	2.89	52.80	2.20	53.40	1.78
60	61.68	5.14	62.46	3.47	63.36	2.64	64.20	2.14
70	72.00	6.00	72.90	4.05	73.92	3.08	74.70	2.49
80	82.32	6.86	83.34	4.63	84.48	3.52	85.50	2.85
90	92.64	7.72	93.78	5.21	95.04	3.96	96.30	3.21
100	102.84	8.57	104.22	5.79	105.60	4.40	107.10	3.57
200	205.80	17.15	208.62	11.59	211.44	8.81	214.20	7.14
300	308.76	25.73	312.84	17.38	317.04	13.21	321.30	10.71
400	411.72	34.31	417.24	23.18	422.88	17.62	428.40	14.28
500	514.68	42.89	521.64	28.98	528.48	22.02	535.50	17.85
600	617.64	51.47	625.86	34.77	634.32	26.43	642.60	21.42
700	720.60	60.05	730.26	40.57	739.92	30.83	749.70	24.99
800	823.56	68.63	834.48	46.36	845.76	35.24	856.80	28.56
900	926.52	77.21	938.88	52.16	951.36	39.64	963.90	32.13
1000	1029.48	85.79	1043.28	57.96	1057.20	44.05	1071.00	35.70
1500	1544.16	128.68	1564.92	86.94	1585.68	66.07	1606.80	53.56
2000	2058.96	171.58	2086.56	115.92	2114.40	88.10	2142.30	71.41
2500	2573.64	214.47	2608.20	144.90	2642.88	110.12	2678.10	89.27
3000	3088.44	257.37	3129.84	173.88	3171.60	132.15	3213.60	107.12
3500	3603.12	300.26	3651.48	202.86	3700.08	154.17	3749.40	124.98
4000	4117.92	343.16	4173.12	231.84	4228.80	176.20	4284.90	142.83
4500	4632.60	386.05	4694.76	260.82	4757.28	198.22	4820.40	160.68
5000	5147.40	428.95	5216.04	289.80	5286.00	220.25	5356.20	178.54
5500	5662.08	471.84	5738.04	318.78	5814.48	242.27	5891.70	196.39
6000	6176.88	514.74	6259.68	347.76	6343.20	264.30	6427.50	214.25
6500	6691.68	557.64	6781.32	376.74	6871.68	286.32	6963.00	232.10
7000	7206.36	600.53	7302.96	405.72	7400.40	308.35	7498.80	249.96
7500	7721.16	643.43	7824.60	434.70	7929.12	330.38	8034.30	267.81
8000	8235.84	686.32	8346.24	463.68	8457.60	352.40	8570.10	285.67
8500	8750.64	729.22	8867.88	492.66	8986.32	374.43	9105.60	303.52
9000	9265.32	772.11	9389.52	521.64	9514.80	396.45	9641.10	321.37
10000	10294.80	857.90	10432.80	579.60	10572.00	440.50	10712.40	357.08
11000	11324.28	943.69	11476.08	637.56	11629.20	484.55	11783.70	392.79
12000	12353.88	1029.49	12519.36	695.52	12686.40	528.60	12855.00	428.50
13000	13383.36	1115.28	13562.64	753.48	13743.60	572.65	13926.30	464.21
14000	14412.84	1201.07	14606.10	811.45	14801.04	616.71	14997.60	499.92
15000	15442.32	1286.86	15649.38	869.41	15858.24	660.76	16068.90	535.63
16000	16471.80	1372.65	16692.66	927.37	16915.44	704.81	17140.20	571.34
17000	17501.28	1458.44	17735.94	985.33	17972.64	748.86	18211.20	607.04
18000	18530.76	1544.23	18779.22	1043.29	19029.84	792.91	19282.50	642.75
19000	19560.24	1630.02	19822.50	1101.25	20087.04	836.96	20353.80	678.46
20000	20589.72	1715.81	20865.78	1159.21	21144.24	881.01	21425.10	714.17
21000	21619.20	1801.60	21909.06	1217.17	22201.44	925.06	22496.40	749.88
22000	22648.68	1887.39	22952.34	1275.13	23258.64	969.11	23567.70	785.59
23000	23678.28	1973.19	23995.62	1333.09	24315.84	1013.16	24639.00	821.30
24000	24707.76	2058.98	25038.90	1391.05	25373.04	1057.21	25710.30	857.01
25000	25737.24	2144.77	26082.18	1449.01	26430.24	1101.26	26781.30	892.71

ANNUAL PERCENTAGE RATE **5.40%**

LOAN AMT	36 MONTHS TOTAL NOTE	36 MONTHS MONTHLY PAYMENT	42 MONTHS TOTAL NOTE	42 MONTHS MONTHLY PAYMENT	48 MONTHS TOTAL NOTE	48 MONTHS MONTHLY PAYMENT	60 MONTHS TOTAL NOTE	60 MONTHS MONTHLY PAYMENT
1	1.08	.03	.84	.02	.96	.02	.60	.01
2	2.16	.06	2.10	.05	1.92	.04	1.80	.03
3	3.24	.09	2.94	.07	2.88	.06	3.00	.05
4	4.32	.12	4.20	.10	4.32	.09	4.20	.07
5	5.40	.15	5.46	.13	5.28	.11	5.40	.09
6	6.48	.18	6.30	.15	6.24	.13	6.60	.11
7	7.56	.21	7.56	.18	7.68	.16	7.80	.13
8	8.64	.24	8.40	.20	8.64	.18	9.00	.15
9	9.72	.27	9.66	.23	9.60	.20	10.20	.17
10	10.80	.30	10.92	.26	11.04	.23	11.40	.19
20	21.60	.60	21.84	.52	22.08	.46	22.80	.38
30	32.40	.90	32.76	.78	33.12	.69	34.20	.57
40	43.20	1.20	43.68	1.04	44.16	.92	45.60	.76
50	54.00	1.50	54.60	1.30	55.68	1.16	57.00	.95
60	64.80	1.80	65.94	1.57	66.72	1.39	68.40	1.14
70	75.96	2.11	76.86	1.83	77.76	1.62	79.80	1.33
80	86.76	2.41	87.78	2.09	88.80	1.85	91.20	1.52
90	97.56	2.71	98.70	2.35	99.84	2.08	102.60	1.71
100	108.36	3.01	109.62	2.61	111.36	2.32	114.00	1.90
200	217.08	6.03	219.66	5.23	222.72	4.64	228.60	3.81
300	325.44	9.04	329.70	7.85	334.08	6.96	342.60	5.71
400	434.16	12.06	439.74	10.47	445.44	9.28	457.20	7.62
500	542.52	15.07	549.78	13.09	556.80	11.60	571.20	9.52
600	651.24	18.09	659.82	15.71	668.16	13.92	685.80	11.43
700	759.60	21.10	769.44	18.32	779.52	16.24	799.80	13.33
800	868.32	24.12	879.48	20.94	890.88	18.56	914.40	15.24
900	976.68	27.13	989.52	23.56	1002.24	20.88	1028.40	17.14
1000	1085.40	30.15	1099.56	26.18	1114.08	23.21	1143.00	19.05
1500	1627.92	45.22	1649.34	39.27	1670.88	34.81	1714.80	28.58
2000	2170.80	60.30	2199.12	52.36	2228.16	46.42	2286.60	38.11
2500	2713.32	75.37	2748.90	65.45	2784.96	58.02	2857.80	47.63
3000	3256.20	90.45	3299.10	78.55	3342.24	69.63	3429.60	57.16
3500	3798.72	105.52	3848.88	91.64	3899.04	81.23	4001.40	66.69
4000	4341.60	120.60	4398.66	104.73	4456.32	92.84	4573.20	76.22
4500	4884.12	135.67	4948.44	117.82	5013.12	104.44	5144.40	85.74
5000	5427.00	150.75	5498.22	130.91	5570.40	116.05	5716.20	95.27
5500	5969.52	165.82	6048.42	144.01	6127.68	127.66	6288.00	104.80
6000	6512.40	180.90	6598.20	157.10	6684.48	139.26	6859.80	114.33
6500	7055.28	195.98	7147.98	170.19	7241.76	150.87	7431.00	123.85
7000	7597.80	211.05	7697.76	183.28	7798.56	162.47	8002.80	133.38
7500	8140.68	226.13	8247.54	196.37	8355.84	174.08	8574.60	142.91
8000	8683.20	241.20	8797.32	209.46	8912.64	185.68	9146.40	152.44
8500	9226.08	256.28	9347.52	222.56	9469.92	197.29	9717.60	161.96
9000	9768.60	271.35	9897.30	235.65	10026.72	208.89	10289.40	171.49
10000	10854.00	301.50	10996.86	261.83	11140.80	232.10	11433.00	190.55
11000	11939.40	331.65	12096.84	288.02	12255.36	255.32	12576.00	209.60
12000	13024.80	361.80	13196.40	314.20	13369.44	278.53	13719.60	228.66
13000	14110.56	391.96	14295.96	340.38	14483.52	301.74	14862.60	247.71
14000	15195.96	422.11	15395.94	366.57	15597.60	324.95	16006.20	266.77
15000	16281.36	452.26	16495.50	392.75	16711.68	348.16	17149.20	285.82
16000	17366.76	482.41	17595.06	418.93	17825.76	371.37	18292.80	304.88
17000	18452.16	512.56	18695.04	445.12	18939.84	394.58	19435.80	323.93
18000	19537.56	542.71	19794.60	471.30	20053.92	417.79	20579.40	342.99
19000	20622.96	572.86	20894.58	497.49	21168.00	441.00	21722.40	362.04
20000	21708.36	603.01	21994.14	523.67	22282.08	464.21	22866.00	381.10
21000	22793.76	633.16	23093.70	549.85	23396.16	487.42	24009.00	400.15
22000	23879.16	663.31	24193.68	576.04	24510.72	510.64	25152.60	419.21
23000	24964.56	693.46	25293.24	602.22	25624.80	533.85	26295.60	438.26
24000	26049.96	723.61	26392.80	628.40	26738.88	557.06	27439.20	457.32
25000	27135.72	753.77	27492.78	654.59	27852.96	580.27	28582.20	476.37

5.50% ANNUAL PERCENTAGE RATE

LOAN AMT	12 MONTHS TOTAL NOTE	MONTHLY PAYMENT	18 MONTHS TOTAL NOTE	MONTHLY PAYMENT	24 MONTHS TOTAL NOTE	MONTHLY PAYMENT	30 MONTHS TOTAL NOTE	MONTHLY PAYMENT
1	.96	.08	.90	.05	.96	.04	.90	.03
2	2.04	.17	1.98	.11	1.92	.08	2.10	.07
3	3.00	.25	3.06	.17	3.12	.13	3.00	.10
4	4.08	.34	4.14	.23	4.08	.17	4.20	.14
5	5.04	.42	5.22	.29	5.28	.22	5.10	.17
6	6.12	.51	6.12	.34	6.24	.26	6.30	.21
7	7.20	.60	7.20	.40	7.20	.30	7.50	.25
8	8.16	.68	8.28	.46	8.40	.35	8.40	.28
9	9.24	.77	9.36	.52	9.36	.39	9.60	.32
10	10.20	.85	10.44	.58	10.56	.44	10.50	.35
20	20.52	1.71	20.88	1.16	21.12	.88	21.30	.71
30	30.84	2.57	31.32	1.74	31.68	1.32	32.10	1.07
40	41.16	3.43	41.76	2.32	42.24	1.76	42.90	1.43
50	51.48	4.29	52.20	2.90	52.80	2.20	53.40	1.78
60	61.80	5.15	62.64	3.48	63.36	2.64	64.20	2.14
70	72.00	6.00	73.08	4.06	73.92	3.08	75.00	2.50
80	82.32	6.86	83.52	4.64	84.48	3.52	85.80	2.86
90	92.64	7.72	93.96	5.22	95.04	3.96	96.30	3.21
100	102.96	8.58	104.40	5.80	105.60	4.40	107.10	3.57
200	205.92	17.16	208.80	11.60	211.44	8.81	214.50	7.15
300	309.00	25.75	313.20	17.40	317.28	13.22	321.60	10.72
400	411.96	34.33	417.60	23.20	423.12	17.63	429.00	14.30
500	514.92	42.91	522.00	29.00	528.96	22.04	536.10	17.87
600	618.00	51.50	626.40	34.80	634.80	26.45	643.50	21.45
700	720.96	60.08	730.80	40.60	740.64	30.86	750.60	25.02
800	823.92	68.66	835.20	46.40	846.48	35.27	858.00	28.60
900	927.00	77.25	939.60	52.20	952.32	39.68	965.10	32.17
1000	1029.96	85.83	1044.00	58.00	1058.16	44.09	1072.50	35.75
1500	1545.00	128.75	1566.00	87.00	1587.36	66.14	1608.90	53.63
2000	2060.04	171.67	2088.18	116.01	2116.56	88.19	2145.00	71.50
2500	2575.08	214.59	2610.18	145.01	2645.52	110.23	2681.40	89.38
3000	3090.12	257.51	3132.18	174.01	3174.72	132.28	3217.80	107.26
3500	3605.04	300.42	3654.36	203.02	3703.92	154.33	3753.90	125.13
4000	4120.08	343.34	4176.36	232.02	4233.12	176.38	4290.30	143.01
4500	4635.12	386.26	4698.36	261.02	4762.32	198.43	4826.70	160.89
5000	5150.16	429.18	5220.36	290.02	5291.28	220.47	5362.80	178.76
5500	5665.20	472.10	5742.54	319.03	5820.48	242.52	5899.20	196.64
6000	6180.24	515.02	6264.54	348.03	6349.68	264.57	6435.60	214.52
6500	6695.16	557.93	6786.54	377.03	6878.88	286.62	6971.70	232.39
7000	7210.20	600.85	7308.72	406.04	7407.84	308.66	7508.10	250.27
7500	7725.24	643.77	7830.72	435.04	7937.04	330.71	8044.50	268.15
8000	8240.28	686.69	8352.72	464.04	8466.24	352.76	8580.60	286.02
8500	8755.32	729.61	8874.72	493.04	8995.44	374.81	9117.00	303.90
9000	9270.36	772.53	9396.90	522.05	9524.64	396.86	9653.40	321.78
10000	10300.32	858.36	10440.90	580.05	10582.80	440.95	10725.90	357.53
11000	11330.40	944.20	11485.08	638.06	11641.20	485.05	11798.70	393.29
12000	12360.48	1030.04	12529.26	696.07	12699.36	529.14	12871.20	429.04
13000	13390.44	1115.87	13573.26	754.07	13757.76	573.24	13943.70	464.79
14000	14420.52	1201.71	14617.44	812.08	14815.92	617.33	15016.50	500.55
15000	15450.60	1287.55	15661.44	870.08	15874.32	661.43	16089.00	536.30
16000	16480.56	1373.38	16705.62	928.09	16932.72	705.53	17161.50	572.05
17000	17510.64	1459.22	17749.62	986.09	17990.88	749.62	18234.30	607.81
18000	18540.72	1545.06	18793.80	1044.10	19049.28	793.72	19306.80	643.56
19000	19570.68	1630.89	19837.98	1102.11	20107.44	837.81	20379.60	679.32
20000	20600.76	1716.73	20881.98	1160.11	21165.84	881.91	21452.10	715.07
21000	21630.84	1802.57	21926.16	1218.12	22224.00	926.00	22524.60	750.82
22000	22660.80	1888.40	22970.16	1276.12	23282.40	970.10	23597.40	786.58
23000	23690.88	1974.24	24014.34	1334.13	24340.80	1014.20	24669.90	822.33
24000	24720.96	2060.08	25058.52	1392.14	25398.96	1058.29	25742.40	858.08
25000	25750.92	2145.91	26102.52	1450.14	26457.36	1102.39	26815.20	893.84

ANNUAL PERCENTAGE RATE **5.50%**

LOAN AMT	36 MONTHS TOTAL NOTE	36 MONTHS MONTHLY PAYMENT	42 MONTHS TOTAL NOTE	42 MONTHS MONTHLY PAYMENT	48 MONTHS TOTAL NOTE	48 MONTHS MONTHLY PAYMENT	60 MONTHS TOTAL NOTE	60 MONTHS MONTHLY PAYMENT
1	1.08	.03	.84	.02	.96	.02	.60	.01
2	2.16	.06	2.10	.05	1.92	.04	1.80	.03
3	3.24	.09	2.94	.07	2.88	.06	3.00	.05
4	4.32	.12	4.20	.10	4.32	.09	4.20	.07
5	5.40	.15	5.46	.13	5.28	.11	5.40	.09
6	6.48	.18	6.30	.15	6.24	.13	6.60	.11
7	7.56	.21	7.56	.18	7.68	.16	7.80	.13
8	8.64	.24	8.40	.20	8.64	.18	9.00	.15
9	9.72	.27	9.66	.23	9.60	.20	10.20	.17
10	10.80	.30	10.92	.26	11.04	.23	11.40	.19
20	21.60	.60	21.84	.52	22.08	.46	22.80	.38
30	32.40	.90	32.76	.78	33.12	.69	34.20	.57
40	43.20	1.20	43.68	1.04	44.64	.93	45.60	.76
50	54.00	1.50	55.02	1.31	55.68	1.16	57.00	.95
60	65.16	1.81	65.94	1.57	66.72	1.39	68.40	1.14
70	75.96	2.11	76.86	1.83	77.76	1.62	79.80	1.33
80	86.76	2.41	87.78	2.09	89.28	1.86	91.20	1.52
90	97.56	2.71	99.12	2.36	100.32	2.09	102.60	1.71
100	108.36	3.01	110.04	2.62	111.36	2.32	114.60	1.91
200	217.08	6.03	220.08	5.24	223.20	4.65	229.20	3.82
300	325.80	9.05	330.12	7.86	334.56	6.97	343.80	5.73
400	434.52	12.07	440.58	10.49	446.40	9.30	458.40	7.64
500	543.24	15.09	550.62	13.11	557.76	11.62	573.00	9.55
600	651.96	18.11	660.66	15.73	669.60	13.95	687.60	11.46
700	760.68	21.13	771.12	18.36	780.96	16.27	802.20	13.37
800	869.40	24.15	881.16	20.98	892.80	18.60	916.80	15.28
900	978.12	27.17	991.20	23.60	1004.64	20.93	1031.40	17.19
1000	1086.84	30.19	1101.24	26.22	1116.00	23.25	1146.00	19.10
1500	1630.44	45.29	1652.28	39.34	1674.24	34.88	1719.00	28.65
2000	2174.04	60.39	2202.90	52.45	2232.48	46.51	2292.00	38.20
2500	2717.28	75.48	2753.94	65.57	2790.72	58.14	2865.00	47.75
3000	3260.88	90.58	3304.56	78.68	3348.48	69.76	3438.00	57.30
3500	3804.48	105.68	3855.60	91.80	3906.72	81.39	4011.00	66.85
4000	4348.08	120.78	4406.22	104.91	4464.96	93.02	4584.00	76.40
4500	4891.68	135.88	4957.26	118.03	5023.20	104.65	5157.00	85.95
5000	5434.92	150.97	5507.88	131.14	5581.44	116.28	5730.00	95.50
5500	5978.52	166.07	6058.50	144.25	6139.68	127.91	6303.00	105.05
6000	6522.12	181.17	6609.54	157.37	6697.44	139.53	6876.00	114.60
6500	7065.72	196.27	7160.16	170.48	7255.68	151.16	7449.00	124.15
7000	7609.32	211.37	7711.20	183.60	7813.92	162.79	8022.00	133.70
7500	8152.56	226.46	8261.82	196.71	8372.16	174.42	8595.00	143.25
8000	8696.16	241.56	8812.86	209.83	8930.40	186.05	9168.00	152.80
8500	9239.76	256.66	9363.48	222.94	9488.64	197.68	9741.00	162.35
9000	9783.36	271.76	9914.52	236.06	10046.40	209.30	10314.60	171.91
10000	10870.20	301.95	11016.18	262.29	11162.88	232.56	11460.60	191.01
11000	11957.40	332.15	12117.42	288.51	12279.36	255.82	12606.60	210.11
12000	13044.60	362.35	13219.08	314.74	13395.36	279.07	13752.60	229.21
13000	14131.44	392.54	14320.74	340.97	14511.84	302.33	14898.60	248.31
14000	15218.64	422.74	15422.40	367.20	15628.32	325.59	16044.60	267.41
15000	16305.48	452.93	16524.06	393.43	16744.32	348.84	17190.60	286.51
16000	17392.68	483.13	17625.72	419.66	17860.80	372.10	18336.60	305.61
17000	18479.88	513.33	18727.38	445.89	18977.28	395.36	19482.60	324.71
18000	19566.72	543.52	19829.04	472.12	20093.28	418.61	20629.20	343.82
19000	20653.92	573.72	20930.70	498.35	21209.76	441.87	21775.20	362.92
20000	21740.76	603.91	22032.36	524.58	22325.76	465.12	22921.20	382.02
21000	22827.96	634.11	23133.60	550.80	23442.24	488.38	24067.20	401.12
22000	23914.80	664.30	24235.26	577.03	24558.72	511.64	25213.20	420.22
23000	25002.00	694.50	25336.92	603.26	25674.72	534.89	26359.20	439.32
24000	26089.20	724.70	26438.58	629.49	26791.20	558.15	27505.20	458.42
25000	27176.04	754.89	27540.24	655.72	27907.68	581.41	28651.20	477.52

5.60% ANNUAL PERCENTAGE RATE

	12 MONTHS		18 MONTHS		24 MONTHS		30 MONTHS	
LOAN AMT	TOTAL NOTE	MONTHLY PAYMENT	TOTAL NOTE	MONTHLY PAYMENT	TOTAL NOTE	MONTHLY PAYMENT	TOTAL NOTE	MONTHLY PAYMENT
1	.96	.08	.90	.05	.96	.04	.90	.03
2	2.04	.17	1.98	.11	1.92	.08	2.10	.07
3	3.00	.25	3.06	.17	3.12	.13	3.00	.10
4	4.08	.34	4.14	.23	4.08	.17	4.20	.14
5	5.04	.42	5.22	.29	5.28	.22	5.10	.17
6	6.12	.51	6.12	.34	6.24	.26	6.30	.21
7	7.20	.60	7.20	.40	7.20	.30	7.50	.25
8	8.16	.68	8.28	.46	8.40	.35	8.40	.28
9	9.24	.77	9.36	.52	9.36	.39	9.60	.32
10	10.20	.85	10.44	.58	10.56	.44	10.50	.35
20	20.52	1.71	20.88	1.16	21.12	.88	21.30	.71
30	30.84	2.57	31.32	1.74	31.68	1.32	32.10	1.07
40	41.16	3.43	41.76	2.32	42.24	1.76	42.90	1.43
50	51.48	4.29	52.20	2.90	52.80	2.20	53.40	1.78
60	61.80	5.15	62.64	3.48	63.36	2.64	64.20	2.14
70	72.12	6.01	73.08	4.06	73.92	3.08	75.00	2.50
80	82.44	6.87	83.52	4.64	84.72	3.53	85.80	2.86
90	92.64	7.72	93.96	5.22	95.28	3.97	96.60	3.22
100	102.96	8.58	104.40	5.80	105.84	4.41	107.10	3.57
200	206.04	17.17	208.98	11.61	211.68	8.82	214.50	7.15
300	309.12	25.76	313.38	17.41	317.76	13.24	321.90	10.73
400	412.20	34.35	417.96	23.22	423.60	17.65	429.30	14.31
500	515.28	42.94	522.36	29.02	529.68	22.07	536.70	17.89
600	618.24	51.52	626.94	34.83	635.52	26.48	644.10	21.47
700	721.32	60.11	731.34	40.63	741.36	30.89	751.50	25.05
800	824.40	68.70	835.92	46.44	847.44	35.31	858.90	28.63
900	927.48	77.29	940.32	52.24	953.28	39.72	966.30	32.21
1000	1030.56	85.88	1044.90	58.05	1059.36	44.14	1073.70	35.79
1500	1545.84	128.82	1567.26	87.07	1589.04	66.21	1610.70	53.69
2000	2061.12	171.76	2089.80	116.10	2118.72	88.28	2147.70	71.59
2500	2576.40	214.70	2612.16	145.12	2648.40	110.35	2684.70	89.49
3000	3091.68	257.64	3134.70	174.15	3178.08	132.42	3221.70	107.39
3500	3606.96	300.58	3657.06	203.17	3707.76	154.49	3758.70	125.29
4000	4122.36	343.53	4179.60	232.20	4237.44	176.56	4295.70	143.19
4500	4637.64	386.47	4701.96	261.22	4767.12	198.63	4832.70	161.09
5000	5152.92	429.41	5224.50	290.25	5296.80	220.70	5369.70	178.99
5500	5668.20	472.35	5747.04	319.28	5826.48	242.77	5906.70	196.89
6000	6183.48	515.29	6269.40	348.30	6356.16	264.84	6443.70	214.79
6500	6698.76	558.23	6791.94	377.33	6885.84	286.91	6980.70	232.69
7000	7214.04	601.17	7314.30	406.35	7415.52	308.98	7517.70	250.59
7500	7729.44	644.12	7836.84	435.38	7945.20	331.05	8054.70	268.49
8000	8244.72	687.06	8359.20	464.40	8474.88	353.12	8591.40	286.38
8500	8760.00	730.00	8881.74	493.43	9004.56	375.19	9128.40	304.28
9000	9275.28	772.94	9404.10	522.45	9534.24	397.26	9665.40	322.18
10000	10305.84	858.82	10449.18	580.51	10593.60	441.40	10739.40	357.98
11000	11336.40	944.70	11494.08	638.56	11652.96	485.54	11813.40	393.78
12000	12367.08	1030.59	12538.98	696.61	12712.32	529.68	12887.40	429.58
13000	13397.64	1116.47	13583.88	754.66	13771.68	573.82	13961.40	465.38
14000	14428.20	1202.35	14628.78	812.71	14831.04	617.96	15035.40	501.18
15000	15458.88	1288.24	15673.68	870.76	15890.40	662.10	16109.40	536.98
16000	16489.44	1374.12	16718.58	928.81	16949.76	706.24	17183.10	572.77
17000	17520.00	1460.00	17763.48	986.86	18009.36	750.39	18257.10	608.57
18000	18550.56	1545.88	18808.38	1044.91	19068.72	794.53	19331.10	644.37
19000	19581.24	1631.77	19853.28	1102.96	20128.08	838.67	20405.10	680.17
20000	20611.80	1717.65	20898.36	1161.02	21187.44	882.81	21479.10	715.97
21000	21642.36	1803.53	21943.26	1219.07	22246.80	926.95	22553.10	751.77
22000	22672.92	1889.41	22988.16	1277.12	23306.16	971.09	23627.10	787.57
23000	23703.60	1975.30	24033.06	1335.17	24365.52	1015.23	24700.80	823.36
24000	24734.16	2061.18	25077.96	1393.22	25424.88	1059.37	25774.80	859.16
25000	25764.72	2147.06	26122.86	1451.27	26484.24	1103.51	26848.80	894.96

ANNUAL PERCENTAGE RATE **5.60%**

LOAN	36 MONTHS		42 MONTHS		48 MONTHS		60 MONTHS	
AMT	TOTAL NOTE	MONTHLY PAYMENT	TOTAL NOTE	MONTHLY PAYMENT	TOTAL NOTE	MONTHLY PAYMENT	TOTAL NOTE	MONTHLY PAYMENT
1	1.08	.03	.84	.02	.96	.02	.60	.01
2	2.16	.06	2.10	.05	1.92	.04	1.80	.03
3	3.24	.09	2.94	.07	2.88	.06	3.00	.05
4	4.32	.12	4.20	.10	4.32	.09	4.20	.07
5	5.40	.15	5.46	.13	5.28	.11	5.40	.09
6	6.48	.18	6.30	.15	6.24	.13	6.60	.11
7	7.56	.21	7.56	.18	7.68	.16	7.80	.13
8	8.64	.24	8.82	.21	8.64	.18	9.00	.15
9	9.72	.27	9.66	.23	9.60	.20	10.20	.17
10	10.80	.30	10.92	.26	11.04	.23	11.40	.19
20	21.60	.60	21.84	.52	22.08	.46	22.80	.38
30	32.40	.90	32.76	.78	33.12	.69	34.20	.57
40	43.20	1.20	44.10	1.05	44.64	.93	45.60	.76
50	54.36	1.51	55.02	1.31	55.68	1.16	57.00	.95
60	65.16	1.81	65.94	1.57	66.72	1.39	68.40	1.14
70	75.96	2.11	76.86	1.83	78.24	1.63	80.40	1.34
80	86.76	2.41	88.20	2.10	89.28	1.86	91.80	1.53
90	97.92	2.72	99.12	2.36	100.32	2.09	103.20	1.72
100	108.72	3.02	110.04	2.62	111.84	2.33	114.60	1.91
200	217.44	6.04	220.50	5.25	223.68	4.66	229.20	3.82
300	326.52	9.07	330.96	7.88	335.52	6.99	344.40	5.74
400	435.24	12.09	441.00	10.50	447.36	9.32	459.00	7.65
500	544.32	15.12	551.46	13.13	559.20	11.65	574.20	9.57
600	653.04	18.14	661.92	15.76	671.04	13.98	688.80	11.48
700	761.76	21.16	772.38	18.39	782.88	16.31	804.00	13.40
800	870.84	24.19	882.42	21.01	894.72	18.64	918.60	15.31
900	979.56	27.21	992.88	23.64	1006.56	20.97	1033.80	17.23
1000	1088.64	30.24	1103.34	26.27	1118.40	23.30	1148.40	19.14
1500	1632.96	45.36	1655.22	39.41	1677.60	34.95	1723.20	28.72
2000	2177.28	60.48	2206.68	52.54	2236.80	46.60	2297.40	38.29
2500	2721.60	75.60	2758.56	65.68	2796.00	58.25	2871.60	47.86
3000	3265.92	90.72	3310.44	78.82	3355.20	69.90	3446.40	57.44
3500	3810.24	105.84	3862.32	91.96	3914.40	81.55	4020.60	67.01
4000	4354.56	120.96	4413.78	105.09	4473.60	93.20	4594.80	76.58
4500	4898.88	136.08	4965.66	118.23	5032.80	104.85	5169.60	86.16
5000	5443.20	151.20	5517.54	131.37	5592.48	116.51	5743.80	95.73
5500	5987.52	166.32	6069.00	144.50	6151.68	128.16	6318.60	105.31
6000	6531.84	181.44	6620.88	157.64	6710.88	139.81	6892.80	114.88
6500	7076.16	196.56	7172.76	170.78	7270.08	151.46	7467.00	124.45
7000	7620.48	211.68	7724.64	183.92	7829.28	163.11	8041.80	134.03
7500	8164.80	226.80	8276.10	197.05	8388.48	174.76	8616.00	143.60
8000	8709.12	241.92	8827.98	210.19	8947.68	186.41	9190.20	153.17
8500	9253.44	257.04	9379.86	223.33	9506.88	198.06	9765.00	162.75
9000	9797.76	272.16	9931.32	236.46	10066.08	209.71	10339.20	172.32
10000	10886.76	302.41	11035.08	262.74	11184.96	233.02	11488.20	191.47
11000	11975.40	332.65	12138.42	289.01	12303.36	256.32	12637.20	210.62
12000	13064.04	362.89	13242.18	315.29	13421.76	279.62	13785.60	229.76
13000	14152.68	393.13	14345.52	341.56	14540.16	302.92	14934.60	248.91
14000	15241.32	423.37	15449.28	367.84	15658.56	326.22	16083.60	268.06
15000	16329.96	453.61	16552.62	394.11	16777.44	349.53	17232.60	287.21
16000	17418.60	483.85	17655.96	420.38	17895.84	372.83	18381.00	306.35
17000	18507.24	514.09	18759.72	446.66	19014.24	396.13	19530.00	325.50
18000	19595.88	544.33	19863.06	472.93	20132.64	419.43	20679.00	344.65
19000	20684.52	574.57	20966.82	499.21	21251.04	442.73	21827.40	363.79
20000	21773.52	604.82	22070.16	525.48	22369.92	466.04	22976.40	382.94
21000	22862.16	635.06	23173.92	551.76	23488.32	489.34	24125.40	402.09
22000	23950.80	665.30	24277.26	578.03	24606.72	512.64	25274.40	421.24
23000	25039.44	695.54	25381.02	604.31	25725.12	535.94	26422.80	440.38
24000	26128.08	725.78	26484.36	630.58	26843.52	559.24	27571.80	459.53
25000	27216.72	756.02	27587.70	656.85	27962.40	582.55	28720.80	478.68

5.70% ANNUAL PERCENTAGE RATE

LOAN AMT	12 MONTHS TOTAL NOTE	12 MONTHS MONTHLY PAYMENT	18 MONTHS TOTAL NOTE	18 MONTHS MONTHLY PAYMENT	24 MONTHS TOTAL NOTE	24 MONTHS MONTHLY PAYMENT	30 MONTHS TOTAL NOTE	30 MONTHS MONTHLY PAYMENT
1	.96	.08	.90	.05	.96	.04	.90	.03
2	2.04	.17	1.98	.11	1.92	.08	2.10	.07
3	3.00	.25	3.06	.17	3.12	.13	3.00	.10
4	4.08	.34	4.14	.23	4.08	.17	4.20	.14
5	5.04	.42	5.22	.29	5.28	.22	5.10	.17
6	6.12	.51	6.12	.34	6.24	.26	6.30	.21
7	7.20	.60	7.20	.40	7.20	.30	7.50	.25
8	8.16	.68	8.28	.46	8.40	.35	8.40	.28
9	9.24	.77	9.36	.52	9.36	.39	9.60	.32
10	10.20	.85	10.44	.58	10.56	.44	10.50	.35
20	20.52	1.71	20.88	1.16	21.12	.88	21.30	.71
30	30.84	2.57	31.32	1.74	31.68	1.32	32.10	1.07
40	41.16	3.43	41.76	2.32	42.24	1.76	42.90	1.43
50	51.48	4.29	52.20	2.90	52.80	2.20	53.70	1.79
60	61.80	5.15	62.64	3.48	63.60	2.65	64.50	2.15
70	72.12	6.01	73.08	4.06	74.16	3.09	75.00	2.50
80	82.44	6.87	83.52	4.64	84.72	3.53	85.80	2.86
90	92.76	7.73	93.96	5.22	95.28	3.97	96.60	3.22
100	103.08	8.59	104.40	5.80	105.84	4.41	107.40	3.58
200	206.16	17.18	208.98	11.61	211.92	8.83	214.80	7.16
300	309.24	25.77	313.56	17.42	318.00	13.25	322.50	10.75
400	412.44	34.37	418.14	23.23	424.08	17.67	429.90	14.33
500	515.52	42.96	522.72	29.04	530.16	22.09	537.60	17.92
600	618.60	51.55	627.30	34.85	636.24	26.51	645.00	21.50
700	721.80	60.15	731.88	40.66	742.08	30.92	752.70	25.09
800	824.88	68.74	836.46	46.47	848.16	35.34	860.10	28.67
900	927.96	77.33	941.04	52.28	954.24	39.76	967.50	32.25
1000	1031.04	85.92	1045.62	58.09	1060.32	44.18	1075.20	35.84
1500	1546.68	128.89	1568.52	87.14	1590.48	66.27	1612.80	53.76
2000	2062.20	171.85	2091.42	116.19	2120.88	88.37	2150.40	71.68
2500	2577.84	214.82	2614.32	145.24	2651.04	110.46	2688.00	89.60
3000	3093.36	257.78	3137.04	174.28	3181.20	132.55	3225.90	107.53
3500	3609.00	300.75	3659.94	203.33	3711.36	154.64	3763.50	125.45
4000	4124.52	343.71	4182.84	232.38	4241.76	176.74	4301.10	143.37
4500	4640.04	386.67	4705.74	261.43	4771.92	198.83	4838.70	161.29
5000	5155.68	429.64	5228.64	290.48	5302.08	220.92	5376.30	179.21
5500	5671.20	472.60	5751.36	319.52	5832.48	243.02	5914.20	197.14
6000	6186.84	515.57	6274.26	348.57	6362.64	265.11	6451.80	215.06
6500	6702.36	558.53	6797.16	377.62	6892.80	287.20	6989.40	232.98
7000	7218.00	601.50	7320.06	406.67	7422.96	309.29	7527.00	250.90
7500	7733.52	644.46	7842.96	435.72	7953.36	331.39	8064.60	268.82
8000	8249.04	687.42	8365.68	464.76	8483.52	353.48	8602.20	286.74
8500	8764.68	730.39	8888.58	493.81	9013.68	375.57	9140.10	304.67
9000	9280.20	773.35	9411.48	522.86	9543.84	397.66	9677.70	322.59
10000	10311.36	859.28	10457.28	580.96	10604.40	441.85	10752.90	358.43
11000	11342.52	945.21	11502.90	639.05	11664.96	486.04	11828.40	394.28
12000	12373.68	1031.14	12548.70	697.15	12725.28	530.22	12903.60	430.12
13000	13404.84	1117.07	13594.50	755.25	13785.84	574.41	13978.80	465.96
14000	14436.00	1203.00	14640.12	813.34	14846.16	618.59	15054.30	501.81
15000	15467.04	1288.92	15685.92	871.44	15906.72	662.78	16129.50	537.65
16000	16498.20	1374.85	16731.54	929.53	16967.04	706.96	17204.70	573.49
17000	17529.36	1460.78	17777.34	987.63	18027.60	751.15	18280.20	609.34
18000	18560.52	1546.71	18823.14	1045.73	19087.92	795.33	19355.40	645.18
19000	19591.68	1632.64	19868.76	1103.82	20148.48	839.52	20430.90	681.03
20000	20622.84	1718.57	20914.56	1161.92	21209.04	883.71	21506.10	716.87
21000	21654.00	1804.50	21960.18	1220.01	22269.36	927.89	22581.30	752.71
22000	22685.04	1890.42	23005.98	1278.11	23329.92	972.08	23656.80	788.56
23000	23716.20	1976.35	24051.78	1336.21	24390.24	1016.26	24732.00	824.40
24000	24747.36	2062.28	25097.40	1394.30	25450.80	1060.45	25807.20	860.24
25000	25778.52	2148.21	26143.20	1452.40	26511.12	1104.63	26882.70	896.09

ANNUAL PERCENTAGE RATE **5.70%**

LOAN AMT	36 MONTHS TOTAL NOTE	36 MONTHS MONTHLY PAYMENT	42 MONTHS TOTAL NOTE	42 MONTHS MONTHLY PAYMENT	48 MONTHS TOTAL NOTE	48 MONTHS MONTHLY PAYMENT	60 MONTHS TOTAL NOTE	60 MONTHS MONTHLY PAYMENT
1	1.08	.03	.84	.02	.96	.02	.60	.01
2	2.16	.06	2.10	.05	1.92	.04	1.80	.03
3	3.24	.09	2.94	.07	3.36	.07	3.00	.05
4	4.32	.12	4.20	.10	4.32	.09	4.20	.07
5	5.40	.15	5.46	.13	5.28	.11	5.40	.09
6	6.48	.18	6.30	.15	6.72	.14	6.60	.11
7	7.56	.21	7.56	.18	7.68	.16	7.80	.13
8	8.64	.24	8.82	.21	8.64	.18	9.00	.15
9	9.72	.27	9.66	.23	10.08	.21	10.20	.17
10	10.80	.30	10.92	.26	11.04	.23	11.40	.19
20	21.60	.60	21.84	.52	22.08	.46	22.80	.38
30	32.40	.90	32.76	.78	33.60	.70	34.20	.57
40	43.56	1.21	44.10	1.05	44.64	.93	45.60	.76
50	54.36	1.51	55.02	1.31	55.68	1.16	57.00	.95
60	65.16	1.81	65.94	1.57	67.20	1.40	69.00	1.15
70	76.32	2.12	77.28	1.84	78.24	1.63	80.40	1.34
80	87.12	2.42	88.20	2.10	89.28	1.86	91.80	1.53
90	97.92	2.72	99.12	2.36	100.80	2.10	103.20	1.72
100	108.72	3.02	110.46	2.63	111.84	2.33	114.60	1.91
200	217.80	6.05	220.92	5.26	223.68	4.66	229.80	3.83
300	326.88	9.08	331.38	7.89	336.00	7.00	345.00	5.75
400	435.96	12.11	441.84	10.52	447.84	9.33	460.20	7.67
500	545.04	15.14	552.30	13.15	560.16	11.67	575.40	9.59
600	654.12	18.17	663.18	15.79	672.00	14.00	690.60	11.51
700	763.20	21.20	773.64	18.42	784.32	16.34	805.80	13.43
800	871.92	24.22	884.10	21.05	896.16	18.67	921.00	15.35
900	981.00	27.25	994.56	23.68	1008.48	21.01	1036.20	17.27
1000	1090.08	30.28	1105.02	26.31	1120.32	23.34	1151.40	19.19
1500	1635.12	45.42	1657.74	39.47	1680.96	35.02	1727.40	28.79
2000	2180.52	60.57	2210.46	52.63	2241.12	46.69	2302.80	38.38
2500	2725.56	75.71	2763.18	65.79	2801.28	58.36	2878.80	47.98
3000	3270.60	90.85	3315.90	78.95	3361.92	70.04	3454.80	57.58
3500	3816.00	106.00	3868.62	92.11	3922.08	81.71	4030.20	67.17
4000	4361.04	121.14	4421.34	105.27	4482.72	93.39	4606.20	76.77
4500	4906.08	136.28	4974.06	118.43	5042.88	105.06	5182.20	86.37
5000	5451.48	151.43	5526.78	131.59	5603.04	116.73	5757.60	95.96
5500	5996.52	166.57	6079.50	144.75	6163.68	128.41	6333.60	105.56
6000	6541.56	181.71	6632.22	157.91	6723.84	140.08	6909.60	115.16
6500	7086.96	196.86	7184.94	171.07	7284.48	151.76	7485.00	124.75
7000	7632.00	212.00	7737.66	184.23	7844.64	163.43	8061.00	134.35
7500	8177.04	227.14	8290.38	197.39	8404.80	175.10	8637.00	143.95
8000	8722.08	242.28	8843.10	210.55	8965.44	186.78	9212.40	153.54
8500	9267.48	257.43	9395.82	223.71	9525.60	198.45	9788.40	163.14
9000	9812.52	272.57	9948.54	236.87	10085.76	210.12	10364.40	172.74
10000	10902.96	302.86	11053.98	263.19	11206.56	233.47	11515.80	191.93
11000	11993.04	333.14	12159.42	289.51	12327.36	256.82	12667.20	211.12
12000	13083.48	363.43	13264.86	315.83	13448.16	280.17	13819.20	230.32
13000	14173.92	393.72	14370.30	342.15	14568.96	303.52	14970.60	249.51
14000	15264.00	424.00	15475.74	368.47	15689.28	326.86	16122.60	268.71
15000	16354.44	454.29	16581.18	394.79	16810.08	350.21	17274.00	287.90
16000	17444.52	484.57	17686.62	421.11	17930.88	373.56	18425.40	307.09
17000	18534.96	514.86	18792.06	447.43	19051.68	396.91	19577.40	326.29
18000	19625.40	545.15	19897.50	473.75	20172.00	420.25	20728.80	345.48
19000	20715.48	575.43	21002.94	500.07	21292.80	443.60	21880.20	364.67
20000	21805.92	605.72	22108.38	526.39	22413.60	466.95	23032.20	383.87
21000	22896.36	636.01	23213.82	552.71	23534.40	490.30	24183.60	403.06
22000	23986.44	666.29	24319.26	579.03	24655.20	513.65	25335.00	422.25
23000	25076.88	696.58	25424.70	605.35	25775.52	536.99	26487.00	441.45
24000	26166.96	726.86	26530.14	631.67	26896.32	560.34	27638.40	460.64
25000	27257.40	757.15	27635.58	657.99	28017.12	583.69	28790.40	479.84

5.75% ANNUAL PERCENTAGE RATE

LOAN AMT	12 MONTHS TOTAL NOTE	12 MONTHS MONTHLY PAYMENT	18 MONTHS TOTAL NOTE	18 MONTHS MONTHLY PAYMENT	24 MONTHS TOTAL NOTE	24 MONTHS MONTHLY PAYMENT	30 MONTHS TOTAL NOTE	30 MONTHS MONTHLY PAYMENT
1	.96	.08	.90	.05	.96	.04	.90	.03
2	2.04	.17	1.98	.11	1.92	.08	2.10	.07
3	3.00	.25	3.06	.17	3.12	.13	3.00	.10
4	4.08	.34	4.14	.23	4.08	.17	4.20	.14
5	5.04	.42	5.22	.29	5.28	.22	5.10	.17
6	6.12	.51	6.12	.34	6.24	.26	6.30	.21
7	7.20	.60	7.20	.40	7.20	.30	7.50	.25
8	8.16	.68	8.28	.46	8.40	.35	8.40	.28
9	9.24	.77	9.36	.52	9.36	.39	9.60	.32
10	10.20	.85	10.44	.58	10.56	.44	10.50	.35
20	20.52	1.71	20.88	1.16	21.12	.88	21.30	.71
30	30.84	2.57	31.32	1.74	31.68	1.32	32.10	1.07
40	41.16	3.43	41.76	2.32	42.24	1.76	42.90	1.43
50	51.48	4.29	52.20	2.90	53.04	2.21	53.70	1.79
60	61.80	5.15	62.64	3.48	63.60	2.65	64.50	2.15
70	72.12	6.01	73.08	4.06	74.16	3.09	75.30	2.51
80	82.44	6.87	83.52	4.64	84.72	3.53	85.80	2.86
90	92.76	7.73	94.14	5.23	95.28	3.97	96.60	3.22
100	103.08	8.59	104.58	5.81	106.08	4.42	107.40	3.58
200	206.28	17.19	209.16	11.62	212.16	8.84	215.10	7.17
300	309.36	25.78	313.74	17.43	318.24	13.26	322.50	10.75
400	412.56	34.38	418.32	23.24	424.32	17.68	430.20	14.34
500	515.64	42.97	522.90	29.05	530.40	22.10	537.90	17.93
600	618.84	51.57	627.66	34.87	636.48	26.52	645.30	21.51
700	721.92	60.16	732.24	40.68	742.56	30.94	753.00	25.10
800	825.12	68.76	836.82	46.49	848.64	35.36	860.70	28.69
900	928.20	77.35	941.40	52.30	954.72	39.78	968.10	32.27
1000	1031.40	85.95	1045.98	58.11	1060.80	44.20	1075.80	35.86
1500	1547.04	128.92	1569.06	87.17	1591.44	66.31	1613.70	53.79
2000	2062.80	171.90	2092.14	116.23	2121.84	88.41	2151.90	71.73
2500	2578.44	214.87	2615.22	145.29	2652.48	110.52	2689.80	89.66
3000	3094.20	257.85	3138.30	174.35	3182.88	132.62	3227.70	107.59
3500	3609.96	300.83	3661.38	203.41	3713.28	154.72	3765.90	125.53
4000	4125.60	343.80	4184.46	232.47	4243.92	176.83	4303.80	143.46
4500	4641.36	386.78	4707.54	261.53	4774.32	198.93	4841.70	161.39
5000	5157.00	429.75	5230.62	290.59	5304.96	221.04	5379.90	179.33
5500	5672.76	472.73	5753.70	319.65	5835.36	243.14	5917.80	197.26
6000	6188.40	515.70	6276.78	348.71	6365.76	265.24	6455.70	215.19
6500	6704.16	558.68	6799.86	377.77	6896.40	287.35	6993.90	233.13
7000	7219.92	601.66	7322.94	406.83	7426.80	309.45	7531.80	251.06
7500	7735.56	644.63	7846.02	435.89	7957.44	331.56	8069.70	268.99
8000	8251.32	687.61	8368.92	464.94	8487.84	353.66	8607.60	286.92
8500	8766.96	730.58	8892.00	494.00	9018.24	375.76	9145.80	304.86
9000	9282.72	773.56	9415.08	523.06	9548.88	397.87	9683.70	322.79
10000	10314.12	859.51	10461.24	581.18	10609.92	442.08	10759.80	358.66
11000	11345.52	945.46	11507.40	639.30	11670.72	486.28	11835.60	394.52
12000	12376.92	1031.41	12553.56	697.42	12731.76	530.49	12911.70	430.39
13000	13408.44	1117.37	13599.72	755.54	13792.80	574.70	13987.80	466.26
14000	14439.84	1203.32	14645.88	813.66	14853.84	618.91	15063.60	502.12
15000	15471.24	1289.27	15692.04	871.78	15914.88	663.12	16139.70	537.99
16000	16502.64	1375.22	16738.02	929.89	16975.68	707.32	17215.50	573.85
17000	17534.04	1461.17	17784.18	988.01	18036.72	751.53	18291.60	609.72
18000	18565.44	1547.12	18830.34	1046.13	19097.76	795.74	19367.70	645.59
19000	19596.84	1633.07	19876.50	1104.25	20158.80	839.95	20443.50	681.45
20000	20628.36	1719.03	20922.66	1162.37	21219.84	884.16	21519.60	717.32
21000	21659.76	1804.98	21968.82	1220.49	22280.64	928.36	22595.70	753.19
22000	22691.16	1890.93	23014.98	1278.61	23341.68	972.57	23671.50	789.05
23000	23722.56	1976.88	24061.14	1336.73	24402.72	1016.78	24747.60	824.92
24000	24753.96	2062.83	25107.12	1394.84	25463.76	1060.99	25823.40	860.78
25000	25785.36	2148.78	26153.28	1452.96	26524.80	1105.20	26899.50	896.65

ANNUAL PERCENTAGE RATE **5.75%**

LOAN AMT	36 MONTHS TOTAL NOTE	36 MONTHS MONTHLY PAYMENT	42 MONTHS TOTAL NOTE	42 MONTHS MONTHLY PAYMENT	48 MONTHS TOTAL NOTE	48 MONTHS MONTHLY PAYMENT	60 MONTHS TOTAL NOTE	60 MONTHS MONTHLY PAYMENT
1	1.08	.03	.84	.02	.96	.02	.60	.01
2	2.16	.06	2.10	.05	1.92	.04	1.80	.03
3	3.24	.09	2.94	.07	3.36	.07	3.00	.05
4	4.32	.12	4.20	.10	4.32	.09	4.20	.07
5	5.40	.15	5.46	.13	5.28	.11	5.40	.09
6	6.48	.18	6.30	.15	6.72	.14	6.60	.11
7	7.56	.21	7.56	.18	7.68	.16	7.80	.13
8	8.64	.24	8.82	.21	8.64	.18	9.00	.15
9	9.72	.27	9.66	.23	10.08	.21	10.20	.17
10	10.80	.30	10.92	.26	11.04	.23	11.40	.19
20	21.60	.60	21.84	.52	22.08	.46	22.80	.38
30	32.40	.90	33 18	.79	33.60	.70	34.20	.57
40	43.56	1.21	44.10	1.05	44.64	.93	45.60	.76
50	54.36	1.51	55.02	1.31	55.68	1.16	57.60	.96
60	65.16	1.81	66.36	1.58	67.20	1.40	69.00	1.15
70	76.32	2.12	77.28	1.84	78.24	1.63	80.40	1.34
80	87.12	2.42	88.20	2.10	89.28	1.86	91.80	1.53
90	97.92	2.72	99.54	2.37	100.80	2.10	103.20	1.72
100	109.08	3.03	110.46	2.63	111.84	2.33	115.20	1.92
200	218.16	6.06	220.92	5.26	224.16	4.67	230.40	3.84
300	327.24	9.09	331.80	7.90	336.48	7.01	345.60	5.76
400	436.32	12.12	442.26	10.53	448.32	9.34	460.80	7.68
500	545.40	15.15	553.14	13.17	560.64	11.68	576.00	9.60
600	654.48	18.18	663.60	15.80	672.96	14.02	691.80	11.53
700	763.56	21.21	774.06	18.43	784.80	16.35	807.00	13.45
800	872.64	24.24	884.94	21.07	897.12	18.69	922.20	15.37
900	981.72	27.27	995.40	23.70	1009.44	21.03	1037.40	17.29
1000	1090.80	30.30	1106.28	26.34	1121.76	23.37	1152.60	19.21
1500	1636.56	45.46	1659.42	39.51	1682.40	35.05	1729.20	28.82
2000	2181.96	60.61	2212.56	52.68	2243.52	46.74	2305.80	38.43
2500	2727.72	75.77	2765.70	65.85	2804.16	58.42	2882.40	48.04
3000	3273.12	90.92	3318.84	79.02	3365.28	70.11	3459.00	57.65
3500	3818.88	106.08	3871.98	92.19	3925.92	81.79	4035.00	67.25
4000	4364.28	121.23	4425.12	105.36	4487.04	93.48	4611.60	76.86
4500	4909.68	136.38	4978.68	118.54	5047.68	105.16	5188.20	86.47
5000	5455.44	151.54	5531.82	131.71	5608.80	116.85	5764.80	96.08
5500	6000.84	166.69	6084.96	144.88	6169.44	128.53	6341.40	105.69
6000	6546.60	181.85	6638.10	158.05	6730.56	140.22	6918.00	115.30
6500	7092.00	197.00	7191.24	171.22	7291.20	151.90	7494.00	124.90
7000	7637.76	212.16	7744.38	184.39	7852.32	163.59	8070.60	134.51
7500	8183.16	227.31	8297.52	197.56	8412.96	175.27	8647.20	144.12
8000	8728.92	242.47	8850.66	210.73	8974.08	186.96	9223.80	153.73
8500	9274.32	257.62	9404.22	223.91	9534.72	198.64	9800.40	163.34
9000	9819.72	272.77	9957.36	237.08	10095.84	210.33	10377.00	172.95
10000	10910.88	303.08	11063.64	263.42	11217.60	233.70	11529.60	192.16
11000	12002.04	333.39	12169.92	289.76	12339.36	257.07	12682.80	211.38
12000	13093.20	363.70	13276.20	316.10	13461.12	280.44	13836.00	230.60
13000	14184.36	394.01	14382.90	342.45	14582.88	303.81	14988.60	249.81
14000	15275.52	424.32	15489.18	368.79	15704.64	327.18	16141.80	269.03
15000	16366.68	454.63	16595.46	395.13	16826.40	350.55	17295.00	288.25
16000	17457.84	484.94	17701.74	421.47	17948.16	373.92	18447.60	307.46
17000	18548.64	515.24	18808.44	447.82	19069.92	397.29	19600.80	326.68
18000	19639.80	545.55	19914.72	474.16	20192.16	420.67	20754.00	345.90
19000	20730.96	575.86	21021.00	500.50	21313.92	444.04	21906.60	365.11
20000	21822.12	606.17	22127.28	526.84	22435.68	467.41	23059.80	384.33
21000	22913.28	636.48	23233.98	553.19	23557.44	490.78	24213.00	403.55
22000	24004.44	666.79	24340.26	579.53	24679.20	514.15	25365.60	422.76
23000	25095.60	697.10	25446.54	605.87	25800.96	537.52	26518.80	441.98
24000	26186.76	727.41	26552.82	632.21	26922.72	560.89	27672.00	461.20
25000	27277.56	757.71	27659.52	658.56	28044.48	584.26	28824.60	480.41

5.80% ANNUAL PERCENTAGE RATE

LOAN AMT	12 MONTHS TOTAL NOTE	12 MONTHS MONTHLY PAYMENT	18 MONTHS TOTAL NOTE	18 MONTHS MONTHLY PAYMENT	24 MONTHS TOTAL NOTE	24 MONTHS MONTHLY PAYMENT	30 MONTHS TOTAL NOTE	30 MONTHS MONTHLY PAYMENT
1	.96	.08	.90	.05	.96	.04	.90	.03
2	2.04	.17	1.98	.11	1.92	.08	2.10	.07
3	3.00	.25	3.06	.17	3.12	.13	3.00	.10
4	4.08	.34	4.14	.23	4.08	.17	4.20	.14
5	5.04	.42	5.22	.29	5.28	.22	5.10	.17
6	6.12	.51	6.12	.34	6.24	.26	6.30	.21
7	7.20	.60	7.20	.40	7.20	.30	7.50	.25
8	8.16	.68	8.28	.46	8.40	.35	8.40	.28
9	9.24	.77	9.36	.52	9.36	.39	9.60	.32
10	10.20	.85	10.44	.58	10.56	.44	10.50	.35
20	20.52	1.71	20.88	1.16	21.12	.88	21.30	.71
30	30.84	2.57	31.32	1.74	31.68	1.32	32.10	1.07
40	41.16	3.43	41.76	2.32	42.24	1.76	42.90	1.43
50	51.48	4.29	52.20	2.90	53.04	2.21	53.70	1.79
60	61.80	5.15	62.64	3.48	63.60	2.65	64.50	2.15
70	72.12	6.01	73.08	4.06	74.16	3.09	75.30	2.51
80	82.44	6.87	83.70	4.65	84.72	3.53	86.10	2.87
90	92.76	7.73	94.14	5.23	95.52	3.98	96.60	3.22
100	103.08	8.59	104.58	5.81	106.08	4.42	107.40	3.58
200	206.28	17.19	209.16	11.62	212.16	8.84	215.10	7.17
300	309.48	25.79	313.92	17.44	318.24	13.26	322.80	10.76
400	412.56	34.38	418.50	23.25	424.56	17.69	430.50	14.35
500	515.76	42.98	523.26	29.07	530.64	22.11	538.20	17.94
600	618.96	51.58	627.84	34.88	636.72	26.53	645.90	21.53
700	722.16	60.18	732.42	40.69	743.04	30.96	753.60	25.12
800	825.24	68.77	837.18	46.51	849.12	35.38	861.30	28.71
900	928.44	77.37	941.76	52.32	955.20	39.80	968.70	32.29
1000	1031.64	85.97	1046.52	58.14	1061.52	44.23	1076.40	35.88
1500	1547.52	128.96	1569.78	87.21	1592.16	66.34	1614.90	53.83
2000	2063.28	171.94	2093.04	116.28	2123.04	88.46	2153.10	71.77
2500	2579.16	214.93	2616.30	145.35	2653.68	110.57	2691.60	89.72
3000	3095.04	257.92	3139.56	174.42	3184.56	132.69	3229.80	107.66
3500	3610.92	300.91	3662.82	203.49	3715.20	154.80	3768.30	125.61
4000	4126.68	343.89	4186.08	232.56	4246.08	176.92	4306.50	143.55
4500	4642.56	386.88	4709.34	261.63	4776.72	199.03	4844.70	161.49
5000	5158.44	429.87	5232.60	290.70	5307.60	221.15	5383.20	179.44
5500	5674.20	472.85	5755.86	319.77	5838.24	243.26	5921.40	197.38
6000	6190.08	515.84	6279.12	348.84	6369.12	265.38	6459.90	215.33
6500	6705.96	558.83	6802.38	377.91	6899.76	287.49	6998.10	233.27
7000	7221.84	601.82	7325.64	406.98	7430.64	309.61	7536.60	251.22
7500	7737.60	644.80	7848.90	436.05	7961.28	331.72	8074.80	269.16
8000	8253.48	687.79	8372.34	465.13	8492.16	353.84	8613.00	287.10
8500	8769.36	730.78	8895.60	494.20	9022.80	375.95	9151.50	305.05
9000	9285.24	773.77	9418.86	523.27	9553.68	398.07	9689.70	322.99
10000	10316.88	859.74	10465.38	581.41	10615.20	442.30	10766.40	358.88
11000	11348.52	945.71	11511.90	639.55	11676.72	486.53	11843.10	394.77
12000	12380.28	1031.69	12558.42	697.69	12738.24	530.76	12919.80	430.66
13000	13411.92	1117.66	13604.94	755.83	13799.76	574.99	13996.50	466.55
14000	14443.68	1203.64	14651.46	813.97	14861.28	619.22	15073.20	502.44
15000	15475.32	1289.61	15697.98	872.11	15922.80	663.45	16149.90	538.33
16000	16507.08	1375.59	16744.68	930.26	16984.32	707.68	17226.30	574.21
17000	17538.72	1461.56	17791.20	988.40	18045.84	751.91	18303.00	610.10
18000	18570.48	1547.54	18837.72	1046.54	19107.36	796.14	19379.70	645.99
19000	19602.12	1633.51	19884.24	1104.68	20169.12	840.38	20456.40	681.88
20000	20633.88	1719.49	20930.76	1162.82	21230.64	884.61	21533.10	717.77
21000	21665.52	1805.46	21977.28	1220.96	22292.16	928.84	22609.80	753.66
22000	22697.16	1891.43	23023.80	1279.10	23353.68	973.07	23686.50	789.55
23000	23728.92	1977.41	24070.50	1337.25	24415.20	1017.30	24763.20	825.44
24000	24760.56	2063.38	25117.02	1395.39	25476.72	1061.53	25839.60	861.32
25000	25792.32	2149.36	26163.54	1453.53	26538.24	1105.76	26916.30	897.21

ANNUAL PERCENTAGE RATE **5.80%**

LOAN AMT	36 MONTHS TOTAL NOTE	36 MONTHS MONTHLY PAYMENT	42 MONTHS TOTAL NOTE	42 MONTHS MONTHLY PAYMENT	48 MONTHS TOTAL NOTE	48 MONTHS MONTHLY PAYMENT	60 MONTHS TOTAL NOTE	60 MONTHS MONTHLY PAYMENT
1	1.08	.03	.84	.02	.96	.02	.60	.01
2	2.16	.06	2.10	.05	1.92	.04	1.80	.03
3	3.24	.09	2.94	.07	3.36	.07	3.00	.05
4	4.32	.12	4.20	.10	4.32	.09	4.20	.07
5	5.40	.15	5.46	.13	5.28	.11	5.40	.09
6	6.48	.18	6.30	.15	6.72	.14	6.60	.11
7	7.56	.21	7.56	.18	7.68	.16	7.80	.13
8	8.64	.24	8.82	.21	8.64	.18	9.00	.15
9	9.72	.27	9.66	.23	10.08	.21	10.20	.17
10	10.80	.30	10.92	.26	11.04	.23	11.40	.19
20	21.60	.60	21.84	.52	22.08	.46	22.80	.38
30	32.40	.90	33.18	.79	33.60	.70	34.20	.57
40	43.56	1.21	44.10	1.05	44.64	.93	45.60	.76
50	54.36	1.51	55.02	1.31	55.68	1.16	57.60	.96
60	65.16	1.81	66.36	1.58	67.20	1.40	69.00	1.15
70	76.32	2.12	77.28	1.84	78.24	1.63	80.40	1.34
80	87.12	2.42	88.20	2.10	89.76	1.87	91.80	1.53
90	97.92	2.72	99.54	2.37	100.80	2.10	103.80	1.73
100	109.08	3.03	110.46	2.63	111.84	2.33	115.20	1.92
200	218.16	6.06	221.34	5.27	224.16	4.67	230.40	3.84
300	327.24	9.09	331.80	7.90	336.48	7.01	346.20	5.77
400	436.68	12.13	442.68	10.54	448.80	9.35	461.40	7.69
500	545.76	15.16	553.56	13.18	561.12	11.69	576.60	9.61
600	654.84	18.19	664.02	15.81	673.44	14.03	692.40	11.54
700	764.28	21.23	774.90	18.45	785.76	16.37	807.60	13.46
800	873.36	24.26	885.78	21.09	898.08	18.71	923.40	15.39
900	982.44	27.29	996.24	23.72	1010.40	21.05	1038.60	17.31
1000	1091.88	30.33	1107.12	26.36	1122.72	23.39	1153.80	19.23
1500	1637.64	45.49	1660.68	39.54	1684.32	35.09	1731.00	28.85
2000	2183.76	60.66	2214.66	52.73	2245.44	46.78	2308.20	38.47
2500	2729.52	75.82	2768.22	65.91	2807.04	58.48	2885.40	48.09
3000	3275.64	90.99	3321.78	79.09	3368.64	70.18	3462.60	57.71
3500	3821.40	106.15	3875.34	92.27	3929.76	81.87	4039.80	67.33
4000	4367.52	121.32	4429.32	105.46	4491.36	93.57	4617.00	76.95
4500	4913.64	136.49	4982.88	118.64	5052.96	105.27	5194.20	86.57
5000	5459.40	151.65	5536.44	131.82	5614.08	116.96	5771.40	96.19
5500	6005.52	166.82	6090.00	145.00	6175.68	128.66	6348.60	105.81
6000	6551.28	181.98	6643.98	158.19	6737.28	140.36	6925.80	115.43
6500	7097.40	197.15	7197.54	171.37	7298.40	152.05	7503.00	125.05
7000	7643.16	212.31	7751.10	184.55	7860.00	163.75	8080.20	134.67
7500	8189.28	227.48	8304.66	197.73	8421.60	175.45	8657.40	144.29
8000	8735.40	242.65	8858.64	210.92	8982.72	187.14	9234.60	153.91
8500	9281.16	257.81	9412.20	224.10	9544.32	198.84	9811.80	163.53
9000	9827.28	272.98	9965.76	237.28	10105.92	210.54	10389.00	173.15
10000	10919.16	303.31	11073.30	263.65	11228.64	233.93	11543.40	192.39
11000	12011.04	333.64	12180.42	290.01	12351.36	257.32	12697.80	211.63
12000	13102.92	363.97	13287.96	316.38	13474.56	280.72	13852.20	230.87
13000	14194.80	394.30	14395.08	342.74	14597.28	304.11	15006.60	250.11
14000	15286.68	424.63	15502.62	369.11	15720.00	327.50	16161.00	269.35
15000	16378.92	454.97	16609.74	395.47	16843.20	350.90	17315.40	288.59
16000	17470.80	485.30	17717.28	421.84	17965.92	374.29	18469.80	307.83
17000	18562.68	515.63	18824.40	448.20	19088.64	397.68	19624.20	327.07
18000	19654.56	545.96	19931.94	474.57	20211.84	421.08	20778.60	346.31
19000	20746.44	576.29	21039.06	500.93	21334.56	444.47	21933.00	365.55
20000	21838.32	606.62	22146.60	527.30	22457.28	467.86	23087.40	384.79
21000	22930.20	636.95	23253.72	553.66	23580.48	491.26	24241.80	404.03
22000	24022.44	667.29	24361.26	580.03	24703.20	514.65	25396.20	423.27
23000	25114.32	697.62	25468.38	606.39	25825.92	538.04	26550.60	442.51
24000	26206.20	727.95	26575.92	632.76	26949.12	561.44	27705.00	461.75
25000	27298.08	758.28	27683.04	659.12	28071.84	584.83	28859.40	480.99

5.90% ANNUAL PERCENTAGE RATE

LOAN AMT	12 MONTHS TOTAL NOTE	12 MONTHS MONTHLY PAYMENT	18 MONTHS TOTAL NOTE	18 MONTHS MONTHLY PAYMENT	24 MONTHS TOTAL NOTE	24 MONTHS MONTHLY PAYMENT	30 MONTHS TOTAL NOTE	30 MONTHS MONTHLY PAYMENT
1	.96	.08	.90	.05	.96	.04	.90	.03
2	2.04	.17	1.98	.11	1.92	.08	2.10	.07
3	3.00	.25	3.06	.17	3.12	.13	3.00	.10
4	4.08	.34	4.14	.23	4.08	.17	4.20	.14
5	5.16	.43	5.22	.29	5.28	.22	5.10	.17
6	6.12	.51	6.12	.34	6.24	.26	6.30	.21
7	7.20	.60	7.20	.40	7.20	.30	7.50	.25
8	8.16	.68	8.28	.46	8.40	.35	8.40	.28
9	9.24	.77	9.36	.52	9.36	.39	9.60	.32
10	10.32	.86	10.44	.58	10.56	.44	10.50	.35
20	20.64	1.72	20.88	1.16	21.12	.88	21.30	.71
30	30.96	2.58	31.32	1.74	31.68	1.32	32.10	1.07
40	41.28	3.44	41.76	2.32	42.48	1.77	42.90	1.43
50	51.60	4.30	52.20	2.90	53.04	2.21	53.70	1.79
60	61.92	5.16	62.82	3.49	63.60	2.65	64.50	2.15
70	72.24	6.02	73.26	4.07	74.16	3.09	75.30	2.51
80	82.56	6.88	83.70	4.65	84.96	3.54	86.10	2.87
90	92.88	7.74	94.14	5.23	95.52	3.98	96.90	3.23
100	103.20	8.60	104.58	5.81	106.08	4.42	107.70	3.59
200	206.40	17.20	209.34	11.63	212.40	8.85	215.40	7.18
300	309.60	25.80	314.10	17.45	318.72	13.28	323.40	10.78
400	412.80	34.40	418.86	23.27	425.04	17.71	431.10	14.37
500	516.12	43.01	523.62	29.09	531.12	22.13	538.80	17.96
600	619.32	51.61	628.38	34.91	637.44	26.56	646.80	21.56
700	722.52	60.21	733.14	40.73	743.76	30.99	754.50	25.15
800	825.72	68.81	837.72	46.54	850.08	35.42	862.20	28.74
900	928.92	77.41	942.48	52.36	956.16	39.84	970.20	32.34
1000	1032.24	86.02	1047.24	58.18	1062.48	44.27	1077.90	35.93
1500	1548.36	129.03	1570.86	87.27	1593.84	66.41	1617.00	53.90
2000	2064.48	172.04	2094.66	116.37	2125.20	88.55	2155.80	71.86
2500	2580.60	215.05	2618.28	145.46	2656.32	110.68	2694.90	89.83
3000	3096.72	258.06	3141.90	174.55	3187.68	132.82	3234.00	107.80
3500	3612.84	301.07	3665.70	203.65	3719.04	154.96	3772.80	125.76
4000	4128.96	344.08	4189.32	232.74	4250.40	177.10	4311.90	143.73
4500	4645.08	387.09	4712.94	261.83	4781.76	199.24	4851.00	161.70
5000	5161.20	430.10	5236.74	290.93	5312.88	221.37	5389.80	179.66
5500	5677.32	473.11	5760.36	320.02	5844.24	243.51	5928.90	197.63
6000	6193.44	516.12	6283.98	349.11	6375.60	265.65	6468.00	215.60
6500	6709.56	559.13	6807.78	378.21	6906.96	287.79	7006.80	233.56
7000	7225.68	602.14	7331.40	407.30	7438.08	309.92	7545.90	251.53
7500	7741.80	645.15	7855.02	436.39	7969.44	332.06	8085.00	269.50
8000	8257.92	688.16	8378.82	465.49	8500.80	354.20	8624.10	287.47
8500	8774.04	731.17	8902.44	494.58	9032.16	376.34	9162.90	305.43
9000	9290.16	774.18	9426.06	523.67	9563.52	398.48	9702.00	323.40
10000	10322.40	860.20	10473.48	581.86	10626.00	442.75	10779.90	359.33
11000	11354.64	946.22	11520.90	640.05	11688.72	487.03	11858.10	395.27
12000	12386.88	1032.24	12568.14	698.23	12751.20	531.30	12936.00	431.20
13000	13419.12	1118.26	13615.56	756.42	13813.92	575.58	14013.90	467.13
14000	14451.36	1204.28	14662.98	814.61	14876.40	619.85	15092.10	503.07
15000	15483.60	1290.30	15710.22	872.79	15939.12	664.13	16170.00	539.00
16000	16515.84	1376.32	16757.64	930.98	17001.60	708.40	17248.20	574.94
17000	17548.08	1462.34	17805.06	989.17	18064.32	752.68	18326.10	610.87
18000	18580.32	1548.36	18852.30	1047.35	19127.04	796.96	19404.00	646.80
19000	19612.56	1634.38	19899.72	1105.54	20189.52	841.23	20482.20	682.74
20000	20644.80	1720.40	20947.14	1163.73	21252.24	885.51	21560.10	718.67
21000	21677.04	1806.42	21994.38	1221.91	22314.72	929.78	22638.00	754.60
22000	22709.40	1892.45	23041.80	1280.10	23377.44	974.06	23716.20	790.54
23000	23741.64	1978.47	24089.04	1338.28	24439.92	1018.33	24794.10	826.47
24000	24773.88	2064.49	25136.46	1396.47	25502.64	1062.61	25872.30	862.41
25000	25806.12	2150.51	26183.88	1454.66	26565.12	1106.88	26950.20	898.34

ANNUAL PERCENTAGE RATE **5.90%**

LOAN AMT	36 MONTHS TOTAL NOTE	MONTHLY PAYMENT	42 MONTHS TOTAL NOTE	MONTHLY PAYMENT	48 MONTHS TOTAL NOTE	MONTHLY PAYMENT	60 MONTHS TOTAL NOTE	MONTHLY PAYMENT
1	1.08	.03	.84	.02	.96	.02	.60	.01
2	2.16	.06	2.10	.05	1.92	.04	1.80	.03
3	3.24	.09	2.94	.07	3.36	.07	3.00	.05
4	4.32	.12	4.20	.10	4.32	.09	4.20	.07
5	5.40	.15	5.46	.13	5.28	.11	5.40	.09
6	6.48	.18	6.30	.15	6.72	.14	6.60	.11
7	7.56	.21	7.56	.18	7.68	.16	7.80	.13
8	8.64	.24	8.82	.21	8.64	.18	9.00	.15
9	9.72	.27	9.66	.23	10.08	.21	10.20	.17
10	10.80	.30	10.92	.26	11.04	.23	11.40	.19
20	21.60	.60	21.84	.52	22.08	.46	22.80	.38
30	32.76	.91	33.18	.79	33.60	.70	34.20	.57
40	43.56	1.21	44.10	1.05	44.64	.93	46.20	.77
50	54.36	1.51	55.44	1.32	56.16	1.17	57.60	.96
60	65.52	1.82	66.36	1.58	67.20	1.40	69.00	1.15
70	76.32	2.12	77.28	1.84	78.72	1.64	81.00	1.35
80	87.48	2.43	88.62	2.11	89.76	1.87	92.40	1.54
90	98.28	2.73	99.54	2.37	100.80	2.10	103.80	1.73
100	109.08	3.03	110.88	2.64	112.32	2.34	115.20	1.92
200	218.52	6.07	221.76	5.28	224.64	4.68	231.00	3.85
300	327.96	9.11	332.64	7.92	337.44	7.03	346.80	5.78
400	437.40	12.15	443.52	10.56	449.76	9.37	462.60	7.71
500	546.48	15.18	554.40	13.20	562.08	11.71	578.40	9.64
600	655.92	18.22	665.28	15.84	674.88	14.06	694.20	11.57
700	765.36	21.26	776.16	18.48	787.20	16.40	810.00	13.50
800	874.80	24.30	887.04	21.12	900.00	18.75	925.20	15.42
900	983.88	27.33	997.92	23.76	1012.32	21.09	1041.00	17.35
1000	1093.32	30.37	1109.22	26.41	1124.64	23.43	1156.80	19.28
1500	1640.16	45.56	1663.62	39.61	1687.20	35.15	1735.20	28.92
2000	2187.00	60.75	2218.44	52.82	2249.76	46.87	2314.20	38.57
2500	2733.84	75.94	2772.84	66.02	2812.32	58.59	2892.60	48.21
3000	3280.32	91.12	3327.66	79.23	3374.88	70.31	3471.00	57.85
3500	3827.16	106.31	3882.06	92.43	3937.44	82.03	4050.00	67.50
4000	4374.00	121.50	4436.88	105.64	4500.00	93.75	4628.40	77.14
4500	4920.84	136.69	4991.28	118.84	5062.56	105.47	5206.80	86.78
5000	5467.68	151.88	5546.10	132.05	5625.12	117.19	5785.80	96.43
5500	6014.52	167.07	6100.50	145.25	6187.68	128.91	6364.20	106.07
6000	6561.00	182.25	6655.32	158.46	6750.24	140.63	6942.60	115.71
6500	7107.84	197.44	7209.72	171.66	7312.80	152.35	7521.60	125.36
7000	7654.68	212.63	7764.54	184.87	7875.36	164.07	8100.00	135.00
7500	8201.52	227.82	8319.36	198.08	8437.92	175.79	8678.40	144.64
8000	8748.36	243.01	8873.76	211.28	9000.48	187.51	9257.40	154.29
8500	9295.20	258.20	9428.58	224.49	9563.04	199.23	9835.80	163.93
9000	9841.68	273.38	9982.98	237.69	10125.60	210.95	10414.20	173.57
10000	10935.36	303.76	11092.20	264.10	11250.72	234.39	11571.60	192.86
11000	12029.04	334.14	12201.42	290.51	12375.84	257.83	12728.40	212.14
12000	13122.36	364.51	13310.64	316.92	13500.96	281.27	13885.80	231.43
13000	14216.04	394.89	14419.86	343.33	14625.60	304.70	15043.20	250.72
14000	15309.72	425.27	15529.08	369.74	15750.72	328.14	16200.00	270.00
15000	16403.04	455.64	16638.72	396.16	16875.84	351.58	17357.40	289.29
16000	17496.72	486.02	17747.94	422.57	18000.96	375.02	18514.80	308.58
17000	18590.40	516.40	18857.16	448.98	19126.08	398.46	19671.60	327.86
18000	19683.72	546.77	19966.38	475.39	20251.20	421.90	20829.00	347.15
19000	20777.40	577.15	21075.60	501.80	21376.32	445.34	21986.40	366.44
20000	21871.08	607.53	22184.82	528.21	22501.44	468.78	23143.20	385.72
21000	22964.40	637.90	23294.04	554.62	23626.56	492.22	24300.60	405.01
22000	24058.08	668.28	24403.26	581.03	24751.68	515.66	25457.40	424.29
23000	25151.76	698.66	25512.48	607.44	25876.80	539.10	26614.80	443.58
24000	26245.08	729.03	26621.70	633.85	27001.92	562.54	27772.20	462.87
25000	27338.76	759.41	27730.92	660.26	28127.04	585.98	28929.00	482.15

6.00% ANNUAL PERCENTAGE RATE

LOAN AMT	12 MONTHS TOTAL NOTE	12 MONTHS MONTHLY PAYMENT	18 MONTHS TOTAL NOTE	18 MONTHS MONTHLY PAYMENT	24 MONTHS TOTAL NOTE	24 MONTHS MONTHLY PAYMENT	30 MONTHS TOTAL NOTE	30 MONTHS MONTHLY PAYMENT
1	.96	.08	.90	.05	.96	.04	.90	.03
2	2.04	.17	1.98	.11	1.92	.08	2.10	.07
3	3.00	.25	3.06	.17	3.12	.13	3.00	.10
4	4.08	.34	4.14	.23	4.08	.17	4.20	.14
5	5.16	.43	5.22	.29	5.28	.22	5.10	.17
6	6.12	.51	6.12	.34	6.24	.26	6.30	.21
7	7.20	.60	7.20	.40	7.44	.31	7.50	.25
8	8.16	.68	8.28	.46	8.40	.35	8.40	.28
9	9.24	.77	9.36	.52	9.36	.39	9.60	.32
10	10.32	.86	10.44	.58	10.56	.44	10.50	.35
20	20.64	1.72	20.88	1.16	21.12	.88	21.30	.71
30	30.96	2.58	31.32	1.74	31.68	1.32	32.10	1.07
40	41.28	3.44	41.76	2.32	42.48	1.77	42.90	1.43
50	51.60	4.30	52.38	2.91	53.04	2.21	53.70	1.79
60	61.92	5.16	62.82	3.49	63.60	2.65	64.50	2.15
70	72.24	6.02	73.26	4.07	74.40	3.10	75.30	2.51
80	82.56	6.88	83.70	4.65	84.96	3.54	86.10	2.87
90	92.88	7.74	94.32	5.24	95.52	3.98	96.90	3.23
100	103.20	8.60	104.76	5.82	106.32	4.43	107.70	3.59
200	206.52	17.21	209.52	11.64	212.64	8.86	215.70	7.19
300	309.72	25.81	314.28	17.46	318.96	13.29	323.70	10.79
400	413.04	34.42	419.22	23.29	425.28	17.72	431.70	14.39
500	516.36	43.03	523.98	29.11	531.84	22.16	539.40	17.98
600	619.56	51.63	628.74	34.93	638.16	26.59	647.40	21.58
700	722.88	60.24	733.68	40.76	744.48	31.02	755.40	25.18
800	826.20	68.85	838.44	46.58	850.80	35.45	863.40	28.78
900	929.40	77.45	943.20	52.40	957.12	39.88	971.40	32.38
1000	1032.72	86.06	1048.14	58.23	1063.68	44.32	1079.10	35.97
1500	1549.08	129.09	1572.12	87.34	1595.52	66.48	1618.80	53.96
2000	2065.56	172.13	2096.28	116.46	2127.36	88.64	2158.50	71.95
2500	2581.92	215.16	2620.26	145.57	2659.20	110.80	2698.20	89.94
3000	3098.28	258.19	3144.42	174.69	3191.04	132.96	3237.90	107.93
3500	3614.76	301.23	3668.58	203.81	3722.88	155.12	3777.60	125.92
4000	4131.12	344.26	4192.56	232.92	4254.72	177.28	4317.30	143.91
4500	4647.48	387.29	4716.72	262.04	4786.56	199.44	4857.00	161.90
5000	5163.96	430.33	5240.70	291.15	5318.40	221.60	5396.70	179.89
5500	5680.32	473.36	5764.86	320.27	5850.24	243.76	5936.40	197.88
6000	6196.68	516.39	6289.02	349.39	6382.08	265.92	6476.10	215.87
6500	6713.16	559.43	6813.00	378.50	6913.92	288.08	7015.80	233.86
7000	7229.52	602.46	7337.16	407.62	7445.76	310.24	7555.50	251.85
7500	7745.88	645.49	7861.14	436.73	7977.60	332.40	8095.20	269.84
8000	8262.36	688.53	8385.30	465.85	8509.44	354.56	8634.90	287.83
8500	8778.72	731.56	8909.28	494.96	9041.28	376.72	9174.60	305.82
9000	9295.08	774.59	9433.44	524.08	9573.12	398.88	9714.30	323.81
10000	10327.92	860.66	10481.58	582.31	10636.80	443.20	10793.40	359.78
11000	11360.76	946.73	11529.72	640.54	11700.48	487.52	11872.80	395.76
12000	12393.48	1032.79	12578.04	698.78	12764.16	531.84	12952.20	431.74
13000	13426.32	1118.86	13626.18	757.01	13827.84	576.16	14031.60	467.72
14000	14459.16	1204.93	14674.32	815.24	14891.52	620.48	15111.00	503.70
15000	15491.88	1290.99	15722.46	873.47	15955.20	664.80	16190.40	539.68
16000	16524.72	1377.06	16770.60	931.70	17018.88	709.12	17269.80	575.66
17000	17557.44	1463.12	17818.74	989.93	18082.80	753.45	18349.20	611.64
18000	18590.28	1549.19	18867.06	1048.17	19146.48	797.77	19428.60	647.62
19000	19623.12	1635.26	19915.20	1106.40	20210.16	842.09	20507.70	683.59
20000	20655.84	1721.32	20963.34	1164.63	21273.84	886.41	21587.10	719.57
21000	21688.68	1807.39	22011.48	1222.86	22337.52	930.73	22666.50	755.55
22000	22721.52	1893.46	23059.62	1281.09	23401.20	975.05	23745.90	791.53
23000	23754.24	1979.52	24107.76	1339.32	24464.88	1019.37	24825.30	827.51
24000	24787.08	2065.59	25156.08	1397.56	25528.56	1063.69	25904.70	863.49
25000	25819.92	2151.66	26204.22	1455.79	26592.24	1108.01	26984.10	899.47

ANNUAL PERCENTAGE RATE **6.00%**

LOAN AMT	36 MONTHS TOTAL NOTE	36 MONTHS MONTHLY PAYMENT	42 MONTHS TOTAL NOTE	42 MONTHS MONTHLY PAYMENT	48 MONTHS TOTAL NOTE	48 MONTHS MONTHLY PAYMENT	60 MONTHS TOTAL NOTE	60 MONTHS MONTHLY PAYMENT
1	1.08	.03	.84	.02	.96	.02	.60	.01
2	2.16	.06	2.10	.05	1.92	.04	1.80	.03
3	3.24	.09	2.94	.07	3.36	.07	3.00	.05
4	4.32	.12	4.20	.10	4.32	.09	4.20	.07
5	5.40	.15	5.46	.13	5.28	.11	5.40	.09
6	6.48	.18	6.30	.15	6.72	.14	6.60	.11
7	7.56	.21	7.56	.18	7.68	.16	7.80	.13
8	8.64	.24	8.82	.21	8.64	.18	9.00	.15
9	9.72	.27	9.66	.23	10.08	.21	10.20	.17
10	10.80	.30	10.92	.26	11.04	.23	11.40	.19
20	21.60	.60	21.84	.52	22.08	.46	22.80	.38
30	32.76	.91	33.18	.79	33.60	.70	34.20	.57
40	43.56	1.21	44.10	1.05	44.64	.93	46.20	.77
50	54.72	1.52	55.44	1.32	56.16	1.17	57.60	.96
60	65.52	1.82	66.36	1.58	67.20	1.40	69.00	1.15
70	76.32	2.12	77.70	1.85	78.72	1.64	81.00	1.35
80	87.48	2.43	88.62	2.11	89.76	1.87	92.40	1.54
90	98.28	2.73	99.96	2.38	101.28	2.11	103.80	1.73
100	109.44	3.04	110.88	2.64	112.32	2.34	115.80	1.93
200	218.88	6.08	222.18	5.29	225.12	4.69	231.60	3.86
300	328.32	9.12	333.06	7.93	337.92	7.04	347.40	5.79
400	437.76	12.16	444.36	10.58	450.72	9.39	463.80	7.73
500	547.56	15.21	555.24	13.22	563.52	11.74	579.60	9.66
600	657.00	18.25	666.54	15.87	676.32	14.09	695.40	11.59
700	766.44	21.29	777.42	18.51	788.64	16.43	811.80	13.53
800	875.88	24.33	888.72	21.16	901.44	18.78	927.60	15.46
900	985.32	27.37	1000.02	23.81	1014.24	21.13	1043.40	17.39
1000	1095.12	30.42	1110.90	26.45	1127.04	23.48	1159.80	19.33
1500	1642.68	45.63	1666.56	39.68	1690.56	35.22	1739.40	28.99
2000	2190.24	60.84	2222.22	52.91	2254.56	46.97	2319.60	38.66
2500	2737.80	76.05	2777.88	66.14	2818.08	58.71	2899.80	48.33
3000	3285.36	91.26	3333.12	79.36	3381.60	70.45	3479.40	57.99
3500	3832.92	106.47	3888.78	92.59	3945.12	82.19	4059.60	67.66
4000	4380.48	121.68	4444.44	105.82	4509.12	93.94	4639.80	77.33
4500	4928.04	136.89	5000.10	119.05	5072.64	105.68	5219.40	86.99
5000	5475.60	152.10	5555.76	132.28	5636.16	117.42	5799.60	96.66
5500	6023.52	167.32	6111.00	145.50	6199.68	129.16	6379.80	106.33
6000	6571.08	182.53	6666.66	158.73	6763.68	140.91	6959.40	115.99
6500	7118.64	197.74	7222.32	171.96	7327.20	152.65	7539.60	125.66
7000	7666.20	212.95	7777.98	185.19	7890.72	164.39	8119.20	135.32
7500	8213.76	228.16	8333.64	198.42	8454.24	176.13	8699.40	144.99
8000	8761.32	243.37	8888.88	211.64	9018.24	187.88	9279.60	154.66
8500	9308.88	258.58	9444.54	224.87	9581.76	199.62	9859.20	164.32
9000	9856.44	273.79	10000.20	238.10	10145.28	211.36	10439.40	173.99
10000	10951.56	304.21	11111.52	264.56	11272.80	234.85	11599.20	193.32
11000	12047.04	334.64	12222.42	291.01	12399.84	258.33	12759.60	212.66
12000	13142.16	365.06	13333.74	317.47	13527.36	281.82	13919.40	231.99
13000	14237.28	395.48	14445.06	343.93	14654.40	305.30	15079.20	251.32
14000	15332.40	425.90	15555.96	370.38	15781.92	328.79	16239.00	270.65
15000	16427.52	456.32	16667.28	396.84	16908.96	352.27	17399.40	289.99
16000	17523.00	486.75	17778.18	423.29	18036.48	375.76	18559.20	309.32
17000	18618.12	517.17	18889.50	449.75	19163.52	399.24	19719.00	328.65
18000	19713.24	547.59	20000.82	476.21	20291.04	422.73	20879.40	347.99
19000	20808.36	578.01	21111.72	502.66	21418.08	446.21	22039.20	367.32
20000	21903.48	608.43	22223.04	529.12	22545.60	469.70	23199.00	386.65
21000	22998.96	638.86	23334.36	555.58	23672.64	493.18	24358.80	405.98
22000	24094.08	669.28	24445.26	582.03	24800.16	516.67	25519.20	425.32
23000	25189.20	699.70	25556.58	608.49	25927.20	540.15	26679.00	444.65
24000	26284.32	730.12	26667.48	634.94	27054.72	563.64	27838.80	463.98
25000	27379.44	760.54	27778.80	661.40	28181.76	587.12	28999.20	483.32

6.10% ANNUAL PERCENTAGE RATE

LOAN AMT	12 MONTHS TOTAL NOTE	12 MONTHS MONTHLY PAYMENT	18 MONTHS TOTAL NOTE	18 MONTHS MONTHLY PAYMENT	24 MONTHS TOTAL NOTE	24 MONTHS MONTHLY PAYMENT	30 MONTHS TOTAL NOTE	30 MONTHS MONTHLY PAYMENT
1	.96	.08	.90	.05	.96	.04	.90	.03
2	2.04	.17	1.98	.11	1.92	.08	2.10	.07
3	3.00	.25	3.06	.17	3.12	.13	3.00	.10
4	4.08	.34	4.14	.23	4.08	.17	4.20	.14
5	5.16	.43	5.22	.29	5.28	.22	5.40	.18
6	6.12	.51	6.12	.34	6.24	.26	6.30	.21
7	7.20	.60	7.20	.40	7.44	.31	7.50	.25
8	8.16	.68	8.28	.46	8.40	.35	8.40	.28
9	9.24	.77	9.36	.52	9.36	.39	9.60	.32
10	10.32	.86	10.44	.58	10.56	.44	10.80	.36
20	20.64	1.72	20.88	1.16	21.12	.88	21.60	.72
30	30.96	2.58	31.32	1.74	31.92	1.33	32.40	1.08
40	41.28	3.44	41.94	2.33	42.48	1.77	43.20	1.44
50	51.60	4.30	52.38	2.91	53.04	2.21	54.00	1.80
60	61.92	5.16	62.82	3.49	63.84	2.66	64.80	2.16
70	72.24	6.02	73.26	4.07	74.40	3.10	75.60	2.52
80	82.56	6.88	83.88	4.66	84.96	3.54	86.40	2.88
90	93.00	7.75	94.32	5.24	95.76	3.99	97.20	3.24
100	103.32	8.61	104.76	5.82	106.32	4.43	108.00	3.60
200	206.64	17.22	209.70	11.65	212.88	8.87	216.00	7.20
300	309.96	25.83	314.64	17.48	319.20	13.30	324.00	10.80
400	413.28	34.44	419.58	23.31	425.76	17.74	432.00	14.40
500	516.60	43.05	524.34	29.13	532.32	22.18	540.30	18.01
600	619.92	51.66	629.28	34.96	638.64	26.61	648.30	21.61
700	723.24	60.27	734.22	40.79	745.20	31.05	756.30	25.21
800	826.56	68.88	839.16	46.62	851.76	35.49	864.30	28.81
900	930.00	77.50	943.92	52.44	958.08	39.92	972.60	32.42
1000	1033.32	86.11	1048.86	58.27	1064.64	44.36	1080.60	36.02
1500	1549.92	129.16	1573.38	87.41	1596.96	66.54	1620.90	54.03
2000	2066.64	172.22	2097.90	116.55	2129.52	88.73	2161.20	72.04
2500	2583.36	215.28	2622.42	145.69	2661.84	110.91	2701.80	90.06
3000	3099.96	258.33	3146.94	174.83	3194.16	133.09	3242.10	108.07
3500	3616.68	301.39	3671.28	203.96	3726.48	155.27	3782.40	126.08
4000	4133.28	344.44	4195.80	233.10	4259.04	177.46	4322.70	144.09
4500	4650.00	387.50	4720.32	262.24	4791.36	199.64	4863.00	162.10
5000	5166.72	430.56	5244.84	291.38	5323.68	221.82	5403.60	180.12
5500	5683.32	473.61	5769.36	320.52	5856.24	244.01	5943.90	198.13
6000	6200.04	516.67	6293.88	349.66	6388.56	266.19	6484.20	216.14
6500	6716.76	559.73	6818.40	378.80	6920.88	288.37	7024.50	234.15
7000	7233.36	602.78	7342.74	407.93	7453.20	310.55	7564.80	252.16
7500	7750.08	645.84	7867.26	437.07	7985.76	332.74	8105.40	270.18
8000	8266.68	688.89	8391.78	466.21	8518.08	354.92	8645.70	288.19
8500	8783.40	731.95	8916.30	495.35	9050.40	377.10	9186.00	306.20
9000	9300.12	775.01	9440.82	524.49	9582.96	399.29	9726.30	324.21
10000	10333.44	861.12	10489.68	582.76	10647.60	443.65	10807.20	360.24
11000	11366.76	947.23	11538.72	641.04	11712.48	488.02	11887.80	396.26
12000	12400.08	1033.34	12587.76	699.32	12777.12	532.38	12968.40	432.28
13000	13433.52	1119.46	13636.80	757.60	13842.00	576.75	14049.30	468.31
14000	14466.84	1205.57	14685.66	815.87	14906.64	621.11	15129.90	504.33
15000	15500.16	1291.68	15734.70	874.15	15971.52	665.48	16210.80	540.36
16000	16533.48	1377.79	16783.74	932.43	17036.40	709.85	17291.40	576.38
17000	17566.92	1463.91	17832.60	990.70	18101.04	754.21	18372.00	612.40
18000	18600.24	1550.02	18881.64	1048.98	19165.92	798.58	19452.90	648.43
19000	19633.56	1636.13	19930.68	1107.26	20230.56	842.94	20533.50	684.45
20000	20666.88	1722.24	20979.54	1165.53	21295.44	887.31	21614.40	720.48
21000	21700.32	1808.36	22028.58	1223.81	22360.08	931.67	22695.00	756.50
22000	22733.64	1894.47	23077.62	1282.09	23424.96	976.04	23775.60	792.52
23000	23766.96	1980.58	24126.66	1340.37	24489.84	1020.41	24856.50	828.55
24000	24800.28	2066.69	25175.52	1398.64	25554.48	1064.77	25937.10	864.57
25000	25833.60	2152.80	26224.56	1456.92	26619.36	1109.14	27018.00	900.60

ANNUAL PERCENTAGE RATE **6.10%**

LOAN AMT	36 MONTHS TOTAL NOTE	36 MONTHS MONTHLY PAYMENT	42 MONTHS TOTAL NOTE	42 MONTHS MONTHLY PAYMENT	48 MONTHS TOTAL NOTE	48 MONTHS MONTHLY PAYMENT	60 MONTHS TOTAL NOTE	60 MONTHS MONTHLY PAYMENT
1	1.08	.03	.84	.02	.96	.02	.60	.01
2	2.16	.06	2.10	.05	1.92	.04	1.80	.03
3	3.24	.09	2.94	.07	3.36	.07	3.00	.05
4	4.32	.12	4.20	.10	4.32	.09	4.20	.07
5	5.40	.15	5.46	.13	5.28	.11	5.40	.09
6	6.48	.18	6.30	.15	6.72	.14	6.60	.11
7	7.56	.21	7.56	.18	7.68	.16	7.80	.13
8	8.64	.24	8.82	.21	8.64	.18	9.00	.15
9	9.72	.27	9.66	.23	10.08	.21	10.20	.17
10	10.80	.30	10.92	.26	11.04	.23	11.40	.19
20	21.60	.60	22.26	.53	22.56	.47	22.80	.38
30	32.76	.91	33.18	.79	33.60	.70	34.80	.58
40	43.56	1.21	44.52	1.06	45.12	.94	46.20	.77
50	54.72	1.52	55.44	1.32	56.16	1.17	57.60	.96
60	65.52	1.82	66.78	1.59	67.68	1.41	69.60	1.16
70	76.68	2.13	77.70	1.85	78.72	1.64	81.00	1.35
80	87.48	2.43	89.04	2.12	90.24	1.88	93.00	1.55
90	98.64	2.74	99.96	2.38	101.28	2.11	104.40	1.74
100	109.44	3.04	111.30	2.65	112.80	2.35	115.80	1.93
200	219.24	6.09	222.60	5.30	225.60	4.70	232.20	3.87
300	329.04	9.14	333.90	7.95	338.40	7.05	348.60	5.81
400	438.48	12.18	445.20	10.60	451.68	9.41	465.00	7.75
500	548.28	15.23	556.50	13.25	564.48	11.76	580.80	9.68
600	658.08	18.28	667.80	15.90	677.28	14.11	697.20	11.62
700	767.52	21.32	779.10	18.55	790.56	16.47	813.60	13.56
800	877.32	24.37	890.40	21.20	903.36	18.82	930.00	15.50
900	987.12	27.42	1001.70	23.85	1016.16	21.17	1046.40	17.44
1000	1096.56	30.46	1113.00	26.50	1129.44	23.53	1162.20	19.37
1500	1645.20	45.70	1669.50	39.75	1693.92	35.29	1743.60	29.06
2000	2193.48	60.93	2226.00	53.00	2258.88	47.06	2325.00	38.75
2500	2741.76	76.16	2782.50	66.25	2823.36	58.82	2906.40	48.44
3000	3290.40	91.40	3339.00	79.50	3388.32	70.59	3487.80	58.13
3500	3838.68	106.63	3895.50	92.75	3952.80	82.35	4069.20	67.82
4000	4386.96	121.86	4452.00	106.00	4517.76	94.12	4650.60	77.51
4500	4935.60	137.10	5008.50	119.25	5082.24	105.88	5232.00	87.20
5000	5483.88	152.33	5565.00	132.50	5647.20	117.65	5813.40	96.89
5500	6032.16	167.56	6121.50	145.75	6211.68	129.41	6394.80	106.58
6000	6580.80	182.80	6678.42	159.01	6776.64	141.18	6976.20	116.27
6500	7129.08	198.03	7234.92	172.26	7341.60	152.95	7557.60	125.96
7000	7677.72	213.27	7791.42	185.51	7906.08	164.71	8139.00	135.65
7500	8226.00	228.50	8347.92	198.76	8471.04	176.48	8720.40	145.34
8000	8774.28	243.73	8904.42	212.01	9035.52	188.24	9301.80	155.03
8500	9322.92	258.97	9460.92	225.26	9600.48	200.01	9883.20	164.72
9000	9871.20	274.20	10017.42	238.51	10164.96	211.77	10464.60	174.41
10000	10968.12	304.67	11130.42	265.01	11294.40	235.30	11627.40	193.79
11000	12064.68	335.13	12243.42	291.51	12423.84	258.83	12790.20	213.17
12000	13161.60	365.60	13356.84	318.02	13553.76	282.37	13953.00	232.55
13000	14258.52	396.07	14469.84	344.52	14683.20	305.90	15115.80	251.93
14000	15355.44	426.54	15582.84	371.02	15812.64	329.43	16278.60	271.31
15000	16452.00	457.00	16695.84	397.52	16942.08	352.96	17441.40	290.69
16000	17548.92	487.47	17808.84	424.02	18071.52	376.49	18603.60	310.06
17000	18645.84	517.94	18922.26	450.53	19200.96	400.02	19766.40	329.44
18000	19742.76	548.41	20035.26	477.03	20330.40	423.55	20929.20	348.82
19000	20839.32	578.87	21148.26	503.53	21459.84	447.08	22092.00	368.20
20000	21936.24	609.34	22261.26	530.03	22589.28	470.61	23254.80	387.58
21000	23033.16	639.81	23374.26	556.53	23718.72	494.14	24417.60	406.96
22000	24129.72	670.27	24487.26	583.03	24848.16	517.67	25580.40	426.34
23000	25226.64	700.74	25600.68	609.54	25978.08	541.21	26743.20	445.72
24000	26323.56	731.21	26713.68	636.04	27107.52	564.74	27906.00	465.10
25000	27420.48	761.68	27826.68	662.54	28236.96	588.27	29068.80	484.48

6.20% ANNUAL PERCENTAGE RATE

	12 MONTHS		18 MONTHS		24 MONTHS		30 MONTHS	
LOAN AMT	TOTAL NOTE	MONTHLY PAYMENT	TOTAL NOTE	MONTHLY PAYMENT	TOTAL NOTE	MONTHLY PAYMENT	TOTAL NOTE	MONTHLY PAYMENT
1	.96	.08	.90	.05	.96	.04	.90	.03
2	2.04	.17	1.98	.11	1.92	.08	2.10	.07
3	3.00	.25	3.06	.17	3.12	.13	3.00	.10
4	4.08	.34	4.14	.23	4.08	.17	4.20	.14
5	5.16	.43	5.22	.29	5.28	.22	5.40	.18
6	6.12	.51	6.12	.34	6.24	.26	6.30	.21
7	7.20	.60	7.20	.40	7.44	.31	7.50	.25
8	8.16	.68	8.28	.46	8.40	.35	8.40	.28
9	9.24	.77	9.36	.52	9.36	.39	9.60	.32
10	10.32	.86	10.44	.58	10.56	.44	10.80	.36
20	20.64	1.72	20.88	1.16	21.12	.88	21.60	.72
30	30.96	2.58	31.32	1.74	31.92	1.33	32.40	1.08
40	41.28	3.44	41.94	2.33	42.48	1.77	43.20	1.44
50	51.60	4.30	52.38	2.91	53.28	2.22	54.00	1.80
60	61.92	5.16	62.82	3.49	63.84	2.66	64.80	2.16
70	72.36	6.03	73.44	4.08	74.40	3.10	75.60	2.52
80	82.68	6.89	83.88	4.66	85.20	3.55	86.40	2.88
90	93.00	7.75	94.32	5.24	95.76	3.99	97.20	3.24
100	103.32	8.61	104.94	5.83	106.56	4.44	108.00	3.60
200	206.76	17.23	209.88	11.66	213.12	8.88	216.30	7.21
300	310.08	25.84	314.82	17.49	319.68	13.32	324.60	10.82
400	413.52	34.46	419.76	23.32	426.24	17.76	432.60	14.42
500	516.84	43.07	524.88	29.16	532.80	22.20	540.90	18.03
600	620.28	51.69	629.82	34.99	639.36	26.64	649.20	21.64
700	723.72	60.31	734.76	40.82	745.92	31.08	757.20	25.24
800	827.04	68.92	839.70	46.65	852.48	35.52	865.50	28.85
900	930.48	77.54	944.64	52.48	959.04	39.96	973.80	32.46
1000	1033.80	86.15	1049.76	58.32	1065.84	44.41	1081.80	36.06
1500	1550.76	129.23	1574.64	87.48	1598.64	66.61	1623.00	54.10
2000	2067.72	172.31	2099.52	116.64	2131.68	88.82	2163.90	72.13
2500	2584.68	215.39	2624.40	145.80	2664.48	111.02	2705.10	90.17
3000	3101.64	258.47	3149.28	174.96	3197.52	133.23	3246.00	108.20
3500	3618.60	301.55	3674.16	204.12	3730.32	155.43	3787.20	126.24
4000	4135.56	344.63	4199.04	233.28	4263.36	177.64	4328.10	144.27
4500	4652.52	387.71	4723.92	262.44	4796.16	199.84	4869.30	162.31
5000	5169.48	430.79	5248.98	291.61	5329.20	222.05	5410.20	180.34
5500	5686.44	473.87	5773.86	320.77	5862.00	244.25	5951.40	198.38
6000	6203.40	516.95	6298.74	349.93	6395.04	266.46	6492.30	216.41
6500	6720.24	560.02	6823.62	379.09	6928.08	288.67	7033.50	234.45
7000	7237.20	603.10	7348.50	408.25	7460.88	310.87	7574.40	252.48
7500	7754.16	646.18	7873.38	437.41	7993.92	333.08	8115.30	270.51
8000	8271.12	689.26	8398.26	466.57	8526.72	355.28	8656.50	288.55
8500	8788.08	732.34	8923.14	495.73	9059.76	377.49	9197.40	306.58
9000	9305.04	775.42	9448.02	524.89	9592.56	399.69	9738.60	324.62
10000	10338.96	861.58	10497.96	583.22	10658.40	444.10	10820.70	360.69
11000	11372.88	947.74	11547.72	641.54	11724.24	488.51	11902.80	396.76
12000	12406.80	1033.90	12597.48	699.86	12790.08	532.92	12984.90	432.83
13000	13440.60	1120.05	13647.24	758.18	13856.16	577.34	14067.00	468.90
14000	14474.52	1206.21	14697.18	816.51	14922.00	621.75	15148.80	504.96
15000	15508.44	1292.37	15746.94	874.83	15987.84	666.16	16230.90	541.03
16000	16542.36	1378.53	16796.70	933.15	17053.68	710.57	17313.00	577.10
17000	17576.28	1464.69	17846.46	991.47	18119.52	754.98	18395.10	613.17
18000	18610.20	1550.85	18896.22	1049.79	19185.36	799.39	19477.20	649.24
19000	19644.00	1637.00	19946.16	1108.12	20251.20	843.80	20559.30	685.31
20000	20677.92	1723.16	20995.92	1166.44	21317.04	888.21	21641.40	721.38
21000	21711.84	1809.32	22045.68	1224.76	22382.88	932.62	22723.50	757.45
22000	22745.76	1895.48	23095.44	1283.08	23448.72	977.03	23805.60	793.52
23000	23779.68	1981.64	24145.38	1341.41	24514.56	1021.44	24887.70	829.59
24000	24813.60	2067.80	25195.14	1399.73	25580.40	1065.85	25969.80	865.66
25000	25847.40	2153.95	26244.90	1458.05	26646.24	1110.26	27051.90	901.73

ANNUAL PERCENTAGE RATE **6.20%**

LOAN AMT	36 MONTHS TOTAL NOTE	36 MONTHS MONTHLY PAYMENT	42 MONTHS TOTAL NOTE	42 MONTHS MONTHLY PAYMENT	48 MONTHS TOTAL NOTE	48 MONTHS MONTHLY PAYMENT	60 MONTHS TOTAL NOTE	60 MONTHS MONTHLY PAYMENT
1	1.08	.03	.84	.02	.96	.02	.60	.01
2	2.16	.06	2.10	.05	1.92	.04	1.80	.03
3	3.24	.09	2.94	.07	3.36	.07	3.00	.05
4	4.32	.12	4.20	.10	4.32	.09	4.20	.07
5	5.40	.15	5.46	.13	5.28	.11	5.40	.09
6	6.48	.18	6.30	.15	6.72	.14	6.60	.11
7	7.56	.21	7.56	.18	7.68	.16	7.80	.13
8	8.64	.24	8.82	.21	8.64	.18	9.00	.15
9	9.72	27	9.66	.23	10.08	.21	10.20	.17
10	10.80	.30	10.92	.26	11.04	.23	11.40	.19
20	21.96	.61	22.26	.53	22.56	.47	22.80	.38
30	32.76	.91	33.18	.79	33.60	.70	34.80	.58
40	43.92	1.22	44.52	1.06	45.12	.94	46.20	.77
50	54.72	1.52	55.44	1.32	56.16	1.17	58.20	.97
60	65.88	1.83	66.78	1.59	67.68	1.41	69.60	1.16
70	76.68	2.13	77.70	1.85	79.20	1.65	81.00	1.35
80	87.84	2.44	89.04	2.12	90.24	1.88	93.00	1.55
90	98.64	2.74	99.96	2.38	101.76	2.12	104.40	1.74
100	109.80	3.05	111.30	2.65	112.80	2.35	116.40	1.94
200	219.60	6.10	222.60	5.30	226.08	4.71	232.80	3.88
300	329.40	9.15	334.32	7.96	339.36	7.07	349.20	5.82
400	439.20	12.20	445.62	10.61	452.64	9.43	466.20	7.77
500	549.00	15.25	557.34	13.27	565.44	11.78	582.60	9.71
600	658.80	18.30	668.64	15.92	678.72	14.14	699.00	11.65
700	768.60	21.35	780.36	18.58	792.00	16.50	815.40	13.59
800	878.76	24.41	891.66	21.23	905.28	18.86	932.40	15.54
900	988.56	27.46	1003.38	23.89	1018.08	21.21	1048.80	17.48
1000	1098.36	30.51	1114.68	26.54	1131.36	23.57	1165.20	19.42
1500	1647.36	45.76	1672.44	39.82	1697.28	35.36	1747.80	29.13
2000	2196.72	61.02	2229.78	53.09	2263.20	47.15	2331.00	38.85
2500	2746.08	76.28	2787.12	66.36	2829.12	58.94	2913.60	48.56
3000	3295.08	91.53	3344.88	79.64	3395.04	70.73	3496.20	58.27
3500	3844.44	106.79	3902.22	92.91	3960.48	82.51	4079.40	67.99
4000	4393.80	122.05	4459.56	106.18	4526.40	94.30	4662.00	77.70
4500	4942.80	137.30	5017.32	119.46	5092.32	106.09	5244.60	87.41
5000	5492.16	152.56	5574.66	132.73	5658.24	117.88	5827.20	97.12
5500	6041.16	167.81	6132.42	146.01	6224.16	129.67	6410.40	106.84
6000	6590.52	183.07	6689.76	159.28	6790.08	141.46	6993.00	116.55
6500	7139.88	198.33	7247.10	172.55	7355.52	153.24	7575.60	126.26
7000	7688.88	213.58	7804.86	185.83	7921.44	165.03	8158.80	135.98
7500	8238.24	228.84	8362.20	199.10	8487.36	176.82	8741.40	145.69
8000	8787.60	244.10	8919.54	212.37	9053.28	188.61	9324.00	155.40
8500	9336.60	259.35	9477.30	225.65	9619.20	200.40	9907.20	165.12
9000	9885.96	274.61	10034.64	238.92	10185.12	212.19	10489.80	174.83
10000	10984.32	305.12	11149.74	265.47	11316.48	235.76	11655.00	194.25
11000	12082.68	335.63	12264.84	292.02	12448.32	259.34	12820.80	213.68
12000	13181.04	366.15	13379.52	318.56	13580.16	282.92	13986.60	233.11
13000	14279.76	396.66	14494.62	345.11	14711.52	306.49	15151.80	252.53
14000	15378.12	427.17	15609.72	371.66	15843.36	330.07	16317.60	271.96
15000	16476.48	457.68	16724.82	398.21	16975.20	353.65	17482.80	291.38
16000	17575.20	488.20	17839.50	424.75	18106.56	377.22	18648.60	310.81
17000	18673.56	518.71	18954.60	451.30	19238.40	400.80	19814.40	330.24
18000	19771.92	549.22	20069.70	477.85	20370.24	424.38	20979.60	349.66
19000	20870.64	579.74	21184.80	504.40	21501.60	447.95	22145.40	369.09
20000	21969.00	610.25	22299.48	530.94	22633.44	471.53	23310.60	388.51
21000	23067.36	640.76	23414.58	557.49	23765.28	495.11	24476.40	407.94
22000	24165.72	671.27	24529.68	584.04	24897.12	518.69	25642.20	427.37
23000	25264.44	701.79	25644.78	610.59	26028.48	542.26	26807.40	446.79
24000	26362.80	732.30	26759.46	637.13	27160.32	565.84	27973.20	466.22
25000	27461.16	762.81	27874.56	663.68	28292.16	589.42	29138.40	485.64

6.25% ANNUAL PERCENTAGE RATE

LOAN AMT	12 MONTHS TOTAL NOTE	12 MONTHS MONTHLY PAYMENT	18 MONTHS TOTAL NOTE	18 MONTHS MONTHLY PAYMENT	24 MONTHS TOTAL NOTE	24 MONTHS MONTHLY PAYMENT	30 MONTHS TOTAL NOTE	30 MONTHS MONTHLY PAYMENT
1	.96	.08	.90	.05	.96	.04	.90	.03
2	2.04	.17	1.98	.11	1.92	.08	2.10	.07
3	3.00	.25	3.06	.17	3.12	.13	3.00	.10
4	4.08	.34	4.14	.23	4.08	.17	4.20	.14
5	5.16	.43	5.22	.29	5.28	.22	5.40	.18
6	6.12	.51	6.30	.35	6.24	.26	6.30	.21
7	7.20	.60	7.20	.40	7.44	.31	7.50	.25
8	8.16	.68	8.28	.46	8.40	.35	8.40	.28
9	9.24	.77	9.36	.52	9.36	.39	9.60	.32
10	10.32	.86	10.44	.58	10.56	.44	10.80	.36
20	20.64	1.72	20.88	1.16	21.12	.88	21.60	.72
30	30.96	2.58	31.50	1.75	31.92	1.33	32.40	1.08
40	41.28	3.44	41.94	2.33	42.48	1.77	43.20	1.44
50	51.60	4.30	52.38	2.91	53.28	2.22	54.00	1.80
60	62.04	5.17	63.00	3.50	63.84	2.66	64.80	2.16
70	72.36	6.03	73.44	4.08	74.64	3.11	75.60	2.52
80	82.68	6.89	83.88	4.66	85.20	3.55	86.40	2.88
90	93.00	7.75	94.50	5.25	95.76	3.99	97.20	3.24
100	103.32	8.61	104.94	5.83	106.56	4.44	108.00	3.60
200	206.76	17.23	209.88	11.66	213.12	8.88	216.30	7.21
300	310.20	25.85	315.00	17.50	319.92	13.33	324.60	10.82
400	413.64	34.47	419.94	23.33	426.48	17.77	432.90	14.43
500	517.08	43.09	525.06	29.17	533.04	22.21	541.20	18.04
600	620.40	51.70	630.00	35.00	639.84	26.66	649.50	21.65
700	723.84	60.32	735.12	40.84	746.40	31.10	757.80	25.26
800	827.28	68.94	840.06	46.67	852.96	35.54	866.10	28.87
900	930.72	77.56	945.18	52.51	959.76	39.99	974.40	32.48
1000	1034.16	86.18	1050.12	58.34	1066.32	44.43	1082.70	36.09
1500	1551.24	129.27	1575.18	87.51	1599.60	66.65	1623.90	54.13
2000	2068.32	172.36	2100.24	116.68	2132.64	88.86	2165.40	72.18
2500	2585.40	215.45	2625.48	145.86	2665.92	111.08	2706.60	90.22
3000	3102.48	258.54	3150.54	175.03	3199.20	133.30	3248.10	108.27
3500	3619.56	301.63	3675.60	204.20	3732.24	155.51	3789.60	126.32
4000	4136.64	344.72	4200.66	233.37	4265.52	177.73	4330.80	144.36
4500	4653.72	387.81	4725.90	262.55	4798.80	199.95	4872.30	162.41
5000	5170.04	430.90	5250.96	291.72	5331.84	222.16	5413.50	180.45
5500	5687.88	473.99	5776.02	320.89	5865.12	244.38	5955.00	198.50
6000	6204.96	517.08	6301.08	350.06	6398.40	266.60	6496.50	216.55
6500	6722.04	560.17	6826.32	379.24	6931.44	288.81	7037.70	234.59
7000	7239.12	603.26	7351.38	408.41	7464.72	311.03	7579.20	252.64
7500	7756.32	646.36	7876.44	437.58	7998.00	333.25	8120.40	270.68
8000	8273.40	689.45	8401.50	466.75	8531.04	355.46	8661.90	288.73
8500	8790.48	732.54	8926.74	495.93	9064.32	377.68	9203.40	306.78
9000	9307.56	775.63	9451.80	525.10	9597.60	399.90	9744.60	324.82
10000	10341.72	861.81	10501.92	583.44	10663.92	444.33	10827.30	360.91
11000	11375.88	947.99	11552.22	641.79	11730.24	488.76	11910.30	397.01
12000	12410.04	1034.17	12602.34	700.13	12796.80	533.20	12993.00	433.10
13000	13444.20	1120.35	13652.64	758.48	13863.12	577.63	14075.70	469.19
14000	14478.36	1206.53	14702.76	816.82	14929.44	622.06	15158.40	505.28
15000	15512.64	1292.72	15753.06	875.17	15996.00	666.50	16241.10	541.37
16000	16546.80	1378.90	16803.18	933.51	17062.32	710.93	17323.80	577.46
17000	17580.96	1465.08	17853.48	991.86	18128.64	755.36	18406.80	613.56
18000	18615.12	1551.26	18903.60	1050.20	19195.20	799.80	19489.50	649.65
19000	19649.28	1637.44	19953.90	1108.55	20261.52	844.23	20572.20	685.74
20000	20683.44	1723.62	21004.02	1166.89	21327.84	888.66	21654.90	721.83
21000	21717.60	1809.80	22054.32	1225.24	22394.40	933.10	22737.60	757.92
22000	22751.88	1895.99	23104.44	1283.58	23460.72	977.53	23820.60	794.02
23000	23786.04	1982.17	24154.74	1341.93	24527.04	1021.96	24903.30	830.11
24000	24820.20	2068.35	25204.86	1400.27	25593.60	1066.40	25986.00	866.20
25000	25854.36	2154.53	26255.16	1458.62	26659.92	1110.83	27068.70	902.29

ANNUAL PERCENTAGE RATE **6.25%**

LOAN AMT	36 MONTHS TOTAL NOTE	36 MONTHS MONTHLY PAYMENT	42 MONTHS TOTAL NOTE	42 MONTHS MONTHLY PAYMENT	48 MONTHS TOTAL NOTE	48 MONTHS MONTHLY PAYMENT	60 MONTHS TOTAL NOTE	60 MONTHS MONTHLY PAYMENT
1	1.08	.03	.84	.02	.96	.02	.60	.01
2	2.16	.06	2.10	.05	1.92	.04	1.80	.03
3	3.24	.09	2.94	.07	3.36	.07	3.00	.05
4	4.32	.12	4.20	.10	4.32	.09	4.20	.07
5	5.40	.15	5.46	.13	5.28	.11	5.40	.09
6	6.48	.18	6.30	.15	6.72	.14	6.60	.11
7	7.56	.21	7.56	.18	7.68	.16	7.80	.13
8	8.64	.24	8.82	.21	8.64	.18	9.00	.15
9	9.72	.27	9.66	.23	10.08	.21	10.20	.17
10	10.80	.30	10.92	.26	11.04	.23	11.40	.19
20	21.96	.61	22.26	.53	22.56	.47	22.80	.38
30	32.76	.91	33.18	.79	33.60	.70	34.80	.58
40	43.92	1.22	44.52	1.06	45.12	.94	46.20	.77
50	54.72	1.52	55.44	1.32	56.16	1.17	58.20	.97
60	65.88	1.83	66.78	1.59	67.68	1.41	69.60	1.16
70	76.68	2.13	77.70	1.85	79.20	1.65	81.60	1.36
80	87.84	2.44	89.04	2.12	90.24	1.88	93.00	1.55
90	98.64	2.74	100.38	2.39	101.76	2.12	105.00	1.75
100	109.80	3.05	111.30	2.65	112.80	2.35	116.40	1.94
200	219.60	6.10	223.02	5.31	226.08	4.71	232.80	3.88
300	329.76	9.16	334.74	7.97	339.36	7.07	349.80	5.83
400	439.56	12.21	446.04	10.62	452.64	9.43	466.20	7.77
500	549.36	15.26	557.76	13.28	565.92	11.79	583.20	9.72
600	659.52	18.32	669.48	15.94	679.20	14.15	699.60	11.66
700	769.32	21.37	780.78	18.59	792.48	16.51	816.60	13.61
800	879.12	24.42	892.50	21.25	905.76	18.87	933.00	15.55
900	989.28	27.48	1004.22	23.91	1019.04	21.23	1050.00	17.50
1000	1099.08	30.53	1115.94	26.57	1132.32	23.59	1166.40	19.44
1500	1648.80	45.80	1673.70	39.85	1698.72	35.39	1750.20	29.17
2000	2198.52	61.07	2231.88	53.14	2265.12	47.19	2333.40	38.89
2500	2747.88	76.33	2789.64	66.42	2831 52	58.99	2917.20	48.62
3000	3297.60	91.60	3347.82	79.71	3397.92	70.79	3500.40	58.34
3500	3847.32	106.87	3905.58	92.99	3964.32	82.59	4084.20	68.07
4000	4397.04	122.14	4463.76	106.28	4530.72	94.39	4667.40	77.79
4500	4946.40	137.40	5021.52	119.56	5097.12	106.19	5251.20	87.52
5000	5496.12	152.67	5579.70	132.85	5663.52	117.99	5834.40	97.24
5500	6045.84	167.94	6137.46	146.13	6229.92	129.79	6418.20	106.97
6000	6595.56	183.21	6695.64	159.42	6796.32	141.59	7001.40	116.69
6500	7144.92	198.47	7253.40	172.70	7362.72	153.39	7585.20	126.42
7000	7694.64	213.74	7811.58	185.99	7929.12	165.19	8168.40	136.14
7500	8244.36	229.01	8369.34	199.27	8495.52	176.99	8751.60	145.86
8000	8794.08	244.28	8927.52	212.56	9061.92	188.79	9335.40	155.59
8500	9343.80	259.55	9485.28	225.84	9628.32	200.59	9918.60	165.31
9000	9893.16	274.81	10043.46	239.13	10194.72	212.39	10502.40	175.04
10000	10992.60	305.35	11159.40	265.70	11327.52	235.99	11669.40	194.49
11000	12091.68	335.88	12275.34	292.27	12460.32	259.59	12836.40	213.94
12000	13191.12	366.42	13391.28	318.84	13593.12	283.19	14003.40	233.39
13000	14290.20	396.95	14507.22	345.41	14725.92	306.79	15170.40	252.84
14000	15389.64	427.49	15623.16	371.98	15858.72	330.39	16336.80	272.28
15000	16489.08	458.03	16739.10	398.55	16991.52	353.99	17503.80	291.73
16000	17588.16	488.56	17855.04	425.12	18124.32	377.59	18670.80	311.18
17000	18687.60	519.10	18970.98	451.69	19257.12	401.19	19837.80	330.63
18000	19786.68	549.63	20086.92	478.26	20389.92	424.79	21004.80	350.08
19000	20886.12	580.17	21202.86	504.83	21522.72	448.39	22171.80	369.53
20000	21985.20	610.70	22318.80	531.40	22655.52	471.99	23338.80	388.98
21000	23084.64	641.24	23434.74	557.97	23788.32	495.59	24505.80	408.43
22000	24183.72	671.77	24550.68	584.54	24921.12	519.19	25672.80	427.88
23000	25283.16	702.31	25666.62	611.11	26053.92	542.79	26839.80	447.33
24000	26382.24	732.84	26782.56	637.68	27186.72	566.39	28006.80	466.78
25000	27481.68	763.38	27898.50	664.25	28319.52	589.99	29173.80	486.23

6.30% ANNUAL PERCENTAGE RATE

LOAN AMT	12 MONTHS TOTAL NOTE	MONTHLY PAYMENT	18 MONTHS TOTAL NOTE	MONTHLY PAYMENT	24 MONTHS TOTAL NOTE	MONTHLY PAYMENT	30 MONTHS TOTAL NOTE	MONTHLY PAYMENT
1	.96	.08	.90	.05	.96	.04	.90	.03
2	2.04	.17	1.98	.11	1.92	.08	2.10	.07
3	3.00	.25	3.06	.17	3.12	.13	3.00	.10
4	4.08	.34	4.14	.23	4.08	.17	4.20	.14
5	5.16	.43	5.22	.29	5.28	.22	5.40	.18
6	6.12	.51	6.30	.35	6.24	.26	6.30	.21
7	7.20	.60	7.20	.40	7.44	.31	7.50	.25
8	8.16	.68	8.28	.46	8.40	.35	8.40	.28
9	9.24	.77	9.36	.52	9.60	.40	9.60	.32
10	10.32	.86	10.44	.58	10.56	.44	10.80	.36
20	20.64	1.72	20.88	1.16	21.12	.88	21.60	.72
30	30.96	2.58	31.50	1.75	31.92	1.33	32.40	1.08
40	41.28	3.44	41.94	2.33	42.48	1.77	43.20	1.44
50	51.72	4.31	52.38	2.91	53.28	2.22	54.00	1.80
60	62.04	5.17	63.00	3.50	63.84	2.66	64.80	2.16
70	72.36	6.03	73.44	4.08	74.64	3.11	75.60	2.52
80	82.68	6.89	83.88	4.66	85.20	3.55	86.40	2.88
90	93.00	7.75	94.50	5.25	96.00	4.00	97.50	3.25
100	103.44	8.62	104.94	5.83	106.56	4.44	108.30	3.61
200	206.88	17.24	210.06	11.67	213.36	8.89	216.60	7.22
300	310.32	25.86	315.18	17.51	319.92	13.33	324.90	10.83
400	413.76	34.48	420.12	23.34	426.72	17.78	433.20	14.44
500	517.20	43.10	525.24	29.18	533.28	22.22	541.50	18.05
600	620.64	51.72	630.36	35.02	640.08	26.67	649.80	21.66
700	724.08	60.34	735.30	40.85	746.64	31.11	758.40	25.28
800	827.52	68.96	840.42	46.69	853.44	35.56	866.70	28.89
900	930.96	77.58	945.54	52.53	960.24	40.01	975.00	32.50
1000	1034.40	86.20	1050.48	58.36	1066.80	44.45	1083.30	36.11
1500	1551.60	129.30	1575.90	87.55	1600.32	66.68	1625.10	54.17
2000	2068.80	172.40	2101.14	116.73	2133.84	88.91	2166.60	72.22
2500	2586.12	215.51	2626.38	145.91	2667.12	111.13	2708.40	90.28
3000	3103.32	258.61	3151.80	175.10	3200.64	133.36	3250.20	108.34
3500	3620.52	301.71	3677.04	204.28	3734.16	155.59	3792.00	126.40
4000	4137.72	344.81	4202.28	233.46	4267.68	177.82	4333.50	144.45
4500	4654.92	387.91	4727.70	262.65	4801.20	200.05	4875.30	162.51
5000	5172.24	431.02	5252.94	291.83	5334.48	222.27	5417.10	180.57
5500	5689.44	474.12	5778.36	321.02	5868.00	244.50	5958.60	198.62
6000	6206.64	517.22	6303.60	350.20	6401.52	266.73	6500.40	216.68
6500	6723.84	560.32	6828.84	379.38	6935.04	288.96	7042.20	234.74
7000	7241.16	603.43	7354.26	408.57	7468.56	311.19	7584.00	252.80
7500	7758.36	646.53	7879.50	437.75	8001.84	333.41	8125.50	270.85
8000	8275.56	689.63	8404.74	466.93	8535.36	355.64	8667.30	288.91
8500	8792.76	732.73	8930.16	496.12	9068.88	377.87	9209.10	306.97
9000	9309.96	775.83	9455.40	525.30	9602.40	400.10	9750.90	325.03
10000	10344.48	862.04	10506.06	583.67	10669.20	444.55	10834.20	361.14
11000	11378.88	948.24	11556.72	642.04	11736.24	489.01	11917.50	397.25
12000	12413.40	1034.45	12607.20	700.40	12803.28	533.47	13001.10	433.37
13000	13447.80	1120.65	13657.86	758.77	13870.08	577.92	14084.40	469.48
14000	14482.32	1206.86	14708.52	817.14	14937.12	622.38	15168.00	505.60
15000	15516.72	1293.06	15759.18	875.51	16003.92	666.83	16251.30	541.71
16000	16551.24	1379.27	16809.66	933.87	17070.96	711.29	17334.90	577.83
17000	17585.64	1465.47	17860.32	992.24	18138.00	755.75	18418.20	613.94
18000	18620.04	1551.67	18910.98	1050.61	19204.80	800.20	19501.80	650.06
19000	19654.56	1637.88	19961.64	1108.98	20271.84	844.66	20585.10	686.17
20000	20688.96	1724.08	21012.12	1167.34	21338.64	889.11	21668.40	722.28
21000	21723.48	1810.29	22062.78	1225.71	22405.68	933.57	22752.00	758.40
22000	22757.88	1896.49	23113.44	1284.08	23472.72	978.03	23835.30	794.51
23000	23792.40	1982.70	24164.10	1342.45	24539.52	1022.48	24918.90	830.63
24000	24826.80	2068.90	25214.58	1400.81	25606.56	1066.94	26002.20	866.74
25000	25861.20	2155.10	26265.24	1459.18	26673.36	1111.39	27085.80	902.86

ANNUAL PERCENTAGE RATE **6.30%**

LOAN AMT	36 MONTHS TOTAL NOTE	36 MONTHS MONTHLY PAYMENT	42 MONTHS TOTAL NOTE	42 MONTHS MONTHLY PAYMENT	48 MONTHS TOTAL NOTE	48 MONTHS MONTHLY PAYMENT	60 MONTHS TOTAL NOTE	60 MONTHS MONTHLY PAYMENT
1	1.08	.03	.84	.02	.96	.02	.60	.01
2	2.16	.06	2.10	.05	1.92	.04	1.80	.03
3	3.24	.09	2.94	.07	3.36	.07	3.00	.05
4	4.32	.12	4.20	.10	4.32	.09	4.20	.07
5	5.40	.15	5.46	.13	5.28	.11	5.40	.09
6	6.48	.18	6.30	.15	6.72	.14	6.60	.11
7	7.56	.21	7.56	.18	7.68	.16	7.80	.13
8	8.64	.24	8.82	.21	8.64	.18	9.00	.15
9	9.72	.27	9.66	.23	10.08	.21	10.20	.17
10	10.80	.30	10.92	.26	11.04	.23	11.40	.19
20	21.96	.61	22.26	.53	22.56	.47	22.80	.38
30	32.76	.91	33.18	.79	33.60	.70	34.80	.58
40	43.92	1.22	44.52	1.06	45.12	.94	46.20	.77
50	54.72	1.52	55.44	1.32	56.64	1.18	58.20	.97
60	65.88	1.83	66.78	1.59	67.68	1.41	69.60	1.16
70	76.68	2.13	78.12	1.86	79.20	1.65	81.60	1.36
80	87.84	2.44	89.04	2.12	90.24	1.88	93.00	1.55
90	99.00	2.75	100.38	2.39	101.76	2.12	105.00	1.75
100	109.80	3.05	111.30	2.65	113.28	2.36	116.40	1.94
200	219.96	6.11	223.02	5.31	226.56	4.72	233.40	3.89
300	329.76	9.16	334.74	7.97	339.84	7.08	350.40	5.84
400	439.92	12.22	446.46	10.63	453.12	9.44	466.80	7.78
500	549.72	15.27	558.18	13.29	566.88	11.81	583.80	9.73
600	659.88	18.33	669.90	15.95	680.16	14.17	700.80	11.68
700	770.04	21.39	781.62	18.61	793.44	16.53	817.80	13.63
800	879.84	24.44	893.34	21.27	906.72	18.89	934.20	15.57
900	990.00	27.50	1005.06	23.93	1020.48	21.26	1051.20	17.52
1000	1099.80	30.55	1116.78	26.59	1133.76	23.62	1168.20	19.47
1500	1649.88	45.83	1674.96	39.88	1700.64	35.43	1752.00	29.20
2000	2199.96	61.11	2233.56	53.18	2267.52	47.24	2336.40	38.94
2500	2750.04	76.39	2792.16	66.48	2834.40	59.05	2920.80	48.68
3000	3300.12	91.67	3350.34	79.77	3401.28	70.86	3504.60	58.41
3500	3850.20	106.95	3908.94	93.07	3968.16	82.67	4089.00	68.15
4000	4400.28	122.23	4467.54	106.37	4535.52	94.49	4673.40	77.89
4500	4950.36	137.51	5025.72	119.66	5102.40	106.30	5257.20	87.62
5000	5500.44	152.79	5584.32	132.96	5669.28	118.11	5841.60	97.36
5500	6050.16	168.06	6142.92	146.26	6236.16	129.92	6425.40	107.09
6000	6600.24	183.34	6701.10	159.55	6803.04	141.73	7009.80	116.83
6500	7150.32	198.62	7259.70	172.85	7369.92	153.54	7594.20	126.57
7000	7700.40	213.90	7818.30	186.15	7936.80	165.35	8178.00	136.30
7500	8250.48	229.18	8376.48	199.44	8504.16	177.17	8762.40	146.04
8000	8800.56	244.46	8935.08	212.74	9071.04	188.98	9346.80	155.78
8500	9350.64	259.74	9493.68	226.04	9637.92	200.79	9930.60	165.51
9000	9900.72	275.02	10051.86	239.33	10204.80	212.60	10515.00	175.25
10000	11000.88	305.58	11169.06	265.93	11338.56	236.22	11683.20	194.72
11000	12100.68	336.13	12285.84	292.52	12472.80	259.85	12851.40	214.19
12000	13200.84	366.69	13402.62	319.11	13606.56	283.47	14020.20	233.67
13000	14301.00	397.25	14519.82	345.71	14740.32	307.09	15188.40	253.14
14000	15401.16	427.81	15636.60	372.30	15874.08	330.71	16356.60	272.61
15000	16501.32	458.37	16753.38	398.89	17008.32	354.34	17524.80	292.08
16000	17601.12	488.92	17870.16	425.48	18142.08	377.96	18693.60	311.56
17000	18701.28	519.48	18987.36	452.08	19275.84	401.58	19861.80	331.03
18000	19801.44	550.04	20104.14	478.67	20410.08	425.21	21030.00	350.50
19000	20901.60	580.60	21220.92	505.26	21543.84	448.83	22198.20	369.97
20000	22001.76	611.16	22338.12	531.86	22677.60	472.45	23367.00	389.45
21000	23101.56	641.71	23454.90	558.45	23811.36	496.07	24535.20	408.92
22000	24201.72	672.27	24571.68	585.04	24945.60	519.70	25703.40	428.39
23000	25301.88	702.83	25688.88	611.64	26079.36	543.32	26871.60	447.86
24000	26402.04	733.39	26805.66	638.23	27213.12	566.94	28040.40	467.34
25000	27502.20	763.95	27922.44	664.82	28347.36	590.57	29208.60	486.81

6.40% ANNUAL PERCENTAGE RATE

	12 MONTHS		18 MONTHS		24 MONTHS		30 MONTHS	
LOAN AMT	TOTAL NOTE	MONTHLY PAYMENT	TOTAL NOTE	MONTHLY PAYMENT	TOTAL NOTE	MONTHLY PAYMENT	TOTAL NOTE	MONTHLY PAYMENT
1	.96	.08	.90	.05	.96	.04	.90	.03
2	2.04	.17	1.98	.11	1.92	.08	2.10	.07
3	3.00	.25	3.06	.17	3.12	.13	3.00	.10
4	4.08	.34	4.14	.23	4.08	.17	4.20	.14
5	5.16	.43	5.22	.29	5.28	.22	5.40	.18
6	6.12	.51	6.30	.35	6.24	.26	6.30	.21
7	7.20	.60	7.20	.40	7.44	.31	7.50	.25
8	8.28	.69	8.28	.46	8.40	.35	8.40	.28
9	9.24	.77	9.36	.52	9.60	.40	9.60	.32
10	10.32	.86	10.44	.58	10.56	.44	10.80	.36
20	20.64	1.72	20.88	1.16	21.36	.89	21.60	.72
30	30.96	2.58	31.50	1.75	31.92	1.33	32.40	1.08
40	41.40	3.45	41.94	2.33	42.72	1.78	43.20	1.44
50	51.72	4.31	52.56	2.92	53.28	2.22	54.00	1.80
60	62.04	5.17	63.00	3.50	64.08	2.67	64.80	2.16
70	72.36	6.03	73.44	4.08	74.64	3.11	75.90	2.53
80	82.80	6.90	84.06	4.67	85.44	3.56	86.70	2.89
90	93.12	7.76	94.50	5.25	96.00	4.00	97.50	3.25
100	103.44	8.62	105.12	5.84	106.80	4.45	108.30	3.61
200	207.00	17.25	210.24	11.68	213.60	8.90	216.90	7.23
300	310.44	25.87	315.36	17.52	320.40	13.35	325.20	10.84
400	414.00	34.50	420.48	23.36	427.20	17.80	433.80	14.46
500	517.44	43.12	525.60	29.20	534.00	22.25	542.10	18.07
600	621.00	51.75	630.72	35.04	640.80	26.70	650.70	21.69
700	724.44	60.37	735.84	40.88	747.60	31.15	759.30	25.31
800	828.00	69.00	841.14	46.73	854.40	35.60	867.60	28.92
900	931.44	77.62	946.26	52.57	961.20	40.05	976.20	32.54
1000	1035.00	86.25	1051.38	58.41	1068.00	44.50	1084.50	36.15
1500	1552.44	129.37	1576.98	87.61	1602.00	66.75	1626.90	54.23
2000	2070.00	172.50	2102.76	116.82	2136.00	89.00	2169.30	72.31
2500	2587.44	215.62	2628.54	146.03	2670.00	111.25	2711.70	90.39
3000	3105.00	258.75	3154.14	175.23	3204.00	133.50	3254.10	108.47
3500	3622.44	301.87	3679.92	204.44	3738.00	155.75	3796.50	126.55
4000	4140.00	345.00	4205.70	233.65	4272.00	178.00	4338.90	144.63
4500	4657.44	388.12	4731.30	262.85	4806.00	200.25	4881.30	162.71
5000	5175.00	431.25	5257.08	292.06	5340.00	222.50	5423.70	180.79
5500	5692.44	474.37	5782.86	321.27	5874.00	244.75	5966.10	198.87
6000	6210.00	517.50	6308.46	350.47	6408.00	267.00	6508.50	216.95
6500	6727.44	560.62	6834.24	379.68	6942.00	289.25	7050.90	235.03
7000	7245.00	603.75	7359.84	408.88	7476.00	311.50	7593.30	253.11
7500	7762.44	646.87	7885.62	438.09	8010.00	333.75	8135.70	271.19
8000	8280.00	690.00	8411.40	467.30	8544.00	356.00	8678.10	289.27
8500	8797.44	733.12	8937.00	496.50	9078.00	378.25	9220.50	307.35
9000	9315.00	776.25	9462.78	525.71	9612.00	400.50	9762.90	325.43
10000	10350.00	862.50	10514.16	584.12	10680.24	445.01	10847.70	361.59
11000	11385.00	948.75	11565.72	642.54	11748.24	489.51	11932.50	397.75
12000	12420.00	1035.00	12617.10	700.95	12816.24	534.01	13017.30	433.91
13000	13455.00	1121.25	13668.48	759.36	13884.24	578.51	14102.10	470.07
14000	14490.00	1207.50	14719.86	817.77	14952.24	623.01	15186.90	506.23
15000	15525.00	1293.75	15771.42	876.19	16020.24	667.51	16271.70	542.39
16000	16560.00	1380.00	16822.80	934.60	17088.24	712.01	17356.50	578.55
17000	17595.00	1466.25	17874.18	993.01	18156.24	756.51	18441.30	614.71
18000	18630.00	1552.50	18925.74	1051.43	19224.24	801.01	19526.10	650.87
19000	19665.00	1638.75	19977.12	1109.84	20292.48	845.52	20610.90	687.03
20000	20700.00	1725.00	21028.50	1168.25	21360.48	890.02	21695.70	723.19
21000	21735.00	1811.25	22079.88	1226.66	22428.48	934.52	22780.50	759.35
22000	22770.00	1897.50	23131.44	1285.08	23496.48	979.02	23865.30	795.51
23000	23805.00	1983.75	24182.82	1343.49	24564.48	1023.52	24950.10	831.67
24000	24840.00	2070.00	25234.20	1401.90	25632.48	1068.02	26034.90	867.83
25000	25875.00	2156.25	26285.58	1460.31	26700.48	1112.52	27119.70	903.99

ANNUAL PERCENTAGE RATE **6.40%**

LOAN AMT	36 MONTHS TOTAL NOTE	36 MONTHS MONTHLY PAYMENT	42 MONTHS TOTAL NOTE	42 MONTHS MONTHLY PAYMENT	48 MONTHS TOTAL NOTE	48 MONTHS MONTHLY PAYMENT	60 MONTHS TOTAL NOTE	60 MONTHS MONTHLY PAYMENT
1	1.08	.03	.84	.02	.96	.02	.60	.01
2	2.16	.06	2.10	.05	1.92	.04	1.80	.03
3	3.24	.09	2.94	.07	3.36	.07	3.00	.05
4	4.32	.12	4.20	.10	4.32	.09	4.20	.07
5	5.40	.15	5.46	.13	5.28	.11	5.40	.09
6	6.48	.18	6.30	.15	6.72	.14	6.60	.11
7	7.56	.21	7.56	.18	7.68	.16	7.80	.13
8	8.64	.24	8.82	.21	8.64	.18	9.00	.15
9	9.72	.27	9.66	.23	10.08	.21	10.20	.17
10	10.80	.30	10.92	.26	11.04	.23	11.40	.19
20	21.96	.61	22.26	.53	22.56	.47	23.40	.39
30	32.76	.91	33.18	.79	34.08	.71	34.80	.58
40	43.92	1.22	44.52	1.06	45.12	.94	46.80	.78
50	55.08	1.53	55.86	1.33	56.64	1.18	58.20	.97
60	65.88	1.83	66.78	1.59	68.16	1.42	70.20	1.17
70	77.04	2.14	78.12	1.86	79.20	1.65	81.60	1.36
80	87.84	2.44	89.46	2.13	90.72	1.89	93.60	1.56
90	99.00	2.75	100.38	2.39	102.24	2.13	105.00	1.75
100	110.16	3.06	111.72	2.66	113.28	2.36	117.00	1.95
200	220.32	6.12	223.44	5.32	227.04	4.73	234.00	3.90
300	330.48	9.18	335.58	7.99	340.80	7.10	351.00	5.85
400	440.64	12.24	447.30	10.65	454.08	9.46	468.00	7.80
500	550.80	15.30	559.02	13.31	567.84	11.83	585.00	9.75
600	660.96	18.36	671.16	15.98	681.60	14.20	702.60	11.71
700	771.12	21.42	782.88	18.64	794.88	16.56	819.60	13.66
800	881.28	24.48	895.02	21.31	908.64	18.93	936.60	15.61
900	991.44	27.54	1006.74	23.97	1022.40	21.30	1053.60	17.56
1000	1101.60	30.60	1118.46	26.63	1135.68	23.66	1170.60	19.51
1500	1652.40	45.90	1677.90	39.95	1704.00	35.50	1756.20	29.27
2000	2203.20	61.20	2237.34	53.27	2271.84	47.33	2341.80	39.03
2500	2754.00	76.50	2796.78	66.59	2840.16	59.17	2927.40	48.79
3000	3305.16	91.81	3356.22	79.91	3408.00	71.00	3513.00	58.55
3500	3855.96	107.11	3915.66	93.23	3976.32	82.84	4098.60	68.31
4000	4406.76	122.41	4475.10	106.55	4544.16	94.67	4684.20	78.07
4500	4957.56	137.71	5034.54	119.87	5112.00	106.50	5269.80	87.83
5000	5508.36	153.01	5593.98	133.19	5680.32	118.34	5855.40	97.59
5500	6059.16	168.31	6153.42	146.51	6248.16	130.17	6441.00	107.35
6000	6610.32	183.62	6712.86	159.83	6816.48	142.01	7026.60	117.11
6500	7161.12	198.92	7272.30	173.15	7384.32	153.84	7612.20	126.87
7000	7711.92	214.22	7831.74	186.47	7952.64	165.68	8197.80	136.63
7500	8262.72	229.52	8391.18	199.79	8520.48	177.51	8783.40	146.39
8000	8813.52	244.82	8950.62	213.11	9088.80	189.35	9369.00	156.15
8500	9364.32	260.12	9510.06	226.43	9656.64	201.18	9954.60	165.91
9000	9915.48	275.43	10069.08	239.74	10224.48	213.01	10540.20	175.67
10000	11017.08	306.03	11187.96	266.38	11360.64	236.68	11711.40	195.19
11000	12118.68	336.63	12306.84	293.02	12496.80	260.35	12882.60	214.71
12000	13220.64	367.24	13425.72	319.66	13632.96	284.02	14053.80	234.23
13000	14322.24	397.84	14544.60	346.30	14769.12	307.69	15225.00	253.75
14000	15423.84	428.44	15663.48	372.94	15905.28	331.36	16396.20	273.27
15000	16525.80	459.05	16782.36	399.58	17041.44	355.03	17567.40	292.79
16000	17627.40	489.65	17901.24	426.22	18177.60	378.70	18738.00	312.30
17000	18729.00	520.25	19020.12	452.86	19313.76	402.37	19909.20	331.82
18000	19830.96	550.86	20138.58	479.49	20449.44	426.03	21080.40	351.34
19000	20932.56	581.46	21257.46	506.13	21585.60	449.70	22251.60	370.86
20000	22034.52	612.07	22376.34	532.77	22721.76	473.37	23422.80	390.38
21000	23136.12	642.67	23495.22	559.41	23857.92	497.04	24594.00	409.90
22000	24237.72	673.27	24614.10	586.05	24994.08	520.71	25765.20	429.42
23000	25339.68	703.88	25732.98	612.69	26130.24	544.38	26936.40	448.94
24000	26441.28	734.48	26851.86	639.33	27266.40	568.05	28107.60	468.46
25000	27542.88	765.08	27970.74	665.97	28402.56	591.72	29278.80	487.98

6.50% ANNUAL PERCENTAGE RATE

LOAN AMT	12 MONTHS TOTAL NOTE	12 MONTHS MONTHLY PAYMENT	18 MONTHS TOTAL NOTE	18 MONTHS MONTHLY PAYMENT	24 MONTHS TOTAL NOTE	24 MONTHS MONTHLY PAYMENT	30 MONTHS TOTAL NOTE	30 MONTHS MONTHLY PAYMENT
1	.96	.08	.90	.05	.96	.04	.90	.03
2	2.04	.17	1.98	.11	1.92	.08	2.10	.07
3	3.00	.25	3.06	.17	3.12	.13	3.00	.10
4	4.08	.34	4.14	.23	4.08	.17	4.20	.14
5	5.16	.43	5.22	.29	5.28	.22	5.40	.18
6	6.12	.51	6.30	.35	6.24	.26	6.30	.21
7	7.20	.60	7.20	.40	7.44	.31	7.50	.25
8	8.28	.69	8.28	.46	8.40	.35	8.40	.28
9	9.24	.77	9.36	.52	9.60	.40	9.60	.32
10	10.32	.86	10.44	.58	10.56	.44	10.80	.36
20	20.64	1.72	20.88	1.16	21.36	.89	21.60	.72
30	30.96	2.58	31.50	1.75	31.92	1.33	32.40	1.08
40	41.40	3.45	41.94	2.33	42.72	1.78	43.20	1.44
50	51.72	4.31	52.56	2.92	53.28	2.22	54.30	1.81
60	62.04	5.17	63.00	3.50	64.08	2.67	65.10	2.17
70	72.48	6.04	73.62	4.09	74.64	3.11	75.90	2.53
80	82.80	6.90	84.06	4.67	85.44	3.56	86.70	2.89
90	93.12	7.76	94.68	5.26	96.00	4.00	97.50	3.25
100	103.44	8.62	105.12	5.84	106.80	4.45	108.60	3.62
200	207.00	17.25	210.42	11.69	213.60	8.90	217.20	7.24
300	310.56	25.88	315.54	17.53	320.64	13.36	325.80	10.86
400	414.12	34.51	420.84	23.38	427.44	17.81	434.40	14.48
500	517.68	43.14	525.96	29.22	534.48	22.27	543.00	18.10
600	621.24	51.77	631.26	35.07	641.28	26.72	651.60	21.72
700	724.80	60.40	736.56	40.92	748.32	31.18	760.20	25.34
800	828.36	69.03	841.68	46.76	855.12	35.63	868.80	28.96
900	931.92	77.66	946.98	52.61	962.16	40.09	977.40	32.58
1000	1035.48	86.29	1052.10	58.45	1068.96	44.54	1086.00	36.20
1500	1553.28	129.44	1578.24	87.68	1603.44	66.81	1629.00	54.30
2000	2071.08	172.59	2104.38	116.91	2138.16	89.09	2172.00	72.40
2500	2588.88	215.74	2630.52	146.14	2672.64	111.36	2715.30	90.51
3000	3106.56	258.88	3156.66	175.37	3207.12	133.63	3258.30	108.61
3500	3624.36	302.03	3682.80	204.60	3741.84	155.91	3801.30	126.71
4000	4142.16	345.18	4208.94	233.83	4276.32	178.18	4344.30	144.81
4500	4659.96	388.33	4735.08	263.06	4810.80	200.45	4887.60	162.92
5000	5177.76	431.48	5261.22	292.29	5345.52	222.73	5430.60	181.02
5500	5695.56	474.63	5787.18	321.51	5880.00	245.00	5973.60	199.12
6000	6213.24	517.77	6313.32	350.74	6414.48	267.27	6516.60	217.22
6500	6731.04	560.92	6839.46	379.97	6949.20	289.55	7059.90	235.33
7000	7248.84	604.07	7365.60	409.20	7483.68	311.82	7602.90	253.43
7500	7766.64	647.22	7891.74	438.43	8018.16	334.09	8145.90	271.53
8000	8284.44	690.37	8417.88	467.66	8552.88	356.37	8688.90	289.63
8500	8802.12	733.51	8944.02	496.89	9087.36	378.64	9232.20	307.74
9000	9319.92	776.66	9470.16	526.12	9621.84	400.91	9775.20	325.84
10000	10355.52	862.96	10522.44	584.58	10691.04	445.46	10861.20	362.04
11000	11391.12	949.26	11574.54	643.03	11760.00	490.00	11947.50	398.25
12000	12426.60	1035.55	12626.82	701.49	12829.20	534.55	13033.50	434.45
13000	13462.20	1121.85	13679.10	759.95	13898.40	579.10	14119.80	470.66
14000	14497.68	1208.14	14731.38	818.41	14967.36	623.64	15205.80	506.86
15000	15533.28	1294.44	15783.66	876.87	16036.56	668.19	16292.10	543.07
16000	16568.88	1380.74	16835.76	935.32	17105.76	712.74	17378.10	579.27
17000	17604.36	1467.03	17888.04	993.78	18174.72	757.28	18464.40	615.48
18000	18639.96	1553.33	18940.32	1052.24	19243.92	801.83	19550.40	651.68
19000	19675.56	1639.63	19992.60	1110.70	20312.88	846.37	20636.70	687.89
20000	20711.04	1725.92	21044.88	1169.16	21382.08	890.92	21722.70	724.09
21000	21746.64	1812.22	22097.16	1227.62	22451.28	935.47	22809.00	760.30
22000	22782.24	1898.52	23149.26	1286.07	23520.24	980.01	23895.00	796.50
23000	23817.72	1984.81	24201.54	1344.53	24589.44	1024.56	24981.30	832.71
24000	24853.32	2071.11	25253.82	1402.99	25658.64	1069.11	26067.30	868.91
25000	25888.92	2157.41	26306.10	1461.45	26727.60	1113.65	27153.60	905.12

ANNUAL PERCENTAGE RATE **6.50%**

LOAN AMT	36 MONTHS TOTAL NOTE	36 MONTHS MONTHLY PAYMENT	42 MONTHS TOTAL NOTE	42 MONTHS MONTHLY PAYMENT	48 MONTHS TOTAL NOTE	48 MONTHS MONTHLY PAYMENT	60 MONTHS TOTAL NOTE	60 MONTHS MONTHLY PAYMENT
1	1.08	.03	.84	.02	.96	.02	.60	.01
2	2.16	.06	2.10	.05	1.92	.04	1.80	.03
3	3.24	.09	3.36	.08	3.36	.07	3.00	.05
4	4.32	.12	4.20	.10	4.32	.09	4.20	.07
5	5.40	.15	5.46	.13	5.28	.11	5.40	.09
6	6.48	.18	6.72	.16	6.72	.14	6.60	.11
7	7.56	.21	7.56	.18	7.68	.16	7.80	.13
8	8.64	.24	8.82	.21	8.64	.18	9.00	.15
9	9.72	.27	10.08	.24	10.08	.21	10.20	.17
10	10.80	.30	10.92	.26	11.04	.23	11.40	.19
20	21.96	.61	22.26	.53	22.56	.47	23.40	.39
30	32.76	.91	33.60	.80	34.08	.71	34.80	.58
40	43.92	1.22	44.52	1.06	45.12	.94	46.80	.78
50	55.08	1.53	55.86	1.33	56.64	1.18	58.20	.97
60	65.88	1.83	67.20	1.60	68.16	1.42	70.20	1.17
70	77.04	2.14	78.12	1.86	79.68	1.66	81.60	1.36
80	88.20	2.45	89.46	2.13	90.72	1.89	93.60	1.56
90	99.00	2.75	100.80	2.40	102.24	2.13	105.60	1.76
100	110.16	3.06	111.72	2.66	113.76	2.37	117.00	1.95
200	220.32	6.12	223.86	5.33	227.52	4.74	234.60	3.91
300	330.84	9.19	336.00	8.00	341.28	7.11	351.60	5.86
400	441.00	12.25	448.14	10.67	455.04	9.48	469.20	7.82
500	551.52	15.32	560.28	13.34	568.80	11.85	586.80	9.78
600	661.68	18.38	672.42	16.01	682.56	14.22	703.80	11.73
700	772.20	21.45	784.14	18.67	796.80	16.60	821.40	13.69
800	882.36	24.51	896.28	21.34	910.56	18.97	939.00	15.65
900	992.88	27.58	1008.42	24.01	1024.32	21.34	1056.00	17.60
1000	1103.04	30.64	1120.56	26.68	1138.08	23.71	1173.60	19.56
1500	1654.92	45.97	1680.84	40.02	1707.36	35.57	1760.40	29.34
2000	2206.44	61.29	2241.12	53.36	2276.16	47.42	2347.80	39.13
2500	2758.32	76.62	2801.82	66.71	2845.44	59.28	2934.60	48.91
3000	3309.84	91.94	3362.10	80.05	3414.72	71.14	3521.40	58.69
3500	3861.72	107.27	3922.38	93.39	3984.00	83.00	4108.80	68.48
4000	4413.24	122.59	4482.66	106.73	4552.80	94.85	4695.60	78.26
4500	4965.12	137.92	5043.36	120.08	5122.08	106.71	5282.40	88.04
5000	5516.64	153.24	5603.64	133.42	5691.36	118.57	5869.80	97.83
5500	6068.16	168.56	6163.92	146.76	6260.64	130.43	6456.60	107.61
6000	6620.04	183.89	6724.20	160.10	6829.44	142.28	7043.40	117.39
6500	7171.56	199.21	7284.48	173.44	7398.72	154.14	7630.20	127.17
7000	7723.44	214.54	7845.18	186.79	7968.00	166.00	8217.60	136.96
7500	8274.96	229.86	8405.46	200.13	8537.28	177.86	8804.40	146.74
8000	8826.84	245.19	8965.74	213.47	9106.08	189.71	9391.20	156.52
8500	9378.36	260.51	9526.02	226.81	9675.36	201.57	9978.60	166.31
9000	9930.24	275.84	10086.72	240.16	10244.64	213.43	10565.40	176.09
10000	11033.64	306.49	11207.28	266.84	11382.72	237.14	11739.60	195.66
11000	12136.68	337.13	12328.26	293.53	12521.28	260.86	12913.20	215.22
12000	13240.08	367.78	13448.82	320.21	13659.36	284.57	14087.40	234.79
13000	14343.48	398.43	14569.38	346.89	14797.92	308.29	15261.00	254.35
14000	15446.88	429.08	15690.36	373.58	15936.00	332.00	16435.20	273.92
15000	16550.28	459.73	16810.92	400.26	17074.56	355.72	17609.40	293.49
16000	17653.68	490.38	17931.90	426.95	18212.64	379.43	18783.00	313.05
17000	18757.08	521.03	19052.46	453.63	19351.20	403.15	19957.20	332.62
18000	19860.48	551.68	20173.44	480.32	20489.28	426.86	21131.40	352.19
19000	20963.88	582.33	21294.00	507.00	21627.84	450.58	22305.00	371.75
20000	22067.28	612.98	22414.98	533.69	22765.92	474.29	23479.20	391.32
21000	23170.32	643.62	23535.54	560.37	23904.48	498.01	24652.80	410.88
22000	24273.72	674.27	24656.52	587.06	25042.56	521.72	25827.00	430.45
23000	25377.12	704.92	25777.08	613.74	26181.12	545.44	27001.20	450.02
24000	26480.52	735.57	26898.06	640.43	27319.20	569.15	28174.80	469.58
25000	27583.92	766.22	28018.62	667.11	28457.76	592.87	29349.00	489.15

6.60% ANNUAL PERCENTAGE RATE

LOAN AMT	12 MONTHS TOTAL NOTE	12 MONTHS MONTHLY PAYMENT	18 MONTHS TOTAL NOTE	18 MONTHS MONTHLY PAYMENT	24 MONTHS TOTAL NOTE	24 MONTHS MONTHLY PAYMENT	30 MONTHS TOTAL NOTE	30 MONTHS MONTHLY PAYMENT
1	.96	.08	.90	.05	.96	.04	.90	.03
2	2.04	.17	1.98	.11	1.92	.08	2.10	.07
3	3.00	.25	3.06	.17	3.12	.13	3.00	.10
4	4.08	.34	4.14	.23	4.08	.17	4.20	.14
5	5.16	.43	5.22	.29	5.28	.22	5.40	.18
6	6.12	.51	6.30	.35	6.24	.26	6.30	.21
7	7.20	.60	7.20	.40	7.44	.31	7.50	.25
8	8.28	.69	8.28	.46	8.40	.35	8.70	.29
9	9.24	.77	9.36	.52	9.60	.40	9.60	.32
10	10.32	.86	10.44	.58	10.56	.44	10.80	.36
20	20.64	1.72	21.06	1.17	21.36	.89	21.60	.72
30	31.08	2.59	31.50	1.75	31.92	1.33	32.40	1.08
40	41.40	3.45	42.12	2.34	42.72	1.78	43.50	1.45
50	51.72	4.31	52.56	2.92	53.28	2.22	54.30	1.81
60	62.16	5.18	63.18	3.51	64.08	2.67	65.10	2.17
70	72.48	6.04	73.62	4.09	74.88	3.12	75.90	2.53
80	82.80	6.90	84.24	4.68	85.44	3.56	87.00	2.90
90	93.24	7.77	94.68	5.26	96.24	4.01	97.80	3.26
100	103.56	8.63	105.30	5.85	106.80	4.45	108.60	3.62
200	207.12	17.26	210.60	11.70	213.84	8.91	217.50	7.25
300	310.80	25.90	315.90	17.55	320.88	13.37	326.10	10.87
400	414.36	34.53	421.20	23.40	427.92	17.83	435.00	14.50
500	518.04	43.17	526.50	29.25	534.96	22.29	543.60	18.12
600	621.60	51.80	631.80	35.10	642.00	26.75	652.50	21.75
700	725.16	60.43	737.10	40.95	749.04	31.21	761.10	25.37
800	828.84	69.07	842.40	46.80	856.08	35.67	870.00	29.00
900	932.40	77.70	947.70	52.65	963.12	40.13	978.60	32.62
1000	1036.08	86.34	1053.00	58.50	1070.16	44.59	1087.50	36.25
1500	1554.12	129.51	1579.50	87.75	1605.12	66.88	1631.10	54.37
2000	2072.16	172.68	2106.00	117.00	2140.32	89.18	2175.00	72.50
2500	2590.20	215.85	2632.50	146.25	2675.28	111.47	2718.60	90.62
3000	3108.24	259.02	3159.18	175.51	3210.48	133.77	3262.50	108.75
3500	3626.28	302.19	3685.68	204.76	3745.68	156.07	3806.10	126.87
4000	4144.32	345.36	4212.18	234.01	4280.64	178.36	4350.00	145.00
4500	4662.48	388.54	4738.68	263.26	4815.84	200.66	4893.60	163.12
5000	5180.52	431.71	5265.18	292.51	5350.80	222.95	5437.50	181.25
5500	5698.56	474.88	5791.68	321.76	5886.00	245.25	5981.10	199.37
6000	6216.60	518.05	6318.36	351.02	6420.96	267.54	6525.00	217.50
6500	6734.64	561.22	6844.86	380.27	6956.16	289.84	7068.60	235.62
7000	7252.68	604.39	7371.36	409.52	7491.36	312.14	7612.50	253.75
7500	7770.72	647.56	7897.86	438.77	8026.32	334.43	8156.10	271.87
8000	8288.76	690.73	8424.36	468.02	8561.52	356.73	8700.00	290.00
8500	8806.92	733.91	8950.86	497.27	9096.48	379.02	9243.60	308.12
9000	9324.96	777.08	9477.54	526.53	9631.68	401.32	9787.50	326.25
10000	10361.04	863.42	10530.54	585.03	10701.84	445.91	10875.00	362.50
11000	11397.12	949.76	11583.54	643.53	11772.00	490.50	11962.50	398.75
12000	12433.20	1036.10	12636.72	702.04	12842.16	535.09	13050.00	435.00
13000	13469.40	1122.45	13689.72	760.54	13912.32	579.68	14137.50	471.25
14000	14505.48	1208.79	14742.72	819.04	14982.72	624.28	15225.00	507.50
15000	15541.56	1295.13	15795.90	877.55	16052.88	668.87	16312.50	543.75
16000	16577.64	1381.47	16848.90	936.05	17123.04	713.46	17400.00	580.00
17000	17613.84	1467.82	17901.90	994.55	18193.20	758.05	18487.50	616.25
18000	18649.92	1554.16	18955.08	1053.06	19263.36	802.64	19575.00	652.50
19000	19686.00	1640.50	20008.08	1111.56	20333.52	847.23	20662.50	688.75
20000	20722.08	1726.84	21061.08	1170.06	21403.68	891.82	21750.00	725.00
21000	21758.28	1813.19	22114.26	1228.57	22474.08	936.42	22837.50	761.25
22000	22794.36	1899.53	23167.26	1287.07	23544.24	981.01	23925.00	797.50
23000	23830.44	1985.87	24220.26	1345.57	24614.40	1025.60	25012.50	833.75
24000	24866.52	2072.21	25273.44	1404.08	25684.56	1070.19	26100.00	870.00
25000	25902.72	2158.56	26326.44	1462.58	26754.72	1114.78	27187.50	906.25

Appendix "D"

169

ANNUAL PERCENTAGE RATE **6.60%**

LOAN AMT	36 MONTHS TOTAL NOTE	36 MONTHS MONTHLY PAYMENT	42 MONTHS TOTAL NOTE	42 MONTHS MONTHLY PAYMENT	48 MONTHS TOTAL NOTE	48 MONTHS MONTHLY PAYMENT	60 MONTHS TOTAL NOTE	60 MONTHS MONTHLY PAYMENT
1	1.08	.03	.84	.02	.96	.02	.60	.01
2	2.16	.06	2.10	.05	1.92	.04	1.80	.03
3	3.24	.09	3.36	.08	3.36	.07	3.00	.05
4	4.32	.12	4.20	.10	4.32	.09	4.20	.07
5	5.40	.15	5.46	.13	5.28	.11	5.40	.09
6	6.48	.18	6.72	.16	6.72	.14	6.60	.11
7	7.56	.21	7.56	.18	7.68	.16	7.80	.13
8	8.64	.24	8.82	.21	9.12	.19	9.00	.15
9	9.72	.27	10.08	.24	10.08	.21	10.20	.17
10	10.80	.30	10.92	.26	11.04	.23	11.40	.19
20	21.96	.61	22.26	.53	22.56	.47	23.40	.39
30	33.12	.92	33.60	.80	34.08	.71	34.80	.58
40	43.92	1.22	44.52	1.06	45.60	.95	46.80	.78
50	55.08	1.53	55.86	1.33	56.64	1.18	58.80	.98
60	66.24	1.84	67.20	1.60	68.16	1.42	70.20	1.17
70	77.04	2.14	78.54	1.87	79.68	1.66	82.20	1.37
80	88.20	2.45	89.46	2.13	91.20	1.90	93.60	1.56
90	99.36	2.76	100.80	2.40	102.24	2.13	105.60	1.76
100	110.16	3.06	112.14	2.67	113.76	2.37	117.60	1.96
200	220.68	6.13	224.28	5.34	228.00	4.75	235.20	3.92
300	331.20	9.20	336.42	8.01	341.76	7.12	352.80	5.88
400	441.72	12.27	448.98	10.69	456.00	9.50	470.40	7.84
500	552.24	15.34	561.12	13.36	570.24	11.88	588.00	9.80
600	662.76	18.41	673.26	16.03	684.00	14.25	705.60	11.76
700	773.28	21.48	785.82	18.71	798.24	16.63	823.20	13.72
800	883.80	24.55	897.96	21.38	912.00	19.00	941.40	15.69
900	994.32	27.62	1010.10	24.05	1026.24	21.38	1059.00	17.65
1000	1104.84	30.69	1122.66	26.73	1140.48	23.76	1176.60	19.61
1500	1657.44	46.04	1683.78	40.09	1710.72	35.64	1764.60	29.41
2000	2209.68	61.38	2245.32	53.46	2280.96	47.52	2353.20	39.22
2500	2762.28	76.73	2806.44	66.82	2851.20	59.40	2941.80	49.03
3000	3314.88	92.08	3367.98	80.19	3421.44	71.28	3529.80	58.83
3500	3867.48	107.43	3929.10	93.55	3991.68	83.16	4118.40	68.64
4000	4419.72	122.77	4490.64	106.92	4561.92	95.04	4707.00	78.45
4500	4972.32	138.12	5051.76	120.28	5132.16	106.92	5295.00	88.25
5000	5524.92	153.47	5613.30	133.65	5702.40	118.80	5883.60	98.06
5500	6077.16	168.81	6174.42	147.01	6272.64	130.68	6472.20	107.87
6000	6629.76	184.16	6735.96	160.38	6842.88	142.56	7060.20	117.67
6500	7182.36	199.51	7297.08	173.74	7413.12	154.44	7648.80	127.48
7000	7734.96	214.86	7858.62	187.11	7983.36	166.32	8237.40	137.29
7500	8287.20	230.20	8419.74	200.47	8553.60	178.20	8825.40	147.09
8000	8839.80	245.55	8981.28	213.84	9123.84	190.08	9414.00	156.90
8500	9392.40	260.90	9542.40	227.20	9694.08	201.96	10002.60	166.71
9000	9945.00	276.25	10103.94	240.57	10264.32	213.84	10590.60	176.51
10000	11049.84	306.94	11226.60	267.30	11405.28	237.61	11767.80	196.13
11000	12154.68	337.63	12349.26	294.03	12545.76	261.37	12944.40	215.74
12000	13259.88	368.33	13471.92	320.76	13686.24	285.13	14121.00	235.35
13000	14364.72	399.02	14594.58	347.49	14826.72	308.89	15297.60	254.96
14000	15469.92	429.72	15717.24	374.22	15967.20	332.65	16474.80	274.58
15000	16574.76	460.41	16839.90	400.95	17107.68	356.41	17651.40	294.19
16000	17679.96	491.11	17962.56	427.68	18248.16	380.17	18828.00	313.80
17000	18784.80	521.80	19085.22	454.41	19388.64	403.93	20005.20	333.42
18000	19890.00	552.50	20207.88	481.14	20529.12	427.69	21181.80	353.03
19000	20994.84	583.19	21330.54	507.87	21670.08	451.46	22358.40	372.64
20000	22100.04	613.89	22453.20	534.60	22810.56	475.22	23535.60	392.26
21000	23204.88	644.58	23575.86	561.33	23951.04	498.98	24712.20	411.87
22000	24309.72	675.27	24698.52	588.06	25091.52	522.74	25888.80	431.48
23000	25414.92	705.97	25821.18	614.79	26232.00	546.50	27065.40	451.09
24000	26519.76	736.66	26944.26	641.53	27372.48	570.26	28242.60	470.71
25000	27624.96	767.36	28066.92	668.26	28512.96	594.02	29419.20	490.32

6.70% ANNUAL PERCENTAGE RATE

LOAN AMT	12 MONTHS TOTAL NOTE	12 MONTHS MONTHLY PAYMENT	18 MONTHS TOTAL NOTE	18 MONTHS MONTHLY PAYMENT	24 MONTHS TOTAL NOTE	24 MONTHS MONTHLY PAYMENT	30 MONTHS TOTAL NOTE	30 MONTHS MONTHLY PAYMENT
1	.96	.08	.90	.05	.96	.04	.90	.03
2	2.04	.17	1.98	.11	1.92	.08	2.10	.07
3	3.00	.25	3.06	.17	3.12	.13	3.00	.10
4	4.08	.34	4.14	.23	4.08	.17	4.20	.14
5	5.16	.43	5.22	.29	5.28	.22	5.40	.18
6	6.12	.51	6.30	.35	6.24	.26	6.30	.21
7	7.20	.60	7.20	.40	7.44	.31	7.50	.25
8	8.28	.69	8.28	.46	8.40	.35	8.70	.29
9	9.24	.77	9.36	.52	9.60	.40	9.60	.32
10	10.32	.86	10.44	.58	10.56	.44	10.80	.36
20	20.64	1.72	21.06	1.17	21.36	.89	21.60	.72
30	31.08	2.59	31.50	1.75	31.92	1.33	32.40	1.08
40	41.40	3.45	42.12	2.34	42.72	1.78	43.50	1.45
50	51.72	4.31	52.56	2.92	53.52	2.23	54.30	1.81
60	62.16	5.18	63.18	3.51	64.08	2.67	65.10	2.17
70	72.48	6.04	73.62	4.09	74.88	3.12	76.20	2.54
80	82.92	6.91	84.24	4.68	85.68	3.57	87.00	2.90
90	93.24	7.77	94.68	5.26	96.24	4.01	97.80	3.26
100	103.56	8.63	105.30	5.85	107.04	4.46	108.60	3.62
200	207.24	17.27	210.60	11.70	214.08	8.92	217.50	7.25
300	310.92	25.91	316.08	17.56	321.36	13.39	326.40	10.88
400	414.60	34.55	421.38	23.41	428.40	17.85	435.30	14.51
500	518.28	43.19	526.86	29.27	535.44	22.31	544.20	18.14
600	621.96	51.83	632.16	35.12	642.72	26.78	653.10	21.77
700	725.64	60.47	737.64	40.98	749.76	31.24	762.00	25.40
800	829.32	69.11	842.94	46.83	856.80	35.70	870.90	29.03
900	932.88	77.74	948.42	52.69	964.08	40.17	979.80	32.66
1000	1036.56	86.38	1053.72	58.54	1071.12	44.63	1088.70	36.29
1500	1554.96	129.58	1580.76	87.82	1606.80	66.95	1633.20	54.44
2000	2073.24	172.77	2107.62	117.09	2142.48	89.27	2177.70	72.59
2500	2591.64	215.97	2634.66	146.37	2678.16	111.59	2721.90	90.73
3000	3109.92	259.16	3161.52	175.64	3213.84	133.91	3266.40	108.88
3500	3628.20	302.35	3688.56	204.92	3749.28	156.22	3810.90	127.03
4000	4146.60	345.55	4215.42	234.19	4284.96	178.54	4355.40	145.18
4500	4664.88	388.74	4742.28	263.46	4820.64	200.86	4899.90	163.33
5000	5183.28	431.94	5269.32	292.74	5356.32	223.18	5444.10	181.47
5500	5701.56	475.13	5796.18	322.01	5892.00	245.50	5988.60	199.62
6000	6219.96	518.33	6323.22	351.29	6427.68	267.82	6533.10	217.77
6500	6738.24	561.52	6850.08	380.56	6963.12	290.13	7077.60	235.92
7000	7256.52	604.71	7377.12	409.84	7498.80	312.45	7621.80	254.06
7500	7774.92	647.91	7903.98	439.11	8034.48	334.77	8166.30	272.21
8000	8293.20	691.10	8431.02	468.39	8570.16	357.09	8710.80	290.36
8500	8811.60	734.30	8957.88	497.66	9105.84	379.41	9255.30	308.51
9000	9329.88	777.49	9484.74	526.93	9641.52	401.73	9799.80	326.66
10000	10366.56	863.88	10538.64	585.48	10712.64	446.36	10888.50	362.95
11000	11403.24	950.27	11592.54	644.03	11784.00	491.00	11977.50	399.25
12000	12439.92	1036.66	12646.44	702.58	12855.36	535.64	13066.20	435.54
13000	13476.60	1123.05	13700.34	761.13	13926.48	580.27	14155.20	471.84
14000	14513.16	1209.43	14754.24	819.68	14997.84	624.91	15243.90	508.13
15000	15549.84	1295.82	15808.14	878.23	16069.20	669.55	16332.90	544.43
16000	16586.52	1382.21	16862.04	936.78	17140.32	714.18	17421.90	580.73
17000	17623.20	1468.60	17915.76	995.32	18211.68	758.82	18510.60	617.02
18000	18659.88	1554.99	18969.66	1053.87	19283.04	803.46	19599.60	653.32
19000	19696.56	1641.38	20023.56	1112.42	20354.16	848.09	20688.30	689.61
20000	20733.24	1727.77	21077.46	1170.97	21425.52	892.73	21777.30	725.91
21000	21769.80	1814.15	22131.36	1229.52	22496.88	937.37	22866.00	762.20
22000	22806.48	1900.54	23185.26	1288.07	23568.00	982.00	23955.00	798.50
23000	23843.16	1986.93	24239.16	1346.62	24639.36	1026.64	25043.70	834.79
24000	24879.84	2073.32	25293.06	1405.17	25710.72	1071.28	26132.70	871.09
25000	25916.52	2159.71	26346.78	1463.71	26781.84	1115.91	27221.70	907.39

ANNUAL PERCENTAGE RATE **6.70%**

LOAN AMT	36 MONTHS TOTAL NOTE	36 MONTHS MONTHLY PAYMENT	42 MONTHS TOTAL NOTE	42 MONTHS MONTHLY PAYMENT	48 MONTHS TOTAL NOTE	48 MONTHS MONTHLY PAYMENT	60 MONTHS TOTAL NOTE	60 MONTHS MONTHLY PAYMENT
1	1.08	.03	.84	.02	.96	.02	.60	.01
2	2.16	.06	2.10	.05	1.92	.04	1.80	.03
3	3.24	.09	3.36	.08	3.36	.07	3.00	.05
4	4.32	.12	4.20	.10	4.32	.09	4.20	.07
5	5.40	.15	5.46	.13	5.28	.11	5.40	.09
6	6.48	.18	6.72	.16	6.72	.14	6.60	.11
7	7.56	.21	7.56	.18	7.68	.16	7.80	.13
8	8.64	.24	8.82	.21	9.12	.19	9.00	.15
9	9.72	.27	10.08	.24	10.08	.21	10.20	.17
10	10.80	.30	10.92	.26	11.04	.23	11.40	.19
20	21.96	.61	22.26	.53	22.56	.47	23.40	.39
30	33.12	.92	33.60	.80	34.08	.71	34.80	.58
40	43.92	1.22	44.94	1.07	45.60	.95	46.80	.78
50	55.08	1.53	55.86	1.33	57.12	1.19	58.80	.98
60	66.24	1.84	67.20	1.60	68.16	1.42	70.20	1.17
70	77.40	2.15	78.54	1.87	79.68	1.66	82.20	1.37
80	88.20	2.45	89.88	2.14	91.20	1.90	94.20	1.57
90	99.36	2.76	100.80	2.40	102.72	2.14	105.60	1.76
100	110.52	3.07	112.14	2.67	114.24	2.38	117.60	1.96
200	221.04	6.14	224.70	5.35	228.48	4.76	235.80	3.93
300	331.92	9.22	337.26	8.03	342.72	7.14	353.40	5.89
400	442.44	12.29	449.82	10.71	456.96	9.52	471.60	7.86
500	553.32	15.37	561.96	13.38	571.20	11.90	589.20	9.82
600	663.84	18.44	674.52	16.06	685.44	14.28	707.40	11.79
700	774.36	21.51	787.08	18.74	799.68	16.66	825.60	13.76
800	885.24	24.59	899.64	21.42	913.92	19.04	943.20	15.72
900	995.76	27.66	1011.78	24.09	1028.16	21.42	1061.40	17.69
1000	1106.64	30.74	1124.34	26.77	1142.40	23.80	1179.00	19.65
1500	1659.96	46.11	1686.72	40.16	1714.08	35.71	1768.80	29.48
2000	2213.28	61.48	2249.10	53.55	2285.28	47.61	2358.60	39.31
2500	2766.60	76.85	2811.48	66.94	2856.48	59.51	2948.40	49.14
3000	3319.92	92.22	3373.44	80.32	3428.16	71.42	3538.20	58.97
3500	3873.24	107.59	3935.82	93.71	3999.36	83.32	4128.00	68.80
4000	4426.56	122.96	4498.20	107.10	4570.56	95.22	4717.80	78.63
4500	4979.88	138.33	5060.58	120.49	5142.24	107.13	5307.60	88.46
5000	5533.20	153.70	5622.96	133.88	5713.44	119.03	5897.40	98.29
5500	6086.52	169.07	6184.92	147.26	6285.12	130.94	6487.20	108.12
6000	6639.84	184.44	6747.30	160.65	6856.32	142.84	7077.00	117.95
6500	7193.16	199.81	7309.68	174.04	7427.52	154.74	7666.80	127.78
7000	7746.48	215.18	7872.06	187.43	7999.20	166.65	8256.60	137.61
7500	8299.80	230.55	8434.44	200.82	8570.40	178.55	8846.40	147.44
8000	8853.12	245.92	8996.82	214.21	9141.60	190.45	9436.20	157.27
8500	9406.44	261.29	9558.78	227.59	9713.28	202.36	10026.00	167.10
9000	9959.76	276.66	10121.16	240.98	10284.48	214.26	10615.80	176.93
10000	11066.40	307.40	11245.92	267.76	11427.36	238.07	11795.40	196.59
11000	12173.04	338.14	12370.26	294.53	12570.24	261.88	12975.00	216.25
12000	13279.68	368.88	13495.02	321.31	13712.64	285.68	14154.60	235.91
13000	14386.32	399.62	14619.78	348.09	14855.52	309.49	15334.20	255.57
14000	15492.96	430.36	15744.12	374.86	15998.40	333.30	16513.80	275.23
15000	16599.60	461.10	16868.88	401.64	17140.80	357.10	17693.40	294.89
16000	17706.24	491.84	17993.64	428.42	18283.68	380.91	18873.00	314.55
17000	18812.88	522.58	19117.98	455.19	19426.56	404.72	20052.60	334.21
18000	19919.52	553.32	20242.74	481.97	20569.44	428.53	21232.20	353.87
19000	21026.16	584.06	21367.08	508.74	21711.84	452.33	22411.80	373.53
20000	22132.80	614.80	22491.84	535.52	22854.72	476.14	23591.40	393.19
21000	23239.44	645.54	23616.60	562.30	23997.60	499.95	24771.00	412.85
22000	24346.08	676.28	24740.94	589.07	25140.48	523.76	25950.60	432.51
23000	25452.72	707.02	25865.70	615.85	26282.88	547.56	27130.20	452.17
24000	26559.36	737.76	26990.46	642.63	27425.76	571.37	28309.80	471.83
25000	27666.00	768.50	28114.80	669.40	28568.64	595.18	29489.40	491.49

6.75% ANNUAL PERCENTAGE RATE

LOAN AMT	12 MONTHS TOTAL NOTE	12 MONTHS MONTHLY PAYMENT	18 MONTHS TOTAL NOTE	18 MONTHS MONTHLY PAYMENT	24 MONTHS TOTAL NOTE	24 MONTHS MONTHLY PAYMENT	30 MONTHS TOTAL NOTE	30 MONTHS MONTHLY PAYMENT
1	.96	.08	.90	.05	.96	.04	.90	.03
2	2.04	.17	1.98	.11	1.92	.08	2.10	.07
3	3.00	.25	3.06	.17	3.12	.13	3.00	.10
4	4.08	.34	4.14	.23	4.08	.17	4.20	.14
5	5.16	.43	5.22	.29	5.28	.22	5.40	.18
6	6.12	.51	6.30	.35	6.24	.26	6.30	.21
7	7.20	.60	7.38	.41	7.44	.31	7.50	.25
8	8.28	.69	8.28	.46	8.40	.35	8.70	.29
9	9.24	.77	9.36	.52	9.60	.40	9.60	.32
10	10.32	.86	10.44	.58	10.56	.44	10.80	.36
20	20.64	1.72	21.06	1.17	21.36	.89	21.60	.72
30	31.08	2.59	31.50	1.75	31.92	1.33	32.40	1.08
40	41.40	3.45	42.12	2.34	42.72	1.78	43.50	1.45
50	51.84	4.32	52.56	2.92	53.52	2.23	54.30	1.81
60	62.16	5.18	63.18	3.51	64.08	2.67	65.10	2.17
70	72.48	6.04	73.80	4.10	74.88	3.12	76.20	2.54
80	82.92	6.91	84.24	4.68	85.68	3.57	87.00	2.90
90	93.24	7.77	94.86	5.27	96.24	4.01	97.80	3.26
100	103.68	8.64	105.30	5.85	107.04	4.46	108.90	3.63
200	207.36	17.28	210.78	11.71	214.32	8.93	217.80	7.26
300	311.04	25.92	316.26	17.57	321.36	13.39	326.70	10.89
400	414.72	34.56	421.56	23.42	428.64	17.86	435.60	14.52
500	518.40	43.20	527.04	29.28	535.68	22.32	544.50	18.15
600	622.08	51.84	632.52	35.14	642.96	26.79	653.70	21.79
700	725.76	60.48	738.00	41.00	750.24	31.26	762.60	25.42
800	829.44	69.12	843.30	46.85	857.28	35.72	871.50	29.05
900	933.24	77.77	948.78	52.71	964.56	40.19	980.40	32.68
1000	1036.92	86.41	1054.26	58.57	1071.60	44.65	1089.30	36.31
1500	1555.32	129.61	1581.30	87.85	1607.52	66.98	1634.10	54.47
2000	2073.84	172.82	2108.52	117.14	2143.44	89.31	2178.90	72.63
2500	2592.24	216.02	2635.56	146.42	2679.36	111.64	2723.70	90.79
3000	3110.76	259.23	3162.78	175.71	3215.28	133.97	3268.50	108.95
3500	3629.28	302.44	3690.00	205.00	3751.20	156.30	3813.30	127.11
4000	4147.68	345.64	4217.04	234.28	4287.12	178.63	4358.10	145.27
4500	4666.20	388.85	4744.26	263.57	4823.04	200.96	4902.90	163.43
5000	5184.60	432.05	5271.30	292.85	5358.96	223.29	5447.70	181.59
5500	5703.12	475.26	5798.52	322.14	5894.88	245.62	5992.50	199.75
6000	6221.52	518.46	6325.56	351.42	6430.80	267.95	6537.30	217.91
6500	6740.04	561.67	6852.78	380.71	6966.72	290.28	7081.80	236.06
7000	7258.56	604.88	7380.00	410.00	7502.64	312.61	7626.60	254.22
7500	7776.96	648.08	7907.04	439.28	8038.56	334.94	8171.40	272.38
8000	8295.48	691.29	8434.26	468.57	8574.48	357.27	8716.20	290.54
8500	8813.88	734.49	8961.30	497.85	9110.40	379.60	9261.00	308.70
9000	9332.40	777.70	9488.52	527.14	9646.32	401.93	9805.80	326.86
10000	10369.32	864.11	10542.78	585.71	10718.16	446.59	10895.40	363.18
11000	11406.24	950.52	11597.04	644.28	11790.00	491.25	11985.00	399.50
12000	12443.16	1036.93	12651.30	702.85	12861.84	535.91	13074.60	435.82
13000	13480.20	1123.35	13705.56	761.42	13933.68	580.57	14163.90	472.13
14000	14517.12	1209.76	14760.00	820.00	15005.52	625.23	15253.50	508.45
15000	15554.04	1296.17	15814.26	878.57	16077.12	669.88	16343.10	544.77
16000	16590.96	1382.58	16868.52	937.14	17148.96	714.54	17432.70	581.09
17000	17627.88	1468.99	17922.78	995.71	18220.80	759.20	18522.30	617.41
18000	18664.80	1555.40	18977.04	1054.28	19292.64	803.86	19611.90	653.73
19000	19701.72	1641.81	20031.30	1112.85	20364.48	848.52	20701.20	690.04
20000	20738.76	1728.23	21085.56	1171.42	21436.32	893.18	21790.80	726.36
21000	21775.68	1814.64	22140.00	1230.00	22508.16	937.84	22880.40	762.68
22000	22812.60	1901.05	23194.26	1288.57	23580.00	982.50	23970.00	799.00
23000	23849.52	1987.46	24248.52	1347.14	24651.84	1027.16	25059.60	835.32
24000	24886.44	2073.87	25302.78	1405.71	25723.68	1071.82	26149.20	871.64
25000	25923.36	2160.28	26357.04	1464.28	26795.52	1116.48	27238.50	907.95

ANNUAL PERCENTAGE RATE **6.75%**

LOAN AMT	36 MONTHS TOTAL NOTE	36 MONTHS MONTHLY PAYMENT	42 MONTHS TOTAL NOTE	42 MONTHS MONTHLY PAYMENT	48 MONTHS TOTAL NOTE	48 MONTHS MONTHLY PAYMENT	60 MONTHS TOTAL NOTE	60 MONTHS MONTHLY PAYMENT
1	1.08	.03	.84	.02	.96	.02	.60	.01
2	2.16	.06	2.10	.05	1.92	.04	1.80	.03
3	3.24	.09	3.36	.08	3.36	.07	3.00	.05
4	4.32	.12	4.20	.10	4.32	.09	4.20	.07
5	5.40	.15	5.46	.13	5.28	.11	5.40	.09
6	6.48	.18	6.72	.16	6.72	.14	6.60	.11
7	7.56	.21	7.56	.18	7.68	.16	7.80	.13
8	8.64	.24	8.82	.21	9.12	.19	9.00	.15
9	9.72	.27	10.08	.24	10.08	.21	10.20	.17
10	10.80	.30	10.92	.26	11.04	.23	11.40	.19
20	21.96	.61	22.26	.53	22.56	.47	23.40	.39
30	33.12	.92	33.60	.80	34.08	.71	35.40	.59
40	44.28	1.23	44.94	1.07	45.60	.95	46.80	.78
50	55.08	1.53	55.86	1.33	57.12	1.19	58.80	.98
60	66.24	1.84	67.20	1.60	68.16	1.42	70.80	1.18
70	77.40	2.15	78.54	1.87	79.68	1.66	82.20	1.37
80	88.56	2.46	89.88	2.14	91.20	1.90	94.20	1.57
90	99.36	2.76	101.22	2.41	102.72	2.14	106.20	1.77
100	110.52	3.07	112.14	2.67	114.24	2.38	117.60	1.96
200	221.40	6.15	224.70	5.35	228.48	4.76	235.80	3.93
300	331.92	9.22	337.26	8.03	342.72	7.14	354.00	5.90
400	442.80	12.30	449.82	10.71	457.44	9.53	472.20	7.87
500	553.68	15.38	562.38	13.39	571.68	11.91	590.40	9.84
600	664.20	18.45	674.94	16.07	685.92	14.29	708.60	11.81
700	775.08	21.53	787.50	18.75	800.64	16.68	826.20	13.77
800	885.96	24.61	900.06	21.43	914.88	19.06	944.40	15.74
900	996.48	27.68	1012.62	24.11	1029.12	21.44	1062.60	17.71
1000	1107.36	30.76	1125.18	26.79	1143.84	23.83	1180.80	19.68
1500	1661.04	46.14	1687.98	40.19	1715.52	35.74	1771.20	29.52
2000	2214.72	61.52	2250.78	53.59	2287.68	47.66	2361.60	39.36
2500	2768.40	76.90	2813.58	66.99	2859.36	59.57	2952.00	49.20
3000	3322.08	92.28	3376.38	80.39	3431.52	71.49	3543.00	59.05
3500	3876.12	107.67	3939.18	93.79	4003.20	83.40	4133.40	68.89
4000	4429.80	123.05	4501.98	107.19	4575.36	95.32	4723.80	78.73
4500	4983.48	138.43	5064.78	120.59	5147.04	107.23	5314.20	88.57
5000	5537.16	153.81	5627.58	133.99	5719.20	119.15	5904.60	98.41
5500	6090.84	169.19	6190.38	147.39	6290.88	131.06	6495.00	108.25
6000	6644.52	184.57	6753.18	160.79	6863.04	142.98	7086.00	118.10
6500	7198.20	199.95	7315.98	174.19	7434.72	154.89	7676.40	127.94
7000	7752.24	215.34	7878.78	187.59	8006.88	166.81	8266.80	137.78
7500	8305.92	230.72	8441.58	200.99	8578.56	178.72	8857.20	147.62
8000	8859.60	246.10	9004.38	214.39	9150.72	190.64	9447.60	157.46
8500	9413.28	261.48	9567.18	227.79	9722.40	202.55	10038.00	167.30
9000	9966.96	276.86	10129.98	241.19	10294.56	214.47	10629.00	177.15
10000	11074.32	307.62	11255.58	267.99	11438.40	238.30	11809.80	196.83
11000	12182.04	338.39	12381.18	294.79	12582.24	262.13	12990.60	216.51
12000	13289.40	369.15	13506.78	321.59	13726.08	285.96	14172.00	236.20
13000	14396.76	399.91	14632.38	348.39	14869.92	309.79	15352.80	255.88
14000	15504.48	430.68	15757.56	375.18	16013.76	333.62	16533.60	275.56
15000	16611.84	461.44	16883.16	401.98	17157.60	357.45	17715.00	295.25
16000	17719.20	492.20	18008.76	428.78	18301.44	381.28	18895.80	314.93
17000	18826.56	522.96	19134.36	455.58	19445.28	405.11	20076.60	334.61
18000	19934.28	553.73	20259.96	482.38	20589.12	428.94	21258.00	354.30
19000	21041.64	584.49	21385.56	509.18	21732.96	452.77	22438.80	373.98
20000	22149.00	615.25	22511.16	535.98	22876.80	476.60	23619.60	393.66
21000	23256.72	646.02	23636.76	562.78	24020.64	500.43	24801.00	413.35
22000	24364.08	676.78	24762.36	589.58	25164.48	524.26	25981.80	433.03
23000	25471.44	707.54	25887.96	616.38	26308.32	548.09	27162.60	452.71
24000	26579.16	738.31	27013.56	643.18	27452.64	571.93	28344.00	472.40
25000	27686.52	769.07	28139.16	669.98	28596.48	595.76	29524.80	492.08

6.80% ANNUAL PERCENTAGE RATE

LOAN AMT	12 MONTHS TOTAL NOTE	12 MONTHS MONTHLY PAYMENT	18 MONTHS TOTAL NOTE	18 MONTHS MONTHLY PAYMENT	24 MONTHS TOTAL NOTE	24 MONTHS MONTHLY PAYMENT	30 MONTHS TOTAL NOTE	30 MONTHS MONTHLY PAYMENT
1	.96	.08	.90	.05	.96	.04	.90	.03
2	2.04	.17	1.98	.11	1.92	.08	2.10	.07
3	3.00	.25	3.06	.17	3.12	.13	3.00	.10
4	4.08	.34	4.14	.23	4.08	.17	4.20	.14
5	5.16	.43	5.22	.29	5.28	.22	5.40	.18
6	6.12	.51	6.30	.35	6.24	.26	6.30	.21
7	7.20	.60	7.38	.41	7.44	.31	7.50	.25
8	8.28	.69	8.28	.46	8.40	.35	8.70	.29
9	9.24	.77	9.36	.52	9.60	.40	9.60	.32
10	10.32	.86	10.44	.58	10.56	.44	10.80	.36
20	20.64	1.72	21.06	1.17	21.36	.89	21.60	.72
30	31.08	2.59	31.50	1.75	32.16	1.34	32.70	1.09
40	41.40	3.45	42.12	2.34	42.72	1.78	43.50	1.45
50	51.84	4.32	52.56	2.92	53.52	2.23	54.30	1.81
60	62.16	5.18	63.18	3.51	64.32	2.68	65.40	2.18
70	72.60	6.05	73.80	4.10	74.88	3.12	76.20	2.54
80	82.92	6.91	84.24	4.68	85.68	3.57	87.00	2.90
90	93.24	7.77	94.86	5.27	96.48	4.02	98.10	3.27
100	103.68	8.64	105.30	5.85	107.04	4.46	108.90	3.63
200	207.36	17.28	210.78	11.71	214.32	8.93	217.80	7.26
300	311.16	25.93	316.26	17.57	321.60	13.40	327.00	10.90
400	414.84	34.57	421.74	23.43	428.88	17.87	435.90	14.53
500	518.52	43.21	527.22	29.29	536.16	22.34	545.10	18.17
600	622.32	51.86	632.70	35.15	643.20	26.80	654.00	21.80
700	726.00	60.50	738.18	41.01	750.48	31.27	762.90	25.43
800	829.68	69.14	843.66	46.87	857.76	35.74	872.10	29.07
900	933.48	77.79	949.14	52.73	965.04	40.21	981.00	32.70
1000	1037.16	86.43	1054.62	58.59	1072.32	44.68	1090.20	36.34
1500	1555.80	129.65	1582.02	87.89	1608.48	67.02	1635.30	54.51
2000	2074.32	172.86	2109.24	117.18	2144.64	89.36	2180.40	72.68
2500	2592.96	216.08	2636.64	146.48	2680.80	111.70	2725.50	90.85
3000	3111.60	259.30	3164.04	175.78	3216.96	134.04	3270.60	109.02
3500	3630.24	302.52	3691.26	205.07	3753.12	156.38	3815.70	127.19
4000	4148.76	345.73	4218.66	234.37	4289.28	178.72	4360.80	145.36
4500	4667.40	388.95	4746.06	263.67	4825.44	201.06	4905.90	163.53
5000	5186.04	432.17	5273.46	292.97	5361.60	223.40	5451.00	181.70
5500	5704.68	475.39	5800.68	322.26	5898.00	245.75	5996.10	199.87
6000	6223.20	518.60	6328.08	351.56	6434.16	268.09	6541.20	218.04
6500	6741.84	561.82	6855.48	380.86	6970.32	290.43	7086.30	236.21
7000	7260.48	605.04	7382.70	410.15	7506.48	312.77	7631.40	254.38
7500	7779.00	648.25	7910.10	439.45	8042.64	335.11	8176.50	272.55
8000	8297.64	691.47	8437.50	468.75	8578.80	357.45	8721.60	290.72
8500	8816.28	734.69	8964.90	498.05	9114.96	379.79	9266.70	308.89
9000	9334.92	777.91	9492.12	527.34	9651.12	402.13	9811.80	327.06
10000	10372.08	864.34	10546.92	585.94	10723.44	446.81	10902.30	363.41
11000	11409.36	950.78	11601.54	644.53	11796.00	491.50	11992.50	399.75
12000	12446.52	1037.21	12656.34	703.13	12868.32	536.18	13082.70	436.09
13000	13483.68	1123.64	13710.96	761.72	13940.64	580.86	14172.90	472.43
14000	14520.96	1210.08	14765.58	820.31	15012.96	625.54	15263.10	508.77
15000	15558.12	1296.51	15820.38	878.91	16085.28	670.22	16353.30	545.11
16000	16595.40	1382.95	16875.00	937.50	17157.84	714.91	17443.50	581.45
17000	17632.56	1469.38	17929.80	996.10	18230.16	759.59	18533.70	617.79
18000	18669.84	1555.82	18984.42	1054.69	19302.48	804.27	19623.90	654.13
19000	19707.00	1642.25	20039.04	1113.28	20374.80	848.95	20714.10	690.47
20000	20744.28	1728.69	21093.84	1171.88	21447.12	893.63	21804.60	726.82
21000	21781.44	1815.12	22148.46	1230.47	22519.68	938.32	22894.80	763.16
22000	22818.72	1901.56	23203.26	1289.07	23592.00	983.00	23985.00	799.50
23000	23855.88	1987.99	24257.88	1347.66	24664.32	1027.68	25075.20	835.84
24000	24893.04	2074.42	25312.68	1406.26	25736.64	1072.36	26165.40	872.18
25000	25930.32	2160.86	26367.30	1464.85	26808.96	1117.04	27255.60	908.52

ANNUAL PERCENTAGE RATE **6.80%**

LOAN AMT	36 MONTHS TOTAL NOTE	36 MONTHS MONTHLY PAYMENT	42 MONTHS TOTAL NOTE	42 MONTHS MONTHLY PAYMENT	48 MONTHS TOTAL NOTE	48 MONTHS MONTHLY PAYMENT	60 MONTHS TOTAL NOTE	60 MONTHS MONTHLY PAYMENT
1	1.08	.03	.84	.02	.96	.02	.60	.01
2	2.16	.06	2.10	.05	1.92	.04	1.80	.03
3	3.24	.09	3.36	.08	3.36	.07	3.00	.05
4	4.32	.12	4.20	.10	4.32	.09	4.20	.07
5	5.40	.15	5.46	.13	5.28	.11	5.40	.09
6	6.48	.18	6.72	.16	6.72	.14	6.60	.11
7	7.56	.21	7.56	.18	7.68	.16	7.80	.13
8	8.64	.24	8.82	.21	9.12	.19	9.00	.15
9	9.72	.27	10.08	.24	10.08	.21	10.20	.17
10	10.80	.30	10.92	.26	11.04	.23	11.40	.19
20	21.96	.61	22.26	.53	22.56	.47	23.40	.39
30	33.12	.92	33.60	.80	34.08	.71	35.40	.59
40	44.28	1.23	44.94	1.07	45.60	.95	46.80	.78
50	55.08	1.53	56.28	1.34	57.12	1.19	58.80	.98
60	66.24	1.84	67.20	1.60	68.64	1.43	70.80	1.18
70	77.40	2.15	78.54	1.87	79.68	1.66	82.20	1.37
80	88.56	2.46	89.88	2.14	91.20	1.90	94.20	1.57
90	99.72	2.77	101.22	2.41	102.72	2.14	106.20	1.77
100	110.52	3.07	112.56	2.68	114.24	2.38	118.20	1.97
200	221.40	6.15	225.12	5.36	228.96	4.77	236.40	3.94
300	332.28	9.23	337.68	8.04	343.20	7.15	354.60	5.91
400	443.16	12.31	450.24	10.72	457.92	9.54	472.80	7.88
500	554.04	15.39	563.22	13.41	572.16	11.92	591.00	9.85
600	664.92	18.47	675.78	16.09	686.88	14.31	709.20	11.82
700	775.80	21.55	788.34	18.77	801.12	16.69	827.40	13.79
800	886.32	24.62	900.90	21.45	915.84	19.08	945.60	15.76
900	997.20	27.70	1013.46	24.13	1030.08	21.46	1063.80	17.73
1000	1108.08	30.78	1126.44	26.82	1144.80	23.85	1182.00	19.70
1500	1662.12	46.17	1689.66	40.23	1717.44	35.78	1773.60	29.56
2000	2216.52	61.57	2252.88	53.64	2289.60	47.70	2364.60	39.41
2500	2770.56	76.96	2816.10	67.05	2862.24	59.63	2955.60	49.26
3000	3324.60	92.35	3379.32	80.46	3434.88	71.56	3547.20	59.12
3500	3879.00	107.75	3942.54	93.87	4007.04	83.48	4138.20	68.97
4000	4433.04	123.14	4505.76	107.28	4579.68	95.41	4729.20	78.82
4500	4987.08	138.53	5068.98	120.69	5152.32	107.34	5320.80	88.68
5000	5541.12	153.92	5632.62	134.11	5724.48	119.26	5911.80	98.53
5500	6095.52	169.32	6195.84	147.52	6297.12	131.19	6502.80	108.38
6000	6649.56	184.71	6759.06	160.93	6869.76	143.12	7094.40	118.24
6500	7203.60	200.10	7322.28	174.34	7441.92	155.04	7685.40	128.09
7000	7758.00	215.50	7885.50	187.75	8014.56	166.97	8276.40	137.94
7500	8312.04	230.89	8448.72	201.16	8587.20	178.90	8868.00	147.80
8000	8866.08	246.28	9011.94	214.57	9159.36	190.82	9459.00	157.65
8500	9420.12	261.67	9575.16	227.98	9732.00	202.75	10050.00	167.50
9000	9974.52	277.07	10138.38	241.39	10304.64	214.68	10641.60	177.36
10000	11082.60	307.85	11265.24	268.22	11449.44	238.53	11823.60	197.06
11000	12191.04	338.64	12391.68	295.04	12594.24	262.38	13006.20	216.77
12000	13299.12	369.42	13518.12	321.86	13739.52	286.24	14188.80	236.48
13000	14407.56	400.21	14644.56	348.68	14884.32	310.09	15371.40	256.19
14000	15516.00	431.00	15771.42	375.51	16029.12	333.94	16553.40	275.89
15000	16624.08	461.78	16897.86	402.33	17174.40	357.80	17736.00	295.60
16000	17732.52	492.57	18024.30	429.15	18319.20	381.65	18918.60	315.31
17000	18840.60	523.35	19150.74	455.97	19464.48	405.51	20100.60	335.01
18000	19949.04	554.14	20277.18	482.79	20609.28	429.36	21283.20	354.72
19000	21057.12	584.92	21404.04	509.62	21754.08	453.21	22465.80	374.43
20000	22165.56	615.71	22530.48	536.44	22899.36	477.07	23647.80	394.13
21000	23274.00	646.50	23656.92	563.26	24044.16	500.92	24830.40	413.84
22000	24382.08	677.28	24783.36	590.08	25188.96	524.77	26013.00	433.55
23000	25490.52	708.07	25910.22	616.91	26334.24	548.63	27195.60	453.26
24000	26598.60	738.85	27036.66	643.73	27479.04	572.48	28377.60	472.96
25000	27707.04	769.64	28163.10	670.55	28623.84	596.33	29560.20	492.67

6.90% ANNUAL PERCENTAGE RATE

	12 MONTHS		18 MONTHS		24 MONTHS		30 MONTHS	
LOAN AMT	TOTAL NOTE	MONTHLY PAYMENT	TOTAL NOTE	MONTHLY PAYMENT	TOTAL NOTE	MONTHLY PAYMENT	TOTAL NOTE	MONTHLY PAYMENT
1	.96	.08	.90	.05	.96	.04	.90	.03
2	2.04	.17	1.98	.11	1.92	.08	2.10	.07
3	3.00	.25	3.06	.17	3.12	.13	3.00	.10
4	4.08	.34	4.14	.23	4.08	.17	4.20	.14
5	5.16	.43	5.22	.29	5.28	.22	5.40	.18
6	6.12	.51	6.30	.35	6.24	.26	6.30	.21
7	7.20	.60	7.38	.41	7.44	.31	7.50	.25
8	8.28	.69	8.28	.46	8.40	.35	8.70	.29
9	9.24	.77	9.36	.52	9.60	.40	9.60	.32
10	10.32	.86	10.44	.58	10.56	.44	10.80	.36
20	20.64	1.72	21.06	1.17	21.36	.89	21.60	.72
30	31.08	2.59	31.50	1.75	32.16	1.34	32.70	1.09
40	41.40	3.45	42.12	2.34	42.72	1.78	43.50	1.45
50	51.84	4.32	52.74	2.93	53.52	2.23	54.30	1.81
60	62.16	5.18	63.18	3.51	64.32	2.68	65.40	2.18
70	72.60	6.05	73.80	4.10	75.12	3.13	76.20	2.54
80	82.92	6.91	84.42	4.69	85.68	3.57	87.30	2.91
90	93.36	7.78	94.86	5.27	96.48	4.02	98.10	3.27
100	103.68	8.64	105.48	5.86	107.28	4.47	108.90	3.63
200	207.48	17.29	210.96	11.72	214.56	8.94	218.10	7.27
300	311.28	25.94	316.62	17.59	321.84	13.41	327.30	10.91
400	415.08	34.59	422.10	23.45	429.36	17.89	436.50	14.55
500	518.88	43.24	527.58	29.31	536.64	22.36	545.70	18.19
600	622.56	51.88	633.24	35.18	643.92	26.83	654.90	21.83
700	726.36	60.53	738.72	41.04	751.20	31.30	764.10	25.47
800	830.16	69.18	844.38	46.91	858.72	35.78	873.00	29.10
900	933.96	77.83	949.86	52.77	966.00	40.25	982.20	32.74
1000	1037.76	86.48	1055.34	58.63	1073.28	44.72	1091.40	36.38
1500	1556.64	129.72	1583.10	87.95	1610.16	67.09	1637.10	54.57
2000	2075.52	172.96	2110.86	117.27	2146.80	89.45	2183.10	72.77
2500	2594.40	216.20	2638.62	146.59	2683.44	111.81	2728.80	90.96
3000	3113.28	259.44	3166.38	175.91	3220.32	134.18	3274.50	109.15
3500	3632.16	302.68	3694.14	205.23	3756.96	156.54	3820.50	127.35
4000	4151.04	345.92	4221.90	234.55	4293.60	178.90	4366.20	145.54
4500	4669.92	389.16	4749.66	263.87	4830.48	201.27	4911.90	163.73
5000	5188.80	432.40	5277.42	293.19	5367.12	223.63	5457.90	181.93
5500	5707.68	475.64	5805.18	322.51	5903.76	245.99	6003.60	200.12
6000	6226.56	518.88	6332.94	351.83	6440.64	268.36	6549.30	218.31
6500	6745.44	562.12	6860.70	381.15	6977.28	290.72	7095.30	236.51
7000	7264.32	605.36	7388.46	410.47	7514.16	313.09	7641.00	254.70
7500	7783.20	648.60	7916.22	439.79	8050.80	335.45	8186.70	272.89
8000	8302.08	691.84	8443.98	469.11	8587.44	357.81	8732.70	291.09
8500	8820.96	735.08	8971.74	498.43	9124.32	380.18	9278.40	309.28
9000	9339.84	778.32	9499.50	527.75	9660.96	402.54	9824.10	327.47
10000	10377.60	864.80	10555.02	586.39	10734.48	447.27	10915.80	363.86
11000	11415.36	951.28	11610.54	645.03	11807.76	491.99	12007.50	400.25
12000	12453.12	1037.76	12666.06	703.67	12881.28	536.72	13098.90	436.63
13000	13490.88	1124.24	13721.58	762.31	13954.80	581.45	14190.60	473.02
14000	14528.64	1210.72	14777.10	820.95	15028.32	626.18	15282.30	509.41
15000	15566.40	1297.20	15832.62	879.59	16101.60	670.90	16373.70	545.79
16000	16604.28	1383.69	16888.14	938.23	17175.12	715.63	17465.40	582.18
17000	17642.04	1470.17	17943.66	996.87	18248.64	760.36	18556.80	618.56
18000	18679.80	1556.65	18999.18	1055.51	19322.16	805.09	19648.50	654.95
19000	19717.56	1643.13	20054.70	1114.15	20395.44	849.81	20740.20	691.34
20000	20755.32	1729.61	21110.22	1172.79	21468.96	894.54	21831.60	727.72
21000	21793.08	1816.09	22165.74	1231.43	22542.48	939.27	22923.30	764.11
22000	22830.84	1902.57	23221.26	1290.07	23615.76	983.99	24015.00	800.50
23000	23868.60	1989.05	24276.78	1348.71	24689.28	1028.72	25106.40	836.88
24000	24906.36	2075.53	25332.12	1407.34	25762.80	1073.45	26198.10	873.27
25000	25944.12	2162.01	26387.64	1465.98	26836.32	1118.18	27289.80	909.66

ANNUAL PERCENTAGE RATE **6.90%**

LOAN AMT	36 MONTHS TOTAL NOTE	36 MONTHS MONTHLY PAYMENT	42 MONTHS TOTAL NOTE	42 MONTHS MONTHLY PAYMENT	48 MONTHS TOTAL NOTE	48 MONTHS MONTHLY PAYMENT	60 MONTHS TOTAL NOTE	60 MONTHS MONTHLY PAYMENT
1	1.08	.03	.84	.02	.96	.02	.60	.01
2	2.16	.06	2.10	.05	1.92	.04	1.80	.03
3	3.24	.09	3.36	.08	3.36	.07	3.00	.05
4	4.32	.12	4.20	.10	4.32	.09	4.20	.07
5	5.40	.15	5.46	.13	5.28	.11	5.40	.09
6	6.48	.18	6.72	.16	6.72	.14	6.60	.11
7	7.56	.21	7.56	.18	7.68	.16	7.80	.13
8	8.64	.24	8.82	.21	9.12	.19	9.00	.15
9	9.72	.27	10.08	.24	10.08	.21	10.20	.17
10	10.80	.30	10.92	.26	11.04	.23	11.40	.19
20	21.96	.61	22.26	.53	22.56	.47	23.40	.39
30	33.12	.92	33.60	.80	34.08	.71	35.40	.59
40	44.28	1.23	44.94	1.07	45.60	.95	47.40	.79
50	55.44	1.54	56.28	1.34	57.12	1.19	58.80	.98
60	66.24	1.84	67.62	1.61	68.64	1.43	70.80	1.18
70	77.40	2.15	78.96	1.88	80.16	1.67	82.80	1.38
80	88.56	2.46	89.88	2.14	91.68	1.91	94.80	1.58
90	99.72	2.77	101.22	2.41	103.20	2.15	106.20	1.77
100	110.88	3.08	112.56	2.68	114.24	2.38	118.20	1.97
200	221.76	6.16	225.54	5.37	228.96	4.77	237.00	3.95
300	332.64	9.24	338.52	8.06	343.68	7.16	355.20	5.92
400	443.88	12.33	451.08	10.74	458.40	9.55	474.00	7.90
500	554.76	15.41	564.06	13.43	573.12	11.94	592.20	9.87
600	665.64	18.49	677.04	16.12	687.84	14.33	711.00	11.85
700	776.88	21.58	789.60	18.80	802.56	16.72	829.20	13.82
800	887.76	24.66	902.58	21.49	917.28	19.11	948.00	15.80
900	998.64	27.74	1015.56	24.18	1032.00	21.50	1066.20	17.77
1000	1109.88	30.83	1128.12	26.86	1146.72	23.89	1185.00	19.75
1500	1664.64	46.24	1692.60	40.30	1720.32	35.84	1777.80	29.63
2000	2219.76	61.66	2256.66	53.73	2293.92	47.79	2370.00	39.50
2500	2774.52	77.07	2821.14	67.17	2867.52	59.74	2962.80	49.38
3000	3329.64	92.49	3385.20	80.60	3441.12	71.69	3555.60	59.26
3500	3884.40	107.90	3949.26	94.03	4014.72	83.64	4147.80	69.13
4000	4439.52	123.32	4513.74	107.47	4588.32	95.59	4740.60	79.01
4500	4994.64	138.74	5077.80	120.90	5161.92	107.54	5333.40	88.89
5000	5549.40	154.15	5642.28	134.34	5735.52	119.49	5926.20	98.77
5500	6104.52	169.57	6206.34	147.77	6309.12	131.44	6518.40	108.64
6000	6659.28	184.98	6770.40	161.20	6882.72	143.39	7111.20	118.52
6500	7214.40	200.40	7334.88	174.64	7456.32	155.34	7704.00	128.40
7000	7769.16	215.81	7898.94	188.07	8029.92	167.29	8296.20	138.27
7500	8324.28	231.23	8463.42	201.51	8603.52	179.24	8889.00	148.15
8000	8879.40	246.65	9027.48	214.94	9177.12	191.19	9481.80	158.03
8500	9434.16	262.06	9591.54	228.37	9750.72	203.14	10074.00	167.90
9000	9989.28	277.48	10156.02	241.81	10324.32	215.09	10666.80	177.78
10000	11099.16	308.31	11284.56	268.68	11471.52	238.99	11852.40	197.54
11000	12209.04	339.14	12413.10	295.55	12618.72	262.89	13037.40	217.29
12000	13318.92	369.97	13541.22	322.41	13765.92	286.79	14222.40	237.04
13000	14428.80	400.80	14669.76	349.28	14913.12	310.69	15408.00	256.80
14000	15538.68	431.63	15798.30	376.15	16060.32	334.59	16593.00	276.55
15000	16648.92	462.47	16926.84	403.02	17207.52	358.49	17778.60	296.31
16000	17758.80	493.30	18055.38	429.89	18354.72	382.39	18963.60	316.06
17000	18868.68	524.13	19183.50	456.75	19501.92	406.29	20148.60	335.81
18000	19978.56	554.96	20312.04	483.62	20649.12	430.19	21334.20	355.57
19000	21088.44	585.79	21440.58	510.49	21796.32	454.09	22519.20	375.32
20000	22198.32	616.62	22569.12	537.36	22943.52	477.99	23704.80	395.08
21000	23308.20	647.45	23697.66	564.23	24090.72	501.89	24889.80	414.83
22000	24418.44	678.29	24826.20	591.10	25237.92	525.79	26074.80	434.58
23000	25528.32	709.12	25954.32	617.96	26385.12	549.69	27260.40	454.34
24000	26638.20	739.95	27082.86	644.83	27532.32	573.59	28445.40	474.09
25000	27748.08	770.78	28211.40	671.70	28679.52	597.49	29631.00	493.85

7.00% ANNUAL PERCENTAGE RATE

LOAN AMT	12 MONTHS TOTAL NOTE	12 MONTHS MONTHLY PAYMENT	18 MONTHS TOTAL NOTE	18 MONTHS MONTHLY PAYMENT	24 MONTHS TOTAL NOTE	24 MONTHS MONTHLY PAYMENT	30 MONTHS TOTAL NOTE	30 MONTHS MONTHLY PAYMENT
1	.96	.08	.90	.05	.96	.04	.90	.03
2	2.04	.17	1.98	.11	1.92	.08	2.10	.07
3	3.00	.25	3.06	.17	3.12	.13	3.00	.10
4	4.08	.34	4.14	.23	4.08	.17	4.20	.14
5	5.16	.43	5.22	.29	5.28	.22	5.40	.18
6	6.12	.51	6.30	.35	6.24	.26	6.30	.21
7	7.20	.60	7.38	.41	7.44	.31	7.50	.25
8	8.28	.69	8.28	.46	8.40	.35	8.70	.29
9	9.24	.77	9.36	.52	9.60	.40	9.60	.32
10	10.32	.86	10.44	.58	10.56	.44	10.80	.36
20	20.76	1.73	21.06	1.17	21.36	.89	21.60	.72
30	31.08	2.59	31.68	1.76	32.16	1.34	32.70	1.09
40	41.52	3.46	42.12	2.34	42.96	1.79	43.50	1.45
50	51.84	4.32	52.74	2.93	53.52	2.23	54.60	1.82
60	62.28	5.19	63.36	3.52	64.32	2.68	65.40	2.18
70	72.60	6.05	73.80	4.10	75.12	3.13	76.50	2.55
80	83.04	6.92	84.42	4.69	85.92	3.58	87.30	2.91
90	93.36	7.78	95.04	5.28	96.48	4.02	98.10	3.27
100	103.80	8.65	105.48	5.86	107.28	4.47	109.20	3.64
200	207.60	17.30	211.14	11.73	214.80	8.95	218.40	7.28
300	311.40	25.95	316.80	17.60	322.32	13.43	327.60	10.92
400	415.32	34.61	422.46	23.47	429.60	17.90	437.10	14.57
500	519.12	43.26	528.12	29.34	537.12	22.38	546.30	18.21
600	622.92	51.91	633.78	35.21	644.64	26.86	655.50	21.85
700	726.72	60.56	739.26	41.07	752.16	31.34	765.00	25.50
800	830.64	69.22	844.92	46.94	859.44	35.81	874.20	29.14
900	934.44	77.87	950.58	52.81	966.96	40.29	983.40	32.78
1000	1038.24	86.52	1056.24	58.68	1074.48	44.77	1092.90	36.43
1500	1557.48	129.79	1584.36	88.02	1611.60	67.15	1639.20	54.64
2000	2076.60	173.05	2112.48	117.36	2148.96	89.54	2185.80	72.86
2500	2595.72	216.31	2640.78	146.71	2686.32	111.93	2732.10	91.07
3000	3114.96	259.58	3168.90	176.05	3223.44	134.31	3278.70	109.29
3500	3634.08	302.84	3697.02	205.39	3760.80	156.70	3825.30	127.51
4000	4153.20	346.10	4225.14	234.73	4298.16	179.09	4371.60	145.72
4500	4672.44	389.37	4753.44	264.08	4835.28	201.47	4918.20	163.94
5000	5191.56	432.63	5281.56	293.42	5372.64	223.86	5464.50	182.15
5500	5710.68	475.89	5809.68	322.76	5909.76	246.24	6011.10	200.37
6000	6229.92	519.16	6337.80	352.10	6447.12	268.63	6557.70	218.59
6500	6749.04	562.42	6866.10	381.45	6984.48	291.02	7104.00	236.80
7000	7268.16	605.68	7394.22	410.79	7521.60	313.40	7650.60	255.02
7500	7787.40	648.95	7922.34	440.13	8058.96	335.79	8196.90	273.23
8000	8306.52	692.21	8450.46	469.47	8596.32	358.18	8743.50	291.45
8500	8825.64	735.47	8978.76	498.82	9133.44	380.56	9290.10	309.67
9000	9344.88	778.74	9506.88	528.16	9670.80	402.95	9836.40	327.88
10000	10383.12	865.26	10563.12	586.84	10745.28	447.72	10929.30	364.31
11000	11421.48	951.79	11619.54	645.53	11819.76	492.49	12022.50	400.75
12000	12459.84	1038.32	12675.78	704.21	12894.48	537.27	13115.40	437.18
13000	13498.08	1124.84	13732.20	762.90	13968.96	582.04	14208.30	473.61
14000	14536.44	1211.37	14788.44	821.58	15043.44	626.81	15301.20	510.04
15000	15574.80	1297.90	15844.86	880.27	16117.92	671.58	16394.10	546.47
16000	16613.04	1384.42	16901.10	938.95	17192.64	716.36	17487.30	582.91
17000	17651.40	1470.95	17957.52	997.64	18267.12	761.13	18580.20	619.34
18000	18689.76	1557.48	19013.76	1056.32	19341.60	805.90	19673.10	655.77
19000	19728.00	1644.00	20070.18	1115.01	20416.08	850.67	20766.00	692.20
20000	20766.36	1730.53	21126.42	1173.69	21490.80	895.45	21858.90	728.63
21000	21804.72	1817.06	22182.84	1232.38	22565.28	940.22	22952.10	765.07
22000	22842.96	1903.58	23239.08	1291.06	23639.76	984.99	24045.00	801.50
23000	23881.32	1990.11	24295.50	1349.75	24714.24	1029.76	25137.90	837.93
24000	24919.68	2076.64	25351.74	1408.43	25788.96	1074.54	26230.80	874.36
25000	25957.92	2163.16	26408.16	1467.12	26863.44	1119.31	27323.70	910.79

ANNUAL PERCENTAGE RATE **7.00%**

	36 MONTHS		42 MONTHS		48 MONTHS		60 MONTHS	
LOAN AMT	TOTAL NOTE	MONTHLY PAYMENT	TOTAL NOTE	MONTHLY PAYMENT	TOTAL NOTE	MONTHLY PAYMENT	TOTAL NOTE	MONTHLY PAYMENT
1	1.08	.03	.84	.02	.96	.02	.60	.01
2	2.16	.06	2.10	.05	1.92	.04	1.80	.03
3	3.24	.09	3.36	.08	3.36	.07	3.00	.05
4	4.32	.12	4.20	.10	4.32	.09	4.20	.07
5	5.40	.15	5.46	.13	5.28	.11	5.40	.09
6	6.48	.18	6.72	.16	6.72	.14	6.60	.11
7	7.56	.21	7.56	.18	7.68	.16	7.80	.13
8	8.64	.24	8.82	.21	9.12	.19	9.00	.15
9	9.72	.27	10.08	.24	10.08	.21	10.20	.17
10	10.80	.30	10.92	.26	11.04	.23	11.40	.19
20	21.96	.61	22.26	.53	22.56	.47	23.40	.39
30	33.12	.92	33.60	.80	34.08	.71	35.40	.59
40	44.28	1.23	44.94	1.07	45.60	.95	47.40	.79
50	55.44	1.54	56.28	1.34	57.12	1.19	59.40	.99
60	66.60	1.85	67.62	1.61	68.64	1.43	70.80	1.18
70	77.76	2.16	78.96	1.88	80.16	1.67	82.80	1.38
80	88.92	2.47	90.30	2.15	91.68	1.91	94.80	1.58
90	99.72	2.77	101.64	2.42	103.20	2.15	106.80	1.78
100	110.88	3.08	112.98	2.69	114.72	2.39	118.80	1.98
200	222.12	6.17	225.96	5.38	229.44	4.78	237.60	3.96
300	333.36	9.26	338.94	8.07	344.64	7.18	356.40	5.94
400	444.60	12.35	451.92	10.76	459.36	9.57	475.20	7.92
500	555.48	15.43	564.90	13.45	574.56	11.97	594.00	9.90
600	666.72	18.52	677.88	16.14	689.28	14.36	712.80	11.88
700	777.96	21.61	790.86	18.83	804.48	16.76	831.60	13.86
800	889.20	24.70	904.26	21.53	919.20	19.15	950.40	15.84
900	1000.08	27.78	1017.24	24.22	1034.40	21.55	1069.20	17.82
1000	1111.32	30.87	1130.22	26.91	1149.12	23.94	1188.00	19.80
1500	1667.16	46.31	1695.54	40.37	1723.68	35.91	1782.00	29.70
2000	2223.00	61.75	2260.44	53.82	2298.72	47.89	2376.00	39.60
2500	2778.84	77.19	2825.76	67.28	2873.28	59.86	2970.00	49.50
3000	3334.68	92.63	3391.08	80.74	3447.84	71.83	3564.00	59.40
3500	3890.16	108.06	3955.98	94.19	4022.88	83.81	4158.00	69.30
4000	4446.00	123.50	4521.30	107.65	4597.44	95.78	4752.00	79.20
4500	5001.84	138.94	5086.62	121.11	5172.00	107.75	5346.00	89.10
5000	5557.68	154.38	5651.94	134.57	5747.04	119.73	5940.00	99.00
5500	6113.52	169.82	6216.84	148.02	6321.60	131.70	6534.00	108.90
6000	6669.36	185.26	6782.16	161.48	6896.16	143.67	7128.00	118.80
6500	7225.20	200.70	7347.48	174.94	7471.20	155.65	7722.00	128.70
7000	7780.68	216.13	7912.38	188.39	8045.76	167.62	8316.00	138.60
7500	8336.52	231.57	8477.70	201.85	8620.32	179.59	8910.00	148.50
8000	8892.36	247.01	9043.02	215.31	9194.88	191.56	9504.00	158.40
8500	9448.20	262.45	9608.34	228.77	9769.92	203.54	10098.60	168.31
9000	10004.04	277.89	10173.24	242.22	10344.48	215.51	10692.60	178.21
10000	11115.72	308.77	11303.88	269.14	11494.08	239.46	11880.60	198.01
11000	12227.04	339.64	12434.10	296.05	12643.20	263.40	13068.60	217.81
12000	13338.72	370.52	13564.74	322.97	13792.80	287.35	14256.60	237.61
13000	14450.40	401.40	14694.96	349.88	14942.40	311.30	15444.60	257.41
14000	15561.72	432.27	15825.18	376.79	16091.52	335.24	16632.60	277.21
15000	16673.40	463.15	16955.82	403.71	17241.12	359.19	17820.60	297.01
16000	17785.08	494.03	18086.04	430.62	18390.24	383.13	19008.60	316.81
17000	18896.76	524.91	19216.68	457.54	19539.84	407.08	20197.20	336.62
18000	20008.08	555.78	20346.90	484.45	20689.44	431.03	21385.20	356.42
19000	21119.76	586.66	21477.12	511.36	21838.56	454.97	22573.20	376.22
20000	22231.44	617.54	22607.76	538.28	22988.16	478.92	23761.20	396.02
21000	23342.76	648.41	23737.98	565.19	24137.76	502.87	24949.20	415.82
22000	24454.44	679.29	24868.62	592.11	25286.88	526.81	26137.20	435.62
23000	25566.12	710.17	25998.84	619.02	26436.48	550.76	27325.20	455.42
24000	26677.80	741.05	27129.48	645.94	27585.60	574.70	28513.20	475.22
25000	27789.12	771.92	28259.70	672.85	28735.20	598.65	29701.20	495.02

7.10% ANNUAL PERCENTAGE RATE

LOAN AMT	12 MONTHS TOTAL NOTE	12 MONTHS MONTHLY PAYMENT	18 MONTHS TOTAL NOTE	18 MONTHS MONTHLY PAYMENT	24 MONTHS TOTAL NOTE	24 MONTHS MONTHLY PAYMENT	30 MONTHS TOTAL NOTE	30 MONTHS MONTHLY PAYMENT
1	.96	.08	.90	.05	.96	.04	.90	.03
2	2.04	.17	1.98	.11	1.92	.08	2.10	.07
3	3.00	.25	3.06	.17	3.12	.13	3.00	.10
4	4.08	.34	4.14	.23	4.08	.17	4.20	.14
5	5.16	.43	5.22	.29	5.28	.22	5.40	.18
6	6.12	.51	6.30	.35	6.24	.26	6.30	.21
7	7.20	.60	7.38	.41	7.44	.31	7.50	.25
8	8.28	.69	8.28	.46	8.40	.35	8.70	.29
9	9.24	.77	9.36	.52	9.60	.40	9.60	.32
10	10.32	.86	10.44	.58	10.56	.44	10.80	.36
20	20.76	1.73	21.06	1.17	21.36	.89	21.60	.72
30	31.08	2.59	31.68	1.76	32.16	1.34	32.70	1.09
40	41.52	3.46	42.12	2.34	42.96	1.79	43.50	1.45
50	51.84	4.32	52.74	2.93	53.76	2.24	54.60	1.82
60	62.28	5.19	63.36	3.52	64.32	2.68	65.40	2.18
70	72.72	6.06	73.98	4.11	75.12	3.13	76.50	2.55
80	83.04	6.92	84.42	4.69	85.92	3.58	87.30	2.91
90	93.48	7.79	95.04	5.28	96.72	4.03	98.40	3.28
100	103.80	8.65	105.66	5.87	107.52	4.48	109.20	3.64
200	207.72	17.31	211.32	11.74	215.04	8.96	218.70	7.29
300	311.64	25.97	316.98	17.61	322.56	13.44	328.20	10.94
400	415.44	34.62	422.82	23.49	430.08	17.92	437.70	14.59
500	519.36	43.28	528.48	29.36	537.60	22.40	546.90	18.23
600	623.28	51.94	634.14	35.23	645.36	26.89	656.40	21.88
700	727.20	60.60	739.98	41.11	752.88	31.37	765.90	25.53
800	831.00	69.25	845.64	46.98	860.40	35.85	875.40	29.18
900	934.92	77.91	951.30	52.85	967.92	40.33	984.60	32.82
1000	1038.84	86.57	1057.14	58.73	1075.44	44.81	1094.10	36.47
1500	1558.20	129.85	1585.62	88.09	1613.28	67.22	1641.30	54.71
2000	2077.68	173.14	2114.28	117.46	2151.12	89.63	2188.50	72.95
2500	2597.16	216.43	2642.76	146.82	2688.96	112.04	2735.70	91.19
3000	3116.52	259.71	3171.42	176.19	3226.80	134.45	3282.90	109.43
3500	3636.00	303.00	3699.90	205.55	3764.64	156.86	3830.10	127.67
4000	4155.48	346.29	4228.56	234.92	4302.48	179.27	4377.00	145.90
4500	4674.84	389.57	4757.04	264.28	4840.32	201.68	4924.20	164.14
5000	5194.32	432.86	5285.70	293.65	5377.92	224.08	5471.40	182.38
5500	5713.80	476.15	5814.18	323.01	5915.76	246.49	6018.60	200.62
6000	6233.16	519.43	6342.84	352.38	6453.60	268.90	6565.80	218.86
6500	6752.64	562.72	6871.32	381.74	6991.44	291.31	7113.00	237.10
7000	7272.00	606.00	7399.98	411.11	7529.28	313.72	7660.20	255.34
7500	7791.48	649.29	7928.46	440.47	8067.12	336.13	8207.40	273.58
8000	8310.96	692.58	8457.12	469.84	8604.96	358.54	8754.30	291.81
8500	8830.32	735.86	8985.60	499.20	9142.80	380.95	9301.50	310.05
9000	9349.80	779.15	9514.26	528.57	9680.64	403.36	9848.70	328.29
10000	10388.64	865.72	10571.40	587.30	10756.08	448.17	10943.10	364.77
11000	11427.60	952.30	11628.54	646.03	11831.76	492.99	12037.50	401.25
12000	12466.44	1038.87	12685.68	704.76	12907.44	537.81	13131.60	437.72
13000	13505.28	1125.44	13742.82	763.49	13983.12	582.63	14226.00	474.20
14000	14544.12	1212.01	14799.96	822.22	15058.80	627.45	15320.40	510.68
15000	15583.08	1298.59	15857.10	880.95	16134.24	672.26	16414.80	547.16
16000	16621.92	1385.16	16914.24	939.68	17209.92	717.08	17508.90	583.63
17000	17660.76	1471.73	17971.38	998.41	18285.60	761.90	18603.30	620.11
18000	18699.72	1558.31	19028.52	1057.14	19361.28	806.72	19697.70	656.59
19000	19738.56	1644.88	20085.66	1115.87	20436.96	851.54	20792.10	693.07
20000	20777.40	1731.45	21142.80	1174.60	21512.40	896.35	21886.20	729.54
21000	21816.24	1818.02	22199.94	1233.33	22588.08	941.17	22980.60	766.02
22000	22855.20	1904.60	23257.08	1292.06	23663.76	985.99	24075.00	802.50
23000	23894.04	1991.17	24314.22	1350.79	24739.44	1030.81	25169.40	838.98
24000	24932.88	2077.74	25371.54	1409.53	25815.12	1075.63	26263.50	875.45
25000	25971.84	2164.32	26428.68	1468.26	26890.56	1120.44	27357.90	911.93

ANNUAL PERCENTAGE RATE **7.10%**

LOAN AMT	36 MONTHS		42 MONTHS		48 MONTHS		60 MONTHS	
	TOTAL NOTE	MONTHLY PAYMENT	TOTAL NOTE	MONTHLY PAYMENT	TOTAL NOTE	MONTHLY PAYMENT	TOTAL NOTE	MONTHLY PAYMENT
1	1.08	.03	.84	.02	.96	.02	.60	.01
2	2.16	.06	2.10	.05	1.92	.04	1.80	.03
3	3.24	.09	3.36	.08	3.36	.07	3.00	.05
4	4.32	.12	4.20	.10	4.32	.09	4.20	.07
5	5.40	.15	5.46	.13	5.28	.11	5.40	.09
6	6.48	.18	6.72	.16	6.72	.14	6.60	.11
7	7.56	.21	7.56	.18	7.68	.16	7.80	.13
8	8.64	.24	8.82	.21	9.12	.19	9.00	.15
9	9.72	.27	10.08	.24	10.08	.21	10.20	.17
10	10.80	.30	10.92	.26	11.04	.23	11.40	.19
20	21.96	.61	22.26	.53	22.56	.47	23.40	.39
30	33.12	.92	33.60	.80	34.08	.71	35.40	.59
40	44.28	1.23	44.94	1.07	45.60	.95	47.40	.79
50	55.44	1.54	56.28	1.34	57.12	1.19	59.40	.99
60	66.60	1.85	67.62	1.61	68.64	1.43	71.40	1.19
70	77.76	2.16	78.96	1.88	80.16	1.67	82.80	1.38
80	88.92	2.47	90.30	2.15	91.68	1.91	94.80	1.58
90	100.08	2.78	101.64	2.42	103.20	2.15	106.80	1.78
100	111.24	3.09	112.98	2.69	114.72	2.39	118.80	1.98
200	222.48	6.18	226.38	5.39	229.92	4.79	237.60	3.96
300	333.72	9.27	339.36	8.08	345.12	7.19	357.00	5.95
400	444.96	12.36	452.76	10.78	460.32	9.59	475.80	7.93
500	556.56	15.46	566.16	13.48	575.52	11.99	595.20	9.92
600	667.80	18.55	679.14	16.17	690.72	14.39	714.00	11.90
700	779.04	21.64	792.54	18.87	805.92	16.79	833.40	13.89
800	890.28	24.73	905.52	21.56	921.12	19.19	952.20	15.87
900	1001.88	27.83	1018.92	24.26	1036.32	21.59	1071.60	17.86
1000	1113.12	30.92	1132.32	26.96	1151.52	23.99	1190.40	19.84
1500	1669.68	46.38	1698.48	40.44	1727.04	35.98	1786.20	29.77
2000	2226.24	61.84	2264.64	53.92	2303.04	47.98	2381.40	39.69
2500	2782.80	77.30	2830.80	67.40	2879.04	59.98	2977.20	49.62
3000	3339.36	92.76	3396.96	80.88	3454.56	71.97	3572.40	59.54
3500	3895.92	108.22	3963.12	94.36	4030.56	83.97	4167.60	69.46
4000	4452.84	123.69	4529.28	107.84	4606.56	95.97	4763.40	79.39
4500	5009.40	139.15	5095.44	121.32	5182.08	107.96	5358.60	89.31
5000	5565.96	154.61	5661.60	134.80	5758.08	119.96	5954.40	99.24
5500	6122.52	170.07	6227.76	148.28	6333.60	131.95	6549.60	109.16
6000	6679.08	185.53	6793.92	161.76	6909.60	143.95	7145.40	119.09
6500	7235.64	200.99	7360.08	175.24	7485.60	155.95	7740.60	129.01
7000	7792.20	216.45	7926.24	188.72	8061.12	167.94	8335.80	138.93
7500	8349.12	231.92	8492.40	202.20	8637.12	179.94	8931.60	148.86
8000	8905.68	247.38	9058.56	215.68	9213.12	191.94	9526.80	158.78
8500	9462.24	262.84	9624.72	229.16	9788.64	203.93	10122.60	168.71
9000	10018.80	278.30	10190.88	242.64	10364.64	215.93	10717.80	178.63
10000	11131.92	309.22	11323.20	269.60	11516.16	239.92	11908.80	198.48
11000	12245.40	340.15	12455.52	296.56	12667.68	263.91	13099.80	218.33
12000	13358.52	371.07	13587.84	323.52	13819.68	287.91	14290.80	238.18
13000	14471.64	401.99	14720.16	350.48	14971.20	311.90	15481.20	258.02
14000	15584.76	432.91	15852.48	377.44	16122.72	335.89	16672.20	277.87
15000	16698.24	463.84	16984.80	404.40	17274.72	359.89	17863.20	297.72
16000	17811.36	494.76	18117.12	431.36	18426.24	383.88	19054.20	317.57
17000	18924.48	525.68	19249.44	458.32	19577.76	407.87	20245.20	337.42
18000	20037.96	556.61	20381.76	485.28	20729.28	431.86	21436.20	357.27
19000	21151.08	587.53	21514.08	512.24	21881.28	455.86	22626.60	377.11
20000	22264.20	618.45	22646.40	539.20	23032.80	479.85	23817.60	396.96
21000	23377.32	649.37	23778.72	566.16	24184.32	503.84	25008.60	416.81
22000	24490.80	680.30	24911.04	593.12	25335.84	527.83	26199.60	436.66
23000	25603.92	711.22	26043.36	620.08	26487.84	551.83	27390.60	456.51
24000	26717.04	742.14	27175.68	647.04	27639.36	575.82	28581.60	476.36
25000	27830.52	773.07	28308.00	674.00	28790.88	599.81	29772.60	496.21

7.20% ANNUAL PERCENTAGE RATE

	12 MONTHS		18 MONTHS		24 MONTHS		30 MONTHS	
LOAN AMT	TOTAL NOTE	MONTHLY PAYMENT	TOTAL NOTE	MONTHLY PAYMENT	TOTAL NOTE	MONTHLY PAYMENT	TOTAL NOTE	MONTHLY PAYMENT
1	.96	.08	.90	.05	.96	.04	.90	.03
2	2.04	.17	1.98	.11	1.92	.08	2.10	.07
3	3.00	.25	3.06	.17	3.12	.13	3.00	.10
4	4.08	.34	4.14	.23	4.08	.17	4.20	.14
5	5.16	.43	5.22	.29	5.28	.22	5.40	.18
6	6.12	.51	6.30	.35	6.24	.26	6.30	.21
7	7.20	.60	7.38	.41	7.44	.31	7.50	.25
8	8.28	.69	8.46	.47	8.40	.35	8.70	.29
9	9.24	.77	9.36	.52	9.60	.40	9.60	.32
10	10.32	.86	10.44	.58	10.56	.44	10.80	.36
20	20.76	1.73	21.06	1.17	21.36	.89	21.90	.73
30	31.08	2.59	31.68	1.76	32.16	1.34	32.70	1.09
40	41.52	3.46	42.30	2.35	42.96	1.79	43.80	1.46
50	51.96	4.33	52.74	2.93	53.76	2.24	54.60	1.82
60	62.28	5.19	63.36	3.52	64.56	2.69	65.70	2.19
70	72.72	6.06	73.98	4.11	75.36	3.14	76.50	2.55
80	83.04	6.92	84.60	4.70	85.92	3.58	87.60	2.92
90	93.48	7.79	95.04	5.28	96.72	4.03	98.40	3.28
100	103.92	8.66	105.66	5.87	107.52	4.48	109.50	3.65
200	207.84	17.32	211.50	11.75	215.28	8.97	219.00	7.30
300	311.76	25.98	317.34	17.63	322.80	13.45	328.50	10.95
400	415.68	34.64	423.18	23.51	430.56	17.94	438.00	14.60
500	519.60	43.30	528.84	29.38	538.32	22.43	547.80	18.26
600	623.64	51.97	634.68	35.26	645.84	26.91	657.30	21.91
700	727.56	60.63	740.52	41.14	753.60	31.40	766.80	25.56
800	831.48	69.29	846.36	47.02	861.36	35.89	876.30	29.21
900	935.40	77.95	952.02	52.89	968.88	40.37	986.10	32.87
1000	1039.32	86.61	1057.86	58.77	1076.64	44.86	1095.60	36.52
1500	1559.04	129.92	1586.88	88.16	1614.96	67.29	1643.40	54.78
2000	2078.76	173.23	2115.90	117.55	2153.28	89.72	2191.20	73.04
2500	2598.48	216.54	2644.74	146.93	2691.60	112.15	2739.00	91.30
3000	3118.20	259.85	3173.76	176.32	3229.92	134.58	3286.80	109.56
3500	3637.92	303.16	3702.78	205.71	3768.48	157.02	3834.90	127.83
4000	4157.64	346.47	4231.80	235.10	4306.80	179.45	4382.70	146.09
4500	4677.36	389.78	4760.82	264.49	4845.12	201.88	4930.50	164.35
5000	5197.08	433.09	5289.66	293.87	5383.44	224.31	5478.30	182.61
5500	5716.80	476.40	5818.68	323.26	5921.76	246.74	6026.10	200.87
6000	6236.52	519.71	6347.70	352.65	6460.08	269.17	6573.90	219.13
6500	6756.24	563.02	6876.72	382.04	6998.64	291.61	7121.70	237.39
7000	7275.96	606.33	7405.74	411.43	7536.96	314.04	7669.80	255.66
7500	7795.68	649.64	7934.58	440.81	8075.28	336.47	8217.60	273.92
8000	8315.40	692.95	8463.60	470.20	8613.60	358.90	8765.40	292.18
8500	8835.12	736.26	8992.62	499.59	9151.92	381.33	9313.20	310.44
9000	9354.84	779.57	9521.64	528.98	9690.24	403.76	9861.00	328.70
10000	10394.16	866.18	10579.50	587.75	10767.12	448.63	10956.60	365.22
11000	11433.60	952.80	11637.54	646.53	11843.76	493.49	12052.50	401.75
12000	12473.04	1039.42	12695.58	705.31	12920.40	538.35	13148.10	438.27
13000	13512.48	1126.04	13753.44	764.08	13997.28	583.22	14243.70	474.79
14000	14551.92	1212.66	14811.48	822.86	15073.92	628.08	15339.60	511.32
15000	15591.36	1299.28	15869.34	881.63	16150.56	672.94	16435.20	547.84
16000	16630.80	1385.90	16927.38	940.41	17227.44	717.81	17530.80	584.36
17000	17670.24	1472.52	17985.42	999.19	18304.08	762.67	18626.40	620.88
18000	18709.68	1559.14	19043.28	1057.96	19380.72	807.53	19722.30	657.41
19000	19749.12	1645.76	20101.32	1116.74	20457.60	852.40	20817.90	693.93
20000	20788.44	1732.37	21159.18	1175.51	21534.24	897.26	21913.50	730.45
21000	21827.88	1818.99	22217.22	1234.29	22610.88	942.12	23009.40	766.98
22000	22867.32	1905.61	23275.08	1293.06	23687.76	986.99	24105.00	803.50
23000	23906.76	1992.23	24333.12	1351.84	24764.40	1031.85	25200.60	840.02
24000	24946.20	2078.85	25391.16	1410.62	25841.04	1076.71	26296.20	876.54
25000	25985.64	2165.47	26449.02	1469.39	26917.92	1121.58	27392.10	913.07

ANNUAL PERCENTAGE RATE **7.20%**

LOAN	36 MONTHS		42 MONTHS		48 MONTHS		60 MONTHS	
AMT	TOTAL NOTE	MONTHLY PAYMENT	TOTAL NOTE	MONTHLY PAYMENT	TOTAL NOTE	MONTHLY PAYMENT	TOTAL NOTE	MONTHLY PAYMENT
1	1.08	.03	.84	.02	.96	.02	.60	.01
2	2.16	.06	2.10	.05	1.92	.04	1.80	.03
3	3.24	.09	3.36	.08	3.36	.07	3.00	.05
4	4.32	.12	4.20	.10	4.32	.09	4.20	.07
5	5.40	.15	5.46	.13	5.76	.12	5.40	.09
6	6.48	.18	6.72	.16	6.72	.14	6.60	.11
7	7.56	.21	7.56	.18	7.68	.16	7.80	.13
8	8.64	.24	8.82	.21	9.12	.19	9.00	.15
9	9.72	.27	10.08	.24	10.08	.21	10.20	.17
10	10.80	.30	11.34	.27	11.52	.24	11.40	.19
20	21.96	.61	22.68	.54	23.04	.48	23.40	.39
30	33.12	.92	34.02	.81	34.56	.72	35.40	.59
40	44.28	1.23	45.36	1.08	46.08	.96	47.40	.79
50	55.44	1.54	56.70	1.35	57.60	1.20	59.40	.99
60	66.60	1.85	68.04	1.62	69.12	1.44	71.40	1.19
70	77.76	2.16	79.38	1.89	80.64	1.68	83.40	1.39
80	88.92	2.47	90.72	2.16	92.16	1.92	95.40	1.59
90	100.08	2.78	102.06	2.43	103.68	2.16	107.40	1.79
100	111.24	3.09	113.40	2.70	115.20	2.40	118.80	1.98
200	222.84	6.19	226.80	5.40	230.40	4.80	238.20	3.97
300	334.44	9.29	340.20	8.10	346.08	7.21	357.60	5.96
400	445.68	12.38	453.60	10.80	461.28	9.61	477.00	7.95
500	557.28	15.48	567.00	13.50	576.48	12.01	596.40	9.94
600	668.88	18.58	680.40	16.20	692.16	14.42	715.80	11.93
700	780.12	21.67	793.80	18.90	807.36	16.82	835.20	13.92
800	891.72	24.77	907.20	21.60	923.04	19.23	954.60	15.91
900	1003.32	27.87	1020.60	24.30	1038.24	21.63	1074.00	17.90
1000	1114.56	30.96	1134.00	27.00	1153.44	24.03	1193.40	19.89
1500	1672.20	46.45	1701.00	40.50	1730.40	36.05	1790.40	29.84
2000	2229.48	61.93	2268.42	54.01	2307.36	48.07	2387.40	39.79
2500	2787.12	77.42	2835.42	67.51	2884.32	60.09	2983.80	49.73
3000	3344.40	92.90	3402.42	81.01	3461.28	72.11	3580.80	59.68
3500	3902.04	108.39	3969.84	94.52	4038.24	84.13	4177.80	69.63
4000	4459.32	123.87	4536.84	108.02	4615.20	96.15	4774.80	79.58
4500	5016.60	139.35	5103.84	121.52	5192.16	108.17	5371.80	89.53
5000	5574.24	154.84	5671.26	135.03	5769.12	120.19	5968.20	99.47
5500	6131.52	170.32	6238.26	148.53	6346.08	132.21	6565.20	109.42
6000	6689.16	185.81	6805.26	162.03	6923.04	144.23	7162.20	119.37
6500	7246.44	201.29	7372.68	175.54	7500.00	156.25	7759.20	129.32
7000	7804.08	216.78	7939.68	189.04	8076.96	168.27	8355.60	139.26
7500	8361.36	232.26	8506.68	202.54	8653.92	180.29	8952.60	149.21
8000	8918.64	247.74	9074.10	216.05	9230.88	192.31	9549.60	159.16
8500	9476.28	263.23	9641.10	229.55	9807.84	204.33	10146.60	169.11
9000	10033.56	278.71	10208.10	243.05	10384.80	216.35	10743.60	179.06
10000	11148.48	309.68	11342.52	270.06	11538.72	240.39	11937.00	198.95
11000	12263.40	340.65	12476.94	297.07	12692.64	264.43	13131.00	218.85
12000	13378.32	371.62	13610.94	324.07	13846.08	288.46	14324.40	238.74
13000	14493.24	402.59	14745.36	351.08	15000.00	312.50	15518.40	258.64
14000	15608.16	433.56	15879.36	378.08	16153.92	336.54	16711.80	278.53
15000	16722.72	464.52	17013.78	405.09	17307.84	360.58	17905.80	298.43
16000	17837.64	495.49	18148.20	432.10	18461.76	384.62	19099.80	318.33
17000	18952.56	526.46	19282.20	459.10	19615.68	408.66	20293.20	338.22
18000	20067.48	557.43	20416.62	486.11	20769.60	432.70	21487.20	358.12
19000	21182.40	588.40	21551.04	513.12	21923.52	456.74	22680.60	378.01
20000	22297.32	619.37	22685.04	540.12	23077.44	480.78	23874.60	397.91
21000	23412.24	650.34	23819.46	567.13	24231.36	504.82	25068.00	417.80
22000	24526.80	681.30	24953.88	594.14	25385.28	528.86	26262.00	437.70
23000	25641.72	712.27	26087.88	621.14	26539.20	552.90	27456.00	457.60
24000	26756.64	743.24	27222.30	648.15	27692.64	576.93	28649.40	477.49
25000	27871.56	774.21	28356.30	675.15	28846.56	600.97	29843.40	497.39

7.25% ANNUAL PERCENTAGE RATE

LOAN AMT	12 MONTHS TOTAL NOTE	12 MONTHS MONTHLY PAYMENT	18 MONTHS TOTAL NOTE	18 MONTHS MONTHLY PAYMENT	24 MONTHS TOTAL NOTE	24 MONTHS MONTHLY PAYMENT	30 MONTHS TOTAL NOTE	30 MONTHS MONTHLY PAYMENT
1	.96	.08	.90	.05	.96	.04	.90	.03
2	2.04	.17	1.98	.11	1.92	.08	2.10	.07
3	3.00	.25	3.06	.17	3.12	.13	3.00	.10
4	4.08	.34	4.14	.23	4.08	.17	4.20	.14
5	5.16	.43	5.22	.29	5.28	.22	5.40	.18
6	6.12	.51	6.30	.35	6.24	.26	6.30	.21
7	7.20	.60	7.38	.41	7.44	.31	7.50	.25
8	8.28	.69	8.46	.47	8.40	.35	8.70	.29
9	9.24	.77	9.36	.52	9.60	.40	9.60	.32
10	10.32	.86	10.44	.58	10.56	.44	10.80	.36
20	20.76	1.73	21.06	1.17	21.36	.89	21.90	.73
30	31.08	2.59	31.68	1.76	32.16	1.34	32.70	1.09
40	41.52	3.46	42.30	2.35	42.96	1.79	43.80	1.46
50	51.96	4.33	52.74	2.93	53.76	2.24	54.60	1.82
60	62.28	5.19	63.36	3.52	64.56	2.69	65.70	2.19
70	72.72	6.06	73.98	4.11	75.36	3.14	76.50	2.55
80	83.16	6.93	84.60	4.70	86.16	3.59	87.60	2.92
90	93.48	7.79	95.22	5.29	96.72	4.03	98.40	3.28
100	103.92	8.66	105.66	5.87	107.52	4.48	109.50	3.65
200	207.84	17.32	211.50	11.75	215.28	8.97	219.00	7.30
300	311.88	25.99	317.34	17.63	323.04	13.46	328.80	10.96
400	415.80	34.65	423.18	23.51	430.80	17.95	438.30	14.61
500	519.84	43.32	529.02	29.39	538.56	22.44	548.10	18.27
600	623.76	51.98	634.86	35.27	646.32	26.93	657.60	21.92
700	727.68	60.64	740.70	41.15	754.08	31.42	767.40	25.58
800	831.72	69.31	846.54	47.03	861.60	35.90	876.90	29.23
900	935.64	77.97	952.38	52.91	969.36	40.39	986.70	32.89
1000	1039.68	86.64	1058.22	58.79	1077.12	44.88	1096.20	36.54
1500	1559.52	129.96	1587.42	88.19	1615.68	67.32	1644.30	54.81
2000	2079.36	173.28	2116.62	117.59	2154.48	89.77	2192.70	73.09
2500	2599.20	216.60	2645.82	146.99	2693.04	112.21	2740.80	91.36
3000	3119.04	259.92	3175.02	176.39	3231.60	134.65	3288.90	109.63
3500	3638.88	303.24	3704.22	205.79	3770.40	157.10	3837.00	127.90
4000	4158.72	346.56	4233.42	235.19	4308.96	179.54	4385.40	146.18
4500	4678.56	389.88	4762.62	264.59	4847.52	201.98	4933.50	164.45
5000	5198.52	433.21	5291.82	293.99	5386.32	224.43	5481.60	182.72
5500	5718.36	476.53	5821.02	323.39	5924.88	246.87	6030.00	201.00
6000	6238.20	519.85	6350.22	352.79	6463.44	269.31	6578.10	219.27
6500	6758.04	563.17	6879.42	382.19	7002.00	291.75	7126.20	237.54
7000	7277.88	606.49	7408.62	411.59	7540.80	314.20	7674.30	255.81
7500	7797.72	649.81	7937.64	440.98	8079.36	336.64	8222.70	274.09
8000	8317.56	693.13	8466.84	470.38	8617.92	359.08	8770.80	292.36
8500	8837.40	736.45	8996.04	499.78	9156.72	381.53	9318.90	310.63
9000	9357.24	779.77	9525.24	529.18	9695.28	403.97	9867.30	328.91
10000	10397.04	866.42	10583.64	587.98	10772.64	448.86	10963.50	365.45
11000	11436.72	953.06	11642.04	646.78	11849.76	493.74	12060.00	402.00
12000	12476.40	1039.70	12700.44	705.58	12927.12	538.63	13156.20	438.54
13000	13516.08	1126.34	13758.84	764.38	14004.24	583.51	14252.70	475.09
14000	14555.76	1212.98	14817.24	823.18	15081.60	628.40	15348.90	511.63
15000	15595.56	1299.63	15875.46	881.97	16158.96	673.29	16445.40	548.18
16000	16635.24	1386.27	16933.86	940.77	17236.08	718.17	17541.90	584.73
17000	17674.92	1472.91	17992.26	999.57	18313.44	763.06	18638.10	621.27
18000	18714.60	1559.55	19050.66	1058.37	19390.56	807.94	19734.60	657.82
19000	19754.28	1646.19	20109.06	1117.17	20467.92	852.83	20830.80	694.36
20000	20794.08	1732.84	21167.46	1175.97	21545.28	897.72	21927.30	730.91
21000	21833.76	1819.48	22225.86	1234.77	22622.40	942.60	23023.50	767.45
22000	22873.44	1906.12	23284.08	1293.56	23699.76	987.49	24120.00	804.00
23000	23913.12	1992.76	24342.48	1352.36	24776.88	1032.37	25216.50	840.55
24000	24952.80	2079.40	25400.88	1411.16	25854.24	1077.26	26312.70	877.09
25000	25992.60	2166.05	26459.28	1469.96	26931.60	1122.15	27409.20	913.64

ANNUAL PERCENTAGE RATE **7.25%**

	36 MONTHS		42 MONTHS		48 MONTHS		60 MONTHS	
LOAN AMT	TOTAL NOTE	MONTHLY PAYMENT	TOTAL NOTE	MONTHLY PAYMENT	TOTAL NOTE	MONTHLY PAYMENT	TOTAL NOTE	MONTHLY PAYMENT
1	1.08	.03	.84	.02	.96	.02	.60	.01
2	2.16	.06	2.10	.05	1.92	.04	1.80	.03
3	3.24	.09	3.36	.08	3.36	.07	3.00	.05
4	4.32	.12	4.20	.10	4.32	.09	4.20	.07
5	5.40	.15	5.46	.13	5.76	.12	5.40	.09
6	6.48	.18	6.72	.16	6.72	.14	6.60	.11
7	7.56	.21	7.56	.18	7.68	.16	7.80	.13
8	8.64	.24	8.82	.21	9.12	.19	9.00	.15
9	9.72	.27	10.08	.24	10.08	.21	10.20	.17
10	10.80	.30	11.34	.27	11.52	.24	11.40	.19
20	21.96	.61	22.68	.54	23.04	.48	23.40	.39
30	33.12	.92	34.02	.81	34.56	.72	35.40	.59
40	44.28	1.23	45.36	1.08	46.08	.96	47.40	.79
50	55.44	1.54	56.70	1.35	57.60	1.20	59.40	.99
60	66.60	1.85	68.04	1.62	69.12	1.44	71.40	1.19
70	77.76	2.16	79.38	1.89	80.64	1.68	83.40	1.39
80	88.92	2.47	90.72	2.16	92.16	1.92	95.40	1.59
90	100.08	2.78	102.06	2.43	103.68	2.16	107.40	1.79
100	111.24	3.09	113.40	2.70	115.20	2.40	119.40	1.99
200	222.84	6.19	226.80	5.40	230.88	4.81	238.80	3.98
300	334.44	9.29	340.20	8.10	346.08	7.21	358.20	5.97
400	446.04	12.39	454.02	10.81	461.76	9.62	477.60	7.96
500	557.64	15.49	567.42	13.51	577.44	12.03	597.00	9.95
600	669.24	18.59	680.82	16.21	692.64	14.43	717.00	11.95
700	780.84	21.69	794.64	18.92	808.32	16.84	836.40	13.94
800	892.44	24.79	908.04	21.62	923.52	19.24	955.80	15.93
900	1004.04	27.89	1021.44	24.32	1039.20	21.65	1075.20	17.92
1000	1115.64	30.99	1134.84	27.02	1154.88	24.06	1194.60	19.91
1500	1673.28	46.48	1702.68	40.54	1732.32	36.09	1792.20	29.87
2000	2231.28	61.98	2270.10	54.05	2309.76	48.12	2389.80	39.83
2500	2788.92	77.47	2837.94	67.57	2887.20	60.15	2987.40	49.79
3000	3346.92	92.97	3405.36	81.08	3464.64	72.18	3585.00	59.75
3500	3904.92	108.47	3973.20	94.60	4042.08	84.21	4182.60	69.71
4000	4462.56	123.96	4540.62	108.11	4619.52	96.24	4780.20	79.67
4500	5020.56	139.46	5108.46	121.63	5197.44	108.28	5377.80	89.63
5000	5578.20	154.95	5675.88	135.14	5774.88	120.31	5975.40	99.59
5500	6136.20	170.45	6243.72	148.66	6352.32	132.34	6573.00	109.55
6000	6693.84	185.94	6811.14	162.17	6929.76	144.37	7170.60	119.51
6500	7251.84	201.44	7378.98	175.69	7507.20	156.40	7768.20	129.47
7000	7809.84	216.94	7946.40	189.20	8084.64	168.43	8365.80	139.43
7500	8367.48	232.43	8514.24	202.72	8662.08	180.46	8963.40	149.39
8000	8925.48	247.93	9081.66	216.23	9239.52	192.49	9561.00	159.35
8500	9483.12	263.42	9649.50	229.75	9817.44	204.53	10158.60	169.31
9000	10041.12	278.92	10216.92	243.26	10394.88	216.56	10756.20	179.27
10000	11156.76	309.91	11352.18	270.29	11549.76	240.62	11951.40	199.19
11000	12272.40	340.90	12487.44	297.32	12704.64	264.68	13146.60	219.11
12000	13388.04	371.89	13622.70	324.35	13859.52	288.74	14341.80	239.03
13000	14503.68	402.88	14757.96	351.38	15014.88	312.81	15537.00	258.95
14000	15619.68	433.88	15893.22	378.41	16169.76	336.87	16732.20	278.87
15000	16735.32	464.87	17028.48	405.44	17324.64	360.93	17927.40	298.79
16000	17850.96	495.86	18163.74	432.47	18479.52	384.99	19122.00	318.70
17000	18966.60	526.85	19299.00	459.50	19634.88	409.06	20317.20	338.62
18000	20082.24	557.84	20434.26	486.53	20789.76	433.12	21512.40	358.54
19000	21197.88	588.83	21569.10	513.55	21944.64	457.18	22707.60	378.46
20000	22313.88	619.83	22704.36	540.58	23099.52	481.24	23902.80	398.38
21000	23429.52	650.82	23839.62	567.61	24254.88	505.31	25098.00	418.30
22000	24545.16	681.81	24974.88	594.64	25409.76	529.37	26293.20	438.22
23000	25660.80	712.80	26110.14	621.67	26564.64	553.43	27488.40	458.14
24000	26776.44	743.79	27245.40	648.70	27719.52	577.49	28683.60	478.06
25000	27892.08	774.78	28380.66	675.73	28874.88	601.56	29878.80	497.98

7.30% ANNUAL PERCENTAGE RATE

LOAN AMT	12 MONTHS TOTAL NOTE	12 MONTHS MONTHLY PAYMENT	18 MONTHS TOTAL NOTE	18 MONTHS MONTHLY PAYMENT	24 MONTHS TOTAL NOTE	24 MONTHS MONTHLY PAYMENT	30 MONTHS TOTAL NOTE	30 MONTHS MONTHLY PAYMENT
1	.96	.08	.90	.05	.96	.04	.90	.03
2	2.04	.17	1.98	.11	1.92	.08	2.10	.07
3	3.00	.25	3.06	.17	3.12	.13	3.00	.10
4	4.08	.34	4.14	.23	4.08	.17	4.20	.14
5	5.16	.43	5.22	.29	5.28	.22	5.40	.18
6	6.12	.51	6.30	.35	6.24	.26	6.30	.21
7	7.20	.60	7.38	.41	7.44	.31	7.50	.25
8	8.28	.69	8.46	.47	8.40	.35	8.70	.29
9	9.24	.77	9.36	.52	9.60	.40	9.60	.32
10	10.32	.86	10.44	.58	10.56	.44	10.80	.36
20	20.76	1.73	21.06	1.17	21.36	.89	21.90	.73
30	31.08	2.59	31.68	1.76	32.16	1.34	32.70	1.09
40	41.52	3.46	42.30	2.35	42.96	1.79	43.80	1.46
50	51.96	4.33	52.92	2.94	53.76	2.24	54.60	1.82
60	62.28	5.19	63.36	3.52	64.56	2.69	65.70	2.19
70	72.72	6.06	73.98	4.11	75.36	3.14	76.50	2.55
80	83.16	6.93	84.60	4.70	86.16	3.59	87.60	2.92
90	93.48	7.79	95.22	5.29	96.96	4.04	98.70	3.29
100	103.92	8.66	105.84	5.88	107.76	4.49	109.50	3.65
200	207.96	17.33	211.68	11.76	215.52	8.98	219.30	7.31
300	311.88	25.99	317.52	17.64	323.28	13.47	329.10	10.97
400	415.92	34.66	423.36	23.52	431.04	17.96	438.60	14.62
500	519.96	43.33	529.38	29.41	538.80	22.45	548.40	18.28
600	623.88	51.99	635.22	35.29	646.56	26.94	658.20	21.94
700	727.92	60.66	741.06	41.17	754.32	31.43	767.70	25.59
800	831.96	69.33	846.90	47.05	862.08	35.92	877.50	29.25
900	935.88	77.99	952.74	52.93	969.84	40.41	987.30	32.91
1000	1039.92	86.66	1058.76	58.82	1077.60	44.90	1096.80	36.56
1500	1559.88	129.99	1588.14	88.23	1616.64	67.36	1645.50	54.85
2000	2079.96	173.33	2117.52	117.64	2155.44	89.81	2193.90	73.13
2500	2599.92	216.66	2646.90	147.05	2694.48	112.27	2742.60	91.42
3000	3119.88	259.99	3176.28	176.46	3233.28	134.72	3291.00	109.70
3500	3639.84	303.32	3705.66	205.87	3772.32	157.18	3839.40	127.98
4000	4159.92	346.66	4235.04	235.28	4311.12	179.63	4388.10	146.27
4500	4679.88	389.99	4764.42	264.69	4849.92	202.08	4936.50	164.55
5000	5199.84	433.32	5293.80	294.10	5388.96	224.54	5485.20	182.84
5500	5719.80	476.65	5823.18	323.51	5927.76	246.99	6033.60	201.12
6000	6239.88	519.99	6352.56	352.92	6466.80	269.45	6582.30	219.41
6500	6759.84	563.32	6881.94	382.33	7005.60	291.90	7130.70	237.69
7000	7279.80	606.65	7411.32	411.74	7544.64	314.36	7679.10	255.97
7500	7799.76	649.98	7940.88	441.16	8083.44	336.81	8227.80	274.26
8000	8319.84	693.32	8470.26	470.57	8622.24	359.26	8776.20	292.54
8500	8839.80	736.65	8999.64	499.98	9161.28	381.72	9324.90	310.83
9000	9359.76	779.98	9529.02	529.39	9700.08	404.17	9873.30	329.11
10000	10399.80	866.65	10587.78	588.21	10777.92	449.08	10970.40	365.68
11000	11439.72	953.31	11646.54	647.03	11855.76	493.99	12067.50	402.25
12000	12479.76	1039.98	12705.30	705.85	12933.60	538.90	13164.60	438.82
13000	13519.68	1126.64	13764.06	764.67	14011.44	583.81	14261.70	475.39
14000	14559.72	1213.31	14822.82	823.49	15089.28	628.72	15358.50	511.95
15000	15599.64	1299.97	15881.76	882.32	16167.12	673.63	16455.60	548.52
16000	16639.68	1386.64	16940.52	941.14	17244.72	718.53	17552.70	585.09
17000	17679.60	1473.30	17999.28	999.96	18322.56	763.44	18649.80	621.66
18000	18719.64	1559.97	19058.04	1058.78	19400.40	808.35	19746.90	658.23
19000	19759.56	1646.63	20116.80	1117.60	20478.24	853.26	20844.00	694.80
20000	20799.60	1733.30	21175.56	1176.42	21556.08	898.17	21940.80	731.36
21000	21839.52	1819.96	22234.32	1235.24	22633.92	943.08	23037.90	767.93
22000	22879.56	1906.63	23293.26	1294.07	23711.76	987.99	24135.00	804.50
23000	23919.48	1993.29	24352.02	1352.89	24789.60	1032.90	25232.10	841.07
24000	24959.52	2079.96	25410.78	1411.71	25867.20	1077.80	26329.20	877.64
25000	25999.44	2166.62	26469.54	1470.53	26945.04	1122.71	27426.30	914.21

ANNUAL PERCENTAGE RATE **7.30%**

LOAN AMT	36 MONTHS TOTAL NOTE	36 MONTHS MONTHLY PAYMENT	42 MONTHS TOTAL NOTE	42 MONTHS MONTHLY PAYMENT	48 MONTHS TOTAL NOTE	48 MONTHS MONTHLY PAYMENT	60 MONTHS TOTAL NOTE	60 MONTHS MONTHLY PAYMENT
1	1.08	.03	.84	.02	.96	.02	.60	.01
2	2.16	.06	2.10	.05	1.92	.04	1.80	.03
3	3.24	.09	3.36	.08	3.36	.07	3.00	.05
4	4.32	.12	4.20	.10	4.32	.09	4.20	.07
5	5.40	.15	5.46	.13	5.76	.12	5.40	.09
6	6.48	.18	6.72	.16	6.72	.14	6.60	.11
7	7.56	.21	7.56	.18	7.68	.16	7.80	.13
8	8.64	.24	8.82	.21	9.12	.19	9.00	.15
9	9.72	.27	10.08	.24	10.08	.21	10.20	.17
10	11.16	.31	11.34	.27	11.52	.24	11.40	.19
20	22.32	.62	22.68	.54	23.04	.48	23.40	.39
30	33.48	.93	34.02	.81	34.56	.72	35.40	.59
40	44.64	1.24	45.36	1.08	46.08	.96	47.40	.79
50	55.80	1.55	56.70	1.35	57.60	1.20	59.40	.99
60	66.96	1.86	68.04	1.62	69.12	1.44	71.40	1.19
70	78.12	2.17	79.38	1.89	80.64	1.68	83.40	1.39
80	89.28	2.48	90.72	2.16	92.16	1.92	95.40	1.59
90	100.44	2.79	102.06	2.43	103.68	2.16	107.40	1.79
100	111.60	3.10	113.40	2.70	115.20	2.40	119.40	1.99
200	223.20	6.20	227.22	5.41	230.88	4.81	238.80	3.98
300	334.80	9.30	340.62	8.11	346.56	7.22	358.80	5.98
400	446.40	12.40	454.44	10.82	462.24	9.63	478.20	7.97
500	558.00	15.50	567.84	13.52	577.92	12.04	598.20	9.97
600	669.60	18.60	681.66	16.23	693.60	14.45	717.60	11.96
700	781.56	21.71	795.06	18.93	808.80	16.85	837.60	13.96
800	893.16	24.81	908.88	21.64	924.48	19.26	957.00	15.95
900	1004.76	27.91	1022.28	24.34	1040.16	21.67	1076.40	17.94
1000	1116.36	31.01	1136.10	27.05	1155.84	24.08	1196.40	19.94
1500	1674.72	46.52	1703.94	40.57	1733.76	36.12	1794.60	29.91
2000	2232.72	62.02	2272.20	54.10	2312.16	48.17	2392.80	39.88
2500	2791.08	77.53	2840.46	67.63	2890.08	60.21	2991.00	49.85
3000	3349.44	93.04	3408.30	81.15	3468.00	72.25	3589.20	59.82
3500	3907.80	108.55	3976.56	94.68	4045.92	84.29	4188.00	69.80
4000	4465.80	124.05	4544.82	108.21	4624.32	96.34	4786.20	79.77
4500	5024.16	139.56	5112.66	121.73	5202.24	108.38	5384.40	89.74
5000	5582.52	155.07	5680.92	135.26	5780.16	120.42	5982.60	99.71
5500	6140.52	170.57	6248.76	148.78	6358.56	132.47	6580.80	109.68
6000	6698.88	186.08	6817.02	162.31	6936.48	144.51	7179.00	119.65
6500	7257.24	201.59	7385.28	175.84	7514.40	156.55	7777.20	129.62
7000	7815.60	217.10	7953.12	189.36	8092.32	168.59	8376.00	139.60
7500	8373.60	232.60	8521.38	202.89	8670.72	180.64	8974.20	149.57
8000	8931.96	248.11	9089.64	216.42	9248.64	192.68	9572.40	159.54
8500	9490.32	263.62	9657.48	229.94	9826.56	204.72	10170.60	169.51
9000	10048.68	279.13	10225.74	243.47	10404.96	216.77	10768.80	179.48
10000	11165.04	310.14	11361.84	270.52	11560.80	240.85	11965.80	199.43
11000	12281.40	341.15	12497.94	297.57	12717.12	264.94	13162.20	219.37
12000	13398.12	372.17	13634.46	324.63	13872.96	289.02	14358.60	239.31
13000	14514.48	403.18	14770.56	351.68	15029.28	313.11	15555.00	259.25
14000	15631.20	434.20	15906.66	378.73	16185.12	337.19	16752.00	279.20
15000	16747.56	465.21	17042.76	405.78	17341.44	361.28	17948.40	299.14
16000	17864.28	496.23	18179.28	432.84	18497.76	385.37	19144.80	319.08
17000	18980.64	527.24	19315.38	459.89	19653.60	409.45	20341.80	339.03
18000	20097.36	558.26	20451.48	486.94	20809.92	433.54	21538.20	358.97
19000	21213.72	589.27	21587.58	513.99	21965.76	457.62	22734.60	378.91
20000	22330.08	620.28	22724.10	541.05	23122.08	481.71	23931.60	398.86
21000	23446.80	651.30	23860.20	568.10	24277.92	505.79	25128.00	418.80
22000	24563.16	682.31	24996.30	595.15	25434.24	529.88	26324.40	438.74
23000	25679.88	713.33	26132.40	622.20	26590.56	553.97	27521.40	458.69
24000	26796.24	744.34	27268.92	649.26	27746.40	578.05	28717.80	478.63
25000	27912.96	775.36	28405.02	676.31	28902.72	602.14	29914.20	498.57

7.40% ANNUAL PERCENTAGE RATE

LOAN AMT	12 MONTHS TOTAL NOTE	12 MONTHS MONTHLY PAYMENT	18 MONTHS TOTAL NOTE	18 MONTHS MONTHLY PAYMENT	24 MONTHS TOTAL NOTE	24 MONTHS MONTHLY PAYMENT	30 MONTHS TOTAL NOTE	30 MONTHS MONTHLY PAYMENT
1	.96	.08	.90	.05	.96	.04	.90	.03
2	2.04	.17	1.98	.11	1.92	.08	2.10	.07
3	3.12	.26	3.06	.17	3.12	.13	3.00	.10
4	4.08	.34	4.14	.23	4.08	.17	4.20	.14
5	5.16	.43	5.22	.29	5.28	.22	5.40	.18
6	6.24	.52	6.30	.35	6.24	.26	6.30	.21
7	7.20	.60	7.38	.41	7.44	.31	7.50	.25
8	8.28	.69	8.46	.47	8.40	.35	8.70	.29
9	9.36	.78	9.36	.52	9.60	.40	9.60	.32
10	10.32	.86	10.44	.58	10.56	.44	10.80	.36
20	20.76	1.73	21.06	1.17	21.36	.89	21.90	.73
30	31.20	2.60	31.68	1.76	32.16	1.34	32.70	1.09
40	41.52	3.46	42.30	2.35	42.96	1.79	43.80	1.46
50	51.96	4.33	52.92	2.94	53.76	2.24	54.90	1.83
60	62.40	5.20	63.54	3.53	64.56	2.69	65.70	2.19
70	72.72	6.06	74.16	4.12	75.36	3.14	76.80	2.56
80	83.16	6.93	84.60	4.70	86.16	3.59	87.60	2.92
90	93.60	7.80	95.22	5.29	96.96	4.04	98.70	3.29
100	104.04	8.67	105.84	5.88	107.76	4.49	109.80	3.66
200	208.08	17.34	211.86	11.77	215.76	8.99	219.60	7.32
300	312.12	26.01	317.88	17.66	323.52	13.48	329.40	10.98
400	416.16	34.68	423.72	23.54	431.52	17.98	439.20	14.64
500	520.20	43.35	529.74	29.43	539.28	22.47	549.00	18.30
600	624.24	52.02	635.76	35.32	647.28	26.97	658.80	21.96
700	728.28	60.69	741.60	41.20	755.04	31.46	768.60	25.62
800	832.32	69.36	847.62	47.09	863.04	35.96	878.70	29.29
900	936.48	78.04	953.64	52.98	970.80	40.45	988.50	32.95
1000	1040.52	86.71	1059.48	58.86	1078.80	44.95	1098.30	36.61
1500	1560.72	130.06	1589.40	88.30	1618.32	67.43	1647.60	54.92
2000	2081.04	173.42	2119.14	117.73	2157.60	89.90	2196.60	73.22
2500	2601.24	216.77	2648.88	147.16	2697.12	112.38	2745.90	91.53
3000	3121.56	260.13	3178.80	176.60	3236.64	134.86	3295.20	109.84
3500	3641.76	303.48	3708.54	206.03	3775.92	157.33	3844.20	128.14
4000	4162.08	346.84	4238.28	235.46	4315.44	179.81	4393.50	146.45
4500	4682.40	390.20	4768.20	264.90	4854.96	202.29	4942.80	164.76
5000	5202.60	433.55	5297.94	294.33	5394.48	224.77	5492.10	183.07
5500	5722.92	476.91	5827.68	323.76	5933.76	247.24	6041.10	201.37
6000	6243.12	520.26	6357.60	353.20	6473.28	269.72	6590.40	219.68
6500	6763.44	563.62	6887.34	382.63	7012.80	292.20	7139.70	237.99
7000	7283.64	606.97	7417.08	412.06	7552.08	314.67	7688.70	256.29
7500	7803.96	650.33	7947.00	441.50	8091.60	337.15	8238.00	274.60
8000	8324.28	693.69	8476.74	470.93	8631.12	359.63	8787.30	292.91
8500	8844.48	737.04	9006.48	500.36	9170.64	382.11	9336.30	311.21
9000	9364.80	780.40	9536.46	529.80	9709.92	404.58	9885.60	329.52
10000	10405.32	867.11	10595.88	588.66	10788.96	449.54	10984.20	366.14
11000	11445.84	953.82	11655.54	647.53	11867.76	494.49	12082.50	402.75
12000	12486.36	1040.53	12715.20	706.40	12946.56	539.44	13180.80	439.36
13000	13526.88	1127.24	13774.68	765.26	14025.60	584.40	14279.40	475.98
14000	14567.40	1213.95	14834.34	824.13	15104.40	629.35	15377.70	512.59
15000	15607.92	1300.66	15894.00	883.00	16183.44	674.31	16476.30	549.21
16000	16648.56	1387.38	16953.48	941.86	17262.24	719.26	17574.60	585.82
17000	17689.08	1474.09	18013.14	1000.73	18341.28	764.22	18672.90	622.43
18000	18729.60	1560.80	19072.80	1059.60	19420.08	809.17	19771.50	659.05
19000	19770.12	1647.51	20132.46	1118.47	20498.88	854.12	20869.80	695.66
20000	20810.64	1734.22	21191.94	1177.33	21577.92	899.08	21968.40	732.28
21000	21851.16	1820.93	22251.60	1236.20	22656.72	944.03	23066.70	768.89
22000	22891.68	1907.64	23311.26	1295.07	23735.76	988.99	24165.00	805.50
23000	23932.20	1994.35	24370.74	1353.93	24814.56	1033.94	25263.60	842.12
24000	24972.84	2081.07	25430.40	1412.80	25893.36	1078.89	26361.90	878.73
25000	26013.36	2167.78	26490.06	1471.67	26972.40	1123.85	27460.50	915.35

ANNUAL PERCENTAGE RATE **7.40%**

LOAN AMT	36 MONTHS TOTAL NOTE	36 MONTHS MONTHLY PAYMENT	42 MONTHS TOTAL NOTE	42 MONTHS MONTHLY PAYMENT	48 MONTHS TOTAL NOTE	48 MONTHS MONTHLY PAYMENT	60 MONTHS TOTAL NOTE	60 MONTHS MONTHLY PAYMENT
1	1.08	.03	.84	.02	.96	.02	.60	.01
2	2.16	.06	2.10	.05	1.92	.04	1.80	.03
3	3.24	.09	3.36	.08	3.36	.07	3.00	.05
4	4.32	.12	4.20	.10	4.32	.09	4.20	.07
5	5.40	.15	5.46	.13	5.76	.12	5.40	.09
6	6.48	.18	6.72	.16	6.72	.14	6.60	.11
7	7.56	.21	7.56	.18	7.68	.16	7.80	.13
8	8.64	.24	8.82	.21	9.12	.19	9.00	.15
9	9.72	.27	10.08	.24	10.08	.21	10.20	.17
10	11.16	.31	11.34	.27	11.52	.24	11.40	.19
20	22.32	.62	22.68	.54	23.04	.48	23.40	.39
30	33.48	.93	34.02	.81	34.56	.72	35.40	.59
40	44.64	1.24	45.36	1.08	46.08	.96	47.40	.79
50	55.80	1.55	56.70	1.35	57.60	1.20	59.40	.99
60	66.96	1.86	68.04	1.62	69.12	1.44	71.40	1.19
70	78.12	2.17	79.38	1.89	80.64	1.68	83.40	1.39
80	89.28	2.48	90.72	2.16	92.64	1.93	95.40	1.59
90	100.44	2.79	102.06	2.43	104.16	2.17	107.40	1.79
100	111.60	3.10	113.40	2.70	115.68	2.41	119.40	1.99
200	223.56	6.21	227.22	5.41	231.36	4.82	239.40	3.99
300	335.16	9.31	341.04	8.12	347.04	7.23	359.40	5.99
400	447.12	12.42	454.86	10.83	463.20	9.65	479.40	7.99
500	559.08	15.53	568.68	13.54	578.88	12.06	599.40	9.99
600	670.68	18.63	682.50	16.25	694.56	14.47	719.40	11.99
700	782.64	21.74	796.32	18.96	810.72	16.89	839.40	13.99
800	894.24	24.84	910.14	21.67	926.40	19.30	959.40	15.99
900	1006.20	27.95	1023.96	24.38	1042.08	21.71	1079.40	17.99
1000	1118.16	31.06	1137.78	27.09	1158.24	24.13	1199.40	19.99
1500	1677.24	46.59	1706.88	40.64	1737.12	36.19	1798.80	29.98
2000	2236.32	62.12	2275.98	54.19	2316.48	48.26	2398.80	39.98
2500	2795.40	77.65	2845.08	67.74	2895.84	60.33	2998.20	49.97
3000	3354.48	93.18	3414.18	81.29	3474.72	72.39	3598.20	59.97
3500	3913.56	108.71	3983.28	94.84	4054.08	84.46	4197.60	69.96
4000	4472.64	124.24	4552.38	108.39	4632.96	96.52	4797.60	79.96
4500	5031.72	139.77	5121.48	121.94	5212.32	108.59	5397.00	89.95
5000	5590.80	155.30	5690.58	135.49	5791.68	120.66	5997.00	99.95
5500	6149.88	170.83	6259.68	149.04	6370.56	132.72	6596.40	109.94
6000	6708.96	186.36	6828.78	162.59	6949.92	144.79	7196.40	119.94
6500	7268.04	201.89	7397.88	176.14	7528.80	156.85	7795.80	129.93
7000	7827.12	217.42	7966.98	189.69	8108.16	168.92	8395.80	139.93
7500	8386.20	232.95	8536.08	203.24	8687.52	180.99	8995.20	149.92
8000	8945.28	248.48	9104.76	216.78	9266.40	193.05	9595.20	159.92
8500	9504.36	264.01	9673.86	230.33	9845.76	205.12	10194.60	169.91
9000	10063.44	279.54	10242.96	243.88	10425.12	217.19	10794.60	179.91
10000	11181.60	310.60	11381.16	270.98	11583.36	241.32	11994.00	199.90
11000	12299.76	341.66	12519.36	298.08	12741.60	265.45	13193.40	219.89
12000	13417.92	372.72	13657.56	325.18	13899.84	289.58	14392.80	239.88
13000	14536.08	403.78	14795.76	352.28	15058.08	313.71	15592.20	259.87
14000	15654.24	434.84	15933.96	379.38	16216.80	337.85	16791.60	279.86
15000	16772.40	465.90	17072.16	406.48	17375.04	361.98	17991.00	299.85
16000	17890.56	496.96	18209.94	433.57	18533.28	386.11	19190.40	319.84
17000	19008.72	528.02	19348.14	460.67	19691.52	410.24	20389.80	339.83
18000	20126.88	559.08	20486.34	487.77	20850.24	434.38	21589.20	359.82
19000	21245.04	590.14	21624.54	514.87	22008.48	458.51	22788.60	379.81
20000	22363.20	621.20	22762.74	541.97	23166.72	482.64	23988.00	399.80
21000	23481.36	652.26	23900.94	569.07	24324.96	506.77	25187.40	419.79
22000	24599.52	683.32	25039.14	596.17	25483.20	530.90	26387.40	439.79
23000	25717.68	714.38	26177.34	623.27	26641.92	555.04	27586.80	459.78
24000	26835.84	745.44	27315.12	650.36	27800.16	579.17	28786.20	479.77
25000	27954.00	776.50	28453.32	677.46	28958.40	603.30	29985.60	499.76

7.50% ANNUAL PERCENTAGE RATE

	12 MONTHS		18 MONTHS		24 MONTHS		30 MONTHS	
LOAN AMT	TOTAL NOTE	MONTHLY PAYMENT	TOTAL NOTE	MONTHLY PAYMENT	TOTAL NOTE	MONTHLY PAYMENT	TOTAL NOTE	MONTHLY PAYMENT
1	.96	.08	.90	.05	.96	.04	.90	.03
2	2.04	.17	1.98	.11	1.92	.08	2.10	.07
3	3.12	.26	3.06	.17	3.12	.13	3.00	.10
4	4.08	.34	4.14	.23	4.08	.17	4.20	.14
5	5.16	.43	5.22	.29	5.28	.22	5.40	.18
6	6.24	.52	6.30	.35	6.24	.26	6.30	.21
7	7.20	.60	7.38	.41	7.44	.31	7.50	.25
8	8.28	.69	8.46	.47	8.40	.35	8.70	.29
9	9.36	.78	9.54	.53	9.60	.40	9.60	.32
10	10.32	.86	10.44	.58	10.56	.44	10.80	.36
20	20.76	1.73	21.06	1.17	21.36	.89	21.90	.73
30	31.20	2.60	31.68	1.76	32.16	1.34	32.70	1.09
40	41.64	3.47	42.30	2.35	42.96	1.79	43.80	1.46
50	51.96	4.33	52.92	2.94	53.76	2.24	54.90	1.83
60	62.40	5.20	63.54	3.53	64.56	2.69	65.70	2.19
70	72.84	6.07	74.16	4.12	75.36	3.14	76.80	2.56
80	83.28	6.94	84.78	4.71	86.16	3.59	87.90	2.93
90	93.60	7.80	95.40	5.30	96.96	4.04	98.70	3.29
100	104.04	8.67	106.02	5.89	107.76	4.49	109.80	3.66
200	208.20	17.35	212.04	11.78	215.76	8.99	219.90	7.33
300	312.24	26.02	318.06	17.67	323.76	13.49	329.70	10.99
400	416.40	34.70	424.08	23.56	431.76	17.99	439.80	14.66
500	520.44	43.37	530.10	29.45	539.76	22.49	549.60	18.32
600	624.60	52.05	636.12	35.34	647.76	26.99	659.70	21.99
700	728.76	60.73	742.14	41.23	755.76	31.49	769.80	25.66
800	832.80	69.40	848.16	47.12	863.76	35.99	879.60	29.32
900	936.96	78.08	954.36	53.02	971.76	40.49	989.70	32.99
1000	1041.00	86.75	1060.38	58.91	1079.76	44.99	1099.50	36.65
1500	1561.56	130.13	1590.48	88.36	1619.76	67.49	1649.40	54.98
2000	2082.12	173.51	2120.76	117.82	2159.76	89.99	2199.30	73.31
2500	2602.68	216.89	2651.04	147.28	2699.76	112.49	2749.20	91.64
3000	3123.24	260.27	3181.14	176.73	3239.76	134.99	3299.10	109.97
3500	3643.80	303.65	3711.42	206.19	3779.76	157.49	3849.00	128.30
4000	4164.24	347.02	4241.52	235.64	4319.76	179.99	4398.90	146.63
4500	4684.80	390.40	4771.80	265.10	4859.76	202.49	4948.80	164.96
5000	5205.36	433.78	5302.08	294.56	5399.76	224.99	5498.70	183.29
5500	5725.92	477.16	5832.18	324.01	5939.76	247.49	6048.60	201.62
6000	6246.48	520.54	6362.46	353.47	6479.76	269.99	6598.50	219.95
6500	6767.04	563.92	6892.74	382.93	7019.76	292.49	7148.40	238.28
7000	7287.60	607.30	7422.84	412.38	7559.76	314.99	7698.30	256.61
7500	7808.16	650.68	7953.12	441.84	8099.76	337.49	8248.20	274.94
8000	8328.60	694.05	8483.22	471.29	8639.76	359.99	8798.10	293.27
8500	8849.16	737.43	9013.50	500.75	9179.76	382.49	9348.00	311.60
9000	9369.72	780.81	9543.78	530.21	9719.76	404.99	9897.90	329.93
10000	10410.84	867.57	10604.16	589.12	10799.76	449.99	10997.70	366.59
11000	11451.96	954.33	11664.54	648.03	11879.76	494.99	12097.50	403.25
12000	12492.96	1041.08	12724.92	706.94	12959.76	539.99	13197.30	439.91
13000	13534.08	1127.84	13785.48	765.86	14039.76	584.99	14297.10	476.57
14000	14575.20	1214.60	14845.86	824.77	15119.76	629.99	15396.90	513.23
15000	15616.32	1301.36	15906.24	883.68	16199.76	674.99	16496.70	549.89
16000	16657.32	1388.11	16966.62	942.59	17279.76	719.99	17596.50	586.55
17000	17698.44	1474.87	18027.18	1001.51	18359.76	764.99	18696.30	623.21
18000	18739.56	1561.63	19087.56	1060.42	19439.76	809.99	19796.10	659.87
19000	19780.68	1648.39	20147.94	1119.33	20519.76	854.99	20895.90	696.53
20000	20821.68	1735.14	21208.32	1178.24	21599.76	899.99	21995.70	733.19
21000	21862.80	1821.90	22268.88	1237.16	22679.76	944.99	23095.50	769.85
22000	22903.92	1908.66	23329.26	1296.07	23759.76	989.99	24195.30	806.51
23000	23945.04	1995.42	24389.64	1354.98	24839.76	1034.99	25295.10	843.17
24000	24986.04	2082.17	25450.02	1413.89	25919.76	1079.99	26394.90	879.83
25000	26027.16	2168.93	26510.40	1472.80	26999.52	1124.98	27494.70	916.49

ANNUAL PERCENTAGE RATE **7.50%**

LOAN AMT	36 MONTHS TOTAL NOTE	MONTHLY PAYMENT	42 MONTHS TOTAL NOTE	MONTHLY PAYMENT	48 MONTHS TOTAL NOTE	MONTHLY PAYMENT	60 MONTHS TOTAL NOTE	MONTHLY PAYMENT
1	1.08	.03	.84	.02	.96	.02	1.20	.02
2	2.16	.06	2.10	.05	1.92	.04	2.40	.04
3	3.24	.09	3.36	.08	3.36	.07	3.60	.06
4	4.32	.12	4.20	.10	4.32	.09	4.80	.08
5	5.40	.15	5.46	.13	5.76	.12	6.00	.10
6	6.48	.18	6.72	.16	6.72	.14	7.20	.12
7	7.56	.21	7.98	.19	7.68	.16	8.40	.14
8	8.64	.24	8.82	.21	9.12	.19	9.60	.16
9	9.72	.27	10.08	.24	10.08	.21	10.80	.18
10	11.16	.31	11.34	.27	11.52	.24	12.00	.20
20	22.32	.62	22.68	.54	23.04	.48	24.00	.40
30	33.48	.93	34.02	.81	34.56	.72	36.00	.60
40	44.64	1.24	45.36	1.08	46.08	.96	48.00	.80
50	55.80	1.55	56.70	1.35	57.60	1.20	60.00	1.00
60	66.96	1.86	68.04	1.62	69.60	1.45	72.00	1.20
70	78.12	2.17	79.80	1.90	81.12	1.69	84.00	1.40
80	89.28	2.48	91.14	2.17	92.64	1.93	96.00	1.60
90	100.44	2.79	102.48	2.44	104.16	2.17	108.00	1.80
100	111.96	3.11	113.82	2.71	115.68	2.41	120.00	2.00
200	223.92	6.22	227.64	5.42	231.84	4.83	240.00	4.00
300	335.88	9.33	341.88	8.14	348.00	7.25	360.60	6.01
400	447.84	12.44	455.70	10.85	464.16	9.67	480.60	8.01
500	559.80	15.55	569.94	13.57	579.84	12.08	600.60	10.01
600	671.76	18.66	683.76	16.28	696.00	14.50	721.20	12.02
700	783.72	21.77	798.00	19.00	812.16	16.92	841.20	14.02
800	895.68	24.88	911.82	21.71	928.32	19.34	961.80	16.03
900	1007.64	27.99	1026.06	24.43	1044.48	21.76	1081.80	18.03
1000	1119.60	31.10	1139.88	27.14	1160.16	24.17	1201.80	20.03
1500	1679.40	46.65	1709.82	40.71	1740.48	36.26	1803.00	30.05
2000	2239.56	62.21	2279.76	54.28	2320.80	48.35	2404.20	40.07
2500	2799.36	77.76	2850.12	67.86	2901.12	60.44	3005.40	50.09
3000	3359.16	93.31	3420.06	81.43	3481.44	72.53	3606.60	60.11
3500	3919.32	108.87	3990.00	95.00	4061.76	84.62	4207.80	70.13
4000	4479.12	124.42	4559.94	108.57	4642.08	96.71	4809.00	80.15
4500	5038.92	139.97	5130.30	122.15	5222.40	108.80	5410.20	90.17
5000	5599.08	155.53	5700.24	135.72	5802.72	120.89	6010.80	100.18
5500	6158.88	171.08	6270.18	149.29	6383.04	132.98	6612.00	110.20
6000	6718.68	186.63	6840.12	162.86	6963.36	145.07	7213.20	120.22
6500	7278.84	202.19	7410.48	176.44	7543.68	157.16	7814.40	130.24
7000	7838.64	217.74	7980.42	190.01	8124.00	169.25	8415.60	140.26
7500	8398.44	233.29	8550.36	203.58	8704.32	181.34	9016.80	150.28
8000	8958.24	248.84	9120.30	217.15	9284.64	193.43	9618.00	160.30
8500	9518.40	264.40	9690.66	230.73	9864.96	205.52	10219.20	170.32
9000	10078.20	279.95	10260.60	244.30	10445.28	217.61	10820.40	180.34
10000	11198.16	311.06	11400.48	271.44	11605.44	241.78	12022.20	200.37
11000	12317.76	342.16	12540.78	298.59	12766.08	265.96	13224.60	220.41
12000	13437.72	373.27	13680.66	325.73	13926.72	290.14	14427.00	240.45
13000	14557.68	404.38	14820.96	352.88	15087.36	314.32	15629.40	260.49
14000	15677.28	435.48	15960.84	380.02	16248.00	338.50	16831.80	280.53
15000	16797.24	466.59	17101.14	407.17	17408.64	362.68	18033.60	300.56
16000	17916.84	497.69	18241.02	434.31	18569.28	386.86	19236.00	320.60
17000	19036.80	528.80	19381.32	461.46	19729.92	411.04	20438.40	340.64
18000	20156.76	559.91	20521.20	488.60	20890.56	435.22	21640.80	360.68
19000	21276.36	591.01	21661.50	515.75	22050.72	459.39	22843.20	380.72
20000	22396.32	622.12	22801.38	542.89	23211.36	483.57	24045.00	400.75
21000	23516.28	653.23	23941.68	570.04	24372.00	507.75	25247.40	420.79
22000	24635.88	684.33	25081.56	597.18	25532.64	531.93	26449.80	440.83
23000	25755.84	715.44	26221.86	624.33	26693.28	556.11	27652.20	460.87
24000	26875.44	746.54	27361.74	651.47	27853.92	580.29	28854.60	480.91
25000	27995.40	777.65	28502.04	678.62	29014.56	604.47	30056.40	500.94

7.60% ANNUAL PERCENTAGE RATE

LOAN AMT	12 MONTHS TOTAL NOTE	12 MONTHS MONTHLY PAYMENT	18 MONTHS TOTAL NOTE	18 MONTHS MONTHLY PAYMENT	24 MONTHS TOTAL NOTE	24 MONTHS MONTHLY PAYMENT	30 MONTHS TOTAL NOTE	30 MONTHS MONTHLY PAYMENT
1	.96	.08	.90	.05	.96	.04	.90	.03
2	2.04	.17	1.98	.11	2.16	.09	2.10	.07
3	3.12	.26	3.06	.17	3.12	.13	3.30	.11
4	4.08	.34	4.14	.23	4.32	.18	4.20	.14
5	5.16	.43	5.22	.29	5.28	.22	5.40	.18
6	6.24	.52	6.30	.35	6.48	.27	6.60	.22
7	7.20	.60	7.38	.41	7.44	.31	7.50	.25
8	8.28	.69	8.46	.47	8.64	.36	8.70	.29
9	9.36	.78	9.54	.53	9.60	.40	9.90	.33
10	10.32	.86	10.44	.58	10.80	.45	10.80	.36
20	20.76	1.73	21.06	1.17	21.60	.90	21.90	.73
30	31.20	2.60	31.68	1.76	32.40	1.35	33.00	1.10
40	41.64	3.47	42.30	2.35	43.20	1.80	43.80	1.46
50	52.08	4.34	52.92	2.94	54.00	2.25	54.90	1.83
60	62.40	5.20	63.54	3.53	64.80	2.70	66.00	2.20
70	72.84	6.07	74.16	4.12	75.60	3.15	76.80	2.56
80	83.28	6.94	84.78	4.71	86.40	3.60	87.90	2.93
90	93.72	7.81	95.40	5.30	97.20	4.05	99.00	3.30
100	104.16	8.68	106.02	5.89	108.00	4.50	110.10	3.67
200	208.32	17.36	212.22	11.79	216.00	9.00	220.20	7.34
300	312.48	26.04	318.24	17.68	324.24	13.51	330.30	11.01
400	416.64	34.72	424.44	23.58	432.24	18.01	440.40	14.68
500	520.80	43.40	530.46	29.47	540.48	22.52	550.50	18.35
600	624.96	52.08	636.66	35.37	648.48	27.02	660.60	22.02
700	729.12	60.76	742.86	41.27	756.72	31.53	770.70	25.69
800	833.28	69.44	848.88	47.16	864.72	36.03	880.80	29.36
900	937.44	78.12	955.08	53.06	972.96	40.54	990.90	33.03
1000	1041.60	86.80	1061.10	58.95	1080.96	45.04	1101.00	36.70
1500	1562.40	130.20	1591.74	88.43	1621.44	67.56	1651.50	55.05
2000	2083.20	173.60	2122.38	117.91	2162.16	90.09	2202.30	73.41
2500	2604.00	217.00	2653.02	147.39	2702.64	112.61	2752.80	91.76
3000	3124.92	260.41	3183.66	176.87	3243.12	135.13	3303.30	110.11
3500	3645.72	303.81	3714.30	206.35	3783.60	157.65	3853.80	128.46
4000	4166.52	347.21	4244.94	235.83	4324.32	180.18	4404.60	146.82
4500	4687.32	390.61	4775.58	265.31	4864.80	202.70	4955.10	165.17
5000	5208.12	434.01	5306.04	294.78	5405.28	225.22	5505.60	183.52
5500	5728.92	477.41	5836.68	324.26	5945.76	247.74	6056.10	201.87
6000	6249.84	520.82	6367.32	353.74	6486.48	270.27	6606.90	220.23
6500	6770.64	564.22	6897.96	383.22	7026.96	292.79	7157.40	238.58
7000	7291.44	607.62	7428.60	412.70	7567.44	315.31	7707.90	256.93
7500	7812.24	651.02	7959.24	442.18	8107.92	337.83	8258.70	275.29
8000	8333.04	694.42	8489.88	471.66	8648.64	360.36	8809.20	293.64
8500	8853.96	737.83	9020.52	501.14	9189.12	382.88	9359.70	311.99
9000	9374.76	781.23	9551.16	530.62	9729.60	405.40	9910.20	330.34
10000	10416.36	868.03	10612.26	589.57	10810.80	450.45	11011.50	367.05
11000	11457.96	954.83	11673.54	648.53	11891.76	495.49	12112.50	403.75
12000	12499.68	1041.64	12734.82	707.49	12972.96	540.54	13213.80	440.46
13000	13541.28	1128.44	13796.10	766.45	14053.92	585.58	14314.80	477.16
14000	14583.00	1215.25	14857.38	825.41	15135.12	630.63	15416.10	513.87
15000	15624.60	1302.05	15918.48	884.36	16216.08	675.67	16517.40	550.58
16000	16666.20	1388.85	16979.76	943.32	17297.28	720.72	17618.40	587.28
17000	17707.92	1475.66	18041.04	1002.28	18378.24	765.76	18719.70	623.99
18000	18749.52	1562.46	19102.32	1061.24	19459.44	810.81	19820.70	660.69
19000	19791.12	1649.26	20163.60	1120.20	20540.40	855.85	20922.00	697.40
20000	20832.84	1736.07	21224.70	1179.15	21621.60	900.90	22023.00	734.10
21000	21874.44	1822.87	22285.98	1238.11	22702.56	945.94	23124.30	770.81
22000	22916.04	1909.67	23347.26	1297.07	23783.76	990.99	24225.30	807.51
23000	23957.76	1996.48	24408.54	1356.03	24864.72	1036.03	25326.60	844.22
24000	24999.36	2083.28	25469.82	1414.99	25945.92	1081.08	26427.60	880.92
25000	26040.96	2170.08	26530.92	1473.94	27026.88	1126.12	27528.90	917.63

ANNUAL PERCENTAGE RATE **7.60%**

LOAN AMT	36 MONTHS TOTAL NOTE	36 MONTHS MONTHLY PAYMENT	42 MONTHS TOTAL NOTE	42 MONTHS MONTHLY PAYMENT	48 MONTHS TOTAL NOTE	48 MONTHS MONTHLY PAYMENT	60 MONTHS TOTAL NOTE	60 MONTHS MONTHLY PAYMENT
1	1.08	.03	.84	.02	.96	.02	1.20	.02
2	2.16	.06	2.10	.05	1.92	.04	2.40	.04
3	3.24	.09	3.36	.08	3.36	.07	3.60	.06
4	4.32	.12	4.20	.10	4.32	.09	4.80	.08
5	5.40	.15	5.46	.13	5.76	.12	6.00	.10
6	6.48	.18	6.72	.16	6.72	.14	7.20	.12
7	7.56	.21	7.98	.19	7.68	.16	8.40	.14
8	8.64	.24	8.82	.21	9.12	.19	9.60	.16
9	10.08	.28	10.08	.24	10.08	.21	10.80	.18
10	11.16	.31	11.34	.27	11.52	.24	12.00	.20
20	22.32	.62	22.68	.54	23.04	.48	24.00	.40
30	33.48	.93	34.02	.81	34.56	.72	36.00	.60
40	44.64	1.24	45.36	1.08	46.08	.96	48.00	.80
50	55.80	1.55	56.70	1.35	58.08	1.21	60.00	1.00
60	66.96	1.86	68.46	1.63	69.60	1.45	72.00	1.20
70	78.48	2.18	79.80	1.90	81.12	1.69	84.00	1.40
80	89.64	2.49	91.14	2.17	92.64	1.93	96.00	1.60
90	100.80	2.80	102.48	2.44	104.64	2.18	108.00	1.80
100	111.96	3.11	113.82	2.71	116.16	2.42	120.00	2.00
200	224.28	6.23	228.06	5.43	232.32	4.84	240.60	4.01
300	336.24	9.34	342.30	8.15	348.48	7.26	361.20	6.02
400	448.56	12.46	456.54	10.87	465.12	9.69	481.80	8.03
500	560.52	15.57	570.78	13.59	581.28	12.11	602.40	10.04
600	672.84	18.69	685.02	16.31	697.44	14.53	723.00	12.05
700	784.80	21.80	799.26	19.03	813.60	16.95	843.00	14.05
800	897.12	24.92	913.50	21.75	930.24	19.38	963.60	16.06
900	1009.08	28.03	1027.74	24.47	1046.40	21.80	1084.20	18.07
1000	1121.40	31.15	1141.98	27.19	1162.56	24.22	1204.80	20.08
1500	1681.92	46.72	1712.76	40.78	1743.84	36.33	1807.20	30.12
2000	2242.80	62.30	2283.96	54.38	2325.60	48.45	2410.20	40.17
2500	2803.68	77.88	2854.74	67.97	2906.88	60.56	3012.60	50.21
3000	3364.20	93.45	3425.94	81.57	3488.16	72.67	3615.00	60.25
3500	3925.08	109.03	3996.72	95.16	4069.44	84.78	4217.40	70.29
4000	4485.60	124.60	4567.92	108.76	4651.20	96.90	4820.40	80.34
4500	5046.48	140.18	5139.12	122.36	5232.48	109.01	5422.80	90.38
5000	5607.36	155.76	5709.90	135.95	5813.76	121.12	6025.20	100.42
5500	6167.88	171.33	6281.10	149.55	6395.52	133.24	6628.20	110.47
6000	6728.76	186.91	6851.88	163.14	6976.80	145.35	7230.60	120.51
6500	7289.28	202.48	7423.08	176.74	7558.08	157.46	7833.00	130.55
7000	7850.16	218.06	7993.86	190.33	8139.36	169.57	8435.40	140.59
7500	8411.04	233.64	8565.06	203.93	8721.12	181.69	9038.40	150.64
8000	8971.56	249.21	9136.26	217.53	9302.40	193.80	9640.80	160.68
8500	9532.44	264.79	9707.04	231.12	9883.68	205.91	10243.20	170.72
9000	10092.96	280.36	10278.24	244.72	10465.44	218.03	10845.60	180.76
10000	11214.72	311.52	11420.22	271.91	11628.00	242.25	12051.00	200.85
11000	12336.12	342.67	12562.20	299.10	12791.04	266.48	13256.40	220.94
12000	13457.52	373.82	13704.18	326.29	13953.60	290.70	14461.20	241.02
13000	14578.92	404.97	14846.16	353.48	15116.64	314.93	15666.60	261.11
14000	15700.68	436.13	15988.14	380.67	16279.20	339.15	16871.40	281.19
15000	16822.08	467.28	17130.12	407.86	17442.24	363.38	18076.80	301.28
16000	17943.48	498.43	18272.52	435.06	18604.80	387.60	19281.60	321.36
17000	19064.88	529.58	19414.50	462.25	19767.84	411.83	20487.00	341.45
18000	20186.28	560.73	20556.48	489.44	20930.88	436.06	21691.80	361.53
19000	21308.04	591.89	21698.46	516.63	22093.44	460.28	22897.20	381.62
20000	22429.44	623.04	22840.44	543.82	23256.48	484.51	24102.60	401.71
21000	23550.84	654.19	23982.42	571.01	24419.04	508.73	25307.40	421.79
22000	24672.24	685.34	25124.40	598.20	25582.08	532.96	26512.80	441.88
23000	25793.64	716.49	26266.38	625.39	26744.64	557.18	27717.60	461.96
24000	26915.40	747.65	27408.78	652.59	27907.68	581.41	28923.00	482.05
25000	28036.80	778.80	28550.76	679.78	29070.24	605.63	30127.80	502.13

7.70% ANNUAL PERCENTAGE RATE

LOAN AMT	12 MONTHS TOTAL NOTE	MONTHLY PAYMENT	18 MONTHS TOTAL NOTE	MONTHLY PAYMENT	24 MONTHS TOTAL NOTE	MONTHLY PAYMENT	30 MONTHS TOTAL NOTE	MONTHLY PAYMENT
1	.96	.08	.90	.05	.96	.04	.90	.03
2	2.04	.17	1.98	.11	2.16	.09	2.10	.07
3	3.12	.26	3.06	.17	3.12	.13	3.30	.11
4	4.08	.34	4.14	.23	4.32	.18	4.20	.14
5	5.16	.43	5.22	.29	5.28	.22	5.40	.18
6	6.24	.52	6.30	.35	6.48	.27	6.60	.22
7	7.20	.60	7.38	.41	7.44	.31	7.50	.25
8	8.28	.69	8.46	.47	8.64	.36	8.70	.29
9	9.36	.78	9.54	.53	9.60	.40	9.90	.33
10	10.32	.86	10.62	.59	10.80	.45	10.80	.36
20	20.76	1.73	21.24	1.18	21.60	.90	21.90	.73
30	31.20	2.60	31.86	1.77	32.40	1.35	33.00	1.10
40	41.64	3.47	42.48	2.36	43.20	1.80	44.10	1.47
50	52.08	4.34	53.10	2.95	54.00	2.25	54.90	1.83
60	62.52	5.21	63.72	3.54	64.80	2.70	66.00	2.20
70	72.84	6.07	74.34	4.13	75.60	3.15	77.10	2.57
80	83.28	6.94	84.96	4.72	86.40	3.60	88.20	2.94
90	93.72	7.81	95.58	5.31	97.20	4.05	99.00	3.30
100	104.16	8.68	106.20	5.90	108.00	4.50	110.10	3.67
200	208.32	17.36	212.40	11.80	216.24	9.01	220.50	7.35
300	312.60	26.05	318.60	17.70	324.48	13.52	330.60	11.02
400	416.76	34.73	424.80	23.60	432.72	18.03	441.00	14.70
500	521.04	43.42	531.00	29.50	540.96	22.54	551.10	18.37
600	625.20	52.10	637.20	35.40	649.20	27.05	661.50	22.05
700	729.48	60.79	743.40	41.30	757.44	31.56	771.60	25.72
800	833.64	69.47	849.60	47.20	865.68	36.07	882.00	29.40
900	937.92	78.16	955.80	53.10	973.92	40.58	992.10	33.07
1000	1042.08	86.84	1062.00	59.00	1082.16	45.09	1102.50	36.75
1500	1563.24	130.27	1593.00	88.50	1623.12	67.63	1653.60	55.12
2000	2084.28	173.69	2124.00	118.00	2164.32	90.18	2205.00	73.50
2500	2605.44	217.12	2655.00	147.50	2705.28	112.72	2756.10	91.87
3000	3126.48	260.54	3186.18	177.01	3246.48	135.27	3307.50	110.25
3500	3647.64	303.97	3717.18	206.51	3787.44	157.81	3858.60	128.62
4000	4168.68	347.39	4248.18	236.01	4328.64	180.36	4410.00	147.00
4500	4689.84	390.82	4779.18	265.51	4869.60	202.90	4961.10	165.37
5000	5210.88	434.24	5310.18	295.01	5410.80	225.45	5512.50	183.75
5500	5732.04	477.67	5841.18	324.51	5951.76	247.99	6063.90	202.13
6000	6253.08	521.09	6372.36	354.02	6492.96	270.54	6615.00	220.50
6500	6774.24	564.52	6903.36	383.52	7033.92	293.08	7166.40	238.88
7000	7295.28	607.94	7434.36	413.02	7575.12	315.63	7717.50	257.25
7500	7816.44	651.37	7965.36	442.52	8116.08	338.17	8268.90	275.63
8000	8337.48	694.79	8496.36	472.02	8657.28	360.72	8820.00	294.00
8500	8858.64	738.22	9027.36	501.52	9198.48	383.27	9371.40	312.38
9000	9379.68	781.64	9558.54	531.03	9739.44	405.81	9922.50	330.75
10000	10421.88	868.49	10620.54	590.03	10821.60	450.90	11025.30	367.51
11000	11464.08	955.34	11682.54	649.03	11903.76	495.99	12127.80	404.26
12000	12506.28	1042.19	12744.72	708.04	12985.92	541.08	13230.30	441.01
13000	13548.48	1129.04	13806.72	767.04	14068.08	586.17	14332.80	477.76
14000	14590.68	1215.89	14868.72	826.04	15150.24	631.26	15435.30	514.51
15000	15632.88	1302.74	15930.90	885.05	16232.40	676.35	16537.80	551.26
16000	16675.08	1389.59	16992.90	944.05	17314.56	721.44	17640.30	588.01
17000	17717.28	1476.44	18054.90	1003.05	18396.96	766.54	18742.80	624.76
18000	18759.48	1563.29	19117.08	1062.06	19479.12	811.63	19845.30	661.51
19000	19801.68	1650.14	20179.08	1121.06	20561.28	856.72	20947.80	698.26
20000	20843.88	1736.99	21241.08	1180.06	21643.44	901.81	22050.60	735.02
21000	21886.08	1823.84	22303.26	1239.07	22725.60	946.90	23153.10	771.77
22000	22928.28	1910.69	23365.26	1298.07	23807.76	991.99	24255.60	808.52
23000	23970.48	1997.54	24427.44	1357.08	24889.92	1037.08	25358.10	845.27
24000	25012.68	2084.39	25489.44	1416.08	25972.08	1082.17	26460.60	882.02
25000	26054.88	2171.24	26551.44	1475.08	27054.24	1127.26	27563.10	918.77

ANNUAL PERCENTAGE RATE **7.70%**

	36 MONTHS		42 MONTHS		48 MONTHS		60 MONTHS	
LOAN AMT	TOTAL NOTE	MONTHLY PAYMENT	TOTAL NOTE	MONTHLY PAYMENT	TOTAL NOTE	MONTHLY PAYMENT	TOTAL NOTE	MONTHLY PAYMENT
1	1.08	.03	.84	.02	.96	.02	1.20	.02
2	2.16	.06	2.10	.05	1.92	.04	2.40	.04
3	3.24	.09	3.36	.08	3.36	.07	3.60	.06
4	4.32	.12	4.20	.10	4.32	.09	4.80	.08
5	5.40	.15	5.46	.13	5.76	.12	6.00	.10
6	6.48	.18	6.72	.16	6.72	.14	7.20	.12
7	7.56	.21	7.98	.19	7.68	.16	8.40	.14
8	8.64	.24	8.82	.21	9.12	.19	9.60	.16
9	10.08	.28	10.08	.24	10.08	.21	10.80	.18
10	11.16	.31	11.34	.27	11.52	.24	12.00	.20
20	22.32	.62	22.68	.54	23.04	.48	24.00	.40
30	33.48	.93	34.02	.81	34.56	.72	36.00	.60
40	44.64	1.24	45.36	1.08	46.56	.97	48.00	.80
50	55.80	1.55	57.12	1.36	58.08	1.21	60.00	1.00
60	67.32	1.87	68.46	1.63	69.60	1.45	72.00	1.20
70	78.48	2.18	79.80	1.90	81.12	1.69	84.00	1.40
80	89.64	2.49	91.14	2.17	93.12	1.94	96.60	1.61
90	100.80	2.80	102.90	2.45	104.64	2.18	108.60	1.81
100	111.96	3.11	114.24	2.72	116.16	2.42	120.60	2.01
200	224.28	6.23	228.48	5.44	232.80	4.85	241.20	4.02
300	336.60	9.35	343.14	8.17	349.44	7.28	361.80	6.03
400	448.92	12.47	457.38	10.89	465.60	9.70	483.00	8.05
500	561.24	15.59	571.62	13.61	582.24	12.13	603.60	10.06
600	673.56	18.71	686.28	16.34	698.88	14.56	724.20	12.07
700	785.88	21.83	800.52	19.06	815.52	16.99	845.40	14.09
800	898.20	24.95	915.18	21.79	931.68	19.41	966.00	16.10
900	1010.52	28.07	1029.42	24.51	1048.32	21.84	1086.60	18.11
1000	1122.84	31.19	1143.66	27.23	1164.96	24.27	1207.80	20.13
1500	1684.44	46.79	1715.70	40.85	1747.20	36.40	1811.40	30.19
2000	2246.04	62.39	2287.74	54.47	2329.92	48.54	2415.60	40.26
2500	2807.64	77.99	2859.78	68.09	2912.64	60.68	3019.80	50.33
3000	3369.24	93.59	3431.82	81.71	3494.88	72.81	3623.40	60.39
3500	3930.84	109.19	4003.86	95.33	4077.60	84.95	4227.60	70.46
4000	4492.44	124.79	4575.90	108.95	4659.84	97.08	4831.80	80.53
4500	5054.04	140.39	5147.52	122.56	5242.56	109.22	5435.40	90.59
5000	5615.64	155.99	5719.56	136.18	5825.28	121.36	6039.60	100.66
5500	6176.88	171.58	6291.60	149.80	6407.52	133.49	6643.80	110.73
6000	6738.48	187.18	6863.64	163.42	6990.24	145.63	7247.40	120.79
6500	7300.08	202.78	7435.68	177.04	7572.96	157.77	7851.60	130.86
7000	7861.68	218.38	8007.72	190.66	8155.20	169.90	8455.80	140.93
7500	8423.28	233.98	8579.76	204.28	8737.92	182.04	9059.40	150.99
8000	8984.88	249.58	9151.80	217.90	9320.16	194.17	9663.60	161.06
8500	9546.48	265.18	9723.42	231.51	9902.88	206.31	10267.80	171.13
9000	10108.08	280.78	10295.46	245.13	10485.60	218.45	10871.40	181.19
10000	11231.28	311.98	11439.54	272.37	11650.56	242.72	12079.80	201.33
11000	12354.12	343.17	12583.62	299.61	12815.52	266.99	13287.60	221.46
12000	13477.32	374.37	13727.70	326.85	13980.48	291.26	14495.40	241.59
13000	14600.52	405.57	14871.36	354.08	15145.92	315.54	15703.80	261.73
14000	15723.72	436.77	16015.44	381.32	16310.88	339.81	16911.60	281.86
15000	16846.92	467.97	17159.52	408.56	17475.84	364.08	18119.40	301.99
16000	17970.12	499.17	18303.60	435.80	18640.80	388.35	19327.20	322.12
17000	19092.96	530.36	19447.26	463.03	19805.76	412.62	20535.60	342.26
18000	20216.16	561.56	20591.34	490.27	20971.20	436.90	21743.40	362.39
19000	21339.36	592.76	21735.42	517.51	22136.16	461.17	22951.20	382.52
20000	22462.56	623.96	22879.50	544.75	23301.12	485.44	24159.60	402.66
21000	23585.76	655.16	24023.58	571.99	24466.08	509.71	25367.40	422.79
22000	24708.60	686.35	25167.24	599.22	25631.52	533.99	26575.20	442.92
23000	25831.80	717.55	26311.32	626.46	26796.48	558.26	27783.60	463.06
24000	26955.00	748.75	27455.40	653.70	27961.44	582.53	28991.40	483.19
25000	28078.20	779.95	28599.48	680.94	29126.40	606.80	30199.20	503.32

7.75% ANNUAL PERCENTAGE RATE

LOAN AMT	12 MONTHS TOTAL NOTE	12 MONTHS MONTHLY PAYMENT	18 MONTHS TOTAL NOTE	18 MONTHS MONTHLY PAYMENT	24 MONTHS TOTAL NOTE	24 MONTHS MONTHLY PAYMENT	30 MONTHS TOTAL NOTE	30 MONTHS MONTHLY PAYMENT
1	.96	.08	.90	.05	.96	.04	.90	.03
2	2.04	.17	1.98	.11	2.16	.09	2.10	.07
3	3.12	.26	3.06	.17	3.12	.13	3.30	.11
4	4.08	.34	4.14	.23	4.32	.18	4.20	.14
5	5.16	.43	5.22	.29	5.28	.22	5.40	.18
6	6.24	.52	6.30	.35	6.48	.27	6.60	.22
7	7.20	.60	7.38	.41	7.44	.31	7.50	.25
8	8.28	.69	8.46	.47	8.64	.36	8.70	.29
9	9.36	.78	9.54	.53	9.60	.40	9.90	.33
10	10.32	.86	10.62	.59	10.80	.45	10.80	.36
20	20.76	1.73	21.24	1.18	21.60	.90	21.90	.73
30	31.20	2.60	31.86	1.77	32.40	1.35	33.00	1.10
40	41.64	3.47	42.48	2.36	43.20	1.80	44.10	1.47
50	52.08	4.34	53.10	2.95	54.00	2.25	54.90	1.83
60	62.52	5.21	63.72	3.54	64.80	2.70	66.00	2.20
70	72.96	6.08	74.34	4.13	75.60	3.15	77.10	2.57
80	83.28	6.94	84.96	4.72	86.40	3.60	88.20	2.94
90	93.72	7.81	95.58	5.31	97.44	4.06	99.00	3.30
100	104.16	8.68	106.20	5.90	108.24	4.51	110.10	3.67
200	208.44	17.37	212.40	11.80	216.48	9.02	220.50	7.35
300	312.72	26.06	318.60	17.70	324.72	13.53	330.90	11.03
400	416.88	34.74	424.98	23.61	432.96	18.04	441.00	14.70
500	521.16	43.43	531.18	29.51	541.20	22.55	551.40	18.38
600	625.44	52.12	637.38	35.41	649.44	27.06	661.80	22.06
700	729.72	60.81	743.58	41.31	757.68	31.57	772.20	25.74
800	833.88	69.49	849.96	47.22	866.16	36.09	882.30	29.41
900	938.16	78.18	956.16	53.12	974.40	40.60	992.70	33.09
1000	1042.44	86.87	1062.36	59.02	1082.64	45.11	1103.10	36.77
1500	1563.60	130.30	1593.54	88.53	1624.08	67.67	1654.80	55.16
2000	2084.88	173.74	2124.90	118.05	2165.28	90.22	2206.20	73.54
2500	2606.16	217.18	2656.08	147.56	2706.72	112.78	2757.90	91.93
3000	3127.32	260.61	3187.26	177.07	3248.16	135.34	3309.60	110.32
3500	3648.60	304.05	3718.62	206.59	3789.36	157.89	3861.00	128.70
4000	4169.88	347.49	4249.80	236.10	4330.80	180.45	4412.70	147.09
4500	4691.04	390.92	4780.98	265.61	4872.24	203.01	4964.40	165.48
5000	5212.32	434.36	5312.34	295.13	5413.44	225.56	5515.80	183.86
5500	5733.60	477.80	5843.52	324.64	5954.88	248.12	6067.50	202.25
6000	6254.76	521.23	6374.70	354.15	6496.32	270.68	6619.20	220.64
6500	6776.04	564.67	6906.06	383.67	7037.52	293.23	7170.90	239.03
7000	7297.32	608.11	7437.24	413.18	7578.96	315.79	7722.30	257.41
7500	7818.48	651.54	7968.42	442.69	8120.40	338.35	8274.00	275.80
8000	8339.76	694.98	8499.78	472.21	8661.60	360.90	8825.70	294.19
8500	8860.92	738.41	9030.96	501.72	9203.04	383.46	9377.10	312.57
9000	9382.20	781.85	9562.14	531.23	9744.48	406.02	9928.80	330.96
10000	10424.64	868.72	10624.68	590.26	10827.12	451.13	11031.90	367.73
11000	11467.20	955.60	11687.04	649.28	11909.76	496.24	12135.30	404.51
12000	12509.64	1042.47	12749.58	708.31	12992.64	541.36	13238.40	441.28
13000	13552.08	1129.34	13812.12	767.34	14075.28	586.47	14341.80	478.06
14000	14594.64	1216.22	14874.48	826.36	15157.92	631.58	15444.90	514.83
15000	15637.08	1303.09	15937.02	885.39	16240.80	676.70	16548.00	551.60
16000	16679.52	1389.96	16999.56	944.42	17323.44	721.81	17651.40	588.38
17000	17721.96	1476.83	18061.92	1003.44	18406.08	766.92	18754.50	625.15
18000	18764.52	1563.71	19124.46	1062.47	19488.96	812.04	19857.90	661.93
19000	19806.96	1650.58	20186.82	1121.49	20571.60	857.15	20961.00	698.70
20000	20849.40	1737.45	21249.36	1180.52	21654.24	902.26	22064.10	735.47
21000	21891.96	1824.33	22311.90	1239.55	22737.12	947.38	23167.50	772.25
22000	22934.40	1911.20	23374.26	1298.57	23819.76	992.49	24270.60	809.02
23000	23976.84	1998.07	24436.80	1357.60	24902.40	1037.60	25373.70	845.79
24000	25019.28	2084.94	25499.34	1416.63	25985.28	1082.72	26477.10	882.57
25000	26061.84	2171.82	26561.70	1475.65	27067.92	1127.83	27580.20	919.34

ANNUAL PERCENTAGE RATE **7.75%**

	36 MONTHS		42 MONTHS		48 MONTHS		60 MONTHS	
LOAN AMT	TOTAL NOTE	MONTHLY PAYMENT	TOTAL NOTE	MONTHLY PAYMENT	TOTAL NOTE	MONTHLY PAYMENT	TOTAL NOTE	MONTHLY PAYMENT
1	1.08	.03	.84	.02	.96	.02	1.20	.02
2	2.16	.06	2.10	.05	1.92	.04	2.40	.04
3	3.24	.09	3.36	.08	3.36	.07	3.60	.06
4	4.32	.12	4.20	.10	4.32	.09	4.80	.08
5	5.40	.15	5.46	.13	5.76	.12	6.00	.10
6	6.48	.18	6.72	.16	6.72	.14	7.20	.12
7	7.56	.21	7.98	.19	8.16	.17	8.40	.14
8	8.64	.24	8.82	.21	9.12	.19	9.60	.16
9	10.08	.28	10.08	.24	10.08	.21	10.80	.18
10	11.16	.31	11.34	.27	11.52	.24	12.00	.20
20	22.32	.62	22.68	.54	23.04	.48	24.00	.40
30	33.48	.93	34.02	.81	34.56	.72	36.00	.60
40	44.64	1.24	45.78	1.09	46.56	.97	48.00	.80
50	56.16	1.56	57.12	1.36	58.08	1.21	60.00	1.00
60	67.32	1.87	68.46	1.63	69.60	1.45	72.00	1.20
70	78.48	2.18	79.80	1.90	81.60	1.70	84.60	1.41
80	89.64	2.49	91.56	2.18	93.12	1.94	96.60	1.61
90	100.80	2.80	102.90	2.45	104.64	2.18	108.60	1.81
100	112.32	3.12	114.24	2.72	116.16	2.42	120.60	2.01
200	224.64	6.24	228.90	5.45	232.80	4.85	241.80	4.03
300	336.96	9.36	343.14	8.17	349.44	7.28	362.40	6.04
400	449.28	12.48	457.80	10.90	466.08	9.71	483.60	8.06
500	561.96	15.61	572.46	13.63	582.72	12.14	604.20	10.07
600	674.28	18.73	686.70	16.35	699.36	14.57	725.40	12.09
700	786.60	21.85	801.36	19.08	816.00	17.00	846.00	14.10
800	898.92	24.97	915.60	21.80	932.64	19.43	967.20	16.12
900	1011.24	28.09	1030.26	24.53	1049.28	21.86	1088.40	18.14
1000	1123.92	31.22	1144.92	27.26	1165.92	24.29	1209.00	20.15
1500	1685.88	46.83	1717.38	40.89	1749.12	36.44	1813.80	30.23
2000	2247.84	62.44	2289.84	54.52	2332.32	48.59	2418.60	40.31
2500	2809.80	78.05	2862.30	68.15	2915.04	60.73	3023.40	50.39
3000	3371.76	93.66	3434.76	81.78	3498.24	72.88	3628.20	60.47
3500	3933.72	109.27	4007.22	95.41	4081.44	85.03	4232.40	70.54
4000	4495.68	124.88	4579.68	109.04	4664.64	97.18	4837.20	80.62
4500	5057.64	140.49	5152.14	122.67	5247.84	109.33	5442.00	90.70
5000	5619.60	156.10	5724.60	136.30	5830.56	121.47	6046.80	100.78
5500	6181.56	171.71	6297.06	149.93	6413.76	133.62	6651.60	110.86
6000	6743.52	187.32	6869.52	163.56	6996.96	145.77	7256.40	120.94
6500	7305.48	202.93	7441.98	177.19	7580.16	157.92	7861.20	131.02
7000	7867.44	218.54	8014.44	190.82	8163.36	170.07	8465.40	141.09
7500	8429.40	234.15	8586.90	204.45	8746.08	182.21	9070.20	151.17
8000	8991.36	249.76	9159.36	218.08	9329.28	194.36	9675.00	161.25
8500	9553.32	265.37	9731.82	231.71	9912.48	206.51	10279.80	171.33
9000	10115.64	280.99	10304.28	245.34	10495.68	218.66	10884.60	181.41
10000	11239.56	312.21	11449.20	272.60	11661.60	242.95	12093.60	201.56
11000	12363.48	343.43	12594.12	299.86	12828.00	267.25	13303.20	221.72
12000	13487.40	374.65	13739.04	327.12	13993.92	291.54	14512.80	241.88
13000	14611.32	405.87	16029.30	354.39	15160.32	315.84	15722.40	262.04
14000	15735.24	437.09	16029.30	381.65	16326.72	340.14	16931.40	282.19
15000	16859.16	468.31	17174.22	408.91	17492.64	364.43	18141.00	302.35
16000	17983.08	499.53	18319.14	436.17	18659.04	388.73	19350.60	322.51
17000	19107.00	530.75	19464.06	463.43	19824.96	413.02	20559.60	342.66
18000	20231.28	561.98	20608.98	490.69	20991.36	437.32	21769.20	362.82
19000	21355.20	593.20	21753.90	517.95	22157.28	461.61	22978.80	382.98
20000	22479.12	624.42	22898.82	545.21	23323.68	485.91	24187.80	403.13
21000	23603.04	655.64	24043.74	572.47	24490.08	510.21	25397.40	423.29
22000	24726.96	686.86	25188.66	599.73	25656.00	534.50	26607.00	443.45
23000	25850.88	718.08	26333.58	626.99	26822.40	558.80	27816.60	463.61
24000	26974.80	749.30	27478.50	654.25	27988.32	583.09	29025.60	483.76
25000	28098.72	780.52	28623.84	681.52	29154.72	607.39	30235.20	503.92

7.80% ANNUAL PERCENTAGE RATE

LOAN AMT	12 MONTHS TOTAL NOTE	12 MONTHS MONTHLY PAYMENT	18 MONTHS TOTAL NOTE	18 MONTHS MONTHLY PAYMENT	24 MONTHS TOTAL NOTE	24 MONTHS MONTHLY PAYMENT	30 MONTHS TOTAL NOTE	30 MONTHS MONTHLY PAYMENT
1	.96	.08	.90	.05	.96	.04	.90	.03
2	2.04	.17	1.98	.11	2.16	.09	2.10	.07
3	3.12	.26	3.06	.17	3.12	.13	3.30	.11
4	4.08	.34	4.14	.23	4.32	.18	4.20	.14
5	5.16	.43	5.22	.29	5.28	.22	5.40	.18
6	6.24	.52	6.30	.35	6.48	.27	6.60	.22
7	7.20	.60	7.38	.41	7.44	.31	7.50	.25
8	8.28	.69	8.46	.47	8.64	.36	8.70	.29
9	9.36	.78	9.54	.53	9.60	.40	9.90	.33
10	10.32	.86	10.62	.59	10.80	.45	10.80	.36
20	20.76	1.73	21.24	1.18	21.60	.90	21.90	.73
30	31.20	2.60	31.86	1.77	32.40	1.35	33.00	1.10
40	41.64	3.47	42.48	2.36	43.20	1.80	44.10	1.47
50	52.08	4.34	53.10	2.95	54.00	2.25	54.90	1.83
60	62.52	5.21	63.72	3.54	64.80	2.70	66.00	2.20
70	72.96	6.08	74.34	4.13	75.60	3.15	77.10	2.57
80	83.40	6.95	84.96	4.72	86.64	3.61	88.20	2.94
90	93.84	7.82	95.58	5.31	97.44	4.06	99.30	3.31
100	104.16	8.68	106.20	5.90	108.24	4.51	110.10	3.67
200	208.44	17.37	212.40	11.80	216.48	9.02	220.50	7.35
300	312.72	26.06	318.78	17.71	324.96	13.54	330.90	11.03
400	417.00	34.75	424.98	23.61	433.20	18.05	441.30	14.71
500	521.28	43.44	531.36	29.52	541.44	22.56	551.70	18.39
600	625.56	52.13	637.56	35.42	649.92	27.08	662.10	22.07
700	729.84	60.82	743.94	41.33	758.16	31.59	772.50	25.75
800	834.12	69.51	850.14	47.23	866.40	36.10	882.90	29.43
900	938.40	78.20	956.52	53.14	974.88	40.62	993.30	33.11
1000	1042.68	86.89	1062.72	59.04	1083.12	45.13	1103.70	36.79
1500	1564.08	130.34	1594.26	88.57	1624.80	67.70	1655.70	55.19
2000	2085.48	173.79	2125.62	118.09	2166.48	90.27	2207.70	73.59
2500	2606.76	217.23	2657.16	147.62	2708.16	112.84	2759.70	91.99
3000	3128.16	260.68	3188.52	177.14	3249.60	135.40	3311.70	110.39
3500	3649.56	304.13	3720.06	206.67	3791.28	157.97	3863.40	128.78
4000	4170.96	347.58	4251.42	236.19	4332.96	180.54	4415.40	147.18
4500	4692.36	391.03	4782.96	265.72	4874.64	203.11	4967.40	165.58
5000	5213.64	434.47	5314.32	295.24	5416.32	225.68	5519.40	183.98
5500	5735.04	477.92	5845.68	324.76	5957.76	248.24	6071.40	202.38
6000	6256.44	521.37	6377.22	354.29	6499.44	270.81	6623.40	220.78
6500	6777.84	564.82	6908.58	383.81	7041.12	293.38	7175.10	239.17
7000	7299.24	608.27	7440.12	413.34	7582.80	315.95	7727.10	257.57
7500	7820.52	651.71	7971.48	442.86	8124.48	338.52	8279.10	275.97
8000	8341.92	695.16	8503.02	472.39	8665.92	361.08	8831.10	294.37
8500	8863.32	738.61	9034.38	501.91	9207.60	383.65	9383.10	312.77
9000	9384.72	782.06	9565.92	531.44	9749.28	406.22	9935.10	331.17
10000	10427.40	868.95	10628.82	590.49	10832.64	451.36	11038.80	367.96
11000	11470.20	955.85	11691.54	649.53	11915.76	496.49	12142.80	404.76
12000	12513.00	1042.75	12754.44	708.58	12999.12	541.63	13246.80	441.56
13000	13555.68	1129.64	13817.34	767.63	14082.24	586.76	14350.50	478.35
14000	14598.48	1216.54	14880.24	826.68	15165.60	631.90	15454.50	515.15
15000	15641.16	1303.43	15943.14	885.73	16248.96	677.04	16558.50	551.95
16000	16683.96	1390.33	17006.04	944.78	17332.08	722.17	17662.20	588.74
17000	17726.76	1477.23	18068.94	1003.83	18415.44	767.31	18766.20	625.54
18000	18769.44	1564.12	19131.84	1062.88	19498.80	812.45	19870.20	662.34
19000	19812.24	1651.02	20194.74	1121.93	20581.92	857.58	20973.90	699.13
20000	20854.92	1737.91	21257.64	1180.98	21665.28	902.72	22077.90	735.93
21000	21897.72	1824.81	22320.54	1240.03	22748.40	947.85	23181.90	772.73
22000	22940.52	1911.71	23383.26	1299.07	23831.76	992.99	24285.60	809.52
23000	23983.20	1998.60	24446.16	1358.12	24915.12	1038.13	25389.60	846.32
24000	25026.00	2085.50	25509.06	1417.17	25998.24	1083.26	26493.60	883.12
25000	26068.68	2172.39	26571.96	1476.22	27081.60	1128.40	27597.30	919.91

ANNUAL PERCENTAGE RATE **7.80%**

LOAN AMT	36 MONTHS TOTAL NOTE	36 MONTHS MONTHLY PAYMENT	42 MONTHS TOTAL NOTE	42 MONTHS MONTHLY PAYMENT	48 MONTHS TOTAL NOTE	48 MONTHS MONTHLY PAYMENT	60 MONTHS TOTAL NOTE	60 MONTHS MONTHLY PAYMENT
1	1.08	.03	.84	.02	.96	.02	1.20	.02
2	2.16	.06	2.10	.05	1.92	.04	2.40	.04
3	3.24	.09	3.36	.08	3.36	.07	3.60	.06
4	4.32	.12	4.20	.10	4.32	.09	4.80	.08
5	5.40	.15	5.46	.13	5.76	.12	6.00	.10
6	6.48	.18	6.72	.16	6.72	.14	7.20	.12
7	7.56	.21	7.98	.19	8.16	.17	8.40	.14
8	8.64	.24	8.82	.21	9.12	.19	9.60	.16
9	10.08	.28	10.08	.24	10.08	.21	10.80	.18
10	11.16	.31	11.34	.27	11.52	.24	12.00	.20
20	22.32	.62	22.68	.54	23.04	.48	24.00	.40
30	33.48	.93	34.02	.81	34.56	.72	36.00	.60
40	44.64	1.24	45.78	1.09	46.56	.97	48.00	.80
50	56.16	1.56	57.12	1.36	58.08	1.21	60.00	1.00
60	67.32	1.87	68.46	1.63	69.60	1.45	72.60	1.21
70	78.48	2.18	79.80	1.90	81.60	1.70	84.60	1.41
80	89.64	2.49	91.56	2.18	93.12	1.94	96.60	1.61
90	101.16	2.81	102.90	2.45	104.64	2.18	108.60	1.81
100	112.32	3.12	114.24	2.72	116.64	2.43	120.60	2.01
200	224.64	6.24	228.90	5.45	233.28	4.86	241.80	4.03
300	337.32	9.37	343.56	8.18	349.92	7.29	363.00	6.05
400	449.64	12.49	458.22	10.91	466.56	9.72	484.20	8.07
500	562.32	15.62	572.88	13.64	583.20	12.15	605.40	10.09
600	674.64	18.74	687.54	16.37	700.32	14.59	726.00	12.10
700	787.32	21.87	801.78	19.09	816.96	17.02	847.20	14.12
800	899.64	24.99	916.44	21.82	933.60	19.45	968.40	16.14
900	1011.96	28.11	1031.10	24.55	1050.24	21.88	1089.60	18.16
1000	1124.64	31.24	1145.76	27.28	1166.88	24.31	1210.80	20.18
1500	1686.96	46.86	1718.64	40.92	1750.56	36.47	1816.20	30.27
2000	2249.28	62.48	2291.52	54.56	2334.24	48.63	2421.60	40.36
2500	2811.96	78.11	2864.82	68.21	2917.92	60.79	3027.00	50.45
3000	3374.28	93.73	3437.70	81.85	3501.60	72.95	3632.40	60.54
3500	3936.60	109.35	4010.58	95.49	4085.28	85.11	4237.80	70.63
4000	4498.92	124.97	4583.46	109.13	4668.96	97.27	4843.20	80.72
4500	5061.24	140.59	5156.34	122.77	5252.64	109.43	5448.60	90.81
5000	5623.92	156.22	5729.64	136.42	5836.32	121.59	6054.00	100.90
5500	6186.24	171.84	6302.52	150.06	6420.00	133.75	6659.40	110.99
6000	6748.56	187.46	6875.40	163.70	7003.68	145.91	7264.80	121.08
6500	7310.88	203.08	7448.28	177.34	7587.36	158.07	7870.20	131.17
7000	7873.20	218.70	8021.16	190.98	8171.04	170.23	8475.60	141.26
7500	8435.88	234.33	8594.46	204.63	8754.72	182.39	9081.00	151.35
8000	8998.20	249.95	9167.34	218.27	9338.40	194.55	9686.40	161.44
8500	9560.52	265.57	9740.22	231.91	9922.08	206.71	10291.80	171.53
9000	10122.84	281.19	10313.10	245.55	10505.76	218.87	10897.20	181.62
10000	11247.84	312.44	11459.28	272.84	11673.12	243.19	12108.00	201.80
11000	12372.48	343.68	12605.04	300.12	12840.48	267.51	13318.80	221.98
12000	13497.48	374.93	13750.80	327.40	14007.36	291.82	14529.60	242.16
13000	14622.12	406.17	14896.98	354.69	15174.72	316.14	15741.00	262.35
14000	15746.76	437.41	16042.74	381.97	16342.08	340.46	16951.80	282.53
15000	16871.76	468.66	17188.92	409.26	17509.44	364.78	18162.60	302.71
16000	17996.40	499.90	18334.68	436.54	18676.80	389.10	19373.40	322.89
17000	19121.40	531.15	19480.44	463.82	19844.16	413.42	20584.20	343.07
18000	20246.04	562.39	20626.62	491.11	21011.52	437.74	21795.00	363.25
19000	21370.68	593.63	21772.38	518.39	22178.88	462.06	23005.80	383.43
20000	22495.68	624.88	22918.56	545.68	23346.24	486.38	24216.60	403.61
21000	23620.32	656.12	24064.32	572.96	24513.60	510.70	25427.40	423.79
22000	24745.32	687.37	25210.08	600.24	25680.96	535.02	26638.20	443.97
23000	25869.96	718.61	26356.26	627.53	26848.32	559.34	27849.00	464.15
24000	26994.96	749.86	27502.02	654.81	28015.20	583.65	29059.80	484.33
25000	28119.60	781.10	28648.20	682.10	29182.56	607.97	30271.20	504.52

7.90% ANNUAL PERCENTAGE RATE

LOAN AMT	12 MONTHS TOTAL NOTE	12 MONTHS MONTHLY PAYMENT	18 MONTHS TOTAL NOTE	18 MONTHS MONTHLY PAYMENT	24 MONTHS TOTAL NOTE	24 MONTHS MONTHLY PAYMENT	30 MONTHS TOTAL NOTE	30 MONTHS MONTHLY PAYMENT
1	.96	.08	.90	.05	.96	.04	.90	.03
2	2.04	.17	1.98	.11	2.16	.09	2.10	.07
3	3.12	.26	3.06	.17	3.12	.13	3.30	.11
4	4.08	.34	4.14	.23	4.32	.18	4.20	.14
5	5.16	.43	5.22	.29	5.28	.22	5.40	.18
6	6.24	.52	6.30	.35	6.48	.27	6.60	.22
7	7.20	.60	7.38	.41	7.44	.31	7.50	.25
8	8.28	.69	8.46	.47	8.64	.36	8.70	.29
9	9.36	.78	9.54	.53	9.60	.40	9.90	.33
10	10.32	.86	10.62	.59	10.80	.45	10.80	.36
20	20.76	1.73	21.24	1.18	21.60	.90	21.90	.73
30	31.20	2.60	31.86	1.77	32.40	1.35	33.00	1.10
40	41.64	3.47	42.48	2.36	43.20	1.80	44.10	1.47
50	52.08	4.34	53.10	2.95	54.00	2.25	55.20	1.84
60	62.52	5.21	63.72	3.54	65.04	2.71	66.30	2.21
70	72.96	6.08	74.34	4.13	75.84	3.16	77.10	2.57
80	83.40	6.95	84.96	4.72	86.64	3.61	88.20	2.94
90	93.84	7.82	95.58	5.31	97.44	4.06	99.30	3.31
100	104.28	8.69	106.20	5.90	108.24	4.51	110.40	3.68
200	208.56	17.38	212.58	11.81	216.72	9.03	220.80	7.36
300	312.96	26.08	318.96	17.72	325.20	13.55	331.50	11.05
400	417.24	34.77	425.34	23.63	433.68	18.07	441.90	14.73
500	521.64	43.47	531.72	29.54	542.16	22.59	552.60	18.42
600	625.92	52.16	638.10	35.45	650.40	27.10	663.00	22.10
700	730.20	60.85	744.48	41.36	758.88	31.62	773.40	25.78
800	834.60	69.55	850.86	47.27	867.36	36.14	884.10	29.47
900	938.88	78.24	957.24	53.18	975.84	40.66	994.50	33.15
1000	1043.28	86.94	1063.62	59.09	1084.32	45.18	1105.20	36.84
1500	1564.92	130.41	1595.52	88.64	1626.48	67.77	1657.80	55.26
2000	2086.56	173.88	2127.24	118.18	2168.64	90.36	2210.40	73.68
2500	2608.20	217.35	2659.14	147.73	2710.80	112.95	2763.00	92.10
3000	3129.84	260.82	3191.04	177.28	3252.96	135.54	3315.60	110.52
3500	3651.48	304.29	3722.94	206.83	3795.12	158.13	3868.20	128.94
4000	4173.12	347.76	4254.66	236.37	4337.28	180.72	4421.10	147.37
4500	4694.76	391.23	4786.56	265.92	4879.44	203.31	4973.70	165.79
5000	5216.52	434.71	5318.46	295.47	5421.60	225.90	5526.30	184.21
5500	5738.16	478.18	5850.36	325.02	5963.76	248.49	6078.90	202.63
6000	6259.80	521.65	6382.08	354.56	6506.16	271.09	6631.50	221.05
6500	6781.44	565.12	6913.98	384.11	7048.32	293.68	7184.10	239.47
7000	7303.08	608.59	7445.88	413.66	7590.48	316.27	7736.70	257.89
7500	7824.72	652.06	7977.78	443.21	8132.64	338.86	8289.30	276.31
8000	8346.36	695.53	8509.50	472.75	8674.80	361.45	8842.20	294.74
8500	8868.00	739.00	9041.40	502.30	9216.96	384.04	9394.80	313.16
9000	9389.64	782.47	9573.30	531.85	9759.12	406.63	9947.40	331.58
10000	10433.04	869.42	10636.92	590.94	10843.44	451.81	11052.60	368.42
11000	11476.32	956.36	11700.72	650.04	11927.76	496.99	12157.80	405.26
12000	12519.60	1043.30	12764.34	709.13	13012.32	542.18	13263.30	442.11
13000	13562.88	1130.24	13828.14	768.23	14096.64	587.36	14368.50	478.95
14000	14606.28	1217.19	14891.76	827.32	15180.96	632.54	15473.70	515.79
15000	15649.56	1304.13	15955.56	886.42	16265.28	677.72	16578.90	552.63
16000	16692.84	1391.07	17019.18	945.51	17349.60	722.90	17684.40	589.48
17000	17736.12	1478.01	18082.80	1004.60	18433.92	768.08	18789.60	626.32
18000	18779.40	1564.95	19146.60	1063.70	19518.48	813.27	19894.80	663.16
19000	19822.80	1651.90	20210.22	1122.79	20602.80	858.45	21000.00	700.00
20000	20866.08	1738.84	21274.02	1181.89	21687.12	903.63	22105.50	736.85
21000	21909.36	1825.78	22337.64	1240.98	22771.44	948.81	23210.70	773.69
22000	22952.64	1912.72	23401.44	1300.08	23855.76	993.99	24315.90	810.53
23000	23996.04	1999.67	24465.06	1359.17	24940.08	1039.17	25421.10	847.37
24000	25039.32	2086.61	25528.86	1418.27	26024.64	1084.36	26526.60	884.22
25000	26082.60	2173.55	26592.48	1477.36	27108.96	1129.54	27631.80	921.06

ANNUAL PERCENTAGE RATE **7.90%**

LOAN AMT	36 MONTHS		42 MONTHS		48 MONTHS		60 MONTHS	
	TOTAL NOTE	MONTHLY PAYMENT	TOTAL NOTE	MONTHLY PAYMENT	TOTAL NOTE	MONTHLY PAYMENT	TOTAL NOTE	MONTHLY PAYMENT
1	1.08	.03	.84	.02	.96	.02	1.20	.02
2	2.16	.06	2.10	.05	1.92	.04	2.40	.04
3	3.24	.09	3.36	.08	3.36	.07	3.60	.06
4	4.32	.12	4.20	.10	4.32	.09	4.80	.08
5	5.40	.15	5.46	.13	5.76	.12	6.00	.10
6	6.48	.18	6.72	.16	6.72	.14	7.20	.12
7	7.56	.21	7.98	.19	8.16	.17	8.40	.14
8	9.00	.25	8.82	.21	9.12	.19	9.60	.16
9	10.08	.28	10.08	.24	10.08	.21	10.80	.18
10	11.16	.31	11.34	.27	11.52	.24	12.00	.20
20	22.32	.62	22.68	.54	23.04	.48	24.00	.40
30	33.48	.93	34.02	.81	35.04	.73	36.00	.60
40	45.00	1.25	45.78	1.09	46.56	.97	48.00	.80
50	56.16	1.56	57.12	1.36	58.08	1.21	60.60	1.01
60	67.32	1.87	68.46	1.63	70.08	1.46	72.60	1.21
70	78.84	2.19	80.22	1.91	81.60	1.70	84.60	1.41
80	90.00	2.50	91.56	2.18	93.12	1.94	96.60	1.61
90	101.16	2.81	102.90	2.45	105.12	2.19	109.20	1.82
100	112.32	3.12	114.66	2.73	116.64	2.43	121.20	2.02
200	225.00	6.25	229.32	5.46	233.76	4.87	242.40	4.04
300	337.68	9.38	343.98	8.19	350.40	7.30	363.60	6.06
400	450.36	12.51	459.06	10.93	467.52	9.74	485.40	8.09
500	563.04	15.64	573.72	13.66	584.64	12.18	606.60	10.11
600	675.72	18.77	688.38	16.39	701.28	14.61	727.80	12.13
700	788.40	21.90	803.46	19.13	818.40	17.05	849.00	14.15
800	901.08	25.03	918.12	21.86	935.52	19.49	970.80	16.18
900	1013.76	28.16	1032.78	24.59	1052.16	21.92	1092.00	18.20
1000	1126.44	31.29	1147.86	27.33	1169.28	24.36	1213.20	20.22
1500	1689.48	46.93	1721.58	40.99	1753.92	36.54	1820.40	30.34
2000	2252.88	62.58	2295.72	54.66	2339.04	48.73	2427.00	40.45
2500	2815.92	78.22	2869.44	68.32	2923.68	60.91	3034.20	50.57
3000	3379.32	93.87	3443.58	81.99	3508.32	73.09	3640.80	60.68
3500	3942.36	109.51	4017.30	95.65	4093.44	85.28	4247.40	70.79
4000	4505.76	125.16	4591.44	109.32	4678.08	97.46	4854.60	80.91
4500	5068.80	140.80	5165.16	122.98	5262.72	109.64	5461.20	91.02
5000	5632.20	156.45	5739.30	136.65	5847.84	121.83	6068.40	101.14
5500	6195.24	172.09	6313.02	150.31	6432.48	134.01	6675.00	111.25
6000	6758.64	187.74	6887.16	163.98	7017.12	146.19	7282.20	121.37
6500	7321.68	203.38	7460.88	177.64	7601.76	158.37	7888.80	131.48
7000	7885.08	219.03	8035.02	191.31	8186.88	170.56	8495.40	141.59
7500	8448.12	234.67	8608.74	204 97	8771.52	182.74	9102.60	151.71
8000	9011.52	250.32	9182.88	218.64	9356.16	194.92	9709.20	161.82
8500	9574.56	265.96	9756.60	232.30	9941.28	207.11	10316.40	171.94
9000	10137.96	281.61	10330.74	245.97	10525.92	219.29	10923.00	182.05
10000	11264.40	312.90	11478.60	273.30	11695.68	243.66	12136.80	202.28
11000	12390.84	344.19	12626.46	300.63	12864.96	268.02	13350.60	222.51
12000	13517.28	375.48	13774.32	327.96	14034.72	292.39	14564.40	242.74
13000	14643.72	406.77	14922.18	355.29	15204.00	316.75	15778.20	262.97
14000	15770.16	438.06	16070.04	382.62	16373.76	341.12	16991.40	283.19
15000	16896.60	469.35	17217.90	409.95	17543.52	365.49	18205.20	303.42
16000	18023.04	500.64	18365.76	437.28	18712.80	389.85	19419.00	323.65
17000	19149.48	531.93	19513.62	464.61	19882.56	414.22	20632.80	343.88
18000	20275.92	563.22	20661.48	491.94	21051.84	438.58	21846.60	364.11
19000	21402.36	594.51	21809.34	519.27	22221.60	462.95	23060.40	384.34
20000	22528.80	625.80	22957.20	546.60	23391.36	487.32	24274.20	404.57
21000	23655.24	657.09	24105.48	573.94	24560.64	511.68	25487.40	424.79
22000	24781.68	688.38	25253.34	601.27	25730.40	536.05	26701.20	445.02
23000	25908.12	719.67	26401.20	628.60	26899.68	560.41	27915.00	465.25
24000	27034.56	750.96	27549.06	655.93	28069.44	584.78	29128.80	485.48
25000	28161.00	782.25	28696.92	683.26	29239.20	609.15	30342.60	505.71

8.00% ANNUAL PERCENTAGE RATE

LOAN AMT	12 MONTHS TOTAL NOTE	MONTHLY PAYMENT	18 MONTHS TOTAL NOTE	MONTHLY PAYMENT	24 MONTHS TOTAL NOTE	MONTHLY PAYMENT	30 MONTHS TOTAL NOTE	MONTHLY PAYMENT
1	.96	.08	.90	.05	.96	.04	.90	.03
2	2.04	.17	1.98	.11	2.16	.09	2.10	.07
3	3.12	.26	3.06	.17	3.12	.13	3.30	.11
4	4.08	.34	4.14	.23	4.32	.18	4.20	.14
5	5.16	.43	5.22	.29	5.28	.22	5.40	.18
6	6.24	.52	6.30	.35	6.48	.27	6.60	.22
7	7.20	.60	7.38	.41	7.44	.31	7.50	.25
8	8.28	.69	8.46	.47	8.64	.36	8.70	.29
9	9.36	.78	9.54	.53	9.60	.40	9.90	.33
10	10.32	.86	10.62	.59	10.80	.45	10.80	.36
20	20 76	1.73	21.24	1.18	21.60	.90	21.90	.73
30	31.20	2.60	31.86	1.77	32.40	1.35	33.00	1.10
40	41.64	3.47	42.48	2.36	43.20	1.80	44.10	1.47
50	52.08	4.34	53.10	2.95	54.24	2.26	55.20	1.84
60	62.52	5.21	63.72	3.54	65.04	2.71	66.30	2.21
70	72.96	6.08	74.34	4.13	75.84	3.16	77.40	2.58
80	83.40	6.95	85.14	4.73	86.64	3.61	88.50	2.95
90	93.84	7.82	95.76	5.32	97.68	4.07	99.30	3.31
100	104.28	8.69	106.38	5.91	108.48	4.52	110.40	3.68
200	208.68	17.39	212.76	11.82	216.96	9.04	221.10	7.37
300	313.08	26.09	319.32	17.74	325.44	13.56	331.80	11.06
400	417.48	34.79	425.70	23.65	434.16	18.09	442.50	14.75
500	521.88	43.49	532.26	29.57	542.64	22.61	553.20	18.44
600	626.28	52.19	638.64	35.48	651.12	27.13	663.90	22.13
700	730.68	60.89	745.02	41.39	759.60	31.65	774.60	25.82
800	835.08	69.59	851.58	47.31	868.32	36.18	885.30	29.51
900	939.36	78.28	957.96	53.22	976.80	40.70	995.70	33.19
1000	1043.76	86.98	1064.52	59.14	1085.28	45.22	1106.40	36.88
1500	1565.76	130.48	1596.78	88.71	1628.16	67.84	1659.90	55.33
2000	2087.64	173.97	2129.04	118.28	2170.80	90.45	2213.10	73.77
2500	2609.64	217.47	2661.30	147.85	2713.44	113.06	2766.60	92.22
3000	3131.52	260.96	3193.56	177.42	3256.32	135.68	3319.80	110.66
3500	3653.40	304.45	3725.82	206.99	3798.96	158.29	3873.00	129.10
4000	4175.40	347.95	4258.08	236.56	4341.60	180.90	4426.50	147.55
4500	4697.28	391.44	4790.34	266.13	4884.48	203.52	4979.70	165.99
5000	5219.28	434.94	5322.60	295.70	5427.12	226.13	5533.20	184.44
5500	5741.16	478.43	5854.86	325.27	5970.00	248.75	6086.40	202.88
6000	6263.16	521.93	6387.12	354.84	6512.64	271.36	6639.60	221.32
6500	6785.04	565.42	6919.38	384.41	7055.28	293.97	7193.10	239.77
7000	7306.92	608.91	7451.64	413.98	7598.16	316.59	7746.30	258.21
7500	7828.92	652.41	7983.90	443.55	8140.80	339.20	8299.80	276.66
8000	8350.80	695.90	8516.16	473.12	8683.44	361.81	8853.00	295.10
8500	8872.80	739.40	9048.42	502.69	9226.32	384.43	9406.50	313.55
9000	9394.68	782.89	9580.68	532.26	9768.96	407.04	9959.70	331.99
10000	10438.56	869.88	10645.20	591.40	10854.48	452.27	11066.40	368.88
11000	11482.44	956.87	11709.72	650.54	11940.00	497.50	12173.10	405.77
12000	12526.32	1043.86	12774.24	709.68	13025.28	542.72	13279.50	442.65
13000	13570.08	1130.84	13838.76	768.82	14110.80	587.95	14386.20	479.54
14000	14613.96	1217.83	14903.28	827.96	15196.32	633.18	15492.90	516.43
15000	15657.84	1304.82	15967.80	887.10	16281.60	678.40	16599.60	553.32
16000	16701.72	1391.81	17032.32	946.24	17367.12	723.63	17706.30	590.21
17000	17745.60	1478.80	18096.84	1005.38	18452.64	768.86	18813.00	627.10
18000	18789.48	1565.79	19161.36	1064.52	19538.16	814.09	19919.40	663.98
19000	19833.36	1652.78	20225.88	1123.66	20623.44	859.31	21026.10	700.87
20000	20877.12	1739.76	21290.40	1182.80	21708.96	904.54	22132.80	737.76
21000	21921.00	1826.75	22354.92	1241.94	22794.48	949.77	23239.50	774.65
22000	22964.88	1913.74	23419.44	1301.08	23880.00	995.00	24346.20	811.54
23000	24008.76	2000.73	24483.96	1360.22	24965.28	1040.22	25452.90	848.43
24000	25052.64	2087.72	25548.48	1419.36	26050.80	1085.45	26559.30	885.31
25000	26096.52	2174.71	26613.00	1478.50	27136.32	1130.68	27666.00	922.20

ANNUAL PERCENTAGE RATE **8.00%**

LOAN	36 MONTHS		42 MONTHS		48 MONTHS		60 MONTHS	
AMT	TOTAL NOTE	MONTHLY PAYMENT	TOTAL NOTE	MONTHLY PAYMENT	TOTAL NOTE	MONTHLY PAYMENT	TOTAL NOTE	MONTHLY PAYMENT
1	1.08	.03	.84	.02	.96	.02	1.20	.02
2	2.16	.06	2.10	.05	1.92	.04	2.40	.04
3	3.24	.09	3.36	.08	3.36	.07	3.60	.06
4	4.32	.12	4.20	.10	4.32	.09	4.80	.08
5	5.40	.15	5.46	.13	5.76	.12	6.00	.10
6	6.48	.18	6.72	.16	6.72	.14	7.20	.12
7	7.56	.21	7.98	.19	8.16	.17	8.40	.14
8	9.00	.25	8.82	.21	9.12	.19	9.60	.16
9	10.08	.28	10.08	.24	10.08	.21	10.80	.18
10	11.16	.31	11.34	.27	11.52	.24	12.00	.20
20	22.32	.62	22.68	.54	23.04	.48	24.00	.40
30	33.84	.94	34.44	.82	35.04	.73	36.00	.60
40	45.00	1.25	45.78	1.09	46.56	.97	48.60	.81
50	56.16	1.56	57.12	1.36	58.56	1.22	60.60	1.01
60	67.68	1.88	68.88	1.64	70.08	1.46	72.60	1.21
70	78.84	2.19	80.22	1.91	81.60	1.70	84.60	1.41
80	90.00	2.50	91.98	2.19	93.60	1.95	97.20	1.62
90	101.52	2.82	103.32	2.46	105.12	2.19	109.20	1.82
100	112.68	3.13	114.66	2.73	117.12	2.44	121.20	2.02
200	225.36	6.26	229.74	5.47	234.24	4.88	243.00	4.05
300	338.40	9.40	344.82	8.21	351.36	7.32	364.80	6.08
400	451.08	12.53	459.90	10.95	468.48	9.76	486.60	8.11
500	563.76	15.66	574.56	13.68	585.60	12.20	607.80	10.13
600	676.80	18.80	689.64	16.42	702.72	14.64	729.60	12.16
700	789.48	21.93	804.72	19.16	819.84	17.08	851.40	14.19
800	902.16	25.06	919.80	21.90	937.44	19.53	973.20	16.22
900	1015.20	28.20	1034.46	24.63	1054.56	21.97	1094.40	18.24
1000	1127.88	31.33	1149.54	27.37	1171.68	24.41	1216.20	20.27
1500	1692.00	47.00	1724.52	41.06	1757.28	36.61	1824.60	30.41
2000	2256.12	62.67	2299.50	54.75	2343.36	48.82	2433.00	40.55
2500	2820.24	78.34	2874.48	68.44	2929.44	61.03	3041.40	50.69
3000	3384.00	94.00	3449.46	82.13	3515.04	73.23	3649.20	60.82
3500	3948.12	109.67	4024.02	95.81	4101.12	85.44	4257.60	70.96
4000	4512.24	125.34	4599.00	109.50	4687.20	97.65	4866.00	81.10
4500	5076.36	141.01	5173.98	123.19	5272.80	109.85	5474.40	91.24
5000	5640.48	156.68	5748.96	136.88	5858.88	122.06	6082.80	101.38
5500	6204.60	172.35	6323.94	150.57	6444.96	134.27	6691.20	111.52
6000	6768.36	188.01	6898.92	164.26	7030.56	146.47	7299.00	121.65
6500	7332.48	203.68	7473.90	177.95	7616.64	158.68	7907.40	131.79
7000	7896.60	219.35	8048.46	191.63	8202.72	170.89	8515.80	141.93
7500	8460.72	235.02	8623.44	205.32	8788.32	183.09	9124.20	152.07
8000	9024.84	250.69	9198.42	219.01	9374.40	195.30	9732.60	162.21
8500	9588.60	266.35	9773.40	232.70	9960.00	207.50	10340.40	172.34
9000	10152.72	282.02	10348.38	246.39	10546.08	219.71	10948.80	182.48
10000	11280.96	313.36	11497.92	273.76	11717.76	244.12	12165.60	202.76
11000	12409.20	344.70	12647.88	301.14	12889.92	268.54	13382.40	223.04
12000	13537.08	376.03	13797.84	328.52	14061.60	292.95	14598.60	243.31
13000	14665.32	407.37	14947.80	355.90	15233.28	317.36	15815.40	263.59
14000	15793.20	438.70	16097.34	383.27	16405.44	341.78	17031.60	283.86
15000	16921.44	470.04	17247.30	410.65	17577.12	366.19	18248.40	304.14
16000	18049.68	501.38	18397.26	438.03	18748.80	390.60	19465.20	324.42
17000	19177.56	532.71	19546.80	465.40	19920.48	415.01	20681.40	344.69
18000	20305.80	564.05	20696.76	492.78	21092.64	439.43	21898.20	364.97
19000	21434.04	595.39	21846.72	520.16	22264.32	463.84	23115.00	385.25
20000	22561.92	626.72	22996.26	547.53	23436.00	488.25	24331.20	405.52
21000	23690.16	658.06	24146.22	574.91	24608.16	512.67	25548.00	425.80
22000	24818.40	689.40	25296.18	602.29	25779.84	537.08	26764.80	446.08
23000	25946.28	720.73	26446.14	629.67	26951.52	561.49	27981.00	466.35
24000	27074.52	752.07	27595.68	657.04	28123.68	585.91	29197.80	486.63
25000	28202.40	783.40	28745.64	684.42	29295.36	610.32	30414.00	506.90

8.10% ANNUAL PERCENTAGE RATE

LOAN AMT	12 MONTHS		18 MONTHS		24 MONTHS		30 MONTHS	
	TOTAL NOTE	MONTHLY PAYMENT	TOTAL NOTE	MONTHLY PAYMENT	TOTAL NOTE	MONTHLY PAYMENT	TOTAL NOTE	MONTHLY PAYMENT
1	.96	.08	.90	.05	.96	.04	.90	.03
2	2.04	.17	1.98	.11	2.16	.09	2.10	.07
3	3.12	.26	3.06	.17	3.12	.13	3.30	.11
4	4.08	.34	4.14	.23	4.32	.18	4.20	.14
5	5.16	.43	5.22	.29	5.28	.22	5.40	.18
6	6.24	.52	6.30	.35	6.48	.27	6.60	.22
7	7.20	.60	7.38	.41	7.44	.31	7.50	.25
8	8.28	.69	8.46	.47	8.64	.36	8.70	.29
9	9.36	.78	9.54	.53	9.60	.40	9.90	.33
10	10.44	.87	10.62	.59	10.80	.45	10.80	.36
20	20.88	1.74	21.24	1.18	21.60	.90	21.90	.73
30	31.32	2.61	31.86	1.77	32.40	1.35	33.00	1.10
40	41.76	3.48	42.48	2.36	43.44	1.81	44.10	1.47
50	52.20	4.35	53.10	2.95	54.24	2.26	55.20	1.84
60	62.64	5.22	63.90	3.55	65.04	2.71	66.30	2.21
70	73.08	6.09	74.52	4.14	75.84	3.16	77.40	2.58
80	83.52	6.96	85.14	4.73	86.88	3.62	88.50	2.95
90	93.96	7.83	95.76	5.32	97.68	4.07	99.60	3.32
100	104.40	8.70	106.38	5.91	108.48	4.52	110.70	3.69
200	208.80	17.40	212.94	11.83	217.20	9.05	221.40	7.38
300	313.32	26.11	319.50	17.75	325.92	13.58	332.40	11.08
400	417.72	34.81	426.06	23.67	434.40	18.10	443.10	14.77
500	522.12	43.51	532.62	29.59	543.12	22.63	553.80	18.46
600	626.64	52.22	639.18	35.51	651.84	27.16	664.80	22.16
700	731.04	60.92	745.74	41.43	760.56	31.69	775.50	25.85
800	835.44	69.62	852.12	47.34	869.04	36.21	886.20	29.54
900	939.96	78.33	958.68	53.26	977.76	40.74	997.20	33.24
1000	1044.36	87.03	1065.24	59.18	1086.48	45.27	1107.90	36.93
1500	1566.60	130.55	1597.86	88.77	1629.60	67.90	1662.00	55.40
2000	2088.72	174.06	2130.66	118.37	2172.96	90.54	2215.80	73.86
2500	2610.96	217.58	2663.28	147.96	2716.32	113.18	2769.90	92.33
3000	3133.20	261.10	3195.90	177.55	3259.44	135.81	3324.00	110.80
3500	3655.44	304.62	3728.70	207.15	3802.80	158.45	3877.80	129.26
4000	4177.56	348.13	4261.32	236.74	4346.16	181.09	4431.90	147.73
4500	4699.80	391.65	4793.94	266.33	4889.28	203.72	4986.00	166.20
5000	5222.04	435.17	5326.56	295.92	5432.64	226.36	5540.10	184.67
5500	5744.28	478.69	5859.36	325.52	5976.00	249.00	6093.90	203.13
6000	6266.40	522.20	6391.98	355.11	6519.12	271.63	6648.00	221.60
6500	6788.64	565.72	6924.60	384.70	7062.48	294.27	7202.10	240.07
7000	7310.88	609.24	7457.40	414.30	7605.84	316.91	7755.90	258.53
7500	7833.12	652.76	7990.02	443.89	8148.96	339.54	8310.00	277.00
8000	8355.24	696.27	8522.64	473.48	8692.32	362.18	8864.10	295.47
8500	8877.48	739.79	9055.44	503.08	9235.44	384.81	9418.20	313.94
9000	9399.72	783.31	9588.06	532.67	9778.80	407.45	9972.00	332.40
10000	10444.08	870.34	10653.30	591.85	10865.28	452.72	11080.20	369.34
11000	11488.56	957.38	11718.72	651.04	11952.00	498.00	12188.10	406.27
12000	12532.92	1044.41	12784.14	710.23	13038.48	543.27	13296.00	443.20
13000	13577.40	1131.45	13849.38	769.41	14124.96	588.54	14404.20	480.14
14000	14621.76	1218.48	14914.80	828.60	15211.68	633.82	15512.10	517.07
15000	15666.24	1305.52	15980.04	887.78	16298.16	679.09	16620.30	554.01
16000	16710.60	1392.55	17045.46	946.97	17384.64	724.36	17728.20	590.94
17000	17754.96	1479.58	18110.88	1006.16	18471.12	769.63	18836.40	627.88
18000	18799.44	1566.62	19176.12	1065.34	19557.84	814.91	19944.30	664.81
19000	19843.80	1653.65	20241.54	1124.53	20644.32	860.18	21052.20	701.74
20000	20888.28	1740.69	21306.78	1183.71	21730.80	905.45	22160.40	738.68
21000	21932.64	1827.72	22372.20	1242.90	22817.52	950.73	23268.30	775.61
22000	22977.12	1914.76	23437.62	1302.09	23904.00	996.00	24376.50	812.55
23000	24021.48	2001.79	24502.86	1361.27	24990.48	1041.27	25484.40	849.48
24000	25065.96	2088.83	25568.28	1420.46	26076.96	1086.54	26592.30	886.41
25000	26110.32	2175.86	26633.52	1479.64	27163.68	1131.82	27700.50	923.35

ANNUAL PERCENTAGE RATE **8.10%**

LOAN AMT	36 MONTHS TOTAL NOTE	MONTHLY PAYMENT	42 MONTHS TOTAL NOTE	MONTHLY PAYMENT	48 MONTHS TOTAL NOTE	MONTHLY PAYMENT	60 MONTHS TOTAL NOTE	MONTHLY PAYMENT
1	1.08	.03	.84	.02	.96	.02	1.20	.02
2	2.16	.06	2.10	.05	1.92	.04	2.40	.04
3	3.24	.09	3.36	.08	3.36	.07	3.60	.06
4	4.32	.12	4.20	.10	4.32	.09	4.80	.08
5	5.40	.15	5.46	.13	5.76	.12	6.00	.10
6	6.48	.18	6.72	.16	6.72	.14	7.20	.12
7	7.56	.21	7.98	.19	8.16	.17	8.40	.14
8	9.00	.25	8.82	.21	9.12	.19	9.60	.16
9	10.08	.28	10.08	.24	10.56	.22	10.80	.18
10	11.16	.31	11.34	.27	11.52	.24	12.00	.20
20	22.32	.62	22.68	.54	23.04	.48	24.00	.40
30	33.84	.94	34.44	.82	35.04	.73	36.00	.60
40	45.00	1.25	45.78	1.09	46.56	.97	48.60	.81
50	56.16	1.56	57.54	1.37	58.56	1.22	60.60	1.01
60	67.68	1.88	68.88	1.64	70.08	1.46	72.60	1.21
70	78.84	2.19	80.22	1.91	82.08	1.71	85.20	1.42
80	90.36	2.51	91.98	2.19	93.60	1.95	97.20	1.62
90	101.52	2.82	103.32	2.46	105.60	2.20	109.20	1.82
100	112.68	3.13	115.08	2.74	117.12	2.44	121.80	2.03
200	225.72	6.27	230.16	5.48	234.72	4.89	243.60	4.06
300	338.76	9.41	345.24	8.22	351.84	7.33	365.40	6.09
400	451.80	12.55	460.32	10.96	469.44	9.78	487.20	8.12
500	564.84	15.69	575.82	13.71	586.56	12.22	609.60	10.16
600	677.52	18.82	690.90	16.45	704.16	14.67	731.40	12.19
700	790.56	21.96	805.98	19.19	821.76	17.12	853.20	14.22
800	903.60	25.10	921.06	21.93	938.88	19.56	975.00	16.25
900	1016.64	28.24	1036.56	24.68	1056.48	22.01	1097.40	18.29
1000	1129.68	31.38	1151.64	27.42	1173.60	24.45	1219.20	20.32
1500	1694.52	47.07	1727.46	41.13	1760.64	36.68	1828.80	30.48
2000	2259.36	62.76	2303.28	54.84	2347.68	48.91	2438.40	40.64
2500	2824.20	78.45	2879.10	68.55	2934.72	61.14	3048.60	50.81
3000	3389.04	94.14	3455.34	82.27	3521.76	73.37	3658.20	60.97
3500	3953.88	109.83	4031.16	95.98	4108.80	85.60	4267.80	71.13
4000	4519.08	125.53	4606.98	109.69	4695.84	97.83	4877.40	81.29
4500	5083.92	141.22	5182.80	123.40	5282.88	110.06	5487.00	91.45
5000	5648.76	156.91	5758.62	137.11	5869.92	122.29	6097.20	101.62
5500	6213.60	172.60	6334.44	150.82	6456.96	134.52	6706.80	111.78
6000	6778.44	188.29	6910.68	164.54	7044.00	146.75	7316.40	121.94
6500	7343.28	203.98	7486.50	178.25	7631.04	158.98	7926.00	132.10
7000	7908.12	219.67	8062.32	191.96	8218.08	171.21	8536.20	142.27
7500	8472.96	235.36	8638.14	205.67	8805.12	183.44	9145.80	152.43
8000	9038.16	251.06	9213.96	219.38	9392.16	195.67	9755.40	162.59
8500	9603.00	266.75	9789.78	233.09	9979.20	207.90	10365.00	172.75
9000	10167.84	282.44	10366.02	246.81	10566.24	220.13	10974.60	182.91
10000	11297.52	313.82	11517.66	274.23	11740.32	244.59	12194.40	203.24
11000	12427.20	345.20	12669.30	301.65	12914.40	269.05	13413.60	223.56
12000	13557.24	376.59	13821.36	329.08	14088.48	293.51	14633.40	243.89
13000	14686.92	407.97	14973.00	356.50	15262.56	317.97	15852.60	264.21
14000	15816.60	439.35	16124.64	383.92	16436.64	342.43	17072.40	284.54
15000	16946.28	470.73	17276.70	411.35	17610.72	366.89	18291.60	304.86
16000	18076.32	502.12	18428.34	438.77	18784.80	391.35	19510.80	325.18
17000	19206.00	533.50	19579.98	466.19	19958.88	415.81	20730.60	345.51
18000	20335.68	564.88	20732.04	493.62	21132.96	440.27	21949.80	365.83
19000	21465.36	596.26	21883.68	521.04	22307.04	464.73	23169.60	386.16
20000	22595.40	627.65	23035.74	548.47	23481.12	489.19	24388.80	406.48
21000	23725.08	659.03	24187.38	575.89	24655.20	513.65	25608.60	426.81
22000	24854.76	690.41	25339.02	603.31	25829.28	538.11	26827.80	447.13
23000	25984.44	721.79	26491.08	630.74	27003.36	562.57	28047.00	467.45
24000	27114.48	753.18	27642.72	658.16	28177.44	587.03	29266.80	487.78
25000	28244.16	784.56	28794.36	685.58	29351.52	611.49	30486.00	508.10

8.20% ANNUAL PERCENTAGE RATE

LOAN AMT	12 MONTHS TOTAL NOTE	12 MONTHS MONTHLY PAYMENT	18 MONTHS TOTAL NOTE	18 MONTHS MONTHLY PAYMENT	24 MONTHS TOTAL NOTE	24 MONTHS MONTHLY PAYMENT	30 MONTHS TOTAL NOTE	30 MONTHS MONTHLY PAYMENT
1	.96	.08	.90	.05	.96	.04	.90	.03
2	2.04	.17	1.98	.11	2.16	.09	2.10	.07
3	3.12	.26	3.06	.17	3.12	.13	3.30	.11
4	4.08	.34	4.14	.23	4.32	.18	4.20	.14
5	5.16	.43	5.22	.29	5.28	.22	5.40	.18
6	6.24	.52	6.30	.35	6.48	.27	6.60	.22
7	7.20	.60	7.38	.41	7.44	.31	7.50	.25
8	8.28	.69	8.46	.47	8.64	.36	8.70	.29
9	9.36	.78	9.54	.53	9.60	.40	9.90	.33
10	10.44	.87	10.62	.59	10.80	.45	10.80	.36
20	20.88	1.74	21.24	1.18	21.60	.90	21.90	.73
30	31.32	2.61	31.86	1.77	32.40	1.35	33.00	1.10
40	41.76	3.48	42.48	2.36	43.44	1.81	44.10	1.47
50	52.20	4.35	53.28	2.96	54.24	2.26	55.20	1.84
60	62.64	5.22	63.90	3.55	65.04	2.71	66.30	2.21
70	73.08	6.09	74.52	4.14	76.08	3.17	77.40	2.58
80	83.52	6.96	85.14	4.73	86.88	3.62	88.50	2.95
90	93.96	7.83	95.94	5.33	97.68	4.07	99.60	3.32
100	104.40	8.70	106.56	5.92	108.72	4.53	110.70	3.69
200	208.92	17.41	213.12	11.84	217.44	9.06	221.70	7.39
300	313.44	26.12	319.68	17.76	326.16	13.59	332.70	11.09
400	417.96	34.83	426.42	23.69	434.88	18.12	443.70	14.79
500	522.48	43.54	532.98	29.61	543.60	22.65	554.70	18.49
600	626.88	52.24	639.54	35.53	652.56	27.19	665.40	22.18
700	731.40	60.95	746.28	41.46	761.28	31.72	776.40	25.88
800	835.92	69.66	852.84	47.38	870.00	36.25	887.40	29.58
900	940.44	78.37	959.40	53.30	978.72	40.78	998.40	33.28
1000	1044.96	87.08	1066.14	59.23	1087.44	45.31	1109.40	36.98
1500	1567.44	130.62	1599.12	88.84	1631.28	67.97	1664.10	55.47
2000	2089.92	174.16	2132.28	118.46	2175.12	90.63	2218.80	73.96
2500	2612.40	217.70	2665.26	148.07	2718.96	113.29	2773.50	92.45
3000	3134.88	261.24	3198.42	177.69	3262.80	135.95	3328.20	110.94
3500	3657.36	304.78	3731.58	207.31	3806.64	158.61	3882.90	129.43
4000	4179.84	348.32	4264.56	236.92	4350.48	181.27	4437.60	147.92
4500	4702.32	391.86	4797.72	266.54	4894.32	203.93	4992.30	166.41
5000	5224.80	435.40	5330.70	296.15	5438.16	226.59	5547.00	184.90
5500	5747.28	478.94	5863.86	325.77	5982.00	249.25	6101.70	203.39
6000	6269.76	522.48	6396.84	355.38	6525.84	271.91	6656.40	221.88
6500	6792.24	566.02	6930.00	385.00	7069.68	294.57	7211.10	240.37
7000	7314.72	609.56	7463.16	414.62	7613.28	317.22	7765.80	258.86
7500	7837.20	653.10	7996.14	444.23	8157.12	339.88	8320.50	277.35
8000	8359.68	696.64	8529.30	473.85	8700.96	362.54	8875.20	295.84
8500	8882.16	740.18	9062.28	503.46	9244.80	385.20	9429.90	314.33
9000	9404.64	783.72	9595.44	533.08	9788.64	407.86	9984.60	332.82
10000	10449.60	870.80	10661.58	592.31	10876.32	453.18	11094.00	369.80
11000	11494.68	957.89	11727.72	651.54	11964.00	498.50	12203.40	406.78
12000	12539.64	1044.97	12793.86	710.77	13051.68	543.82	13312.80	443.76
13000	13584.60	1132.05	13860.18	770.01	14139.36	589.14	14422.20	480.74
14000	14629.56	1219.13	14926.32	829.24	15226.80	634.45	15531.60	517.72
15000	15674.52	1306.21	15992.46	888.47	16314.48	679.77	16641.00	554.70
16000	16719.48	1393.29	17058.60	947.70	17402.16	725.09	17750.40	591.68
17000	17764.44	1480.37	18124.74	1006.93	18489.84	770.41	18859.80	628.66
18000	18809.40	1567.45	19190.88	1066.16	19577.52	815.73	19969.20	665.64
19000	19854.36	1654.53	20257.20	1125.40	20665.20	861.05	21078.60	702.62
20000	20899.32	1741.61	21323.34	1184.63	21752.88	906.37	22188.00	739.60
21000	21944.28	1828.69	22389.48	1243.86	22840.32	951.68	23297.40	776.58
22000	22989.36	1915.78	23455.62	1303.09	23928.00	997.00	24406.80	813.56
23000	24034.32	2002.86	24521.76	1362.32	25015.68	1042.32	25516.20	850.54
24000	25079.28	2089.94	25587.90	1421.55	26103.36	1087.64	26625.60	887.52
25000	26124.24	2177.02	26654.22	1480.79	27191.04	1132.96	27735.00	924.50

ANNUAL PERCENTAGE RATE **8.20%**

LOAN AMT	36 MONTHS TOTAL NOTE	36 MONTHS MONTHLY PAYMENT	42 MONTHS TOTAL NOTE	42 MONTHS MONTHLY PAYMENT	48 MONTHS TOTAL NOTE	48 MONTHS MONTHLY PAYMENT	60 MONTHS TOTAL NOTE	60 MONTHS MONTHLY PAYMENT
1	1.08	.03	.84	.02	.96	.02	1.20	.02
2	2.16	.06	2.10	.05	1.92	.04	2.40	.04
3	3.24	.09	3.36	.08	3.36	.07	3.60	.06
4	4.32	.12	4.20	.10	4.32	.09	4.80	.08
5	5.40	.15	5.46	.13	5.76	.12	6.00	.10
6	6.48	.18	6.72	.16	6.72	.14	7.20	.12
7	7.92	.22	7.98	.19	8.16	.17	8.40	.14
8	9.00	.25	8.82	.21	9.12	.19	9.60	.16
9	10.08	.28	10.08	.24	10.56	.22	10.80	.18
10	11.16	.31	11.34	.27	11.52	.24	12.00	.20
20	22.32	.62	22.68	.54	23.52	.49	24.00	.40
30	33.84	.94	34.44	.82	35.04	.73	36.60	.61
40	45.00	1.25	45.78	1.09	47.04	.98	48.60	.81
50	56.52	1.57	57.54	1.37	58.56	1.22	60.60	1.01
60	67.68	1.88	68.88	1.64	70.56	1.47	73.20	1.22
70	79.20	2.20	80.64	1.92	82.08	1.71	85.20	1.42
80	90.36	2.51	91.98	2.19	94.08	1.96	97.20	1.62
90	101.52	2.82	103.74	2.47	105.60	2.20	109.80	1.83
100	113.04	3.14	115.08	2.74	117.60	2.45	121.80	2.03
200	226.08	6.28	230.58	5.49	235.20	4.90	244.20	4.07
300	339.12	9.42	346.08	8.24	352.80	7.35	366.60	6.11
400	452.52	12.57	461.16	10.98	470.40	9.80	488.40	8.14
500	565.56	15.71	576.66	13.73	588.00	12.25	610.80	10.18
600	678.60	18.85	692.16	16.48	705.60	14.70	733.20	12.22
700	792.00	22.00	807.24	19.22	823.20	17.15	855.60	14.26
800	905.04	25.14	922.74	21.97	940.80	19.60	977.40	16.29
900	1018.08	28.28	1038.24	24.72	1058.40	22.05	1099.80	18.33
1000	1131.12	31.42	1153.74	27.47	1176.00	24.50	1222.20	20.37
1500	1697.04	47.14	1730.40	41.20	1764.48	36.76	1833.00	30.55
2000	2262.60	62.85	2307.48	54.94	2352.48	49.01	2444.40	40.74
2500	2828.52	78.57	2884.14	68.67	2940.48	61.26	3055.80	50.93
3000	3394.08	94.28	3461.22	82.41	3528.96	73.52	3666.60	61.11
3500	3960.00	110.00	4037.88	96.14	4116.96	85.77	4278.00	71.30
4000	4525.56	125.71	4614.96	109.88	4704.96	98.02	4888.80	81.48
4500	5091.12	141.42	5191.62	123.61	5293.44	110.28	5500.20	91.67
5000	5657.04	157.14	5768.70	137.35	5881.44	122.53	6111.60	101.86
5500	6222.60	172.85	6345.36	151.08	6469.44	134.78	6722.40	112.04
6000	6788.52	188.57	6922.44	164.82	7057.92	147.04	7333.80	122.23
6500	7354.08	204.28	7499.10	178.55	7645.92	159.29	7944.80	132.41
7000	7920.00	220.00	8076.18	192.29	8233.92	171.54	8556.00	142.60
7500	8485.56	235.71	8652.84	206.02	8822.40	183.80	9167.40	152.79
8000	9051.12	251.42	9229.92	219.76	9410.40	196.05	9778.20	162.97
8500	9617.04	267.14	9806.58	233.49	9998.40	208.30	10389.60	173.16
9000	10182.60	282.85	10383.66	247.23	10586.88	220.56	11001.00	183.35
10000	11314.08	314.28	11537.40	274.70	11762.88	245.06	12223.20	203.72
11000	12445.56	345.71	12691.14	302.17	12939.36	269.57	13445.40	224.09
12000	13577.04	377.14	13844.88	329.64	14115.84	294.08	14667.60	244.46
13000	14708.52	408.57	14998.62	357.11	15291.84	318.58	15889.80	264.83
14000	15840.00	440.00	16152.36	384.58	16468.32	343.09	17112.60	285.21
15000	16971.48	471.43	17306.10	412.05	17644.80	367.60	18334.80	305.58
16000	18102.60	502.85	18459.84	439.52	18821.28	392.11	19557.00	325.95
17000	19234.08	534.28	19613.58	466.99	19997.28	416.61	20779.20	346.32
18000	20365.56	565.71	20767.32	494.46	21173.76	441.12	22002.00	366.70
19000	21497.04	597.14	21921.06	521.93	22350.24	465.63	23224.20	387.07
20000	22628.52	628.57	23074.80	549.40	23526.24	490.13	24446.40	407.44
21000	23760.00	660.00	24228.54	576.87	24702.72	514.64	25668.60	427.81
22000	24891.48	691.43	25382.28	604.34	25879.20	539.15	26890.80	448.18
23000	26022.96	722.86	26536.02	631.81	27055.20	563.65	28113.60	468.56
24000	27154.08	754.28	27689.76	659.28	28231.68	588.16	29335.80	488.93
25000	28285.56	785.71	28843.50	686.75	29408.16	612.67	30558.00	509.30

8.25% ANNUAL PERCENTAGE RATE

LOAN AMT	12 MONTHS TOTAL NOTE	12 MONTHS MONTHLY PAYMENT	18 MONTHS TOTAL NOTE	18 MONTHS MONTHLY PAYMENT	24 MONTHS TOTAL NOTE	24 MONTHS MONTHLY PAYMENT	30 MONTHS TOTAL NOTE	30 MONTHS MONTHLY PAYMENT
1	.96	.08	.90	.05	.96	.04	.90	.03
2	2.04	.17	1.98	.11	2.16	.09	2.10	.07
3	3.12	.26	3.06	.17	3.12	.13	3.30	.11
4	4.08	.34	4.14	.23	4.32	.18	4.20	.14
5	5.16	.43	5.22	.29	5.28	.22	5.40	.18
6	6.24	.52	6.30	.35	6.48	.27	6.60	.22
7	7.20	.60	7.38	.41	7.44	.31	7.50	.25
8	8.28	.69	8.46	.47	8.64	.36	8.70	.29
9	9.36	.78	9.54	.53	9.60	.40	9.90	.33
10	10.44	.87	10.62	.59	10.80	.45	11.10	.37
20	20.88	1.74	21.24	1.18	21.60	.90	22.20	.74
30	31.32	2.61	31.86	1.77	32.64	1.36	33.30	1.11
40	41.76	3.48	42.66	2.37	43.44	1.81	44.40	1.48
50	52.20	4.35	53.28	2.96	54.24	2.26	55.50	1.85
60	62.64	5.22	63.90	3.55	65.28	2.72	66.60	2.22
70	73.08	6.09	74.52	4.14	76.08	3.17	77.70	2.59
80	83.52	6.96	85.32	4.74	86.88	3.62	88.80	2.96
90	93.96	7.83	95.94	5.33	97.92	4.08	99.90	3.33
100	104.52	8.71	106.56	5.92	108.72	4.53	111.00	3.70
200	209.04	17.42	213.30	11.85	217.44	9.06	222.00	7.40
300	313.56	26.13	319.86	17.77	326.40	13.60	333.00	11.10
400	418.08	34.84	426.60	23.70	435.12	18.13	444.00	14.80
500	522.60	43.55	533.16	29.62	544.08	22.67	555.00	18.50
600	627.12	52.26	639.90	35.55	652.80	27.20	666.00	22.20
700	731.64	60.97	746.46	41.47	761.52	31.73	777.00	25.90
800	836.16	69.68	853.20	47.40	870.48	36.27	888.00	29.60
900	940.68	78.39	959.76	53.32	979.20	40.80	999.00	33.30
1000	1045.20	87.10	1066.50	59.25	1088.16	45.34	1110.00	37.00
1500	1567.80	130.65	1599.84	88.88	1632.24	68.01	1665.00	55.50
2000	2090.40	174.20	2133.00	118.50	2176.32	90.68	2220.00	74.00
2500	2613.12	217.76	2666.34	148.13	2720.40	113.35	2775.00	92.50
3000	3135.72	261.31	3199.68	177.76	3264.48	136.02	3330.00	111.00
3500	3658.32	304.86	3733.02	207.39	3808.56	158.69	3885.30	129.51
4000	4180.92	348.41	4266.18	237.01	4352.64	181.36	4440.30	148.01
4500	4703.52	391.96	4799.52	266.64	4896.72	204.03	4995.30	166.51
5000	5226.24	435.52	5332.86	296.27	5440.80	226.70	5550.30	185.01
5500	5748.84	479.07	5866.02	325.89	5984.88	249.37	6105.30	203.51
6000	6271.44	522.62	6399.36	355.52	6528.96	272.04	6660.30	222.01
6500	6794.04	566.17	6932.70	385.15	7073.04	294.71	7215.30	240.51
7000	7316.64	609.72	7466.04	414.78	7617.12	317.38	7770.60	259.02
7500	7839.36	653.28	7999.20	444.40	8161.44	340.06	8325.60	277.52
8000	8361.96	696.83	8532.54	474.03	8705.52	362.73	8880.60	296.02
8500	8884.56	740.38	9065.88	503.66	9249.60	385.40	9435.60	314.52
9000	9407.16	783.93	9599.22	533.29	9793.68	408.07	9990.60	333.02
10000	10452.48	871.04	10665.72	592.54	10881.84	453.41	11100.60	370.02
11000	11497.68	958.14	11732.22	651.79	11970.00	498.75	12210.90	407.03
12000	12542.88	1045.24	12798.90	711.05	13058.16	544.09	13320.90	444.03
13000	13588.20	1132.35	13865.40	770.30	14146.32	589.43	14430.90	481.03
14000	14633.40	1219.45	14932.08	829.56	15234.48	634.77	15541.20	518.04
15000	15678.72	1306.56	15998.58	888.81	16322.88	680.12	16651.20	555.04
16000	16723.92	1393.66	17065.26	948.07	17411.04	725.46	17761.20	592.04
17000	17769.12	1480.76	18131.76	1007.32	18499.20	770.80	18871.50	629.05
18000	18814.44	1567.87	19198.44	1066.58	19587.36	816.14	19981.50	666.05
19000	19859.64	1654.97	20264.94	1125.83	20675.52	861.48	21091.50	703.05
20000	20904.96	1742.08	21331.44	1185.08	21763.68	906.82	22201.50	740.05
21000	21950.16	1829.18	22398.12	1244.34	22851.84	952.16	23311.80	777.06
22000	22995.36	1916.28	23464.62	1303.59	23940.24	997.51	24421.80	814.06
23000	24040.68	2003.39	24531.30	1362.85	25028.40	1042.85	25531.80	851.06
24000	25085.88	2090.49	25597.80	1422.10	26116.56	1088.19	26642.10	888.07
25000	26131.20	2177.60	26664.48	1481.36	27204.72	1133.53	27752.10	925.07

ANNUAL PERCENTAGE RATE **8.25%**

LOAN AMT	36 MONTHS TOTAL NOTE	36 MONTHS MONTHLY PAYMENT	42 MONTHS TOTAL NOTE	42 MONTHS MONTHLY PAYMENT	48 MONTHS TOTAL NOTE	48 MONTHS MONTHLY PAYMENT	60 MONTHS TOTAL NOTE	60 MONTHS MONTHLY PAYMENT
1	1.08	.03	.84	.02	.96	.02	1.20	.02
2	2.16	.06	2.10	.05	1.92	.04	2.40	.04
3	3.24	.09	3.36	.08	3.36	.07	3.60	.06
4	4.32	.12	4.20	.10	4.32	.09	4.80	.08
5	5.40	.15	5.46	.13	5.76	.12	6.00	.10
6	6.48	.18	6.72	.16	6.72	.14	7.20	.12
7	7.92	.22	7.98	.19	8.16	.17	8.40	.14
8	9.00	.25	8.82	.21	9.12	.19	9.60	.16
9	10.08	.28	10.08	.24	10.56	.22	10.80	.18
10	11.16	.31	11.34	.27	11.52	.24	12.00	.20
20	22.32	.62	22.68	.54	23.52	.49	24.00	.40
30	33.84	.94	34.44	.82	35.04	.73	36.60	.61
40	45.00	1.25	45.78	1.09	47.04	.98	48.60	.81
50	56.52	1.57	57.54	1.37	58.56	1.22	60.60	1.01
60	67.68	1.88	68.88	1.64	70.56	1.47	73.20	1.22
70	79.20	2.20	80.64	1.92	82.08	1.71	85.20	1.42
80	90.36	2.51	91.98	2.19	94.08	1.96	97.80	1.63
90	101.88	2.83	103.74	2.47	105.60	2.20	109.80	1.83
100	113.04	3.14	115.08	2.74	117.60	2.45	121.80	2.03
200	226.44	6.29	230.58	5.49	235.20	4.90	244.20	4.07
300	339.48	9.43	346.08	8.24	352.80	7.35	366.60	6.11
400	452.88	12.58	461.58	10.99	470.88	9.81	489.00	8.15
500	565.92	15.72	577.08	13.74	588.48	12.26	611.40	10.19
600	679.32	18.87	692.58	16.49	706.08	14.71	733.80	12.23
700	792.36	22.01	808.08	19.24	824.16	17.17	856.20	14.27
800	905.76	25.16	923.58	21.99	941.76	19.62	978.60	16.31
900	1018.80	28.30	1039.08	24.74	1059.36	22.07	1101.00	18.35
1000	1132.20	31.45	1154.58	27.49	1177.44	24.53	1223.40	20.39
1500	1698.12	47.17	1732.08	41.24	1765.92	36.79	1835.40	30.59
2000	2264.40	62.90	2309.16	54.98	2354.88	49.06	2447.40	40.79
2500	2830.32	78.62	2886.66	68.73	2943.36	61.32	3059.40	50.99
3000	3396.60	94.35	3464.16	82.48	3532.32	73.59	3670.80	61.18
3500	3962.88	110.08	4041.24	96.22	4120.80	85.85	4282.80	71.38
4000	4528.80	125.80	4618.74	109.97	4709.76	98.12	4894.80	81.58
4500	5095.08	141.53	5196.24	123.72	5298.24	110.38	5506.80	91.78
5000	5661.00	157.25	5773.32	137.46	5887.20	122.65	6118.80	101.98
5500	6227.28	172.98	6350.82	151.21	6475.68	134.91	6730.20	112.17
6000	6793.56	188.71	6928.32	164.96	7064.64	147.18	7342.20	122.37
6500	7359.48	204.43	7505.40	178.70	7653.12	159.44	7954.20	132.57
7000	7925.76	220.16	8082.90	192.45	8242.08	171.71	8566.20	142.77
7500	8491.68	235.88	8660.40	206.20	8830.56	183.97	9178.20	152.97
8000	9057.96	251.61	9237.48	219.94	9419.52	196.24	9790.20	163.17
8500	9624.24	267.34	9814.98	233.69	10008.00	208.50	10401.60	173.36
9000	10190.16	283.06	10392.48	247.44	10596.96	220.77	11013.60	183.56
10000	11322.36	314.51	11547.06	274.93	11774.40	245.30	12237.60	203.96
11000	12454.92	345.97	12701.64	302.42	12951.84	269.83	13461.00	224.35
12000	13587.12	377.42	13856.64	329.92	14129.28	294.36	14685.00	244.75
13000	14719.32	408.87	15011.22	357.41	15306.72	318.89	15909.00	265.15
14000	15851.52	440.32	16165.80	384.90	16484.16	343.42	17132.40	285.54
15000	16983.72	471.77	17320.80	412.40	17661.60	367.95	18356.40	305.94
16000	18115.92	503.22	18475.38	439.89	18839.04	392.48	19580.40	326.34
17000	19248.48	534.68	19629.96	467.38	20016.48	417.01	20803.80	346.73
18000	20380.68	566.13	20784.96	494.88	21193.92	441.54	22027.80	367.13
19000	21512.88	597.58	21939.54	522.37	22371.36	466.07	23251.20	387.52
20000	22645.08	629.03	23094.12	549.86	23548.80	490.60	24475.20	407.92
21000	23777.28	660.48	24249.12	577.36	24726.24	515.13	25699.20	428.32
22000	24909.84	691.94	25403.70	604.85	25903.68	539.66	26922.60	448.71
23000	26042.04	723.39	26558.28	632.34	27081.60	564.20	28146.60	469.11
24000	27174.24	754.84	27713.28	659.84	28259.04	588.73	29370.60	489.51
25000	28306.44	786.29	28867.86	687.33	29436.48	613.26	30594.00	509.90

8.30% ANNUAL PERCENTAGE RATE

LOAN AMT	12 MONTHS TOTAL NOTE	12 MONTHS MONTHLY PAYMENT	18 MONTHS TOTAL NOTE	18 MONTHS MONTHLY PAYMENT	24 MONTHS TOTAL NOTE	24 MONTHS MONTHLY PAYMENT	30 MONTHS TOTAL NOTE	30 MONTHS MONTHLY PAYMENT
1	.96	.08	.90	.05	.96	.04	.90	.03
2	2.04	.17	1.98	.11	2.16	.09	2.10	.07
3	3.12	.26	3.06	.17	3.12	.13	3.30	.11
4	4.08	.34	4.14	.23	4.32	.18	4.20	.14
5	5.16	.43	5.22	.29	5.28	.22	5.40	.18
6	6.24	.52	6.30	.35	6.48	.27	6.60	.22
7	7.20	.60	7.38	.41	7.44	.31	7.50	.25
8	8.28	.69	8.46	.47	8.64	.36	8.70	.29
9	9.36	.78	9.54	.53	9.60	.40	9.90	.33
10	10.44	.87	10.62	.59	10.80	.45	11.10	.37
20	20.88	1.74	21.24	1.18	21.60	.90	22.20	.74
30	31.32	2.61	31.86	1.77	32.64	1.36	33.30	1.11
40	41.76	3.48	42.66	2.37	43.44	1.81	44.40	1.48
50	52.20	4.35	53.28	2.96	54.24	2.26	55.50	1.85
60	62.64	5.22	63.90	3.55	65.28	2.72	66.60	2.22
70	73.08	6.09	74.52	4.14	76.08	3.17	77.70	2.59
80	83.64	6.97	85.32	4.74	86.88	3.62	88.80	2.96
90	94.08	7.84	95.94	5.33	97.92	4.08	99.90	3.33
100	104.52	8.71	106.56	5.92	108.72	4.53	111.00	3.70
200	209.04	17.42	213.30	11.85	217.68	9.07	222.00	7.40
300	313.56	26.13	320.04	17.78	326.40	13.60	333.00	11.10
400	418.20	34.85	426.78	23.71	435.36	18.14	444.30	14.81
500	522.72	43.56	533.34	29.63	544.32	22.68	555.30	18.51
600	627.24	52.27	640.08	35.56	653.04	27.21	666.30	22.21
700	731.76	60.98	746.82	41.49	762.00	31.75	777.30	25.91
800	836.40	69.70	853.56	47.42	870.96	36.29	888.60	29.62
900	940.92	78.41	960.12	53.34	979.68	40.82	999.60	33.32
1000	1045.44	87.12	1066.86	59.27	1088.64	45.36	1110.60	37.02
1500	1568.28	130.69	1600.38	88.91	1632.96	68.04	1665.90	55.53
2000	2091.00	174.25	2133.90	118.55	2177.28	90.72	2221.50	74.05
2500	2613.72	217.81	2667.42	148.19	2721.84	113.41	2776.80	92.56
3000	3136.56	261.38	3200.94	177.83	3266.16	136.09	3332.10	111.07
3500	3659.28	304.94	3734.46	207.47	3810.48	158.77	3887.70	129.59
4000	4182.00	348.50	4267.80	237.10	4354.80	181.45	4443.00	148.10
4500	4704.84	392.07	4801.32	266.74	4899.12	204.13	4998.30	166.61
5000	5227.56	435.63	5334.84	296.38	5443.68	226.82	5553.60	185.12
5500	5750.28	479.19	5868.36	326.02	5988.00	249.50	6109.20	203.64
6000	6273.12	522.76	6401.88	355.66	6532.32	272.18	6664.50	222.15
6500	6795.84	566.32	6935.40	385.30	7076.64	294.86	7219.80	240.66
7000	7318.68	609.89	7468.92	414.94	7620.96	317.54	7775.40	259.18
7500	7841.40	653.45	8002.26	444.57	8165.52	340.23	8330.70	277.69
8000	8364.12	697.01	8535.78	474.21	8709.84	362.91	8886.00	296.20
8500	8886.96	740.58	9069.30	503.85	9254.16	385.59	9441.60	314.72
9000	9409.68	784.14	9602.82	533.49	9798.48	408.27	9996.90	333.23
10000	10455.24	871.27	10669.86	592.77	10887.36	453.64	11107.50	370.25
11000	11500.68	958.39	11736.90	652.05	11976.00	499.00	12218.40	407.28
12000	12546.24	1045.52	12803.76	711.32	13064.88	544.37	13329.30	444.31
13000	13591.80	1132.65	13870.80	770.60	14153.52	589.73	14439.90	481.33
14000	14637.36	1219.78	14937.84	829.88	15242.16	635.09	15550.80	518.36
15000	15682.80	1306.90	16004.70	889.15	16331.04	680.46	16661.40	555.38
16000	16728.36	1394.03	17071.74	948.43	17419.68	725.82	17772.30	592.41
17000	17773.92	1481.16	18138.78	1007.71	18508.56	771.19	18883.20	629.44
18000	18819.36	1568.28	19205.82	1066.99	19597.20	816.55	19993.80	666.46
19000	19864.92	1655.41	20272.68	1126.26	20686.08	861.92	21104.70	703.49
20000	20910.48	1742.54	21339.72	1185.54	21774.72	907.28	22215.30	740.51
21000	21956.04	1829.67	22406.76	1244.82	22863.36	952.64	23326.20	777.54
22000	23001.48	1916.79	23473.80	1304.10	23952.24	998.01	24437.10	814.57
23000	24047.04	2003.92	24540.66	1363.37	25040.88	1043.37	25547.70	851.59
24000	25092.60	2091.05	25607.70	1422.65	26129.76	1088.74	26658.60	888.62
25000	26138.16	2178.18	26674.74	1481.93	27218.40	1134.10	27769.20	925.64

ANNUAL PERCENTAGE RATE **8.30%**

LOAN AMT	36 MONTHS TOTAL NOTE	36 MONTHS MONTHLY PAYMENT	42 MONTHS TOTAL NOTE	42 MONTHS MONTHLY PAYMENT	48 MONTHS TOTAL NOTE	48 MONTHS MONTHLY PAYMENT	60 MONTHS TOTAL NOTE	60 MONTHS MONTHLY PAYMENT
1	1.08	.03	.84	.02	.96	.02	1.20	.02
2	2.16	.06	2.10	.05	1.92	.04	2.40	.04
3	3.24	.09	3.36	.08	3.36	.07	3.60	.06
4	4.32	.12	4.62	.11	4.32	.09	4.80	.08
5	5.40	.15	5.46	.13	5.76	.12	6.00	.10
6	6.48	.18	6.72	.16	6.72	.14	7.20	.12
7	7.92	.22	7.98	.19	8.16	.17	8.40	.14
8	9.00	.25	9.24	.22	9.12	.19	9.60	.16
9	10.08	.28	10.08	.24	10.56	.22	10.80	.18
10	11.16	.31	11.34	.27	11.52	.24	12.00	.20
20	22.32	.62	23.10	.55	23.52	.49	24.00	.40
30	33.84	.94	34.44	.82	35.04	.73	36.60	.61
40	45.00	1.25	46.20	1.10	47.04	.98	48.60	.81
50	56.52	1.57	57.54	1.37	58.56	1.22	61.20	1.02
60	67.68	1.88	69.30	1.65	70.56	1.47	73.20	1.22
70	79.20	2.20	80.64	1.92	82.08	1.71	85.20	1.42
80	90.36	2.51	92.40	2.20	94.08	1.96	97.80	1.63
90	101.88	2.83	103.74	2.47	105.60	2.20	109.80	1.83
100	113.04	3.14	115.50	2.75	117.60	2.45	122.40	2.04
200	226.44	6.29	231.00	5.50	235.68	4.91	244.80	4.08
300	339.84	9.44	346.50	8.25	353.28	7.36	367.20	6.12
400	452.88	12.58	462.00	11.00	471.36	9.82	489.60	8.16
500	566.28	15.73	577.50	13.75	588.96	12.27	612.60	10.21
600	679.68	18.88	693.42	16.51	707.04	14.73	735.00	12.25
700	793.08	22.03	808.92	19.26	824.64	17.18	857.40	14.29
800	906.12	25.17	924.42	22.01	942.72	19.64	979.80	16.33
900	1019.52	28.32	1039.92	24.76	1060.32	22.09	1102.20	18.37
1000	1132.92	31.47	1155.42	27.51	1178.40	24.55	1225.20	20.42
1500	1699.56	47.21	1733.34	41.27	1767.84	36.83	1837.80	30.63
2000	2265.84	62.94	2311.26	55.03	2356.80	49.10	2450.40	40.84
2500	2832.48	78.68	2889.18	68.79	2946.24	61.38	3063.00	51.05
3000	3399.12	94.42	3467.10	82.55	3535.68	73.66	3675.60	61.26
3500	3965.76	110.16	4044.60	96.30	4124.64	85.93	4288.20	71.47
4000	4532.04	125.89	4622.52	110.06	4714.08	98.21	4900.80	81.68
4500	5098.68	141.63	5200.44	123.82	5303.52	110.49	5513.40	91.89
5000	5665.32	157.37	5778.36	137.58	5892.48	122.76	6126.00	102.10
5500	6231.96	173.11	6356.28	151.34	6481.92	135.04	6738.60	112.31
6000	6798.24	188.84	6934.20	165.10	7071.36	147.32	7351.20	122.52
6500	7364.88	204.58	7511.70	178.85	7660.80	159.60	7963.80	132.73
7000	7931.52	220.32	8089.62	192.61	8249.76	171.87	8576.40	142.94
7500	8498.16	236.06	8667.54	206.37	8839.20	184.15	9189.00	153.15
8000	9064.44	251.79	9245.46	220.13	9428.64	196.43	9801.60	163.36
8500	9631.08	267.53	9823.38	233.89	10017.60	208.70	10414.20	173.57
9000	10197.72	283.27	10401.30	247.65	10607.04	220.98	11026.80	183.78
10000	11330.64	314.74	11556.72	275.16	11785.44	245.53	12252.00	204.20
11000	12463.92	346.22	12712.56	302.68	12964.32	270.09	13477.20	224.62
12000	13596.84	377.69	13868.40	330.20	14142.72	294.64	14702.40	245.04
13000	14730.12	409.17	15023.82	357.71	15321.60	319.20	15927.60	265.46
14000	15863.04	440.64	16179.66	385.23	16500.00	343.75	17152.80	285.88
15000	16996.32	472.12	17335.50	412.75	17678.40	368.30	18378.00	306.30
16000	18129.24	503.59	18490.92	440.26	18857.28	392.86	19603.20	326.72
17000	19262.52	535.07	19646.76	467.78	20035.68	417.41	20828.40	347.14
18000	20395.44	566.54	20802.60	495.30	21214.56	441.97	22053.60	367.56
19000	21528.72	598.02	21958.02	522.81	22392.96	466.52	23278.80	387.98
20000	22661.64	629.49	23113.86	550.33	23571.36	491.07	24504.00	408.40
21000	23794.92	660.97	24269.70	577.85	24750.24	515.63	25729.20	428.82
22000	24927.84	692.44	25425.12	605.36	25928.64	540.18	26954.40	449.24
23000	26061.12	723.92	26580.96	632.88	27107.52	564.74	28179.60	469.66
24000	27194.04	755.39	27736.80	660.40	28285.92	589.29	29404.80	490.08
25000	28327.32	786.87	28892.22	687.91	29464.32	613.84	30630.00	510.50

8.40% ANNUAL PERCENTAGE RATE

LOAN AMT	12 MONTHS TOTAL NOTE	12 MONTHS MONTHLY PAYMENT	18 MONTHS TOTAL NOTE	18 MONTHS MONTHLY PAYMENT	24 MONTHS TOTAL NOTE	24 MONTHS MONTHLY PAYMENT	30 MONTHS TOTAL NOTE	30 MONTHS MONTHLY PAYMENT
1	.96	.08	.90	.05	.96	.04	.90	.03
2	2.04	.17	1.98	.11	2.16	.09	2.10	.07
3	3.12	.26	3.06	.17	3.12	.13	3.30	.11
4	4.08	.34	4.14	.23	4.32	.18	4.20	.14
5	5.16	.43	5.22	.29	5.28	.22	5.40	.18
6	6.24	.52	6.30	.35	6.48	.27	6.60	.22
7	7.32	.61	7.38	.41	7.44	.31	7.50	.25
8	8.28	.69	8.46	.47	8.64	.36	8.70	.29
9	9.36	.78	9.54	.53	9.60	.40	9.90	.33
10	10.44	.87	10.62	.59	10.80	.45	11.10	.37
20	20.88	1.74	21.24	1.18	21.60	.90	22.20	.74
30	31.32	2.61	31.86	1.77	32.64	1.36	33.30	1.11
40	41.76	3.48	42.66	2.37	43.44	1.81	44.40	1.48
50	52.20	4.35	53.28	2.96	54.48	2.27	55.50	1.85
60	62.76	5.23	63.90	3.55	65.28	2.72	66.60	2.22
70	73.20	6.10	74.70	4.15	76.08	3.17	77.70	2.59
80	83.64	6.97	85.32	4.74	87.12	3.63	88.80	2.96
90	94.08	7.84	95.94	5.33	97.92	4.08	99.90	3.33
100	104.52	8.71	106.74	5.93	108.96	4.54	111.00	3.70
200	209.16	17.43	213.48	11.86	217.92	9.08	222.30	7.41
300	313.80	26.15	320.22	17.79	326.88	13.62	333.60	11.12
400	418.32	34.86	426.96	23.72	435.84	18.16	444.60	14.82
500	522.96	43.58	533.88	29.66	544.80	22.70	555.90	18.53
600	627.60	52.30	640.62	35.59	653.76	27.24	667.20	22.24
700	732.24	61.02	747.36	41.52	762.72	31.78	778.50	25.95
800	836.76	69.73	854.10	47.45	871.68	36.32	889.50	29.65
900	941.40	78.45	961.02	53.39	980.64	40.86	1000.80	33.36
1000	1046.04	87.17	1067.76	59.32	1089.60	45.40	1112.10	37.07
1500	1569.12	130.76	1601.64	88.98	1634.64	68.11	1668.00	55.60
2000	2092.08	174.34	2135.52	118.64	2179.44	90.81	2224.20	74.14
2500	2615.16	217.93	2669.40	148.30	2724.48	113.52	2780.10	92.67
3000	3138.24	261.52	3203.28	177.96	3269.28	136.22	3336.30	111.21
3500	3661.20	305.10	3737.34	207.63	3814.32	158.93	3892.50	129.75
4000	4184.28	348.69	4271.22	237.29	4359.12	181.63	4448.40	148.28
4500	4707.36	392.28	4805.10	266.95	4904.16	204.34	5004.60	166.82
5000	5230.32	435.86	5338.98	296.61	5448.96	227.04	5560.50	185.35
5500	5753.40	479.45	5872.86	326.27	5994.00	249.75	6116.70	203.89
6000	6276.48	523.04	6406.74	355.93	6538.80	272.45	6672.90	222.43
6500	6799.44	566.62	6940.62	385.59	7083.84	295.16	7228.80	240.96
7000	7322.52	610.21	7474.68	415.26	7628.64	317.86	7785.00	259.50
7500	7845.60	653.80	8008.56	444.92	8173.68	340.57	8340.90	278.03
8000	8368.56	697.38	8542.44	474.58	8718.48	363.27	8897.10	296.57
8500	8891.64	740.97	9076.32	504.24	9263.52	385.98	9453.30	315.11
9000	9414.72	784.56	9610.20	533.90	9808.32	408.68	10009.20	333.64
10000	10460.76	871.73	10677.96	593.22	10898.16	454.09	11121.30	370.71
11000	11506.80	958.90	11745.90	652.55	11988.00	499.50	12233.70	407.79
12000	12552.96	1046.08	12813.66	711.87	13077.84	544.91	13345.80	444.86
13000	13599.00	1133.25	13881.42	771.19	14167.68	590.32	14457.90	481.93
14000	14645.04	1220.42	14949.36	830.52	15257.52	635.73	15570.00	519.00
15000	15691.20	1307.60	16017.12	889.84	16347.36	681.14	16682.10	556.07
16000	16737.24	1394.77	17084.88	949.16	17437.20	726.55	17794.20	593.14
17000	17783.28	1481.94	18152.82	1008.49	18527.04	771.96	18906.60	630.22
18000	18829.44	1569.12	19220.58	1067.81	19616.88	817.37	20018.70	667.29
19000	19875.48	1656.29	20288.34	1127.13	20706.72	862.78	21130.80	704.36
20000	20921.52	1743.46	21356.10	1186.45	21796.56	908.19	22242.90	741.43
21000	21967.68	1830.64	22424.04	1245.78	22886.40	953.60	23355.00	778.50
22000	23013.72	1917.81	23491.80	1305.10	23976.24	999.01	24467.40	815.58
23000	24059.88	2004.99	24559.56	1364.42	25066.08	1044.42	25579.50	852.65
24000	25105.92	2092.16	25627.50	1423.75	26155.92	1089.83	26691.60	889.72
25000	26151.96	2179.33	26695.26	1483.07	27245.76	1135.24	27803.70	926.79

ANNUAL PERCENTAGE RATE **8.40%**

LOAN AMT	36 MONTHS TOTAL NOTE	36 MONTHS MONTHLY PAYMENT	42 MONTHS TOTAL NOTE	42 MONTHS MONTHLY PAYMENT	48 MONTHS TOTAL NOTE	48 MONTHS MONTHLY PAYMENT	60 MONTHS TOTAL NOTE	60 MONTHS MONTHLY PAYMENT
1	1.08	.03	.84	.02	.96	.02	1.20	.02
2	2.16	.06	2.10	.05	1.92	.04	2.40	.04
3	3.24	.09	3.36	.08	3.36	.07	3.60	.06
4	4.32	.12	4.62	.11	4.32	.09	4.80	.08
5	5.40	.15	5.46	.13	5.76	.12	6.00	.10
6	6.48	.18	6.72	.16	6.72	.14	7.20	.12
7	7.92	.22	7.98	.19	8.16	.17	8.40	.14
8	9.00	.25	9.24	.22	9.12	.19	9.60	.16
9	10.08	.28	10.08	.24	10.56	.22	10.80	.18
10	11.16	.31	11.34	.27	11.52	.24	12.00	.20
20	22.68	.63	23.10	.55	23.52	.49	24.00	.40
30	33.84	.94	34.44	.82	35.04	.73	36.60	.61
40	45.36	1.26	46.20	1.10	47.04	.98	48.60	.81
50	56.52	1.57	57.54	1.37	59.04	1.23	61.20	1.02
60	68.04	1.89	69.30	1.65	70.56	1.47	73.20	1.22
70	79.20	2.20	80.64	1.92	82.56	1.72	85.80	1.43
80	90.72	2.52	92.40	2.20	94.08	1.96	97.80	1.63
90	101.88	2.83	104.16	2.48	106.08	2.21	110.40	1.84
100	113.40	3.15	115.50	2.75	118.08	2.46	122.40	2.04
200	226.80	6.30	231.42	5.51	236.16	4.92	245.40	4.09
300	340.20	9.45	346.92	8.26	354.24	7.38	368.40	6.14
400	453.60	12.60	462.84	11.02	472.32	9.84	490.80	8.18
500	567.36	15.76	578.76	13.78	590.40	12.30	613.80	10.23
600	680.76	18.91	694.26	16.53	708.48	14.76	736.80	12.28
700	794.16	22.06	810.18	19.29	826.56	17.22	859.20	14.32
800	907.56	25.21	926.10	22.05	944.64	19.68	982.20	16.37
900	1020.96	28.36	1041.60	24.80	1062.72	22.14	1105.20	18.42
1000	1134.72	31.52	1157.52	27.56	1180.80	24.60	1227.60	20.46
1500	1702.08	47.28	1736.28	41.34	1771.20	36.90	1842.00	30.70
2000	2269.44	63.04	2315.04	55.12	2361.60	49.20	2455.80	40.93
2500	2836.80	78.80	2893.80	68.90	2952.00	61.50	3070.20	51.17
3000	3404.16	94.56	3472.98	82.69	3542.40	73.80	3684.00	61.40
3500	3971.52	110.32	4051.74	96.47	4132.80	86.10	4297.80	71.63
4000	4538.88	126.08	4630.50	110.25	4723.20	98.40	4912.20	81.87
4500	5106.24	141.84	5209.26	124.03	5313.60	110.70	5526.00	92.10
5000	5673.60	157.60	5788.02	137.81	5904.00	123.00	6140.40	102.34
5500	6240.96	173.36	6366.78	151.59	6494.40	135.30	6754.20	112.57
6000	6808.32	189.12	6945.96	165.38	7084.80	147.60	7368.60	122.81
6500	7375.68	204.88	7524.72	179.16	7675.20	159.90	7982.40	133.04
7000	7943.04	220.64	8103.48	192.94	8265.60	172.20	8596.20	143.27
7500	8510.40	236.40	8682.24	206.72	8856.00	184.50	9210.60	153.51
8000	9077.76	252.16	9261.00	220.50	9446.40	196.80	9824.40	163.74
8500	9645.48	267.93	9839.76	234.28	10036.80	209.10	10438.80	173.98
9000	10212.84	283.69	10418.94	248.07	10627.68	221.41	11052.60	184.21
10000	11347.56	315.21	11576.46	275.63	11808.48	246.01	12280.80	204.68
11000	12482.28	346.73	12733.98	303.19	12989.28	270.61	13509.00	225.15
12000	13617.00	378.25	13891.92	330.76	14170.08	295.21	14737.20	245.62
13000	14751.72	409.77	15049.44	358.32	15350.88	319.81	15964.80	266.08
14000	15886.44	441.29	16206.96	385.88	16531.68	344.41	17193.00	286.55
15000	17021.16	472.81	17364.90	413.45	17712.48	369.01	18421.20	307.02
16000	18155.88	504.33	18522.42	441.01	18893.28	393.61	19649.40	327.49
17000	19290.96	535.86	19679.94	468.57	20074.08	418.21	20877.60	347.96
18000	20425.68	567.38	20837.88	496.14	21255.36	442.82	22105.80	368.43
19000	21560.40	598.90	21995.40	523.70	22436.16	467.42	23333.40	388.89
20000	22695.12	630.42	23152.92	551.26	23616.96	492.02	24561.60	409.36
21000	23829.84	661.94	24310.86	578.83	24797.76	516.62	25789.80	429.83
22000	24964.56	693.46	25468.38	606.39	25978.56	541.22	27018.00	450.30
23000	26099.28	724.98	26625.90	633.95	27159.36	565.82	28246.20	470.77
24000	27234.00	756.50	27783.84	661.52	28340.16	590.42	29474.40	491.24
25000	28369.08	788.03	28941.36	689.08	29520.96	615.02	30702.00	511.70

8.50% ANNUAL PERCENTAGE RATE

LOAN AMT	12 MONTHS TOTAL NOTE	12 MONTHS MONTHLY PAYMENT	18 MONTHS TOTAL NOTE	18 MONTHS MONTHLY PAYMENT	24 MONTHS TOTAL NOTE	24 MONTHS MONTHLY PAYMENT	30 MONTHS TOTAL NOTE	30 MONTHS MONTHLY PAYMENT
1	.96	.08	.90	.05	.96	.04	.90	.03
2	2.04	.17	1.98	.11	2.16	.09	2.10	.07
3	3.12	.26	3.06	.17	3.12	.13	3.30	.11
4	4.08	.34	4.14	.23	4.32	.18	4.20	.14
5	5.16	.43	5.22	.29	5.28	.22	5.40	.18
6	6.24	.52	6.30	.35	6.48	.27	6.60	.22
7	7.32	.61	7.38	.41	7.44	.31	7.50	.25
8	8.28	.69	8.46	.47	8.64	.36	8.70	.29
9	9.36	.78	9.54	.53	9.60	.40	9.90	.33
10	10.44	.87	10.62	.59	10.80	.45	11.10	.37
20	20.88	1.74	21.24	1.18	21.60	.90	22.20	.74
30	31.32	2.61	32.04	1.78	32.64	1.36	33.30	1.11
40	41.76	3.48	42.66	2.37	43.44	1.81	44.40	1.48
50	52.32	4.36	53.28	2.96	54.48	2.27	55.50	1.85
60	62.76	5.23	64.08	3.56	65.28	2.72	66.60	2.22
70	73.20	6.10	74.70	4.15	76.32	3.18	77.70	2.59
80	83.64	6.97	85.32	4.74	87.12	3.63	88.80	2.96
90	94.08	7.84	96.12	5.34	98.16	4.09	100.20	3.34
100	104.64	8.72	106.74	5.93	108.96	4.54	111.30	3.71
200	209.28	17.44	213.66	11.87	218.16	9.09	222.60	7.42
300	313.92	26.16	320.58	17.81	327.12	13.63	333.90	11.13
400	418.56	34.88	427.32	23.74	436.32	18.18	445.20	14.84
500	523.20	43.60	534.24	29.68	545.28	22.72	556.50	18.55
600	627.96	52.33	641.16	35.62	654.48	27.27	668.10	22.27
700	732.60	61.05	747.90	41.55	763.44	31.81	779.40	25.98
800	837.24	69.77	854.82	47.49	872.64	36.36	890.70	29.69
900	941.88	78.49	961.74	53.43	981.84	40.91	1002.00	33.40
1000	1046.52	87.21	1068.48	59.36	1090.80	45.45	1113.30	37.11
1500	1569.84	130.82	1602.90	89.05	1636.32	68.18	1670.10	55.67
2000	2093.16	174.43	2137.14	118.73	2181.84	90.91	2226.90	74.23
2500	2616.48	218.04	2671.56	148.42	2727.12	113.63	2783.70	92.79
3000	3139.80	261.65	3205.80	178.10	3272.64	136.36	3340.50	111.35
3500	3663.12	305.26	3740.22	207.79	3818.16	159.09	3897.30	129.91
4000	4186.44	348.87	4274.46	237.47	4363.68	181.82	4454.10	148.47
4500	4709.76	392.48	4808.70	267.15	4909.20	204.55	5010.90	167.03
5000	5233.08	436.09	5343.12	296.84	5454.48	227.27	5567.40	185.58
5500	5756.40	479.70	5877.36	326.52	6000.00	250.00	6124.20	204.14
6000	6279.72	523.31	6411.78	356.21	6545.52	272.73	6681.00	222.70
6500	6803.04	566.92	6946.02	385.89	7091.04	295.46	7237.80	241.26
7000	7326.36	610.53	7480.44	415.58	7636.32	318.18	7794.60	259.82
7500	7849.68	654.14	8014.68	445.26	8181.84	340.91	8351.40	278.38
8000	8373.00	697.75	8548.92	474.94	8727.36	363.64	8908.20	296.94
8500	8896.32	741.36	9083.34	504.63	9272.88	386.37	9465.00	315.50
9000	9419.64	784.97	9617.58	534.31	9818.40	409.10	10021.80	334.06
10000	10466.28	872.19	10686.24	593.68	10909.20	454.55	11135.10	371.17
11000	11512.92	959.41	11754.90	653.05	12000.24	500.01	12248.70	408.29
12000	12559.56	1046.63	12823.56	712.42	13091.04	545.46	13362.30	445.41
13000	13606.20	1133.85	13892.22	771.79	14182.08	590.92	14475.90	482.53
14000	14652.84	1221.07	14960.88	831.16	15272.88	636.37	15589.20	519.64
15000	15699.48	1308.29	16029.54	890.53	16363.92	681.83	16702.80	556.76
16000	16746.12	1395.51	17098.02	949.89	17454.96	727.29	17816.40	593.88
17000	17792.76	1482.73	18166.68	1009.26	18545.76	772.74	18930.00	631.00
18000	18839.40	1569.95	19235.34	1068.63	19636.80	818.20	20043.60	668.12
19000	19886.04	1657.17	20304.00	1128.00	20727.60	863.65	21156.90	705.23
20000	20932.68	1744.39	21372.66	1187.37	21818.64	909.11	22270.50	742.35
21000	21979.32	1831.61	22441.32	1246.74	22909.44	954.56	23384.10	779.47
22000	23025.96	1918.83	23509.98	1306.11	24000.48	1000.02	24497.70	816.59
23000	24072.60	2006.05	24578.64	1365.48	25091.52	1045.48	25611.00	853.70
24000	25119.24	2093.27	25647.12	1424.84	26182.32	1090.93	26724.60	890.82
25000	26165.88	2180.49	26715.78	1484.21	27273.36	1136.39	27838.20	927.94

ANNUAL PERCENTAGE RATE **8.50%**

	36 MONTHS		42 MONTHS		48 MONTHS		60 MONTHS	
LOAN AMT	TOTAL NOTE	MONTHLY PAYMENT	TOTAL NOTE	MONTHLY PAYMENT	TOTAL NOTE	MONTHLY PAYMENT	TOTAL NOTE	MONTHLY PAYMENT
1	1.08	.03	.84	.02	.96	.02	1.20	.02
2	2.16	.06	2.10	.05	1.92	.04	2.40	.04
3	3.24	.09	3.36	.08	3.36	.07	3.60	.06
4	4.32	.12	4.62	.11	4.32	.09	4.80	.08
5	5.40	.15	5.46	.13	5.76	.12	6.00	.10
6	6.48	.18	6.72	.16	6.72	.14	7.20	.12
7	7.92	.22	7.98	.19	8.16	.17	8.40	.14
8	9.00	.25	9.24	.22	9.12	.19	9.60	.16
9	10.08	.28	10.08	.24	10.56	.22	10.80	.18
10	11.16	.31	11.34	.27	11.52	.24	12.00	.20
20	22.68	.63	23.10	.55	23.52	.49	24.60	.41
30	33.84	.94	34.44	.82	35.04	.73	36.60	.61
40	45.36	1.26	46.20	1.10	47.04	.98	49.20	.82
50	56.52	1.57	57.96	1.38	59.04	1.23	61.20	1.02
60	68.04	1.89	69.30	1.65	70.56	1.47	73.80	1.23
70	79.20	2.20	81.06	1.93	82.56	1.72	85.80	1.43
80	90.72	2.52	92.40	2.20	94.56	1.97	98.40	1.64
90	102.24	2.84	104.16	2.48	106.08	2.21	110.40	1.84
100	113.40	3.15	115.92	2.76	118.08	2.46	123.00	2.05
200	227.16	6.31	231.84	5.52	236.16	4.92	246.00	4.10
300	340.92	9.47	347.76	8.28	354.72	7.39	369.00	6.15
400	454.32	12.62	463.68	11.04	472.80	9.85	492.00	8.20
500	568.08	15.78	579.60	13.80	591.36	12.32	615.00	10.25
600	681.84	18.94	695.52	16.56	709.44	14.78	738.00	12.30
700	795.24	22.09	811.44	19.32	828.00	17.25	861.60	14.36
800	909.00	25.25	927.36	22.08	946.08	19.71	984.60	16.41
900	1022.76	28.41	1043.28	24.84	1064.64	22.18	1107.60	18.46
1000	1136.16	31.56	1159.62	27.61	1182.72	24.64	1230.60	20.51
1500	1704.60	47.35	1739.22	41.41	1774.56	36.97	1846.20	30.77
2000	2272.68	63.13	2319.24	55.22	2365.92	49.29	2461.80	41.03
2500	2840.76	78.91	2898.84	69.02	2957.76	61.62	3077.40	51.29
3000	3409.20	94.70	3478.86	82.83	3549.12	73.94	3692.40	61.54
3500	3977.28	110.48	4058.46	96.63	4140.48	86.26	4308.00	71.80
4000	4545.72	126.27	4638.48	110.44	4732.32	98.59	4923.60	82.06
4500	5113.80	142.05	5218.08	124.24	5323.68	110.91	5539.20	92.32
5000	5681.88	157.83	5798.10	138.05	5915.52	123.24	6154.80	102.58
5500	6250.32	173.62	6377.70	151.85	6506.88	135.56	6770.40	112.84
6000	6818.40	189.40	6957.72	165.66	7098.24	147.88	7385.40	123.09
6500	7386.48	205.18	7537.32	179.46	7690.08	160.21	8001.00	133.35
7000	7954.92	220.97	8117.34	193.27	8281.44	172.53	8616.60	143.61
7500	8523.00	236.75	8696.94	207.07	8873.28	184.86	9232.20	153.87
8000	9091.44	252.54	9276.96	220.88	9464.64	197.18	9847.80	164.13
8500	9659.52	268.32	9856.56	234.68	10056.48	209.51	10463.40	174.39
9000	10227.60	284.10	10436.58	248.49	10647.84	221.83	11078.40	184.64
10000	11364.12	315.67	11596.20	276.10	11831.04	246.48	12309.60	205.16
11000	12500.64	347.24	12755.82	303.71	13014.24	271.13	13540.80	225.68
12000	13637.16	378.81	13915.44	331.32	14196.96	295.77	14771.40	246.19
13000	14773.32	410.37	15075.06	358.93	15380.16	320.42	16002.60	266.71
14000	15909.84	441.94	16234.68	386.54	16563.36	345.07	17233.80	287.23
15000	17046.36	473.51	17394.30	414.15	17746.56	369.72	18464.40	307.74
16000	18182.88	505.08	18553.92	441.76	18929.76	394.37	19695.60	328.26
17000	19319.04	536.64	19713.54	469.37	20112.96	419.02	20926.80	348.78
18000	20455.56	568.21	20873.16	496.98	21295.68	443.66	22157.40	369.29
19000	21592.08	599.78	22032.78	524.59	22478.88	468.31	23388.60	389.81
20000	22728.60	631.35	23192.40	552.20	23662.08	492.96	24619.80	410.33
21000	23864.76	662.91	24352.02	579.81	24845.28	517.61	25850.40	430.84
22000	25001.28	694.48	25511.64	607.42	26028.48	542.26	27081.60	451.36
23000	26137.80	726.05	26671.26	635.03	27211.68	566.91	28312.80	471.88
24000	27274.32	757.62	27830.88	662.64	28394.40	591.55	29543.40	492.39
25000	28410.48	789.18	28990.50	690.25	29577.60	616.20	30774.60	512.91

8.60% ANNUAL PERCENTAGE RATE

LOAN AMT	12 MONTHS TOTAL NOTE	12 MONTHS MONTHLY PAYMENT	18 MONTHS TOTAL NOTE	18 MONTHS MONTHLY PAYMENT	24 MONTHS TOTAL NOTE	24 MONTHS MONTHLY PAYMENT	30 MONTHS TOTAL NOTE	30 MONTHS MONTHLY PAYMENT
1	.96	.08	.90	.05	.96	.04	.90	.03
2	2.04	.17	1.98	.11	2.16	.09	2.10	.07
3	3.12	.26	3.06	.17	3.12	.13	3.30	.11
4	4.08	.34	4.14	.23	4.32	.18	4.20	.14
5	5.16	.43	5.22	.29	5.28	.22	5.40	.18
6	6.24	.52	6.30	.35	6.48	.27	6.60	.22
7	7.32	.61	7.38	.41	7.44	.31	7.80	.26
8	8.28	.69	8.46	.47	8.64	.36	8.70	.29
9	9.36	.78	9.54	.53	9.60	.40	9.90	.33
10	10.44	.87	10.62	.59	10.80	.45	11.10	.37
20	20.88	1.74	21.24	1.18	21.84	.91	22.20	.74
30	31.32	2.61	32.04	1.78	32.64	1.36	33.30	1.11
40	41.88	3.49	42.66	2.37	43.68	1.82	44.40	1.48
50	52.32	4.36	53.46	2.97	54.48	2.27	55.50	1.85
60	62.76	5.23	64.08	3.56	65.52	2.73	66.60	2.22
70	73.20	6.10	74.70	4.15	76.32	3.18	78.00	2.60
80	83.76	6.98	85.50	4.75	87.36	3.64	89.10	2.97
90	94.20	7.85	96.12	5.34	98.16	4.09	100.20	3.34
100	104.64	8.72	106.92	5.94	109.20	4.55	111.30	3.71
200	209.40	17.45	213.84	11.88	218.40	9.10	222.90	7.43
300	314.04	26.17	320.76	17.82	327.60	13.65	334.20	11.14
400	418.80	34.90	427.68	23.76	436.80	18.20	445.80	14.86
500	523.56	43.63	534.60	29.70	546.00	22.75	557.40	18.58
600	628.20	52.35	641.52	35.64	655.20	27.30	668.70	22.29
700	732.96	61.08	748.62	41.59	764.40	31.85	780.30	26.01
800	837.72	69.81	855.54	47.53	873.60	36.40	891.90	29.73
900	942.36	78.53	962.46	53.47	982.80	40.95	1003.20	33.44
1000	1047.12	87.26	1069.38	59.41	1092.00	45.50	1114.80	37.16
1500	1570.68	130.89	1604.16	89.12	1638.00	68.25	1672.20	55.74
2000	2094.36	174.53	2138.76	118.82	2184.00	91.00	2229.60	74.32
2500	2617.92	218.16	2673.54	148.53	2730.00	113.75	2787.00	92.90
3000	3141.48	261.79	3208.32	178.24	3276.00	136.50	3344.70	111.49
3500	3665.16	305.43	3743.10	207.95	3822.00	159.25	3902.10	130.07
4000	4188.72	349.06	4277.70	237.65	4368.00	182.00	4459.50	148.65
4500	4712.28	392.69	4812.48	267.36	4914.00	204.75	5016.90	167.23
5000	5235.96	436.33	5347.26	297.07	5460.00	227.50	5574.30	185.81
5500	5759.52	479.96	5881.86	326.77	6006.00	250.25	6132.00	204.40
6000	6283.08	523.59	6416.64	356.48	6552.00	273.00	6689.40	222.98
6500	6806.64	567.22	6951.42	386.19	7098.00	295.75	7246.80	241.56
7000	7330.32	610.86	7486.20	415.90	7644.24	318.51	7804.20	260.14
7500	7853.88	654.49	8020.80	445.60	8190.24	341.26	8361.60	278.72
8000	8377.44	698.12	8555.58	475.31	8736.24	364.01	8919.30	297.31
8500	8901.12	741.76	9090.36	505.02	9282.24	386.76	9476.70	315.89
9000	9424.68	785.39	9625.14	534.73	9828.24	409.51	10034.10	334.47
10000	10471.92	872.66	10694.52	594.14	10920.24	455.01	11148.90	371.63
11000	11519.04	959.92	11763.90	653.55	12012.24	500.51	12264.00	408.80
12000	12566.28	1047.19	12833.46	712.97	13104.24	546.01	13378.80	445.96
13000	13613.40	1134.45	13902.84	772.38	14196.24	591.51	14493.60	483.12
14000	14660.64	1221.72	14972.40	831.80	15288.48	637.02	15608.70	520.29
15000	15707.88	1308.99	16041.78	891.21	16380.48	682.52	16723.50	557.45
16000	16755.00	1396.25	17111.34	950.63	17472.48	728.02	17838.60	594.62
17000	17802.24	1483.52	18180.72	1010.04	18564.48	773.52	18953.40	631.78
18000	18849.36	1570.78	19250.28	1069.46	19656.48	819.02	20068.20	668.94
19000	19896.60	1658.05	20319.66	1128.87	20748.48	864.52	21183.30	706.11
20000	20943.84	1745.32	21389.04	1188.28	21840.48	910.02	22298.10	743.27
21000	21990.96	1832.58	22458.60	1247.70	22932.72	955.53	23413.20	780.44
22000	23038.20	1919.85	23527.98	1307.11	24024.72	1001.03	24528.00	817.60
23000	24085.44	2007.12	24597.54	1366.53	25116.72	1046.53	25642.80	854.76
24000	25132.56	2094.38	25666.92	1425.94	26208.72	1092.03	26757.90	891.93
25000	26179.80	2181.65	26736.48	1485.36	27300.72	1137.53	27872.70	929.09

Appendix "D"

ANNUAL PERCENTAGE RATE **8.60%**

LOAN AMT	36 MONTHS TOTAL NOTE	MONTHLY PAYMENT	42 MONTHS TOTAL NOTE	MONTHLY PAYMENT	48 MONTHS TOTAL NOTE	MONTHLY PAYMENT	60 MONTHS TOTAL NOTE	MONTHLY PAYMENT
1	1.08	.03	.84	.02	.96	.02	1.20	.02
2	2.16	.06	2.10	.05	1.92	.04	2.40	.04
3	3.24	.09	3.36	.08	3.36	.07	3.60	.06
4	4.32	.12	4.62	.11	4.32	.09	4.80	.08
5	5.40	.15	5.46	.13	5.76	.12	6.00	.10
6	6.48	.18	6.72	.16	6.72	.14	7.20	.12
7	7.92	.22	7.98	.19	8.16	.17	8.40	.14
8	9.00	.25	9.24	.22	9.12	.19	9.60	.16
9	10.08	.28	10.08	.24	10.56	.22	10.80	.18
10	11.16	.31	11.34	.27	11.52	.24	12.00	.20
20	22.68	.63	23.10	.55	23.52	.49	24.60	.41
30	33.84	.94	34.44	.82	35.52	.74	36.60	.61
40	45.36	1.26	46.20	1.10	47.04	.98	49.20	.82
50	56.88	1.58	57.96	1.38	59.04	1.23	61.20	1.02
60	68.04	1.89	69.30	1.65	71.04	1.48	73.80	1.23
70	79.56	2.21	81.06	1.93	82.56	1.72	85.80	1.43
80	90.72	2.52	92.82	2.21	94.56	1.97	98.40	1.64
90	102.24	2.84	104.16	2.48	106.56	2.22	111.00	1.85
100	113.76	3.16	115.92	2.76	118.08	2.46	123.00	2.05
200	227.52	6.32	232.26	5.53	236.64	4.93	246.60	4.11
300	341.28	9.48	348.18	8.29	355.20	7.40	369.60	6.16
400	455.04	12.64	464.52	11.06	473.76	9.87	493.20	8.22
500	568.80	15.80	580.44	13.82	592.32	12.34	616.80	10.28
600	682.56	18.96	696.78	16.59	710.88	14.81	739.80	12.33
700	796.32	22.12	812.70	19.35	829.44	17.28	863.40	14.39
800	910.44	25.29	929.04	22.12	948.00	19.75	987.00	16.45
900	1024.20	28.45	1045.38	24.89	1066.56	22.22	1110.00	18.50
1000	1137.96	31.61	1161.30	27.65	1185.12	24.69	1233.60	20.56
1500	1707.12	47.42	1742.16	41.48	1777.92	37.04	1850.40	30.84
2000	2275.92	63.22	2323.02	55.31	2370.72	49.39	2467.20	41.12
2500	2845.08	79.03	2903.88	69.14	2963.04	61.73	3084.60	51.41
3000	3414.24	94.84	3484.74	82.97	3555.84	74.08	3701.40	61.69
3500	3983.04	110.64	4065.18	96.79	4148.64	86.43	4318.20	71.97
4000	4552.20	126.45	4646.04	110.62	4741.44	98.78	4935.00	82.25
4500	5121.36	142.26	5226.90	124.45	5333.76	111.12	5552.40	92.54
5000	5690.16	158.06	5807.76	138.28	5926.56	123.47	6169.20	102.82
5500	6259.32	173.87	6388.62	152.11	6519.36	135.82	6786.00	113.10
6000	6828.48	189.68	6969.48	165.94	7112.16	148.17	7402.80	123.38
6500	7397.64	205.49	7550.34	179.77	7704.96	160.52	8020.20	133.67
7000	7966.44	221.29	8130.78	193.59	8297.28	172.86	8637.00	143.95
7500	8535.60	237.10	8711.64	207.42	8890.08	185.21	9253.80	154.23
8000	9104.76	252.91	9292.50	221.25	9482.88	197.56	9870.60	164.51
8500	9673.56	268.71	9873.36	235.08	10075.68	209.91	10488.00	174.80
9000	10242.72	284.52	10454.22	248.91	10668.00	222.25	11104.80	185.08
10000	11380.68	316.13	11615.52	276.56	11853.60	246.95	12338.40	205.64
11000	12519.00	347.75	12777.24	304.22	13039.20	271.65	13572.60	226.21
12000	13656.96	379.36	13938.96	331.88	14224.32	296.34	14806.20	246.77
13000	14795.28	410.98	15100.68	359.54	15409.92	321.04	16040.40	267.34
14000	15933.24	442.59	16261.98	387.19	16595.04	345.73	17274.00	287.90
15000	17071.20	474.20	17423.70	414.85	17780.64	370.43	18508.20	308.47
16000	18209.52	505.82	18585.42	442.51	18965.76	395.12	19741.80	329.03
17000	19347.48	537.43	19746.72	470.16	20151.36	419.82	20976.00	349.60
18000	20485.80	569.05	20908.44	497.82	21336.48	444.51	22209.60	370.16
19000	21623.76	600.66	22070.16	525.48	22522.08	469.21	23443.80	390.73
20000	22761.72	632.27	23231.46	553.13	23707.68	493.91	24677.40	411.29
21000	23900.04	663.89	24393.18	580.79	24892.80	518.60	25911.00	431.85
22000	25038.00	695.50	25554.90	608.45	26078.40	543.30	27145.20	452.42
23000	26175.96	727.11	26716.20	636.10	27263.52	567.99	28378.80	472.98
24000	27314.28	758.73	27877.92	663.76	28449.12	592.69	29613.00	493.55
25000	28452.24	790.34	29039.64	691.42	29634.24	617.38	30846.60	514.11

8.70% ANNUAL PERCENTAGE RATE

LOAN AMT	12 MONTHS TOTAL NOTE	MONTHLY PAYMENT	18 MONTHS TOTAL NOTE	MONTHLY PAYMENT	24 MONTHS TOTAL NOTE	MONTHLY PAYMENT	30 MONTHS TOTAL NOTE	MONTHLY PAYMENT
1	.96	.08	.90	.05	.96	.04	.90	.03
2	2.04	.17	1.98	.11	2.16	.09	2.10	.07
3	3.12	.26	3.06	.17	3.12	.13	3.30	.11
4	4.08	.34	4.14	.23	4.32	.18	4.20	.14
5	5.16	.43	5.22	.29	5.28	.22	5.40	.18
6	6.24	.52	6.30	.35	6.48	.27	6.60	.22
7	7.32	.61	7.38	.41	7.44	.31	7.80	.26
8	8.28	.69	8.46	.47	8.64	.36	8.70	.29
9	9.36	.78	9.54	.53	9.60	.40	9.90	.33
10	10.44	.87	10.62	.59	10.80	.45	11.10	.37
20	20.88	1.74	21.24	1.18	21.84	.91	22.20	.74
30	31.32	2.61	32.04	1.78	32.64	1.36	33.30	1.11
40	41.88	3.49	42.66	2.37	43.68	1.82	44.40	1.48
50	52.32	4.36	53.46	2.97	54.48	2.27	55.80	1.86
60	62.76	5.23	64.08	3.56	65.52	2.73	66.90	2.23
70	73.32	6.11	74.88	4.16	76.32	3.18	78.00	2.60
80	83.76	6.98	85.50	4.75	87.36	3.64	89.10	2.97
90	94.20	7.85	96.30	5.35	98.16	4.09	100.20	3.34
100	104.76	8.73	106.92	5.94	109.20	4.55	111.60	3.72
200	209.52	17.46	214.02	11.89	218.40	9.10	223.20	7.44
300	314.28	26.19	320.94	17.83	327.84	13.66	334.80	11.16
400	419.04	34.92	428.04	23.78	437.04	18.21	446.40	14.88
500	523.80	43.65	535.14	29.73	546.48	22.77	558.00	18.60
600	628.56	52.38	642.06	35.67	655.68	27.32	669.60	22.32
700	733.32	61.11	749.16	41.62	765.12	31.88	781.20	26.04
800	838.08	69.84	856.08	47.56	874.32	36.43	892.80	29.76
900	942.96	78.58	963.18	53.51	983.76	40.99	1004.40	33.48
1000	1047.72	87.31	1070.28	59.46	1092.96	45.54	1116.00	37.20
1500	1571.52	130.96	1605.42	89.19	1639.68	68.32	1674.30	55.81
2000	2095.44	174.62	2140.56	118.92	2186.16	91.09	2232.30	74.41
2500	2619.36	218.28	2675.70	148.65	2732.64	113.86	2790.60	93.02
3000	3143.16	261.93	3210.84	178.38	3279.36	136.64	3348.60	111.62
3500	3667.08	305.59	3745.98	208.11	3825.84	159.41	3906.90	130.23
4000	4190.88	349.24	4281.12	237.84	4372.32	182.18	4464.90	148.83
4500	4714.80	392.90	4816.26	267.57	4919.04	204.96	5023.20	167.44
5000	5238.72	436.56	5351.40	297.30	5465.52	227.73	5581.20	186.04
5500	5762.52	480.21	5886.54	327.03	6012.00	250.50	6139.50	204.65
6000	6286.44	523.87	6421.68	356.76	6558.72	273.28	6697.50	223.25
6500	6810.36	567.53	6956.82	386.49	7105.20	296.05	7255.80	241.86
7000	7334.16	611.18	7491.96	416.22	7651.92	318.83	7813.80	260.46
7500	7858.08	654.84	8027.10	445.95	8198.40	341.60	8372.10	279.07
8000	8381.88	698.49	8562.24	475.68	8744.88	364.37	8930.10	297.67
8500	8905.80	742.15	9097.38	505.41	9291.60	387.15	9488.40	316.28
9000	9429.72	785.81	9632.52	535.14	9838.08	409.92	10046.40	334.88
10000	10477.44	873.12	10702.80	594.60	10931.28	455.47	11162.70	372.09
11000	11525.16	960.43	11773.08	654.06	12024.24	501.01	12279.00	409.30
12000	12572.88	1047.74	12843.36	713.52	13117.44	546.56	13395.30	446.51
13000	13620.72	1135.06	13913.64	772.98	14210.64	592.11	14511.60	483.72
14000	14668.44	1222.37	14983.92	832.44	15303.84	637.66	15627.90	520.93
15000	15716.16	1309.68	16054.20	891.90	16396.80	683.20	16744.20	558.14
16000	16763.88	1396.99	17124.48	951.36	17490.00	728.75	17860.50	595.35
17000	17811.72	1484.31	18194.76	1010.82	18583.20	774.30	18976.80	632.56
18000	18859.44	1571.62	19265.04	1070.28	19676.16	819.84	20093.10	669.77
19000	19907.16	1658.93	20335.32	1129.74	20769.36	865.39	21209.40	706.98
20000	20954.88	1746.24	21405.60	1189.20	21862.56	910.94	22325.70	744.19
21000	22002.72	1833.56	22475.88	1248.66	22955.76	956.49	23442.00	781.40
22000	23050.44	1920.87	23546.16	1308.12	24048.72	1002.03	24558.30	818.61
23000	24098.16	2008.18	24616.44	1367.58	25141.92	1047.58	25674.60	855.82
24000	25145.88	2095.49	25686.72	1427.04	26235.12	1093.13	26790.90	893.03
25000	26193.72	2182.81	26757.00	1486.50	27328.32	1138.68	27907.20	930.24

ANNUAL PERCENTAGE RATE **8.70%**

LOAN AMT	36 MONTHS TOTAL NOTE	36 MONTHS MONTHLY PAYMENT	42 MONTHS TOTAL NOTE	42 MONTHS MONTHLY PAYMENT	48 MONTHS TOTAL NOTE	48 MONTHS MONTHLY PAYMENT	60 MONTHS TOTAL NOTE	60 MONTHS MONTHLY PAYMENT
1	1.08	.03	.84	.02	.96	.02	1.20	.02
2	2.16	.06	2.10	.05	1.92	.04	2.40	.04
3	3.24	.09	3.36	.08	3.36	.07	3.60	.06
4	4.32	.12	4.62	.11	4.32	.09	4.80	.08
5	5.40	.15	5.46	.13	5.76	.12	6.00	.10
6	6.48	.18	6.72	.16	6.72	.14	7.20	.12
7	7.92	.22	7.98	.19	8.16	.17	8.40	.14
8	9.00	.25	9.24	.22	9.12	.19	9.60	.16
9	10.08	.28	10.08	.24	10.56	.22	10.80	.18
10	11.16	.31	11.34	.27	11.52	.24	12.00	.20
20	22.68	.63	23.10	.55	23.52	.49	24.60	.41
30	33.84	.94	34.86	.83	35.52	.74	36.60	.61
40	45.36	1.26	46.20	1.10	47.04	.98	49.20	.82
50	56.88	1.58	57.96	1.38	59.04	1.23	61.80	1.03
60	68.04	1.89	69.72	1.66	71.04	1.48	73.80	1.23
70	79.56	2.21	81.06	1.93	83.04	1.73	86.40	1.44
80	91.08	2.53	92.82	2.21	94.56	1.97	98.40	1.64
90	102.24	2.84	104.58	2.49	106.56	2.22	111.00	1.85
100	113.76	3.16	116.34	2.77	118.56	2.47	123.60	2.06
200	227.88	6.33	232.68	5.54	237.12	4.94	247.20	4.12
300	341.64	9.49	349.02	8.31	356.16	7.42	370.80	6.18
400	455.76	12.66	465.36	11.08	474.72	9.89	494.40	8.24
500	569.88	15.83	581.70	13.85	593.76	12.37	618.00	10.30
600	683.64	18.99	698.04	16.62	712.32	14.84	741.60	12.36
700	797.76	22.16	814.38	19.39	830.88	17.31	865.20	14.42
800	911.52	25.32	930.72	22.16	949.92	19.79	989.40	16.49
900	1025.64	28.49	1047.06	24.93	1068.48	22.26	1113.00	18.55
1000	1139.76	31.66	1163.40	27.70	1187.52	24.74	1236.60	20.61
1500	1709.64	47.49	1745.10	41.55	1781.28	37.11	1854.60	30.91
2000	2279.52	63.32	2326.80	55.40	2375.04	49.48	2473.20	41.22
2500	2849.40	79.15	2908.50	69.25	2968.80	61.85	3091.80	51.53
3000	3419.28	94.98	3490.62	83.11	3562.56	74.22	3709.80	61.83
3500	3989.16	110.81	4072.32	96.96	4156.32	86.59	4328.40	72.14
4000	4559.04	126.64	4654.02	110.81	4750.56	98.97	4947.00	82.45
4500	5128.92	142.47	5235.72	124.66	5344.32	111.34	5565.00	92.75
5000	5698.80	158.30	5817.42	138.51	5938.08	123.71	6183.60	103.06
5500	6268.68	174.13	6399.54	152.37	6531.84	136.08	6802.20	113.37
6000	6838.56	189.96	6981.24	166.22	7125.60	148.45	7420.20	123.67
6500	7408.44	205.79	7562.94	180.07	7719.36	160.82	8038.80	133.98
7000	7978.32	221.62	8144.64	193.92	8313.12	173.19	8657.40	144.29
7500	8548.20	237.45	8726.34	207.77	8907.36	185.57	9275.40	154.59
8000	9118.08	253.28	9308.46	221.63	9501.12	197.94	9894.00	164.90
8500	9687.96	269.11	9890.16	235.48	10094.88	210.31	10512.60	175.21
9000	10257.84	284.94	10471.86	249.33	10688.64	222.68	11130.60	185.51
10000	11397.60	316.60	11635.26	277.03	11876.16	247.42	12367.80	206.13
11000	12537.36	348.26	12799.08	304.74	13064.16	272.17	13604.40	226.74
12000	13677.12	379.92	13962.48	332.44	14251.68	296.91	14841.00	247.35
13000	14816.88	411.58	15125.88	360.14	15439.20	321.65	16077.60	267.96
14000	15956.64	443.24	16289.70	387.85	16626.72	346.39	17314.80	288.58
15000	17096.40	474.90	17453.10	415.55	17814.72	371.14	18551.40	309.19
16000	18236.16	506.56	18616.92	443.26	19002.24	395.88	19788.00	329.80
17000	19375.92	538.22	19780.32	470.96	20189.76	420.62	21025.20	350.42
18000	20515.68	569.88	20943.72	498.66	21377.76	445.37	22261.80	371.03
19000	21655.44	601.54	22107.54	526.37	22565.28	470.11	23498.40	391.64
20000	22795.20	633.20	23270.94	554.07	23752.80	494.85	24735.60	412.26
21000	23934.96	664.86	24434.34	581.77	24940.32	519.59	25972.20	432.87
22000	25074.72	696.52	25598.16	609.48	26128.32	544.34	27208.80	453.48
23000	26214.48	728.18	26761.56	637.18	27315.84	569.08	28446.00	474.10
24000	27354.24	759.84	27925.38	664.89	28503.36	593.82	29682.60	494.71
25000	28494.00	791.50	29088.78	692.59	29691.36	618.57	30919.20	515.32

8.75% ANNUAL PERCENTAGE RATE

LOAN AMT	12 MONTHS TOTAL NOTE	12 MONTHS MONTHLY PAYMENT	18 MONTHS TOTAL NOTE	18 MONTHS MONTHLY PAYMENT	24 MONTHS TOTAL NOTE	24 MONTHS MONTHLY PAYMENT	30 MONTHS TOTAL NOTE	30 MONTHS MONTHLY PAYMENT
1	.96	.08	.90	.05	.96	.04	.90	.03
2	2.04	.17	1.98	.11	2.16	.09	2.10	.07
3	3.12	.26	3.06	.17	3.12	.13	3.30	.11
4	4.08	.34	4.14	.23	4.32	.18	4.20	.14
5	5.16	.43	5.22	.29	5.28	.22	5.40	.18
6	6.24	.52	6.30	.35	6.48	.27	6.60	.22
7	7.32	.61	7.38	.41	7.44	.31	7.80	.26
8	8.28	.69	8.46	.47	8.64	.36	8.70	.29
9	9.36	.78	9.54	.53	9.84	.41	9.90	.33
10	10.44	.87	10.62	.59	10.80	.45	11.10	.37
20	20.88	1.74	21.24	1.18	21.84	.91	22.20	.74
30	31.44	2.62	32.04	1.78	32.64	1.36	33.30	1.11
40	41.88	3.49	42.66	2.37	43.68	1.82	44.40	1.48
50	52.32	4.36	53.46	2.97	54.48	2.27	55.80	1.86
60	62.88	5.24	64.08	3.56	65.52	2.73	66.90	2.23
70	73.32	6.11	74.88	4.16	76.32	3.18	78.00	2.60
80	83.76	6.98	85.50	4.75	87.36	3.64	89.10	2.97
90	94.32	7.86	96.30	5.35	98.40	4.10	100.50	3.35
100	104.76	8.73	106.92	5.94	109.20	4.55	111.60	3.72
200	209.52	17.46	214.02	11.89	218.64	9.11	223.20	7.44
300	314.40	26.20	321.12	17.84	328.08	13.67	334.80	11.16
400	419.16	34.93	428.22	23.79	437.28	18.22	446.70	14.89
500	523.92	43.66	535.32	29.74	546.72	22.78	558.30	18.61
600	628.80	52.40	642.24	35.68	656.16	27.34	669.90	22.33
700	733.56	61.13	749.34	41.63	765.36	31.89	781.80	26.06
800	838.32	69.86	856.44	47.58	874.80	36.45	893.40	29.78
900	943.20	78.60	963.54	53.53	984.24	41.01	1005.00	33.50
1000	1047.96	87.33	1070.64	59.48	1093.68	45.57	1116.90	37.23
1500	1572.00	131.00	1605.96	89.22	1640.40	68.35	1675.20	55.84
2000	2096.04	174.67	2141.28	118.96	2187.36	91.14	2233.80	74.46
2500	2619.96	218.33	2676.60	148.70	2734.08	113.92	2792.40	93.08
3000	3144.00	262.00	3211.92	178.44	3281.04	136.71	3350.70	111.69
3500	3668.04	305.67	3747.42	208.19	3827.76	159.49	3909.30	130.31
4000	4192.08	349.34	4282.74	237.93	4374.72	182.28	4467.90	148.93
4500	4716.12	393.01	4818.06	267.67	4921.44	205.06	5026.20	167.54
5000	5240.04	436.67	5353.38	297.41	5468.40	227.85	5584.80	186.16
5500	5764.08	480.34	5888.70	327.15	6015.12	250.63	6143.40	204.78
6000	6288.12	524.01	6424.02	356.89	6562.08	273.42	6701.70	223.39
6500	6812.16	567.68	6959.52	386.64	7108.80	296.20	7260.30	242.01
7000	7336.08	611.34	7494.84	416.38	7655.76	318.99	7818.90	260.63
7500	7860.12	655.01	8030.16	446.12	8202.48	341.77	8377.20	279.24
8000	8384.16	698.68	8565.48	475.86	8749.44	364.56	8935.80	297.86
8500	8908.20	742.35	9100.80	505.60	9296.16	387.34	9494.10	316.47
9000	9432.24	786.02	9636.12	535.34	9843.12	410.13	10052.70	335.09
10000	10480.20	873.35	10706.94	594.83	10936.80	455.70	11169.60	372.32
11000	11528.28	960.69	11777.58	654.31	12030.48	501.27	12286.80	409.56
12000	12576.24	1048.02	12848.22	713.79	13124.16	546.84	13403.70	446.79
13000	13624.32	1135.36	13919.04	773.28	14217.84	592.41	14520.60	484.02
14000	14672.28	1222.69	14989.68	832.76	15311.52	637.98	15637.80	521.26
15000	15720.36	1310.03	16060.32	892.24	16405.20	683.55	16754.70	558.49
16000	16768.32	1397.36	17131.14	951.73	17498.88	729.12	17871.60	595.72
17000	17816.40	1484.70	18201.78	1011.21	18592.56	774.69	18988.50	632.95
18000	18864.48	1572.04	19272.42	1070.69	19686.24	820.26	20105.70	670.19
19000	19912.44	1659.37	20343.06	1130.17	20779.92	865.83	21222.60	707.42
20000	20960.52	1746.71	21413.88	1189.66	21873.60	911.40	22339.50	744.65
21000	22008.48	1834.04	22484.52	1249.14	22967.28	956.97	23456.70	781.89
22000	23056.56	1921.38	23555.16	1308.62	24060.96	1002.54	24573.60	819.12
23000	24104.52	2008.71	24625.98	1368.11	25154.64	1048.11	25690.50	856.35
24000	25152.60	2096.05	25696.62	1427.59	26248.32	1093.68	26807.40	893.58
25000	26200.56	2183.38	26767.26	1487.07	27342.00	1139.25	27924.60	930.82

ANNUAL PERCENTAGE RATE **8.75%**

LOAN AMT	36 MONTHS TOTAL NOTE	36 MONTHS MONTHLY PAYMENT	42 MONTHS TOTAL NOTE	42 MONTHS MONTHLY PAYMENT	48 MONTHS TOTAL NOTE	48 MONTHS MONTHLY PAYMENT	60 MONTHS TOTAL NOTE	60 MONTHS MONTHLY PAYMENT
1	1.08	.03	.84	.02	.96	.02	1.20	.02
2	2.16	.06	2.10	.05	1.92	.04	2.40	.04
3	3.24	.09	3.36	.08	3.36	.07	3.60	.06
4	4.32	.12	4.62	.11	4.32	.09	4.80	.08
5	5.40	.15	5.46	.13	5.76	.12	6.00	.10
6	6.84	.19	6.72	.16	6.72	.14	7.20	.12
7	7.92	.22	7.98	.19	8.16	.17	8.40	.14
8	9.00	.25	9.24	.22	9.12	.19	9.60	.16
9	10.08	.28	10.08	.24	10.56	.22	10.80	.18
10	11.16	.31	11.34	.27	11.52	.24	12.00	.20
20	22.68	.63	23.10	.55	23.52	.49	24.60	.41
30	34.20	.95	34.86	.83	35.52	.74	36.60	.61
40	45.36	1.26	46.20	1.10	47.52	.99	49.20	.82
50	56.88	1.58	57.96	1.38	59.04	1.23	61.80	1.03
60	68.40	1.90	69.72	1.66	71.04	1.48	73.80	1.23
70	79.56	2.21	81.48	1.94	83.04	1.73	86.40	1.44
80	91.08	2.53	92.82	2.21	95.04	1.98	99.00	1.65
90	102.60	2.85	104.58	2.49	106.56	2.22	111.00	1.85
100	113.76	3.16	116.34	2.77	118.56	2.47	123.60	2.06
200	227.88	6.33	232.68	5.54	237.60	4.95	247.20	4.12
300	342.00	9.50	349.02	8.31	356.16	7.42	371.40	6.19
400	456.12	12.67	465.78	11.09	475.20	9.90	495.00	8.25
500	570.24	15.84	582.12	13.86	594.24	12.38	618.60	10.31
600	684.36	19.01	698.46	16.63	712.80	14.85	742.80	12.38
700	798.12	22.17	814.80	19.40	831.84	17.33	866.40	14.44
800	912.24	25.34	931.56	22.18	950.88	19.81	990.00	16.50
900	1026.36	28.51	1047.90	24.95	1069.44	22.28	1114.20	18.57
1000	1140.48	31.68	1164.24	27.72	1188.48	24.76	1237.80	20.63
1500	1710.72	47.52	1746.78	41.59	1782.72	37.14	1857.00	30.95
2000	2280.96	63.36	2328.90	55.45	2377.44	49.53	2476.20	41.27
2500	2851.20	79.20	2911.02	69.31	2971.68	61.91	3095.40	51.59
3000	3421.80	95.05	3493.56	83.18	3565.92	74.29	3714.60	61.91
3500	3992.04	110.89	4075.68	97.04	4160.64	86.68	4333.80	72.23
4000	4562.28	126.73	4657.80	110.90	4754.88	99.06	4952.40	82.54
4500	5132.52	142.57	5240.34	124.77	5349.12	111.44	5571.60	92.86
5000	5702.76	158.41	5822.46	138.63	5943.84	123.83	6190.80	103.18
5500	6273.00	174.25	6404.58	152.49	6538.08	136.21	6810.00	113.50
6000	6843.60	190.10	6987.12	166.36	7132.32	148.59	7429.20	123.82
6500	7413.84	205.94	7569.24	180.22	7727.04	160.98	8048.40	134.14
7000	7984.08	221.78	8151.78	194.09	8321.28	173.36	8667.60	144.46
7500	8554.32	237.62	8733.90	207.95	8915.52	185.74	9286.20	154.77
8000	9124.56	253.46	9316.02	221.81	9510.24	198.13	9905.40	165.09
8500	9694.80	269.30	9898.56	235.68	10104.48	210.51	10524.60	175.41
9000	10265.40	285.15	10480.68	249.54	10698.72	222.89	11143.80	185.73
10000	11405.88	316.83	11645.34	277.27	11887.68	247.66	12382.20	206.37
11000	12546.36	348.51	12809.58	304.99	13076.64	272.43	13620.00	227.00
12000	13687.20	380.20	13974.24	332.72	14265.12	297.19	14858.40	247.64
13000	14827.68	411.88	15138.90	360.45	15454.08	321.96	16096.80	268.28
14000	15968.16	443.56	16303.56	388.18	16643.04	346.73	17335.20	288.92
15000	17109.00	475.25	17467.80	415.90	17831.52	371.49	18573.00	309.55
16000	18249.48	506.93	18632.46	443.63	19020.48	396.26	19811.40	330.19
17000	19389.96	538.61	19797.12	471.36	20209.44	421.03	21049.80	350.83
18000	20530.80	570.30	20961.36	499.08	21397.92	445.79	22288.20	371.47
19000	21671.28	601.98	22126.02	526.81	22586.88	470.56	23526.00	392.10
20000	22812.12	633.67	23290.68	554.54	23775.84	495.33	24764.40	412.74
21000	23952.60	665.35	24455.34	582.27	24964.32	520.09	26002.80	433.38
22000	25093.08	697.03	25619.58	609.99	26153.28	544.86	27240.60	454.01
23000	26233.92	728.72	26784.24	637.72	27341.76	569.62	28479.00	474.65
24000	27374.40	760.40	27948.90	665.45	28530.72	594.39	29717.40	495.29
25000	28514.88	792.08	29113.14	693.17	29719.68	619.16	30955.80	515.93

8.80% ANNUAL PERCENTAGE RATE

LOAN AMT	12 MONTHS TOTAL NOTE	12 MONTHS MONTHLY PAYMENT	18 MONTHS TOTAL NOTE	18 MONTHS MONTHLY PAYMENT	24 MONTHS TOTAL NOTE	24 MONTHS MONTHLY PAYMENT	30 MONTHS TOTAL NOTE	30 MONTHS MONTHLY PAYMENT
1	.96	.08	.90	.05	.96	.04	.90	.03
2	2.04	.17	1.98	.11	2.16	.09	2.10	.07
3	3.12	.26	3.06	.17	3.12	.13	3.30	.11
4	4.08	.34	4.14	.23	4.32	.18	4.20	.14
5	5.16	.43	5.22	.29	5.28	.22	5.40	.18
6	6.24	.52	6.30	.35	6.48	.27	6.60	.22
7	7.32	.61	7.38	.41	7.44	.31	7.80	.26
8	8.28	.69	8.46	.47	8.64	.36	8.70	.29
9	9.36	.78	9.54	.53	9.84	.41	9.90	.33
10	10.44	.87	10.62	.59	10.80	.45	11.10	.37
20	20.88	1.74	21.42	1.19	21.84	.91	22.20	.74
30	31.44	2.62	32.04	1.78	32.64	1.36	33.30	1.11
40	41.88	3.49	42.84	2.38	43.68	1.82	44.70	1.49
50	52.32	4.36	53.46	2.97	54.48	2.27	55.80	1.86
60	62.88	5.24	64.26	3.57	65.52	2.73	66.90	2.23
70	73.32	6.11	74.88	4.16	76.56	3.19	78.00	2.60
80	83.76	6.98	85.68	4.76	87.36	3.64	89.40	2.98
90	94.32	7.86	96.30	5.35	98.40	4.10	100.50	3.35
100	104.76	8.73	107.10	5.95	109.20	4.55	111.60	3.72
200	209.64	17.47	214.20	11.90	218.64	9.11	223.50	7.45
300	314.40	26.20	321.30	17.85	328.08	13.67	335.10	11.17
400	419.28	34.94	428.40	23.80	437.52	18.23	447.00	14.90
500	524.04	43.67	535.50	29.75	546.96	22.79	558.60	18.62
600	628.92	52.41	642.60	35.70	656.40	27.35	670.50	22.35
700	733.80	61.15	749.70	41.65	765.84	31.91	782.10	26.07
800	838.56	69.88	856.80	47.60	875.28	36.47	894.00	29.80
900	943.44	78.62	963.90	53.55	984.72	41.03	1005.90	33.53
1000	1048.20	87.35	1071.00	59.50	1094.16	45.59	1117.50	37.25
1500	1572.36	131.03	1606.50	89.25	1641.12	68.38	1676.40	55.88
2000	2096.52	174.71	2142.18	119.01	2188.32	91.18	2235.30	74.51
2500	2620.68	218.39	2677.68	148.76	2735.52	113.98	2793.90	93.13
3000	3144.84	262.07	3213.18	178.51	3282.48	136.77	3352.80	111.76
3500	3669.00	305.75	3748.86	208.27	3829.68	159.57	3911.70	130.39
4000	4193.16	349.43	4284.36	238.02	4376.88	182.37	4470.60	149.02
4500	4717.32	393.11	4819.86	267.77	4923.84	205.16	5029.50	167.65
5000	5241.48	436.79	5355.54	297.53	5471.04	227.96	5588.10	186.27
5500	5765.64	480.47	5891.04	327.28	6018.24	250.76	6147.00	204.90
6000	6289.80	524.15	6426.54	357.03	6565.20	273.55	6705.90	223.53
6500	6813.96	567.83	6962.04	386.78	7112.40	296.35	7264.80	242.16
7000	7338.12	611.51	7497.72	416.54	7659.60	319.15	7823.70	260.79
7500	7862.28	655.19	8033.22	446.29	8206.56	341.94	8382.30	279.41
8000	8386.44	698.87	8568.72	476.04	8753.76	364.74	8941.20	298.04
8500	8910.48	742.54	9104.40	505.80	9300.96	387.54	9500.10	316.67
9000	9434.64	786.22	9639.90	535.55	9847.92	410.33	10059.00	335.30
10000	10482.96	873.58	10711.08	595.06	10942.32	455.93	11176.50	372.55
11000	11531.28	960.94	11782.08	654.56	12036.48	501.52	12294.30	409.81
12000	12579.60	1048.30	12853.26	714.07	13130.64	547.11	13412.10	447.07
13000	13627.92	1135.66	13924.26	773.57	14224.80	592.70	14529.60	484.32
14000	14676.24	1223.02	14995.44	833.08	15319.20	638.30	15647.40	521.58
15000	15724.56	1310.38	16066.62	892.59	16413.36	683.89	16764.90	558.83
16000	16772.88	1397.74	17137.62	952.09	17507.52	729.48	17882.70	596.09
17000	17821.08	1485.09	18208.80	1011.60	18601.92	775.08	19000.50	633.35
18000	18869.40	1572.45	19279.80	1071.10	19696.08	820.67	20118.00	670.60
19000	19917.72	1659.81	20350.98	1130.61	20790.24	866.26	21235.80	707.86
20000	20966.04	1747.17	21422.16	1190.12	21884.64	911.86	22353.30	745.11
21000	22014.36	1834.53	22493.16	1249.62	22978.80	957.45	23471.10	782.37
22000	23062.68	1921.89	23564.34	1309.13	24072.96	1003.04	24588.90	819.63
23000	24111.00	2009.25	24635.34	1368.63	25167.12	1048.63	25706.40	856.88
24000	25159.32	2096.61	25706.52	1428.14	26261.52	1094.23	26824.20	894.14
25000	26207.52	2183.96	26777.70	1487.65	27355.68	1139.82	27941.70	931.39

ANNUAL PERCENTAGE RATE **8.80%**

LOAN AMT	36 MONTHS TOTAL NOTE	36 MONTHS MONTHLY PAYMENT	42 MONTHS TOTAL NOTE	42 MONTHS MONTHLY PAYMENT	48 MONTHS TOTAL NOTE	48 MONTHS MONTHLY PAYMENT	60 MONTHS TOTAL NOTE	60 MONTHS MONTHLY PAYMENT
1	1.08	.03	.84	.02	.96	.02	1.20	.02
2	2.16	.06	2.10	.05	1.92	.04	2.40	.04
3	3.24	.09	3.36	.08	3.36	.07	3.60	.06
4	4.32	.12	4.62	.11	4.32	.09	4.80	.08
5	5.40	.15	5.46	.13	5.76	.12	6.00	.10
6	6.84	.19	6.72	.16	6.72	.14	7.20	.12
7	7.92	.22	7.98	.19	8.16	.17	8.40	.14
8	9.00	.25	9.24	.22	9.12	.19	9.60	.16
9	10.08	.28	10.08	.24	10.56	.22	10.80	.18
10	11.16	.31	11.34	.27	11.52	.24	12.00	.20
20	22.68	.63	23.10	.55	23.52	.49	24.60	.41
30	34.20	.95	34.86	.83	35.52	.74	36.60	.61
40	45.36	1.26	46.62	1.11	47.52	.99	49.20	.82
50	56.88	1.58	57.96	1.38	59.04	1.23	61.80	1.03
60	68.40	1.90	69.72	1.66	71.04	1.48	73.80	1.23
70	79.56	2.21	81.48	1.94	83.04	1.73	86.40	1.44
80	91.08	2.53	93.24	2.22	95.04	1.98	99.00	1.65
90	102.60	2.85	104.58	2.49	107.04	2.23	111.00	1.85
100	114.12	3.17	116.34	2.77	118.56	2.47	123.60	2.06
200	228.24	6.34	233.10	5.55	237.60	4.95	247.80	4.13
300	342.36	9.51	349.44	8.32	356.64	7.43	371.40	6.19
400	456.48	12.68	466.20	11.10	475.68	9.91	495.60	8.26
500	570.60	15.85	582.54	13.87	594.72	12.39	619.80	10.33
600	684.72	19.02	699.30	16.65	713.76	14.87	743.40	12.39
700	798.84	22.19	815.64	19.42	832.80	17.35	867.60	14.46
800	912.96	25.36	932.40	22.20	951.84	19.83	991.20	16.52
900	1027.08	28.53	1048.74	24.97	1070.88	22.31	1115.40	18.59
1000	1141.20	31.70	1165.50	27.75	1189.92	24.79	1239.60	20.66
1500	1712.16	47.56	1748.04	41.62	1784.64	37.18	1859.40	30.99
2000	2282.76	63.41	2331.00	55.50	2379.84	49.58	2479.20	41.32
2500	2853.36	79.26	2913.54	69.37	2974.56	61.97	3099.00	51.65
3000	3424.32	95.12	3496.50	83.25	3569.76	74.37	3718.80	61.98
3500	3994.92	110.97	4079.04	97.12	4164.48	86.76	4338.60	72.31
4000	4565.52	126.82	4662.00	111.00	4759.68	99.16	4958.40	82.64
4500	5136.48	142.68	5244.54	124.87	5354.40	111.55	5578.20	92.97
5000	5707.08	158.53	5827.50	138.75	5949.60	123.95	6198.00	103.30
5500	6277.68	174.38	6410.04	152.62	6544.32	136.34	6817.80	113.63
6000	6848.64	190.24	6993.00	166.50	7139.52	148.74	7437.60	123.96
6500	7419.24	206.09	7575.54	180.37	7734.24	161.13	8057.40	134.29
7000	7989.84	221.94	8158.50	194.25	8329.44	173.53	8677.20	144.62
7500	8560.80	237.80	8741.04	208.12	8924.16	185.92	9297.60	154.96
8000	9131.40	253.65	9324.00	222.00	9519.36	198.32	9917.40	165.29
8500	9702.00	269.50	9906.96	235.88	10114.08	210.71	10537.20	175.62
9000	10272.96	285.36	10489.50	249.75	10709.28	223.11	11157.00	185.95
10000	11414.16	317.06	11655.00	277.50	11899.20	247.90	12396.60	206.61
11000	12555.72	348.77	12820.50	305.25	13089.12	272.69	13636.20	227.27
12000	13697.28	380.48	13986.00	333.00	14279.04	297.48	14875.80	247.93
13000	14838.48	412.18	15151.50	360.75	15468.96	322.27	16115.40	268.59
14000	15980.04	443.89	16317.00	388.50	16658.88	347.06	17355.00	289.25
15000	17121.60	475.60	17482.50	416.25	17848.80	371.85	18595.20	309.92
16000	18262.80	507.30	18648.42	444.01	19038.72	396.64	19834.80	330.58
17000	19404.36	539.01	19813.92	471.76	20228.64	421.43	21074.40	351.24
18000	20545.92	570.72	20979.42	499.51	21418.56	446.22	22314.00	371.90
19000	21687.12	602.42	22144.92	527.26	22608.48	471.01	23553.60	392.56
20000	22828.68	634.13	23310.42	555.01	23798.40	495.80	24793.20	413.22
21000	23970.24	665.84	24475.92	582.76	24988.32	520.59	26032.80	433.88
22000	25111.44	697.54	25641.42	610.51	26178.24	545.38	27273.00	454.55
23000	26253.00	729.25	26806.92	638.26	27368.16	570.17	28512.60	475.21
24000	27394.56	760.96	27972.42	666.01	28558.08	594.96	29752.20	495.87
25000	28535.76	792.66	29137.92	693.76	29748.00	619.75	30991.80	516.53

8.90% ANNUAL PERCENTAGE RATE

LOAN AMT	12 MONTHS TOTAL NOTE	12 MONTHS MONTHLY PAYMENT	18 MONTHS TOTAL NOTE	18 MONTHS MONTHLY PAYMENT	24 MONTHS TOTAL NOTE	24 MONTHS MONTHLY PAYMENT	30 MONTHS TOTAL NOTE	30 MONTHS MONTHLY PAYMENT
1	.96	.08	.90	.05	.96	.04	.90	.03
2	2.04	.17	1.98	.11	2.16	.09	2.10	.07
3	3.12	.26	3.06	.17	3.12	.13	3.30	.11
4	4.08	.34	4.14	.23	4.32	.18	4.20	.14
5	5.16	.43	5.22	.29	5.28	.22	5.40	.18
6	6.24	.52	6.30	.35	6.48	.27	6.60	.22
7	7.32	.61	7.38	.41	7.44	.31	7.80	.26
8	8.28	.69	8.46	.47	8.64	.36	8.70	.29
9	9.36	.78	9.54	.53	9.84	.41	9.90	.33
10	10.44	.87	10.62	.59	10.80	.45	11.10	.37
20	20.88	1.74	21.42	1.19	21.84	.91	22.20	.74
30	31.44	2.62	32.04	1.78	32.64	1.36	33.30	1.11
40	41.88	3.49	42.84	2.38	43.68	1.82	44.70	1.49
50	52.44	4.37	53.46	2.97	54.72	2.28	55.80	1.86
60	62.88	5.24	64.26	3.57	65.52	2.73	66.90	2.23
70	73.32	6.11	74.88	4.16	76.56	3.19	78.30	2.61
80	83.88	6.99	85.68	4.76	87.60	3.65	89.40	2.98
90	94.32	7.86	96.30	5.35	98.40	4.10	100.50	3.35
100	104.88	8.74	107.10	5.95	109.44	4.56	111.90	3.73
200	209.76	17.48	214.38	11.91	218.88	9.12	223.80	7.46
300	314.64	26.22	321.48	17.86	328.56	13.69	335.70	11.19
400	419.52	34.96	428.76	23.82	438.00	18.25	447.60	14.92
500	524.40	43.70	535.86	29.77	547.44	22.81	559.50	18.65
600	629.28	52.44	643.14	35.73	657.12	27.38	671.40	22.38
700	734.16	61.18	750.24	41.68	766.56	31.94	783.30	26.11
800	839.04	69.92	857.52	47.64	876.24	36.51	895.20	29.84
900	943.92	78.66	964.62	53.59	985.68	41.07	1007.10	33.57
1000	1048.80	87.40	1071.90	59.55	1095.12	45.63	1119.00	37.30
1500	1573.20	131.10	1607.76	89.32	1642.80	68.45	1678.50	55.95
2000	2097.72	174.81	2143.80	119.10	2190.48	91.27	2238.00	74.60
2500	2622.12	218.51	2679.66	148.87	2738.16	114.09	2797.50	93.25
3000	3146.52	262.21	3215.70	178.65	3285.84	136.91	3357.00	111.90
3500	3670.92	305.91	3751.74	208.43	3833.52	159.73	3916.50	130.55
4000	4195.44	349.62	4287.60	238.20	4381.20	182.55	4476.00	149.20
4500	4719.84	393.32	4823.64	267.98	4928.88	205.37	5035.50	167.85
5000	5244.24	437.02	5359.50	297.75	5476.56	228.19	5595.30	186.51
5500	5768.64	480.72	5895.54	327.53	6024.24	251.01	6154.80	205.16
6000	6293.16	524.43	6431.58	357.31	6571.92	273.83	6714.30	223.81
6500	6817.56	568.13	6967.44	387.08	7119.60	296.65	7273.80	242.46
7000	7341.96	611.83	7503.48	416.86	7667.28	319.47	7833.30	261.11
7500	7866.36	655.53	8039.34	446.63	8214.96	342.29	8392.80	279.76
8000	8390.88	699.24	8575.38	476.41	8762.64	365.11	8952.30	298.41
8500	8915.28	742.94	9111.42	506.19	9310.32	387.93	9511.80	317.06
9000	9439.68	786.64	9647.28	535.96	9857.76	410.74	10071.30	335.71
10000	10488.60	874.05	10719.18	595.51	10953.12	456.38	11190.60	373.02
11000	11537.40	961.45	11791.26	655.07	12048.48	502.02	12309.60	410.32
12000	12586.32	1048.86	12863.16	714.62	13143.84	547.66	13428.60	447.62
13000	13635.12	1136.26	13935.06	774.17	14239.20	593.30	14547.60	484.92
14000	14684.04	1223.67	15006.96	833.72	15334.56	638.94	15666.60	522.22
15000	15732.84	1311.07	16078.86	893.27	16429.92	684.58	16785.90	559.53
16000	16781.76	1398.48	17150.76	952.82	17525.28	730.22	17904.90	596.83
17000	17830.56	1485.88	18222.84	1012.38	18620.64	775.86	19023.90	634.13
18000	18879.48	1573.29	19294.74	1071.93	19715.76	821.49	20142.90	671.43
19000	19928.28	1660.69	20366.64	1131.48	20811.12	867.13	21261.90	708.73
20000	20977.20	1748.10	21438.54	1191.03	21906.48	912.77	22381.20	746.04
21000	22026.00	1835.50	22510.44	1250.58	23001.84	958.41	23500.20	783.34
22000	23074.92	1922.91	23582.52	1310.14	24097.20	1004.05	24619.20	820.64
23000	24123.72	2010.31	24654.42	1369.69	25192.56	1049.69	25738.20	857.94
24000	25172.64	2097.72	25726.32	1429.24	26287.92	1095.33	26857.20	895.24
25000	26221.44	2185.12	26798.22	1488.79	27383.28	1140.97	27976.50	932.55

ANNUAL PERCENTAGE RATE **8.90%**

LOAN AMT	36 MONTHS TOTAL NOTE	MONTHLY PAYMENT	42 MONTHS TOTAL NOTE	MONTHLY PAYMENT	48 MONTHS TOTAL NOTE	MONTHLY PAYMENT	60 MONTHS TOTAL NOTE	MONTHLY PAYMENT
1	1.08	.03	.84	.02	.96	.02	1.20	.02
2	2.16	.06	2.10	.05	1.92	.04	2.40	.04
3	3.24	.09	3.36	.08	3.36	.07	3.60	.06
4	4.32	.12	4.62	.11	4.32	.09	4.80	.08
5	5.40	.15	5.46	.13	5.76	.12	6.00	.10
6	6.84	.19	6.72	.16	6.72	.14	7.20	.12
7	7.92	.22	7.98	.19	8.16	.17	8.40	.14
8	9.00	.25	9.24	.22	9.12	.19	9.60	.16
9	10.08	.28	10.50	.25	10.56	.22	10.80	.18
10	11.16	.31	11.34	.27	11.52	.24	12.00	.20
20	22.68	.63	23.10	.55	23.52	.49	24.60	.41
30	34.20	.95	34.86	.83	35.52	.74	37.20	.62
40	45.72	1.27	46.62	1.11	47.52	.99	49.20	.82
50	56.88	1.58	57.96	1.38	59.52	1.24	61.80	1.03
60	68.40	1.90	69.72	1.66	71.52	1.49	74.40	1.24
70	79.92	2.22	81.48	1.94	83.04	1.73	86.40	1.44
80	91.44	2.54	93.24	2.22	95.04	1.98	99.00	1.65
90	102.60	2.85	105.00	2.50	107.04	2.23	111.60	1.86
100	114.12	3.17	116.34	2.77	119.04	2.48	124.20	2.07
200	228.60	6.35	233.10	5.55	238.08	4.96	248.40	4.14
300	342.72	9.52	349.86	8.33	357.60	7.45	372.60	6.21
400	457.20	12.70	466.62	11.11	476.64	9.93	496.80	8.28
500	571.32	15.87	583.38	13.89	595.68	12.41	621.00	10.35
600	685.80	19.05	700.14	16.67	715.20	14.90	745.20	12.42
700	799.92	22.22	816.90	19.45	834.24	17.38	869.40	14.49
800	914.40	25.40	933.66	22.23	953.76	19.87	993.60	16.56
900	1028.52	28.57	1050.42	25.01	1072.80	22.35	1117.80	18.63
1000	1143.00	31.75	1167.18	27.79	1191.84	24.83	1242.00	20.70
1500	1714.32	47.62	1750.98	41.69	1788.00	37.25	1863.60	31.06
2000	2286.00	63.50	2334.78	55.59	2384.16	49.67	2484.60	41.41
2500	2857.68	79.38	2918.58	69.49	2980.32	62.09	3106.20	51.77
3000	3429.00	95.25	3502.38	83.39	3576.48	74.51	3727.20	62.12
3500	4000.68	111.13	4086.18	97.29	4172.64	86.93	4348.80	72.48
4000	4572.36	127.01	4669.98	111.19	4768.80	99.35	4969.80	82.83
4500	5143.68	142.88	5253.36	125.08	5364.48	111.76	5591.40	93.19
5000	5715.36	158.76	5837.16	138.98	5960.64	124.18	6212.40	103.54
5500	6287.04	174.64	6420.96	152.88	6556.80	136.60	6834.00	113.90
6000	6858.36	190.51	7004.76	166.78	7152.96	149.02	7455.00	124.25
6500	7430.04	206.39	7588.56	180.68	7749.12	161.44	8076.60	134.61
7000	8001.72	222.27	8172.36	194.58	8345.28	173.86	8697.60	144.96
7500	8573.04	238.14	8756.16	208.48	8941.44	186.28	9319.20	155.32
8000	9144.72	254.02	9339.96	222.38	9537.60	198.70	9940.20	165.67
8500	9716.40	269.90	9923.34	236.27	10133.28	211.11	10561.80	176.03
9000	10287.72	285.77	10507.14	250.17	10729.44	223.53	11182.80	186.38
10000	11431.08	317.53	11674.74	277.97	11921.76	248.37	12425.40	207.09
11000	12574.08	349.28	12842.34	305.77	13114.08	273.21	13668.00	227.80
12000	13717.08	381.03	14009.94	333.57	14306.40	298.05	14910.60	248.51
13000	14860.44	412.79	15177.12	361.36	15498.24	322.88	16153.20	269.22
14000	16003.44	444.54	16344.72	389.16	16690.56	347.72	17395.80	289.93
15000	17146.44	476.29	17512.32	416.96	17882.88	372.56	18638.40	310.64
16000	18289.80	508.05	18679.92	444.76	19075.20	397.40	19881.00	331.35
17000	19432.80	539.80	19847.10	472.55	20267.04	422.23	21123.60	352.06
18000	20575.80	571.55	21014.70	500.35	21459.36	447.07	22366.20	372.77
19000	21719.16	603.31	22182.30	528.15	22651.68	471.91	23608.80	393.48
20000	22862.16	635.06	23349.90	555.95	23844.00	496.75	24851.40	414.19
21000	24005.16	666.81	24517.08	583.74	25035.84	521.58	26094.00	434.90
22000	25148.52	698.57	25684.68	611.54	26228.16	546.42	27336.60	455.61
23000	26291.52	730.32	26852.28	639.34	27420.48	571.26	28579.20	476.32
24000	27434.52	762.07	28019.88	667.14	28612.80	596.10	29821.80	497.03
25000	28577.88	793.83	29187.06	694.93	29804.64	620.93	31064.40	517.74

9.00% ANNUAL PERCENTAGE RATE

LOAN AMT	12 MONTHS TOTAL NOTE	12 MONTHS MONTHLY PAYMENT	18 MONTHS TOTAL NOTE	18 MONTHS MONTHLY PAYMENT	24 MONTHS TOTAL NOTE	24 MONTHS MONTHLY PAYMENT	30 MONTHS TOTAL NOTE	30 MONTHS MONTHLY PAYMENT
1	.96	.08	.90	.05	.96	.04	.90	.03
2	2.04	.17	1.98	.11	2.16	.09	2.10	.07
3	3.12	.26	3.06	.17	3.12	.13	3.30	.11
4	4.08	.34	4.14	.23	4.32	.18	4.20	.14
5	5.16	.43	5.22	.29	5.28	.22	5.40	.18
6	6.24	.52	6.30	.35	6.48	.27	6.60	.22
7	7.32	.61	7.38	.41	7.44	.31	7.80	.26
8	8.28	.69	8.46	.47	8.64	.36	8.70	.29
9	9.36	.78	9.54	.53	9.84	.41	9.90	.33
10	10.44	.87	10.62	.59	10.80	.45	11.10	.37
20	20.88	1.74	21.42	1.19	21.84	.91	22.20	.74
30	31.44	2.62	32.04	1.78	32.88	1.37	33.60	1.12
40	41.88	3.49	42.84	2.38	43.68	1.82	44.70	1.49
50	52.44	4.37	53.46	2.97	54.72	2.28	55.80	1.86
60	62.88	5.24	64.26	3.57	65.76	2.74	67.20	2.24
70	73.44	6.12	75.06	4.17	76.56	3.19	78.30	2.61
80	83.88	6.99	85.68	4.76	87.60	3.65	89.40	2.98
90	94.44	7.87	96.48	5.36	98.64	4.11	100.80	3.36
100	104.88	8.74	107.10	5.95	109.44	4.56	111.90	3.73
200	209.88	17.49	214.38	11.91	219.12	9.13	223.80	7.46
300	314.76	26.23	321.66	17.87	328.80	13.70	336.00	11.20
400	419.76	34.98	428.94	23.83	438.48	18.27	447.90	14.93
500	524.64	43.72	536.22	29.79	548.16	22.84	560.10	18.67
600	629.64	52.47	643.50	35.75	657.84	27.41	672.00	22.40
700	734.52	61.21	750.78	41.71	767.28	31.97	784.20	26.14
800	839.52	69.96	858.06	47.67	876.96	36.54	896.10	29.87
900	944.40	78.70	965.34	53.63	986.64	41.11	1008.30	33.61
1000	1049.40	87.45	1072.62	59.59	1096.32	45.68	1120.20	37.34
1500	1574.04	131.17	1609.02	89.39	1644.48	68.52	1680.60	56.02
2000	2098.80	174.90	2145.42	119.19	2192.64	91.36	2240.70	74.69
2500	2623.44	218.62	2681.82	148.99	2741.04	114.21	2801.10	93.37
3000	3148.20	262.35	3218.22	178.79	3289.20	137.05	3361.20	112.04
3500	3672.96	306.08	3754.62	208.59	3837.36	159.89	3921.30	130.71
4000	4197.60	349.80	4291.02	238.39	4385.52	182.73	4481.70	149.39
4500	4722.36	393.53	4827.24	268.18	4933.92	205.58	5041.80	168.06
5000	5247.00	437.25	5363.64	297.98	5482.08	228.42	5602.20	186.74
5500	5771.76	480.98	5900.04	327.78	6030.24	251.26	6162.30	205.41
6000	6296.40	524.70	6436.44	357.58	6578.40	274.10	6722.40	224.08
6500	6821.16	568.43	6972.84	387.38	7126.80	296.95	7282.80	242.76
7000	7345.92	612.16	7509.24	417.18	7674.96	319.79	7842.90	261.43
7500	7870.56	655.88	8045.64	446.98	8223.12	342.63	8403.30	280.11
8000	8395.32	699.61	8582.04	476.78	8771.28	365.47	8963.40	298.78
8500	8919.96	743.33	9118.44	506.58	9319.68	388.32	9523.50	317.45
9000	9444.72	787.06	9654.66	536.37	9867.84	411.16	10083.90	336.13
10000	10494.12	874.51	10727.46	595.97	10964.16	456.84	11204.40	373.48
11000	11543.52	961.96	11800.26	655.57	12060.72	502.53	12324.60	410.82
12000	12592.92	1049.41	12873.06	715.17	13157.04	548.21	13445.10	448.17
13000	13642.32	1136.86	13945.68	774.76	14253.60	593.90	14565.60	485.52
14000	14691.84	1224.32	15018.48	834.36	15349.92	639.58	15686.10	522.87
15000	15741.24	1311.77	16091.28	893.96	16446.48	685.27	16806.60	560.22
16000	16790.64	1399.22	17164.08	953.56	17542.80	730.95	17927.10	597.57
17000	17840.04	1486.67	18236.88	1013.16	18639.36	776.64	19047.30	634.91
18000	18889.44	1574.12	19309.50	1072.75	19735.68	822.32	20167.80	672.26
19000	19938.84	1661.57	20382.30	1132.35	20832.24	868.01	21288.30	709.61
20000	20988.24	1749.02	21455.10	1191.95	21928.56	913.69	22408.80	746.96
21000	22037.76	1836.48	22527.90	1251.55	23024.88	959.37	23529.30	784.31
22000	23087.16	1923.93	23600.52	1311.14	24121.44	1005.06	24649.50	821.65
23000	24136.56	2011.38	24673.32	1370.74	25217.76	1050.74	25770.00	859.00
24000	25185.96	2098.83	25746.12	1430.34	26314.32	1096.43	26890.50	896.35
25000	26235.36	2186.28	26818.92	1489.94	27410.64	1142.11	28011.00	933.70

ANNUAL PERCENTAGE RATE **9.00%**

LOAN AMT	36 MONTHS TOTAL NOTE	36 MONTHS MONTHLY PAYMENT	42 MONTHS TOTAL NOTE	42 MONTHS MONTHLY PAYMENT	48 MONTHS TOTAL NOTE	48 MONTHS MONTHLY PAYMENT	60 MONTHS TOTAL NOTE	60 MONTHS MONTHLY PAYMENT
1	1.08	.03	.84	.02	.96	.02	1.20	.02
2	2.16	.06	2.10	.05	1.92	.04	2.40	.04
3	3.24	.09	3.36	.08	3.36	.07	3.60	.06
4	4.32	.12	4.62	.11	4.32	.09	4.80	.08
5	5.40	.15	5.46	.13	5.76	.12	6.00	.10
6	6.84	.19	6.72	.16	6.72	.14	7.20	.12
7	7.92	.22	7.98	.19	8.16	.17	8.40	.14
8	9.00	.25	9.24	.22	9.12	.19	9.60	.16
9	10.08	.28	10.50	.25	10.56	.22	10.80	.18
10	11.16	.31	11.34	.27	11.52	.24	12.00	.20
20	22.68	.63	23.10	.55	23.52	.49	24.60	.41
30	34.20	.95	34.86	.83	35.52	.74	37.20	.62
40	45.72	1.27	46.62	1.11	47.52	.99	49.80	.83
50	56.88	1.58	58.38	1.39	59.52	1.24	61.80	1.03
60	68.40	1.90	70.14	1.67	71.52	1.49	74.40	1.24
70	79.92	2.22	81.48	1.94	83.52	1.74	87.00	1.45
80	91.44	2.54	93.24	2.22	95.52	1.99	99.60	1.66
90	102.96	2.86	105.00	2.50	107.04	2.23	111.60	1.86
100	114.12	3.17	116.76	2.78	119.04	2.48	124.20	2.07
200	228.60	6.35	233.52	5.56	238.56	4.97	249.00	4.15
300	343.08	9.53	350.70	8.35	358.08	7.46	373.20	6.22
400	457.56	12.71	467.46	11.13	477.60	9.95	498.00	8.30
500	572.04	15.89	584.64	13.92	597.12	12.44	622.20	10.37
600	686.52	19.07	701.40	16.70	716.64	14.93	747.00	12.45
700	801.00	22.25	818.58	19.49	835.68	17.41	871.80	14.53
800	915.48	25.43	935.34	22.27	955.20	19.90	996.00	16.60
900	1029.96	28.61	1052.52	25.06	1074.72	22.39	1120.80	18.68
1000	1144.44	31.79	1169.28	27.84	1194.24	24.88	1245.00	20.75
1500	1716.84	47.69	1753.92	41.76	1791.36	37.32	1867.80	31.13
2000	2289.24	63.59	2338.56	55.68	2388.96	49.77	2490.60	41.51
2500	2861.64	79.49	2923.62	69.61	2986.08	62.21	3113.40	51.89
3000	3434.04	95.39	3508.26	83.53	3583.20	74.65	3736.20	62.27
3500	4006.44	111.29	4092.90	97.45	4180.32	87.09	4359.00	72.65
4000	4578.84	127.19	4677.54	111.37	4777.92	99.54	4981.80	83.03
4500	5151.24	143.09	5262.60	125.30	5375.04	111.98	5604.60	93.41
5000	5723.64	158.99	5847.24	139.22	5972.16	124.42	6227.40	103.79
5500	6296.04	174.89	6431.88	153.14	6569.28	136.86	6850.20	114.17
6000	6868.44	190.79	7016.52	167.06	7166.88	149.31	7473.00	124.55
6500	7440.84	206.69	7601.16	180.98	7764.00	161.75	8095.20	134.92
7000	8013.24	222.59	8186.22	194.91	8361.12	174.19	8718.00	145.30
7500	8585.64	238.49	8770.86	208.83	8958.24	186.63	9340.80	155.68
8000	9158.04	254.39	9355.50	222.75	9555.84	199.08	9963.60	166.06
8500	9730.44	270.29	9940.14	236.67	10152.96	211.52	10586.40	176.44
9000	10302.84	286.19	10525.20	250.60	10750.08	223.96	11209.20	186.82
10000	11447.64	317.99	11694.48	278.44	11944.80	248.85	12454.80	207.58
11000	12592.44	349.79	12863.76	306.28	13139.04	273.73	13700.40	228.34
12000	13737.24	381.59	14033.46	334.13	14333.76	298.62	14946.00	249.10
13000	14882.04	413.39	15202.74	361.97	15528.00	323.50	16191.00	269.85
14000	16026.84	445.19	16372.44	389.82	16722.72	348.39	17436.60	290.61
15000	17171.64	476.99	17541.72	417.66	17916.96	373.27	18682.20	311.37
16000	18316.44	508.79	18711.42	445.51	19111.68	398.16	19927.80	332.13
17000	19461.24	540.59	19880.70	473.35	20305.92	423.04	21173.40	352.89
18000	20606.04	572.39	21050.40	501.20	21500.64	447.93	22419.00	373.65
19000	21750.84	604.19	22219.68	529.04	22694.88	472.81	23664.00	394.40
20000	22895.64	635.99	23389.38	556.89	23889.60	497.70	24909.60	415.16
21000	24040.04	667.79	24558.66	584.73	25083.84	522.58	26155.20	435.92
22000	25185.24	699.59	25727.94	612.57	26278.56	547.47	27400.80	456.68
23000	26330.04	731.39	26897.64	640.42	27472.80	572.35	28646.40	477.44
24000	27474.84	763.19	28066.92	668.26	28667.52	597.24	29892.00	498.20
25000	28619.64	794.99	29236.62	696.11	29861.76	622.12	31137.00	518.95

9.10% ANNUAL PERCENTAGE RATE

LOAN AMT	12 MONTHS TOTAL NOTE	12 MONTHS MONTHLY PAYMENT	18 MONTHS TOTAL NOTE	18 MONTHS MONTHLY PAYMENT	24 MONTHS TOTAL NOTE	24 MONTHS MONTHLY PAYMENT	30 MONTHS TOTAL NOTE	30 MONTHS MONTHLY PAYMENT
1	.96	.08	.90	.05	.96	.04	.90	.03
2	2.04	.17	1.98	.11	2.16	.09	2.10	.07
3	3.12	.26	3.06	.17	3.12	.13	3.30	.11
4	4.08	.34	4.14	.23	4.32	.18	4.20	.14
5	5.16	.43	5.22	.29	5.28	.22	5.40	.18
6	6.24	.52	6.30	.35	6.48	.27	6.60	.22
7	7.32	.61	7.38	.41	7.68	.32	7.80	.26
8	8.28	.69	8.46	.47	8.64	.36	8.70	.29
9	9.36	.78	9.54	.53	9.84	.41	9.90	.33
10	10.44	.87	10.62	.59	10.80	.45	11.10	.37
20	20.88	1.74	21.42	1.19	21.84	.91	22.20	.74
30	31.44	2.62	32.04	1.78	32.88	1.37	33.60	1.12
40	41.88	3.49	42.84	2.38	43.68	1.82	44.70	1.49
50	52.44	4.37	53.64	2.98	54.72	2.28	55.80	1.86
60	62.88	5.24	64.26	3.57	65.76	2.74	67.20	2.24
70	73.44	6.12	75.06	4.17	76.80	3.20	78.30	2.61
80	83.88	6.99	85.86	4.77	87.60	3.65	89.70	2.99
90	94.44	7.87	96.48	5.36	98.64	4.11	100.80	3.36
100	104.88	8.74	107.28	5.96	109.68	4.57	111.90	3.73
200	209.88	17.49	214.56	11.92	219.36	9.14	224.10	7.47
300	314.88	26.24	322.02	17.89	329.04	13.71	336.30	11.21
400	419.88	34.99	429.30	23.85	438.96	18.29	448.50	14.95
500	524.88	43.74	536.76	29.82	548.64	22.86	560.70	18.69
600	629.88	52.49	644.04	35.78	658.32	27.43	672.90	22.43
700	734.88	61.24	751.50	41.75	768.24	32.01	785.10	26.17
800	839.88	69.99	858.78	47.71	877.92	36.58	897.30	29.91
900	944.88	78.74	966.06	53.67	987.60	41.15	1009.50	33.65
1000	1049.88	87.49	1073.52	59.64	1097.52	45.73	1121.70	37.39
1500	1574.88	131.24	1610.28	89.46	1646.16	68.59	1682.70	56.09
2000	2099.88	174.99	2147.04	119.28	2195.04	91.46	2243.40	74.78
2500	2624.88	218.74	2683.80	149.10	2743.68	114.32	2804.40	93.48
3000	3149.88	262.49	3220.74	178.93	3292.56	137.19	3365.40	112.18
3500	3674.88	306.24	3757.50	208.75	3841.20	160.05	3926.40	130.88
4000	4199.88	349.99	4294.26	238.57	4390.08	182.92	4487.10	149.57
4500	4724.88	393.74	4831.02	268.39	4938.72	205.78	5048.10	168.27
5000	5249.76	437.48	5367.78	298.21	5487.60	228.65	5609.10	186.97
5500	5774.76	481.23	5904.54	328.03	6036.24	251.51	6169.80	205.66
6000	6299.76	524.98	6441.48	357.86	6585.12	274.38	6730.80	224.36
6500	6824.76	568.73	6978.24	387.68	7133.76	297.24	7291.80	243.06
7000	7349.76	612.48	7515.00	417.50	7682.64	320.11	7852.80	261.76
7500	7874.76	656.23	8051.76	447.32	8231.28	342.97	8413.50	280.45
8000	8399.76	699.98	8588.52	477.14	8780.16	365.84	8974.50	299.15
8500	8924.76	743.73	9125.28	506.96	9329.04	388.71	9535.50	317.85
9000	9449.76	787.48	9662.22	536.79	9877.68	411.57	10096.20	336.54
10000	10499.64	874.97	10735.74	596.43	10975.20	457.30	11218.20	373.94
11000	11549.64	962.47	11809.26	656.07	12072.72	503.03	12339.90	411.33
12000	12599.64	1049.97	12882.96	715.72	13170.24	548.76	13461.90	448.73
13000	13649.64	1137.47	13956.48	775.36	14267.76	594.49	14583.60	486.12
14000	14699.52	1224.96	15030.00	835.00	15365.28	640.22	15705.60	523.52
15000	15749.52	1312.46	16103.70	894.65	16462.80	685.95	16827.30	560.91
16000	16799.52	1399.96	17177.22	954.29	17560.56	731.69	17949.00	598.30
17000	17849.52	1487.46	18250.74	1013.93	18658.08	777.42	19071.00	635.70
18000	18899.52	1574.96	19324.44	1073.58	19755.60	823.15	20192.70	673.09
19000	19949.40	1662.45	20397.96	1133.22	20853.12	868.88	21314.70	710.49
20000	20999.40	1749.95	21471.66	1192.87	21950.64	914.61	22436.40	747.88
21000	22049.40	1837.45	22545.18	1252.51	23048.16	960.34	23558.40	785.28
22000	23099.40	1924.95	23618.70	1312.15	24145.68	1006.07	24680.10	822.67
23000	24149.40	2012.45	24692.40	1371.80	25243.20	1051.80	25801.80	860.06
24000	25199.28	2099.94	25765.92	1431.44	26340.72	1097.53	26923.80	897.46
25000	26249.28	2187.44	26839.44	1491.08	27438.24	1143.26	28045.50	934.85

ANNUAL PERCENTAGE RATE **9.10%**

LOAN AMT	36 MONTHS TOTAL NOTE	36 MONTHS MONTHLY PAYMENT	42 MONTHS TOTAL NOTE	42 MONTHS MONTHLY PAYMENT	48 MONTHS TOTAL NOTE	48 MONTHS MONTHLY PAYMENT	60 MONTHS TOTAL NOTE	60 MONTHS MONTHLY PAYMENT
1	1.08	.03	.84	.02	.96	.02	1.20	.02
2	2.16	.06	2.10	.05	1.92	.04	2.40	.04
3	3.24	.09	3.36	.08	3.36	.07	3.60	.06
4	4.32	.12	4.62	.11	4.32	.09	4.80	.08
5	5.40	.15	5.46	.13	5.76	.12	6.00	.10
6	6.84	.19	6.72	.16	6.72	.14	7.20	.12
7	7.92	.22	7.98	.19	8.16	.17	8.40	.14
8	9.00	.25	9.24	.22	9.12	.19	9.60	.16
9	10.08	.28	10.50	.25	10.56	.22	10.80	.18
10	11.16	.31	11.34	.27	11.52	.24	12.00	.20
20	22.68	.63	23.10	.55	23.52	.49	24.60	.41
30	34.20	.95	34.86	.83	35.52	.74	37.20	.62
40	45.72	1.27	46.62	1.11	47.52	.99	49.80	.83
50	57.24	1.59	58.38	1.39	59.52	1.24	62.40	1.04
60	68.76	1.91	70.14	1.67	71.52	1.49	74.40	1.24
70	79.92	2.22	81.90	1.95	83.52	1.74	87.00	1.45
80	91.44	2.54	93.66	2.23	95.52	1.99	99.60	1.66
90	102.96	2.86	105.42	2.51	107.52	2.24	112.20	1.87
100	114.48	3.18	116.76	2.78	119.52	2.49	124.80	2.08
200	228.96	6.36	233.94	5.57	239.04	4.98	249.60	4.16
300	343.80	9.55	351.12	8.36	358.56	7.47	374.40	6.24
400	458.28	12.73	468.30	11.15	478.56	9.97	499.20	8.32
500	573.12	15.92	585.48	13.94	598.08	12.46	624.00	10.40
600	687.60	19.10	702.66	16.73	717.60	14.95	748.80	12.48
700	802.44	22.29	819.84	19.52	837.60	17.45	873.60	14.56
800	916.92	25.47	937.02	22.31	957.12	19.94	998.40	16.64
900	1031.76	28.66	1054.20	25.10	1076.64	22.43	1123.20	18.72
1000	1146.24	31.84	1171.38	27.89	1196.64	24.93	1248.00	20.80
1500	1719.36	47.76	1756.86	41.83	1794.72	37.39	1872.60	31.21
2000	2292.84	63.69	2342.76	55.78	2393.28	49.86	2496.60	41.61
2500	2865.96	79.61	2928.24	69.72	2991.84	62.33	3120.60	52.01
3000	3439.08	95.53	3514.14	83.67	3589.92	74.79	3745.20	62.42
3500	4012.56	111.46	4100.04	97.62	4188.48	87.26	4369.20	72.82
4000	4585.68	127.38	4685.52	111.56	4787.04	99.73	4993.20	83.22
4500	5158.80	143.30	5271.42	125.51	5385.12	112.19	5617.80	93.63
5000	5732.28	159.23	5856.90	139.45	5983.68	124.66	6241.80	104.03
5500	6305.40	175.15	6442.80	153.40	6581.76	137.12	6865.80	114.43
6000	6878.52	191.07	7028.28	167.34	7180.32	149.59	7490.40	124.84
6500	7452.00	207.00	7614.18	181.29	7778.88	162.06	8114.40	135.24
7000	8025.12	222.92	8200.08	195.24	8376.96	174.52	8738.40	145.64
7500	8598.24	238.84	8785.56	209.18	8975.52	186.99	9363.00	156.05
8000	9171.72	254.77	9371.46	223.13	9574.08	199.46	9987.00	166.45
8500	9744.84	270.69	9956.94	237.07	10172.16	211.92	10611.00	176.85
9000	10317.96	286.61	10542.84	251.02	10770.72	224.39	11235.60	187.26
10000	11464.56	318.46	11714.22	278.91	11967.36	249.32	12483.60	208.06
11000	12610.80	350.30	12885.60	306.80	13164.00	274.25	13732.20	228.87
12000	13757.40	382.15	14056.98	334.69	14361.12	299.19	14980.80	249.68
13000	14904.00	414.00	15228.36	362.58	15557.76	324.12	16228.80	270.48
14000	16050.24	445.84	16400.16	390.48	16754.40	349.05	17477.40	291.29
15000	17196.84	477.69	17571.54	418.37	17951.04	373.98	18725.00	312.10
16000	18343.44	509.54	18742.92	446.26	19148.16	398.92	19974.60	332.91
17000	19489.68	541.38	19914.30	474.15	20344.80	423.85	21222.60	353.71
18000	20636.28	573.23	21085.68	502.04	21541.44	448.78	22471.20	374.52
19000	21782.52	605.07	22257.06	529.93	22738.08	473.71	23719.80	395.33
20000	22929.12	636.92	23428.86	557.83	23935.20	498.65	24967.80	416.13
21000	24075.72	668.77	24600.24	585.72	25131.84	523.58	26216.40	436.94
22000	25221.96	700.61	25771.62	613.61	26328.48	548.51	27465.00	457.75
23000	26368.56	732.46	26943.00	641.50	27525.12	573.44	28713.00	478.55
24000	27515.16	764.31	28114.38	669.39	28722.24	598.38	29961.60	499.36
25000	28661.40	796.15	29285.76	697.28	29918.88	623.31	31210.20	520.17

9.20% ANNUAL PERCENTAGE RATE

LOAN AMT	12 MONTHS TOTAL NOTE	12 MONTHS MONTHLY PAYMENT	18 MONTHS TOTAL NOTE	18 MONTHS MONTHLY PAYMENT	24 MONTHS TOTAL NOTE	24 MONTHS MONTHLY PAYMENT	30 MONTHS TOTAL NOTE	30 MONTHS MONTHLY PAYMENT
1	.96	.08	.90	.05	.96	.04	.90	.03
2	2.04	.17	1.98	.11	2.16	.09	2.10	.07
3	3.12	.26	3.06	.17	3.12	.13	3.30	.11
4	4.20	.35	4.14	.23	4.32	.18	4.20	.14
5	5.16	.43	5.22	.29	5.28	.22	5.40	.18
6	6.24	.52	6.30	.35	6.48	.27	6.60	.22
7	7.32	.61	7.38	.41	7.68	.32	7.80	.26
8	8.40	.70	8.46	.47	8.64	.36	8.70	.29
9	9.36	.78	9.54	.53	9.84	.41	9.90	.33
10	10.44	.87	10.62	.59	10.80	.45	11.10	.37
20	21.00	1.75	21.42	1.19	21.84	.91	22.20	.74
30	31.44	2.62	32.22	1.79	32.88	1.37	33.60	1.12
40	42.00	3.50	42.84	2.38	43.92	1.83	44.70	1.49
50	52.44	4.37	53.64	2.98	54.72	2.28	56.10	1.87
60	63.00	5.25	64.44	3.58	65.76	2.74	67.20	2.24
70	73.44	6.12	75.06	4.17	76.80	3.20	78.60	2.62
80	84.00	7.00	85.86	4.77	87.84	3.66	89.70	2.99
90	94.44	7.87	96.66	5.37	98.64	4.11	100.80	3.36
100	105.00	8.75	107.28	5.96	109.68	4.57	112.20	3.74
200	210.00	17.50	214.74	11.93	219.60	9.15	224.40	7.48
300	315.12	26.26	322.20	17.90	329.52	13.73	336.90	11.23
400	420.12	35.01	429.66	23.87	439.44	18.31	449.10	14.97
500	525.24	43.77	537.12	29.84	549.12	22.88	561.60	18.72
600	630.24	52.52	644.58	35.81	659.04	27.46	673.80	22.46
700	735.36	61.28	752.04	41.78	768.96	32.04	786.00	26.20
800	840.36	70.03	859.50	47.75	878.88	36.62	898.50	29.95
900	945.36	78.78	966.96	53.72	988.56	41.19	1010.70	33.69
1000	1050.48	87.54	1074.24	59.68	1098.48	45.77	1123.20	37.44
1500	1575.72	131.31	1611.54	89.53	1647.84	68.66	1684.80	56.16
2000	2100.96	175.08	2148.66	119.37	2197.20	91.55	2246.40	74.88
2500	2626.32	218.86	2685.96	149.22	2746.56	114.44	2808.00	93.60
3000	3151.56	262.63	3223.08	179.06	3295.68	137.32	3369.60	112.32
3500	3676.80	306.40	3760.38	208.91	3845.04	160.21	3931.20	131.04
4000	4202.04	350.17	4297.50	238.75	4394.40	183.10	4492.80	149.76
4500	4727.28	393.94	4834.80	268.60	4943.76	205.99	5054.40	168.48
5000	5252.64	437.72	5371.92	298.44	5493.12	228.88	5616.00	187.20
5500	5777.88	481.49	5909.22	328.29	6042.48	251.77	6177.60	205.92
6000	6303.12	525.26	6446.34	358.13	6591.60	274.65	6739.20	224.64
6500	6828.36	569.03	6983.64	387.98	7140.96	297.54	7300.80	243.36
7000	7353.60	612.80	7520.76	417.82	7690.32	320.43	7862.40	262.08
7500	7878.96	656.58	8058.06	447.67	8239.68	343.32	8424.00	280.80
8000	8404.20	700.35	8595.18	477.51	8789.04	366.21	8985.60	299.52
8500	8929.44	744.12	9132.30	507.35	9338.40	389.10	9547.20	318.24
9000	9454.68	787.89	9669.60	537.20	9887.52	411.98	10108.80	336.96
10000	10505.28	875.44	10744.02	596.89	10986.24	457.76	11232.00	374.40
11000	11555.76	962.98	11818.44	656.58	12084.96	503.54	12355.20	411.84
12000	12606.36	1050.53	12892.86	716.27	13183.44	549.31	13478.40	449.28
13000	13656.84	1138.07	13967.28	775.96	14282.16	595.09	14601.60	486.72
14000	14707.32	1225.61	15041.70	835.65	15380.88	640.87	15724.80	524.16
15000	15757.92	1313.16	16116.12	895.34	16479.36	686.64	16848.00	561.60
16000	16808.40	1400.70	17190.54	955.03	17578.08	732.42	17971.20	599.04
17000	17859.00	1488.25	18264.78	1014.71	18676.80	778.20	19094.40	636.48
18000	18909.48	1575.79	19339.20	1074.40	19775.28	823.97	20217.60	673.92
19000	19960.08	1663.34	20413.62	1134.09	20874.00	869.75	21341.10	711.37
20000	21010.56	1750.88	21488.04	1193.78	21972.72	915.53	22464.30	748.81
21000	22061.04	1838.42	22562.46	1253.47	23071.20	961.30	23587.50	786.25
22000	23111.64	1925.97	23636.88	1313.16	24169.92	1007.08	24710.70	823.69
23000	24162.12	2013.51	24711.30	1372.85	25268.64	1052.86	25833.90	861.13
24000	25212.72	2101.06	25785.72	1432.54	26367.12	1098.63	26957.10	898.57
25000	26263.20	2188.60	26860.14	1492.23	27465.84	1144.41	28080.30	936.01

ANNUAL PERCENTAGE RATE **9.20%**

LOAN AMT	36 MONTHS TOTAL NOTE	36 MONTHS MONTHLY PAYMENT	42 MONTHS TOTAL NOTE	42 MONTHS MONTHLY PAYMENT	48 MONTHS TOTAL NOTE	48 MONTHS MONTHLY PAYMENT	60 MONTHS TOTAL NOTE	60 MONTHS MONTHLY PAYMENT
1	1.08	.03	.84	.02	.96	.02	1.20	.02
2	2.16	.06	2.10	.05	1.92	.04	2.40	.04
3	3.24	.09	3.36	.08	3.36	.07	3.60	.06
4	4.32	.12	4.62	.11	4.32	.09	4.80	.08
5	5.40	.15	5.46	.13	5.76	.12	6.00	.10
6	6.84	.19	6.72	.16	6.72	.14	7.20	.12
7	7.92	.22	7.98	.19	8.16	.17	8.40	.14
8	9.00	.25	9.24	.22	9.12	.19	9.60	.16
9	10.08	.28	10.50	.25	10.56	.22	10.80	.18
10	11.16	.31	11.34	.27	11.52	.24	12.00	.20
20	22.68	.63	23.10	.55	23.52	.49	24.60	.41
30	34.20	.95	34.86	.83	35.52	.74	37.20	.62
40	45.72	1.27	46.62	1.11	47.52	.99	49.80	.83
50	57.24	1.59	58.38	1.39	59.52	1.24	62.40	1.04
60	68.76	1.91	70.14	1.67	71.52	1.49	75.00	1.25
70	80.28	2.23	81.90	1.95	83.52	1.74	87.00	1.45
80	91.80	2.55	93.66	2.23	95.52	1.99	99.60	1.66
90	103.32	2.87	105.42	2.51	107.52	2.24	112.20	1.87
100	114.48	3.18	117.18	2.79	119.52	2.49	124.80	2.08
200	229.32	6.37	234.36	5.58	239.52	4.99	250.20	4.17
300	344.16	9.56	351.96	8.38	359.52	7.49	375.00	6.25
400	459.00	12.75	469.14	11.17	479.52	9.99	500.40	8.34
500	573.84	15.94	586.32	13.96	599.52	12.49	625.20	10.42
600	688.68	19.13	703.92	16.76	719.04	14.98	750.60	12.51
700	803.52	22.32	821.10	19.55	839.04	17.48	875.40	14.59
800	918.36	25.51	938.70	22.35	959.04	19.98	1000.80	16.68
900	1033.20	28.70	1055.88	25.14	1079.04	22.48	1126.20	18.77
1000	1148.04	31.89	1173.06	27.93	1199.04	24.98	1251.00	20.85
1500	1721.88	47.83	1759.80	41.90	1798.56	37.47	1876.80	31.28
2000	2296.08	63.78	2346.54	55.87	2398.08	49.96	2502.60	41.71
2500	2870.28	79.73	2933.28	69.84	2997.60	62.45	3127.80	52.13
3000	3444.12	95.67	3520.02	83.81	3597.12	74.94	3753.60	62.56
3500	4018.32	111.62	4106.76	97.78	4196.64	87.43	4379.40	72.99
4000	4592.52	127.57	4693.50	111.75	4796.16	99.92	5005.20	83.42
4500	5166.36	143.51	5280.24	125.72	5395.68	112.41	5631.00	93.85
5000	5740.56	159.46	5866.98	139.69	5995.20	124.90	6256.20	104.27
5500	6314.76	175.41	6453.72	153.66	6594.72	137.39	6882.00	114.70
6000	6888.60	191.35	7040.46	167.63	7194.24	149.88	7507.80	125.13
6500	7462.80	207.30	7627.20	181.60	7793.76	162.37	8133.60	135.56
7000	8037.00	223.25	8213.94	195.57	8393.28	174.86	8758.80	145.98
7500	8610.84	239.19	8800.26	209.53	8992.80	187.35	9384.60	156.41
8000	9185.04	255.14	9387.00	223.50	9592.32	199.84	10010.40	166.84
8500	9758.88	271.08	9973.74	237.47	10191.84	212.33	10636.20	177.27
9000	10333.08	287.03	10560.48	251.44	10791.36	224.82	11262.00	187.70
10000	11481.12	318.92	11733.96	279.38	11990.40	249.80	12513.00	208.55
11000	12629.52	350.82	12907.44	307.32	13189.44	274.78	13764.60	229.41
12000	13777.56	382.71	14080.92	335.26	14388.48	299.76	15015.60	250.26
13000	14925.60	414.60	15254.40	363.20	15587.52	324.74	16267.20	271.12
14000	16074.00	446.50	16427.88	391.14	16786.56	349.72	17518.20	291.97
15000	17222.04	478.39	17600.94	419.07	17985.60	374.70	18769.80	312.83
16000	18370.08	510.28	18774.42	447.01	19184.64	399.68	20020.80	333.68
17000	19518.12	542.17	19947.90	474.95	20383.68	424.66	21272.40	354.54
18000	20666.52	574.07	21121.38	502.89	21582.72	449.64	22524.00	375.40
19000	21814.56	605.96	22294.86	530.83	22781.76	474.62	23775.00	396.25
20000	22962.60	637.85	23468.34	558.77	23980.80	499.60	25026.60	417.11
21000	24111.00	669.75	24641.82	586.71	25179.84	524.58	26277.60	437.96
22000	25259.04	701.64	25814.88	614.64	26378.88	549.56	27529.20	458.82
23000	26407.08	733.53	26988.36	642.58	27577.92	574.54	28780.20	479.67
24000	27555.12	765.42	28161.84	670.52	28776.96	599.52	30031.80	500.53
25000	28703.52	797.32	29335.32	698.46	29976.00	624.50	31282.80	521.38

9.25% ANNUAL PERCENTAGE RATE

LOAN AMT	12 MONTHS TOTAL NOTE	12 MONTHS MONTHLY PAYMENT	18 MONTHS TOTAL NOTE	18 MONTHS MONTHLY PAYMENT	24 MONTHS TOTAL NOTE	24 MONTHS MONTHLY PAYMENT	30 MONTHS TOTAL NOTE	30 MONTHS MONTHLY PAYMENT
1	.96	.08	.90	.05	.96	.04	.90	.03
2	2.04	.17	1.98	.11	2.16	.09	2.10	.07
3	3.12	.26	3.06	.17	3.12	.13	3.30	.11
4	4.20	.35	4.14	.23	4.32	.18	4.20	.14
5	5.16	.43	5.22	.29	5.28	.22	5.40	.18
6	6.24	.52	6.30	.35	6.48	.27	6.60	.22
7	7.32	.61	7.38	.41	7.68	.32	7.80	.26
8	8.40	.70	8.46	.47	8.64	.36	8.70	.29
9	9.36	.78	9.54	.53	9.84	.41	9.90	.33
10	10.44	.87	10.62	.59	10.80	.45	11.10	.37
20	21.00	1.75	21.42	1.19	21.84	.91	22.20	.74
30	31.44	2.62	32.22	1.79	32.88	1.37	33.60	1.12
40	42.00	3.50	42.84	2.38	43.92	1.83	44.70	1.49
50	52.44	4.37	53.64	2.98	54.72	2.28	56.10	1.87
60	63.00	5.25	64.44	3.58	65.76	2.74	67.20	2.24
70	73.44	6.12	75.06	4.17	76.80	3.20	78.60	2.62
80	84.00	7.00	85.86	4.77	87.84	3.66	89.70	2.99
90	94.56	7.88	96.66	5.37	98.88	4.12	101.10	3.37
100	105.00	8.75	107.46	5.97	109.68	4.57	112.20	3.74
200	210.12	17.51	214.92	11.94	219.60	9.15	224.70	7.49
300	315.24	26.27	322.38	17.91	329.52	13.73	336.90	11.23
400	420.24	35.02	429.84	23.88	439.44	18.31	449.40	14.98
500	525.36	43.78	537.30	29.85	549.36	22.89	561.90	18.73
600	630.48	52.54	644.76	35.82	659.28	27.47	674.10	22.47
700	735.48	61.29	752.22	41.79	769.20	32.05	786.60	26.22
800	840.60	70.05	859.68	47.76	879.12	36.63	899.10	29.97
900	945.72	78.81	967.32	53.74	989.04	41.21	1011.30	33.71
1000	1050.72	87.56	1074.78	59.71	1098.96	45.79	1123.80	37.46
1500	1576.20	131.35	1612.08	89.56	1648.56	68.69	1685.70	56.19
2000	2101.56	175.13	2149.56	119.42	2198.16	91.59	2247.60	74.92
2500	2626.92	218.91	2687.04	149.28	2747.76	114.49	2809.50	93.65
3000	3152.40	262.70	3224.34	179.13	3297.36	137.39	3371.70	112.39
3500	3677.76	306.48	3761.82	208.99	3846.96	160.29	3933.60	131.12
4000	4203.12	350.26	4299.12	238.84	4396.56	183.19	4495.50	149.85
4500	4728.60	394.05	4836.60	268.70	4946.16	206.09	5057.40	168.58
5000	5253.96	437.83	5374.08	298.56	5495.76	228.99	5619.30	187.31
5500	5779.44	481.62	5911.38	328.41	6045.36	251.89	6181.50	206.05
6000	6304.80	525.40	6448.86	358.27	6594.96	274.79	6743.40	224.78
6500	6830.16	569.18	6986.34	388.13	7144.56	297.69	7305.30	243.51
7000	7355.64	612.97	7523.64	417.98	7694.16	320.59	7867.20	262.24
7500	7881.00	656.75	8061.12	447.84	8243.76	343.49	8429.10	280.97
8000	8406.36	700.53	8598.42	477.69	8793.36	366.39	8991.00	299.70
8500	8931.84	744.32	9135.90	507.55	9342.96	389.29	9553.20	318.44
9000	9457.20	788.10	9673.38	537.41	9892.56	412.19	10115.10	337.17
10000	10508.04	875.67	10748.16	597.12	10991.76	457.99	11238.90	374.63
11000	11558.88	963.24	11822.94	656.83	12090.96	503.79	12363.00	412.10
12000	12609.60	1050.80	12897.72	716.54	13190.16	549.59	13486.80	449.56
13000	13660.44	1138.37	13972.68	776.26	14289.36	595.39	14610.60	487.02
14000	14711.28	1225.94	15047.46	835.97	15388.56	641.19	15734.70	524.49
15000	15762.12	1313.51	16122.24	895.68	16487.76	686.99	16858.50	561.95
16000	16812.84	1401.07	17197.02	955.39	17586.96	732.79	17982.30	599.41
17000	17863.68	1488.64	18271.80	1015.10	18686.16	778.59	19106.40	636.88
18000	18914.52	1576.21	19346.76	1074.82	19785.36	824.39	20230.20	674.34
19000	19965.36	1663.78	20421.54	1134.53	20884.56	870.19	21354.00	711.80
20000	21016.08	1751.34	21496.32	1194.24	21983.76	915.99	22478.10	749.27
21000	22066.92	1838.91	22571.10	1253.95	23082.96	961.79	23601.90	786.73
22000	23117.76	1926.48	23646.06	1313.67	24181.92	1007.58	24726.00	824.20
23000	24168.60	2014.05	24720.84	1373.38	25281.12	1053.38	25849.80	861.66
24000	25219.32	2101.61	25795.62	1433.09	26380.32	1099.18	26973.60	899.12
25000	26270.16	2189.18	26870.40	1492.80	27479.52	1144.98	28097.70	936.59

ANNUAL PERCENTAGE RATE **9.25%**

LOAN AMT	36 MONTHS TOTAL NOTE	36 MONTHS MONTHLY PAYMENT	42 MONTHS TOTAL NOTE	42 MONTHS MONTHLY PAYMENT	48 MONTHS TOTAL NOTE	48 MONTHS MONTHLY PAYMENT	60 MONTHS TOTAL NOTE	60 MONTHS MONTHLY PAYMENT
1	1.08	.03	.84	.02	.96	.02	1.20	.02
2	2.16	.06	2.10	.05	2.40	.05	2.40	.04
3	3.24	.09	3.36	.08	3.36	.07	3.60	.06
4	4.32	.12	4.62	.11	4.80	.10	4.80	.08
5	5.40	.15	5.46	.13	5.76	.12	6.00	.10
6	6.84	.19	6.72	.16	7.20	.15	7.20	.12
7	7.92	.22	7.98	.19	8.16	.17	8.40	.14
8	9.00	.25	9.24	.22	9.60	.20	9.60	.16
9	10.08	.28	10.50	.25	10.56	.22	10.80	.18
10	11.16	.31	11.34	.27	12.00	.25	12.00	.20
20	22.68	.63	23.10	.55	24.00	.50	24.60	.41
30	34.20	.95	34.86	.83	36.00	.75	37.20	.62
40	45.72	1.27	46.62	1.11	48.00	1.00	49.80	.83
50	57.24	1.59	58.38	1.39	60.00	1.25	62.40	1.04
60	68.76	1.91	70.14	1.67	72.00	1.50	75.00	1.25
70	80.28	2.23	81.90	1.95	84.00	1.75	87.60	1.46
80	91.80	2.55	93.66	2.23	96.00	2.00	100.20	1.67
90	103.32	2.87	105.42	2.51	108.00	2.25	112.20	1.87
100	114.84	3.19	117.18	2.79	120.00	2.50	124.80	2.08
200	229.68	6.38	234.78	5.59	240.00	5.00	250.20	4.17
300	344.52	9.57	351.96	8.38	360.00	7.50	375.60	6.26
400	459.36	12.76	469.56	11.18	480.00	10.00	501.00	8.35
500	574.20	15.95	587.16	13.98	600.00	12.50	625.80	10.43
600	689.04	19.14	704.34	16.77	720.00	15.00	751.20	12.52
700	804.24	22.34	821.94	19.57	840.00	17.50	876.60	14.61
800	919.08	25.53	939.12	22.36	960.00	20.00	1002.00	16.70
900	1033.92	28.72	1056.72	25.16	1080.00	22.50	1127.40	18.79
1000	1148.76	31.91	1174.32	27.96	1200.00	25.00	1252.20	20.87
1500	1723.32	47.87	1761.48	41.94	1800.00	37.50	1878.60	31.31
2000	2297.88	63.83	2348.64	55.92	2400.00	50.00	2505.00	41.75
2500	2872.44	79.79	2935.80	69.90	3000.00	62.50	3131.40	52.19
3000	3446.64	95.74	3522.96	83.88	3600.48	75.01	3757.80	62.63
3500	4021.20	111.70	4110.12	97.86	4200.48	87.51	4384.20	73.07
4000	4595.76	127.66	4697.28	111.84	4800.48	100.01	5010.60	83.51
4500	5170.32	143.62	5284.44	125.82	5400.48	112.51	5637.00	93.95
5000	5744.88	159.58	5872.02	139.81	6000.48	125.01	6263.40	104.39
5500	6319.08	175.53	6459.18	153.79	6600.96	137.52	6889.80	114.83
6000	6893.64	191.49	7046.34	167.77	7200.96	150.02	7516.20	125.27
6500	7468.20	207.45	7633.50	181.75	7800.96	162.52	8142.60	135.71
7000	8042.76	223.41	8220.66	195.73	8400.96	175.02	8769.00	146.15
7500	8617.32	239.37	8807.82	209.71	9000.96	187.52	9395.40	156.59
8000	9191.52	255.32	9394.98	223.69	9601.44	200.03	10021.80	167.03
8500	9766.08	271.28	9982.14	237.67	10201.44	212.53	10648.20	177.47
9000	10340.64	287.24	10569.30	251.65	10801.44	225.03	11274.60	187.91
10000	11489.76	319.16	11744.04	279.62	12001.44	250.03	12527.40	208.79
11000	12638.52	351.07	12918.36	307.58	13201.92	275.04	13780.20	229.67
12000	13787.64	382.99	14092.68	335.54	14401.92	300.04	15033.00	250.55
13000	14936.76	414.91	15267.00	363.50	15602.40	325.05	16285.80	271.43
14000	16085.52	446.82	16441.74	391.47	16802.40	350.05	17538.60	292.31
15000	17234.64	478.74	17616.06	419.43	18002.40	375.05	18791.40	313.19
16000	18383.40	510.65	18790.38	447.39	19202.88	400.06	20044.20	334.07
17000	19532.52	542.57	19964.70	475.35	20402.88	425.06	21297.00	354.95
18000	20681.64	574.49	21139.02	503.31	21603.36	450.07	22549.80	375.83
19000	21830.40	606.40	22313.76	531.28	22803.36	475.07	23802.60	396.71
20000	22979.52	638.32	23488.08	559.24	24003.36	500.07	25055.40	417.59
21000	24128.64	670.24	24662.40	587.20	25203.84	525.08	26308.20	438.47
22000	25277.40	702.15	25836.72	615.16	26403.84	550.08	27561.00	459.35
23000	26426.52	734.07	27011.04	643.12	27604.32	575.09	28813.80	480.23
24000	27575.28	765.98	28185.78	671.09	28804.32	600.09	30066.60	501.11
25000	28724.40	797.90	29360.10	699.05	30004.32	625.09	31319.40	521.99

9.30% ANNUAL PERCENTAGE RATE

LOAN AMT	12 MONTHS TOTAL NOTE	MONTHLY PAYMENT	18 MONTHS TOTAL NOTE	MONTHLY PAYMENT	24 MONTHS TOTAL NOTE	MONTHLY PAYMENT	30 MONTHS TOTAL NOTE	MONTHLY PAYMENT
1	.96	.08	.90	.05	.96	.04	.90	.03
2	2.04	.17	1.98	.11	2.16	.09	2.10	.07
3	3.12	.26	3.06	.17	3.12	.13	3.30	.11
4	4.20	.35	4.14	.23	4.32	.18	4.20	.14
5	5.16	.43	5.22	.29	5.28	.22	5.40	.18
6	6.24	.52	6.30	.35	6.48	.27	6.60	.22
7	7.32	.61	7.38	.41	7.68	.32	7.80	.26
8	8.40	.70	8.46	.47	8.64	.36	8.70	.29
9	9.36	.78	9.54	.53	9.84	.41	9.90	.33
10	10.44	.87	10.62	.59	10.80	.45	11.10	.37
20	21.00	1.75	21.42	1.19	21.84	.91	22.20	.74
30	31.44	2.62	32.22	1.79	32.88	1.37	33.60	1.12
40	42.00	3.50	42.84	2.38	43.92	1.83	44.70	1.49
50	52.44	4.37	53.64	2.98	54.96	2.29	56.10	1.87
60	63.00	5.25	64.44	3.58	65.76	2.74	67.20	2.24
70	73.56	6.13	75.24	4.18	76.80	3.20	78.60	2.62
80	84.00	7.00	85.86	4.77	87.84	3.66	89.70	2.99
90	94.56	7.88	96.66	5.37	98.88	4.12	101.10	3.37
100	105.00	8.75	107.46	5.97	109.92	4.58	112.20	3.74
200	210.12	17.51	214.92	11.94	219.84	9.16	224.70	7.49
300	315.24	26.27	322.56	17.92	329.76	13.74	337.20	11.24
400	420.36	35.03	430.02	23.89	439.68	18.32	449.70	14.99
500	525.48	43.79	537.48	29.86	549.84	22.91	562.20	18.74
600	630.60	52.55	645.12	35.84	659.76	27.49	674.70	22.49
700	735.72	61.31	752.58	41.81	769.68	32.07	787.20	26.24
800	840.84	70.07	860.04	47.78	879.60	36.65	899.40	29.98
900	945.96	78.83	967.68	53.76	989.76	41.24	1011.90	33.73
1000	1051.08	87.59	1075.14	59.73	1099.68	45.82	1124.40	37.48
1500	1576.56	131.38	1612.80	89.60	1649.52	68.73	1686.90	56.23
2000	2102.16	175.18	2150.46	119.47	2199.36	91.64	2249.10	74.97
2500	2627.64	218.97	2687.94	149.33	2749.20	114.55	2811.30	93.71
3000	3153.24	262.77	3225.60	179.20	3299.04	137.46	3373.80	112.46
3500	3678.72	306.56	3763.26	209.07	3848.88	160.37	3936.00	131.20
4000	4204.32	350.36	4300.92	238.94	4398.96	183.29	4498.20	149.94
4500	4729.80	394.15	4838.40	268.80	4948.80	206.20	5060.70	168.69
5000	5255.04	437.95	5376.06	298.67	5498.64	229.11	5622.90	187.43
5500	5780.88	481.74	5913.72	328.54	6048.48	252.02	6185.10	206.17
6000	6306.48	525.54	6451.38	358.41	6598.32	274.93	6747.60	224.92
6500	6831.96	569.33	6988.86	388.27	7148.16	297.84	7309.80	243.66
7000	7357.56	613.13	7526.52	418.14	7698.00	320.75	7872.00	262.40
7500	7883.04	656.92	8064.18	448.01	8247.84	343.66	8434.50	281.15
8000	8408.64	700.72	8601.84	477.88	8797.92	366.58	8996.70	299.89
8500	8934.24	744.52	9139.32	507.74	9347.76	389.49	9558.90	318.63
9000	9459.72	788.31	9676.98	537.61	9897.60	412.40	10121.40	337.38
10000	10510.80	875.90	10752.30	597.35	10997.28	458.22	11245.80	374.86
11000	11561.88	963.49	11827.44	657.08	12096.96	504.04	12370.50	412.35
12000	12612.96	1051.08	12902.76	716.82	13196.88	549.87	13495.20	449.84
13000	13664.04	1138.67	13977.90	776.55	14296.56	595.69	14619.60	487.32
14000	14715.12	1226.26	15053.22	836.29	15396.24	641.51	15744.30	524.81
15000	15766.20	1313.85	16128.36	896.02	16495.92	687.33	16869.00	562.30
16000	16817.40	1401.45	17203.68	955.76	17595.84	733.16	17993.40	599.78
17000	17868.48	1489.04	18278.82	1015.49	18695.52	778.98	19118.10	637.27
18000	18919.56	1576.63	19354.14	1075.23	19795.20	824.80	20242.80	674.76
19000	19970.64	1664.22	20429.46	1134.97	20894.88	870.62	21367.20	712.24
20000	21021.72	1751.81	21504.60	1194.70	21994.80	916.45	22491.90	749.73
21000	22072.80	1839.40	22579.92	1254.44	23094.48	962.27	23616.60	787.22
22000	23123.88	1926.99	23655.06	1314.17	24194.16	1008.09	24741.00	824.70
23000	24174.96	2014.58	24730.38	1373.91	25293.84	1053.91	25865.70	862.19
24000	25226.04	2102.17	25805.52	1433.64	26393.76	1099.74	26990.40	899.68
25000	26277.12	2189.76	26880.84	1493.38	27493.44	1145.56	28114.80	937.16

ANNUAL PERCENTAGE RATE **9.30%**

LOAN AMT	36 MONTHS TOTAL NOTE	36 MONTHS MONTHLY PAYMENT	42 MONTHS TOTAL NOTE	42 MONTHS MONTHLY PAYMENT	48 MONTHS TOTAL NOTE	48 MONTHS MONTHLY PAYMENT	60 MONTHS TOTAL NOTE	60 MONTHS MONTHLY PAYMENT
1	1.08	.03	.84	.02	.96	.02	1.20	.02
2	2.16	.06	2.10	.05	2.40	.05	2.40	.04
3	3.24	.09	3.36	.08	3.36	.07	3.60	.06
4	4.32	.12	4.62	.11	4.80	.10	4.80	.08
5	5.40	.15	5.46	.13	5.76	.12	6.00	.10
6	6.84	.19	6.72	.16	7.20	.15	7.20	.12
7	7.92	.22	7.98	.19	8.16	.17	8.40	.14
8	9.00	.25	9.24	.22	9.60	.20	9.60	.16
9	10.08	.28	10.50	.25	10.56	.22	10.80	.18
10	11.16	.31	11.34	.27	12.00	.25	12.00	.20
20	22.68	.63	23.10	.55	24.00	.50	24.60	.41
30	34.20	.95	34.86	.83	36.00	.75	37.20	.62
40	45.72	1.27	46.62	1.11	48.00	1.00	49.80	.83
50	57.24	1.59	58.38	1.39	60.00	1.25	62.40	1.04
60	68.76	1.91	70.14	1.67	72.00	1.50	75.00	1.25
70	80.28	2.23	81.90	1.95	84.00	1.75	87.60	1.46
80	91.80	2.55	93.66	2.23	96.00	2.00	100.20	1.67
90	103.32	2.87	105.42	2.51	108.00	2.25	112.80	1.88
100	114.84	3.19	117.18	2.79	120.00	2.50	125.40	2.09
200	229.68	6.38	234.78	5.59	240.00	5.00	250.80	4.18
300	344.88	9.58	352.38	8.39	360.00	7.50	376.20	6.27
400	459.72	12.77	469.98	11.19	480.48	10.01	501.60	8.36
500	574.56	15.96	587.58	13.99	600.48	12.51	627.00	10.45
600	689.76	19.16	705.18	16.79	720.48	15.01	752.40	12.54
700	804.60	22.35	822.36	19.58	840.48	17.51	877.80	14.63
800	919.80	25.55	939.96	22.38	960.96	20.02	1003.20	16.72
900	1034.64	28.74	1057.56	25.18	1080.96	22.52	1128.60	18.81
1000	1149.48	31.93	1175.16	27.98	1200.96	25.02	1254.00	20.90
1500	1724.40	47.90	1762.74	41.97	1801.92	37.54	1881.00	31.35
2000	2299.32	63.87	2350.74	55.97	2402.40	50.05	2508.00	41.80
2500	2874.24	79.84	2938.32	69.96	3002.88	62.56	3135.60	52.26
3000	3449.16	95.81	3525.90	83.95	3603.84	75.08	3762.60	62.71
3500	4024.08	111.78	4113.48	97.94	4204.32	87.59	4389.60	73.16
4000	4599.00	127.75	4701.48	111.94	4805.28	100.11	5016.60	83.61
4500	5173.92	143.72	5289.06	125.93	5405.76	112.62	5643.60	94.06
5000	5748.84	159.69	5876.64	139.92	6006.24	125.13	6271.20	104.52
5500	6323.76	175.66	6464.64	153.92	6607.20	137.65	6898.20	114.97
6000	6898.68	191.63	7052.22	167.91	7207.68	150.16	7525.20	125.42
6500	7473.60	207.60	7639.80	181.90	7808.64	162.68	8152.20	135.87
7000	8048.52	223.57	8227.38	195.89	8409.12	175.19	8779.20	146.32
7500	8623.44	239.54	8815.38	209.89	9009.60	187.70	9406.80	156.78
8000	9198.36	255.51	9402.96	223.88	9610.56	200.22	10033.80	167.23
8500	9773.28	271.48	9990.54	237.87	10211.04	212.73	10660.80	177.68
9000	10348.20	287.45	10578.54	251.87	10811.52	225.24	11287.80	188.13
10000	11498.04	319.39	11753.70	279.85	12012.96	250.27	12542.40	209.04
11000	12647.88	351.33	12929.28	307.84	13214.40	275.30	13796.40	229.94
12000	13797.72	383.27	14104.44	335.82	14415.84	300.33	15051.00	250.85
13000	14947.56	415.21	15280.02	363.81	15617.28	325.36	16305.00	271.75
14000	16097.40	447.15	16455.18	391.79	16818.24	350.38	17559.00	292.65
15000	17247.24	479.09	17630.76	419.78	18019.68	375.41	18813.60	313.56
16000	18397.08	511.03	18806.34	447.77	19221.12	400.44	20067.60	334.46
17000	19546.92	542.97	19981.50	475.75	20422.56	425.47	21322.20	355.37
18000	20696.76	574.91	21157.08	503.74	21623.52	450.49	22576.20	376.27
19000	21846.60	606.85	22332.24	531.72	22824.96	475.52	23830.80	397.18
20000	22996.44	638.79	23507.82	559.71	24026.40	500.55	25084.80	418.08
21000	24146.28	670.73	24682.98	587.69	25227.84	525.58	26338.80	438.98
22000	25295.76	702.66	25858.56	615.68	26429.28	550.61	27593.40	459.89
23000	26445.60	734.60	27034.14	643.67	27630.24	575.63	28847.40	480.79
24000	27595.44	766.54	28209.30	671.65	28831.68	600.66	30102.00	501.70
25000	28745.28	798.48	29384.88	699.64	30033.12	625.69	31356.00	522.60

9.40% ANNUAL PERCENTAGE RATE

LOAN AMT	12 MONTHS TOTAL NOTE	12 MONTHS MONTHLY PAYMENT	18 MONTHS TOTAL NOTE	18 MONTHS MONTHLY PAYMENT	24 MONTHS TOTAL NOTE	24 MONTHS MONTHLY PAYMENT	30 MONTHS TOTAL NOTE	30 MONTHS MONTHLY PAYMENT
1	.96	.08	.90	.05	.96	.04	.90	.03
2	2.04	.17	1.98	.11	2.16	.09	2.10	.07
3	3.12	.26	3.06	.17	3.12	.13	3.30	.11
4	4.20	.35	4.14	.23	4.32	.18	4.50	.15
5	5.16	.43	5.22	.29	5.28	.22	5.40	.18
6	6.24	.52	6.30	.35	6.48	.27	6.60	.22
7	7.32	.61	7.38	.41	7.68	.32	7.80	.26
8	8.40	.70	8.46	.47	8.64	.36	9.00	.30
9	9.36	.78	9.54	.53	9.84	.41	9.90	.33
10	10.44	.87	10.62	.59	10.80	.45	11.10	.37
20	21.00	1.75	21.42	1.19	21.84	.91	22.50	.75
30	31.44	2.62	32.22	1.79	32.88	1.37	33.60	1.12
40	42.00	3.50	43.02	2.39	43.92	1.83	45.00	1.50
50	52.56	4.38	53.64	2.98	54.96	2.29	56.10	1.87
60	63.00	5.25	64.44	3.58	66.00	2.75	67.50	2.25
70	73.56	6.13	75.24	4.18	77.04	3.21	78.60	2.62
80	84.12	7.01	86.04	4.78	87.84	3.66	90.00	3.00
90	94.56	7.88	96.84	5.38	98.88	4.12	101.10	3.37
100	105.12	8.76	107.46	5.97	109.92	4.58	112.50	3.75
200	210.24	17.52	215.10	11.95	220.08	9.17	225.00	7.50
300	315.48	26.29	322.74	17.93	330.24	13.76	337.50	11.25
400	420.60	35.05	430.38	23.91	440.16	18.34	450.30	15.01
500	525.72	43.81	538.02	29.89	550.32	22.93	562.80	18.76
600	630.96	52.58	645.48	35.86	660.48	27.52	675.30	22.51
700	736.08	61.34	753.12	41.84	770.40	32.10	788.10	26.27
800	841.20	70.10	860.76	47.82	880.56	36.69	900.60	30.02
900	946.44	78.87	968.40	53.80	990.72	41.28	1013.10	33.77
1000	1051.56	87.63	1076.04	59.78	1100.64	45.86	1125.90	37.53
1500	1577.40	131.45	1614.06	89.67	1651.20	68.80	1688.70	56.29
2000	2103.24	175.27	2152.08	119.56	2201.52	91.73	2251.80	75.06
2500	2629.08	219.09	2690.10	149.45	2752.08	114.67	2814.90	93.83
3000	3154.92	262.91	3228.12	179.34	3302.40	137.60	3377.70	112.59
3500	3680.64	306.72	3766.14	209.23	3852.72	160.53	3940.80	131.36
4000	4206.48	350.54	4304.16	239.12	4403.28	183.47	4503.90	150.13
4500	4732.32	394.36	4842.18	269.01	4953.60	206.40	5066.70	168.89
5000	5258.16	438.18	5380.20	298.90	5504.16	229.34	5629.80	187.66
5500	5784.00	482.00	5918.22	328.79	6054.48	252.27	6192.90	206.43
6000	6309.84	525.82	6456.24	358.68	6605.04	275.21	6755.70	225.19
6500	6835.68	569.64	6994.26	388.57	7155.36	298.14	7318.80	243.96
7000	7361.40	613.45	7532.28	418.46	7705.68	321.07	7881.90	262.73
7500	7887.24	657.27	8070.30	448.35	8256.24	344.01	8444.70	281.49
8000	8413.08	701.09	8608.32	478.24	8806.56	366.94	9007.80	300.26
8500	8938.92	744.91	9146.52	508.14	9357.12	389.88	9570.90	319.03
9000	9464.76	788.73	9684.54	538.03	9907.44	412.81	10133.70	337.79
10000	10516.44	876.37	10760.58	597.81	11008.32	458.68	11259.90	375.33
11000	11568.00	964.00	11836.62	657.59	12109.20	504.55	12385.80	412.86
12000	12619.68	1051.64	12912.66	717.37	13210.08	550.42	13511.70	450.39
13000	13671.36	1139.28	13988.70	777.15	14310.96	596.29	14637.60	487.92
14000	14722.92	1226.91	15064.74	836.93	15411.60	642.15	15763.80	525.46
15000	15774.60	1314.55	16140.78	896.71	16512.48	688.02	16889.70	562.99
16000	16826.28	1402.19	17216.82	956.49	17613.36	733.89	18015.60	600.52
17000	17877.96	1489.83	18293.04	1016.28	18714.24	779.76	19141.80	638.06
18000	18929.52	1577.46	19369.08	1076.06	19815.12	825.63	20267.70	675.59
19000	19981.20	1665.10	20445.12	1135.84	20916.00	871.50	21393.60	713.12
20000	21032.88	1752.74	21521.16	1195.62	22016.64	917.36	22519.80	750.66
21000	22084.44	1840.37	22597.20	1255.40	23117.52	963.23	23645.70	788.19
22000	23136.12	1928.01	23673.24	1315.18	24218.40	1009.10	24771.60	825.72
23000	24187.80	2015.65	24749.28	1374.96	25319.28	1054.97	25897.80	863.26
24000	25239.36	2103.28	25825.32	1434.74	26420.16	1100.84	27023.70	900.79
25000	26291.04	2190.92	26901.36	1494.52	27521.04	1146.71	28149.60	938.32

ANNUAL PERCENTAGE RATE **9.40%**

LOAN AMT	36 MONTHS TOTAL NOTE	MONTHLY PAYMENT	42 MONTHS TOTAL NOTE	MONTHLY PAYMENT	48 MONTHS TOTAL NOTE	MONTHLY PAYMENT	60 MONTHS TOTAL NOTE	MONTHLY PAYMENT
1	1.08	.03	.84	.02	.96	.02	1.20	.02
2	2.16	.06	2.10	.05	2.40	.05	2.40	.04
3	3.24	.09	3.36	.08	3.36	.07	3.60	.06
4	4.32	.12	4.62	.11	4.80	.10	4.80	.08
5	5.40	.15	5.88	.14	5.76	.12	6.00	.10
6	6.84	.19	6.72	.16	7.20	.15	7.20	.12
7	7.92	.22	7.98	.19	8.16	.17	8.40	.14
8	9.00	.25	9.24	.22	9.60	.20	9.60	.16
9	10.08	.28	10.50	.25	10.56	.22	10.80	.18
10	11.16	.31	11.76	.28	12.00	.25	12.00	.20
20	22.68	.63	23.52	.56	24.00	.50	24.60	.41
30	34.20	.95	35.28	.84	36.00	.75	37.20	.62
40	45.72	1.27	47.04	1.12	48.00	1.00	49.80	.83
50	57.24	1.59	58.80	1.40	60.00	1.25	62.40	1.04
60	68.76	1.91	70.56	1.68	72.00	1.50	75.00	1.25
70	80.28	2.23	82.32	1.96	84.00	1.75	87.60	1.46
80	91.80	2.55	94.08	2.24	96.00	2.00	100.20	1.67
90	103.32	2.87	105.84	2.52	108.00	2.25	112.80	1.88
100	114.84	3.19	117.60	2.80	120.00	2.50	125.40	2.09
200	230.04	6.39	235.20	5.60	240.48	5.01	251.40	4.19
300	345.24	9.59	352.80	8.40	360.96	7.52	376.80	6.28
400	460.44	12.79	470.82	11.21	481.44	10.03	502.80	8.38
500	575.64	15.99	588.42	14.01	601.44	12.53	628.20	10.47
600	690.84	19.19	706.02	16.81	721.92	15.04	754.20	12.57
700	806.04	22.39	824.04	19.62	842.40	17.55	879.60	14.66
800	920.88	25.58	941.64	22.42	962.88	20.06	1005.60	16.76
900	1036.08	28.78	1059.24	25.22	1082.88	22.56	1131.00	18.85
1000	1151.28	31.98	1177.26	28.03	1203.36	25.07	1257.00	20.95
1500	1726.92	47.97	1765.68	42.04	1805.28	37.61	1885.20	31.42
2000	2302.92	63.97	2354.52	56.06	2407.20	50.15	2514.00	41.90
2500	2878.56	79.96	2943.36	70.08	3008.64	62.68	3142.80	52.38
3000	3454.20	95.95	3531.78	84.09	3610.56	75.22	3771.00	62.85
3500	4030.20	111.95	4120.62	98.11	4212.48	87.76	4399.80	73.33
4000	4605.84	127.94	4709.46	112.13	4814.40	100.30	5028.60	83.81
4500	5181.48	143.93	5297.88	126.14	5415.84	112.83	5656.80	94.28
5000	5757.48	159.93	5886.72	140.16	6017.76	125.37	6285.60	104.76
5500	6333.12	175.92	6475.56	154.18	6619.68	137.91	6914.40	115.24
6000	6908.76	191.91	7063.98	168.19	7221.60	150.45	7542.60	125.71
6500	7484.76	207.91	7652.82	182.21	7823.52	162.99	8171.40	136.19
7000	8060.40	223.90	8241.66	196.23	8424.96	175.52	8800.20	146.67
7500	8636.04	239.89	8830.08	210.24	9026.88	188.06	9428.40	157.14
8000	9211.68	255.88	9418.92	224.26	9628.80	200.60	10057.20	167.62
8500	9787.68	271.88	10007.34	238.27	10230.72	213.14	10686.00	178.10
9000	10363.32	287.87	10596.18	252.29	10832.16	225.67	11314.20	188.57
10000	11514.96	319.86	11773.44	280.32	12036.00	250.75	12571.80	209.53
11000	12666.24	351.84	12951.12	308.36	13239.36	275.82	13828.80	230.48
12000	13817.88	383.83	14128.38	336.39	14443.20	300.90	15085.80	251.43
13000	14969.52	415.82	15305.64	364.42	15647.04	325.98	16342.80	272.38
14000	16120.80	447.80	16483.32	392.46	16850.40	351.05	17600.40	293.34
15000	17272.44	479.79	17660.58	420.49	18054.24	376.13	18857.40	314.29
16000	18423.72	511.77	18837.84	448.52	19257.60	401.20	20114.40	335.24
17000	19575.36	543.76	20015.10	476.55	20461.44	426.28	21372.00	356.20
18000	20727.00	575.75	21192.78	504.59	21664.80	451.35	22629.00	377.15
19000	21878.28	607.73	22370.04	532.62	22868.64	476.43	23886.00	398.10
20000	23029.92	639.72	23547.30	560.65	24072.00	501.50	25143.60	419.06
21000	24181.56	671.71	24724.98	588.69	25275.84	526.58	26400.60	440.01
22000	25332.84	703.69	25902.24	616.72	26479.20	551.65	27657.60	460.96
23000	26484.48	735.68	27079.50	644.75	27683.04	576.73	28914.60	481.91
24000	27635.76	767.66	28256.76	672.78	28886.40	601.80	30172.20	502.87
25000	28787.40	799.65	29434.44	700.82	30090.24	626.88	31429.20	523.82

9.50% ANNUAL PERCENTAGE RATE

LOAN AMT	12 MONTHS TOTAL NOTE	12 MONTHS MONTHLY PAYMENT	18 MONTHS TOTAL NOTE	18 MONTHS MONTHLY PAYMENT	24 MONTHS TOTAL NOTE	24 MONTHS MONTHLY PAYMENT	30 MONTHS TOTAL NOTE	30 MONTHS MONTHLY PAYMENT
1	.96	.08	.90	.05	.96	.04	.90	.03
2	2.04	.17	1.98	.11	2.16	.09	2.10	.07
3	3.12	.26	3.06	.17	3.12	.13	3.30	.11
4	4.20	.35	4.14	.23	4.32	.18	4.50	.15
5	5.16	.43	5.22	.29	5.28	.22	5.40	.18
6	6.24	.52	6.30	.35	6.48	.27	6.60	.22
7	7.32	.61	7.38	.41	7.68	.32	7.80	.26
8	8.40	.70	8.46	.47	8.64	.36	9.00	.30
9	9.36	.78	9.54	.53	9.84	.41	9.90	.33
10	10.44	.87	10.62	.59	10.80	.45	11.10	.37
20	21.00	1.75	21.42	1.19	21.84	.91	22.50	.75
30	31.56	2.63	32.22	1.79	32.88	1.37	33.60	1.12
40	42.00	3.50	43.02	2.39	43.92	1.83	45.00	1.50
50	52.56	4.38	53.82	2.99	54.96	2.29	56.10	1.87
60	63.12	5.26	64.44	3.58	66.00	2.75	67.50	2.25
70	73.56	6.13	75.24	4.18	77.04	3.21	78.90	2.63
80	84.12	7.01	86.04	4.78	88.08	3.67	90.00	3.00
90	94.68	7.89	96.84	5.38	99.12	4.13	101.40	3.38
100	105.12	8.76	107.64	5.98	110.16	4.59	112.50	3.75
200	210.36	17.53	215.28	11.96	220.32	9.18	225.30	7.51
300	315.60	26.30	322.92	17.94	330.48	13.77	338.10	11.27
400	420.84	35.07	430.74	23.93	440.64	18.36	450.90	15.03
500	526.08	43.84	538.38	29.91	550.80	22.95	563.40	18.78
600	631.32	52.61	646.02	35.89	660.96	27.54	676.20	22.54
700	736.44	61.37	753.66	41.87	771.36	32.14	789.00	26.30
800	841.68	70.14	861.48	47.86	881.52	36.73	901.80	30.06
900	946.92	78.91	969.12	53.84	991.68	41.32	1014.60	33.82
1000	1052.16	87.68	1076.76	59.82	1101.84	45.91	1127.10	37.57
1500	1578.24	131.52	1615.32	89.74	1652.88	68.87	1690.80	56.36
2000	2104.32	175.36	2153.70	119.65	2203.68	91.82	2254.50	75.15
2500	2630.40	219.20	2692.08	149.56	2754.72	114.78	2818.20	93.94
3000	3156.60	263.05	3230.64	179.48	3305.76	137.74	3381.90	112.73
3500	3682.68	306.89	3769.02	209.39	3856.80	160.70	3945.60	131.52
4000	4208.76	350.73	4307.40	239.30	4407.60	183.65	4509.30	150.31
4500	4734.84	394.57	4845.96	269.22	4958.64	206.61	5073.00	169.10
5000	5260.92	438.41	5384.34	299.13	5509.68	229.57	5636.70	187.89
5500	5787.00	482.25	5922.72	329.04	6060.48	252.52	6200.40	206.68
6000	6313.20	526.10	6461.28	358.96	6611.52	275.48	6764.10	225.47
6500	6839.28	569.94	6999.66	388.87	7162.56	298.44	7327.80	244.26
7000	7365.36	613.78	7538.04	418.78	7713.60	321.40	7891.50	263.05
7500	7891.44	657.62	8076.60	448.70	8264.40	344.35	8455.20	281.84
8000	8417.52	701.46	8614.98	478.61	8815.44	367.31	9018.90	300.63
8500	8943.60	745.30	9153.54	508.53	9366.48	390.27	9582.60	319.42
9000	9469.80	789.15	9691.92	538.44	9917.52	413.23	10146.30	338.21
10000	10521.96	876.83	10768.86	598.27	11019.36	459.14	11273.70	375.79
11000	11574.12	964.51	11845.62	658.09	12121.20	505.05	12401.10	413.37
12000	12626.40	1052.20	12922.56	717.92	13223.28	550.97	13528.50	450.95
13000	13678.56	1139.88	13999.50	777.75	14325.12	596.88	14655.90	488.53
14000	14730.72	1227.56	15076.26	837.57	15427.20	642.80	15783.30	526.11
15000	15783.00	1315.25	16153.20	897.40	16529.04	688.71	16910.70	563.69
16000	16835.16	1402.93	17230.14	957.23	17631.12	734.63	18037.80	601.26
17000	17887.32	1490.61	18307.08	1017.06	18732.96	780.54	19165.20	638.84
18000	18939.60	1578.30	19383.84	1076.88	19835.04	826.46	20292.60	676.42
19000	19991.76	1665.98	20460.78	1136.71	20936.88	872.37	21420.00	714.00
20000	21044.04	1753.67	21537.72	1196.54	22038.72	918.28	22547.40	751.58
21000	22096.20	1841.35	22614.48	1256.36	23140.80	964.20	23674.80	789.16
22000	23148.36	1929.03	23691.42	1316.19	24242.64	1010.11	24802.20	826.74
23000	24200.64	2016.72	24768.36	1376.02	25344.72	1056.03	25929.60	864.32
24000	25252.80	2104.40	25845.30	1435.85	26446.56	1101.94	27057.00	901.90
25000	26304.96	2192.08	26922.06	1495.67	27548.64	1147.86	28184.40	939.48

ANNUAL PERCENTAGE RATE **9.50%**

LOAN AMT	36 MONTHS TOTAL NOTE	36 MONTHS MONTHLY PAYMENT	42 MONTHS TOTAL NOTE	42 MONTHS MONTHLY PAYMENT	48 MONTHS TOTAL NOTE	48 MONTHS MONTHLY PAYMENT	60 MONTHS TOTAL NOTE	60 MONTHS MONTHLY PAYMENT
1	1.08	.03	.84	.02	.96	.02	1.20	.02
2	2.16	.06	2.10	.05	2.40	.05	2.40	.04
3	3.24	.09	3.36	.08	3.36	.07	3.60	.06
4	4.32	.12	4.62	.11	4.80	.10	4.80	.08
5	5.76	.16	5.88	.14	5.76	.12	6.00	.10
6	6.84	.19	6.72	.16	7.20	.15	7.20	.12
7	7.92	.22	7.98	.19	8.16	.17	8.40	.14
8	9.00	.25	9.24	.22	9.60	.20	9.60	.16
9	10.08	.28	10.50	.25	10.56	.22	10.80	.18
10	11.52	.32	11.76	.28	12.00	.25	12.60	.21
20	23.04	.64	23.52	.56	24.00	.50	25.20	.42
30	34.56	.96	35.28	.84	36.00	.75	37.80	.63
40	46.08	1.28	47.04	1.12	48.00	1.00	50.40	.84
50	57.60	1.60	58.80	1.40	60.00	1.25	63.00	1.05
60	69.12	1.92	70.56	1.68	72.00	1.50	75.60	1.26
70	80.64	2.24	82.32	1.96	84.00	1.75	88.20	1.47
80	92.16	2.56	94.08	2.24	96.00	2.00	100.80	1.68
90	103.68	2.88	105.84	2.52	108.48	2.26	113.40	1.89
100	115.20	3.20	117.60	2.80	120.48	2.51	126.00	2.10
200	230.40	6.40	235.62	5.61	240.96	5.02	252.00	4.20
300	345.60	9.60	353.64	8.42	361.44	7.53	378.00	6.30
400	461.16	12.81	471.66	11.23	481.92	10.04	504.00	8.40
500	576.36	16.01	589.68	14.04	602.88	12.56	630.00	10.50
600	691.56	19.21	707.28	16.84	723.36	15.07	756.00	12.60
700	807.12	22.42	825.30	19.65	843.84	17.58	882.00	14.70
800	922.32	25.62	943.32	22.46	964.32	20.09	1008.00	16.80
900	1037.52	28.82	1061.34	25.27	1085.28	22.61	1134.00	18.90
1000	1153.08	32.03	1179.36	28.08	1205.76	25.12	1260.00	21.00
1500	1729.44	48.04	1769.04	42.12	1808.64	37.68	1890.00	31.50
2000	2306.16	64.06	2358.72	56.16	2411.52	50.24	2520.00	42.00
2500	2882.88	80.08	2948.40	70.20	3014.40	62.80	3150.00	52.50
3000	3459.24	96.09	3538.08	84.24	3617.28	75.36	3780.00	63.00
3500	4035.96	112.11	4127.76	98.28	4220.64	87.93	4410.00	73.50
4000	4612.68	128.13	4717.44	112.32	4823.52	100.49	5040.00	84.00
4500	5189.04	144.14	5307.12	126.36	5426.40	113.05	5670.00	94.50
5000	5765.76	160.16	5896.80	140.40	6029.28	125.61	6300.00	105.00
5500	6342.48	176.18	6486.48	154.44	6632.16	138.17	6930.60	115.51
6000	6918.84	192.19	7076.16	168.48	7235.04	150.73	7560.60	126.01
6500	7495.56	208.21	7665.84	182.52	7838.40	163.30	8190.60	136.51
7000	8072.28	224.23	8255.52	196.56	8441.28	175.86	8820.60	147.01
7500	8648.64	240.24	8845.20	210.60	9044.16	188.42	9450.60	157.51
8000	9225.36	256.26	9434.88	224.64	9647.04	200.98	10080.60	168.01
8500	9802.08	272.28	10024.56	238.68	10249.92	213.54	10710.60	178.51
9000	10378.44	288.29	10614.24	252.72	10852.80	226.10	11340.60	189.01
10000	11531.52	320.32	11793.60	280.80	12059.04	251.23	12600.60	210.01
11000	12684.96	352.36	12972.96	308.88	13264.80	276.35	13861.20	231.02
12000	13838.04	384.39	14152.32	336.96	14470.56	301.47	15121.20	252.02
13000	14991.12	416.42	15331.68	365.04	15676.80	326.60	16381.20	273.02
14000	16144.56	448.46	16511.04	393.12	16882.56	351.72	17641.20	294.02
15000	17297.64	480.49	17690.40	421.20	18088.32	376.84	18901.20	315.02
16000	18450.72	512.52	18869.76	449.28	19294.56	401.97	20161.20	336.02
17000	19604.16	544.56	20049.12	477.36	20500.32	427.09	21421.80	357.03
18000	20757.24	576.59	21228.48	505.44	21706.08	452.21	22681.80	378.03
19000	21910.32	608.62	22407.84	533.52	22911.84	477.33	23941.80	399.03
20000	23063.40	640.65	23587.20	561.60	24118.08	502.46	25201.80	420.03
21000	24216.84	672.69	24766.56	589.68	25323.84	527.58	26461.80	441.03
22000	25369.92	704.72	25945.92	617.76	26529.60	552.70	27722.40	462.04
23000	26523.00	736.75	27125.28	645.84	27735.84	577.83	28982.40	483.04
24000	27676.44	768.79	28304.64	673.92	28941.60	602.95	30242.40	504.04
25000	28829.52	800.82	29484.00	702.00	30147.36	628.07	31502.40	525.04

9.60% ANNUAL PERCENTAGE RATE

LOAN AMT	12 MONTHS TOTAL NOTE	12 MONTHS MONTHLY PAYMENT	18 MONTHS TOTAL NOTE	18 MONTHS MONTHLY PAYMENT	24 MONTHS TOTAL NOTE	24 MONTHS MONTHLY PAYMENT	30 MONTHS TOTAL NOTE	30 MONTHS MONTHLY PAYMENT
1	.96	.08	.90	.05	.96	.04	.90	.03
2	2.04	.17	1.98	.11	2.16	.09	2.10	.07
3	3.12	.26	3.06	.17	3.12	.13	3.30	.11
4	4.20	.35	4.14	.23	4.32	.18	4.50	.15
5	5.16	.43	5.22	.29	5.28	.22	5.40	.18
6	6.24	.52	6.30	.35	6.48	.27	6.60	.22
7	7.32	.61	7.38	.41	7.68	.32	7.80	.26
8	8.40	.70	8.46	.47	8.64	.36	9.00	.30
9	9.36	.78	9.54	.53	9.84	.41	9.90	.33
10	10.44	.87	10.62	.59	10.80	.45	11.10	.37
20	21.00	1.75	21.42	1.19	21.84	.91	22.50	.75
30	31.56	2.63	32.22	1.79	32.88	1.37	33.60	1.12
40	42.00	3.50	43.02	2.39	43.92	1.83	45.00	1.50
50	52.56	4.38	53.82	2.99	54.96	2.29	56.40	1.88
60	63.12	5.26	64.62	3.59	66.00	2.75	67.50	2.25
70	73.68	6.14	75.42	4.19	77.04	3.21	78.90	2.63
80	84.12	7.01	86.04	4.78	88.08	3.67	90.30	3.01
90	94.68	7.89	96.84	5.38	99.12	4.13	101.40	3.38
100	105.24	8.77	107.64	5.98	110.16	4.59	112.80	3.76
200	210.48	17.54	215.46	11.97	220.56	9.19	225.60	7.52
300	315.72	26.31	323.28	17.96	330.72	13.78	338.40	11.28
400	421.08	35.09	430.92	23.94	441.12	18.38	451.50	15.05
500	526.32	43.86	538.74	29.93	551.52	22.98	564.30	18.81
600	631.56	52.63	646.56	35.92	661.68	27.57	677.10	22.57
700	736.92	61.41	754.38	41.91	772.08	32.17	789.90	26.33
800	842.16	70.18	862.02	47.89	882.24	36.76	903.00	30.10
900	947.40	78.95	969.84	53.88	992.64	41.36	1015.80	33.86
1000	1052.64	87.72	1077.66	59.87	1103.04	45.96	1128.60	37.62
1500	1579.08	131.59	1616.40	89.80	1654.56	68.94	1692.90	56.43
2000	2105.40	175.45	2155.32	119.74	2206.08	91.92	2257.50	75.25
2500	2631.84	219.32	2694.24	149.68	2757.60	114.90	2821.80	94.06
3000	3158.16	263.18	3232.98	179.61	3309.12	137.88	3386.10	112.87
3500	3684.60	307.05	3771.90	209.55	3860.64	160.86	3950.40	131.68
4000	4210.92	350.91	4310.82	239.49	4412.16	183.84	4515.00	150.50
4500	4737.36	394.78	4849.56	269.42	4963.68	206.82	5079.30	169.31
5000	5263.68	438.64	5388.48	299.36	5515.20	229.80	5643.60	188.12
5500	5790.12	482.51	5927.40	329.30	6066.72	252.78	6208.20	206.94
6000	6316.44	526.37	6466.14	359.23	6618.24	275.76	6772.50	225.75
6500	6842.88	570.24	7005.06	389.17	7169.76	298.74	7336.80	244.56
7000	7369.20	614.10	7543.98	419.11	7721.28	321.72	7901.10	263.37
7500	7895.64	657.97	8082.72	449.04	8272.80	344.70	8465.70	282.19
8000	8421.96	701.83	8621.64	478.98	8824.32	367.68	9030.00	301.00
8500	8948.40	745.70	9160.56	508.92	9375.84	390.66	9594.30	319.81
9000	9474.72	789.56	9699.30	538.85	9927.36	413.64	10158.90	338.63
10000	10527.48	877.29	10777.14	598.73	11030.40	459.60	11287.50	376.25
11000	11580.24	965.02	11854.80	658.60	12133.44	505.56	12416.40	413.88
12000	12633.00	1052.75	12932.46	718.47	13236.48	551.52	13545.00	451.50
13000	13685.76	1140.48	14010.12	778.34	14339.52	597.48	14673.90	489.13
14000	14738.52	1228.21	15087.96	838.22	15442.56	643.44	15802.50	526.75
15000	15791.28	1315.94	16165.62	898.09	16545.60	689.40	16931.40	564.38
16000	16844.04	1403.67	17243.28	957.96	17648.64	735.36	18060.30	602.01
17000	17896.80	1491.40	18321.12	1017.84	18751.68	781.32	19188.90	639.63
18000	18949.56	1579.13	19398.78	1077.71	19854.72	827.28	20317.80	677.26
19000	20002.32	1666.86	20476.44	1137.58	20957.76	873.24	21446.40	714.88
20000	21055.08	1754.59	21554.28	1197.46	22061.04	919.21	22575.30	752.51
21000	22107.84	1842.32	22631.94	1257.33	23164.08	965.17	23703.90	790.13
22000	23160.60	1930.05	23709.60	1317.20	24267.12	1011.13	24832.80	827.76
23000	24213.36	2017.78	24787.44	1377.08	25370.16	1057.09	25961.70	865.39
24000	25266.12	2105.51	25865.10	1436.95	26473.20	1103.05	27090.30	903.01
25000	26318.88	2193.24	26942.76	1496.82	27576.24	1149.01	28219.20	940.64

ANNUAL PERCENTAGE RATE **9.60%**

LOAN AMT	36 MONTHS TOTAL NOTE	36 MONTHS MONTHLY PAYMENT	42 MONTHS TOTAL NOTE	42 MONTHS MONTHLY PAYMENT	48 MONTHS TOTAL NOTE	48 MONTHS MONTHLY PAYMENT	60 MONTHS TOTAL NOTE	60 MONTHS MONTHLY PAYMENT
1	1.08	.03	.84	.02	.96	.02	1.20	.02
2	2.16	.06	2.10	.05	2.40	.05	2.40	.04
3	3.24	.09	3.36	.08	3.36	.07	3.60	.06
4	4.32	.12	4.62	.11	4.80	.10	4.80	.08
5	5.76	.16	5.88	.14	5.76	.12	6.00	.10
6	6.84	.19	6.72	.16	7.20	.15	7.20	.12
7	7.92	.22	7.98	.19	8.16	.17	8.40	.14
8	9.00	.25	9.24	.22	9.60	.20	9.60	.16
9	10.08	.28	10.50	.25	10.56	.22	10.80	.18
10	11.52	.32	11.76	.28	12.00	.25	12.60	.21
20	23.04	.64	23.52	.56	24.00	.50	25.20	.42
30	34.56	.96	35.28	.84	36.00	.75	37.80	.63
40	46.08	1.28	47.04	1.12	48.00	1.00	50.40	.84
50	57.60	1.60	58.80	1.40	60.00	1.25	63.00	1.05
60	69.12	1.92	70.56	1.68	72.48	1.51	75.60	1.26
70	80.64	2.24	82.32	1.96	84.48	1.76	88.20	1.47
80	92.16	2.56	94.50	2.25	96.48	2.01	100.80	1.68
90	103.68	2.88	106.26	2.53	108.48	2.26	113.40	1.89
100	115.20	3.20	118.02	2.81	120.48	2.51	126.00	2.10
200	230.76	6.41	236.04	5.62	241.44	5.03	252.60	4.21
300	346.32	9.62	354.06	8.43	362.40	7.55	378.60	6.31
400	461.88	12.83	472.50	11.25	482.88	10.06	505.20	8.42
500	577.08	16.03	590.52	14.06	603.84	12.58	631.20	10.52
600	692.64	19.24	708.54	16.87	724.80	15.10	757.80	12.63
700	808.20	22.45	826.56	19.68	845.28	17.61	883.80	14.73
800	923.76	25.66	945.00	22.50	966.24	20.13	1010.40	16.84
900	1039.32	28.87	1063.02	25.31	1087.20	22.65	1136.40	18.94
1000	1154.52	32.07	1181.04	28.12	1208.16	25.17	1263.00	21.05
1500	1731.96	48.11	1771.98	42.19	1812.00	37.75	1894.20	31.57
2000	2309.40	64.15	2362.50	56.25	2416.32	50.34	2526.00	42.10
2500	2886.84	80.19	2953.02	70.31	3020.16	62.92	3157.20	52.62
3000	3464.28	96.23	3543.96	84.38	3624.48	75.51	3789.00	63.15
3500	4041.72	112.27	4134.48	98.44	4228.32	88.09	4420.20	73.67
4000	4619.16	128.31	4725.00	112.50	4832.64	100.68	5052.00	84.20
4500	5196.60	144.35	5315.94	126.57	5436.48	113.26	5683.20	94.72
5000	5774.04	160.39	5906.46	140.63	6040.80	125.85	6315.00	105.25
5500	6351.48	176.43	6497.40	154.70	6645.12	138.44	6946.20	115.77
6000	6928.92	192.47	7087.92	168.76	7248.96	151.02	7578.00	126.30
6500	7506.36	208.51	7678.44	182.82	7853.28	163.61	8209.20	136.82
7000	8083.80	224.55	8269.38	196.89	8457.12	176.19	8841.00	147.35
7500	8661.24	240.59	8859.90	210.95	9061.44	188.78	9472.80	157.88
8000	9238.68	256.63	9450.42	225.01	9665.28	201.36	10104.00	168.40
8500	9816.12	272.67	10041.36	239.08	10269.60	213.95	10735.80	178.93
9000	10393.56	288.71	10631.88	253.14	10873.44	226.53	11367.00	189.45
10000	11548.44	320.79	11813.34	281.27	12081.60	251.70	12630.00	210.50
11000	12703.32	352.87	12994.80	309.40	13290.24	276.88	13893.00	231.55
12000	13858.20	384.95	14175.84	337.52	14498.40	302.05	15156.00	252.60
13000	15013.08	417.03	15357.30	365.65	15706.56	327.22	16419.00	273.65
14000	16167.96	449.11	16538.76	393.78	16914.72	352.39	17682.60	294.71
15000	17322.84	481.19	17719.80	421.90	18122.88	377.56	18945.60	315.76
16000	18477.72	513.27	18901.26	450.03	19331.04	402.73	20208.60	336.81
17000	19632.60	545.35	20082.72	478.16	20539.20	427.90	21471.60	357.86
18000	20787.48	577.43	21264.18	506.29	21747.36	453.07	22734.60	378.91
19000	21942.36	609.51	22445.22	534.41	22955.52	478.24	23997.60	399.96
20000	23097.24	641.59	23626.68	562.54	24163.68	503.41	25260.60	421.01
21000	24252.12	673.67	24808.14	590.67	25371.84	528.58	26523.60	442.06
22000	25407.00	705.75	25989.60	618.80	26580.48	553.76	27786.60	463.11
23000	26561.88	737.83	27170.64	646.92	27788.64	578.93	29049.60	484.16
24000	27716.76	769.91	28352.10	675.05	28996.80	604.10	30312.60	505.21
25000	28871.64	801.99	29533.56	703.18	30204.96	629.27	31575.60	526.26

9.70% ANNUAL PERCENTAGE RATE

LOAN AMT	12 MONTHS TOTAL NOTE	MONTHLY PAYMENT	18 MONTHS TOTAL NOTE	MONTHLY PAYMENT	24 MONTHS TOTAL NOTE	MONTHLY PAYMENT	30 MONTHS TOTAL NOTE	MONTHLY PAYMENT
1	.96	.08	.90	.05	.96	.04	.90	.03
2	2.04	.17	1.98	.11	2.16	.09	2.10	.07
3	3.12	.26	3.06	.17	3.12	.13	3.30	.11
4	4.20	.35	4.14	.23	4.32	.18	4.50	.15
5	5.16	.43	5.22	.29	5.52	.23	5.40	.18
6	6.24	.52	6.30	.35	6.48	.27	6.60	.22
7	7.32	.61	7.38	.41	7.68	.32	7.80	.26
8	8.40	.70	8.46	.47	8.64	.36	9.00	.30
9	9.36	.78	9.54	.53	9.84	.41	9.90	.33
10	10.44	.87	10.62	.59	11.04	.46	11.10	.37
20	21.00	1.75	21.42	1.19	22.08	.92	22.50	.75
30	31.56	2.63	32.22	1.79	33.12	1.38	33.90	1.13
40	42.12	3.51	43.02	2.39	44.16	1.84	45.00	1.50
50	52.56	4.38	53.82	2.99	55.20	2.30	56.40	1.88
60	63.12	5.26	64.62	3.59	66.24	2.76	67.80	2.26
70	73.68	6.14	75.42	4.19	77.28	3.22	78.90	2.63
80	84.24	7.02	86.22	4.79	88.32	3.68	90.30	3.01
90	94.68	7.89	97.02	5.39	99.36	4.14	101.70	3.39
100	105.24	8.77	107.82	5.99	110.40	4.60	112.80	3.76
200	210.60	17.55	215.64	11.98	220.80	9.20	225.90	7.53
300	315.96	26.33	323.46	17.97	331.20	13.80	339.00	11.30
400	421.32	35.11	431.28	23.96	441.60	18.40	451.80	15.06
500	526.56	43.88	539.10	29.95	552.00	23.00	564.90	18.83
600	631.92	52.66	647.10	35.95	662.40	27.60	678.00	22.60
700	737.28	61.44	754.92	41.94	772.80	32.20	791.10	26.37
800	842.64	70.22	862.74	47.93	883.20	36.80	903.90	30.13
900	947.88	78.99	970.56	53.92	993.60	41.40	1017.00	33.90
1000	1053.24	87.77	1078.38	59.91	1104.00	46.00	1130.10	37.67
1500	1579.92	131.66	1617.66	89.87	1656.00	69.00	1695.00	56.50
2000	2106.60	175.55	2156.94	119.83	2208.24	92.01	2260.20	75.34
2500	2633.28	219.44	2696.22	149.79	2760.24	115.01	2825.40	94.18
3000	3159.84	263.32	3235.50	179.75	3312.24	138.01	3390.30	113.01
3500	3686.52	307.21	3774.78	209.71	3864.48	161.02	3955.50	131.85
4000	4213.20	351.10	4314.06	239.67	4416.48	184.02	4520.40	150.68
4500	4739.88	394.99	4853.34	269.63	4968.48	207.02	5085.60	169.52
5000	5266.56	438.88	5392.62	299.59	5520.72	230.03	5650.80	188.36
5500	5793.24	482.77	5931.90	329.55	6072.72	253.03	6215.70	207.19
6000	6319.80	526.65	6471.18	359.51	6624.72	276.03	6780.90	226.03
6500	6846.48	570.54	7010.46	389.47	7176.96	299.04	7345.80	244.86
7000	7373.16	614.43	7549.74	419.43	7728.96	322.04	7911.00	263.70
7500	7899.84	658.32	8089.02	449.39	8280.96	345.04	8476.20	282.54
8000	8426.52	702.21	8628.30	479.35	8833.20	368.05	9041.10	301.37
8500	8953.08	746.09	9167.58	509.31	9385.20	391.05	9606.30	320.21
9000	9479.76	789.98	9706.86	539.27	9937.20	414.05	10171.20	339.04
10000	10533.12	877.76	10785.42	599.19	11041.44	460.06	11301.60	376.72
11000	11586.48	965.54	11863.80	659.10	12145.68	506.07	12431.70	414.39
12000	12639.72	1053.31	12942.36	719.02	13249.68	552.07	13561.80	452.06
13000	13693.08	1141.09	14020.92	778.94	14353.92	598.08	14691.90	489.73
14000	14746.32	1228.86	15099.48	838.86	15458.16	644.09	15822.00	527.40
15000	15799.68	1316.64	16178.04	898.78	16562.16	690.09	16952.40	565.08
16000	16853.04	1404.42	17256.60	958.70	17666.40	736.10	18082.50	602.75
17000	17906.28	1492.19	18335.16	1018.62	18770.64	782.11	19212.60	640.42
18000	18959.64	1579.97	19413.72	1078.54	19874.64	828.11	20342.70	678.09
19000	20013.00	1667.75	20492.28	1138.46	20978.88	874.12	21472.80	715.76
20000	21066.24	1755.52	21570.84	1198.38	22083.12	920.13	22603.20	753.44
21000	22119.60	1843.30	22649.22	1258.29	23187.12	966.13	23733.30	791.11
22000	23172.96	1931.08	23727.78	1318.21	24291.36	1012.14	24863.40	828.78
23000	24226.20	2018.85	24806.34	1378.13	25395.60	1058.15	25993.50	866.45
24000	25279.56	2106.63	25884.90	1438.05	26499.60	1104.15	27123.60	904.12
25000	26332.92	2194.41	26963.46	1497.97	27603.84	1150.16	28254.00	941.80

ANNUAL PERCENTAGE RATE **9.70%**

LOAN AMT	36 MONTHS TOTAL NOTE	36 MONTHS MONTHLY PAYMENT	42 MONTHS TOTAL NOTE	42 MONTHS MONTHLY PAYMENT	48 MONTHS TOTAL NOTE	48 MONTHS MONTHLY PAYMENT	60 MONTHS TOTAL NOTE	60 MONTHS MONTHLY PAYMENT
1	1.08	.03	.84	.02	.96	.02	1.20	.02
2	2.16	.06	2.10	.05	2.40	.05	2.40	.04
3	3.24	.09	3.36	.08	3.36	.07	3.60	.06
4	4.32	.12	4.62	.11	4.80	.10	4.80	.08
5	5.76	.16	5.88	.14	5.76	.12	6.00	.10
6	6.84	.19	6.72	.16	7.20	.15	7.20	.12
7	7.92	.22	7.98	.19	8.16	.17	8.40	.14
8	9.00	.25	9.24	.22	9.60	.20	9.60	.16
9	10.08	.28	10.50	.25	10.56	.22	10.80	.18
10	11.52	.32	11.76	.28	12.00	.25	12.60	.21
20	23.04	.64	23.52	.56	24.00	.50	25.20	.42
30	34.56	.96	35.28	.84	36.00	.75	37.80	.63
40	46.08	1.28	47.04	1.12	48.00	1.00	50.40	.84
50	57.60	1.60	58.80	1.40	60.48	1.26	63.00	1.05
60	69.12	1.92	70.98	1.69	72.48	1.51	75.60	1.26
70	80.64	2.24	82.74	1.97	84.48	1.76	88.20	1.47
80	92.52	2.57	94.50	2.25	96.48	2.01	100.80	1.68
90	104.04	2.89	106.26	2.53	108.48	2.26	113.40	1.89
100	115.56	3.21	118.02	2.81	120.96	2.52	126.00	2.10
200	231.12	6.42	236.46	5.63	241.92	5.04	252.60	4.21
300	346.68	9.63	354.90	8.45	362.88	7.56	379.20	6.32
400	462.60	12.85	472.92	11.26	483.84	10.08	505.80	8.43
500	578.16	16.06	591.36	14.08	604.80	12.60	632.40	10.54
600	693.72	19.27	709.80	16.90	726.24	15.13	759.00	12.65
700	809.28	22.48	828.24	19.72	847.20	17.65	885.60	14.76
800	925.20	25.70	946.26	22.53	968.16	20.17	1012.20	16.87
900	1040.76	28.91	1064.70	25.35	1089.12	22.69	1138.80	18.98
1000	1156.32	32.12	1183.14	28.17	1210.08	25.21	1265.40	21.09
1500	1734.48	48.18	1774.92	42.26	1815.36	37.82	1898.40	31.64
2000	2313.00	64.25	2366.28	56.34	2420.64	50.43	2531.40	42.19
2500	2891.16	80.31	2958.06	70.43	3025.92	63.04	3164.40	52.74
3000	3469.32	96.37	3549.84	84.52	3631.20	75.65	3797.40	63.29
3500	4047.84	112.44	4141.62	98.61	4236.48	88.26	4430.40	73.84
4000	4626.00	128.50	4732.98	112.69	4841.76	100.87	5063.40	84.39
4500	5204.16	144.56	5324.76	126.78	5447.04	113.48	5696.40	94.94
5000	5782.68	160.63	5916.54	140.87	6052.32	126.09	6329.40	105.49
5500	6360.84	176.69	6508.32	154.96	6657.60	138.70	6962.40	116.04
6000	6939.00	192.75	7099.68	169.04	7262.88	151.31	7595.40	126.59
6500	7517.52	208.82	7691.46	183.13	7868.16	163.92	8228.40	137.14
7000	8095.68	224.88	8283.24	197.22	8473.44	176.53	8861.40	147.69
7500	8673.84	240.94	8874.60	211.30	9078.72	189.14	9494.40	158.24
8000	9252.36	257.01	9466.38	225.39	9684.00	201.75	10127.40	168.79
8500	9830.52	273.07	10058.16	239.48	10288.80	214.35	10760.40	179.34
9000	10408.68	289.13	10649.94	253.57	10894.08	226.96	11393.40	189.89
10000	11565.36	321.26	11833.08	281.74	12104.64	252.18	12659.40	210.99
11000	12722.04	353.39	13016.64	309.92	13315.20	277.40	13925.40	232.09
12000	13878.36	385.51	14199.78	338.09	14525.76	302.62	15191.40	253.19
13000	15035.04	417.64	15383.34	366.27	15736.32	327.84	16457.40	274.29
14000	16191.72	449.77	16566.48	394.44	16946.88	353.06	17723.40	295.39
15000	17348.04	481.89	17749.62	422.61	18157.44	378.28	18989.40	316.49
16000	18504.72	514.02	18933.18	450.79	19368.00	403.50	20255.40	337.59
17000	19661.40	546.15	20116.32	478.96	20578.08	428.71	21521.40	358.69
18000	20817.72	578.27	21299.88	507.14	21788.64	453.93	22787.40	379.79
19000	21974.40	610.40	22483.02	535.31	22999.20	479.15	24053.40	400.89
20000	23131.08	642.53	23666.58	563.49	24209.76	504.37	25319.40	421.99
21000	24287.40	674.65	24849.72	591.66	25420.32	529.59	26585.40	443.09
22000	25444.08	706.78	26033.28	619.84	26630.88	554.81	27851.40	464.19
23000	26600.76	738.91	27216.42	648.01	27841.44	580.03	29117.40	485.29
24000	27757.08	771.03	28399.98	676.19	29052.00	605.25	30383.40	506.39
25000	28913.76	803.16	29583.12	704.36	30262.08	630.46	31649.40	527.49

9.75% ANNUAL PERCENTAGE RATE

	12 MONTHS		18 MONTHS		24 MONTHS		30 MONTHS	
LOAN AMT	TOTAL NOTE	MONTHLY PAYMENT	TOTAL NOTE	MONTHLY PAYMENT	TOTAL NOTE	MONTHLY PAYMENT	TOTAL NOTE	MONTHLY PAYMENT
1	.96	.08	.90	.05	.96	.04	.90	.03
2	2.04	.17	1.98	.11	2.16	.09	2.10	.07
3	3.12	.26	3.06	.17	3.12	.13	3.30	.11
4	4.20	.35	4.14	.23	4.32	.18	4.50	.15
5	5.16	.43	5.22	.29	5.52	.23	5.40	.18
6	6.24	.52	6.30	.35	6.48	.27	6.60	.22
7	7.32	.61	7.38	.41	7.68	.32	7.80	.26
8	8.40	.70	8.46	.47	8.64	.36	9.00	.30
9	9.48	.79	9.54	.53	9.84	.41	9.90	.33
10	10.44	.87	10.62	.59	11.04	.46	11.10	.37
20	21.00	1.75	21.42	1.19	22.08	.92	22.50	.75
30	31.56	2.63	32.22	1.79	33.12	1.38	33.90	1.13
40	42.12	3.51	43.02	2.39	44.16	1.84	45.00	1.50
50	52.56	4.38	53.82	2.99	55.20	2.30	56.40	1.88
60	63.12	5.26	64.62	3.59	66.24	2.76	67.80	2.26
70	73.68	6.14	75.42	4.19	77.28	3.22	78.90	2.63
80	84.24	7.02	86.22	4.79	88.32	3.68	90.30	3.01
90	94.80	7.90	97.02	5.39	99.36	4.14	101.70	3.39
100	105.24	8.77	107.82	5.99	110.40	4.60	112.80	3.76
200	210.60	17.55	215.64	11.98	220.80	9.20	225.90	7.53
300	315.96	26.33	323.64	17.98	331.20	13.80	339.00	11.30
400	421.32	35.11	431.46	23.97	441.84	18.41	452.10	15.07
500	526.68	43.89	539.46	29.97	552.24	23.01	565.20	18.84
600	632.04	52.67	647.28	35.96	662.64	27.61	678.30	22.61
700	737.40	61.45	755.10	41.95	773.28	32.22	791.40	26.38
800	842.76	70.23	863.10	47.95	883.68	36.82	904.50	30.15
900	948.12	79.01	970.92	53.94	994.08	41.42	1017.60	33.92
1000	1053.48	87.79	1078.92	59.94	1104.48	46.02	1130.70	37.69
1500	1580.28	131.69	1618.38	89.91	1656.96	69.04	1696.20	56.54
2000	2107.08	175.59	2157.84	119.88	2209.20	92.05	2261.70	75.39
2500	2633.88	219.49	2697.30	149.85	2761.68	115.07	2826.90	94.23
3000	3160.68	263.39	3236.76	179.82	3313.92	138.08	3392.40	113.08
3500	3687.48	307.29	3776.22	209.79	3866.40	161.10	3957.90	131.93
4000	4214.28	351.19	4315.68	239.76	4418.64	184.11	4523.40	150.78
4500	4741.08	395.09	4855.14	269.73	4971.12	207.13	5088.60	169.62
5000	5267.88	438.99	5394.78	299.71	5523.36	230.14	5654.10	188.47
5500	5794.68	482.89	5934.24	329.68	6075.84	253.16	6219.60	207.32
6000	6321.48	526.79	6473.70	359.65	6628.08	276.17	6785.10	226.17
6500	6848.28	570.69	7013.16	389.62	7180.56	299.19	7350.30	245.01
7000	7375.08	614.59	7552.62	419.59	7732.80	322.20	7915.80	263.86
7500	7901.88	658.49	8092.08	449.56	8285.28	345.22	8481.30	282.71
8000	8428.68	702.39	8631.54	479.53	8837.52	368.23	9046.80	301.56
8500	8955.48	746.29	9171.00	509.50	9390.00	391.25	9612.00	320.40
9000	9482.28	790.19	9710.46	539.47	9942.24	414.26	10177.50	339.25
10000	10535.88	877.99	10789.56	599.42	11046.96	460.29	11308.50	376.95
11000	11589.48	965.79	11868.48	659.36	12151.68	506.32	12439.20	414.64
12000	12643.08	1053.59	12947.40	719.30	13256.40	552.35	13570.20	452.34
13000	13696.68	1141.39	14026.32	779.24	14361.12	598.38	14700.90	490.03
14000	14750.28	1229.19	15105.24	839.18	15465.84	644.41	15831.90	527.73
15000	15803.88	1316.99	16184.34	899.13	16570.56	690.44	16962.60	565.42
16000	16857.48	1404.79	17263.26	959.07	17675.28	736.47	18093.60	603.12
17000	17911.08	1492.59	18342.18	1019.01	18780.00	782.50	19224.30	640.81
18000	18964.68	1580.39	19421.10	1078.95	19884.72	828.53	20355.30	678.51
19000	20018.28	1668.19	20500.02	1138.89	20989.44	874.56	21486.30	716.21
20000	21071.88	1755.99	21579.12	1198.84	22094.16	920.59	22617.00	753.90
21000	22125.48	1843.79	22658.04	1258.78	23198.88	966.62	23748.00	791.60
22000	23179.08	1931.59	23736.96	1318.72	24303.60	1012.65	24878.70	829.29
23000	24232.68	2019.39	24815.88	1378.66	25408.32	1058.68	26009.70	866.99
24000	25286.28	2107.19	25894.80	1438.60	26513.04	1104.71	27140.40	904.68
25000	26339.88	2194.99	26973.90	1498.55	27617.76	1150.74	28271.40	942.38

ANNUAL PERCENTAGE RATE **9.75%**

LOAN	36 MONTHS		42 MONTHS		48 MONTHS		60 MONTHS	
AMT	TOTAL NOTE	MONTHLY PAYMENT	TOTAL NOTE	MONTHLY PAYMENT	TOTAL NOTE	MONTHLY PAYMENT	TOTAL NOTE	MONTHLY PAYMENT
1	1.08	.03	.84	.02	.96	.02	1.20	.02
2	2.16	.06	2.10	.05	2.40	.05	2.40	.04
3	3.24	.09	3.36	.08	3.36	.07	3.60	.06
4	4.32	.12	4.62	.11	4.80	.10	4.80	.08
5	5.76	.16	5.88	.14	5.76	.12	6.00	.10
6	6.84	.19	6.72	.16	7.20	.15	7.20	.12
7	7.92	.22	7.98	.19	8.16	.17	8.40	.14
8	9.00	.25	9.24	.22	9.60	.20	9.60	.16
9	10.08	.28	10.50	.25	10.56	.22	11.40	.19
10	11.52	.32	11.76	.28	12.00	.25	12.60	.21
20	23.04	.64	23.52	.56	24.00	.50	25.20	.42
30	34.56	.96	35.28	.84	36.00	.75	37.80	.63
40	46.08	1.28	47.04	1.12	48.00	1.00	50.40	.84
50	57.60	1.60	58.80	1.40	60.48	1.26	63.00	1.05
60	69.12	1.92	70.98	1.69	72.48	1.51	75.60	1.26
70	81.00	2.25	82.74	1.97	84.48	1.76	88.20	1.47
80	92.52	2.57	94.50	2.25	96.48	2.01	100.80	1.68
90	104.04	2.89	106.26	2.53	108.96	2.27	114.00	1.90
100	115.56	3.21	118.02	2.81	120.96	2.52	126.60	2.11
200	231.12	6.42	236.46	5.63	241.92	5.04	253.20	4.22
300	347.04	9.64	354.90	8.45	363.36	7.57	379.80	6.33
400	462.60	12.85	473.34	11.27	484.32	10.09	506.40	8.44
500	578.52	16.07	591.78	14.09	605.76	12.62	633.60	10.56
600	694.08	19.28	710.22	16.91	726.72	15.14	760.20	12.67
700	810.00	22.50	828.66	19.73	847.68	17.66	886.80	14.78
800	925.56	25.71	947.10	22.55	969.12	20.19	1013.40	16.89
900	1041.48	28.93	1065.54	25.37	1090.08	22.71	1140.60	19.01
1000	1157.04	32.14	1183.98	28.19	1211.52	25.24	1267.20	21.12
1500	1735.92	48.22	1776.18	42.29	1817.28	37.86	1900.80	31.68
2000	2314.44	64.29	2368.38	56.39	2423.04	50.48	2534.40	42.24
2500	2893.32	80.37	2960.58	70.49	3028.80	63.10	3168.60	52.81
3000	3471.84	96.44	3552.78	84.59	3634.56	75.72	3802.20	63.37
3500	4050.72	112.52	4144.98	98.69	4240.32	88.34	4435.80	73.93
4000	4629.24	128.59	4737.18	112.79	4846.56	100.97	5069.40	84.49
4500	5208.12	144.67	5329.38	126.89	5452.32	113.59	5703.00	95.05
5000	5786.64	160.74	5921.58	140.99	6058.08	126.21	6337.20	105.62
5500	6365.52	176.82	6513.78	155.09	6663.84	138.83	6970.80	116.18
6000	6944.04	192.89	7105.56	169.18	7269.60	151.45	7604.40	126.74
6500	7522.92	208.97	7697.76	183.28	7875.36	164.07	8238.00	137.30
7000	8101.44	225.04	8289.96	197.38	8481.12	176.69	8871.60	147.86
7500	8680.32	241.12	8882.16	211.48	9087.36	189.32	9505.80	158.43
8000	9258.84	257.19	9474.36	225.58	9693.12	201.94	10139.40	168.99
8500	9837.72	273.27	10066.56	239.68	10298.88	214.56	10773.00	179.55
9000	10416.24	289.34	10658.76	253.78	10904.64	227.18	11406.60	190.11
10000	11573.64	321.49	11843.16	281.98	12116.16	252.42	12674.40	211.24
11000	12731.04	353.64	13027.56	310.18	13327.68	277.66	13941.60	232.36
12000	13888.44	385.79	14211.54	338.37	14539.68	302.91	15209.40	253.49
13000	15045.84	417.94	15395.94	366.57	15751.20	328.15	16476.60	274.61
14000	16203.24	450.09	16580.34	394.77	16962.72	353.39	17743.80	295.73
15000	17360.64	482.24	17764.74	422.97	18174.72	378.64	19011.60	316.86
16000	18518.04	514.39	18949.14	451.17	19386.24	403.88	20278.80	337.98
17000	19675.44	546.54	20133.54	479.37	20597.76	429.12	21546.60	359.11
18000	20832.84	578.69	21317.52	507.56	21809.28	454.36	22813.80	380.23
19000	21990.24	610.84	22501.92	535.76	23021.28	479.61	24081.60	401.36
20000	23147.64	642.99	23686.32	563.96	24232.80	504.85	25348.80	422.48
21000	24305.04	675.14	24870.72	592.16	25444.32	530.09	26616.00	443.60
22000	25462.44	707.29	26055.12	620.36	26655.84	555.33	27883.80	464.73
23000	26619.84	739.44	27239.52	648.56	27867.84	580.58	29151.00	485.85
24000	27777.24	771.59	28423.50	676.75	29079.36	605.82	30418.80	506.98
25000	28934.64	803.74	29607.90	704.95	30290.88	631.06	31686.00	528.10

9.80% ANNUAL PERCENTAGE RATE

LOAN AMT	12 MONTHS TOTAL NOTE	MONTHLY PAYMENT	18 MONTHS TOTAL NOTE	MONTHLY PAYMENT	24 MONTHS TOTAL NOTE	MONTHLY PAYMENT	30 MONTHS TOTAL NOTE	MONTHLY PAYMENT
1	.96	.08	.90	.05	.96	.04	.90	.03
2	2.04	.17	1.98	.11	2.16	.09	2.10	.07
3	3.12	.26	3.06	.17	3.12	.13	3.30	.11
4	4.20	.35	4.14	.23	4.32	.18	4.50	.15
5	5.16	.43	5.22	.29	5.52	.23	5.40	.18
6	6.24	.52	6.30	.35	6.48	.27	6.60	.22
7	7.32	.61	7.38	.41	7.68	.32	7.80	.26
8	8.40	.70	8.46	.47	8.64	.36	9.00	.30
9	9.48	.79	9.54	.53	9.84	.41	9.90	.33
10	10.44	.87	10.62	.59	11.04	.46	11.10	.37
20	21.00	1.75	21.42	1.19	22.08	.92	22.50	.75
30	31.56	2.63	32.22	1.79	33.12	1.38	33.90	1.13
40	42.12	3.51	43.02	2.39	44.16	1.84	45.00	1.50
50	52.68	4.39	53.82	2.99	55.20	2.30	56.40	1.88
60	63.12	5.26	64.62	3.59	66.24	2.76	67.80	2.26
70	73.68	6.14	75.42	4.19	77.28	3.22	79.20	2.64
80	84.24	7.02	86.22	4.79	88.32	3.68	90.30	3.01
90	94.80	7.90	97.02	5.39	99.36	4.14	101.70	3.39
100	105.36	8.78	107.82	5.99	110.40	4.60	113.10	3.77
200	210.72	17.56	215.82	11.99	221.04	9.21	226.20	7.54
300	316.08	26.34	323.64	17.98	331.44	13.81	339.30	11.31
400	421.44	35.12	431.64	23.98	442.08	18.42	452.40	15.08
500	526.92	43.91	539.64	29.98	552.48	23.02	565.50	18.85
600	632.28	52.69	647.46	35.97	663.12	27.63	678.90	22.63
700	737.64	61.47	755.46	41.97	773.52	32.23	792.00	26.40
800	843.00	70.25	863.46	47.97	884.16	36.84	905.10	30.17
900	948.48	79.04	971.28	53.96	994.56	41.44	1018.20	33.94
1000	1053.84	87.82	1079.28	59.96	1105.20	46.05	1131.30	37.71
1500	1580.76	131.73	1618.92	89.94	1657.68	69.07	1697.10	56.57
2000	2107.68	175.64	2158.74	119.93	2210.40	92.10	2262.90	75.43
2500	2634.60	219.55	2698.38	149.91	2763.12	115.13	2828.70	94.29
3000	3161.52	263.46	3238.02	179.89	3315.60	138.15	3394.50	113.15
3500	3688.56	307.38	3777.66	209.87	3868.32	161.18	3960.30	132.01
4000	4215.48	351.29	4317.48	239.86	4421.04	184.21	4526.10	150.87
4500	4742.40	395.20	4857.12	269.84	4973.52	207.23	5091.90	169.73
5000	5269.32	439.11	5396.76	299.82	5526.24	230.26	5657.70	188.59
5500	5796.24	483.02	5936.40	329.80	6078.72	253.28	6223.50	207.45
6000	6323.16	526.93	6476.22	359.79	6631.44	276.31	6789.30	226.31
6500	6850.08	570.84	7015.86	389.77	7184.16	299.34	7355.10	245.17
7000	7377.12	614.76	7555.50	419.75	7736.64	322.36	7920.60	264.02
7500	7904.04	658.67	8095.14	449.73	8289.36	345.39	8486.40	282.88
8000	8430.96	702.58	8634.96	479.72	8842.08	368.42	9052.20	301.74
8500	8957.88	746.49	9174.60	509.70	9394.56	391.44	9618.00	320.60
9000	9484.80	790.40	9714.24	539.68	9947.28	414.47	10183.80	339.46
10000	10538.64	878.22	10793.70	599.65	11052.48	460.52	11315.40	377.18
11000	11592.60	966.05	11872.98	659.61	12157.68	506.57	12447.00	414.90
12000	12646.44	1053.87	12952.44	719.58	13263.12	552.63	13578.60	452.62
13000	13700.28	1141.69	14031.72	779.54	14368.32	598.68	14710.20	490.34
14000	14754.24	1229.52	15111.18	839.51	15473.52	644.73	15841.50	528.05
15000	15808.08	1317.34	16190.46	899.47	16578.96	690.79	16973.10	565.77
16000	16861.92	1405.16	17269.92	959.44	17684.16	736.84	18104.70	603.49
17000	17915.76	1492.98	18349.20	1019.40	18789.36	782.89	19236.30	641.21
18000	18969.72	1580.81	19428.66	1079.37	19894.56	828.94	20367.90	678.93
19000	20023.56	1668.63	20507.94	1139.33	21000.00	875.00	21499.50	716.65
20000	21077.40	1756.45	21587.40	1199.30	22105.20	921.05	22630.80	754.36
21000	22131.36	1844.28	22666.68	1259.26	23210.40	967.10	23762.40	792.08
22000	23185.20	1932.10	23746.14	1319.23	24315.60	1013.15	24894.00	829.80
23000	24239.04	2019.92	24825.42	1379.19	25421.04	1059.21	26025.60	867.52
24000	25292.88	2107.74	25904.88	1439.16	26526.24	1105.26	27157.20	905.24
25000	26346.84	2195.57	26984.16	1499.12	27631.44	1151.31	28288.80	942.96

ANNUAL PERCENTAGE RATE **9.80%**

LOAN AMT	36 MONTHS TOTAL NOTE	36 MONTHS MONTHLY PAYMENT	42 MONTHS TOTAL NOTE	42 MONTHS MONTHLY PAYMENT	48 MONTHS TOTAL NOTE	48 MONTHS MONTHLY PAYMENT	60 MONTHS TOTAL NOTE	60 MONTHS MONTHLY PAYMENT
1	1.08	.03	.84	.02	.96	.02	1.20	.02
2	2.16	.06	2.10	.05	2.40	.05	2.40	.04
3	3.24	.09	3.36	.08	3.36	.07	3.60	.06
4	4.32	.12	4.62	.11	4.80	.10	4.80	.08
5	5.76	.16	5.88	.14	5.76	.12	6.00	.10
6	6.84	.19	6.72	.16	7.20	.15	7.20	.12
7	7.92	.22	7.98	.19	8.16	.17	8.40	.14
8	9.00	.25	9.24	.22	9.60	.20	9.60	.16
9	10.08	.28	10.50	.25	10.56	.22	11.40	.19
10	11.52	.32	11.76	.28	12.00	.25	12.60	.21
20	23.04	.64	23.52	.56	24.00	.50	25.20	.42
30	34.56	.96	35.28	.84	36.00	.75	37.80	.63
40	46.08	1.28	47.04	1.12	48.48	1.01	50.40	.84
50	57.60	1.60	59.22	1.41	60.48	1.26	63.00	1.05
60	69.48	1.93	70.98	1.69	72.48	1.51	75.60	1.26
70	81.00	2.25	82.74	1.97	84.48	1.76	88.80	1.48
80	92.52	2.57	94.50	2.25	96.96	2.02	101.40	1.69
90	104.04	2.89	106.26	2.53	108.96	2.27	114.00	1.90
100	115.56	3.21	118.44	2.82	120.96	2.52	126.60	2.11
200	231.48	6.43	236.88	5.64	242.40	5.05	253.20	4.22
300	347.40	9.65	355.32	8.46	363.36	7.57	380.40	6.34
400	462.96	12.86	473.76	11.28	484.80	10.10	507.00	8.45
500	578.88	16.08	592.62	14.11	606.24	12.63	634.20	10.57
600	694.80	19.30	711.06	16.93	727.20	15.15	760.80	12.68
700	810.72	22.52	829.50	19.75	848.64	17.68	888.00	14.80
800	926.28	25.73	947.94	22.57	970.08	20.21	1014.60	16.91
900	1042.20	28.95	1066.38	25.39	1091.04	22.73	1141.80	19.03
1000	1158.12	32.17	1185.24	28.22	1212.48	25.26	1268.40	21.14
1500	1737.36	48.26	1777.86	42.33	1818.72	37.89	1903.20	31.72
2000	2316.24	64.34	2370.48	56.44	2425.44	50.53	2537.40	42.29
2500	2895.48	80.43	2963.10	70.55	3031.68	63.16	3172.20	52.87
3000	3474.72	96.52	3555.72	84.66	3637.92	75.79	3806.40	63.44
3500	4053.60	112.60	4148.34	98.77	4244.64	88.43	4441.20	74.02
4000	4632.84	128.69	4740.96	112.88	4850.88	101.06	5075.40	84.59
4500	5212.08	144.78	5333.58	126.99	5457.12	113.69	5709.60	95.16
5000	5790.96	160.86	5926.20	141.10	6063.84	126.33	6344.40	105.74
5500	6370.20	176.95	6519.24	155.22	6670.08	138.96	6978.60	116.31
6000	6949.44	193.04	7111.86	169.33	7276.32	151.59	7613.40	126.89
6500	7528.32	209.12	7704.48	183.44	7883.04	164.23	8247.60	137.46
7000	8107.56	225.21	8297.10	197.55	8489.28	176.86	8882.40	148.04
7500	8686.80	241.30	8889.72	211.66	9095.52	189.49	9516.60	158.61
8000	9265.68	257.38	9482.34	225.77	9702.24	202.13	10151.40	169.19
8500	9844.92	273.47	10074.96	239.88	10308.48	214.76	10785.60	179.76
9000	10424.16	289.56	10667.58	253.99	10914.72	227.39	11419.80	190.33
10000	11582.28	321.73	11852.82	282.21	12127.68	252.66	12688.80	211.48
11000	12740.40	353.90	13038.48	310.44	13340.64	277.93	13957.80	232.63
12000	13898.88	386.08	14223.72	338.66	14553.12	303.19	15226.80	253.78
13000	15057.00	418.25	15408.96	366.88	15766.08	328.46	16495.80	274.93
14000	16215.12	450.42	16594.20	395.10	16979.04	353.73	17764.80	296.08
15000	17373.60	482.60	17779.44	423.32	18191.52	378.99	19033.80	317.23
16000	18531.72	514.77	18965.10	451.55	19404.48	404.26	20302.80	338.38
17000	19689.84	546.94	20150.34	479.77	20617.44	429.53	21571.20	359.52
18000	20848.32	579.12	21335.58	507.99	21829.92	454.79	22840.20	380.67
19000	22006.44	611.29	22520.82	536.21	23042.88	480.06	24109.20	401.82
20000	23164.56	643.46	23706.06	564.43	24255.84	505.33	25378.20	422.97
21000	24323.04	675.64	24891.72	592.66	25468.32	530.59	26647.20	444.12
22000	25481.16	707.81	26076.96	620.88	26681.28	555.86	27916.20	465.27
23000	26639.28	739.98	27262.20	649.10	27894.24	581.13	29185.20	486.42
24000	27797.76	772.16	28447.44	677.32	29106.72	606.39	30454.20	507.57
25000	28955.88	804.33	29632.68	705.54	30319.68	631.66	31722.60	528.71

9.90% ANNUAL PERCENTAGE RATE

LOAN AMT	12 MONTHS TOTAL NOTE	12 MONTHS MONTHLY PAYMENT	18 MONTHS TOTAL NOTE	18 MONTHS MONTHLY PAYMENT	24 MONTHS TOTAL NOTE	24 MONTHS MONTHLY PAYMENT	30 MONTHS TOTAL NOTE	30 MONTHS MONTHLY PAYMENT
1	.96	.08	1.08	.06	.96	.04	.90	.03
2	2.04	.17	2.16	.12	2.16	.09	2.10	.07
3	3.12	.26	3.24	.18	3.12	.13	3.30	.11
4	4.20	.35	4.32	.24	4.32	.18	4.50	.15
5	5.16	.43	5.40	.30	5.52	.23	5.40	.18
6	6.24	.52	6.48	.36	6.48	.27	6.60	.22
7	7.32	.61	7.56	.42	7.68	.32	7.80	.26
8	8.40	.70	8.64	.48	8.64	.36	9.00	.30
9	9.48	.79	9.72	.54	9.84	.41	9.90	.33
10	10.44	.87	10.80	.60	11.04	.46	11.10	.37
20	21.00	1.75	21.60	1.20	22.08	.92	22.50	.75
30	31.56	2.63	32.40	1.80	33.12	1.38	33.90	1.13
40	42.12	3.51	43.20	2.40	44.16	1.84	45.30	1.51
50	52.68	4.39	54.00	3.00	55.20	2.30	56.40	1.88
60	63.24	5.27	64.80	3.60	66.24	2.76	67.80	2.26
70	73.80	6.15	75.60	4.20	77.28	3.22	79.20	2.64
80	84.24	7.02	86.40	4.80	88.32	3.68	90.60	3.02
90	94.80	7.90	97.20	5.40	99.36	4.14	101.70	3.39
100	105.36	8.78	108.00	6.00	110.40	4.60	113.10	3.77
200	210.84	17.57	216.00	12.00	221.04	9.21	226.50	7.55
300	316.32	26.36	324.00	18.00	331.68	13.82	339.60	11.32
400	421.68	35.14	432.00	24.00	442.32	18.43	453.00	15.10
500	527.16	43.93	540.00	30.00	552.96	23.04	566.40	18.88
600	632.64	52.72	648.00	36.00	663.60	27.65	679.50	22.65
700	738.00	61.50	756.00	42.00	774.24	32.26	792.90	26.43
800	843.48	70.29	864.00	48.00	884.88	36.87	906.30	30.21
900	948.96	79.08	972.00	54.00	995.52	41.48	1019.40	33.98
1000	1054.32	87.86	1080.18	60.01	1106.16	46.09	1132.80	37.76
1500	1581.60	131.80	1620.18	90.01	1659.36	69.14	1699.20	56.64
2000	2108.76	175.73	2160.36	120.02	2212.56	92.19	2265.60	75.52
2500	2636.04	219.67	2700.36	150.02	2765.76	115.24	2832.30	94.41
3000	3163.20	263.60	3240.54	180.03	3318.96	138.29	3398.70	113.29
3500	3690.48	307.54	3780.54	210.03	3872.16	161.34	3965.10	132.17
4000	4217.64	351.47	4320.72	240.04	4425.36	184.39	4531.50	151.05
4500	4744.92	395.41	4860.72	270.04	4978.56	207.44	5098.20	169.94
5000	5272.08	439.34	5400.90	300.05	5531.76	230.49	5664.60	188.82
5500	5799.36	483.28	5941.08	330.06	6084.96	253.54	6231.00	207.70
6000	6326.52	527.21	6481.08	360.06	6638.16	276.59	6797.40	226.58
6500	6853.80	571.15	7021.26	390.07	7191.36	299.64	7364.10	245.47
7000	7380.96	615.08	7561.26	420.07	7744.56	322.69	7930.50	264.35
7500	7908.24	659.02	8101.44	450.08	8297.76	345.74	8496.90	283.23
8000	8435.40	702.95	8641.44	480.08	8850.96	368.79	9063.30	302.11
8500	8962.56	746.88	9181.62	510.09	9403.92	391.83	9630.00	321.00
9000	9489.84	790.82	9721.62	540.09	9957.12	414.88	10196.40	339.88
10000	10544.28	878.69	10801.98	600.11	11063.52	460.98	11329.20	377.64
11000	11598.72	966.56	11882.16	660.12	12169.92	507.08	12462.30	415.41
12000	12653.16	1054.43	12962.34	720.13	13276.32	553.18	13595.10	453.17
13000	13707.60	1142.30	14042.52	780.14	14382.72	599.28	14728.20	490.94
14000	14762.04	1230.17	15122.70	840.15	15489.12	645.38	15861.00	528.70
15000	15816.48	1318.04	16202.88	900.16	16595.52	691.48	16994.10	566.47
16000	16870.92	1405.91	17283.06	960.17	17701.92	737.58	18126.90	604.23
17000	17925.24	1493.77	18363.24	1020.18	18808.08	783.67	19260.00	642.00
18000	18979.68	1581.64	19443.42	1080.19	19914.48	829.77	20392.80	679.76
19000	20034.12	1669.51	20523.60	1140.20	21020.88	875.87	21525.90	717.53
20000	21088.56	1757.38	21603.96	1200.22	22127.28	921.97	22658.70	755.29
21000	22143.00	1845.25	22684.14	1260.23	23233.68	968.07	23791.80	793.06
22000	23197.44	1933.12	23764.32	1320.24	24340.08	1014.17	24924.60	830.82
23000	24251.88	2020.99	24844.50	1380.25	25446.48	1060.27	26057.70	868.59
24000	25306.32	2108.86	25924.68	1440.26	26552.88	1106.37	27190.50	906.35
25000	26360.76	2196.73	27004.86	1500.27	27659.04	1152.46	28323.60	944.12

ANNUAL PERCENTAGE RATE **9.90%**

LOAN AMT	36 MONTHS TOTAL NOTE	36 MONTHS MONTHLY PAYMENT	42 MONTHS TOTAL NOTE	42 MONTHS MONTHLY PAYMENT	48 MONTHS TOTAL NOTE	48 MONTHS MONTHLY PAYMENT	60 MONTHS TOTAL NOTE	60 MONTHS MONTHLY PAYMENT
1	1.08	.03	.84	.02	.96	.02	1.20	.02
2	2.16	.06	2.10	.05	2.40	.05	2.40	.04
3	3.24	.09	3.36	.08	3.36	.07	3.60	.06
4	4.32	.12	4.62	.11	4.80	.10	4.80	.08
5	5.76	.16	5.88	.14	5.76	.12	6.00	.10
6	6.84	.19	6.72	.16	7.20	.15	7.20	.12
7	7.92	.22	7.98	.19	8.16	.17	8.40	.14
8	9.00	.25	9.24	.22	9.60	.20	9.60	.16
9	10.08	.28	10.50	.25	10.56	.22	11.40	.19
10	11.52	.32	11.76	.28	12.00	.25	12.60	.21
20	23.04	.64	23.52	.56	24.00	.50	25.20	.42
30	34.56	.96	35.28	.84	36.00	.75	37.80	.63
40	46.08	1.28	47.46	1.13	48.48	1.01	50.40	.84
50	57.96	1.61	59.22	1.41	60.48	1.26	63.00	1.05
60	69.48	1.93	70.98	1.69	72.48	1.51	76.20	1.27
70	81.00	2.25	82.74	1.97	84.96	1.77	88.80	1.48
80	92.52	2.57	94.92	2.26	96.96	2.02	101.40	1.69
90	104.04	2.89	106.68	2.54	108.96	2.27	114.00	1.90
100	115.92	3.22	118.44	2.82	121.44	2.53	126.60	2.11
200	231.84	6.44	237.30	5.65	242.88	5.06	253.80	4.23
300	347.76	9.66	356.16	8.48	364.32	7.59	381.00	6.35
400	463.68	12.88	474.60	11.30	485.76	10.12	508.20	8.47
500	579.96	16.11	593.46	14.13	607.20	12.65	635.40	10.59
600	695.88	19.33	712.32	16.96	728.64	15.18	762.60	12.71
700	811.80	22.55	830.76	19.78	850.56	17.72	889.80	14.83
800	927.72	25.77	949.62	22.61	972.00	20.25	1017.00	16.95
900	1043.64	28.99	1068.48	25.44	1093.44	22.78	1144.20	19.07
1000	1159.92	32.22	1186.92	28.26	1214.88	25.31	1271.40	21.19
1500	1739.88	48.33	1780.80	42.40	1822.56	37.97	1907.40	31.79
2000	2319.84	64.44	2374.26	56.53	2429.76	50.62	2543.40	42.39
2500	2899.80	80.55	2968.14	70.67	3037.44	63.28	3179.40	52.99
3000	3479.76	96.66	3561.60	84.80	3645.12	75.94	3815.40	63.59
3500	4059.72	112.77	4155.48	98.94	4252.80	88.60	4451.40	74.19
4000	4639.68	128.88	4748.94	113.07	4860.00	101.25	5087.40	84.79
4500	5219.64	144.99	5342.82	127.21	5467.68	113.91	5723.40	95.39
5000	5799.60	161.10	5936.28	141.34	6075.36	126.57	6358.80	105.98
5500	6379.56	177.21	6530.16	155.48	6683.04	139.23	6994.80	116.58
6000	6959.52	193.32	7123.62	169.61	7290.24	151.88	7630.80	127.18
6500	7539.48	209.43	7717.50	183.75	7897.92	164.54	8266.80	137.78
7000	8119.44	225.54	8310.96	197.88	8505.60	177.20	8902.80	148.38
7500	8699.40	241.65	8904.84	212.02	9112.80	189.85	9538.80	158.98
8000	9279.36	257.76	9498.30	226.15	9720.48	202.51	10174.80	169.58
8500	9859.32	273.87	10091.76	240.28	10328.16	215.17	10810.80	180.18
9000	10439.28	289.98	10685.64	254.42	10935.84	227.83	11446.80	190.78
10000	11599.20	322.20	11872.98	282.69	12150.72	253.14	12718.20	211.97
11000	12759.12	354.42	13060.32	310.96	13366.08	278.46	13990.20	233.17
12000	13919.04	386.64	14247.66	339.23	14580.96	303.77	15262.20	254.37
13000	15078.96	418.86	15435.00	367.50	15795.84	329.08	16534.20	275.57
14000	16238.88	451.08	16622.34	395.77	17011.20	354.40	17806.20	296.77
15000	17398.80	483.30	17809.68	424.04	18226.08	379.71	19077.60	317.96
16000	18558.72	515.52	18997.02	452.31	19441.44	405.03	20349.60	339.16
17000	19718.64	547.74	20183.94	480.57	20656.32	430.34	21621.60	360.36
18000	20878.56	579.96	21371.28	508.84	21871.68	455.66	22893.60	381.56
19000	22038.48	612.18	22558.62	537.11	23086.56	480.97	24165.00	402.75
20000	23198.40	644.40	23745.96	565.38	24301.92	506.29	25437.00	423.95
21000	24358.32	676.62	24933.30	593.65	25516.80	531.60	26709.00	445.15
22000	25518.24	708.84	26120.64	621.92	26732.16	556.92	27981.00	466.35
23000	26678.16	741.06	27307.98	650.19	27947.04	582.23	29253.00	487.55
24000	27838.08	773.28	28495.32	678.46	29162.40	607.55	30524.40	508.74
25000	28998.00	805.50	29682.66	706.73	30377.28	632.86	31796.40	529.94

10.00% ANNUAL PERCENTAGE RATE

LOAN AMT	12 MONTHS TOTAL NOTE	12 MONTHS MONTHLY PAYMENT	18 MONTHS TOTAL NOTE	18 MONTHS MONTHLY PAYMENT	24 MONTHS TOTAL NOTE	24 MONTHS MONTHLY PAYMENT	30 MONTHS TOTAL NOTE	30 MONTHS MONTHLY PAYMENT
1	.96	.08	1.08	.06	.96	.04	.90	.03
2	2.04	.17	2.16	.12	2.16	.09	2.10	.07
3	3.12	.26	3.24	.18	3.12	.13	3.30	.11
4	4.20	.35	4.32	.24	4.32	.18	4.50	.15
5	5.16	.43	5.40	.30	5.52	.23	5.40	.18
6	6.24	.52	6.48	.36	6.48	.27	6.60	.22
7	7.32	.61	7.56	.42	7.68	.32	7.80	.26
8	8.40	.70	8.64	.48	8.64	.36	9.00	.30
9	9.48	.79	9.72	.54	9.84	.41	10.20	.34
10	10.44	.87	10.80	.60	11.04	.46	11.10	.37
20	21.00	1.75	21.60	1.20	22.08	.92	22.50	.75
30	31.56	2.63	32.40	1.80	33.12	1.38	33.90	1.13
40	42.12	3.51	43.20	2.40	44.16	1.84	45.30	1.51
50	52.68	4.39	54.00	3.00	55.20	2.30	56.70	1.89
60	63.24	5.27	64.80	3.60	66.24	2.76	67.80	2.26
70	73.80	6.15	75.60	4.20	77.52	3.23	79.20	2.64
80	84.36	7.03	86.40	4.80	88.56	3.69	90.60	3.02
90	94.92	7.91	97.20	5.40	99.60	4.15	102.00	3.40
100	105.48	8.79	108.00	6.00	110.64	4.61	113.40	3.78
200	210.96	17.58	216.18	12.01	221.28	9.22	226.80	7.56
300	316.44	26.37	324.18	18.01	332.16	13.84	340.20	11.34
400	421.92	35.16	432.36	24.02	442.80	18.45	453.60	15.12
500	527.40	43.95	540.36	30.02	553.68	23.07	567.00	18.90
600	632.88	52.74	648.54	36.03	664.32	27.68	680.40	22.68
700	738.48	61.54	756.54	42.03	775.20	32.30	793.80	26.46
800	843.96	70.33	864.72	48.04	885.84	36.91	907.20	30.24
900	949.44	79.12	972.90	54.05	996.72	41.53	1020.90	34.03
1000	1054.92	87.91	1080.90	60.05	1107.36	46.14	1134.30	37.81
1500	1582.44	131.87	1621.44	90.08	1661.04	69.21	1701.30	56.71
2000	2109.96	175.83	2161.98	120.11	2214.72	92.28	2268.60	75.62
2500	2637.36	219.78	2702.52	150.14	2768.64	115.36	2835.60	94.52
3000	3164.88	263.74	3243.06	180.17	3322.32	138.43	3402.90	113.43
3500	3692.40	307.70	3783.42	210.19	3876.00	161.50	3969.90	132.33
4000	4219.92	351.66	4323.96	240.22	4429.68	184.57	4537.20	151.24
4500	4747.44	395.62	4864.50	270.25	4983.60	207.65	5104.50	170.15
5000	5274.84	439.57	5405.04	300.28	5537.28	230.72	5671.50	189.05
5500	5802.36	483.53	5945.58	330.31	6090.96	253.79	6238.80	207.96
6000	6329.88	527.49	6486.12	360.34	6644.64	276.86	6805.80	226.86
6500	6857.40	571.45	7026.66	390.37	7198.56	299.94	7373.10	245.77
7000	7384.92	615.41	7567.02	420.39	7752.24	323.01	7940.10	264.67
7500	7912.32	659.36	8107.56	450.42	8305.92	346.08	8507.40	283.58
8000	8439.84	703.32	8648.10	480.45	8859.60	369.15	9074.70	302.49
8500	8967.36	747.28	9188.64	510.48	9413.52	392.23	9641.70	321.39
9000	9494.88	791.24	9729.18	540.51	9967.20	415.30	10209.00	340.30
10000	10549.80	879.15	10810.26	600.57	11074.56	461.44	11343.30	378.11
11000	11604.84	967.07	11891.16	660.62	12182.16	507.59	12477.60	415.92
12000	12659.88	1054.99	12972.24	720.68	13289.52	553.73	13611.90	453.73
13000	13714.80	1142.90	14053.32	780.74	14397.12	599.88	14746.20	491.54
14000	14769.84	1230.82	15134.22	840.79	15504.48	646.02	15880.50	529.35
15000	15824.76	1318.73	16215.30	900.85	16612.08	692.17	17015.10	567.17
16000	16879.80	1406.65	17296.38	960.91	17719.44	738.31	18149.40	604.98
17000	17934.84	1494.57	18377.46	1020.97	18827.04	784.46	19283.70	642.79
18000	18989.76	1582.48	19458.36	1081.02	19934.40	830.60	20418.00	680.60
19000	20044.80	1670.40	20539.44	1141.08	21042.00	876.75	21552.30	718.41
20000	21099.72	1758.31	21620.52	1201.14	22149.36	922.89	22686.60	756.22
21000	22154.76	1846.23	22701.42	1261.19	23256.96	969.04	23820.90	794.03
22000	23209.68	1934.14	23782.50	1321.25	24364.32	1015.18	24955.50	831.85
23000	24264.72	2022.06	24863.58	1381.31	25471.92	1061.33	26089.80	869.66
24000	25319.76	2109.98	25944.48	1441.36	26579.28	1107.47	27224.10	907.47
25000	26374.68	2197.89	27025.56	1501.42	27686.88	1153.62	28358.40	945.28

ANNUAL PERCENTAGE RATE **10.00%**

LOAN AMT	36 MONTHS TOTAL NOTE	36 MONTHS MONTHLY PAYMENT	42 MONTHS TOTAL NOTE	42 MONTHS MONTHLY PAYMENT	48 MONTHS TOTAL NOTE	48 MONTHS MONTHLY PAYMENT	60 MONTHS TOTAL NOTE	60 MONTHS MONTHLY PAYMENT
1	1.08	.03	.84	.02	.96	.02	1.20	.02
2	2.16	.06	2.10	.05	2.40	.05	2.40	.04
3	3.24	.09	3.36	.08	3.36	.07	3.60	.06
4	4.32	.12	4.62	.11	4.80	.10	4.80	.08
5	5.76	.16	5.88	.14	5.76	.12	6.00	.10
6	6.84	.19	6.72	.16	7.20	.15	7.20	.12
7	7.92	.22	7.98	.19	8.16	.17	8.40	.14
8	9.00	.25	9.24	.22	9.60	.20	9.60	.16
9	10.44	.29	10.50	.25	10.56	.22	11.40	.19
10	11.52	.32	11.76	.28	12.00	.25	12.60	.21
20	23.04	.64	23.52	.56	24.00	.50	25.20	.42
30	34.56	.96	35.28	.84	36.48	.76	37.80	.63
40	46.44	1.29	47.46	1.13	48.48	1.01	50.40	.84
50	57.96	1.61	59.22	1.41	60.48	1.26	63.60	1.06
60	69.48	1.93	70.98	1.69	72.96	1.52	76.20	1.27
70	81.00	2.25	83.16	1.98	84.96	1.77	88.80	1.48
80	92.88	2.58	94.92	2.26	96.96	2.02	101.40	1.69
90	104.40	2.90	106.68	2.54	109.44	2.28	114.60	1.91
100	115.92	3.22	118.86	2.83	121.44	2.53	127.20	2.12
200	232.20	6.45	237.72	5.66	243.36	5.07	254.40	4.24
300	348.48	9.68	356.58	8.49	364.80	7.60	382.20	6.37
400	464.40	12.90	475.44	11.32	486.72	10.14	509.40	8.49
500	580.68	16.13	594.30	14.15	608.64	12.68	637.20	10.62
600	696.96	19.36	713.58	16.99	730.08	15.21	764.40	12.74
700	812.88	22.58	832.44	19.82	852.00	17.75	892.20	14.87
800	929.16	25.81	951.30	22.65	973.92	20.29	1019.40	16.99
900	1045.44	29.04	1070.16	25.48	1095.36	22.82	1147.20	19.12
1000	1161.36	32.26	1189.02	28.31	1217.28	25.36	1274.40	21.24
1500	1742.40	48.40	1783.74	42.47	1825.92	38.04	1912.20	31.87
2000	2323.08	64.53	2378.46	56.63	2434.56	50.72	2549.40	42.49
2500	2903.76	80.66	2973.18	70.79	3043.20	63.40	3186.60	53.11
3000	3484.80	96.80	3567.90	84.95	3651.84	76.08	3824.40	63.74
3500	4065.48	112.93	4162.20	99.10	4260.48	88.76	4461.60	74.36
4000	4646.16	129.06	4756.92	113.26	4869.60	101.45	5098.80	84.98
4500	5227.20	145.20	5351.64	127.42	5478.24	114.13	5736.60	95.61
5000	5807.88	161.33	5946.36	141.58	6086.88	126.81	6373.80	106.23
5500	6388.56	177.46	6541.08	155.74	6695.52	139.49	7011.00	116.85
6000	6969.60	193.60	7135.80	169.90	7304.16	152.17	7648.80	127.48
6500	7550.28	209.73	7730.10	184.05	7912.80	164.85	8286.00	138.10
7000	8131.32	225.87	8324.82	198.21	8521.44	177.53	8923.20	148.72
7500	8712.00	242.00	8919.54	212.37	9130.08	190.21	9561.00	159.35
8000	9292.68	258.13	9514.26	226.53	9739.20	202.90	10198.20	169.97
8500	9873.72	274.27	10108.98	240.69	10347.84	215.58	10835.40	180.59
9000	10454.40	290.40	10703.70	254.85	10956.48	228.26	11473.20	191.22
10000	11616.12	322.67	11892.72	283.16	12173.76	253.62	12748.20	212.47
11000	12777.48	354.93	13082.16	311.48	13391.04	278.98	14022.60	233.71
12000	13939.20	387.20	14271.60	339.80	14608.80	304.35	15297.60	254.96
13000	15100.92	419.47	15460.62	368.11	15826.08	329.71	16572.60	276.21
14000	16262.64	451.74	16650.06	396.43	17043.36	355.07	17847.00	297.45
15000	17424.00	484.00	17839.50	424.75	18260.64	380.43	19122.00	318.70
16000	18585.72	516.27	19028.52	453.06	19478.40	405.80	20397.00	339.95
17000	19747.44	548.54	20217.96	481.38	20695.68	431.16	21671.40	361.19
18000	20908.80	580.80	21407.40	509.70	21912.96	456.52	22946.40	382.44
19000	22070.52	613.07	22596.42	538.01	23130.24	481.88	24221.40	403.69
20000	23232.24	645.34	23785.86	566.33	24348.00	507.25	25496.40	424.94
21000	24393.96	677.61	24975.30	594.65	25565.28	532.61	26770.80	446.18
22000	25555.32	709.87	26164.74	622.97	26782.56	557.97	28045.80	467.43
23000	26717.04	742.14	27353.76	651.28	27999.84	583.33	29320.80	488.68
24000	27878.76	774.41	28543.20	679.60	29217.60	608.70	30595.20	509.92
25000	29040.12	806.67	29732.64	707.92	30434.88	634.06	31870.20	531.17

10.10% ANNUAL PERCENTAGE RATE

LOAN AMT	12 MONTHS TOTAL NOTE	MONTHLY PAYMENT	18 MONTHS TOTAL NOTE	MONTHLY PAYMENT	24 MONTHS TOTAL NOTE	MONTHLY PAYMENT	30 MONTHS TOTAL NOTE	MONTHLY PAYMENT
1	.96	.08	1.08	.06	.96	.04	.90	.03
2	2.04	.17	2.16	.12	2.16	.09	2.10	.07
3	3.12	.26	3.24	.18	3.12	.13	3.30	.11
4	4.20	.35	4.32	.24	4.32	.18	4.50	.15
5	5.16	.43	5.40	.30	5.52	.23	5.40	.18
6	6.24	.52	6.48	.36	6.48	.27	6.60	.22
7	7.32	.61	7.56	.42	7.68	.32	7.80	.26
8	8.40	.70	8.64	.48	8.64	.36	9.00	.30
9	9.48	.79	9.72	.54	9.84	.41	10.20	.34
10	10.44	.87	10.80	.60	11.04	.46	11.10	.37
20	21.00	1.75	21.60	1.20	22.08	.92	22.50	.75
30	31.56	2.63	32.40	1.80	33.12	1.38	33.90	1.13
40	42.12	3.51	43.20	2.40	44.16	1.84	45.30	1.51
50	52.68	4.39	54.00	3.00	55.20	2.30	56.70	1.89
60	63.24	5.27	64.80	3.60	66.48	2.77	68.10	2.27
70	73.80	6.15	75.60	4.20	77.52	3.23	79.50	2.65
80	84.36	7.03	86.40	4.80	88.56	3.69	90.60	3.02
90	94.92	7.91	97.20	5.40	99.60	4.15	102.00	3.40
100	105.48	8.79	108.18	6.01	110.64	4.61	113.40	3.78
200	211.08	17.59	216.36	12.02	221.52	9.23	227.10	7.57
300	316.56	26.38	324.54	18.03	332.40	13.85	340.50	11.35
400	422.16	35.18	432.72	24.04	443.28	18.47	454.20	15.14
500	527.76	43.98	540.90	30.05	554.16	23.09	567.60	18.92
600	633.24	52.77	649.08	36.06	665.04	27.71	681.30	22.71
700	738.84	61.57	757.26	42.07	775.92	32.33	795.00	26.50
800	844.32	70.36	865.44	48.08	886.80	36.95	908.40	30.28
900	949.92	79.16	973.62	54.09	997.68	41.57	1022.10	34.07
1000	1055.52	87.96	1081.80	60.10	1108.56	46.19	1135.50	37.85
1500	1583.28	131.94	1622.70	90.15	1662.72	69.28	1703.40	56.78
2000	2111.04	175.92	2163.60	120.20	2217.12	92.38	2271.30	75.71
2500	2638.80	219.90	2704.50	150.25	2771.28	115.47	2839.20	94.64
3000	3166.56	263.88	3245.40	180.30	3325.68	138.57	3407.10	113.57
3500	3694.32	307.86	3786.48	210.36	3879.84	161.66	3975.00	132.50
4000	4222.08	351.84	4327.38	240.41	4434.24	184.76	4542.90	151.43
4500	4749.96	395.83	4868.28	270.46	4988.40	207.85	5110.80	170.36
5000	5277.72	439.81	5409.18	300.51	5542.80	230.95	5678.40	189.28
5500	5805.48	483.79	5950.08	330.56	6097.20	254.05	6246.30	208.21
6000	6333.24	527.77	6490.98	360.61	6651.36	277.14	6814.20	227.14
6500	6861.00	571.75	7032.06	390.67	7205.76	300.24	7382.10	246.07
7000	7388.76	615.73	7572.96	420.72	7759.92	323.33	7950.00	265.00
7500	7916.52	659.71	8113.86	450.77	8314.32	346.43	8517.90	283.93
8000	8444.28	703.69	8654.76	480.82	8868.48	369.52	9085.80	302.86
8500	8972.16	747.68	9195.66	510.87	9422.88	392.62	9653.70	321.79
9000	9499.92	791.66	9736.56	540.92	9977.04	415.71	10221.60	340.72
10000	10555.44	879.62	10818.54	601.03	11085.84	461.91	11357.10	378.57
11000	11610.96	967.58	11900.34	661.13	12194.40	508.10	12492.90	416.43
12000	12666.48	1055.54	12982.14	721.23	13302.96	554.29	13628.70	454.29
13000	13722.12	1143.51	14064.12	781.34	14411.52	600.48	14764.50	492.15
14000	14777.64	1231.47	15145.92	841.44	15520.08	646.67	15900.30	530.01
15000	15833.16	1319.43	16227.72	901.54	16628.64	692.86	17035.80	567.86
16000	16888.68	1407.39	17309.70	961.65	17737.20	739.05	18171.60	605.72
17000	17944.32	1495.36	18391.50	1021.75	18845.76	785.24	19307.40	643.58
18000	18999.84	1583.32	19473.30	1081.85	19954.32	831.43	20443.20	681.44
19000	20055.36	1671.28	20555.10	1141.95	21063.12	877.63	21579.00	719.30
20000	21110.88	1759.24	21637.08	1202.06	22171.68	923.82	22714.50	757.15
21000	22166.52	1847.21	22718.88	1262.16	23280.24	970.01	23850.30	795.01
22000	23222.04	1935.17	23800.68	1322.26	24388.80	1016.20	24986.10	832.87
23000	24277.56	2023.13	24882.66	1382.37	25497.36	1062.39	26121.90	870.73
24000	25333.08	2111.09	25964.46	1442.47	26605.92	1108.58	27257.70	908.59
25000	26388.72	2199.06	27046.26	1502.57	27714.48	1154.77	28393.20	946.44

ANNUAL PERCENTAGE RATE **10.10%**

LOAN AMT	36 MONTHS TOTAL NOTE	36 MONTHS MONTHLY PAYMENT	42 MONTHS TOTAL NOTE	42 MONTHS MONTHLY PAYMENT	48 MONTHS TOTAL NOTE	48 MONTHS MONTHLY PAYMENT	60 MONTHS TOTAL NOTE	60 MONTHS MONTHLY PAYMENT
1	1.08	.03	.84	.02	.96	.02	1.20	.02
2	2.16	.06	2.10	.05	2.40	.05	2.40	.04
3	3.24	.09	3.36	.08	3.36	.07	3.60	.06
4	4.32	.12	4.62	.11	4.80	.10	4.80	.08
5	5.76	.16	5.88	.14	5.76	.12	6.00	.10
6	6.84	.19	7.14	.17	7.20	.15	7.20	.12
7	7.92	.22	7.98	.19	8.16	.17	8.40	.14
8	9.00	.25	9.24	.22	9.60	.20	10.20	.17
9	10.44	.29	10.50	.25	10.56	.22	11.40	.19
10	11.52	.32	11.76	.28	12.00	.25	12.60	.21
20	23.04	.64	23.52	.56	24.00	.50	25.20	.42
30	34.56	.96	35.70	.85	36.48	.76	37.80	.63
40	46.44	1.29	47.46	1.13	48.48	1.01	51.00	.85
50	57.96	1.61	59.22	1.41	60.96	1.27	63.60	1.06
60	69.48	1.93	71.40	1.70	72.96	1.52	76.20	1.27
70	81.36	2.26	83.16	1.98	84.96	1.77	89.40	1.49
80	92.88	2.58	94.92	2.26	97.44	2.03	102.00	1.70
90	104.40	2.90	107.10	2.55	109.44	2.28	114.60	1.91
100	116.28	3.23	118.86	2.83	121.92	2.54	127.20	2.12
200	232.56	6.46	238.14	5.67	243.84	5.08	255.00	4.25
300	348.84	9.69	357.00	8.50	365.76	7.62	382.80	6.38
400	465.12	12.92	476.28	11.34	487.68	10.16	510.60	8.51
500	581.40	16.15	595.56	14.18	609.60	12.70	638.40	10.64
600	697.68	19.38	714.42	17.01	731.52	15.24	766.20	12.77
700	813.96	22.61	833.70	19.85	853.44	17.78	894.00	14.90
800	930.60	25.85	952.98	22.69	975.36	20.32	1021.80	17.03
900	1046.88	29.08	1071.84	25.52	1097.28	22.86	1149.60	19.16
1000	1163.16	32.31	1191.12	28.36	1219.68	25.41	1277.40	21.29
1500	1744.92	48.47	1786.68	42.54	1829.28	38.11	1916.40	31.94
2000	2326.32	64.62	2382.24	56.72	2439.36	50.82	2555.40	42.59
2500	2908.08	80.78	2978.22	70.91	3048.96	63.52	3194.40	53.24
3000	3489.84	96.94	3573.78	85.09	3659.04	76.23	3832.80	63.88
3500	4071.24	113.09	4169.34	99.27	4268.64	88.93	4471.80	74.53
4000	4653.00	129.25	4764.90	113.45	4878.72	101.64	5110.80	85.18
4500	5234.76	145.41	5360.46	127.63	5488.32	114.34	5749.80	95.83
5000	5816.52	161.57	5956.44	141.82	6098.40	127.05	6388.80	106.48
5500	6397.92	177.72	6552.00	156.00	6708.00	139.75	7027.20	117.12
6000	6979.68	193.88	7147.56	170.18	7318.08	152.46	7666.20	127.77
6500	7561.44	210.04	7743.12	184.36	7927.68	165.16	8305.20	138.42
7000	8142.84	226.19	8339.10	198.55	8537.76	177.87	8944.20	149.07
7500	8724.60	242.35	8934.66	212.73	9147.36	190.57	9583.20	159.72
8000	9306.36	258.51	9530.22	226.91	9757.44	203.28	10222.20	170.37
8500	9888.12	274.67	10125.78	241.09	10367.52	215.99	10860.60	181.01
9000	10469.52	290.82	10721.34	255.27	10977.12	228.69	11499.60	191.66
10000	11633.04	323.14	11912.88	283.64	12196.80	254.10	12777.60	212.96
11000	12796.20	355.45	13104.00	312.00	13416.48	279.51	14055.00	234.25
12000	13959.36	387.76	14295.54	340.37	14636.16	304.92	15333.00	255.55
13000	15122.88	420.08	15486.66	368.73	15855.84	330.33	16611.00	276.85
14000	16286.04	452.39	16678.20	397.10	17075.52	355.74	17888.40	298.14
15000	17449.56	484.71	17869.32	425.46	18295.20	381.15	19166.40	319.44
16000	18612.72	517.02	19060.44	453.82	19515.36	406.57	20444.40	340.74
17000	19776.24	549.34	20251.98	482.19	20735.04	431.98	21721.80	362.03
18000	20939.40	581.65	21443.10	510.55	21954.72	457.39	22999.80	383.33
19000	22102.56	613.96	22634.64	538.92	23174.40	482.80	24277.20	404.62
20000	23266.08	646.28	23825.76	567.28	24394.08	508.21	25555.20	425.92
21000	24429.24	678.59	25017.30	595.65	25613.76	533.62	26833.20	447.22
22000	25592.76	710.91	26208.42	624.01	26833.44	559.03	28110.60	468.51
23000	26755.92	743.22	27399.54	652.37	28053.12	584.44	29388.60	489.81
24000	27919.08	775.53	28591.08	680.74	29272.80	609.85	30666.60	511.11
25000	29082.60	807.85	29782.20	709.10	30492.48	635.26	31944.00	532.40

10.20% ANNUAL PERCENTAGE RATE

LOAN AMT	12 MONTHS TOTAL NOTE	12 MONTHS MONTHLY PAYMENT	18 MONTHS TOTAL NOTE	18 MONTHS MONTHLY PAYMENT	24 MONTHS TOTAL NOTE	24 MONTHS MONTHLY PAYMENT	30 MONTHS TOTAL NOTE	30 MONTHS MONTHLY PAYMENT
1	.96	.08	1.08	.06	.96	.04	.90	.03
2	2.04	.17	2.16	.12	2.16	.09	2.10	.07
3	3.12	.26	3.24	.18	3.12	.13	3.30	.11
4	4.20	.35	4.32	.24	4.32	.18	4.50	.15
5	5.28	.44	5.40	.30	5.52	.23	5.40	.18
6	6.24	.52	6.48	.36	6.48	.27	6.60	.22
7	7.32	.61	7.56	.42	7.68	.32	7.80	.26
8	8.40	.70	8.64	.48	8.64	.36	9.00	.30
9	9.48	.79	9.72	.54	9.84	.41	10.20	.34
10	10.56	.88	10.80	.60	11.04	.46	11.10	.37
20	21.12	1.76	21.60	1.20	22.08	.92	22.50	.75
30	31.68	2.64	32.40	1.80	33.12	1.38	33.90	1.13
40	42.24	3.52	43.20	2.40	44.16	1.84	45.30	1.51
50	52.80	4.40	54.00	3.00	55.44	2.31	56.70	1.89
60	63.36	5.28	64.80	3.60	66.48	2.77	68.10	2.27
70	73.92	6.16	75.78	4.21	77.52	3.23	79.50	2.65
80	84.48	7.04	86.58	4.81	88.56	3.69	90.90	3.03
90	95.04	7.92	97.38	5.41	99.84	4.16	102.30	3.41
100	105.60	8.80	108.18	6.01	110.88	4.62	113.70	3.79
200	211.20	17.60	216.36	12.02	221.76	9.24	227.40	7.58
300	316.80	26.40	324.72	18.04	332.88	13.87	341.10	11.37
400	422.40	35.20	432.90	24.05	443.76	18.49	454.80	15.16
500	528.00	44.00	541.26	30.07	554.64	23.11	568.50	18.95
600	633.60	52.80	649.44	36.08	665.76	27.74	682.20	22.74
700	739.20	61.60	757.80	42.10	776.64	32.36	795.90	26.53
800	844.80	70.40	865.98	48.11	887.52	36.98	909.60	30.32
900	950.40	79.20	974.34	54.13	998.64	41.61	1023.30	34.11
1000	1056.00	88.00	1082.52	60.14	1109.52	46.23	1137.00	37.90
1500	1584.12	132.01	1623.96	90.22	1664.40	69.35	1705.50	56.85
2000	2112.12	176.01	2165.22	120.29	2219.28	92.47	2274.00	75.80
2500	2640.24	220.02	2706.66	150.37	2774.16	115.59	2842.80	94.76
3000	3168.24	264.02	3247.92	180.44	3329.04	138.71	3411.30	113.71
3500	3696.36	308.03	3789.36	210.52	3883.92	161.83	3979.80	132.66
4000	4224.36	352.03	4330.62	240.59	4438.56	184.94	4548.30	151.61
4500	4752.48	396.04	4872.06	270.67	4993.44	208.06	5117.10	170.57
5000	5280.48	440.04	5413.32	300.74	5548.32	231.18	5685.60	189.52
5500	5808.48	484.04	5954.76	330.82	6103.20	254.30	6254.10	208.47
6000	6336.60	528.05	6496.02	360.89	6658.08	277.42	6822.60	227.42
6500	6864.60	572.05	7037.28	390.96	7212.96	300.54	7391.10	246.37
7000	7392.72	616.06	7578.72	421.04	7767.84	323.66	7959.90	265.33
7500	7920.72	660.06	8119.98	451.11	8322.48	346.77	8528.40	284.28
8000	8448.84	704.07	8661.42	481.19	8877.36	369.89	9096.90	303.23
8500	8976.84	748.07	9202.68	511.26	9432.24	393.01	9665.40	322.18
9000	9504.96	792.08	9744.12	541.34	9987.12	416.13	10234.20	341.14
10000	10560.96	880.08	10826.82	601.49	11096.88	462.37	11371.20	379.04
11000	11617.08	968.09	11909.52	661.64	12206.64	508.61	12508.20	416.94
12000	12673.20	1056.10	12992.22	721.79	13316.16	554.84	13645.50	454.85
13000	13729.32	1144.11	14074.74	781.93	14425.92	601.08	14782.50	492.75
14000	14785.44	1232.12	15157.44	842.08	15535.68	647.32	15919.80	530.66
15000	15841.56	1320.13	16240.14	902.23	16645.20	693.55	17056.80	568.56
16000	16897.68	1408.14	17322.84	962.38	17754.96	739.79	18194.10	606.47
17000	17953.80	1496.15	18405.54	1022.53	18864.72	786.03	19331.10	644.37
18000	19009.92	1584.16	19488.24	1082.68	19974.48	832.27	20468.40	682.28
19000	20065.92	1672.16	20570.94	1142.83	21084.00	878.50	21605.40	720.18
20000	21122.04	1760.17	21653.64	1202.98	22193.76	924.74	22742.40	758.08
21000	22178.16	1848.18	22736.34	1263.13	23303.52	970.98	23879.70	795.99
22000	23234.28	1936.19	23819.04	1323.28	24413.28	1017.22	25016.70	833.89
23000	24290.40	2024.20	24901.74	1383.43	25522.80	1063.45	26154.00	871.80
24000	25346.52	2112.21	25984.44	1443.58	26632.56	1109.69	27291.00	909.70
25000	26402.64	2200.22	27067.14	1503.73	27742.32	1155.93	28428.30	947.61

	ANNUAL PERCENTAGE RATE **10.20%**						
	36 MONTHS		**42 MONTHS**		**48 MONTHS**		**60 MONTHS**	
LOAN AMT	TOTAL NOTE	MONTHLY PAYMENT	TOTAL NOTE	MONTHLY PAYMENT	TOTAL NOTE	MONTHLY PAYMENT	TOTAL NOTE	MONTHLY PAYMENT
1	1.08	.03	.84	.02	.96	.02	1.20	.02
2	2.16	.06	2.10	.05	2.40	.05	2.40	.04
3	3.24	.09	3.36	.08	3.36	.07	3.60	.06
4	4.32	.12	4.62	.11	4.80	.10	4.80	.08
5	5.76	.16	5.88	.14	5.76	.12	6.00	.10
6	6.84	.19	7.14	.17	7.20	.15	7.20	.12
7	7.92	.22	7.98	.19	8.16	.17	8.40	.14
8	9.00	.25	9.24	.22	9.60	.20	10.20	.17
9	10.44	.29	10.50	.25	10.56	.22	11.40	.19
10	11.52	.32	11.76	.28	12.00	.25	12.60	.21
20	23.04	.64	23.52	.56	24.00	.50	25.20	.42
30	34.92	.97	35.70	.85	36.48	.76	38.40	.64
40	46.44	1.29	47.46	1.13	48.48	1.01	51.00	.85
50	57.96	1.61	59.64	1.42	60.96	1.27	63.60	1.06
60	69.84	1.94	71.40	1.70	72.96	1.52	76.80	1.28
70	81.36	2.26	83.16	1.98	85.44	1.78	89.40	1.49
80	92.88	2.58	95.34	2.27	97.44	2.03	102.00	1.70
90	104.76	2.91	107.10	2.55	109.92	2.29	115.20	1.92
100	116.28	3.23	119.28	2.84	121.92	2.54	127.80	2.13
200	232.92	6.47	238.56	5.68	244.32	5.09	255.60	4.26
300	349.20	9.70	357.84	8.52	366.24	7.63	384.00	6.40
400	465.84	12.94	477.12	11.36	488.64	10.18	511.80	8.53
500	582.48	16.18	596.40	14.20	610.56	12.72	640.20	10.67
600	698.76	19.41	715.68	17.04	732.96	15.27	768.00	12.80
700	815.40	22.65	834.96	19.88	855.36	17.82	896.40	14.94
800	931.68	25.88	954.24	22.72	977.28	20.36	1024.20	17.07
900	1048.32	29.12	1073.94	25.57	1099.68	22.91	1152.60	19.21
1000	1164.96	32.36	1193.22	28.41	1221.60	25.45	1280.40	21.34
1500	1747.44	48.54	1789.62	42.61	1832.64	38.18	1920.60	32.01
2000	2329.92	64.72	2386.44	56.82	2443.68	50.91	2561.40	42.69
2500	2912.40	80.90	2982.84	71.02	3054.72	63.64	3201.60	53.36
3000	3494.88	97.08	3579.66	85.23	3665.76	76.37	3841.80	64.03
3500	4077.36	113.26	4176.48	99.44	4276.80	89.10	4482.00	74.70
4000	4659.84	129.44	4772.88	113.64	4887.84	101.83	5122.80	85.38
4500	5242.32	145.62	5369.70	127.85	5498.88	114.56	5763.00	96.05
5000	5824.80	161.80	5966.10	142.05	6109.92	127.29	6403.20	106.72
5500	6407.28	177.98	6562.92	156.26	6720.96	140.02	7044.00	117.40
6000	6989.76	194.16	7159.74	170.47	7332.00	152.75	7684.20	128.07
6500	7572.24	210.34	7756.14	184.67	7943.04	165.48	8324.40	138.74
7000	8154.72	226.52	8352.96	198.88	8554.08	178.21	8964.60	149.41
7500	8737.20	242.70	8949.36	213.08	9165.12	190.94	9605.40	160.09
8000	9319.68	258.88	9546.18	227.29	9775.68	203.66	10245.60	170.76
8500	9902.16	275.06	10143.00	241.50	10386.72	216.39	10885.80	181.43
9000	10485.00	291.25	10739.40	255.70	10997.76	229.12	11526.60	192.11
10000	11649.96	323.61	11932.62	284.11	12219.84	254.58	12807.00	213.45
11000	12814.92	355.97	13126.26	312.53	13441.92	280.04	14088.00	234.80
12000	13979.88	388.33	14319.48	340.94	14664.00	305.50	15368.40	256.14
13000	15144.84	420.69	15512.70	369.35	15886.08	330.96	16649.40	277.49
14000	16309.80	453.05	16705.92	397.76	17108.16	356.42	17929.80	298.83
15000	17474.76	485.41	17899.14	426.17	18330.24	381.88	19210.80	320.18
16000	18639.72	517.77	19092.36	454.58	19551.84	407.33	20491.20	341.52
17000	19804.68	550.13	20286.00	483.00	20773.92	432.79	21772.20	362.87
18000	20970.00	582.50	21479.22	511.41	21996.00	458.25	23053.20	384.22
19000	22134.96	614.86	22672.44	539.82	23218.08	483.71	24333.60	405.56
20000	23299.92	647.22	23865.66	568.23	24440.16	509.17	25614.60	426.91
21000	24464.88	679.58	25058.88	596.64	25662.24	534.63	26895.00	448.25
22000	25629.84	711.94	26252.52	625.06	26884.32	560.09	28176.00	469.60
23000	26794.80	744.30	27445.74	653.47	28106.40	585.55	29456.40	490.94
24000	27959.76	776.66	28638.96	681.88	29328.00	611.00	30737.40	512.29
25000	29124.72	809.02	29832.18	710.29	30550.08	636.46	32017.80	533.63

10.25% ANNUAL PERCENTAGE RATE

	12 MONTHS		18 MONTHS		24 MONTHS		30 MONTHS	
LOAN AMT	TOTAL NOTE	MONTHLY PAYMENT	TOTAL NOTE	MONTHLY PAYMENT	TOTAL NOTE	MONTHLY PAYMENT	TOTAL NOTE	MONTHLY PAYMENT
1	.96	.08	1.08	.06	.96	.04	.90	.03
2	2.04	.17	2.16	.12	2.16	.09	2.10	.07
3	3.12	.26	3.24	.18	3.12	.13	3.30	.11
4	4.20	.35	4.32	.24	4.32	.18	4.50	.15
5	5.28	.44	5.40	.30	5.52	.23	5.40	.18
6	6.24	.52	6.48	.36	6.48	.27	6.60	.22
7	7.32	.61	7.56	.42	7.68	.32	7.80	.26
8	8.40	.70	8.64	.48	8.88	.37	9.00	.30
9	9.48	.79	9.72	.54	9.84	.41	10.20	.34
10	10.56	.88	10.80	.60	11.04	.46	11.10	.37
20	21.12	1.76	21.60	1.20	22.08	.92	22.50	.75
30	31.68	2.64	32.40	1.80	33.12	1.38	33.90	1.13
40	42.24	3.52	43.20	2.40	44.40	1.85	45.30	1.51
50	52.80	4.40	54.00	3.00	55.44	2.31	56.70	1.89
60	63.36	5.28	64.98	3.61	66.48	2.77	68.10	2.27
70	73.92	6.16	75.78	4.21	77.52	3.23	79.50	2.65
80	84.48	7.04	86.58	4.81	88.80	3.70	90.90	3.03
90	95.04	7.92	97.38	5.41	99.84	4.16	102.30	3.41
100	105.60	8.80	108.18	6.01	110.88	4.62	113.70	3.79
200	211.20	17.60	216.54	12.03	222.00	9.25	227.40	7.58
300	316.80	26.40	324.90	18.05	332.88	13.87	341.10	11.37
400	422.52	35.21	433.08	24.06	444.00	18.50	455.10	15.17
500	528.12	44.01	541.44	30.08	555.12	23.13	568.80	18.96
600	633.72	52.81	649.80	36.10	666.00	27.75	682.50	22.75
700	739.44	61.62	758.16	42.12	777.12	32.38	796.20	26.54
800	845.04	70.42	866.34	48.13	888.00	37.00	910.20	30.34
900	950.64	79.22	974.70	54.15	999.12	41.63	1023.90	34.13
1000	1056.36	88.03	1083.06	60.17	1110.24	46.26	1137.60	37.92
1500	1584.48	132.04	1624.50	90.25	1665.36	69.39	1706.70	56.89
2000	2112.72	176.06	2166.12	120.34	2220.48	92.52	2275.50	75.85
2500	2640.96	220.08	2707.74	150.43	2775.60	115.65	2844.30	94.81
3000	3169.08	264.09	3249.18	180.51	3330.72	138.78	3413.40	113.78
3500	3697.32	308.11	3790.80	210.60	3885.84	161.91	3982.20	132.74
4000	4225.44	352.12	4332.24	240.68	4440.96	185.04	4551.30	151.71
4500	4753.68	396.14	4873.86	270.77	4996.08	208.17	5120.10	170.67
5000	5281.92	440.16	5415.48	300.86	5551.20	231.30	5688.90	189.63
5500	5810.04	484.17	5956.92	330.94	6106.32	254.43	6258.00	208.60
6000	6338.28	528.19	6498.54	361.03	6661.44	277.56	6826.80	227.56
6500	6866.40	572.20	7039.98	391.11	7216.56	300.69	7395.90	246.53
7000	7394.64	616.22	7581.60	421.20	7771.68	323.82	7964.70	265.49
7500	7922.88	660.24	8123.22	451.29	8326.80	346.95	8533.50	284.45
8000	8451.00	704.25	8664.66	481.37	8881.92	370.08	9102.60	303.42
8500	8979.24	748.27	9206.28	511.46	9437.04	393.21	9671.40	322.38
9000	9507.36	792.28	9747.90	541.55	9992.16	416.34	10240.20	341.34
10000	10563.84	880.32	10830.96	601.72	11102.40	462.60	11378.10	379.27
11000	11620.20	968.35	11914.02	661.89	12212.64	508.86	12516.00	417.20
12000	12676.56	1056.38	12997.08	722.06	13322.88	555.12	13653.90	455.13
13000	13732.92	1144.41	14080.14	782.23	14433.12	601.38	14791.80	493.06
14000	14789.40	1232.45	15163.38	842.41	15543.36	647.64	15929.40	530.98
15000	15845.76	1320.48	16246.44	902.58	16653.60	693.90	17067.30	568.91
16000	16902.12	1408.51	17329.50	962.75	17763.84	740.16	18205.20	606.84
17000	17958.48	1496.54	18412.56	1022.92	18874.08	786.42	19343.10	644.77
18000	19014.84	1584.57	19495.80	1083.10	19984.32	832.68	20480.70	682.69
19000	20071.32	1672.61	20578.86	1143.27	21094.56	878.94	21618.60	720.62
20000	21127.68	1760.64	21661.92	1203.44	22204.80	925.20	22756.50	758.55
21000	22184.04	1848.67	22744.98	1263.61	23315.04	971.46	23894.40	796.48
22000	23240.40	1936.70	23828.04	1323.78	24425.28	1017.72	25032.30	834.41
23000	24296.88	2024.74	24911.28	1383.96	25535.52	1063.98	26169.90	872.33
24000	25353.24	2112.77	25994.34	1444.13	26645.76	1110.24	27307.80	910.26
25000	26409.60	2200.80	27077.40	1504.30	27756.00	1156.50	28445.70	948.19

ANNUAL PERCENTAGE RATE **10.25%**

LOAN AMT	36 MONTHS TOTAL NOTE	36 MONTHS MONTHLY PAYMENT	42 MONTHS TOTAL NOTE	42 MONTHS MONTHLY PAYMENT	48 MONTHS TOTAL NOTE	48 MONTHS MONTHLY PAYMENT	60 MONTHS TOTAL NOTE	60 MONTHS MONTHLY PAYMENT
1	1.08	.03	.84	.02	.96	.02	1.20	.02
2	2.16	.06	2.10	.05	2.40	.05	2.40	.04
3	3.24	.09	3.36	.08	3.36	.07	3.60	.06
4	4.32	.12	4.62	.11	4.80	.10	4.80	.08
5	5.76	.16	5.88	.14	5.76	.12	6.00	.10
6	6.84	.19	7.14	.17	7.20	.15	7.20	.12
7	7.92	.22	7.98	.19	8.16	.17	8.40	.14
8	9.00	.25	9.24	.22	9.60	.20	10.20	.17
9	10.44	.29	10.50	.25	10.56	.22	11.40	.19
10	11.52	.32	11.76	.28	12.00	.25	12.60	.21
20	23.04	.64	23.52	.56	24.00	.50	25.20	.42
30	34.92	.97	35.70	.85	36.48	.76	38.40	.64
40	46.44	1.29	47.46	1.13	48.48	1.01	51.00	.85
50	57.96	1.61	59.64	1.42	60.96	1.27	63.60	1.06
60	69.84	1.94	71.40	1.70	72.96	1.52	76.80	1.28
70	81.36	2.26	83.58	1.99	85.44	1.78	89.40	1.49
80	93.24	2.59	95.34	2.27	97.44	2.03	102.00	1.70
90	104.76	2.91	107.10	2.55	109.92	2.29	115.20	1.92
100	116.28	3.23	119.28	2.84	121.92	2.54	127.80	2.13
200	232.92	6.47	238.56	5.68	244.32	5.09	256.20	4.27
300	349.56	9.71	358.26	8.53	366.72	7.64	384.60	6.41
400	466.20	12.95	477.54	11.37	489.12	10.19	512.40	8.54
500	582.84	16.19	596.82	14.21	611.52	12.74	640.80	10.68
600	699.48	19.43	716.52	17.06	733.44	15.28	769.20	12.82
700	815.76	22.66	835.80	19.90	855.84	17.83	897.00	14.95
800	932.40	25.90	955.08	22.74	978.24	20.38	1025.40	17.09
900	1049.04	29.14	1074.78	25.59	1100.64	22.93	1153.80	19.23
1000	1165.68	32.38	1194.06	28.43	1223.04	25.48	1282.20	21.37
1500	1748.52	48.57	1791.30	42.65	1834.56	38.22	1923.00	32.05
2000	2331.36	64.76	2388.54	56.87	2446.08	50.96	2564.40	42.74
2500	2914.56	80.96	2985.36	71.08	3057.60	63.70	3205.20	53.42
3000	3497.40	97.15	3582.60	85.30	3669.12	76.44	3846.60	64.11
3500	4080.24	113.34	4179.84	99.52	4280.64	89.18	4487.40	74.79
4000	4663.08	129.53	4777.08	113.74	4892.64	101.93	5128.80	85.48
4500	5246.28	145.73	5374.32	127.96	5504.16	114.67	5769.60	96.16
5000	5829.12	161.92	5971.14	142.17	6115.68	127.41	6411.00	106.85
5500	6411.96	178.11	6568.38	156.39	6727.20	140.15	7051.80	117.53
6000	6994.80	194.30	7165.62	170.61	7338.72	152.89	7693.20	128.22
6500	7578.00	210.50	7762.86	184.83	7950.24	165.63	8334.00	138.90
7000	8160.84	226.69	8359.68	199.04	8561.76	178.37	8975.40	149.59
7500	8743.68	242.88	8956.92	213.26	9173.76	191.12	9616.20	160.27
8000	9326.52	259.07	9554.16	227.48	9785.28	203.86	10257.60	170.96
8500	9909.36	275.26	10151.40	241.70	10396.80	216.60	10898.40	181.64
9000	10492.56	291.46	10748.64	255.92	11008.32	229.34	11539.80	192.33
10000	11658.24	323.84	11942.70	284.35	12231.36	254.82	12822.00	213.70
11000	12824.28	356.23	13137.18	312.79	13454.88	280.31	14104.20	235.07
12000	13989.96	388.61	14331.24	341.22	14677.92	305.79	15386.40	256.44
13000	15156.00	421.00	15525.72	369.66	15900.96	331.27	16668.60	277.81
14000	16321.68	453.38	16719.78	398.09	17124.00	356.75	17950.80	299.18
15000	17487.72	485.77	17914.26	426.53	18347.52	382.24	19233.00	320.55
16000	18653.40	518.15	19108.74	454.97	19570.56	407.72	20515.20	341.92
17000	19819.08	550.53	20302.80	483.40	20793.60	433.20	21797.40	363.29
18000	20985.12	582.92	21497.28	511.84	22017.12	458.69	23079.60	384.66
19000	22150.80	615.30	22691.34	540.27	23240.16	484.17	24361.80	406.03
20000	23316.84	647.69	23885.82	568.71	24463.20	509.65	25644.00	427.40
21000	24482.52	680.07	25079.88	597.14	25686.24	535.13	26926.20	448.77
22000	25648.56	712.46	26274.36	625.58	26909.76	560.62	28208.40	470.14
23000	26814.24	744.84	27468.42	654.01	28132.80	586.10	29490.60	491.51
24000	27980.28	777.23	28662.90	682.45	29355.84	611.58	30772.80	512.88
25000	29145.96	809.61	29857.38	710.89	30579.36	637.07	32055.00	534.25

10.30% ANNUAL PERCENTAGE RATE

LOAN AMT	12 MONTHS TOTAL NOTE	MONTHLY PAYMENT	18 MONTHS TOTAL NOTE	MONTHLY PAYMENT	24 MONTHS TOTAL NOTE	MONTHLY PAYMENT	30 MONTHS TOTAL NOTE	MONTHLY PAYMENT
1	.96	.08	1.08	.06	.96	.04	.90	.03
2	2.04	.17	2.16	.12	2.16	.09	2.10	.07
3	3.12	.26	3.24	.18	3.12	.13	3.30	.11
4	4.20	.35	4.32	.24	4.32	.18	4.50	.15
5	5.28	.44	5.40	.30	5.52	.23	5.40	.18
6	6.24	.52	6.48	.36	6.48	.27	6.60	.22
7	7.32	.61	7.56	.42	7.68	.32	7.80	.26
8	8.40	.70	8.64	.48	8.88	.37	9.00	.30
9	9.48	.79	9.72	.54	9.84	.41	10.20	.34
10	10.56	.88	10.80	.60	11.04	.46	11.10	.37
20	21.12	1.76	21.60	1.20	22.08	.92	22.50	.75
30	31.68	2.64	32.40	1.80	33.12	1.38	33.90	1.13
40	42.24	3.52	43.20	2.40	44.40	1.85	45.30	1.51
50	52.80	4.40	54.00	3.00	55.44	2.31	56.70	1.89
60	63.36	5.28	64.98	3.61	66.48	2.77	68.10	2.27
70	73.92	6.16	75.78	4.21	77.52	3.23	79.50	2.65
80	84.48	7.04	86.58	4.81	88.80	3.70	90.90	3.03
90	95.04	7.92	97.38	5.41	99.84	4.16	102.30	3.41
100	105.60	8.80	108.18	6.01	110.88	4.62	113.70	3.79
200	211.32	17.61	216.54	12.03	222.00	9.25	227.70	7.59
300	316.92	26.41	324.90	18.05	333.12	13.88	341.40	11.38
400	422.64	35.22	433.26	24.07	444.24	18.51	455.40	15.18
500	528.24	44.02	541.62	30.09	555.36	23.14	569.10	18.97
600	633.96	52.83	649.98	36.11	666.48	27.77	683.10	22.77
700	739.56	61.63	758.34	42.13	777.36	32.39	796.80	26.56
800	845.28	70.44	866.70	48.15	888.48	37.02	910.80	30.36
900	950.88	79.24	975.06	54.17	999.60	41.65	1024.50	34.15
1000	1056.60	88.05	1083.42	60.19	1110.72	46.28	1138.50	37.95
1500	1584.96	132.08	1625.22	90.29	1666.08	69.42	1707.60	56.92
2000	2113.32	176.11	2167.02	120.39	2221.44	92.56	2277.00	75.90
2500	2641.56	220.13	2708.64	150.48	2776.80	115.70	2846.10	94.87
3000	3169.92	264.16	3250.44	180.58	3332.40	138.85	3415.50	113.85
3500	3698.28	308.19	3792.24	210.68	3887.76	161.99	3984.60	132.82
4000	4226.64	352.22	4334.04	240.78	4443.12	185.13	4554.00	151.80
4500	4754.88	396.24	4875.66	270.87	4998.48	208.27	5123.10	170.77
5000	5283.24	440.27	5417.46	300.97	5553.84	231.41	5692.50	189.75
5500	5811.60	484.30	5959.26	331.07	6109.20	254.55	6261.90	208.73
6000	6339.96	528.33	6501.06	361.17	6664.80	277.70	6831.00	227.70
6500	6868.32	572.36	7042.68	391.26	7220.16	300.84	7400.40	246.68
7000	7396.56	616.38	7584.48	421.36	7775.52	323.98	7969.50	265.65
7500	7924.92	660.41	8126.28	451.46	8330.88	347.12	8538.90	284.63
8000	8453.28	704.44	8668.08	481.56	8886.24	370.26	9108.00	303.60
8500	8981.64	748.47	9209.88	511.66	9441.60	393.40	9677.40	322.58
9000	9509.88	792.49	9751.50	541.75	9997.20	416.55	10246.50	341.55
10000	10566.60	880.55	10835.10	601.95	11107.92	462.83	11385.30	379.51
11000	11623.32	968.61	11918.52	662.14	12218.64	509.11	12523.80	417.46
12000	12679.92	1056.66	13002.12	722.34	13329.60	555.40	13662.30	455.41
13000	13736.64	1144.72	14085.54	782.53	14440.32	601.68	14800.80	493.36
14000	14793.24	1232.77	15169.14	842.73	15551.04	647.96	15939.30	531.31
15000	15849.96	1320.83	16252.56	902.92	16662.00	694.25	17077.80	569.26
16000	16906.56	1408.88	17336.16	963.12	17772.72	740.53	18216.30	607.21
17000	17963.28	1496.94	18419.76	1023.32	18883.44	786.81	19354.80	645.16
18000	19019.88	1584.99	19503.18	1083.51	19994.40	833.10	20493.30	683.11
19000	20076.60	1673.05	20586.78	1143.71	21105.12	879.38	21631.80	721.06
20000	21133.20	1761.10	21670.20	1203.90	22216.08	925.67	22770.60	759.02
21000	22189.92	1849.16	22753.80	1264.10	23326.80	971.95	23909.10	796.97
22000	23246.64	1937.22	23837.22	1324.29	24437.52	1018.23	25047.60	834.92
23000	24303.24	2025.27	24920.82	1384.49	25548.48	1064.52	26186.10	872.87
24000	25359.96	2113.33	26004.24	1444.68	26659.20	1110.80	27324.60	910.82
25000	26416.56	2201.38	27087.84	1504.88	27769.92	1157.08	28463.10	948.77

ANNUAL PERCENTAGE RATE **10.30%**

LOAN AMT	36 MONTHS TOTAL NOTE	36 MONTHS MONTHLY PAYMENT	42 MONTHS TOTAL NOTE	42 MONTHS MONTHLY PAYMENT	48 MONTHS TOTAL NOTE	48 MONTHS MONTHLY PAYMENT	60 MONTHS TOTAL NOTE	60 MONTHS MONTHLY PAYMENT
1	1.08	.03	.84	.02	.96	.02	1.20	.02
2	2.16	.06	2.10	.05	2.40	.05	2.40	.04
3	3.24	.09	3.36	.08	3.36	.07	3.60	.06
4	4.32	.12	4.62	.11	4.80	.10	4.80	.08
5	5.76	.16	5.88	.14	5.76	.12	6.00	.10
6	6.84	.19	7.14	.17	7.20	.15	7.20	.12
7	7.92	.22	7.98	.19	8.16	.17	8.40	.14
8	9.00	.25	9.24	.22	9.60	.20	10.20	.17
9	10.44	.29	10.50	.25	10.56	.22	11.40	.19
10	11.52	.32	11.76	.28	12.00	.25	12.60	.21
20	23.04	.64	23.52	.56	24.48	.51	25.20	.42
30	34.92	.97	35.70	.85	36.48	.76	38.40	.64
40	46.44	1.29	47.46	1.13	48.96	1.02	51.00	.85
50	58.32	1.62	59.64	1.42	60.96	1.27	63.60	1.06
60	69.84	1.94	71.40	1.70	73.44	1.53	76.80	1.28
70	81.36	2.26	83.58	1.99	85.44	1.78	89.40	1.49
80	93.24	2.59	95.34	2.27	97.92	2.04	102.60	1.71
90	104.76	2.91	107.52	2.56	109.92	2.29	115.20	1.92
100	116.64	3.24	119.28	2.84	122.40	2.55	127.80	2.13
200	233.28	6.48	238.98	5.69	244.80	5.10	256.20	4.27
300	349.92	9.72	358.26	8.53	367.20	7.65	384.60	6.41
400	466.56	12.96	477.96	11.38	489.60	10.20	513.00	8.55
500	583.20	16.20	597.24	14.22	612.00	12.75	641.40	10.69
600	699.84	19.44	716.94	17.07	734.40	15.30	769.80	12.83
700	816.48	22.68	836.64	19.92	856.80	17.85	898.20	14.97
800	933.12	25.92	955.92	22.76	979.20	20.40	1026.60	17.11
900	1049.76	29.16	1075.62	25.61	1101.60	22.95	1155.00	19.25
1000	1166.40	32.40	1194.90	28.45	1224.00	25.50	1283.40	21.39
1500	1749.96	48.61	1792.56	42.68	1836.48	38.26	1925.40	32.09
2000	2333.16	64.81	2390.22	56.91	2448.48	51.01	2566.80	42.78
2500	2916.72	81.02	2987.88	71.14	3060.48	63.76	3208.80	53.48
3000	3499.92	97.22	3585.54	85.37	3672.96	76.52	3850.80	64.18
3500	4083.12	113.42	4183.20	99.60	4284.96	89.27	4492.80	74.88
4000	4666.68	129.63	4780.86	113.83	4896.96	102.02	5134.20	85.57
4500	5249.88	145.83	5378.52	128.06	5509.44	114.78	5776.20	96.27
5000	5833.44	162.04	5976.18	142.29	6121.44	127.53	6418.20	106.97
5500	6416.64	178.24	6573.84	156.52	6733.44	140.28	7060.20	117.67
6000	6999.84	194.44	7171.50	170.75	7345.92	153.04	7701.60	128.36
6500	7583.40	210.65	7769.16	184.98	7957.92	165.79	8343.60	139.06
7000	8166.60	226.85	8366.82	199.21	8569.92	178.54	8985.60	149.76
7500	8750.16	243.06	8964.48	213.44	9182.40	191.30	9627.60	160.46
8000	9333.36	259.26	9562.14	227.67	9794.40	204.05	10269.00	171.15
8500	9916.56	275.46	10159.80	241.90	10406.40	216.80	10911.00	181.85
9000	10500.12	291.67	10757.46	256.13	11018.88	229.56	11553.00	192.55
10000	11666.88	324.08	11952.78	284.59	12242.88	255.06	12836.40	213.94
11000	12833.64	356.49	13148.10	313.05	13467.36	280.57	14120.40	235.34
12000	14000.04	388.89	14343.42	341.51	14691.84	306.08	15403.80	256.73
13000	15166.80	421.30	15538.74	369.97	15915.84	331.58	16687.80	278.13
14000	16333.56	453.71	16734.06	398.43	17140.32	357.09	17971.20	299.52
15000	17500.32	486.12	17929.38	426.89	18364.80	382.60	19255.20	320.92
16000	18667.08	518.53	19124.70	455.35	19589.28	408.11	20538.60	342.31
17000	19833.48	550.93	20320.02	483.81	20813.28	433.61	21822.60	363.71
18000	21000.24	583.34	21514.92	512.26	22037.76	459.12	23106.00	385.10
19000	22167.00	615.75	22710.24	540.72	23262.24	484.63	24390.00	406.50
20000	23333.76	648.16	23905.56	569.18	24486.24	510.13	25673.40	427.89
21000	24500.52	680.57	25100.88	597.64	25710.72	535.64	26957.40	449.29
22000	25667.28	712.98	26296.20	626.10	26935.20	561.15	28240.80	470.68
23000	26833.68	745.38	27491.52	654.56	28159.20	586.65	29524.80	492.08
24000	28000.44	777.79	28686.84	683.02	29383.68	612.16	30808.20	513.47
25000	29167.20	810.20	29882.16	711.48	30608.16	637.67	32092.20	534.87

10.40% ANNUAL PERCENTAGE RATE

LOAN AMT	12 MONTHS TOTAL NOTE	12 MONTHS MONTHLY PAYMENT	18 MONTHS TOTAL NOTE	18 MONTHS MONTHLY PAYMENT	24 MONTHS TOTAL NOTE	24 MONTHS MONTHLY PAYMENT	30 MONTHS TOTAL NOTE	30 MONTHS MONTHLY PAYMENT
1	.96	.08	1.08	.06	.96	.04	.90	.03
2	2.04	.17	2.16	.12	2.16	.09	2.10	.07
3	3.12	.26	3.24	.18	3.12	.13	3.30	.11
4	4.20	.35	4.32	.24	4.32	.18	4.50	.15
5	5.28	.44	5.40	.30	5.52	.23	5.40	.18
6	6.24	.52	6.48	.36	6.48	.27	6.60	.22
7	7.32	.61	7.56	.42	7.68	.32	7.80	.26
8	8.40	.70	8.64	.48	8.88	.37	9.00	.30
9	9.48	.79	9.72	.54	9.84	.41	10.20	.34
10	10.56	.88	10.80	.60	11.04	.46	11.10	.37
20	21.12	1.76	21.60	1.20	22.08	.92	22.50	.75
30	31.68	2.64	32.40	1.80	33.12	1.38	33.90	1.13
40	42.24	3.52	43.20	2.40	44.40	1.85	45.30	1.51
50	52.80	4.40	54.18	3.01	55.44	2.31	56.70	1.89
60	63.36	5.28	64.98	3.61	66.48	2.77	68.10	2.27
70	73.92	6.16	75.78	4.21	77.76	3.24	79.50	2.65
80	84.48	7.04	86.58	4.81	88.80	3.70	90.90	3.03
90	95.04	7.92	97.56	5.42	99.84	4.16	102.30	3.41
100	105.72	8.81	108.36	6.02	111.12	4.63	113.70	3.79
200	211.44	17.62	216.72	12.04	222.24	9.26	227.70	7.59
300	317.16	26.43	325.26	18.07	333.36	13.89	341.70	11.39
400	422.88	35.24	433.62	24.09	444.72	18.53	455.70	15.19
500	528.60	44.05	542.16	30.12	555.84	23.16	569.70	18.99
600	634.32	52.86	650.52	36.14	666.96	27.79	683.70	22.79
700	740.04	61.67	758.88	42.16	778.32	32.43	797.70	26.59
800	845.76	70.48	867.42	48.19	889.44	37.06	911.70	30.39
900	951.48	79.29	975.78	54.21	1000.56	41.69	1025.70	34.19
1000	1057.20	88.10	1084.32	60.24	1111.68	46.32	1139.70	37.99
1500	1585.80	132.15	1626.48	90.36	1667.76	69.49	1709.70	56.99
2000	2114.40	176.20	2168.64	120.48	2223.60	92.65	2279.70	75.99
2500	2643.00	220.25	2710.80	150.60	2779.68	115.82	2849.70	94.99
3000	3171.60	264.30	3252.96	180.72	3335.52	138.98	3419.70	113.99
3500	3700.20	308.35	3795.12	210.84	3891.60	162.15	3989.70	132.99
4000	4228.80	352.40	4337.28	240.96	4447.44	185.31	4559.70	151.99
4500	4757.40	396.45	4879.44	271.08	5003.52	208.48	5129.40	170.98
5000	5286.12	440.51	5421.60	301.20	5559.36	231.64	5699.40	189.98
5500	5814.72	484.56	5963.76	331.32	6115.44	254.81	6269.40	208.98
6000	6343.32	528.61	6505.92	361.44	6671.28	277.97	6839.40	227.98
6500	6871.92	572.66	7048.08	391.56	7227.36	301.14	7409.40	246.98
7000	7400.52	616.71	7590.24	421.68	7783.20	324.30	7979.40	265.98
7500	7929.12	660.76	8132.58	451.81	8339.28	347.47	8549.40	284.98
8000	8457.72	704.81	8674.74	481.93	8895.12	370.63	9119.40	303.98
8500	8986.32	748.86	9216.90	512.05	9451.20	393.80	9689.40	322.98
9000	9514.92	792.91	9759.06	542.17	10007.04	416.96	10259.10	341.97
10000	10572.24	881.02	10843.38	602.41	11118.96	463.29	11399.10	379.97
11000	11629.44	969.12	11927.70	662.65	12230.88	509.62	12539.10	417.97
12000	12686.64	1057.22	13012.02	722.89	13342.80	555.95	13679.10	455.97
13000	13743.84	1145.32	14096.34	783.13	14454.72	602.28	14818.80	493.96
14000	14801.04	1233.42	15180.66	843.37	15566.64	648.61	15958.80	531.96
15000	15858.36	1321.53	16265.16	903.62	16678.56	694.94	17098.80	569.96
16000	16915.56	1409.63	17349.48	963.86	17790.48	741.27	18238.80	607.96
17000	17972.76	1497.73	18433.80	1024.10	18902.40	787.60	19378.80	645.96
18000	19029.96	1585.83	19518.12	1084.34	20014.32	833.93	20518.50	683.95
19000	20087.16	1673.93	20602.44	1144.58	21126.24	880.26	21658.50	721.95
20000	21144.48	1762.04	21686.76	1204.82	22238.16	926.59	22798.50	759.95
21000	22201.68	1850.14	22771.08	1265.06	23350.08	972.92	23938.50	797.95
22000	23258.88	1938.24	23855.58	1325.31	24462.00	1019.25	25078.20	835.94
23000	24316.08	2026.34	24939.90	1385.55	25573.92	1065.58	26218.20	873.94
24000	25373.28	2114.44	26024.22	1445.79	26685.84	1111.91	27358.20	911.94
25000	26430.60	2202.55	27108.54	1506.03	27797.76	1158.24	28498.20	949.94

ANNUAL PERCENTAGE RATE **10.40%**

LOAN AMT	36 MONTHS TOTAL NOTE	36 MONTHS MONTHLY PAYMENT	42 MONTHS TOTAL NOTE	42 MONTHS MONTHLY PAYMENT	48 MONTHS TOTAL NOTE	48 MONTHS MONTHLY PAYMENT	60 MONTHS TOTAL NOTE	60 MONTHS MONTHLY PAYMENT
1	1.08	.03	.84	.02	.96	.02	1.20	.02
2	2.16	.06	2.10	.05	2.40	.05	2.40	.04
3	3.24	.09	3.36	.08	3.36	.07	3.60	.06
4	4.32	.12	4.62	.11	4.80	.10	4.80	.08
5	5.76	.16	5.88	.14	5.76	.12	6.00	.10
6	6.84	.19	7.14	.17	7.20	.15	7.20	.12
7	7.92	.22	7.98	.19	8.16	.17	9.00	.15
8	9.00	.25	9.24	.22	9.60	.20	10.20	.17
9	10.44	.29	10.50	.25	10.56	.22	11.40	.19
10	11.52	.32	11.76	.28	12.00	.25	12.60	.21
20	23.04	.64	23.94	.57	24.48	.51	25.20	.42
30	34.92	.97	35.70	.85	36.48	.76	38.40	.64
40	46.44	1.29	47.88	1.14	48.96	1.02	51.00	.85
50	58.32	1.62	59.64	1.42	60.96	1.27	64.20	1.07
60	69.84	1.94	71.82	1.71	73.44	1.53	76.80	1.28
70	81.72	2.27	83.58	1.99	85.44	1.78	90.00	1.50
80	93.24	2.59	95.76	2.28	97.92	2.04	102.60	1.71
90	105.12	2.92	107.52	2.56	109.92	2.29	115.20	1.92
100	116.64	3.24	119.70	2.85	122.40	2.55	128.40	2.14
200	233.64	6.49	239.40	5.70	245.28	5.11	256.80	4.28
300	350.28	9.73	359.10	8.55	367.68	7.66	385.80	6.43
400	467.28	12.98	478.80	11.40	490.56	10.22	514.20	8.57
500	583.92	16.22	598.50	14.25	612.96	12.77	643.20	10.72
600	700.92	19.47	718.20	17.10	735.84	15.33	771.60	12.86
700	817.56	22.71	837.90	19.95	858.24	17.88	900.60	15.01
800	934.56	25.96	957.60	22.80	981.12	20.44	1029.00	17.15
900	1051.20	29.20	1077.30	25.65	1103.52	22.99	1157.40	19.29
1000	1168.20	32.45	1197.00	28.50	1226.40	25.55	1286.40	21.44
1500	1752.48	48.68	1795.92	42.76	1839.84	38.33	1929.60	32.16
2000	2336.76	64.91	2394.42	57.01	2453.28	51.11	2572.80	42.88
2500	2920.68	81.13	2992.92	71.26	3066.24	63.88	3216.60	53.61
3000	3504.96	97.36	3591.84	85.52	3679.68	76.66	3859.80	64.33
3500	4089.24	113.59	4190.34	99.77	4293.12	89.44	4503.00	75.05
4000	4673.52	129.82	4788.84	114.02	4906.56	102.22	5146.20	85.77
4500	5257.44	146.04	5387.76	128.28	5519.52	114.99	5789.40	96.49
5000	5841.72	162.27	5986.26	142.53	6132.96	127.77	6433.20	107.22
5500	6426.00	178.50	6584.76	156.78	6746.40	140.55	7076.40	117.94
6000	7010.28	194.73	7183.68	171.04	7359.84	153.33	7719.60	128.66
6500	7594.20	210.95	7782.18	185.29	7972.80	166.10	8362.80	139.38
7000	8178.48	227.18	8380.68	199.54	8586.24	178.88	9006.60	150.11
7500	8762.76	243.41	8979.60	213.80	9199.68	191.66	9649.80	160.83
8000	9347.04	259.64	9578.10	228.05	9813.12	204.44	10293.00	171.55
8500	9931.32	275.87	10177.02	242.31	10426.08	217.21	10936.20	182.27
9000	10515.24	292.09	10775.52	256.56	11039.52	229.99	11579.40	192.99
10000	11683.80	324.55	11972.94	285.07	12266.40	255.55	12866.40	214.44
11000	12852.00	357.00	13169.94	313.57	13492.80	281.10	14152.80	235.88
12000	14020.56	389.46	14367.36	342.08	14719.68	306.66	15439.80	257.33
13000	15188.76	421.91	15564.78	370.59	15946.08	332.21	16726.20	278.77
14000	16357.32	454.37	16761.78	399.09	17172.96	357.77	18013.20	300.22
15000	17525.52	486.82	17959.20	427.60	18399.36	383.32	19299.60	321.66
16000	18694.08	519.28	19156.62	456.11	19626.24	408.88	20586.60	343.11
17000	19862.64	551.74	20354.04	484.62	20852.64	434.43	21873.00	364.55
18000	21030.84	584.19	21551.04	513.12	22079.52	459.99	23159.40	385.99
19000	22199.40	616.65	22748.46	541.63	23305.92	485.54	24446.40	407.44
20000	23367.60	649.10	23945.88	570.14	24532.80	511.10	25732.80	428.88
21000	24536.16	681.56	25142.88	598.64	25759.20	536.65	27019.80	450.33
22000	25704.36	714.01	26340.30	627.15	26986.08	562.21	28306.20	471.77
23000	26872.92	746.47	27537.72	655.66	28212.48	587.76	29593.20	493.22
24000	28041.12	778.92	28734.72	684.16	29439.36	613.32	30879.60	514.66
25000	29209.68	811.38	29932.14	712.67	30665.76	638.87	32166.00	536.10

10.50% ANNUAL PERCENTAGE RATE

LOAN AMT	12 MONTHS TOTAL NOTE	12 MONTHS MONTHLY PAYMENT	18 MONTHS TOTAL NOTE	18 MONTHS MONTHLY PAYMENT	24 MONTHS TOTAL NOTE	24 MONTHS MONTHLY PAYMENT	30 MONTHS TOTAL NOTE	30 MONTHS MONTHLY PAYMENT
1	.96	.08	1.08	.06	.96	.04	.90	.03
2	2.04	.17	2.16	.12	2.16	.09	2.10	.07
3	3.12	.26	3.24	.18	3.12	.13	3.30	.11
4	4.20	.35	4.32	.24	4.32	.18	4.50	.15
5	5.28	.44	5.40	.30	5.52	.23	5.70	.19
6	6.24	.52	6.48	.36	6.48	.27	6.60	.22
7	7.32	.61	7.56	.42	7.68	.32	7.80	.26
8	8.40	.70	8.64	.48	8.88	.37	9.00	.30
9	9.48	.79	9.72	.54	9.84	.41	10.20	.34
10	10.56	.88	10.80	.60	11.04	.46	11.40	.38
20	21.12	1.76	21.60	1.20	22.08	.92	22.80	.76
30	31.68	2.64	32.40	1.80	33.36	1.39	34.20	1.14
40	42.24	3.52	43.38	2.41	44.40	1.85	45.60	1.52
50	52.80	4.40	54.18	3.01	55.44	2.31	57.00	1.90
60	63.36	5.28	64.98	3.61	66.72	2.78	68.40	2.28
70	74.04	6.17	75.96	4.22	77.76	3.24	79.80	2.66
80	84.60	7.05	86.76	4.82	89.04	3.71	91.20	3.04
90	95.16	7.93	97.56	5.42	100.08	4.17	102.60	3.42
100	105.72	8.81	108.36	6.02	111.12	4.63	114.00	3.80
200	211.44	17.62	216.90	12.05	222.48	9.27	228.00	7.60
300	317.28	26.44	325.44	18.08	333.84	13.91	342.30	11.41
400	423.00	35.25	433.98	24.11	445.20	18.55	456.30	15.21
500	528.84	44.07	542.52	30.14	556.32	23.18	570.60	19.02
600	634.56	52.88	651.06	36.17	667.68	27.82	684.60	22.82
700	740.40	61.70	759.60	42.20	779.04	32.46	798.90	26.63
800	846.12	70.51	868.14	48.23	890.40	37.10	912.90	30.43
900	951.96	79.33	976.50	54.25	1001.52	41.73	1026.90	34.23
1000	1057.68	88.14	1085.04	60.28	1112.88	46.37	1141.20	38.04
1500	1586.64	132.22	1627.74	90.43	1669.44	69.56	1711.80	57.06
2000	2115.48	176.29	2170.26	120.57	2226.00	92.75	2282.40	76.08
2500	2644.44	220.37	2712.78	150.71	2782.56	115.94	2853.30	95.11
3000	3173.28	264.44	3255.48	180.86	3338.88	139.12	3423.90	114.13
3500	3702.24	308.52	3798.00	211.00	3895.44	162.31	3994.50	133.15
4000	4231.08	352.59	4340.70	241.15	4452.00	185.50	4565.10	152.17
4500	4759.92	396.66	4883.22	271.29	5008.56	208.69	5135.70	171.19
5000	5288.88	440.74	5425.74	301.43	5565.12	231.88	5706.60	190.22
5500	5817.72	484.81	5968.44	331.58	6121.44	255.06	6277.20	209.24
6000	6346.68	528.89	6510.96	361.72	6678.00	278.25	6847.80	228.26
6500	6875.52	572.96	7053.48	391.86	7234.56	301.44	7418.40	247.28
7000	7404.48	617.04	7596.18	422.01	7791.12	324.63	7989.30	266.31
7500	7933.32	661.11	8138.70	452.15	8347.68	347.82	8559.90	285.33
8000	8462.16	705.18	8681.40	482.30	8904.00	371.00	9130.50	304.35
8500	8991.12	749.26	9223.92	512.44	9460.56	394.19	9701.10	323.37
9000	9519.96	793.33	9766.44	542.58	10017.12	417.38	10271.70	342.39
10000	10577.76	881.48	10851.66	602.87	11130.24	463.76	11413.20	380.44
11000	11635.56	969.63	11936.88	663.16	12243.12	510.13	12554.40	418.48
12000	12693.36	1057.78	13022.10	723.45	13356.24	556.51	13695.90	456.53
13000	13751.16	1145.93	14107.14	783.73	14469.12	602.88	14837.10	494.57
14000	14808.96	1234.08	15192.36	844.02	15582.24	649.26	15978.60	532.62
15000	15866.64	1322.22	16277.58	904.31	16695.36	695.64	17119.80	570.66
16000	16924.44	1410.37	17362.80	964.60	17808.24	742.01	18261.00	608.70
17000	17982.24	1498.52	18447.84	1024.88	18921.36	788.39	19402.50	646.75
18000	19040.04	1586.67	19533.06	1085.17	20034.24	834.76	20543.70	684.79
19000	20097.84	1674.82	20618.28	1145.46	21147.36	881.14	21685.20	722.84
20000	21155.64	1762.97	21703.50	1205.75	22260.48	927.52	22826.40	760.88
21000	22213.44	1851.12	22788.54	1266.03	23373.36	973.89	23967.90	798.93
22000	23271.12	1939.26	23873.76	1326.32	24486.48	1020.27	25109.10	836.97
23000	24328.92	2027.41	24958.98	1386.61	25599.36	1066.64	26250.30	875.01
24000	25386.72	2115.56	26044.20	1446.90	26712.48	1113.02	27391.80	913.06
25000	26444.52	2203.71	27129.24	1507.18	27825.60	1159.40	28533.00	951.10

ANNUAL PERCENTAGE RATE **10.50%**

LOAN AMT	36 MONTHS TOTAL NOTE	36 MONTHS MONTHLY PAYMENT	42 MONTHS TOTAL NOTE	42 MONTHS MONTHLY PAYMENT	48 MONTHS TOTAL NOTE	48 MONTHS MONTHLY PAYMENT	60 MONTHS TOTAL NOTE	60 MONTHS MONTHLY PAYMENT
1	1.08	.03	.84	.02	.96	.02	1.20	.02
2	2.16	.06	2.10	.05	2.40	.05	2.40	.04
3	3.24	.09	3.36	.08	3.36	.07	3.60	.06
4	4.68	.13	4.62	.11	4.80	.10	4.80	.08
5	5.76	.16	5.88	.14	5.76	.12	6.00	.10
6	6.84	.19	7.14	.17	7.20	.15	7.20	.12
7	7.92	.22	7.98	.19	8.16	.17	9.00	.15
8	9.36	.26	9.24	.22	9.60	.20	10.20	.17
9	10.44	.29	10.50	.25	11.04	.23	11.40	.19
10	11.52	.32	11.76	.28	12.00	.25	12.60	.21
20	23.40	.65	23.94	.57	24.48	.51	25.20	.42
30	34.92	.97	35.70	.85	36.48	.76	38.40	.64
40	46.80	1.30	47.88	1.14	48.96	1.02	51.00	.85
50	58.32	1.62	59.64	1.42	61.44	1.28	64.20	1.07
60	70.20	1.95	71.82	1.71	73.44	1.53	76.80	1.28
70	81.72	2.27	83.58	1.99	85.92	1.79	90.00	1.50
80	93.60	2.60	95.76	2.28	97.92	2.04	102.60	1.71
90	105.12	2.92	107.52	2.56	110.40	2.30	115.80	1.93
100	117.00	3.25	119.70	2.85	122.88	2.56	128.40	2.14
200	234.00	6.50	239.82	5.71	245.76	5.12	257.40	4.29
300	351.00	9.75	359.52	8.56	368.64	7.68	386.40	6.44
400	468.00	13.00	479.64	11.42	491.52	10.24	515.40	8.59
500	585.00	16.25	599.34	14.27	614.40	12.80	644.40	10.74
600	702.00	19.50	719.46	17.13	737.28	15.36	773.40	12.89
700	819.00	22.75	839.16	19.98	860.16	17.92	902.40	15.04
800	936.00	26.00	959.28	22.84	983.04	20.48	1031.40	17.19
900	1053.00	29.25	1078.98	25.69	1105.92	23.04	1160.40	19.34
1000	1170.00	32.50	1199.10	28.55	1228.80	25.60	1289.40	21.49
1500	1755.00	48.75	1798.86	42.83	1843.20	38.40	1934.40	32.24
2000	2340.00	65.00	2398.20	57.10	2457.60	51.20	2578.80	42.98
2500	2925.00	81.25	2997.96	71.38	3072.00	64.00	3223.80	53.73
3000	3510.00	97.50	3597.72	85.66	3686.88	76.81	3868.80	64.48
3500	4095.00	113.75	4197.48	99.94	4301.28	89.61	4513.20	75.22
4000	4680.00	130.00	4796.82	114.21	4915.68	102.41	5158.20	85.97
4500	5265.36	146.26	5396.58	128.49	5530.08	115.21	5803.20	96.72
5000	5850.36	162.51	5996.34	142.77	6144.48	128.01	6447.60	107.46
5500	6435.36	178.76	6596.10	157.05	6758.88	140.81	7092.60	118.21
6000	7020.36	195.01	7195.44	171.32	7373.76	153.62	7737.60	128.96
6500	7605.36	211.26	7795.20	185.60	7988.16	166.42	8382.60	139.71
7000	8190.36	227.51	8394.96	199.88	8602.56	179.22	9027.00	150.45
7500	8775.36	243.76	8994.72	214.16	9216.96	192.02	9672.00	161.20
8000	9360.36	260.01	9594.06	228.43	9831.36	204.82	10317.00	171.95
8500	9945.72	276.27	10193.82	242.71	10445.76	217.62	10961.40	182.69
9000	10530.72	292.52	10793.58	256.99	11060.64	230.43	11606.40	193.44
10000	11700.72	325.02	11992.68	285.54	12289.44	256.03	12895.80	214.93
11000	12870.72	357.52	13192.20	314.10	13518.24	281.63	14185.80	236.43
12000	14040.72	390.02	14391.30	342.65	14747.52	307.24	15475.20	257.92
13000	15211.08	422.53	15590.82	371.21	15976.32	332.84	16765.20	279.42
14000	16381.08	455.03	16789.92	399.76	17205.12	358.44	18054.60	300.91
15000	17551.08	487.53	17989.44	428.32	18434.40	384.05	19344.00	322.40
16000	18721.08	520.03	19188.54	456.87	19663.20	409.65	20634.00	343.90
17000	19891.44	552.54	20388.06	485.43	20892.00	435.25	21923.40	365.39
18000	21061.44	585.04	21587.16	513.98	22121.28	460.86	23213.40	386.89
19000	22231.44	617.54	22786.68	542.54	23350.08	486.46	24502.80	408.38
20000	23401.44	650.04	23985.78	571.09	24578.88	512.06	25792.20	429.87
21000	24571.80	682.55	25184.88	599.64	25808.16	537.67	27082.20	451.37
22000	25741.80	715.05	26384.40	628.20	27036.96	563.27	28371.60	472.86
23000	26911.80	747.55	27583.50	656.75	28265.76	588.87	29661.00	494.35
24000	28081.80	780.05	28783.02	685.31	29495.04	614.48	30951.00	515.85
25000	29252.16	812.56	29982.12	713.86	30723.84	640.08	32240.40	537.34

Checklist for New Cars

1. Cars I want to test drive:

Manufacturer #1 _____

Manufacturer #2 _____

Manufacturer #3 _____

2. The car I want to buy:

Make _____

Model _____

Options _____

Color _____

Type _____

3. Incentives:

Cash rebate or low interest rate financing, if any _____

Factory to dealer incentie, if any _____

Carry over allowance/special sale, if any _____

First time buyer/college graduate, if any _____

Hold back (secret profit) _____

4. Trade (if any)

N.A.D.A. retail price $ _____

Loan value $ _____

Wholesale price $ _____

5. Interest Rate:

Bank Name	Person/Contact	Telephone	Rate of Interest
1. _____	_____	_____	_____
2. _____	_____	_____	_____
3. _____	_____	_____	_____

Credit Union:

_____ _____ _____ _____

Manufacturer's lowest financing rate: _____

Rate of financing through dealer: _____

6. Service Contract:

        5 years or 60,000 miles $_____

        6 years or 70,000 miles $_____

        Major insurance company's cost $_____

        Dealer's cost $_____

7. Down Payment:

        Cash, if any $_____

        Value of trade, if any $_____

8. Price:

        Selling price $_____

        Total price $_____

        Monthly payment $_____

Checklist for Used Cars

1. **The car I want to buy:**

    Make _____

    Model _____

    Type _____

    Year _____

2. **Where I will shop for my car:**

	<u>Name</u>	<u>Telephone No.</u>
Dealer	_____	_____
Bank Auction	_____	_____
Govt. Auction	_____	_____
Other	_____	_____

3. **The price I want to pay is $_____**

4. **Warranty**

    _____

5. **Interest Rate**

    _____%

    Name of Institution and telephone No.

267

Used Car Appraisal

USED CAR APPRAISAL REPORT

(SAMPLE)

Date:		Interested in	
owner's name		Make	
address		Model	
V.I. No.		Type	
Lic. No.		Year	
Mileage		Salesman	

DESCRIPTION	CONDITION	REPAIR COSTS
FINISH		
BODY AND TOP		
FENDERS		
TIRES		
STARTER		
BATTERY		
MOTOR		
TRANSMISSION		
REAR		
AXLE		
INTERIOR		
JACK		
POWER BRAKES		
POWER STEERING		
POWER SEATS		
POWER WINDOWS		
AIR CONDITIONING		

TOTAL COST OF REPAIRS $

USED CAR AVERAGE VALUE $

DEDUCTION FOR RECONDITIONING ALLOWANCE $

APPRAISED BY:

Reader Comments, Suggestions and Questions

I would love to hear any comments, suggestions or questions you may have for future editions of this important book. Please send them to the following address:

Jake Jacobs
P.O. Box 740893
Boynton Beach, Florida 33474

Please contact me as well if you have any questions regarding my seminar and also on my consultation service. And let me if you need me for consultation. Write to me. I love to hear from you.

I wrote "Hassle–Free Car Buying" out of a sincere desire to help people, so that they can eliminate all the problems of purchasing an automobile. In writing it, I have not withheld any 'special secrets,' but have shared with you everything I know.

Car buying is a never-ending process and, as my knowledge deepens, the volume will be updated so that you can keep up with the latest information.

Although I can't guarantee that each and every car dealer, warranty company and financial institution will cooperate with you, if you use the check list provided in this book it will help eliminate much of the frustration car buyers often encounter, and it will save you both time and money.

Index

About the Author

Mr. Jake Jacobs is an experienced and successful dealer for both domestic as well as foreign cars. For over a decade, with his vast experience and extensive research in the business, he has not only been able to help hundreds of people buy motor vehicles of their liking, hassle-free, but to also assist them at every stage to secure adequate financing. His good relationship with his customers has won their confidence and has enabled him to build a high reputation for himself.

Fascinated with cars of various models and designs since his youth, he ventured a career in car dealership after attending the State University of New York (SUNY) at Buffalo. His determination and dedication not only enabled him to make his childhood dream a reality, but also climb the ladder of success rapidly in order to become one of the best salesmen in the country.

Jacobs, with his profound knowledge of the art of car dealership, has thoroughly grasped the hassle and frustration people experience in purchasing a good vehicle suited for their needs and in this profit-oriented world of manufacturers, dealers and financiers in the automobile industry prompted him to venture this book, "Hassle-Free Car Buying." Mr. Jacobs gives very interesting and helpful hints along with lucid insights into the inner secrets, in simple terms, to help genuine car buyers—new or used—to get their money's worth with adequate financing, without being confronted with confusing technical terminology.

Order Form

Yes, I want to invest $14.95 in my future and have a copy of this book.

Send _____ of *Hassle Free Car Buying* by Jake Jacobs.
Please add $2 per book for postage and handling.
Florida residents must include 6% sales tax.
Canadian orders must be accompanied by a postal money order in U.S. funds.

Send check or money order payable to:

Jake Jacobs
P.O. Box 740893
Boynton Beach, FL 33474
or call (561) 731-0160

Name _____ Tele. No. _____

Address _____

City _____ State _____ Zip Code _____

Money Back Guarantee: If not completely satisfied, will refund 100% of your money.

Here's my check/money order for $_____

Bill my _____ Visa _____ Mastercard

Account No. _____ Expires _____

Signature _____

QUANTITY ORDERS INVITED. For Bulk discount prices, please call (561) 731-0160.